*Marriages of*

# MOBILE COUNTY, ALABAMA

1813-1855

# Marriages of

# MOBILE COUNTY, ALABAMA

## 1813-1855

*Compiled and Edited by*

Clinton P. King &
Meriem A. Barlow

*Baltimore*
GENEALOGICAL PUBLISHING CO., INC.
*1985*

**FOREWORD**

This index contains an alphabetical listing of brides and grooms from three sources of information:

1. Marriage & Bond Books #1-14 of Probate Records of Mobile County
2. Index to Marriages, 1813-1855, Direct and Indirect
3. Appendix Z-1, Peter J. Hamilton, Colonial Mobile (1910 ed.)

MARRIAGE AND BOND BOOKS 1-14

```
 1  Marriage License Record   Apr. 1823 - Sept. 1825
 2  Marriage License Record   White   Dec. 1827 - Nov. 1834
 3  Marriage License Record   White   Jan.  1835 - Apr. 1840
 4  Marriage License Bond Record   White   Nov. 1837 - Aug. 1841
 5  Marriage License Record   White   Nov. 1839 - Mar. 1844
 6  Marriage License Bond Record   White   Oct. 1841 - Oct. 1843
 7  Marriage License Bond Record   White   Oct. 1843 - Nov. 1845
 8  Marriage License Record   White   Apr. 1844 - Aug. 1849
 9  Marriage License Bond Record   White   Jun. 1846 - Aug. 1849
10  Marriage License Bond Record   White   Aug. 1849 - Sep. 1852
11  Marriage License Record   White   Aug. 1849 - Sep. 1852
12  Marriage License Bond Record   White   Sep. 1852 - Oct. 1853
13  Marriage License Bond Record   White   Oct. 1853 - Jan. 1855
14  Marriage License Bond Record   White   Jan. 1855 - May 1856
```

The markings on the spines of these volumes are as indicated above but records of marriage of free persons of color are included. These are all Marriage License and Bond Books for the period 1823-1855.

INDEX TO MARRIAGES  WHITE  1813-1855  DIRECT and INDIRECT

These index books, hereinafter referred to as OIB or Old Index Books, are two little-used volumes of the Mobile County Probate Court Records. They were probably compiled about 1853-1855, as the entries for 1854 and 1855 are in a different handwriting than the earlier entries. The handwriting is generally clear and easy to read. These entries contain only the name of bride and groom and year of marriage. Three of these were checked against records of the Catholic church and the record of marriage was found. These are listed in this publication as OIB/ADM (Old Index Book/Archives Diocese of Mobile). Two entries were checked against the manuscript of Rev. Jacob Schroebel, a Baptist minister, which is preserved in the archives of Mobile College. Records of these were found and are listed as OIB/AMC (Old Index Book/Archives Mobile College). The marriages contained in Rev. Schroebel's manuscript were published in the Alabama Genealogical Society Quarterly, Volume 17, #1-4, 1983. Another interesting entry is that of Alvan Robeshaw to Catherine Nicholson. No proof of this marriage has been located but Alvan Robeshaw was appointed Justice of the Peace for Mobile County in 1813. He later served as Chief Justice of the Orphans' Court and performed several marriages which are recorded in Will Book 1. In January 1825, after Robeshaw's death his wife, Catherine, was appointed guardian of their minor daughter. The records of marriage recorded in Will Book 1 are listed as WB 1.

Most of the 8,000 names contained in the Old Index Books also appear in Marriages & Bonds #1-14 or Hamilton's Appendix Z-1. There are, however, 400 entries which appear only in these indices and are designated in this publication as OIB in the Book/Page Column. These entries will help to fill the gaps for the missing years 1822 and 1826, for which there are no marriages, and for other years in which the listings are incomplete. It is recommended that other source material be used for verifying the indicated marriage.

## HAMILTON'S APPENDIX Z-1

This appendix contains the names of 206 brides and grooms, covering the period 1813-1821. In an explanatory note Hamilton states..."entries under each year are taken from the returns by the officers, found mainly on the licenses; ...[others] have no such returns, and including date, are taken from the bond always given against legal impediments. Such bond date may not always be that of marriage. In one case, not given in the list, the bond was dated January, 1820, and the ceremony was not until January, 1822. But, as the licenses and returns are lost, the bond is in these cases the only record evidence tending to show the marriage." Peter J. Hamilton, Colonial Mobile (Cambridge: Riverside Press, 1910) pp.556-559. These entries are marked CM (Colonial Mobile).

## CHURCH AND CIVIL MARRIAGES

Under French and Spanish rule marriage was an ecclesiastical function and was performed by the resident priest after banns of marriage were properly announced. When the Mobile District became a part of the Mississippi Territory, marriage became a civil function and was regulated by the laws of Mississippi Territory, later Alabama Territory and then the state of Alabama. Briefly the regulations under territorial and early statehood were:

1. Act passed 1805: license to be issued by register of orphans' court where bride usually resides; bond to be taken in penal sum of $200; consent of parent or guardian required if groom under twenty-one years of age or bride under eighteen.

2. Marriage, between any free persons within the territory to be solemnized by territorial judge, justice of peace, ordained minister of the gospel, or pastor of religious society. Quakers and Mennonites may be joined by mutual consent.

3. Certificate of marriage to be signed by person celebrating same and to be returned to register of orphans' court for recordation within six months.

4. Regulation regarding degree of kinship within which marriage is forbidden, etc.

5. Act passed 1818: legitimizing all marriages solemnized without license in any county of Alabama Territory before organization of same; that offspring of such marriages are made legitimate.

6. Act passed 1821: that any licensed minister of the gospel of any denomination is authorized to solemnize the rites of matrimony, provided he shall comply with requisites of the law; all marriages so performed are declared legal.

## MOBILE COUNTY BOUNDARIES

On December 18, 1812, the legislature of Mississippi Territory established Mobile County, comprising all the country south of the 31st parallel, extending from the Pearl to Perdido River. Jackson County was created in 1813 and became the western boundary. In 1820 the boundaries were again changed when Washington County became the northern boundary and Mobile River and Bay the eastern boundary. It has remained virtually unchanged to the present time.

## OBTAINING COPIES OF RECORDS

Copies of marriage and bond may be obtained from the Probate Court of Mobile County. As of this writing (November 1984) the cost for copies of official records is $1.00 per page plus postage. If a certificate is desired the cost is $3.40 which includes postage. Only money orders will be accepted as payment when ordering by mail. Orders for copies should be addressed as follows:

Probate Court of Mobile County
(Marriage License Division)
Post Office Box 7
Mobile, AL                          36601

## CODE

| | |
|---|---|
| NSL | No surname listed |
| WB-1 | Will Book 1 |
| CM | Colonial Mobile |
| * | Return of license not properly recorded. Additional sources should be checked to validate these marriages. |
| B | Bond. This generally indicates a separate bond and may contain valuable information, such as parent or other relative of bride. |
| wid | Widow |
| widr | Widower |
| OIB | Old Index Books |
| OIB/ADM | Old Index Book/Archives Diocese of Mobile (Catholic) |
| OIB/AMC | Old Index Book/Archives Mobile College |
| (Name) | Alternative spelling of name. In some cases there are variations in the spelling of names in the records, in others, because of the quality of the penmanship it was thought expedient to suggest alternative spellings of some names. |
| ? | The question mark is used to indicate a questionable spelling if there is no alternative in the records or there was not enough space to list. |

## ACKNOWLEDGMENTS

The compilers wish to thank their respective spouses for help and understanding. Thanks are due, also, to Mrs. Grace Hood and other members of the Probate Court for their invaluable assistance. We are indebted to Mrs. Rachel-Duke Hamilton Cannon, daughter of Peter J. Hamilton, for permission to use and quote Appendix Z-1 from Colonial Mobile.

## A

| BRIDE OR GROOM | SPOUSE | DATE | BK/PAGE |
|---|---|---|---|
| Abbadie, Bertrand | Langloir, Louise | Oct 29 1853 | 12/428 |
| Abels, Samuel W | Ditmar, Mary | Jan 4 1847 | 8/210 |
| Aberich, Margaret | Obering, Frederick | Apr 12 1852 | 11/235 |
| Abernathy, Thomas S | Collins, Ellen | Apr 7 1851 | 11/135 |
| Abrahams, Tobias | Taylor, Mary Ann | Apr 1 1840* | 5/16 |
| Achard, Magdalene | Boniface, Dominique | Nov 2 1829 | 2/100 |
| Acker, Herbert F | Marsh, Mary | Jul 10 1855 | 14/194 |
| Acker, James | Flynn, Margaret | Aug 4 1851 | 11/171 |
| Acre, Elizabeth | Bullock, Jonathan | Mar 2 1833* | 2/1091 |
| Acre, Elizabeth C | Tucker, Joseph | Feb 9 1847 | 8/214 |
| Acre, Mary | Frowner, James | May 3 1839* | 3/176 |
| Adams, Ann | Mann, John H (Marsh) | Feb 11 1842 | 5/179B |
| Adams, Ann | Jones, John | Jan 17 1841* | 5/89B |
| Adams, Jasper | Clark, Ann | Jan 20 1838* | 3/108 |
| Adams, Jasper | Ellsworth, Martha | May 13 1851 | 11/148 |
| Adams, Lewin | Reniga, Margaret | Dec 23 1841* | 5/164B |
| Adams, Lucy | Curlett, George | Apr 11 1848 | 8/298 |
| Adams, Margarett | Carroll, Thomas | Apr 8 1840* | 5/22 |
| Adams, Mary | Roach, John | Oct 17 1844 | 8/44B |
| Adams, Mary E | Williams, Joseph N | Jul 2 1841* | 5/142B |
| Adams, Mary E | Pope, William B | Dec 18 1846 | 8/205 |
| Adams, Mary Josephine | Pitt, William | Oct 10 1840* | 5/53B |
| Adams, Susan | Baptiste, Edward | Nov 17 1841* | 5/157B |
| Adams, William S | Hutchison, Mary | Jun 22 1839* | 3/179 |
| Adams, Wyatt | Dismukes, Lucinda | Sep 13 1843 | 5/297B |
| Adde, William | Turner, Catherine | Apr 14 1852 | 11/237 |
| Addis, Abigal DeWolf | Christian, Thomas | Apr 20 1837* | 3/81 |
| Adelheim, Adel | Cohen, Joel | Jun 9 1853* | 12/312 |
| Adkins, George B | Graves, Eliza | Jan 17 1833* | 2/1211 |
| Adler, Jeannette | John, David | Oct 29 1847 | 8/262 |
| Adolph, Henry | Kokler, Terresa (Kehler) | Feb 15 1849* | 8/357 |
| Adrian, Thomas W | Raridon, Eliza | Feb 22 1847 | 8/219 |
| Adrughn, Benjamin ? | Sebon, Josephine ? | Jun 10 1839* | 3/178 |
| Adrington, Benjamin F ? | Sibon, Josephine ? | 1839* | OIB |
| Aegan, Rosana | Quinn, John | Feb 13 1849* | 8/356 |
| Aesart, Catherine | Wilkie, Ferdinand | Aug 4 1846 | 8/183 |
| Afannor, Ann (O'Connor) | Dwyne, John | Mar 7 1837* | 3/74 |
| Agin, Rosa | Hannon, Michael | Dec 24 1838* | 3/A153 |
| Aggers, William B (Aggus) | Egaleton, Francis | Nov 28 1849 | 11/19 |
| Aggus, William B (Aggers) | Engelson, Francis | Nov 28 1849 | 11/19 |
| Agnew, Thomas S | Woods, Catharine | Feb 2 1846 | 8/143B |
| Ahern, John | McMahon, Catherine | Jul 28 1855 | 14/200 |
| Ahern, Timothy | Carroll, Catherine | May 22 1843 | 5/274B |
| Ahlgreen, John | Shelton, Emeline | May 2 1851 | 11/144 |

| BRIDE OR GROOM | SPOUSE | DATE | BOOK/PAGE |
|---|---|---|---|
| Ahrens, August William | Sendfludt, Johanna | May 5 1851 | 11/46 |
| Aikin, Hugh K | Gayle, Mary | Dec 15 1852 | 12/94 |
| Aikin, John G | Kennedy, Clarissa A | Jun 4 1844* | 8/25B |
| Ainsworth, Sarah | Dade, Robert T Jr | May 16 1844 | 8/21B |
| Aite, George | Gager, Roxana | Sep 6 1845 | 8/117B |
| Akridge, Daniel | Goodwin, Minerva E | Dec 24 1853 | 13/51 |
| Alareer, Julia | Sefeore, Francis A | Apr 19 1838 | 3/119 |
| Albritton, Polly A | Murray, David K | Mar 20 1854 | 13/163 |
| Aldan, Mary | Nilegas, Abbott | Dec 8 1840* | 5/71 |
| Alderson, William S | Gaillard, Lydia H | Dec 5 1854 | 13/400 |
| Aldredge, Green | Dukes, Eliza | Apr 4 1840 | 5/16 |
| Alembert, Willoughby D | Walker, Emma L | Apr 29 1853 | 12/260 |
| Alexander, Ann Eliza | Pritchett, Robert | Feb 10 1845* | 8/71B |
| Alexander, Catherine | Costello, John | Feb 13 1844* | 5/322B |
| Alexander, Eliza | Demerest, John B | Sep 20 1836* | 3/59 |
| Alexander, Elizabeth | Buckanan, William | Feb 27 1839* | 3/158 |
| Alexander, Evelina | Dubroca, Sylvestre | Apr 23 1835* | 3/22 |
| Alexander, Francis | Rester, Anna | Jun 15 1835* | 3/17 |
| Alexander, Frances, Jr | Moore, Martha J | Jul 3 1855 | 14/186 |
| Alexander, Frosine | Kanedy, William | May 29 1841* | 5/133B |
| Alexander, Henry | Pierre, Mary B H | Aug 2 1842 | 5/213B |
| Alexander, James P | Gray, Virginia | May 27 1837* | 3/84 |
| Alexander, Jefferson | Davis, Julia Ann | Jun 18 1836* | 3/51 |
| Alexander, Jefferson B | Gatting, Sarah Ann | Mar 9 1846 | 8/150B |
| Alexander, Joseph | Holmes, Elizabeth | Sep 18 1852 | 12/8 |
| Alexander, Lucretia | Grimsley, William | Feb 26 1845 | 8/76B |
| Alexander, Mary | Mallory, Henry | Sep 19 1854 | 13/338 |
| Alexander, Mary Ann | Patterson, George M | May 22 1837* | 3/83 |
| Alexander, Nancy | Baptiste, Jacob P | Mar 1 1845 | 8/77B |
| Alexander, Obediah | McCarty, Catharine | Aug 25 1841* | 5/149B |
| Alexander, Roselia | Quirk, J D G | Nov 8 1843 | 5/302B |
| Alexander, Sarah | Daily, Alexander | Jul 4 1851 | 11/161 |
| Alexander, Virginia C | Burke, John M | Dec 13 1844 | 8/59B |
| Alford, William C | Pettis, Mary | Apr 30 1852 | 11/244 |
| Allaire, Jane | Cooper, Latham | Mar 5 1831 | 2/152 |
| Allaire, Maria B (L) | Robertson, Richard | Dec 4 1841* | 5/160B |
| Allard, Marie I | Gildemaster, Hugo | Apr 25 1836* | 3/45 |
| Allarnst, Ada ? | Frank, Benedict | Apr 28 1842* | 5/194B |
| Allen, Bridget | Robinson, Samuel | Jul 12 1851 | 11/164 |
| Allen, Charles | Brown, Phillis | Nov 16 1843 | 5/305B |
| Allen, Elizabeth | Johnson, Jamess | Jan 20 1820* | CM |
| Allen, Elizabeth | Smith, Richard Jr | Jul 13 1848* | 8/316 |
| Allen, Elizabeth | McLean, John | Feb 26 1842 | 5/183B |
| Allen, George | McCoy, Julia | Jan 26 1852 | 11/208 |
| Allen, George W | Anderson, Jane A | Jan 16 1854 | 13/82 |
| Allen, Hamilton | Bowers, Henrietta | Nov 18 1839* | 5/1 |
| Allen, Isaac L | Horton, Elizabeth M | Mar 30 1850 | 11/48 |
| Allen, Isabella | German, Robert | Mar 11 1820* | CM |
| Allen, James W | Hart, Hannah | Dec 31 1846 | 8/208 |
| Allen, John B | Drew, Maria | Nov 12 1844* | 8/50B |
| Allen, John E | Howell, Sarah | Nov 29 1849 | 11/20 |
| Allen, Josiah T | Sommers, Barbara | Feb 7 1839* | 3/155 |
| Allen, Mary | Johnson, William | Jun 19 1851 | 11/159 |
| Allen, Mary Ann | Howard, Thomas | Dec 22 1842* | 5/237B |
| Allen, Mary E | Howell, James | Jun 3 1851 | 11/155 |
| Allen, Mary A S | Mahler, Evard | Jul 1 1854 | 13/270 |
| Allen, Minerva (Mrs) | Weaver, John | Apr 8 1853* | 12/223 |
| Allen, Samuel W | Pfister, Amantine R | Aug 12 1834* | 2/201B |
| Allen, Sarah | Barnard, Francis J | Dec 13 1842 | 5/233B |
| Allen, William | Howell, Civility | Mar 20 1851 | 11/130 |
| Allen, William | Snow, Minerva | Jul 4 1849 | 8/396 |
| Allen, William | Colthar, Virginia | Jun 4 1855 | 14/158 |
| Allen, William | Keeley, Nancy | Jun 21 1855 | 14/183 |
| Allen, William B | Cox, Mary L | Mar 25 1828 | 2/18 |

| BRIDE OR GROOM | SPOUSE | DATE | BOOK/PAGE |
|---|---|---|---|
| Allenback, Jacob | Klamon, Barbary (Klarine) | Apr 1 1852 | 11/232 |
| Alleyn, Rosanna (Allain) | Lewis, Thomas F | Apr 29 1820* | CM |
| Alphen, Catherine | Hays, James | Jun 5 1852 | 11/260 |
| Alsferssen, Jacob | Gras, Margaret | May 30 1845 | 8/100B |
| Alstdorfer, Rosina | Britling, Joseph | Mar 30 1843 | 5/256B |
| Alvarez, Alexander E | Moreno, Cecelia M | Dec 16 1853 | 13/42 |
| Alvarez, Citye Rose | Murphy, William E | May 15 1843* | 5/271B |
| Alvarez, Diego | Weathers, Hypolite | Dec 22 1823 | 1/18 |
| Alvarez, Gertrude | Thompson, Joseph P | Jan 6 1842 | 5/169B |
| Alvarez, Henry | Hartley, Sarah | Nov 9 1852 | 12/54 |
| Alvarez, Joseph F | Brannan, Martha E | Nov 9 1853 | 13/10 |
| Alvarez, Louisa M | Towle, Amos | Jan 10 1846 | 8/139B |
| Alvarez, Mary | Pritchard, Daniel M | Jan 14 1836* | 3/36 |
| Alvarez, Mercelete | Van Fossen, Thomas L | Apr 10 1844* | 8/11B |
| Alvarez, Vincent | Morris, Jane | Jul 28 1841* | 5/144B |
| Alvarez, William Henry | Hartley, Irene | Oct 12 1847 | 8/258 |
| Alverez, William | Poor, Mary | Feb 5 1838* | 3/110 |
| Alvirez, Emanuel | Potter, Frances E | Jan 12 1837 | 3/69 |
| Amar, Mary | Ditinar, Auguste | Aug 4 1835* | 3/21 |
| Anderson, Amanda Malvina | Risher, Jacob | Mar 24 1832* | 2/1621 |
| Anderson, Andrew H | Burgess, Jeanie (Jane) | Aug 16 1852 | 11/275 |
| Anderson, Ann | McLelland, Robert J | Aug 16 1851 | 11/172 |
| Anderson, Ann J | Roberts, Henry J | May 18 1853 | 12/290 |
| Anderson, Catherine | Smullhy, William | Feb 1 1841 | 5/83B |
| Anderson, Claes | McDonald, Margaret | Jan 25 1852 | 11/206 |
| Anderson, Clara L | Hargar, John B | Jul 9 1836* | 3/53 |
| Anderson, Elias | O'Connor, Ann | Jan 6 1849* | 8/346 |
| Anderson, Emeline | Pratt, George | Jul 13 1853 | 12/352 |
| Anderson, Isaac A | Knaggs, Martha C | Sep 3 1847 | 8/254 |
| Anderson, James | Ashton, Elizabeth H | Apr 16 1852 | 11/238 |
| Anderson, James H | Patton, Margaret | Apr 16 1844 | 8/14B |
| Anderson, Jane A | Allen, George W | Jan 16 1854 | 13/82 |
| Anderson, John | Giffon, Mary | Nov 4 1829* | 2/101 |
| Anderson, John | Murphy, Bridget | Oct 12 1850 | 11/89 |
| Anderson, John | Hennesy, Margaret | May 26 1847 | 8/237 |
| Anderson, John | Murphy, Jane | May 20 1854 | 13/230 |
| Anderson, John N | McNamara, Ellen | Feb 29 1840* | 5/13 |
| Anderson, Laura Ann | Monk, Wiley | Mar 21 1834* | 2/371 |
| Anderson, Lydia | Pollard, Robert P | Nov 5 1844 | 8/47B |
| Anderson, Lydia Lucinda | Rasher, Jacob | Jul 2 1840* | 5/33 |
| Anderson, Margarette | Wright, Henry | Feb 14 1838* | 3/112 |
| Anderson, Martha | Graham, Walter | May 5 1853 | 12/271 |
| Anderson, Mary Ann (wid) | Hughs, John M (widr) | Jul 2 1853 | 12/339 |
| Anderson, Mary Jane | Tosh, Lewis Prosper | Mar 22 1843 | 5/255B |
| Anderson, Moses S | Shepherd, Sarah D | Jun 30 1845 | 8/107B |
| Anderson, Nelson | Campbell, Mary A | May 4 1846 | 8/163B |
| Anderson, Samuel ? | Garrett, Lydia ? | 1829* | OIB |
| Anderson, Samuel | Garrett, Lydia | Dec 23 1837 | 3/105 |
| Anderson, Solomon | Booth, Eliza | Feb 25 1833* | 2/1111B |
| Anderson, Solomon | Lee, Rebecca | Jan 1 1852 | 11/200 |
| Anderson, Susannah | Taylor, James | Mar 11 1821* | CM |
| Anderson, William H | Witherspoon, Ann L | Dec 24 1851 | 11/197 |
| Andouy, Charles (Andony) | Townsley, Marie | Jul 4 1843 | 5/286B |
| Andre, Claiborne | Hervey, Eliza | Aug 2 1849* | 8/386 |
| Andre, Delphine | Trenier, John Jr | Apr 29 1849* | 8/370 |
| Andre, Felix | NANCY (NSL) | Jul 28 1849* | 8/384 |
| Andre, Louis | Reveno, Artemus | Jun 10 1841* | 5/137B |
| Andre, Modeste | Cook, Alexander | Apr 26 1849 | 8/371 |
| Andre, Outin | Winkler, Eliza | Jan 3 1854 | 13/60 |
| Andre, Patrone | Chastang, Zenon Jr | Aug 17 1844 | 8/39B |
| Andrews, Catherine | Smallhf, William | Jan 1 1841* | 5/83 |
| Andrews, Edmund | Strimple, Mary | Dec 27 1845 | 8/133B |
| Andrews, Elizabeth J | Banes, David J | Apr 30 1853 | 12/262 |
| Andrews, John M | Gallager, Mahala | Aug 17 1850 | 11/80 |

| BRIDE OR GROOM | SPOUSE | DATE | BOOK/PAGE |
|---|---|---|---|
| Andrews, John M | Grimes, Rebecca | Oct 30 1852 | 12/41 |
| Andrews, Lavinia | Mitchell, Frank | Mar 9 1850 | 11/44 |
| Andrews, Martha J | Freeman, Rueben H | Jan 27 1852 | 11/209 |
| Andrews, Sara Ann Eliz | Windham, John | Aug 12 1847* | 8/251 |
| Andrews, Sarah A E | Phillips, William | Jul 10 1850* | 11/72 |
| Andrews, Sarah | Phillips, William | Jul 2 1852* | 11/273 |
| Andry, Alexandrine | Jujean, Roman (Juzan) | Aug 10 1852 | 11/275 |
| Andry, Felix | Dufrenne, Ceolene | Feb 6 1824 | 1/20 |
| Andry, Felix Jr | Bertrand, Ceadile | Sep 2 1852 | 11/281 |
| Andry, Jeane | Collins, Theodore | Mar 15 1828 | 2/17 |
| Andry, Juli | Sauvage, Antoine | Sep 18 1850 | 11/85 |
| Andry, Julia | Chastang, Albert | Jun 18 1850 | 11/67 |
| Andry, Louisa | Chastang, Francis Zeno | Jul 25 1846 | 8/181 |
| Andry, Seymour | Parker, Jane | Sep 28 1854 | 13/343 |
| Andry, Sylvester | Henry, Alexandrine | Apr 8 1830* | 2/121 |
| Angier, Matthew B | Tarvin, Margaret | Apr 27 1813* | WB1/7 |
| Angier, Samuella M.R. | Robertson, Fred. | May 31 1843 | 5/277B |
| Antonio, Betsy | Renova, Francis | Apr 28 1820* | CM |
| Antunes, Joaquim | Girard, Mary | Aug 27 1823 | 1/12 |
| Antunez, Joaquim | Demouy, Merced | Mar 3 1832* | 2/1691 |
| Antunez, Joseph | Imeaub, Eugenia | Aug 10 1854 | 13/309 |
| Anze, Charles A (Auze) | Deas, Margaret | Mar 24 1841* | 5/133 |
| Arbery, George | Fagan, Anne (Hagan) | Nov 4 1841* | 5/155B |
| Archer, Benjamin | Ellison, Ainey | Sep 15 1829 | 2/97 |
| Archer, John | Davis, Sabrina C | Mar 11 1824 | 1/25 |
| Archer, Thomas Fredrick | Phillips, Delphine | Jun 3 1837* | 3/97 |
| Ardoyno, Bartolome | McGarahay, Jane | Oct 30 1854 | 13/364 |
| Argess, Mary | Arto, John | Jun 19 1845 | 8/106B |
| Arguelles, Lewis Deonis | Davis, Emma | Feb 3 1849 | 8/353 |
| Arhart, John | Steinhart, Christina | Apr 19 1851* | 11/140 |
| Armburn, Marie Carmelite | Robertson, Douglas | Feb 8 1840* | 3/193 |
| Armer, Agnes | Burnside, Andrew | Dec 20 1823 | 1/17 |
| Armer, Elizabeth | Lose, Jacob | Apr 12 1844 | 8/12B |
| Armindinger, George | Seek, Susan | Oct 28 1835* | 3/30 |
| Armor, Angeline | Oliver, Frances H | Oct 14 1842 | 5/223B |
| Armour, Annie | Bancroft, Josiah | Nov 7 1854* | 13/371 |
| Armstrong, John | Godet, Leda Marie | Aug 5 1849* | 8/390B |
| Armstrong, Mary | Kerns, David | Aug 31 1849 | 11/1 |
| Armstrong, Mary Ann | Murtaugh, John | Jul 27 1852 | 11/273 |
| Armstrong, Michael | Rankin, Ann | Jan 3 1855 | 13/433 |
| Armstrong, Michael | Welch, Johanna F | Jun 4 1853 | 12/310 |
| Armstrong, William | LeMoine, Henrietta | Jun 17 1841* | 5/138B |
| Arnold, Elizabeth | Barrington, Armstead | Mar 11 1846 | 8/152B |
| Arnold, Elizabeth | Caleb, John | Feb 21 1848 | 8/285 |
| Arnold, Harriet | Cleal, John G | Mar 18 1837* | 3/76 |
| Arnold, Lewis | Fenkerhiel, Cath. | Feb 25 1843 | 6/288B |
| Arnold, Rebecca | Pierce, Z.Davis | Jun 6 1844 | 8/25B |
| Arnold, William | Heaney, Margaret | Oct 1 1855 | 14/243 |
| Arnold, William A | Ludlow, Mary D C | Feb 14 1853 | 12/171 |
| Arrego, John | Lavalle, Mary | Jan 13 1853 | 12/129 |
| Artegus, Valentine | Kirby, Mary | Mar 25 1845* | 8/82B |
| Arto, John | Argess, Mary | Jun 19 1845 | 8/106B |
| Ashburn, Mary | Harrub, Thomas | Feb 23 1854 | 13/135 |
| Ashley, Jane Harriet | Moffatt, Thomas T | Jun 16 1846 | 8/173 |
| Ashley, John (wid) | Wood, Ida S | Mar 23 1853 | 12/202 |
| Ashley, John S | Hays, Rebecca | May 2 1844 | 8/18B |
| Ashley, Mary Ann | Edwards, George M | Mar 16 1850 | 11/46 |
| Ashlock, Mary E | Crippen, William Henry | Feb 25 1851* | 11/124 |
| Assing, Elizabeth | Merz, Charles | Oct 22 1855 | 14/259 |
| Ashton, Elizabeth H | Anderson, James | Apr 16 1852 | 11/238 |
| Ashton, James M | Winship, Lydia | Apr 22 1834* | 2/281 |
| Ashton, Lydia J | Santern, William | May 14 1847 | 8/235 |
| Atkins, David | Cooper, Mary J | Apr 26 1852 | 11/243 |
| Atkinson, Raymond | Holly, Winney | Aug 25 1814 | WB1/25 |

| BRIDE OR GROOM | SPOUSE | DATE | BOOK/PAGE |
|---|---|---|---|
| Attaway, Elsie Amanda | Colthar, William | Apr 10 1830 | 2/122 |
| Attaway, Lucinda | Roach, Joshua H | Feb 16 1836* | 3/40 |
| Attwood, Malberry B | Desmukes, Lydia A | Feb 5 1852 | 11/212 |
| Atwood, Lucinda | Ebletoft, Gabriel | Mar 9 1846 | 8/150B |
| Aubert, Mark Thomas | Mazange, Helene | Feb 13 1830* | 2/111 |
| Aubry, Michael | Dietrich, Barbara | Jan 2 1846 | 8/135B |
| Audrahen, Ellen | McCarthy, Jeremiah | May 20 1838* | 3/129 |
| Aufleger, Albert | Siler, Theresa | Feb 9 1855 | 14/43 |
| Auld, Margaret A | Clemmons, Josephus | Nov 24 1847 | 8/267 |
| Auld, Miss Alison | Couell, Samuel | Feb 21 1837* | 3/72 |
| Ausier, Joseph Jacques | Caubert, Catharine C | Jan 23 1846 | 8/141B |
| Austil, Sarah | Cheesebrough, Hiram | Mar 9 1829* | 2/75 |
| Austin, Charles H | MaCre, Eugenia L | Dec 21 1829* | 2/107 |
| Austin, Clara H | Tardy, Balthazar | Feb 1 1836* | 3/39 |
| Austin, Hiram B | MacNamara, Mary A | May 13 1840* | 5/23 |
| Austin, Jane R | Springer, Mark | Feb 9 1843 | 5/248B |
| Austin, Sarah R | Vail, Lovick B | Apr 5 1830* | 2/120 |
| Austin, Sarah V | Croom, B.F. | Jan 27 1851* | 11/117 |
| Austin, William | Stodder, Marcia | Nov 25 1824 | 1/50 |
| Auston, Amanda | Banifer, John F (widr) | Oct 29 1853 | 12/421 |
| Autrey, Catherine A | Snow, Harvey | May 21 1844 | 8/21B |
| Auzi, A | Deas, John C | Dec 22 1844 | 8/62B |
| Auzy, George | Gallegher, Bridget | Jul 24 1851 | 11/169 |
| Avey, Catherine | Curly, Patrick | Apr 13 1844 | 8/12B |
| Avon, Jerome | Chastang, Louisa | Oct 9 1838* | 3/143 |
| Avril, Martial | Prudhomme, Mary L | Apr 21 1843 | 5/263B |
| Awtrey, Sarah R | Heard, Robert A | Apr 22 1847 | 8/229 |
| Aycock, A.L. (S) | Hendeaberry, Jane | Apr 15 1841* | 5/123 |
| Aycock, Augustus S | Roberts, Minerva | Sep 28 1835* | 3/28 |
| Ayer, Charles A | Dras, Mgante(?) | May 25 1841 | 4/3071B |
| Ayers, Andrew | Deolin, Catherine | Mar 21 1831* | 2/157 |
| Ayers, Jane A | Masterson, Hugh | Aug 9 1853 | 12/377 |
| Ayheir, Dave | Quigly, Ann | May 19 1838* | 3/126 |
| Ayin, Rosa (Agin) | Harenarr, Michael | Dec 24 1838* | 3/A153 |
| Aymard, Adelle E | Clark, James H | May 20 1851 | 11/150 |
| Aymard, Rosalie | Perkins, Henry H | Nov 8 1852 | 12/50 |
| Ayres, Catherine | Mullikin, Benjamin | Jan 16 1840* | 5/8 |
| Ayres, Catherine | Vines, Charles | Dec 25 1837* | 3/105 |

B

| | | | |
|---|---|---|---|
| Baarcke, Charles | Sangrouber, Albertine | Jul 9 1846* | 8/176 |
| Baas, Joseph W | Geandreau, Mary M | May 8 1855 | 14/134 |
| Babbitt, Charles | Mulligan, Elizabeth | Jun 2 1852 | 11/259 |
| Babe, Rosalie | Gordon, Mark | Dec 10 1846 | 8/204 |
| Baccaresse, Charles | Cohen, Augustine L | Oct 19 1840* | 5/55B |
| Bacchos, Mary | March, Edward | Oct 13 1836* | 3/60 |
| Bacchus, Elizabeth | Childers, John | Sep 23 1847* | 8/257 |
| Bachelor, John | Golden, Ellen | Jun 3 1837* | 3/87 |
| Bachus, Elizabeth | Flemming, James | Feb 5 1848* | 8/280 |
| Backus, Crocker | Backus, Eliza (Wid) | Jul 2 1853* | 12/343 |
| Backus, Eliza (wid) | Backus, Crocker | Jul 2 1853* | 12/343 |
| Backus, Eliza E | Kirk, George S | Sep 24 1855 | 14/240 |

| BRIDE OR GROOM | SPOUSE | DATE | BOOK/PAGE |
|---|---|---|---|
| Backus, Joseph B | Taylor, Eliza E | Dec 21 1841 | 5/163B |
| Bacon, Alfred | Bennett, Mary Ann | May 16 1846 | 8/166B |
| Bacon, John D | Kinners, Charlotte | Jul  2 1841* | 5/141 |
| Badgenstos, George W | Hines, Elizabeth E | Dec  6 1851 | 11/192 |
| Badger, Charles H | Percay, Sophia A (Pescay) | Apr 16 1844 | 8/14B |
| Badget, James | Fox, Ann | Jan  3 1852 | 11/201 |
| Badlun, Elizabeth | Brook, Nicholas | 1827* | OIB |
| Bagley, Elmira | Dunn, Samuel J | Jan  1 1851 | 11/107 |
| Baglin, Rosales | Harrison, William | Apr 14 1847 | 8/227 |
| Bailey, Harriett | Brandt, David G | May 29 1840* | 5/24 |
| Bailey, John | LaCoste, Elizabeth | Jun 17 1845 | 8/104B |
| Bailey, Mary | Ronan, James | Nov 24 1854 | 13/391 |
| Bailey, Thomas | O'Brien, Abby | Feb 13 1847 | 8/217 |
| Bailey, William | Pearce, Rebecca | Jun 16 1832* | 2/1451 |
| Baird, Adele | Phillips, C | Aug  6 1844 | 8/38B |
| Baird, James | Simpson, Ellen | Jun 15 1840* | 5/27 |
| Baitl, Saffier | Cleindiest, Catherine | Feb  9 1855 | 14/44 |
| Baiz, Desir | Durand, Aurora | May 10 1834* | 2/271 |
| Baiz, Sea | Murlin, Aulden | Jun  4 1838* | 3/130 |
| Baker, Albert W | Cutler, Frances C | May 15 1844 | 8/21B |
| Baker, Arina | Slaton, William | Nov  5 1844 | 8/47B |
| Baker, Batsey M | Collins, Jacob | 1827* | OIB |
| Baker, Charles | McDermott, Jane (Mrs) | Dec  8 1845 | 8/129B |
| Baker, Exer | Deakle, James A | Feb 27 1852 | 11/222 |
| Baker, George | McDevitt, Hannah | Jan 31 1842* | 5/176B |
| Baker, Irene | Hamilton, Benjamin | Mar 23 1853 | 12/201 |
| Baker, Jefferson | Phillips, Martha | Nov  7 1849* | 11/14 |
| Baker, John H | Nager, T.S. | Feb 23 1850 | 11/42 |
| Baker, Louisa | Geelin, Patrick | Mar 27 1855 | 14/91 |
| Baker, Margaret | Miller, Charles | Oct  6 1847 | 8/257 |
| Baker, Martha Ann | Foster, John | Nov 29 1854 | 13/394 |
| Baker, Mary | O'Brien, Timothy | Jan  7 1843 | 5/241B |
| Baker, Mary | Cooper, Caisin | Jan  9 1828* | 2/3B |
| Baker, Nancy | Baker, Patterson | Dec 27 1842 | 5/238B |
| Baker, Patterson | Baker, Nancy | Dec 27 1842 | 5/238B |
| Baker, Roseanna | O'Brien, Patrick | May 30 1853 | 12/300 |
| Baker, Sarah | Fincher, Fredrick | Sep  4 1854 | 13/328 |
| Baker, Sarah | Collins, Joshua Jr. | Dec  5 1829* | 2/105 |
| Baker, William | Niles, Rosanna | Oct  3 1835* | 3/29 |
| Baker, William  (Batur) | Collins, Sarah | Sep 18 1850 | 11/86 |
| Baker, William G | Martin, Ann Jane | Nov 10 1847 | 8/263 |
| Baklmann, Gerhard | Suhr, Metta Lucie | Nov 26 1851 | 11/190 |
| Balardo, G | Cullian, Bridget | 1852* | OIB |
| Baldo, Leon M | Rovira, Josephine  ? | Apr 18 1854 | 13/191 |
| Baldwin, Emma W | Savage, Obed W | Nov  6 1848* | 8/332 |
| Baldwin, Mary E | Brightman, Latham | Dec 31 1851 | 11/199 |
| Baldwin, Mary P | Fernandez, Henry | May  7 1850 | 11/59 |
| Baldwin, Sarah | Howes, Malchus R | 1825* | OIB |
| Baldwin, William J (I) | Miller, Catherine A | Jun  9 1853 | 12/313 |
| Baldwyn, Henry C | Hartley, Susan M | Jul  2 1844 | 8/31B |
| Baldwyn, Marshall J | Cavallero, Louisa A | Jan 20 1842* | 5/171B |
| Baley, Elizabeth | Shaw, Jepthah | Jun 18 1819 | CM |
| Ball, John | Pinta, Ellen | Apr  2 1855 | 14/95 |
| Ball, John T | Smith, Sarah E.P. | Apr 18 1848* | 8/299 |
| Ball, Joseph | Heyder, Catherine | May 21 1855 | 14/145 |
| Ballantyne, Hamilton | Henry, Josephine E | Mar 31 1851 | 11/133 |
| Ballard, Louisa | Galloway, John | Feb 13 1815* | CM |
| Ballard, Sarah | Campbelle, John | Mar 29 1839* | 3/162 |
| Ballaron, Joseph | Neal, Mary | Feb 15 1847 | 8/217 |
| Ballinger, Charlotte | Gliddon, John S | Jan 30 1840* | 5/10 |
| Ballinger, Elizabeth | Webster, Eden | Feb 19 1835* | 3/9 |
| Ballinger, Mary Jane | Puckett, James | Jun 25 1833* | 2/911 |
| Ballinger, Susannah | Locke, Richard H | Oct  1 1833* | 2/781 |
| Ballisette, Francis A | Meeker, Nathan | Nov 20 1844 | 8/52B |

| BRIDE OR GROOM | SPOUSE | DATE | BOOK/PAGE |
|---|---|---|---|
| Ballos, Eugenia | LaQuaite, Iran B | Apr 6 1850 | 11/51 |
| Bancroft, Anna Margaret | Otis, William | Dec 18 1850 | 11/104 |
| Bancroft, Charles | Weathers, Rebecca | Jan 6 1820* | CM |
| Bancroft, Charles, Jr. | Pollard, Mary L. | Jan 2 1850 | 11/30 |
| Bancroft, Elizabeth | Ramsey, Thomas M | Feb 4 1846 | 8/144B |
| Bancroft, Elmira | Hobart, Calvin G. | Feb 18 1852 | 11/219 |
| Bancroft, George | Cain, Anna Margaret | Jun 25 1833* | 2/921 |
| Bancroft, Harriett | Tisdale, Henry | Feb 3 1846 | 8/144B |
| Bancroft, Josiah | Armour, Annie | Nov 7 1854* | 13/371 |
| Bancroft, Sarah E | Delchamps, John J. | Nov 23 1844* | 8/54B |
| Band, Eleanor J | Gostenhofes, Lewis H | Mar 1 1841 | 5/109B |
| Bandler, Elizabeth | Gillen, Isaac G | Feb 17 1849 | 8/354 |
| Banere, John Emanuel | Fabel, Justin | 1822* | OIB |
| Banes, David J | Andrews, Elizabeth J | Apr 30 1853 | 12/262 |
| Banesse, George (Baresso) | Parker, Mary | May 17 1841* | 5/131B |
| Banfield, John F | Cole, Levera H (Savera) | Mar 11 1840* | 5/15B |
| Bang, Desire | Rabbie, Anatol | Apr 9 1834* | 2/331 |
| Banifer, John F (widr) ? | Auston, Amanda | Oct 20 1853 | 12/421 |
| Bankston, Thomas | Lewis, Susanah | 1826* | OIB |
| Bannon, James | McGrath, Mary | Feb 5 1853 | 12/164 |
| Bant, Maria H | Hyems, Nathaniel | May 9 1836* | 3/46 |
| Bany, Catherine | Welch, Matthew | Jul 8 1835* | 3/19 |
| Bany, Edmund | Churchill, Catherine | Jun 21 1855 | 14/182 |
| Bany, Jacob | Bodro, Angelie | Jan 21 1841* | 5/91 |
| Baptist, Elizabeth A | Kirkbride, Jonathan | Dec 18 1844 | 8/60B |
| Baptiste, Adolphe | Miles, Margaret | Sep 29 1852* | 12/14 |
| Baptiste, Catharine | Strong, Hercules | Sep 7 1847 | 8/255 |
| Baptiste, Catherine | Lborns, Pierre | Oct 7 1854 | 13/346B |
| Baptiste, Edward | Adams, Susan | Nov 17 1841* | 5/157B |
| Baptiste, Edward | Monk, Martha | Dec 19 1839* | 5/4B |
| Baptiste, Isabella | Johnson, William | Nov 4 1853 | 13/6 |
| Baptiste, Jacob Pierre | Alexander, Nancy | Mar 1 1845 | 8/77B |
| Baptiste, John | Blackman, Winnie | Nov 27 1841 | 5/159B |
| Baptiste, John | Rouville, Lucy | May 19 1846 | 8/167B |
| Baptiste, John P | McNellage, Jane M. | Oct 8 1842 | 5/222B |
| Baptiste, John P | Monroe, Margaret | Mar 18 1848 | 8/294 |
| Baptiste, Louisa | Chighezola, Jacob | Jun 4 1814* | CM |
| Baptiste, Louisa | Dean, Henry | Sep 18 1848* | 8/322 |
| Baptiste, Peter | Berrieller, Mary | Jan 16 1828* | 2/5 |
| Baquie, Catherine E M | Baquie, Joseph A | Jun 3 1837* | 3/97 |
| Baquie, Joseph A | Baquie, Catherine | Jun 3 1837* | 3/97 |
| Barante, Martha T | Lemerson, Boyd D | Oct 21 1840* | 5/57B |
| Barboda (NSL) (Barbary) | Roberson, Dones | Feb 5 1842 | 5/177B |
| Barcelonio, Antonio | O'Brien, Ellen | Oct 1 1852 | 12/15 |
| Barckley, Anna | Walton, John M | Jun 29 1854* | 13/269 |
| Barclay, Henry A | Moreno, Genevive | Mar 17 1831* | 2/156 |
| Barclay, Henry W A | Philibert, Josephine | Dec 20 1842 | 5/235B |
| Barclay, Josephine | Revere, John W | Apr 29 1844 | 8/17B |
| Barclay, Mary E. | Townsley, Louis O | Apr 16 1852* | 11/237 |
| Barclay, Sophie E | Sawyer, Enoch | May 12 1852 | 11/249 |
| Barclay, Stephen | Scipes, Ann Thomas | May 3 1842* | 5/197B |
| Bareso, George | Motch, Theresa | May 24 1837* | 3/84 |
| Baresso, George | Parker, Mary | May 17 1841* | 5/131B |
| Barfoot, Robert L | McHugh, Jane | May 15 1835* | 3/14 |
| Barford, Belinda | Kennedy, Patrick | May 21 1852 | 11/253 |
| Barker, Ann Miss | Cummings, George S | Jan 8 1844 | 5/314B |
| Barker, Edy | Kennedy, John | Apr 20 1839* | 3/168 |
| Barker, Elizabeth | Given, Alexander | May 17 1847 | 8/235 |
| Barker, Mary | Mott, Thomas L | 1826* | OIB |
| Barker, William | Middleton, Eadie | May 18 1836* | 3/48 |
| Barlow, Joice | Pollard, William | Mar 1 1820* | CM |
| Barlow, Robert Z | LaCoste, Corinne | Jul 21 1851 | 11/168 |
| Barnard, DeLiede | Long, John | Jun 6 1855 | 14/163 |
| Barnard, Francis J | Allen, Sarah | Dec 13 1842 | 6/238B |

7

| BRIDE OR GROOM | SPOUSE | DATE | BOOK/PAGE |
|---|---|---|---|
| Barnard, James R | Mahony, Mary Jane | Dec 29 1843* | 5/312B |
| Barnard, Jerome W | Wickes, Delphine | May 9 1855 | 14/136 |
| Barnard, Sarah | Stewart, John | Apr 19 1824 | 1/27 |
| Barnes, Adalaide | Leaven, John F | Nov 1 1855 | 14/269 |
| Barnes, David | Shaughnessy, Margaret O | Jul 9 1855 | 14/193 |
| Barnes, Frances L Del | Patterson, William | Mar 4 1848* | 8/291 |
| Barnes, James | Cleveland, Mary | Feb 26 1845 | 8/75B |
| Barnes, James | Courton, Harriet | Jul 3 1854 | 13/271 |
| Barnes, John | Hurter, Mary Ann (Hurtel) | Sep 12 1829 | 2/96 |
| Barnes, Mary (wid) | Marchand, Louis | Jan 2 1855* | 13/432 |
| Barnes, Philipe Margarete | Molden, Nelson | Mar 17 1837* | 3/75 |
| Barnes, Rachel | Benedict, John | 1826* | OIB |
| Barnes, Reuben | Hodge, Mary L | Sep 10 1839* | 3/186 |
| Barnes, Sarah | Walsh, D.R. | Nov 22 1836* | 3/62 |
| Barnes, Sarah E | Thrower, Sterling | Feb 5 1835 | 3/7 |
| Barnes, Thomas | Parker, Chrispe ? | 1826* | OIB |
| Barnett, Betsy | Weathers, Thomas | Aug 25 1819* | CM |
| Barnett, Fanny | Mifflin, David | Apr 20 1854 | 13/198 |
| Barnett, James | Beaslee, Mary M | Jun 8 1854 | 13/245 |
| Barnewall, Henry | Tankersley, Caroline A | Oct 19 1852 | 12/31 |
| Barney, Elizabeth | Stewart, Aloysius | May 13 1819* | CM |
| Barney, Hindrance ? | Deshee, Caroline | Mar 15 1847 | 8/221 |
| Barney, Hinderson ? | Desha, Caroline (Deshee) | Mar 15 1847 | 8/221 |
| Barney, Josiah M | Owen, Susan M | Jun 4 1845 | 8/101B |
| Barney, Susan M | Harris, George W | Nov 6 1854 | 13/368 |
| Barnheart, Nancy | Charles, William H | Nov 8 1834* | 2/21 |
| Barns, Mary V | Turn, John | Feb 22 1841* | 5/108 |
| Barnwell, William Jr | Ingersoll, Helen | Nov 17 1848* | 8/333 |
| Baro, Pierr (Buro) | Taben, Winney (Tasson) | Jul 2 1853 | 12/338 |
| Baron, Elizabeth Jane | March, John | Nov 13 1838* | 3/146 |
| Baron, Francis (Barrow) | Reardon, Joanna | Oct 9 1852 | 12/27 |
| Barr, Charles | Bosard, Rosalie | May 6 1836* | 3/46 |
| Barrath, John H (Banath) | Sanderson, Amanda U | Feb 15 1847 | 8/217 |
| Barren, John W | Galloway, Martha | Jul 13 1843 | 5/288B |
| Barren, Julia | Williams, William F | Nov 15 1840* | 5/63B |
| Barrenos, Joakim | Moffit, Margaret | Apr 12 1841 | 4/91B |
| Barret, Catherine | Gelvan, Patrick | May 18 1852 | 11/250 |
| Barret, John W | DeWalt, Caroline | Jul 19 1854 | 13/289 |
| Barret, Margaret | Sullivan, Cornelius | Feb 19 1855 | 14/59 |
| Barrett, Abigail | Quinlan, James | Mar 3 1851 | 11/127 |
| Barrett, B.T. | Sanford, Frances | May 1 1846 | 8/162B |
| Barrett, Martha T | Simison, B.D. | Oct 20 1840 | 5/261B |
| Barrett, Robert | Griffin, Mary | May 4 1849* | 8/372 |
| Barriel, Joseph | Laurendine, Josephine | Apr 9 1828 | 2/10 |
| Barrington, Armstead W | Arnold, Elizabeth | Mar 17 1846 | 8/152B |
| Barron, John W (Barrow) | Galloway, Martha | Jul 13 1843 | 5/288B |
| Barrow, Jane A | Rowell, Tilman T E L | Jul 19 1853 | 12/361 |
| Barrow, Jeremiah | Bolton, Jane A | May 1 1847 | 8/231 |
| Barrow, Margaret A | Wooley, James | Oct 15 1855 | 14/252 |
| Barrow, Oliver | Pomeroy, Mary | 1837* | OIB |
| Barry, Bridget | Durud, Louis | Oct 20 1852 | 12/32 |
| Barry, Catherine | McCordy, Michael ? | Nov 20 1840* | 5/65B |
| Barry, Catherine | McCarley, Michael ? | Nov 20 1840 | 5/65B |
| Barry, Edmond | Roach, Joanna (Roads) | Feb 22 1841* | 5/106B |
| Barry, Ellen | Gleason, Thomas | Apr 21 1855 | 14/113 |
| Barry, Garrett | Casey, Mary | Feb 10 1852 | 11/215 |
| Barry, Helena | McCarley, Michael | Nov 20 1840* | 5/65 |
| Barry, Honora A | O'Connor, Dennis | Apr 23 1851 | 11/141 |
| Barry, John | Kelly, Ann | Jan 20 1844* | 5/318B |
| Barry, Joseph | Lonegren, Ellen | Aug 15 1840* | 5/41B |
| Barry, Leonore | Sauer, Edward | Jan 21 1841* | 5/91 |
| Barry, Margaret | Byrnes, Moses | Sep 20 1855 | 14/235 |
| Barry, Mary | Finn, John | 1841* | OIB |
| Barry, Samuel D C | Dawson, Elizabeth | Dec 11 1855 | 14/302 |

8

| BRIDE OR GROOM | SPOUSE | DATE | BOOK/PAGE |
|---|---|---|---|
| Barstow, Nathaniel | Page, Annony | Mar 4 1843 | 5/251B |
| Barterigue, Henry ? | Wright, Mary Ann | Jun 12 1847 | 8/241 |
| Bartlett, Helen L | Sanders, William C | May 15 1849* | 8/376 |
| Bartlett, James R | Hall, Patience | Nov 8 1824 | 1/45 |
| Bartlett, John Jr | Purcell, Helen L | Feb 6 1839* | 3/155 |
| Barton, Fanny | MacLary, Edward W | Jun 5 1854 | 13/241 |
| Barton, Julia | Pelerron, William | Dec 15 1837* | 3/103 |
| Barvilli, Joachim | Moffitt, Margaret | Apr 12 1841* | 5/122B |
| Barvoe, Theodore | Green, Anna M | Jul 22 1854* | 13/292 |
| Basing, Julia (Barren) | Williams, William F | Mar 17 1840 | 4/1741B |
| Basford, Margaret | Matthews, Benjamin F | Jan 13 1853 | 12/128 |
| Basley, John | Martin, Sarah | Feb 28 1850 | 11/88 |
| Bass, Ebenezer A | Plumb, Mary | Feb 25 1848 | 8/286 |
| Bass, Henry | Leister, Mary L | Jun 1 1852 | 11/259 |
| Bass, Margaret Matilda | Magee, William | Nov 3 1828 | 2/51 |
| Bass, Mary | McRae, Colmin (Colin) | 1827* | OIB |
| Bassett, Andrew K | Martin, Mary Josephine | Jul 23 1849* | 8/379 |
| Bassett, Mary | West, George | Apr 4 1849 | 8/365 |
| Bassford, Daniel C | Demouy, Isabel (Dumony) | Feb 10 1851 | 11/120 |
| Bassford, Griffith | Martin, Mary | Apr 27 1835* | 3/23 |
| Bastable, Richard | Sweeney, Rose | Jul 27 1852 | 11/273 |
| Bastock, James B | Juden, Eliza Susan | Apr 2 1846 | 7/428B |
| Baston, Joseph O | Glaize, Rebecca | Jan 22 1846 | 7/756B |
| Basworth, Abel H | Weis, Rachel M | Feb 14 1844 | 5/322B |
| Bateman, Cecelia Ann | McDermott, P.H.M. | May 10 1845 | 8/94B |
| Bateman, Elizabeth | Davidson, John | Nov 30 1844 | 8/55B |
| Bateman, Margaret A | Torrance, Thomas | Nov 8 1847* | 8/264B |
| Bateman, Mary Catherine | Mervin, William | Jan 7 1846 | 8/137B |
| Bates, Caroline | Powell, Elijah | Nov 30 1829 | 2/104 |
| Bates, Elizabeth M | Waldrip, Hillen | Feb 4 1828* | 2/7 |
| Bates, James F | Skinner, Anna H | Nov 15 1854* | 13/379 |
| Bates, James P | Bates, Lidia | Feb 15 1821* | CM |
| Bates, Jared | Tulane, Artemise J ? | Mar 17 1842* | 5/186B |
| Bates, John G | Smith, Mary Ann | Feb 11 1839* | 3/156 |
| Bates, Joseph Jr | Fisher, Missle C | Aug 7 1838* | 3/137 |
| Bates, Lidia | Bates, James P | Feb 15 1821* | CM |
| Bates, Maria | Erst, William | Dec 16 1820* | CM |
| Bates, Mary Ann | Harris, Lud W | 1827* | OIB |
| Batiste, Beelo ? | Whately, Mary | 1828* | OIB |
| Batiste, John P | Rue, Rebecca | Dec 22 1844* | 8/61B |
| Batiste, John Pierre | Williams, Nancy | Apr 19 1824 | 1/28 |
| Batre, Adolphus | Chaudron, Jane | Mar 3 1828 | 2/9 |
| Batre, Charles | MaCre, Adele | Dec 25 1824* | 1/59 |
| Batre, Coralie | Henry, Francis | Apr 8 1845 | 8/85B |
| Batre, Zoe | De St Cyr, Hyacinth | Feb 11 1846 | 8/145B |
| Batt, Charles E | Byrne, Elizabeth | Aug 2 1849 | 8/385 |
| Batt, Charles E | Byrne, Elizabeth | Aug 2 1849 | 8/385 |
| Batteaste, Mary | Murphy, Samuel J | Apr 19 1839* | 8/369 |
| Battelle, John A | Schrobel, Juliana A | Jan 28 1843* | 5/246B |
| Battelle, John A | Schroebel, Juliana A | Feb 7 1843 | OIB/AMC |
| Battes, Eugenia | Sagnaile, Jean Baptiste | 1850* | OIB |
| Battle, Annie E | Scott, John | Dec 24 1855 | 14/313 |
| Baudain, Cecile Bozille | Lalande, Charles Jr | Jan 8 1842 | 5/169B |
| Baudain, Judique | Bertrand, Gabriel | May 16 1843 | 5/273 |
| Baudin, Celestin | Colin, Louise | May 13 1834* | 2/261 |
| Bauer, Charles | Young, Mary | Dec 13 1847 | 8/270 |
| Baumann, Elizabeth | Lutz, John | Jul 6 1854* | 13/275 |
| Baumblatt, Aaron | Frank, Rosa | Nov 24 1854 | 13/390 |
| Baumblatt, Sabina | Ellmann, Sigismond | Jan 27 1853* | 12/151 |
| Baumhauer, Andrew | Casper, Catherine | Aug 28 1854 | 13/323 |
| Baun, Alfred | Bennett, Mary Ann | May 16 1846 | 7/486B |
| Bawldin, Francis | Williams, John | Nov 18 1823 | 1/13 |
| Baxter, Andrew | Young, Hellen | Jul 23 1841* | 5/144B |
| Baxter, Harriette | Jones, William | May 28 1839* | 3/174 |

| BRIDE OR GROOM | SPOUSE | DATE | BOOK/PAGE |
|---|---|---|---|
| Baxter, James | Willeford, Charity ? | Jun 14 1828* | 2/34 |
| Baxter, John | Gillespie, Ellen | Apr 14 1853 | 12/240 |
| Baxter, Levine | Jones, Willei | May 19 1823* | 1/4 |
| Baxter, Mary | Collins, Christopher J | Dec 9 1852 | 12/84 |
| Baxter, Mary | Webb, Nathaniel | Nov 5 1855 | 14/272 |
| Baxter, Noble W | Howard, Mary Ann | Oct 19 1854 | 13/352 |
| Baxter, Rachel | Stringfellow, James | Sep 22 1828* | 2/41 |
| Bayle, Dennis (Boyle) | Mulligan, Grace | Jan 24 1843 | 5/244B |
| Bayle, Thomas C (Boyle) | Blume, Cecilia E ? | Nov 25 1846 | 8/201 |
| Bayne, Thomas L | Gayle, Anne M | Dec 21 1853 | 13/44 |
| Bayte, James | Parnell, Margaret | 1826* | 0IB |
| Bayzon, Caroline | Smith, David | Sep 23 1847 | 8/256 |
| Bazemore, William J | Thomas, Amanda J | Mar 1 1854 | 13/147 |
| Bazer, Martha | Garcia, Joseph | Jan 19 1829* | 2/64 |
| Bazile, Bazelice | Trenier, Fermin | Jan 27 1834* | 2/491 |
| Bazile, Catherine | Chastang, Augustus | Apr 28 1851 | 11/142 |
| Beadan, Bridget | Mansfield, Michael | Apr 19 1853 | 12/246 |
| Beal, Louisa B | Leland, Lewis Jr | Feb 8 1829* | 2/71 |
| Beam, Jane Augusta | George, William H | Dec 30 1848 | 8/342 |
| Beam, Jemima C | Mann, Thomas N | Jan 25 1851 | 11/117 |
| Bean, Mary | Fahl, Edward (widr) | Sep 17 1853 | 12/409 |
| Beard, Margarett | Formerville, Charles | Feb 8 1841* | 5/101B |
| Beard, Sarah (Mrs) | Bryant, Adolphus | Dec 9 1840* | 5/73B |
| Beardsley, Cyrus | Johnson, Hepsay | Jan 11 1820* | CM |
| Beardsley, Epsey | Warner, Caleb | Feb 26 1824* | 1/22 |
| Bearzage, Rose M (Bosarge) | Boh, Joseph (Bob) | Apr 20 1846* | 8/158B |
| Beaslee, Mary M | Barnett, James | Jun 8 1854 | 13/245 |
| Beasley, Amanda W | Holliman, Aeson B | May 2 1843 | 5/266B |
| Beatty, James | Chastang, Margaret | Oct 11 1830* | 2/140 |
| Beaudreaux, Zeferan | Jones, Elizabeth | Aug 3 1842* | 5/214B |
| Beaumont, William | Darling, Maria | Sep 2 1843 | 5/294B |
| Beaver, Seaborn Jones | Williams, Louisa | Feb 1 1842 | 5/176B |
| Beck, Louis Nelson | Theben, Marian (Phelan) | Feb 1 1849 | 8/352 |
| Beck, Richard M | Fletcher, Sarah A | Jul 20 1841* | 5/91B |
| Beck, Robert | Travis, Mary S | Jan 29 1846 | 8/142B |
| Beck, Samuel | Straus, Rosina | May 16 1850* | 11/98 |
| Beckler, Louisa | Goss, Adam | Oct 21 1850 | 11/90 |
| Beckler, Margaret | Johnson, Virgil A | Mar 6 1855 | 14/76 |
| Beckley, Aaron | Everett, Marie | Nov 13 1839* | 3/191 |
| Beckman, Dorethea | Mehrtens, George H | Mar 11 1848 | 8/292 |
| Beda, Elizabeth (Boda) | Collins, Joseph | Sep 22 1842 | 6/196B |
| Bedell, John | Mason, Fannie V | Aug 1 1855 | 14/203 |
| Beebe, Gustavus A | Vines, Catherine (Viner) | May 23 1842* | 5/213B |
| Beebe, Leshey | Lewis, Samuel | Jan 25 1841* | 5/93B |
| Beeber, Eliza (Beebe) | Kellogg, Theron | Dec 25 1815* | CM |
| Beeler, George W | Dunnington, Martha J | May 12 1842 | 6/141B |
| Beer, Jetty | Reinach, Frederick M | Apr 9 1847 | 8/225 |
| Beers, Anna M W | Hamilton, Peter | Dec 26 1840* | 5/81B |
| Beers, Caroline E.S.(Burs) | Campbell, William P | Jun 7 1843 | 5/279B |
| Beers, Oliver S | Hogan, Amelia E | Feb 23 1842* | 5/182B |
| Begley, Ellen | Gilgan, Martin | Nov 17 1855 | 14/283 |
| Beielle, Catherine L | Dann, Stamath | Dec 28 1850 | 11/106 |
| Bein, Patrick | Darcy, Bridget | Mar 31 1854 | 13/169 |
| Beline, Philip (Boline) | Calhelm, Ursuline | Jun 3 1841* | 5/135 |
| Belknap, Jackson O | Weir, Sarah J | Apr 10 1851* | 11/136 |
| Belknap, William | McWaine, Margaret | Jun 2 1823* | 1/9 |
| Bell, Charles | Phillips, Virginia | Dec 29 1844 | 8/63B |
| Bell, Gamaliel | Conell, Emily | Dec 19 1819* | CM |
| Bell, Jackson | Fitzgerald, Harriett | Mar 12 1832* | 2/1681 |
| Bell, John J | Miller, Mary | Aug 28 1854 | 13/322 |
| Bell, Josephine F | Royster, Ajax | Feb 25 1847 | 8/220 |
| Bell, Laura | James, Thomas S | Jan 16 1836* | 3/36 |
| Bell, Laura J | Perkins, David | Dec 29 1847 | 8/273 |
| Bell, Luella B | Merrill, Daniel F | May 21 1845 | 8/96B |

| | | | |
|---|---|---|---|
| Bell, Samuel S | Garner, Julia Ann | Dec 14 1852 | 12/89 |
| Bell, William | Doran, Mary | Jan 22 1850* | 11/35 |
| Bell, William | Jarvis, Margaret | Mar 19 1850 | 11/47 |
| Bell, William | Spalding, Laura | 1827* | OIB |
| Bell, William A | Edmond, Mary T | Dec 3 1855 | 14/297 |
| Bellanger, Anastasie | Raymond, Serie | Dec 31 1833* | 2/621 |
| Bellas, Terese | Higinbotham, O | 1833* | OIB |
| Bellew, James | McCabe, Mary | Jan 29 1855 | 14/26 |
| Belloc, Adolphe | Dyer, Gertrude F Moreton | Jun 21 1853 | 12/324 |
| Bellougnet, Louise | Hanemann, William | May 30 1843 | 5/276B |
| Belton, Edmund L (S) | Holden, Bridget | Jan 18 1850 | 11/34 |
| Bemis, Hortense | Colin, Maximillian | Jul 11 1832* | 2/1411 |
| Benal, Francois (Berral) | Dorr, Louie | Jun 7 1841* | 5/136B |
| Bender, John A | Byrnes, Mary | Jul 9 1825* | 1/85 |
| Benedict, John | Barnes, Rachel | 1826* | OIB |
| Benedict, Joseph | Pfeninger, Risalin | Feb 11 1839* | 3/156 |
| Benedict, Rachel | Moor, William | 1826* | OIB |
| Benetes, Manuel | Girard, Sarah | Oct 19 1854 | 13/354 |
| Benhauser, Antoine | Donbach, Maria Louisa | Dec 6 1836* | 3/6B |
| Benite, Euphrazie | Bosage, Joseph | Feb 21 1845 | 8/74B |
| Benite, Mary | Jeantin, Pierre W | Feb 17 1840* | 3/194 |
| Benjamin, Joseph | Sheelby, Eunice (Shultz) | Nov 20 1837* | 3/101 |
| Benjamin, Joseph | Hays, Nancy | Apr 22 1845 | 8/88B |
| Benjamin, Sidney | Berry, Lucy A | Apr 29 1847 | 8/230 |
| Benjamin, Walter C | Stewart, Louisa A | Nov 9 1850 | 11/95 |
| Benners, Edward G | Donaldson, Helen | Dec 16 1844 | 8/60B |
| Bennett, Ellen (wid) | Schock, Philip | Aug 10 1853 | 12/380 |
| Bennett, James H | Kendall, Elizabeth (Mrs) | Aug 12 1843 | 5/292B |
| Bennett, Mary Ann | Bacon, Alfred | May 16 1846 | 8/166B |
| Bennett, Mary E | Clark, John | May 18 1853* | 12/288 |
| Bennett, Robert F | Skinner, Sarah E Mrs | Dec 16 1844 | 8/59B |
| Bensaden, Joseph | Bixler, Adeleni | Feb 24 1841* | 5/109B |
| Benson, Jesse W | Elliott, Maria | Nov 10 1845 | 8/124B |
| Benson, Maria L | Collins, Josiah | Jan 15 1834* | 2/521 |
| Benson, Thomas | Brashears, Eliza | May 16 1818* | CM |
| Bently, Nancy | Brookshire, Manning J | Apr 22 1837* | 3/81 |
| Benton, Victor L | Clark, Elizabeth | Apr 9 1850 | 11/52 |
| Benustein, Nathan | Heidelberg, Rebecca | Mar 16 1850 | 11/46 |
| Berg, Apolonia | Horst, Martin | Dec 28 1854 | 13/421 |
| Berg, Clara E | Davidson, Robert J | Jan 2 1855 | 13/430 |
| Berg, Louisa | Marshall, Jacob | Apr 8 1844 | 8/10B |
| Berg, Tobias | Weinschank, Apalonia | Dec 15 1846 | 8/205 |
| Bergen, Mary Ann | Brannan, Dominick T | May 24 1848* | 8/305 |
| Berger, Joseph | Farante, Catherine | Jan 30 1843 | 5/247B |
| Bergh, Honorine | Foolkes, John | May 23 1835* | 3/16 |
| Berhok, Ann | Walker, John W | Feb 15 1840* | 5/12 |
| Berkhardt, John | Schwars, Elizabeth | Oct 5 1852 | 12/22 |
| Bermen, Christian | King, Ellen | Jan 3 1843 | 5/240 |
| Bermoody, Babaltite | Laluse, Merceill | May 15 1851 | 11/149 |
| Bernard, Mary A | Tranier, Charles W | Apr 5 1851* | 11/134 |
| Bernbrock, Henry | Ewers, Susan | Jun 9 1854 | 13/248 |
| Bernody, Annette | Dubroca, Maximilian | May 4 1831* | 2/166 |
| Bernody, Bretaigne | Dubroca, Nesin | Apr 19 1834* | 2/291 |
| Bernody, Catharine | Dubroca, Basile | Feb 18 1840* | 5/12 |
| Bernody, Catherine | Carderoy, Simon | 1826* | OIB |
| Bernody, Hortense | Colin, Maximillian | Jul 11 1832* | 2/1411 |
| Bernoody, Batille | LaSuse, Mercully (LaLuse) | 1851* | OIB |
| Bernstein, Bertha | Bernstein, Henry | Nov 18 1854 | 13/385 |
| Bernstein, C | Herv, M | Jan 3 1851* | 11/108 |
| Bernstein, Caroline | Kayser, Henry | Jan 31 1853* | 12/158 |
| Bernstein, Henry | Bernstein, Bertha | Nov 18 1854 | 13/385 |
| Beroujon, Claude | O'Neil, Margaret | Feb 22 1837 | OIB/ADM |
| Berral, Francoise (Benal) | Dorn, Lorni | Jun 7 1841 | 4/3241B |
| Berrieller, Mary | Baptiste, Peter | Jan 16 1828* | 2/5 |

11

| BRIDE OR GROOM | SPOUSE | DATE | BOOK/PAGE |
|---|---|---|---|
| Berrien, James William | Casey, Catherine J | May 5 1831* | 2/168 |
| Berry, Jane Louisa | Spillings, James | Apr 17 1845* | 8/87B |
| Berry, John Calvin | Carver, Eliza L (Carves) | Jul 8 1848 | 8/314 |
| Berry, Laura | Lavens, Edward | Jan 2 1841 | 4/1441B |
| Berry, Lucy A | Benjamin, Sidney | Apr 29 1847 | 8/230 |
| Berry, Margaret A | Pope, William | Jun 28 1853 | 12/334 |
| Bertrand, Ceadile | Andry, Felix Jr | Sep 2 1852 | 11/281 |
| Bertrand, Gabriel | Boudini, Judique | May 16 1843 | 5/273B |
| Bertrand, Isaac | Rodgers, Ellen | Feb 7 1846 | 8/146B |
| Besanceney, Rose | Pasqual, Simon | Jun 12 1843 | 5/281B |
| Bescanceny, Christostime | Futz, Bridget (Faty) | Apr 18 1854 | 13/189 |
| Best, Harriett | Brewster, Henry B | May 11 1844 | 8/20B |
| Betbeze, Jeane | Pasqual, Dumont | Sep 27 1848 | 8/325 |
| Betbeze, Justina | Pons, Megile M Y | Oct 20 1854 | 13/356 |
| Bethany, Elizabeth | Ellis, Daniel | May 13 1832* | 2/1471 |
| Bettisworth, James K | Moxton, Elizabeth | May 10 1836* | 3/47 |
| Betz, Margaret | Petzer, John | Apr 3 1834* | 2/351 |
| Bias, Elizabeth | Ludley, William | Apr 28 1846 | 8/160B |
| Bibb, Joseph D | Harrison, Jane V | Apr 2 1845 | 8/83B |
| Bickell, Emaline | Chapman, Robert | Jun 23 1825 | 1/82 |
| Bicknell, John | Smith, Caroline | Aug 6 1852 | 11/274 |
| Biddle, Sidonia | Stikes, Augustus | May 11 1846 | 8/165B |
| Bidgood, Thomas S | Redwood, Martha C | Dec 21 1847 | 8/272 |
| Bidwell, Solomon S | Simpson, Lavinia | Jan 10 1854 | 13/72 |
| Bier, Jenny | Brocher, John | Nov 3 1853 | 13/5 |
| Biers, Henderson | Bryson, Symintha (wid) | Nov 1 1853 | 13/2 |
| Bigley, Bridget | Ellison, Benjamin | Apr 10 1850 | 11/52 |
| Biihler, Frank Jacob | Murphy, Bridget | May 31 1855 | 14/153 |
| Biles, Eunice A | Jones, Edward S | Jan 18 1840* | 5/9 |
| Biley, Lucetta | Horlock, John | Mar 6 1848 | 8/291 |
| Bille, Peter | Ingerman, Conrardina | Aug 31 1847 | 8/254 |
| Billing, Mary | Simmons, Malachi | Apr 25 1818* | CM |
| Billings, Samuel W | Hart, Bridget Ann | Jun 9 1840* | 5/27B |
| Billings, Samuel W | Cunningham, Bridgett | Sep 9 1846 | 8/188 |
| Billirey, Felix | Stephani, Martha | Oct 14 1845 | 8/119B |
| Bimane, Pauline D | Laurent, Michael | Feb 19 1850 | 11/40 |
| Bine, Elianor J (Band) | Gostenhofer, Lewis | Mar 1 1841 | 4/651B |
| Bindge, John | Miller, Eliza | Apr 6 1842* | 5/190B |
| Bingham, Charles | Malone, Louisa H | Sep 7 1829* | 2/94 |
| Bingler, John | Ellenbek, Maelena | Mar 4 1852 | 11/224 |
| Binzer, William E | Hackmier, Wilhelmina | May 28 1847 | 8/239 |
| Birch, Joseph | Mooney, Jane | Jun 26 1852 | 11/266 |
| Birch, Joseph | Rogers, Bridget | Jan 25 1854 | 13/98 |
| Birch, Julia Ann | Russell, John Y | Apr 12 1842* | 5/192 |
| Birch, William H | Jaymes, Elizabeth J | Aug 19 1854 | 13/316 |
| Bird, Catharine | Delamere, Edward J | Jun 26 1849* | 8/393 |
| Bird, Mary | Doyle, Patrick | May 10 1851 | 11/147 |
| Bird, Polly | Langford, Stephen | 1822* | OIB |
| Birk, Peter | Bryan, Amanda J | May 13 1851* | 11/148 |
| Bissardon, John C | Tarrant, Catharine | Oct 20 1848* | 8/328 |
| Bissell, Elijah | Hopkins, Ann | Dec 28 1850 | 11/106 |
| Bitzer, Margaret | Frank, Lawrence | Oct 29 1844 | 8/46B |
| Bixler, Adeleni | Bensaden, Joseph | Feb 24 1841 | 5/109B |
| Bixley, Edward J | Davis, Adeline | Feb 5 1838* | 3/109 |
| Bizascoa, Camilla | Bobe, Thomas | Nov 29 1832* | 2/1291B |
| Blachenship, William | Eutis, Thaney | 1826* | OIB |
| Black, Ann | Collin, Andrew | Aug 14 1855 | 14/211 |
| Black, John | Corbet, Sarah | May 19 1835 | 3/15 |
| Black, William | Huggins, Phoebe E | Feb 28 1855 | 14/72 |
| Blackledge, Martha C | Mason, Powell | Nov 1 1852 | 12/42 |
| Blackman, Sarah | Davidson, Joseph | May 4 1852* | 11/245 |
| Blackman, Winnie | Baptiste, John | Nov 27 1841 | 5/159B |
| Blackmore, Jane | Lewis, John | Dec 31 1849 | 11/30 |
| Blackwell, Dorcas | Randall, Marcus T | Jun 28 1845 | 8/107B |

| BRIDE OR GROOM | SPOUSE | DATE | BOOK/PAGE |
|---|---|---|---|
| Blair, Ellen C | Rugeley, Alphonse J | Dec 28 1855 | 14/319 |
| Blair, Henry D | Saunders, Mary L | Feb 25 1852* | 11/222 |
| Blair, Rosina | Rutherford, Walter | Sep 15 1849 | 11/5 |
| Blair, Thomas | Damoan, Euphrosie | Jun 12 1815* | CM |
| Blakely, Matilda S | Davis, Isaac S | Apr 6 1841 | 5/121B |
| Blakester, George J | Curtis, Mary G | Feb 22 1844 | 5/324B |
| Blakley, Joel | Casey, Olivia | Jan 10 1855 | 14/9 |
| Blaksley, George J | Curtis, Mary G | Feb 22 1844 | 7/147 |
| Blalock, Allen B | Smith, Mary | Oct 8 1855 | 14/248 |
| Blame, Cecilia Eugenia ? | Bayle, Thomas C (Boyle) | Nov 25 1846 | 8/201 |
| Blansford, Eliza Jane | Robins, Stuart | Feb 27 1837* | 3/73 |
| Blatchley, Laura A | Wyatt, William | Aug 16 1837* | 3/91 |
| Bleeker, Eliza M. | Pinkham, George R | May 26 1819* | CM |
| Blevins, George P | Hopkins, Louisa G | May 4 1846 | 8/163B |
| Blish, Cynthia R | Evans, George | Jul 17 1849* | 8/389 |
| Blish, Samuel K | Ellison, Rehamah | Jan 21 1832* | 2/1751 |
| Bliss, Catherine H | Goodwin, James | Feb 23 1832* | 2/1671 |
| Blissfellows, James | Kirk, Adelia Maria | Dec 31 1851* | 11/200 |
| Bloch, Jeanette | Goldsticker, Abram | Apr 29 1850* | 11/57 |
| Bloch, Joseph | Goldstryker, Hammyrhen | Sep 7 1849 | 11/3 |
| Block, Caroline | Leinkauf, William H | Mar 21 1854 | 13/164 |
| Blocker, Julia M. | Montgomery, John A | Nov 15 1849 | 11/17 |
| Blocker, Virginia M | Thomas, John F | May 2 1855 | 14/127 |
| Bloodgood, M. Hildreth | Kennedy, Augusta | Feb 15 1853 | 12/172 |
| Bloomendelf, Anna | Horlock, John | Jun 11 1840 | 4/4161B |
| Blossine, Francisco | Ginochi, Mary | May 8 1852 | 11/247 |
| Blossman, Sampson | Debeupart, Joanna (?) | Mar 19 1838* | 3/115 |
| Blossman, Sampson | Davenport, Joanna | Mar 19 1838* | 3/115 |
| Blount, Felix E | Miller, Mary M | Sep 13 1855* | 14/230 |
| Blount, Frederick S | James, Emily | Dec 10 1835* | 3/33 |
| Blount, Henry G | Chase, Louisa L | Feb 9 1852 | 11/214 |
| Blue, Mary J | Chapman, John A | Jun 19 1845 | 8/105B |
| Blue, Uriah | Sturtevant, Rebecca | 1827* | OIB |
| Blume, Cecilia Eugenia ? | Bayle, Thomas C (Boyle) | Nov 25 1846 | 8/201 |
| Blundell, Sarah | Mack, William | May 18 1852 | 11/251 |
| Blythe, Rachel | Scott, Mathew | May 1 1854 | 13/212 |
| Boardman, Benjamin F | Ticknor, Mary E | Jul 30 1851 | 11/171 |
| Bob, Joseph (Boh)(Bobe) | Beauzage, Rose M | Apr 20 1846 | 7/572B |
| Bobe, Josephine | Bosmanick, Marco | Nov 15 1854 | 13/378 |
| Bobe, Thomas | Bizascoa, Camilla | Nov 29 1852* | 12/1291 |
| Boch, Sebastien | George, Mary | Apr 11 1853 | 12/231 |
| Bock, Moretz | Gage, Mariana | Jun 27 1853* | 12/332 |
| Bock, Sebastian | Moriarty, Mary | Mar 2 1855 | 14/73 |
| Boda, Elizabeth (Beda) | Collins, Joseph | Sep 22 1842 | 5/220B |
| Boddie, Sidney S | Burks, Martha J | Apr 20 1852 | 11/240 |
| Bodelson, Andrew | Johnson, Bridget | Apr 26 1848* | 8/301 |
| Bodro, Angelie | Bany, Jacob | Jan 21 1841* | 5/91 |
| Boe, Paul | Magestra, Caroline | Apr 27 1849 | 8/371 |
| Bogue, Terrance | Monk, Elizabeth (Mack) | Jul 25 1844 | 8/35B |
| Boh, Joseph | Bearzage, Rose M | Apr 20 1846* | 8/158B |
| Boice, George L | Malone, Parnecia E | May 30 1854 | 13/238 |
| Boislandry, Eugene | Chieusse, L (Lazarus) | 1826* | OIB |
| Boissint, Magdalen | Pierry, John B | Jan 30 1829* | 2/67 |
| Bokey, Margaret | Rodregues, Manuel | Feb 20 1849 | 8/359 |
| Boldz, Henry | Younger, Mary | Feb 16 1841* | 5/104B |
| Boline, Philip | Cachelire, Ursuline | Jun 3 1841 | 4/2491B |
| Boling, Henry | Werner, Amalia Elise | Feb 2 1846* | 8/143B |
| Bolles, Mary T | Roberts, Joel A | Feb 17 1840* | 5/12 |
| Bolling, Julia C | Thurber, William K | Dec 23 1848* | 8/340 |
| Bolman, John | Frink, Eliza | Aug 9 1848 | 8/319 |
| Bolton, Artemissa | Wright, Richard | Jan 31 1850 | 11/36 |
| Bolton, Jane A | Barrow, Jeremiah | May 1 1847 | 8/231 |
| Bolton, Lucinda | Jones, John W | Jul 19 1848* | 8/317 |
| Bolton, Martha | Rainwater, William J | Sep 21 1848 | 8/325 |

| BRIDE OR GROOM | SPOUSE | DATE | BOOK/PAGE |
|---|---|---|---|
| Bolton, Mary E | Pollard, William A | Apr 2 1853 | 12/217 |
| Bolton, Matilda A | Pollard, James | Jun 3 1848 | 8/307 |
| Bolz, Henry | Younger, Mary | Feb 16 1841 | 4/1251B |
| Bomheart, Elizabeth | Holloway, James W | Jun 27 1835* | 3/18 |
| Bonan, Margaret | Chonfreon, Joseph | Jul 12 1852 | 11/269 |
| Bonaville, Elizabeth | Domingo, Joseph | Aug 19 1854 | 13/315 |
| Bondlemann, Henry | Weltz, Rika | Sep 13 1852* | 12/1 |
| Bondurant, E A | Perryman, E S | May 17 1853* | 12/287 |
| Bones, Elizabeth | Stephens, William | Apr 15 1835* | 3/22 |
| Boney, Mary Ann | Caldwell, Stephen B | Apr 21 1841* | 5/126B |
| Bonhagan, Frederick | Jane (NSL) | Nov 16 1843 | 5/305B |
| Boniface, Dominique | Achard, Magdalene | Nov 2 1829 | 2/100 |
| Bonifer, John F (widr) | Auston, Amanda | Oct 20 1853 | 12/321 |
| Bonique, Germaine | Richardson, Lucinda | Jan 27 1842 | 5/174B |
| Bonne, Arthur (Bonare) | Patton, Emily | May 1 1849* | 8/372 |
| Bonne, Octave | Bourrelly, Louise | Jun 25 1844* | 8/30B |
| Boone, Frances | Vincent, David H | Oct 24 1854 | 13/361 |
| Boone, George T | Lang, Angelina | Dec 3 1851* | 11/191 |
| Bonner, William | Hartley, Sarah (wid) | Aug 20 1853 | 12/388 |
| Booth, Eliza | Anderson, Solomon | Feb 25 1833* | 2/1111 |
| Booth, Noah | Sims, Elizabeth | Nov 19 1840* | 5/63B |
| Borden, William J | Gosson, Mary E | Aug 17 1855 | 14/212 |
| Borgan, Francis (Borque) | Vilaceca, Marie | Jun 17 1832 | 2/1461 |
| Borguare, Madelaine | Peters, John | 1827* | OIB |
| Borrow, James | Cohen, Sarah | May 9 1848* | 8/303 |
| Borrowsale, Fearon W ? | Thomson, Margaret McR | 1843* | OIB |
| Borrowscale, Fearon W | Thomson, Margaret M | Jun 9 1842* | 5/205B |
| Borum, James C | Grant, Rachel R | Feb 12 1846 | 8/145B |
| Bosage, Alfred | Gurlot, Melissa | Dec 14 1847 | 8/270 |
| Bosage, Joseph | Benite, Euphrazie | Feb 21 1845 | 8/74B |
| Bosage, Victor | Davison, Betsy | Mar 30 1837* | 3/77 |
| Bosard, Rosalie | Barr, Charles | May 6 1836* | 3/46 |
| Bosarge, Artimese | Galle, Louis | Dec 8 1845 | 8/128B |
| Bosarge, Calvin | Grelott, Louise | Dec 21 1854 | 13/417 |
| Bosarge, Maximillian | Miller, Eliza | Mar 26 1855 | 14/89 |
| Bosc, Mary | Walsh, Thomas | Feb 14 1825 | 1/63 |
| Bosech, Geshine | Odoin, Christian | Aug 8 1850 | 11/78 |
| Bosmanick, Marco | Bobe, Josephine | Nov 15 1854 | 13/378 |
| Bossage, Matilda | Diez, Joseph | Jun 27 1844 | 8/29B |
| Bossarge, Onsue | Cassibry, George | Jun 14 1842 | 5/206B |
| Bossorge, Elizabeth | Tiblin, Victor | Nov 20 1839* | 5/1 |
| Bostock, James B | Juden, Eliza Susan | Apr 2 1846 | 8/154 |
| Bostwick, Rebecca Mck | Stockton, Philip A | Jul 14 1836* | 3/53 |
| Bosworth, Abel W | Weir, Rachel M | Feb 14 1844 | 5/322B |
| Bosworth, Harriet | Brown, Calvin J | Jun 26 1849* | 8/393 |
| Bosworth, William | Crocker, Mary | Jan 21 1848 | 8/280 |
| Bottleman, Frederika | Lusher, Bernard | Jan 21 1854* | 13/91 |
| Botto, Columba | Dere, Nicola | Mar 24 1851 | 11/131 |
| Botto, Rosa Sofia | Costa, Stephen | Apr 19 1851 | 11/139 |
| Bou, Mary | Stranber, Gracomo | Mar 6 1838* | 3/114 |
| Bouch, Rachael | Heiser, John (Imheisen) | Jan 13 1846 | 8/140B |
| Boudin, Alexander H | Jean, Estrazila ? | Oct 10 1838* | 3/143 |
| Boudinet, Sebastian | Gues, Maria A | May 31 1852 | 11/258 |
| Boudini, Judique | Bertrand, Gabriel | May 16 1843 | 5/273B |
| Bouigue, Germain (Bonique) | Richardson, Lucinda | Jan 27 1842 | 5/174B |
| Boullemet, Augustus | Kimball, Cornelia A | Dec 18 1854 | 13/413 |
| Boullemils, Milton | Miller, Eliza Ann | Oct 1 1839* | 3/187 |
| Bounds, Mary Ann D | Tilman, Gideon | Aug 13 1832 | 2/1371 |
| Bourch, Virginia | Cazalas, Francois | Sep 9 1842* | 5/218B |
| Bourrelly, Louise | Bonne, Octave | Jun 25 1844* | 8/30B |
| Bousses, Camille | Latorre, Alvarez | Jan 2 1850 | 11/30 |
| Bousson, John A (widr) | Davis, Margaret (Wid) | Dec 30 1853 | 13/57 |
| Boutin, Francis L L | Dempsey, Susan | 1827* | OIB |
| Bouvier, Mariah | Johnson, Samuel | Jun 30 1838 | 3/135 |

| BRIDE OR GROOM | SPOUSE | DATE | BOOK/PAGE |
|---|---|---|---|
| Bowen, Aribella | King, George F | Dec 1 1853 | 13/32 |
| Bowen, Daniel E (Bowers) | Harrison, Cecelia | Feb 4 1854 | 13/109 |
| Bowen, Edward | Colthar, Sarah P | Apr 17 1855 | 14/107 |
| Bowen, John | Stuart, Sarah | Dec 31 1850 | 11/107 |
| Bowen, Margaret P | Kempe, Thomas B | Apr 9 1849* | 8/366 |
| Bowen, Silas | Seawell, Elizabeth G (Mrs) | 1837* | OIB |
| Bower, Eudora C | Nevill, Samuel L | Jun 6 1848* | 8/308 |
| Bower, John | Rittan, Salley | Apr 11 1837* | 3/80 |
| Bower, John | Lips, Terese | Mar 22 1851 | 11/130 |
| Bowers, Catherine A | Raymond, Hubert N | May 27 1833* | 2/991 |
| Bowers, Francis E | Toulmin, Edmund P | Apr 10 1849* | 8/367 |
| Bowers, Helen M | Sheet, Alexander M | Apr 9 1849* | 8/367 |
| Bowers, Henrietta | Allen, Hamilton | Nov 18 1839* | 5/1 |
| Bowers, Laura Margaret | Muller, Frederick W | Jun 23 1845 | 8/106B |
| Bowers, Lloyd | Toulmin, Louisa Anna | Jun 11 1846* | 8/172 |
| Bowers, Samuel | Robertson, Rachael | Mar 12 1836* | 3/42 |
| Bowman, John | Waverly, Mary | Jan 8 1846 | 8/138B |
| Bowman, William | Jones, Margaret | Apr 14 1838* | 3/119 |
| Bowzer, Caroline | McAdams, Harvey | Nov 8 1849 | 11/15 |
| Box, George W | Turner, Martha | Dec 23 1847 | 8/272 |
| Box, Mary Ann | Bruce, Robert | 1826* | OIB |
| Boyce, Gacy | Quinn, Matthew | Aug 17 1836* | 3/56 |
| Boyd, James P | Little, Florah Ann | Apr 30 1852 | 11/244 |
| Boyden, Angelina | Sullivan, Leonard M | May 10 1847 | 8/234 |
| Boykin, John J | Breshiers, Henrietta | Oct 21 1844* | 8/44B |
| Boykin, June | Dorherty, John | Jan 8 1845* | 8/66B |
| Boykin, Mary Ann | Smith, Charles | Dec 8 1843 | 5/308B |
| Boyla, Margaret | Malone, Martin | 1836* | OIB |
| Boyle, Dennis (Bayle) | Mulligan, Grace | Jan 24 1843 | 5/244B |
| Boyle, William | Spaulding, Elizabeth | 1839* | OIB |
| Boyles, Elizabeth S | Desmukes, Henry J | Jul 12 1848* | 8/316 |
| Boyles, Jane E | Peterson, Frederick | Jan 21 1836* | 3/37 |
| Boyls, Euphame | Gabriel, Thomas | Jul 25 1853 | 12/368 |
| Boyne, Barney (Byrne) | Gill, Mary | Mar 18 1844 | 5/328B |
| Boyne, Samuel (Bozone) | Stafford, Nancy | Jan 23 1832* | 2/1721 |
| Boynton, Eli Everett | Cune, Sarah C | May 3 1847 | 8/232 |
| Boynton, Joseph W | Drew, Lucy | May 9 1838* | 3/124 |
| Boyrus, Terrance (Boyne) | Deburrows, Mary | Feb 20 1852 | 11/219 |
| Bozage, Denny | Lanquet, Elizabeth | Jul 30 1853* | 12/374 |
| Bozage, Edward | Goleman, Lucinda | Jul 13 1846 | 8/177 |
| Bozage, Eugene | Galaway, Rita | Jul 27 1852* | 11/272 |
| Bozage, John B | Grelot, Cecile | Aug 20 1851 | 11/173 |
| Bozage, Joseph | Benite, Euphrazie | Feb 21 1845 | 8/74B |
| Bozage, Louise | Ladiner, Emanuel | Jan 24 1853* | 12/142 |
| Bozage, Matilda | Deiz, Joseph | Jun 27 1844 | 8/29B |
| Bozage, Poline | Clark, Thomas J | Jan 11 1851 | 11/111 |
| Bozage, Sidoine | Fournie, Hemelie | Feb 27 1829* | 2/73 |
| Bozans, Lamas (Bozars) | Ladanair, Claris | Aug 12 1841 | 5/147B |
| Bozard, John | Davidson, Rinna | Apr 29 1844 | 8/17B |
| Bozard, Mary | Miller, George | Aug 25 1838* | 3/140 |
| Bozarge, Artimese | Galle, Louis | Dec 8 1845 | 8/128B |
| Bozarge, Mary | Williams, Alfred | Aug 30 1854 | 13/325 |
| Bozarge, Seadwin | Gallowa(y), Maria | Nov 8 1852* | 12/49 |
| Bozars, Mary | Mon, Benito (Mann) | May 21 1842* | 5/202B |
| Bozars, Virginia | Laurendine, Joseph | Feb 10 1840* | 1/193 |
| Bozone, Samuel | Stafford, Nancy | Jan 23 1832* | 2/1721 |
| Brabman, Ann | Robertson, Jzett | Oct 8 1855 | 14/249 |
| Brabner, Judith | Gilchrist, John | Jan 5 1853 | 12/112 |
| Brace, Thomas W | Wintzill, Ellen | Jun 12 1837* | 3/86 |
| Brack, Roxie | Shepherd, Charles J | Mar 16 1853 | 12/194 |
| Bracken, William R | Chandler, Susan | Aug 2 1841* | 5/144B |
| Brackett, Wm R | Chandler, Susan | Aug 2 1841 | 4/501B |
| Bracy, Samuel | Smith, Jane | Dec 10 1836* | 3/64 |
| Bradford, King | Hart, Elizabeth | Aug 4 1849 | 8/390 |

| BRIDE OR GROOM | SPOUSE | DATE | BOOK/PAGE |
|---|---|---|---|
| Bradley, Andrew | Fox, Sarah | Oct 21 1843 | 5/300B |
| Bradley, Martha A | Myrick, George W | Sep 25 1855 | 14/241 |
| Bradling, Miranda | Cleveland, William F | Jul  7 1835* | 3/19 |
| Brados, Charles | Morow, Camillo | Mar 29 1849 | 8/364 |
| Brady, Ellen | Maloney, William | Apr 27 1849* | 8/371 |
| Brady, John | Cody, Ellen | Aug 26 1841* | 5/150 |
| Brady, John | Cavery, Mary | Apr 18 1854 | 13/192 |
| Brady, Mary | Dees, Willis | Feb 19 1851 | 11/123 |
| Brady, Mary | McLaughlin, Thomas | Jun  5 1841* | 5/135B |
| Brady, Michael | Turpey, Winneford | Feb 14 1854 | 13/121 |
| Brady, Roseanna | Giles, William Lion | Nov 18 1844 | 8/51B |
| Bragg, Catharine A | Walton, Laurence | Apr 15 1847 | 8/228 |
| Brainnan, Betsey | Hensling, Lewis | 1826* | OIB |
| Braitlingen, Maria K | Michael, George | Dec 31 1833* | 2/611 |
| Brakes, Milly E J | Payton, Charles | Mar 30 1852 | 11/231 |
| Bramard, James M | Covington, Mary Jane | Feb 22 1839* | 3/158 |
| Branch, Francis S | Capers, Robert F W | Apr 13 1853 | 12/238 |
| Branch, William H | Christon, Margaret E | Aug 14 1854 | 13/312 |
| Brandein, Margaret Noily | Latour, John | Feb  7 1848* | 8/281 |
| Brandt, David G | Bailey, Harriett | May 29 1840* | 5/24 |
| Branham, Nelly | Wiathers, William | Apr 28 1840* | 5/21 |
| Brannam, Sarah | Mason, John | Sep  3 1846 | 8/187 |
| Brannan, Ann | Valpey, Edward | Aug  4 1840* | 5/37B |
| Brannan, Caroline E | Saulnier, Joseph | Feb 10 1854 | 13/116 |
| Brannan, Dominick T | Bergen, Mary Ann | May 24 1848* | 8/305 |
| Brannan, Eliza | Thomas, William M | Mar  6 1855 | 14/74 |
| Brannan, Elizabeth | Ransifer, Ira E | Jan 28 1837* | 3/70 |
| Brannan, James | Mason, Frances | Sep 12 1834* | 2/161 |
| Brannan, Martha E | Alvarez, Joseph F | Nov  9 1853 | 13/10 |
| Brannan, Nancy | Coston, John W | Dec 17 1853 | 13/43 |
| Brannan, Samuel | Weathers, Becky | Aug 21 1819* | CM |
| Brannan, Samuel | Mason, Cely | 1822* | OIB |
| Brannes, Dorothea | Schumacher, Henry | Jan 16 1838* | 3/107 |
| Branning, William | Malone, Anna | Aug 13 1825 | 1/89 |
| Brantley, Ethlebert | Thompson, Eleanor | Apr 30 1831* | 2/164 |
| Brashears, Alexander M | Harmon, Rachel W | Jan 14 1846 | 7/736B |
| Brashears, Eliza | Benson, Thomas | May 16 1818* | CM |
| Brashears, Emeline | Smith, Ira B | Dec 24 1850 | 11/106 |
| Brashears, Louise Z | Smith, Nathaniel J | Jan  4 1850 | 11/31 |
| Brasheirs, Rachael | Daniel, Asa | Jun 12 1846 | 8/172 |
| Brasheur, Alexander M | Harmon, Rachael W | Jan 14 1846 | 7/736B |
| Brasnolran, Joanna | Lucid, John | Nov 27 1855 | 14/290 |
| Brathard, Ruthy | Smith, Isaac | Feb 27 1824* | 1/23 |
| Bray, Anna Mary | Peterson, John R | Mar 16 1846 | 8/152B |
| Bray, Sophia | Mason, Rufus | May 24 1855 | 14/152 |
| Brazill, F G | Breland, Polly | Jan 13 1845 | 8/66B |
| Brazille, Francisco J | Laverty, Catherine | Mar 12 1842* | 5/186B |
| Breadahbin, C M | Dalton, Julia | Jun  5 1837* | 3/81 |
| Breadalline, C M    ? | Dalton, Julia | 1837* | OIB |
| Breen, Breszy | Holloway, James W | Jun  8 1843 | 5/272B |
| Breinkeninn, Charles | Kistler, Magdalina | Apr 29 1848 | 8/302 |
| Breland, Polly (Bruland) | Brazill, F G | Jan 13 1845 | 86B |
| Brennan, Ann | Kelly, Christopher | Feb  1 1854 | 13/106 |
| Brent, R Carrere | Miller, Janet Elliot | Jul 19 1851 | 11/166 |
| Brereton, Elisabeth | Moore, John P | Dec 11 1852 | 12/85 |
| Breshiers, Henrietta | Boykin, John J | Oct 21 1844* | 8/44B |
| Breswitz, Christian F | Turken, Frina | Jul 26 1844 | 8/36B |
| Brett, Michael | Davidson, Margaret | Mar 24 1852 | 11/230 |
| Brewer, Charles | Flynn, Mary | Apr  1 1843 | 5/257B |
| Brewer, Charles (widr) | Burden, Ellen | Jul 14 1853 | 12/355 |
| Brewer, George | Drew, Julia J | Sep 16 1851 | 11/179 |
| Brewer, Henry O | Hull, Angela  (Hall) | Jan  7 1843 | 5/242B |
| Brewster, Catherine | Collings, George | Nov 23 1837* | 3/101 |
| Brewster, Henry B | Best, Harriett | May 11 1844 | 8/20B |

| BRIDE OR GROOM | SPOUSE | DATE | BOOK/PAGE |
|---|---|---|---|
| Bride, James | Milligan, Ellen (Nelegan) | Nov 27 1850 | 11/100 |
| Bridge, Henry (widr) | Haney, Alice | Jan 29 1853 | 12/156 |
| Bridges, Ann M | Stephenson, John | Dec 18 1838* | 3/A152 |
| Bridges, Charles E | McMillan, Mary E | May 5 1852 | 11/246 |
| Bridges, Elizabeth H | Johnson, William J | Dec 18 1844 | 8/60B |
| Bridgewood, B (Mrs) | Fogger, D W | Oct 2 1852 | 12/18 |
| Briedy, Michael | McCune, Catharine | May 19 1848* | 8/305 |
| Brien, Emily | Hall, Daniel E | May 23 1851 | 11/151 |
| Brien, William | Lodge, Jane | Jul 7 1825* | 1/84 |
| Brient, Adolphus | Dees, Sarah Ann | Aug 20 1845 | 8/115B |
| Brigalie, Charles | Dubracar, Josephine | Nov 29 1853 | 13/29 |
| Bright, Charles J S | Woodcock, Caroline M | Mar 5 1841 | 5/112B |
| Bright, Henry | Pinney, Emeline M | Feb 10 1835 | 3/8 |
| Bright, Michael Jr | George, Adele | Nov 28 1851 | 11/190 |
| Brightman, Latham | Baldwin, Mary E | Dec 31 1851 | 11/199 |
| Briody, Judy | Collins, John | Jun 15 1848* | 8/309 |
| Brison, Eliza | Callahan, William | Apr 28 1842 | 5/195 |
| Britling, Joseph | Alstdorfer, Rosina | Mar 30 1843 | 5/256B |
| Britling, Magdelina | Kaufman, Joseph | Jul 29 1847 | 8/248 |
| Britton, Alexander | Towers, Susan | May 21 1832* | 2/1481 |
| Britton, Harriett E | Kener, Fransna | Oct 11 1843* | 5/299B |
| Broades, Mathew | Rowe, Catherine | Sep 19 1854 | 13/339 |
| Broadhurst, Moses | Rogers, Elizabeth | Oct 5 1820* | CM |
| Brochal, Richard | Burns, Margaret | Dec 10 1842* | 5/233 |
| Brocher, John | Bier, Jenny (Boer) | Nov 3 1853 | 13/5 |
| Brocker, John | Swink, Barbary | Feb 10 1852 | 11/214 |
| Broderick, James | Glorinny, Mary Ann J | Mar 28 1851 | 11/132 |
| Broderick, Margaret | Cannon, Arthur | Feb 2 1852 | 11/210 |
| Broderick, Margaret | Flood, Hugh | Apr 29 1854 | 13/209 |
| Broderick, Thomas | Reynolds, Mary Ann | May 15 1851 | 11/149 |
| Brodie, William | Cummins, Hannah | Jan 7 1854 | 13/64 |
| Broduax, Henry W | Gardim, Emma B | Nov 7 1849 | 11/15 |
| Broduax, Sarah S | Duncan, Robert M | Jan 10 1854 | 13/69 |
| Brook, Nicholas | Badlun, Elizabeth | 1827* | OIB |
| Brookery, Peter | Carrigan, Bridgit | Jan 2 1843 | 5/239B |
| Brookey, Ann | Foley, David | Jan 8 1842 | 5/170B |
| Brooks, Augustus | Everitt, Mary | Feb 4 1835* | 3/7 |
| Brooks, James P | Hughs, Aroline | Mar 24 1845 | 8/81B |
| Brooks, John R | Richards, Mary | Nov 16 1852* | 12/64 |
| Brooks, Louisa M | Sager, Edmund M | Sep 18 1852 | 12/6 |
| Brooks, Robert | Russell, Eliza J | Jan 9 1850 | 11/32 |
| Brookshire, Manning J | Bently, Nancy | Apr 22 1837* | 3/81 |
| Brothers, Patience | Evans, Alfred | Dec 26 1844 | 8/63B |
| Brotherson, Mary | Round, George | Feb 22 1838* | 3/113 |
| Broughton, Elsey M | Tardy, Edwin | Jul 20 1852 | 11/270 |
| Broughton, Mary Ann | Turner, William E | Sep 18 1850 | 11/86 |
| Broughton, Peggy | Hartley, Frederick | Dec 24 1814* | CM |
| Broussard, Clelie | Landry, Dorcilly | Jan 22 1851 | 11/115 |
| Browhe, Margaret | Denhew, Daniel | Jan 22 1855 | 14/21 |
| Brown, Alexander | Ruse, Maria Louisa | Jul 28 1847* | 8/248 |
| Brown, Alexander | Connors, Ann | Jan 21 1853 | 12/139 |
| Brown, Alexander G | Pitch, Sarah | Jan 26 1850 | 11/35 |
| Brown, Ann | Haynie, John D | Jun 12 1837* | 3/88 |
| Brown, Ann | Martin, Felix | Nov 22 1843* | 5/306B |
| Brown, Ann Marie | Geller, Jean Marie | Feb 5 1839* | 3/155 |
| Brown, Barbara | Forest, Alexander | Jan 1 1838* | 3/106 |
| Brown, Betsey Lena | Clow, Peter | Apr 30 1847 | 8/231 |
| Brown, Brinkley | Pierce, Matilda | 1827* | OIB |
| Brown, Brinkley J | Tucker, Aceline | Aug 9 1855 | 14/207 |
| Brown, Calvin J | Bosworth, Harriett | Jun 26 1849* | 8/393 |
| Brown, Catharine | DeBoure, John | Mar 22 1849* | 8/363 |
| Brown, Catherine E (Mrs) | Parish, Walter A | Dec 19 1845 | 8/131B |
| Brown, Charles D | Mordecai, Mary E | Jan 18 1854 | 13/86 |
| Brown, Easter | Gleason, John | Jun 18 1853 | 12/322 |

| BRIDE OR GROOM | SPOUSE | DATE | BOOK/PAGE |
|---|---|---|---|
| Brown, Edward | Hagan, Rosannah | May 30 1836* | 3/48 |
| Brown, Edward | Jackson, Catherine | Nov 18 1850 | 11/98 |
| Brown, Eliza | Simmons, Butler | Apr 14 1843* | 5/261B |
| Brown, Eliza | Griffin, William | Nov 13 1852 | 12/62 |
| Brown, Elizabeth | Vandergriff, Earle | Feb 12 1855 | 14/48 |
| Brown, Emily A | Campbell, Alexander | Jul 11 1851 | 11/164 |
| Brown, George | Deese, Creisey (wid) | Oct 19 1853 | 12/419 |
| Brown, George L | Caro, Josephine A | Jan 1 1849* | 8/343 |
| Brown, Herman H | Rush, Eliza | Sep 27 1854 | 13/341 |
| Brown, Hyram W | Buck, Amanda D | Oct 3 1837* | 3/92 |
| Brown, James | McManus, Ann | Apr 20 1854 | 13/197 |
| Brown, Jane | Hughes, Edward | Dec 21 1842 | 5/237B |
| Brown, Jane | Rasher, Redding | Jul 9 1828* | 2/36 |
| Brown, John | Toomey, Margaret | Aug 21 1852 | 11/278 |
| Brown, John | Ritter, Henrietta | Jan 4 1840* | 5/6 |
| Brown, John M | Lord, Rebecca | Feb 11 1835* | 3/8 |
| Brown, John M | Winston, Mary J (Winslow) | Jan 7 1843 | 5/242B |
| Brown, John M | Brown, Sarah M | Nov 15 1849 | 11/16 |
| Brown, Joseph | Robertson, S.J. | Nov 3 1836* | 3/61 |
| Brown, Joshua | Fitzgerald, Eliza | Oct 30 1849 | 11/12 |
| Brown, Josiah I (Jonah) | Downer, Louisa A | May 14 1842 | 5/200B |
| Brown, Laura | Chase, Samuel | Jul 19 1836* | 3/53 |
| Brown, Louisa A | Goodman, James M | Oct 30 1850 | 11/93 |
| Brown, Lucinda | McKay, Charles | Jul 8 1854 | 13/278 |
| Brown, Margaret | Thompson, Jeremiah R | Sep 26 1844 | 8/42B |
| Brown, Martha P | Jennings, William E | Jan 26 1833* | 2/1191 |
| Brown, Mary | Davis, Nicholas | 1837* | 0IB |
| Brown, Mary | Walker, Granville | Nov 27 1843 | 5/307B |
| Brown, Mary | Fulham, Patrick | May 22 1854 | 13/231 |
| Brown, Mary R (wid) | Chastang, Pierre | Mar 15 1833 | 2/1071 |
| Brown, Matilda | Traites, John | Aug 6 1843 | 5/291B |
| Brown, May | Mann, John | Apr 28 1823 | 1/2 |
| Brown, Morgan D | Tompkins, Harriet | Dec 23 1824 | 1/57 |
| Brown, N Harleston | Deas, Mary C | Dec 24 1850 | 11/105 |
| Brown, Noah | Pegin, Lucinda | Nov 6 1844 | 8/48B |
| Brown, P P | Ewing, Cornelia J | Feb 10 1840* | 3/193 |
| Brown, Patrick | Justice, Ann | Dec 6 1844 | 8/56B |
| Brown, Perino | McKern, Georgia B | Oct 24 1850* | 11/92 |
| Brown, Peter | Hurley, Catherine | Jan 12 1854* | 13/75 |
| Brown, Peter L | Dyas, Ann | Aug 27 1851 | 11/173 |
| Brown, Phillis | Allen, Charles | Nov 16 1843 | 5/305B |
| Brown, Rebecca | Clarke, Charles | Aug 13 1838* | 3/138 |
| Brown, Robert S | Richards, Eugenia | Apr 3 1846 | 8/155B |
| Brown, Samuel | Colthu, Elsy A (Colthar) | Mar 19 1839* | 3/161 |
| Brown, Sarah G | Rawls, Thomas H | Oct 27 1853 | 12/425 |
| Brown, Sarah M | Brown, John M | Nov 15 1849 | 11/16 |
| Brown, Susanna | Frazier, John | Oct 19 1846 | 8/195 |
| Brown, Thomas | Roach, Lucinda | Jun 26 1843* | 5/284B |
| Brown, Thomas G | Sanford, Mary A (Emily A) | Aug 5 1840* | 5/39B |
| Brown, Thomas H | Hollowell, Elizabeth | May 4 1847 | 8/233 |
| Brown, Watler C | Labidir, Marlezett | May 29 1839* | 3/175 |
| Brown, William | Tribb, Margaret | May 31 1839* | 3/175 |
| Brown, William | Neville, Hannah | Feb 2 1841* | 5/99B |
| Brown, William L | Lewis, Martha | Aug 10 1842 | 5/215B |
| Brown, Willie B | Rawls, Francis | Dec 22 1841 | 5/164B |
| Brownejohn, Thomas | Souchet, Amelia | Mar 19 1825 | 1/69 |
| Browning, Joseph S | McKeen, Martha A | Oct 19 1846 | 8/194 |
| Browning, Matilda | Slocum, John | Dec 4 1838* | 3/151 |
| Brownjohn, Amelia | Christian, Benjamin R | Aug 31 1832* | 2/1361 |
| Bruce, Elizabeth Welch | Penny, Samuel | May 21 1845 | 8/96B |
| Bruce, James | McCallum, Jane | Feb 28 1840* | 5/13 |
| Bruce, John P | Bullock, Mary F | Mar 12 1849* | 8/361 |
| Bruce, Mary Ann | Johnson, John | Jul 6 1839 | 3/181 |
| Bruce, Robert | Stevenson, Betsey | 1822* | 0IB |

18

| BRIDE OR GROOM | SPOUSE | DATE | BOOK/PAGE |
|---|---|---|---|
| Bruce, Robert | Box, Mary Ann | 1826* | 0IB |
| Bruce, Thomas W | Wintzell, Ellen | Jun 12 1837* | 3/86 |
| Brue, Benoy | Lorant, Matilda | Jun 19 1855 | 14/177 |
| Brue, Lawrence | DuBroca, Josephine | Aug 10 1824 | 1/36 |
| Bruland, Polly | Brazill, F G | Jan 13 1845 | 8/66 |
| Brunsled, Henry B | Havens, Ann | Oct 20 1839* | 3/189 |
| Bruse, William C (Bruce) | Edmond, Cornelia | May  2 1838* | 3/122 |
| Brusenhauer, Ellen | Pierce, Patrick | Jan 22 1852 | 11/207 |
| Brushears, Alexander M | Haverman, Rachel W | Jan 14 1846 | 8/140 |
| Bryan, Amanda J | Birk, Peter | May 13 1851* | 11/148 |
| Bryan, Isaac | Quarles, Julia Ann | Jul 15 1830 | 2/132 |
| Bryan, Martin Hansen | Harris, Elizabeth | Dec 15 1851 | 11/194 |
| Bryan, Mary Louisa | Jones, William B | May 21 1853 | 12/270 |
| Bryan, Rebecca Ann | Williams, Benjamin | Jul  3 1844 | 8/31B |
| Bryant, Adolphus | Beard, Sarah (Mrs) | Dec  9 1840* | 5/73B |
| Bryant, John E | Flanegan, Catherine | Apr 11 1853 | 12/234 |
| Bryant, Joseph | Smith, Catharine A | Oct 17 1842* | 5/224 |
| Bryars, Laz I | Smith, Mary | Oct  4 1816* | CM |
| Bryne, Benny | Gill, Mary | Mar 18 1844 | 5/328B |
| Brynes, Catherine | McGrime, Thomas | May  2 1843 | 5/267 |
| Bryran, George | Rainwater, Eliz. | Dec 13 1845* | 8/130B |
| Bryson, Frances | Pennington, James | Dec 19 1836* | 3/65 |
| Bryson, Symintha (wid) | Biers, Henderson | Nov  1 1853 | 13/2 |
| Buch, Julia Ann (Burch) | Rupall, John G (Russall) | Apr 15 1842 | 6/118B |
| Buchanan, Betsey Ann | Russell, Albert R | Dec 31 1852 | 12/108 |
| Buchanan, Henry | Nixon, Maria L | Apr  6 1841* | 5/121B |
| Buck, Amanda D | Brown, Hyram W | Oct  3 1837* | 3/92 |
| Buck, William A | Langdon, Margaret | Oct 28 1852 | 12/37 |
| Buck, William J | Chastang, Mary L | Jan 10 1854 | 13/68 |
| Buckanan, William | Alexander, Elizabeth | Feb 27 1839* | 3/158 |
| Buckhotts, Martha | Smoot, Joseph H | Jun 12 1855 | 14/171 |
| Buckley, Caroline (Racklus) | Heppler, Charles | Nov 14 1840 | 5/61B |
| Buckley, Catherine | Corbatt, Dennis | Jan 28 1841* | 5/95B |
| Buckley, Ellen | Fitzgerald, Daniel | Jan 20 1841* | 5/97B |
| Buckley, Horace | Martin, Elizabeth | Nov 26 1842 | 5/229B |
| Buckley, Johannah | Ives, John | Apr  9 1853 | 12/225 |
| Buckley, Martha C | Ryan, Moses | Apr 16 1844* | 8/14B |
| Buckley, Mary | Sullivan, David | Dec  3 1837* | 3/102 |
| Buckley, Morris | Conklin, Anne | Apr 13 1847 | 8/227 |
| Buckley, Rebecca | Vines, Charles | Mar  7 1835 | 3/10 |
| Buckley, Rosa | Smith, Sylvester | 1837* | 3/85 |
| Buckman, John | Driscoll, Mary Ann | May 16 1846 | 8/166B |
| Buckman, Mary A H | Whitfield, James K | Feb  1 1848 | 8/280 |
| Budelman, Henry | Weltz, Rika | Sep 13 1852* | 12/1 |
| Budlong, Rebecca A J | Read, Alvin A | Jan 14 1854 | 13/79 |
| Bufkins, Benjamin F | Sullivan, Jemimy | Feb  9 1854 | 13/114 |
| Buler, George W | Dunnington, Martha | May 12 1842 | 5/200B |
| Bull, Alfred | Powers, Mary | Feb  5 1838* | 3/110 |
| Bull, Sarah C | Roberts, William H | Apr 25 1854 | 13/203 |
| Bullard, James | Deakle, Mary | Sep  2 1853* | 12/399 |
| Bullard, Samuel P | Phillips, Mary | Oct 22 1834* | 3/5 |
| Bullard, Samuel P | Converse, Phibe (Phoebe) | Mar 21 1838* | 3/116 |
| Bullock, Erasmus D | Chaney, Helen E | Jan 14 1841* | 5/87 |
| Bullock, Jonathan | Acre, Elizabeth | Mar  2 1833* | 2/1091 |
| Bullock, Mary F | Bruce, John P | Mar 12 1849* | 8/361 |
| Bullock, William F | Smith, Martha E | Apr 18 1848 | 8/299 |
| Buman, Christian (Berman) | King, Ellen | Jan  3 1843 | 5/240B |
| Bumhaur, Alonzo H (Barnham) | Sercy, Eliza (Sarah) | Apr 21 1838* | 3/120 |
| Bunce, Mary E | Carter, William P | Nov  4 1847 | 8/263 |
| Bunce, Thomas | Cox, Eliza | Jan 29 1828 | 2/6 |
| Bunch, Mary | Wolcott, John | Nov  1 1851 | 11/185 |
| Bunch, Richard L | Smith, Margaret | Jul 21 1846 | 8/180 |
| Bunnell, William H | Leeman, Elizabeth | Mar 19 1842* | 5/187B |
| Buquiet, Elizabeth | Sarrouil, Pascal | Nov 24 1846 | 8/201 |

| BRIDE OR GROOM | SPOUSE | DATE | BOOK/PAGE |
|---|---|---|---|
| Burbe, Anne | Gomez, Laurence | Aug 3 1847* | 8/249 |
| Burden, Ellen | Brewer, Charles (widr) | Jul 14 1853 | 12/355 |
| Burgan, Adeline | Stouder, Frances | Sep 26 1844 | 8/41B |
| Burge, John | Hesley, Hannah (Herley) | Aug 14 1851 | 11/172 |
| Burge, John M (Bindge) | Miller, Eliza | Apr 6 1842 | 5/190B |
| Burge, Mary Olevia | Cannon, Alfred W | Dec 28 1839* | 5/5 |
| Burgess, Ann Elizabeth | Ellison, Robert C | Jan 4 1834* | 2/581 |
| Burgess, Jeanie | Anderson, Andrew | Aug 16 1852 | 11/275 |
| Burgess, Joshua P (widr) | Offin, Cecelia J (wid) | Apr 30 1853 | 12/261 |
| Burgess, Phebbe | Thompson, Benjamin | Jul 28 1842 | 5/212B |
| Burgett, Barbara | Fuller, Lewis | Feb 8 1848 | 8/281 |
| Burgmiere, Simon | Ramstein, Agatha | Nov 14 1836* | 3/62 |
| Burguan, Jacob | Stouder, Elizabeth | Jul 2 1844 | 8/31B |
| Burh, Patrick (Burk) | Kelly, Eliza | May 23 1855 | 14/149 |
| Burien, J | Chestang, Clair | 1822* | 0IB |
| Burk, Eliza | Wills, Nelson | Feb 20 1847 | 8/218 |
| Burk, Farley | Hill, Bridget | Feb 7 1852 | 11/213 |
| Burk, Jane | Gomez, Lorenzo | Jun 19 1847 | 8/242 |
| Burk, Martin (Buck) | Ullman, Barbara | Aug 8 1843* | 5/291B |
| Burk, Mary | Cusak, William | May 2 1852 | 11/245 |
| Burk, Patrick | Kelly, Eliza | May 23 1855 | 14/149 |
| Burke, Ann | McDonald, Andrew | Aug 4 1847 | 8/249 |
| Burke, Anna | Wolfe, Udolpho | Jan 11 1842* | 5/170B |
| Burke, Anne | Haggerty, Patrick | Sep 10 1842* | 5/219B |
| Burke, Catherine | Halpan, Matthew | Dec 3 1852 | 12/81 |
| Burke, Charlotte | Orr, Joseph | Oct 23 1846 | 8/195 |
| Burke, Edward K (Edmund) | Hemmingway, Ann | Aug 1 1838* | 3/137 |
| Burke, Eliza | Casey, Owen | Feb 22 1841* | 5/108B |
| Burke, Johanna | Connor, Patrick O' (widr) | Jul 14 1853 | 12/354 |
| Burke, John (Bart) | Morris, Mary | Jun 19 1845* | 8/105B |
| Burke, John | Kain(e), Mary | Apr 2 1853 | 12/215 |
| Burke, John M | Ezell, Eliza | Apr 11 1838 | 3/118 |
| Burke, John M | Alexander, Virginia | Dec 13 1844 | 8/59B |
| Burke, Louise | Hannevig, John | Mar 30 1854 | 13/168 |
| Burke, Margaret | Thompson, Thomas | Jun 24 1835* | 3/18 |
| Burke, Margaret | Elsworth, George L | Feb 15 1847 | 8/218 |
| Burke, Margaret | Collins, William | Jun 14 1854 | 13/255 |
| Burke, Margaret | Diveni, Michael | Aug 13 1853 | 12/381 |
| Burke, Mary | Rahilly, Thomas H | Feb 20 1855 | 14/64 |
| Burke, Mary A | Russell, Adolphus | Jul 17 1854 | 13/286 |
| Burke, Michael | O'Brien, Catherine | Nov 25 1852 | 12/74 |
| Burke, Thomas | Frye, Rosana | Oct 20 1842 | 5/225B |
| Burke, Thomas | Sweeney, Maria | Dec 11 1841 | 5/161B |
| Burkhardt, Charles B | Morgan, Mary | May 8 1841* | 5/129B |
| Burks, Lucretia T | Connoly, Levi | Oct 12 1852 | 12/28 |
| Burks, Martha J | Boddie, Sidney S | Apr 20 1852 | 11/240 |
| Burlison, Sally | Clark, Ebenezer | Oct 7 1828 | 2/43 |
| Burn, Jane (Burr) | Volkining, Fredrick | Jan 24 1842 | 5/173B |
| Burnara, Frances J | Allen, Sarah | Dec 13 1842 | 5/233 |
| Burnes, Eliza | Ryals, Henry | Apr 6 1837* | 3/79 |
| Burnes, Mary | Thompson, Thomas | Mar 7 1849 | 8/360 |
| Burnes, William S | Huxham, Mary | Jul 12 1848* | 8/316 |
| Burnett, Eliza C | Canterbury, Levi B | Jul 15 1854 | 13/283 |
| Burnett, Jane | Cooney, James | Apr 24 1851 | 11/141 |
| Burney, James D | Harris, Elisabeth | May 18 1852 | 11/251 |
| Burnham, Alonzo H | Quinn, Patience | Mar 12 1830* | 2/117 |
| Burns, Alice | Kelly, Joseph | Jan 19 1850 | 11/34 |
| Burns, Anna M (Beers) | Hamilton, Peter | Dec 26 1840* | 5/81B |
| Burns, Catherine | Havens, Joseph | Apr 10 1847 | 8/225 |
| Burns, Ellen | Shield, Cornelius | Jul 25 1840* | 5/37B |
| Burns, Frances | Goode, Garland | Nov 26 1846* | 8/202 |
| Burns, James | Shields, Elizabeth | Dec 30 1840* | 5/71B |
| Burns, James | Lawler, Jane | Mar 18 1854 | 13/161 |
| Burns, Jane (June) | Jones, Nathan | Jul 7 1845 | 8/109B |

| BRIDE OR GROOM | SPOUSE | DATE | BOOK/PAGE |
|---|---|---|---|
| Burns, Margaret | Brochal, Richard | Dec 10 1842* | 5/233 |
| Burns, Margaret | Jarvis, Thomas | Apr 10 1844 | 8/11B |
| Burns, Mary | Martin, Felix | Jan 22 1842 | 5/172B |
| Burns, Mary | Fountain, David | Jul 13 1846* | 8/178 |
| Burns, Oliver S (Beers) | Hogan, Amelia E | Feb 23 1842* | 5/182B |
| Burns, Robert | McDonald, Catherine | Aug 4 1846 | 8/183 |
| Burns, Sarah | Carey, Daniel | May 19 1853 | 12/292 |
| Burns, Susan | Lee, William | Feb 18 1847 | 8/218 |
| Burns, Thomas | Vanatta, Mary E | Feb 3 1851 | 11/119 |
| Burnside, Andrew | Armer, Agnes | Dec 20 1823 | 1/17 |
| Burnstein, Bevert | Markstein, A | Feb 26 1850* | 11/43 |
| Burrows, Elizabeth | Laurendine, Peter | Feb 22 1814* | WB 1/17 |
| Burs, Caroline E S (Beers) | Campbell, William | Jun 7 1843 | 5/279B |
| Burt, Margaret M | Wood, Edwin T | Feb 18 1850 | 11/40 |
| Burwell, John G | DeBose, Rebecca | Jan 1 1849 | 8/343 |
| Burwell, John G | Covington, Matilda | Mar 31 1855 | 14/94 |
| Busbee, Marande | Payne, John | Jan 21 1852 | 11/205 |
| Busby, Maria | Young, Alexander | Aug 30 1852 | 11/280 |
| Busby, Milinda | Stewart, Gershom N | Aug 17 1854 | 13/314 |
| Busby, William | Grimes, Phoebe | Jun 2 1851 | 11/153 |
| Buscail, Francis | Gowrner, Josephine | Aug 13 1840 | 4/2401B |
| Bush, Ann | Bush, Henry | Jun 27 1851 | 11/161 |
| Bush, David | Carrall, Susanna | Jan 17 1849* | 8/348 |
| Bush, Hannah | Vaughner, John | Jan 10 1834* | 2/561 |
| Bush, Henry | Bush, Ann | Jun 27 1851 | 11/161 |
| Bush, Marshall | Page, Martha (Mrs) | Jun 12 1850 | 11/66 |
| Buss, Mary Elizabeth | Mavro, Joseph | Sep 11 1846 | 8/188 |
| Butler, Bridget | Martin, Felix | Nov 12 1842 | 5/227B |
| Butler, Cinderella | Miller, Peter J | Feb 10 1834* | 2/471 |
| Butler, Edward | Mulaugh, Ellen | Jul 15 1853 | 12/358 |
| Butler, Francis | Muxon, Mary (Maxson) | Jan 9 1850 | 11/32 |
| Butler, George B | Tapp, Anna M | Jan 13 1831* | 2/146 |
| Butler, Joseph | Paris, Sarah | Aug 15 1836* | 3/56 |
| Butler, Laird M | Robertson, Maria L | May 16 1850 | 11/61 |
| Butler, Martin | Hines, Mary | Jul 2 1842 | 5/209B |
| Butler, Mary | McDonald, Daniel | Feb 20 1845 | 8/70B |
| Butler, Mary | Felis, Sebastian | May 8 1850 | 11/60 |
| Butler, Mary | Forley, Edwin (Farley) | May 16 1851 | 11/150 |
| Butler, Sage O | Gazzam, Mary A | Jun 10 1833* | 2/941 |
| Butler, Samuel | Stewart, Martha | Sep 2 1853 | 12/398 |
| Butler, William | Tuney, Mary Ann | Apr 5 1847 | 8/224 |
| Butler, William | Larkins, Ann | Jun 1 1855 | 14/156 |
| Butt, Cary W | Heard, Ann B | Aug 22 1849* | 8/399 |
| Butt, Martha A | Seawell, William B | Nov 29 1852 | 12/78 |
| Buzhart, Thomas | Fountain, Polly | Jul 11 1825 | 1/86 |
| Byard, Garrett H | Hogan, Ann M | May 31 1837* | 3/85 |
| Byers, James M | Marshall, Parmelia | May 30 1836* | 3/48 |
| Byran, Patrick C | Haynes, Clara S | Feb 24 1841 | 4/3001B |
| Byrd, Berry | George, Caroline | 1837* | OIB |
| Byrd, Caroline | Byrd, Lemuel | Oct 23 1848 | 8/329 |
| Byrd, Eliza | Clark, Charles | Jul 19 1847 | 8/246 |
| Byrd, James | Harris, Julia A | Aug 6 1845 | 8/115B |
| Byrd, Jesse | Langforth, Judith | 1823* | OIB |
| Byrd, Lemuel | Byrd, Caroline | Oct 23 1848 | 8/329 |
| Byrd, Robert | Lott, Marion | Jul 15 1835* | 3/20 |
| Byrd, Sarah | George, Joseph | Aug 6 1831 | 2/179 |
| Byrde, Elizabeth | Dyas, John | Sep 14 1847* | 8/256 |
| Byrne, Ann | Wilson, James | Dec 11 1823* | 1/15 |
| Byrne, Elizabeth | Batt, Charles E | Aug 2 1849 | 8/385 |
| Byrne, Hugh | Callahan, Sarah | Feb 2 1853 | 12/16C |
| Byrne, James | Dailey, Margarett | Apr 23 1840* | 5/2C |
| Byrne, John | Purtell, Mary | Jan 10 1854 | 13/66 |
| Byrne, Mary | McMahon, James | Nov 28 1848* | 8/335 |
| Byrne, Patrick | Caperton, Catherine (wid) | Feb 1 1816* | CM |

| BRIDE OR GROOM | SPOUSE | DATE | BOOK/PAGE |
|---|---|---|---|
| Byrne, Patrick | Everett, Margaret | Jan 4 1851 | 11/109 |
| Byrne, Patrick Timothy | Mitchell, Rosanna | Dec 17 1841 | 5/163B |
| Byrne, Peter C | Hagnes, Claresa | Feb 24 1841* | 5/109 |
| Byrnes, Andrew | Welsh, Mary | Nov 22 1852 | 12/69 |
| Byrnes, Andrew | Doran, Catherine | Dec 2 1854 | 13/396 |
| Byrnes, Ann | Seaman, John | Jul 14 1854 | 13/281 |
| Byrnes, Ann | Wardue, Patrick | Feb 17 1854 | 13/123 |
| Byrnes, Bridget | Morris, Michael | Aug 14 1843 | 5/292B |
| Byrnes, Catherine | McGraine, Thomas | May 2 1843* | 5/205B |
| Byrnes, Charles | Tracy, Ellen | Apr 30 1855 | 14/125 |
| Byrnes, Denis | McGrath, Ann | May 16 1843 | 5/273B |
| Byrnes, Dennis | Linehan, Fanny | Jan 30 1849* | 8/351 |
| Byrnes, James | McCabe, Catherine | May 25 1846 | 8/169B |
| Byrnes, John | Fitzsimmons, Sarah | Mar 5 1832* | 2/1661 |
| Byrnes, Mary | Bender, John | Jul 9 1825* | 1/85 |
| Byrnes, Mary | Doyle, Andrew | Apr 15 1852 | 11/237 |
| Byrnes, Michael | Keen, Catherine | Dec 2 1835* | 3/32 |
| Byrnes, Moses | Barry, Margaret | Sep 20 1855 | 14/235 |
| Byrnes, Thomas | McAfee, Eliza | Feb 27 1843 | 5/251B |
| Byrnes, William | Whatley, Rebecca | 1827* | OIB |
| Byrns, Margaret | Robinson, Patrick | Oct 2 1852 | 12/17 |

## C

| | | | |
|---|---|---|---|
| Cabaniss, William P | Clark, Annette E | Jun 12 1855 | 14/169 |
| Cachelire, Ursuline | Boline, Philip | Jun 3 1841 | 4/2491 |
| Cade, Joseph | Pollard, Eliza | Oct 3 1833* | 2/741 |
| Cadet, Barbara | Newbold, Thomas G | May 22 1815* | CM |
| Cady, Harriett (Cosey) | Jewell, Robert | Dec 3 1842 | 5/231B |
| Caffie, Alice | Kelly, Peter | Feb 24 1846 | 8/147B |
| Cahall, Alfred B | Sullivan, Ellen B | Aug 20 1855 | 14/214 |
| Cahill, James | Garvey, Margaret (Mrs) | Sep 12 1843* | 5/296B |
| Cahill, Patrick | Leahy, Bridget (Leary) | Jul 3 1854 | 13/272 |
| Caille, Adolphus | Massey, Mary A | 1837* | OIB |
| Caille, Augusta | Read, Quartus M | Jan 9 1855 | 14/6 |
| Cain, Anna | Murphy, John | Apr 14 1853 | 12/239 |
| Cain, Anna Margaret | Bancroft, George | Jun 25 1833* | 2/921 |
| Cain, Jesse | Lassabe, Emma | Dec 2 1841 | 5/160B |
| Cain, John | O'Mealy, Cicily | Apr 10 1854 | 13/177 |
| Cain, Joseph S | Rabby, Elizabeth A | May 15 1855 | 14/141 |
| Cain, Margaret | Norton, Thomas | Jan 14 1843* | 5/243 |
| Cain, Thomas | Jordan, Mary | Mar 17 1845 | 8/79B |
| Caing, John ? | Watson, Agnes | Jun 26 1854 | 13/265 |
| Cairns, Bridget | Smith, Michael | Feb 25 1854 | 13/140 |
| Calahan, Julia | Sullivan, Jeremiah | Mar 23 1842 | 5/187B |
| Calahan, Philip | Cochrane, Ellen | Nov 20 1841* | 5/158B |
| Calahan, Polly | Pollard, William | Jun 2 1834* | 2/241 |
| Calcina, Joseph | Raffin, Delphine | Nov 18 1844 | 8/51B |
| Calderon, Francis | Theodore, Mary | Jun 2 1831 | 2/175 |
| Caldwell, Ariann A | Logan, Benjamin B | Aug 18 1853 | 12/385 |
| Caldwell, Cyrus | Kinney, Ellen | Jun 4 1836* | 3/49 |
| Caldwell, John F | Plum, Mary A | Jul 6 1844 | 8/32 |

| BRIDE OR GROOM | SPOUSE | DATE | BOOK/PAGE |
|---|---|---|---|
| Caldwell, Mary Ann (Mrs) | Peden, John W | Aug  5 1841* | 5/146B |
| Caldwell, Mary A | Travis, John H | May 17 1854 | 13/227 |
| Caldwell, Stephen B | Boney, Mary Ann | Apr 21 1841* | 5/126B |
| Caleb, John  (Calep) | Wilson, Sarah | Feb 28 1843 | 5/251B |
| Caleb, John | Arnold, Elizabeth | Feb 21 1848 | 8/285B |
| Calhelm, Ursuline | Boline, Philip | Jun  5 1841 | 5/135B |
| Callaghan, Catherine | Finner, Patrick | Jan  7 1837* | 3/68 |
| Callaghan, Charlotte F O | Elliott, James  G | Jun  3 1840* | 5/26B |
| Callaghan, Julia | Dally, Michael (Daily) | 1837* | OIB |
| Callaghan, Margarette | McDonald, Thomas | Jun 12 1837* | 3/87 |
| Callaghan, Mary | Nicholson, Charles | Jul 13 1850 | 11/72 |
| Callahan, Amanda | Goodwin, John | Dec 27 1837* | 3/106 |
| Callahan, Bridget | Longhurst, George | Jan 23 1851* | 11/116 |
| Callahan, Catharine | Callahan, Matthias B | Dec  2 1848* | 8/336 |
| Callahan, Catharine | McClenachan, James | Jul 16 1845 | 8/111B |
| Callahan, Joanna | Conner, Patrick | Apr 26 1848* | 8/301 |
| Callahan, John | Phillips, Elizabeth | Dec  9 1839* | 5/3 |
| Callahan, Lucinda | Ellis, Delano | Jul 29 1854* | 13/297 |
| Callahan, Margaret  (wid) | Lyon, Daniel | Jul 23 1853 | 12/366 |
| Callahan, Mary | Pollard, William | Jan 20 1836 | 3/37 |
| Callahan, Mathias B | Callahan, Catharine | Dec  2 1848* | 8/336 |
| Callahan, Sarah | Byrne, Hugh | Feb  2 1853 | 12/160 |
| Callahan, William | Brison, Eliza (Prison) | Apr 28 1842 | 5/195B |
| Callan, James  (Cullan?) | McGrain, Ann | Feb 21 1848* | 8/285 |
| Callan, James | Grinnell, Bridget | May  2 1835* | 3/23 |
| Callan, Patrick | Cassady, Mary | Mar 28 1842 | 5/188B |
| Callaway, George | Cohen, E R | Oct  2 1838* | 3/142 |
| Callen, Ellen | Gwin, Thomas | Jan 28 1842 | 5/175 |
| Calloway, Frances Amanda | Turner, Oliver | Apr 21 1841* | 5/125B |
| Calloway, Mary | Turner, Henry | Aug  4 1835* | 3/21 |
| Calon, Jane S | Cordier, Charles | Jul 18 1848 | 8/317 |
| Calvert, Mary M | Wilkes, William | Aug  1 1840* | 5/37B |
| Calvert, William | Flaut, Caroline | Jun 16 1831* | 2/176 |
| Calvin, Thomas | Riley, Mary Ann | Oct 22 1833* | 2/751 |
| Cambron, Levi | Hull, Hannah | Jun 13 1833* | 2/931 |
| Cameron, Alexander | Toomey, Mary | Jan  4 1845 | 8/65B |
| Cameron, Allen | Clark, Mary | Nov 23 1852 | 12/72 |
| Cameron, John Jr | Thompson, Ann | Dec 14 1846 | 8/205 |
| Cameron, Roderick | Denney, Bridget | Mar 10 1855 | 14/78 |
| Camody, Catherine | McMahon, Michael | Apr  1 1854 | 13/171 |
| Campbell, Agnes | Sheppard, C | Oct 15 1845 | 8/120B |
| Campbell, Alexander | Brown, Emily A | Jul 11 1851 | 11/164 |
| Campbell, Caledonia | Morton, William  S | Nov 20 1852 | 12/65 |
| Campbell, Edward | Hollinger, Margt. | Jul 30 1847 | 8/248 |
| Campbell, Eliza | Spears, Edward | Feb 13 1849* | 8/356 |
| Campbell, Frances | McCloud, Charles | Mar  5 1849* | 8/360 |
| Campbell, Hellen E | George, Edward V | Mar 16 1853 | 12/193 |
| Campbell, James | Toulmin, Mary C | Jan 14 1824 | 1/19 |
| Campbell, James W | Wright, Sarah Ann | Jan  4 1849 | 8/345 |
| Campbell, Jane | Lee, George | Jul 19 1851 | 11/167 |
| Campbell, Mary | Creighton, William | Sep 24 1834* | 2/131 |
| Campbell, Mary | Morris, Mathew | Jul  8 1851 | 11/163 |
| Campbell, Mary | St John, Richard | Sep  5 1854 | 13/331 |
| Campbell, Mary | Gartman, Philip | Jun  2 1855 | 14/157 |
| Campbell, Mary | Dilleport, George | Jan 25 1854 | 13/96 |
| Campbell, Mary Ann | Anderson, Nelson | May  4 1846 | 8/163B |
| Campbell, Michael | McGovern, Margaret | Jul 19 1851 | 11/167 |
| Campbell, Roseanna | Morgan, John | Sep 23 1852 | 12/12 |
| Campbell, Thomas | Meyers, Redia E | May 23 1855 | 14/146 |
| Campbell, Thomas S | Elliott, Nancy A | Jun 23 1855 | 14/185 |
| Campbell, William | Cluninne, Margaret | May 29 1852 | 11/256 |
| Campbell, William P | Beers, Caroline | Jun  7 1843 | 5/279B |
| Campbelle, John | Ballard, Sarah | Mar 29 1839* | 3/162 |
| Camphete, Eliza | Seawell, Joseph | Jun 24 1837* | 3/87 |

| Camphmuller, Catherine | Speth, Ferdinand | Jul 22 1854 | 13/291 |
| Cana, Demetry | Paudely, Helena | Oct 11 1834* | 2/101 |
| Canaher, Alice | Canaher, Bernard | Dec 26 1845* | 7/812B |
| Canaher, Bernard | Canaher, Alice | Dec 26 1845* | 7/812B |
| Canaville, Marie C | Pinto, Antonio | 1826* | OIB |
| Canavillo, Charles F | Dunlap, Sarah J | Mar 18 1834* | 2/391 |
| Canbert, Catherine C | Ausier, Joseph J | Jan 23 1846 | 7/716B |
| Canedy, Jenette B | Smith, Philip A | Dec 21 1841* | 5/163B |
| Canivin, Mary | O'Donaghue, Timothy | Mar 18 1851 | 11/129 |
| Cann, John | Spencer, Margaret | Dec  1 1852 | 12/80 |
| Cannon, Alfred W | Burge, Mary Olevia | Dec 28 1839* | 5/5 |
| Cannon, Arthur | Broderick, Margaret | Feb  2 1852 | 11/210 |
| Cannon, Caroline | Grove, Sylvester | Dec 28 1839* | 5/6 |
| Cannon, Eliza | McIntyre, Thomas | May  5 1842 | 5/199B |
| Cannon, Elizabeth T | Gallup, George | Aug 28 1854 | 13/324 |
| Cannon, Levina | Robinson, William | 1840* | OIB |
| Cannon, Mary | Pernall, John | Jul 20 1836* | 3/54 |
| Cannon, William D | Reach, Abegail (Roach) | Jan 20 1848* | 5/9 |
| Canovan, Anthony | Connor, Mary | Dec 15 1851 | 11/194 |
| Canovan, Anthony | Orme, Charlott | Jun 19 1849* | 8/392 |
| Canovan, Anastasia | O'Connor, Timothy | May  1 1845 | 8/90B |
| Canovin, Ann | Carr, Timothy | Feb 11 1854 | 13/119 |
| Canterbury, Levi B | Burnett, Eliza C | Jul 15 1854 | 13/283 |
| Capas, Ramon | Hervey, Susan | Feb 10 1842* | 5/180B |
| Capell, Harvey S | Eslava, Malvina | Dec 11 1849* | 11/24 |
| Capella, Francisco | Dere, Columba | Nov 10 1853 | 13/11 |
| Capers, Robert F | Branch, Francis S | Apr 13 1853 | 12/238 |
| Caperton, Catherine (wid) | Byrne, Patrick | Feb  1 1816* | CM |
| Capmann, Stephen | Karnar, Mary | Mar 18 1852 | 11/227 |
| Cappick, James | McCowl, Ann (McCloud) | Jul  1 1843* | 5/285B |
| Capps, Bassett | Jones, Mary E | Jan 23 1855 | 14/22 |
| Capuck, Ellen | Rickard, Joseph | May 18 1849* | 8/376 |
| Capus, Raymond | DeCamp, Caroline M | Sep 16 1841 | 4/921B |
| Carby, James | English, Eleanor | Jun 23 1838* | 3/133 |
| Carderon, Benine | Chavana, Corinne | Jan 13 1853 | 12/122 |
| Carderoy, Simon | Bernody, Catherine | 1826* | OIB |
| Care, Henry | McCanner, Ellen | Dec 21 1842* | 5/236 |
| Carey, Daniel | Burns, Sarah | May 19 1853 | 12/292 |
| Carey, Patrick M | Devine, Julia M | Feb  9 1855 | 14/45 |
| Carey, William | Laurendine, Mary | Apr 24 1828 | 2/22 |
| Carl, Thomas H | Perry, Catherine | May 30 1833* | 2/971 |
| Carles, Peter | Serda, Catharine | Jun 12 1846 | 8/172 |
| Carlin, Ann | Reardon, Patrick | Sep  6 1851 | 11/177 |
| Carlin, James | Lynch, Joanna (wid) | Dec 15 1841 | 5/162B |
| Carlin, Joanna (Mrs) | Robb, William | Apr 20 1854 | 13/196 |
| Carlin, John | Ferrell, Ann | Jan 31 1846 | 8/143B |
| Carlin, Mary | Harris, Richmond B | Nov  1 1850 | 11/94 |
| Carlysle, Mary | Harris, James W | May 27 1848 | 8/306 |
| Carman, Claire | Doggett, Thomas | Aug  4 1815* | CM |
| Carmelich, George | Gager, Aretusa | Jan  3 1852 | 11/200 |
| Carmichael, Daniel | Kornegan, Hester | Dec 12 1855 | 14/303 |
| Carminetti, John | Treynor, Martha | Mar 25 1844* | 8/7B |
| Carney, Ann | O'Hara, Charles K | Dec 18 1854 | 13/414 |
| Carnfield, Joseph | Seawell, Mary | Jun  8 1835* | 3/17B |
| Carnhlion, Joanna | Donnlly, Daniel | Jul  3 1842 | 6/172 |
| Carnvella, Sarah Jane | Taggard, Elijah | Oct 11 1849 | 11/9 |
| Caro, Adelia A | Lassabe, John R | Nov 10 1852 | 12/59 |
| Caro, Josephine A | Brown, George L | Jan  1 1849* | 8/343 |
| Caro, Matilda C | Duval, Philip | Dec 28 1844* | 8/63B |
| Carpenter, Emily | Deas, Wiseman | Mar 29 1843 | 5/255B |
| Carpenter, James | Welch, Ann | Oct  5 1840* | 5/51 |
| Carr, Bridget | Jones, William | May  5 1838* | 3/123 |
| Carr, Henrietta | Porter, Arnold W | Jul 31 1854 | 13/298 |
| Carr, Hugh M    (McCan) | Morris, Ann Eliza | Jun 22 1840 | 5/29B |

| BRIDE OR GROOM | SPOUSE | DATE | BOOK/PAGE |
|---|---|---|---|
| Carr, Thomas A | Oliver, Jane | Mar 22 1836* | 3/43 |
| Carr, Timothy | Canovin, Ann | Feb 11 1854 | 13/119 |
| Carragun, Mary | Lindsay, David | Mar 20 1845 | 8/80B |
| Carrall, Susanna | Bush, David | Jan 17 1849* | 8/348 |
| Carrigan, Ann | O'Brien, Thomas | May 13 1844 | 8/20B |
| Carrigan, Bridget | Brookery, Peter | Jan 2 1843* | 5/239B |
| Carroll, Ann | McGill, John | Nov 30 1843* | 5/308B |
| Carroll, Catherine | Ahern, Timothy | May 22 1843 | 5/274B |
| Carroll, Catherine | Wooton, Jesse | Mar 25 1852 | 11/230 |
| Carroll, Elizabeth | Cocklan, Cornelius | Aug 3 1855 | 14/204 |
| Carroll, John | Smith, Eliza | Dec 18 1852 | 12/97 |
| Carroll, Margaret Jane | Stark, Charles R | Apr 5 1849 | 8/365 |
| Carroll, Rosaline | Pretlove, John | Sep 28 1847* | 8/257 |
| Carroll, Thomas (William) | Adams, Margarett | Apr 8 1840* | 5/22 |
| Carroll, William B | Patton, Margarett | Feb 3 1840* | 3/192 |
| Carson, Eliza J | Rice, John | Jul 23 1855 | 14/198 |
| Carson, John P | Fleven, Ann Eliza | Jul 28 1848* | 8/318 |
| Carson, Sarah | Smith, John | Nov 16 1824 | 1/49 |
| Carson, Thomas | Daly, Ellen | Apr 21 1843 | 5/263B |
| Carter, Henry | Cochran, Elizabeth | Apr 4 1851 | 11/134 |
| Carter, Jane | Latourell, Charles | Dec 11 1843 | 5/309B |
| Carter, Jesse | Kennedy, Mary Louise | May 28 1835 | 3/16 |
| Carter, John T | Darrington, Eliza C | Dec 23 1854 | 13/419 |
| Carter, Julia A | LeFevre, Francis A | 1838* | 0IB |
| Carter, Margaret | Pledger, Abel K | Feb 14 1843 | 5/249B |
| Carter, Mary | Jones, John | Jun 26 1851* | 11/160 |
| Carter, Mary | Gerlott, John | Oct 18 1852 | 12/30 |
| Carter, Matthew | Roberts, Exis | Sep 17 1839* | 3/186 |
| Carter, Phebe | Goodson, John A | May 1 1828* | 2/24 |
| Carter, Thomas | Moore, Parmelia | Jul 16 1851* | 11/165 |
| Carter, William P | Bunce, Mary E (Bruce) | Nov 4 1847 | 8/263 |
| Carter, William S | Master, Martha (Martin) | Aug 23 1838* | 3/140 |
| Carthy, Susannah | Martin, Marius | Feb 2 1839* | 3/154 |
| Carthy, Thomas L | Webb, Harriett | Dec 14 1824 | 1/52 |
| Carver, Eliza L | Berry, John Calvin | Jul 8 1848 | 8/314 |
| Carver, John S | Reese, Ellen | May 8 1854 | 13/219 |
| Carver, Thomas J | Strang, Lavinia | Mar 29 1849 | 8/364 |
| Carver, Thomas J | Gales, Emiline (Gates) | Nov 15 1838* | 3/147 |
| Carver, William J | Nelson, Sarah A | Apr 12 1851 | 11/137 |
| Cary, Ellen | Reynolds, John M | Nov 22 1845 | 8/125B |
| Casabuena, Gabriel | Terrenes, Louise | Jun 14 1847 | 8/242 |
| Casal, Joseph | Grady, Catharine | Jul 24 1849* | 8/382 |
| Casbrey, James | Monnahan, Alice | Jul 27 1851 | 11/169 |
| Case, Bridget | Connery, Tarrance H | Feb 11 1851 | 11/120 |
| Case, Henry | McCannen, Ellen | Dec 21 1842 | 6/247B |
| Case, John | Flynn, Ann (wid) | Oct 1 1846 | 8/192 |
| Case, Joseph | Pollard, Eliza | Oct 30 1833* | 2/741 |
| Case, Kate C | Hamilton, James L | Sep 5 1855 | 14/226 |
| Case, Mary Ann | Vlaho, Emanuel | Mar 13 1852 | 11/226 |
| Case, Richard | English, Jane | Feb 1 1840 | 3/192 |
| Casey, Bridget | Delaney, Patrick | Jan 14 1854 | 13/78 |
| Casey, Bridget | Hoey, John | Feb 11 1854 | 13/118 |
| Casey, Catherine J | Berrien, James William | May 5 1831* | 2/168 |
| Casey, Ellen | Grant, John | Jan 28 1841* | 5/95B |
| Casey, Margaret | Noonder, Edward | Apr 5 1847 | 8/224 |
| Casey, Mary | Barry, Garrett | Feb 10 1852 | 11/215 |
| Casey, Mary | Kinney, Richard | Aug 6 1853 | 12/376 |
| Casey, Mary Ann | Phelps, Jefferson | Dec 8 1836* | 3/64 |
| Casey, Mary Jane | Witherspoon, Daniel M | Feb 21 1835 | 3/9 |
| Casey, Michael | Dunaree, Jane | Feb 25 1851 | 11/124 |
| Casey, Michael | St Laurence, Mary A | Oct 23 1855 | 14/263 |
| Casey, Olivia | Blakley, Joel | Jan 10 1855 | 14/9 |
| Casey, Owen | Burke, Eliza | Feb 22 1841* | 5/108B |
| Casey, Richard Thomas | McLauthlin, Anne | Jun 18 1845 | 8/105B |

| BRIDE OR GROOM | SPOUSE | DATE | BOOK/PAGE |
|---|---|---|---|
| Cash, Silas W | Rhodes, Elizabeth | Sep 12 1834* | 2/151 |
| Cashell, Thursby H | Laurine, Adler | Nov 20 1841 | 5/158B |
| Cashin, Denis | Johnson, Sarah | Jan 31 1852 | 11/210 |
| Cashmier, Ellen | Quebeuf, M A Napoleon | Jan 30 1841* | 5/97B |
| Casidy, Lydia | Fagan, Peter | Dec 29 1853 | 13/56 |
| Casper, Catherine | Baumhauer, Andrew | Aug 28 1854 | 13/323 |
| Cassady, Catharine | Fox, Peter | Aug 30 1852 | 11/280 |
| Cassady, Mary | Clifford, Patrick | Dec 19 1840* | 5/77B |
| Cassady, Mary | Callan, Patrick | Mar 28 1842 | 5/188B |
| Cassagne, Francois | Martin, Merthi | Nov 24 1845 | 8/125B |
| Cassanas, Josephine | Cunningham, John | Jan 30 1854* | 13/102 |
| Cassas, Ramon | Henvey, Susan  (Hervey) | Feb 10 1842 | 6/80 |
| Casser, Laveria ? | Ross, Mary Ann | Dec 17 1840* | 5/75B |
| Cassibry, George | Bossarge, Orsan | Jun 14 1842 | 5/206B |
| Cassor, Saverio ? | Ross, Mary Ann | Dec 17 1840 | 4/2561B |
| Cassus, Raymond | Decauss, Lucy C M | Sep 15 1841* | 5/151 |
| Castella, Mary Ann | Kelly, Thomas S | Apr 11 1842 | 5/191 |
| Castello, William | Castillo, Mary | Feb 14 1838* | 3/113 |
| Castello, William  (widr) | Shay, Mary  (wid) | Jan 30 1854* | 13/104 |
| Caster, Holsworth | Peach, Mary L | Nov 27 1838* | 3/149 |
| Castilli, John | Duffie, Jane (Duffy) | Feb 28 1840* | 3/195 |
| Castillo, John | Alexander, Catherine | Feb 13 1844* | 5/322 |
| Castillo, Joseph | Maura, Josephine | Mar 18 1848 | 8/293 |
| Castillo, Mary | Castello, William | Feb 14 1838* | 3/113 |
| Castillo, Walter | McLaughlin, Bridget | Mar 21 1843 | 5/255B |
| Castillo, Walter  (widr) | Conway, Emma  (wid) | Jul 20 1853 | 12/362 |
| Castoneil, Rosaline | Codra, Beltran | Aug 20 1841* | 5/149B |
| Catchett, John | Logan, Mary Ann | Dec  8 1840* | 5/73B |
| Cates, Betsey | Williams, Henry | Nov 26 1852* | 12/76 |
| Cates, Cynthia | Simmons, James E | Apr 10 1851 | 11/136 |
| Cates, Elizabeth | Simmons, John | Nov 29 1852 | 12/79 |
| Catherine (NSL) | Connell, Vincent R | 1838* | OIB |
| Catherine (NSL) | McGrow, James (McGrew) | Jun  8 1842 | 6/157 |
| Cating, Mary Ann | Hurley, Charles | Jan 11 1842 | 5/171B |
| Cato, Alexander | Crosby, Rebecca | Aug  7 1844 | 8/38B |
| Cato, Phillip | King, Rosannah | Nov 22 1821* | CM |
| Cato, Philip | Keyser, Louisa K | Mar 21 1854 | 13/165 |
| Caua, Demetry | Paudley, Helena | Oct 11 1834* | 2/101 |
| Caubertz, Catharine C | Ausies, Joseph J | Jan 23 1846 | 8/241 |
| Caufield, John C | O'Connor, Margaret A | 1838* | OIB |
| Caufman, Sarah | Moser, Samuel | Jul 26 1844* | 8/36 |
| Caughlin, Ellen | Conlon, Patrick | Aug 29 1846 | 8/186B |
| Caughlin, Joanna | Dougherty, Michael | Apr 13 1842 | 5/192B |
| Cauley, Purtzman | Kidd, Martha J | Apr 11 1853 | 12/243 |
| Caunahan, Jane | Goodman, Alex W | May 22 1838* | 3/128 |
| Cavallara, Sarah | Loprester, Salvador | Feb 18 1853 | 12/176 |
| Cavallero, Louisa A | Baldwyn, Marshall J D | Jan 20 1842* | 5/171B |
| Cavanagh, James | Rupell, Matilda (Russell) | Feb  9 1847* | 8/214 |
| Cavendish, Rebecca | Jordan, Isaac S | Jul  5 1836* | 3/52 |
| Cavery, Mary | Brady, John | Apr 18 1854 | 13/192 |
| Caves, Mary Elizabeth | Eslava, Jerome | Jun 24 1851 | 11/159 |
| Cavin, Charlotte | Proctin, Thomas S | Nov 20 1842 | 5/228B |
| Cawfield, William A | Freeman, Pewninah | Mar 25 1835 | 3/12 |
| Cawpano, Felix | Marlen, Madame | Oct  1 1833* | 3/142 |
| Cawthorn, Orville F | Cowan, Sarah A | Feb 27 1855 | 14/71 |
| Cayetanos, Miran | Mulligan, John | Apr  7 1840* | 3/198 |
| Cazalas, Francois | Bourch, Virginia | Sep  9 1842* | 5/218B |
| Cazeaux, Ulysses | Leon, Florence | Jan 30 1851 | 11/119 |
| Cazelos, Mary | Radomich, Stephen | Dec 22 1849 | 11/27 |
| Celburn, James L | Randall, Malvina | Aug 10 1847 | 8/251 |
| Celestine, Josephine | Turner, Lafayette | Mar  3 1851 | 11/126 |
| Centener, George Adam | Ross, Elizabeth | Dec 24 1849 | 11/28 |
| Center, Henry | Pinkham, Eliza | 1822* | OIB |
| Center, Eliza M | Chapman, Samuel | Nov 19 1844 | 8/52B |

| BRIDE OR GROOM | SPOUSE | DATE | BOOK/PAGE |
|---|---|---|---|
| Cerbut, James | Lyles, Mary | Sep 10 1851 | 11/177 |
| Cerulalon, Pierre Isador | Pellet, Mary Ann | May 25 1847* | 8/236 |
| Cesaneny, Chrisostome | Miller, Catherine ? | Apr 21 1843 | 5/262B |
| Chadick, Asa | Goodson, Phoebe | Aug 23 1854 | 13/318 |
| Chailan, James | Goodwin, Sarah | Sep 29 1846 | 8/190 |
| Chaix, Pierre Germueil | Poller, Julie (Potter) | May 20 1839* | 3/173 |
| Chamberlain, Barlett S | Mosely, Lucy A | Dec 13 1854 | 13/412 |
| Chamberlain, Elizabeth R | Wilson, William M H | Jan 30 1849* | 8/350 |
| Chamberlain, Henry | Shipley, Josephine | Jan 28 1842* | 5/175B |
| Chamberlain, Reubanna L | Gibson, John | Dec 18 1845 | 8/131B |
| Chamberlain, Robert T | Rondeau, Mary L | Jan 27 1853 | 12/150 |
| Chambers, Augustus | Norman, Joanna F | Nov 14 1843 | 5/304B |
| Chambers, George A | Johnson, Elizabeth | May 22 1841 | 5/131B |
| Champanois, Simon P | Monk, Harriet C | Dec 19 1848 | 8/339 |
| Champnoise, Issac | Crabtree, Louisa | Nov 3 1845 | 8/123B |
| Chanceller, Mary Ann(Mrs) | Drinkwater, Sewell | May 24 1851 | 11/152 |
| Chandler, Charles G | Gregory, Louisa | Mar 12 1855 | 14/80 |
| Chandler, John B | Ranger, Theresa J | Sep 6 1847 | 8/254 |
| Chandler, Philinda B | Preston, Royal | Jun 5 1851 | 11/156 |
| Chandler, Susan | Brackett, William R | Aug 2 1841 | 5/144B |
| Chaney, Helen Elizabeth | Bullock, Erasmus D | Jan 14 1841* | 5/87B |
| Chaney, William P | Roan, Mary A | Jun 22 1852 | 11/264 |
| Chanpentien, Azile C | Haifleigh, William F | Jul 12 1843 | 5/287B |
| Chantron, Pepin | Dumei, Ernestine | Mar 3 1853* | 12/182 |
| Chapman, Abby Anne | Sperry, John J | Apr 10 1843 | 5/260B |
| Chapman, Antoinette E | Gascoigne, Charles W | Feb 19 1855 | 14/58 |
| Chapman, Hiram | Flowers, Mary | Nov 8 1851 | 11/186 |
| Chapman, Jane | Watson, Artinus J | Jan 30 1854 | 13/103 |
| Chapman, John A | Blue, Mary J | Jun 19 1845 | 8/105B |
| Chapman, Lewis T | Willey, Mary E | Jun 11 1852 | 11/261 |
| Chapman, Mary | Pierce, Jeremiah | Nov 2 1855 | 14/270 |
| Chapman, Patrick | Hennessee, Bridget | Jan 24 1854* | 13/94 |
| Chapman, Robert | Bickell, Emaline | Jun 23 1825 | 1/82 |
| Chapman, Samuel | Center, Eliza M | Nov 19 1844 | 8/52B |
| Chappell, Lewis W | Mitchell, Sarah A | Dec 19 1846 | 8/206 |
| Charbonett, Amelia | Slade, Joseph | Jul 25 1845 | 8/112B |
| Charles, William H | Barnheart, Nancy | Nov 8 1834* | 2/21 |
| Charley, Francis | Trenier, Annette | Mar 22 1841 | 4/701B |
| Charpen, Huldah | Torrans, William H | Jan 16 1851 | 11/113 |
| Charpenter, Mary Delphine | Lenoir, Julius | Jan 4 1845 | 8/65B |
| Charpentier, Raymond | Prudhomme, Josephine | Jun 8 1843 | 5/280B |
| Charpentier, Stephen | Horan, Sarah | May 24 1847* | 8/236 |
| Charpin, Francis | Davis, Huldah | Jul 22 1835* | 3/20 |
| Charray, Etienne | Claude, Jeanne | Jun 4 1855 | 14/160 |
| Chase, Louisa L | Blount, Henry G | Feb 9 1852 | 11/214 |
| Chase, Samuel | Brown, Laura | Jul 19 1836* | 3/53 |
| Chasene, Maria Del Rosano | Ferino, Celso G | Feb 13 1841* | 5/104B |
| Chastang, Albert | Andry, Julia | Jun 18 1850 | 11/67 |
| Chastang, Augustus | Weathers, Harriet | Dec 22 1828 | 2/57 |
| Chastang, Augustus | Bazile, Catherine | Apr 28 1851 | 11/142 |
| Chastang, Augustus | Kennedy, Euphrozine | Jan 12 1854 | 13/762 |
| Chastang, Clare | Namond, H N | Jun 25 1838* | 3/133 |
| Chastang, Corielie | Chastang, Peter | May 15 1854 | 13/223 |
| Chastang, Edward | Petite, Mary | Sep 11 1843 | 5/295B |
| Chastang, Edward | Collins, Celeste | Aug 13 1841 | 5/148B |
| Chastang, Elizabeth | Perrault, Michael | Jul 5 1813* | WB 1/7 |
| Chastang, Fostin | Juzan, Delphine | Aug 14 1848* | 8/320 |
| Chastang, Francis Zeno | Andry, Louisa | Jul 25 1846 | 8/181 |
| Chastang, Gertrude | Juzan, John Baptiste | May 18 1829 | 2/86 |
| Chastang, Isabelle | Lorent, Joseph | Jul 14 1830* | 2/131 |
| Chastang, John | Igg, Nannette | Jul 5 1831* | 2/177 |
| Chastang, John Joshua | Margaret (NSL) | Mar 13 1832* | 2/1651 |
| Chastang, Josaphine | Whyte, William J | Dec 25 1855 | 14/316 |
| Chastang, Julia | Ingram, Thomas | Jun 29 1843 | 6/386 |

| BRIDE OR GROOM | SPOUSE | DATE | BOOK/PAGE |
|---|---|---|---|
| Chastang, Louise | Marnse, Pierre | May 19 1842* | 5/201B |
| Chastang, Louise | Dubroca, Bazil | Jun 27 1832* | 2/1441 |
| Chastang, Louisa | Avon, Jerome | Oct 9 1838* | 3/143 |
| Chastang, Margaret | Beatty, James | Oct 11 1830* | 2/140 |
| Chastang, Margarete | Juzan, Daniel | May 20 1813* | WB 1/7 |
| Chastang, Mary L | Buck, William J | Jan 10 1854 | 13/68 |
| Chastang, Peter | Chastang, Corielie | May 15 1854 | 13/223 |
| Chastang, Pierre | Brown, Mary R (wid) | Mar 15 1833 | 2/1071 |
| Chastang, Salia | Inzcan, Thomas (Juzan) | Jun 29 1843 | 5/284 |
| Chastang, Sidione J | Juzan, Mary M | Jan 15 1846 | 8/141B |
| Chastang, Zenon, Jr | Andre, Patrone | Aug 17 1844 | 8/39B |
| Chastang, Zenon Jr | Patrone, Andre ? | Aug 17 1844 | 8/39B |
| Chatard, John | Poulet, Marie L | Jun 14 1854 | 13/258 |
| Chatham, Rebecca | Holoman, Thomas | Mar 26 1836* | 3/54 |
| Chaudron, Emma | Elliott, John R | Feb 25 1830* | 2/115 |
| Chaudron, Jane | Batre, Adolphus | Mar 3 1828 | 2/9 |
| Chaudron, Julian | Doud, Annette F | Dec 14 1832* | 2/1261 |
| Chaudron, Melanie | Weeks, Nicholas Jr | Feb 21 1833* | 2/1101 |
| Chavana, Corinne | Carderon, Benine | Jan 13 1853 | 12/122 |
| Chavana, Vincent | Dubroca, Catherine | Apr 17 1834* | 2/311 |
| Cheesborough, Catherine | Childres, Nicholas | Oct 17 1842 | 5/2241B |
| Cheesebrough, Hiram | Austil, Sarah | Mar 9 1829* | 2/75 |
| Chenault, William | Felix, Jane | Feb 5 1816* | CM |
| Chenet, Louis | LeBourgeris, Emma | May 2 1853 | 12/264 |
| Cherry, C L | Revoult, Josephine | Feb 14 1838* | 3/112 |
| Cherry, Cornelia | Reilly, James W | Jul 26 1841 | 5/93B |
| Cheseborough, Hiram | Files, Catherine A | Jan 16 1833* | 2/1221 |
| Chestnut, Janie | Smith, Josiah L | Jan 5 1853 | 12/114 |
| Chesnut, William | Drus, Jane | Nov 12 1846 | 8/198 |
| Chestang, Clair | Burien, J | 1822* | OIB |
| Chestang, Gertrude | Dragis, Peter | Nov 26 1846 | 8/202 |
| Chestang, John Joshua | Margaret (NSL) | Mar 13 1832* | 2/1651 |
| Chester, Caroline | Sinnot, John A | Feb 13 1855 | 14/50 |
| Chevalier, Julien | Kestlen, Madaline | Nov 24 1849 | 11/18 |
| Chevealleer, Marie | DiGiovanna, Francois | Apr 25 1854 | 13/205 |
| Cheyse, Mary | Lonsdale, Horatio B | Mar 8 1841 | 5/114B |
| Chieusse, Joseph E | Seymour, Emerant | Mar 19 1849 | 8/362 |
| Chieusse, L (Lazarus) | Boislandry, Eugenie | 1826* | OIB |
| Chighazola, James | Chighazola, Mary | 1837* | OIB |
| Chighezola, Jacob | Baptiste, Louisa | Jun 4 1814* | CM |
| Chighizola, Marie | Monnin, Louis | Sep 9 1848 | 8/323 |
| Chighyola, Giacoma | Sagomagiore, Chiora | Apr 3 1837* | 3/78 |
| Child, Beulah M | Olive, Young B | Dec 18 1850 | 11/103 |
| Child, John V | Crane, A M (Mrs) | Apr 26 1841* | 5/126 |
| Child, Susan | McKinstry, Thomas | Dec 1 1841 | 5/160B |
| Childers, Amanda M (wid) | Mitchell, William M | Dec 13 1853 | 13/37 |
| Childers, John | Bacchus, Elizabeth | Sep 23 1847* | 8/257 |
| Childers, Mary E G | Files, David J | Dec 21 1843 | 5/310B |
| Childers, Nicholas | Cheesborough, Catherine | Oct 17 1842 | 5/2241B |
| Childress, Elizabeth | Deakle, William | Sep 22 1855 | 14/23 |
| Childress, Samuel | Davidson, Mary Ann | Jun 29 1836* | 3/52 |
| Childs, Isabella C | Ulrick, John G | May 17 1842 | 5/201B |
| Childs, John V | Crane, Ann | Apr 26 1841 | 4/2081 |
| Chimps, Andrew | Ibach, Nimpha | Dec 26 1851 | 11/199 |
| Chisholm, Anne E | Ellis, Thomas L | May 6 1851 | 11/146 |
| Chisolm, Jonathan | Normon, Emeline | Jun 5 1828* | 2/32 |
| Chisolm, Jonathan (widr) | Miller, Mary | Dec 31 1853 | 13/59 |
| Chivers, Jane | Miller, James | Nov 6 1843* | 5/302B |
| Chonfreon, Joseph | Bonan, Margaret | Jul 12 1852 | 11/269 |
| Chouifse, Ellis | Juzan, Elizabeth | May 4 1854 | 13/216 |
| Chrelien, Tony (Juny) ? | Nicholson, Sarah | Jun 21 1853 | 12/325 |
| Christain, Amelia (Mrs) | McGowin, Elijah O | Sep 8 1840* | 5/45B |
| Christian, Benjamin R | Brownjohn, Amelia | Aug 31 1832* | 2/1361 |
| Christian, Joseph | Mitaine, Madelene | Mar 17 1842 | 5/186B |

| --- | --- | --- | --- |
| Christian, Mary | Williams, James | Jun 22 1824 | 1/34 |
| Christian, Thomas | Addis, Abigal DeWolf | Apr 20 1837* | 3/81 |
| Christon, Margaret E | Branch, William H | Aug 14 1854 | 13/312 |
| Chumperios, Julia | Sutton, James | Mar 8 1847 | 8/220 |
| Church, James | McPhillips, Ann | May 4 1844 | 8/19B |
| Church, Margaret | Rogers, Thomas | Apr 9 1853 | 12/226 |
| Church, Thomas B | Tatum, Claudia C | May 15 1838* | 3/126 |
| Churchill, Catherine | Bany, Edmund | Jun 21 1855 | 14/182 |
| Churchill, Sarah | Fox, Felix | Nov 29 1854 | 13/393 |
| Cialos, Biena | Molliere, Augustus | Apr 3 1855 | 14/96 |
| Cilbourne, James D | Cole, Harriet | Jul 10 1818* | CM |
| Cilburn, Harriett | Hamilton, Andrew | Feb 21 1832* | 2/1711 |
| Cirode, Daniel W | Smith, Mary Ann | Nov 11 1843 | 5/303B |
| Citron, Jacob | Hirsh, Milco | Apr 1 1854* | 13/170 |
| Clagg, David | Stafford, Susan | 1826* | OIB |
| Clair, John | Keith, Mary (Kris) | Nov 2 1849* | 11/13 |
| Clancy, Jeremiah | Smith, Isabella | Nov 22 1841 | 5/158B |
| Clancy, Michael | Doyle, Rose Anna | Nov 22 1852 | 12/70 |
| Clark, Alafal | Pool, Jechonias P | May 18 1854 | 13/229 |
| Clark, Ann | Adams, Jasper | Jan 20 1838* | 3/108 |
| Clark, Archibald | Crabtree, Milley | Mar 24 1853 | 12/205 |
| Clark, Catharine | Mahony, Michael | Jun 5 1843 | 5/278B |
| Clark, Charles | Byrd, Eliza | Jul 19 1847 | 8/246 |
| Clark, Ebenezer | Burlison, Sally | Oct 7 1828 | 2/43 |
| Clark, Elizabeth | Rounsaville, William | 1825* | OIB |
| Clark, Elizabeth | French, Zerubabel | Oct 4 1849 | 11/8 |
| Clark, Elizabeth | Benton, Victor L | Apr 9 1850 | 11/52 |
| Clark, Elizabeth | Riley, Arthur W | Apr 1 1851 | 11/133 |
| Clark, Francis B | Shepherd, Helen M | Jun 9 1845 | 8/102B |
| Clark, Hezekiah | Odom, Isabella | Aug 17 1852 | 11/276 |
| Clark, James H | Aymard, Adelle E | May 20 1851 | 11/150 |
| Clark, John | Oxendale, Rebecca | Apr 13 1844 | 8/13B |
| Clark, John | Bennett, Mary E | May 18 1853* | 12/288 |
| Clark, Lucinda | Measles, Reubin | Aug 24 1847* | 8/252 |
| Clark, Mary J | Goff, Lorenzo D | Jan 7 1851 | 11/110 |
| Clark, Micajah | Raiford, Susannah | Apr 12 1847 | 8/226 |
| Clark, Milbry | Hudson, Deril | Aug 18 1838* | 3/140 |
| Clark, Moses | Haynes, Sarah Ann | Mar 20 1830* | 2/118 |
| Clark, Nancy | Starkweather, Asher | Dec 1 1831* | 2/1801 |
| Clark, Nancy | Houston, Jesse | Aug 19 1852 | 11/277 |
| Clark, Robert C | McKnight, Margaret | Nov 11 1839* | 3/191 |
| Clark, Sarah Ann | Gayer, Ledyard D | Apr 15 1844 | 8/13B |
| Clark, Spotswood W | Turner, Cordelia | Jan 26 1852 | 11/208 |
| Clark, Thomas J | Bozage, Poline | Jan 11 1851 | 11/111 |
| Clark, William | Manny, Caroline | Feb 10 1847 | 8/215 |
| Clarke, Ann | Tunnage, Henry (Turnage) | 1826* | OIB |
| Clarke, Annette E | Cabaniss, William P | Jun 12 1855 | 14/169 |
| Clarke, Bridget | Huston, Bernard | Feb 17 1844 | 5/323B |
| Clarke, Charles | Brown, Rebecca | Aug 13 1838* | 3/138 |
| Clarke, James | Vink, Martha (Vintz) | Jul 7 1846* | 8/179 |
| Clarke, John B | Clement, Mary | Jul 7 1837* | 3/90 |
| Clarke, John E | Murphy, Eliza | Feb 10 1853 | 12/169 |
| Clarke, Mary | Rooney, John | May 16 1853 | 12/284 |
| Clarke, Mary | Cameron, Allen | Nov 23 1852 | 12/72 |
| Clarke, Mary | May, George | Apr 22 1853* | 12/200 |
| Clarke, Mary A | Glover, John | Nov 21 1854 | 13/386 |
| Clarrson, Peter | Emley, Mary | Oct 9 1843 | 6/21 |
| Clary, P F | McDonald, Mary | Nov 12 1850 | 11/96 |
| Claude, Jeanne | Charray, Etienne | Jun 4 1855 | 14/160 |
| Clauson, Peter | Emley, Mary | Oct 9 1843* | 5/299B |
| Clawdes, Mary | Tomlinson, William | Sep 24 1828 | 2/42 |
| Clawdes, Mary Ann C | Demarest, John | Dec 29 1828 | 2/59 |
| Clay, William H | Harrington, Hannah | Jun 20 1854 | 13/261 |
| Clayton, Charles A | Rabby, Mary | Jun 28 1852 | 11/266 |

| BRIDE OR GROOM | SPOUSE | DATE | BOOK/PAGE |
|---|---|---|---|
| Cleal, John Goppy | Arnold, Harriet | Mar 18 1837* | 3/76 |
| Clegg, Susan | Richardson, John W | Apr 12 1841 | 5/122B |
| Cleindienst, Catherine | Baitl, Saffier | Feb 9 1855 | 14/44 |
| Clement, Joshua | Clement, Polly | 1822* | OIB |
| Clement, Mary | Clarke, John B | Jul 7 1837* | 3/90 |
| Clement, Polly | Clement, Joshua | 1822* | OIB |
| Clements, Anderson | Demouy, Margaret | Dec 21 1831* | 2/1771 |
| Clemmons, George C | Mansker, Margaret S | Oct 23 1855 | 14/262 |
| Clemmons, Josephus | Auld, Margaret A | Nov 24 1847 | 8/267 |
| Cleveland, George A | Owen, Mary E (Oliver) | Jun 14 1845 | 8/103B |
| Cleveland, George Jr | Tensdale, Mary | Jun 9 1841* | 5/136 |
| Cleveland, Harriet | Spriggs, Erastus S | Feb 9 1838* | 3/110 |
| Cleveland, Henderson K | Fowler, Mary C | Nov 29 1855 | 14/293 |
| Cleveland, Isaac M | Ross, Jane | Jun 7 1855 | 14/164 |
| Cleveland, John G | Shepard, Rebecca | Sep 16 1824 | 1/37 |
| Cleveland, John G Jr | Hollinger, Cecelia R | Jun 15 1849 | 8/379 |
| Cleveland, John M | Mimms, Nancy Jane | Jun 10 1852 | 11/261 |
| Cleveland, Martha Ellen | Roulufs, John | Jul 27 1852 | 11/272 |
| Cleveland, Mary | Barnes, James | Feb 26 1845 | 8/75B |
| Cleveland, Mary Alabama | Drummond, Thomas M | Feb 20 1855 | 14/62 |
| Cleveland, Mary E | Reynolds, Jonathan | Mar 10 1835* | 3/11 |
| Cleveland, Palestyne | Fitch, George W | Nov 29 1849 | 11/20 |
| Cleveland, William F | Bradling, Miranda | Jul 7 1835* | 3/19 |
| Clifford, John widr | McKee, Ann (wid) | May 2 1853 | 12/266 |
| Clifford, Patrick | Cassady, Mary | Dec 19 1840* | 5/77B |
| Clint, George | Fisher, Rosina Mary | Oct 19 1846 | 8/194 |
| Clinton, Alice | Gaffney, Michael | Sep 30 1842* | 5/215B |
| Cload, James Joseph | Ivers, Bridget | Mar 12 1840* | 5/15 |
| Cloonin, Michael | Dolin, Bridget | Jul 2 1850 | 11/71 |
| Close, Adeline | Tapineo, Valentine | Mar 8 1849* | 8/360 |
| Cloudis, George W | Ruse, Jane (Mrs) | Oct 31 1840* | 5/59B |
| Clow, Peter | Brown, Betsey Lena | Apr 30 1847 | 8/231 |
| Cluis, Emily A | Deas, States G | Jan 5 1836* | 3/34 |
| Cluis, Frederick V | Wein, Mary E | Nov 1 1851* | 11/185 |
| Cluis, Frederick V | Deboutiere, Florida | Oct 27 1835* | 3/30 |
| Clunin, Ann | Fahay, Michael | Apr 21 1852 | 11/240 |
| Cluninne, Margaret | Campbell, William | May 29 1852 | 11/256 |
| Coan, Mary Ann | Fowler, Daniel Jr | 1826* | OIB |
| Coan, Parnell | Fishe, William | Jun 12 1837* | 3/88 |
| Coates, Esborn | McCarty, Julutte A | Aug 26 1837 | 3/98 |
| Cobb, Oliver S | Wainwright, Nancy M | Feb 9 1848 | 8/282 |
| Cocauape, Anthony | Seger, Maria Agatha | Jul 24 1846 | 8/181 |
| Cochran, Elizabeth | Carter, Henry | Apr 4 1851 | 11/134 |
| Cochran, James M | Cockrum, Sarah | Aug 12 1835* | 3/24 |
| Cochran, Louisa | Martin, Lorris | Feb 25 1840* | 3/194 |
| Cochran, P Malinda | Ronlufts, John | Oct 1 1842* | 5/221B |
| Cochran, Sarah | Davis, William | 1837* | OIB |
| Cochran, William L | Moore, June S | May 9 1835 | 3/14 |
| Cochrane, Ellen | Calahan, Philip | Nov 20 1841* | 5/158 |
| Cocke, Ann E | Redus, Augustus F | Dec 12 1844 | 8/58B |
| Cocklan, Cornelius | Carroll, Elizabeth | Aug 3 1855 | 14/204 |
| Cocklin, Mary | Odrescol, Cornelius | Dec 24 1837 | 3/104 |
| Cocknane, Pricilla M | Roulutz, John | Oct 1 1842 | 6/193 |
| Cockran, Mary | Loften, Van | Jun 29 1833* | 2/891 |
| Cockrum, Sarah | Cochran, James M | Aug 12 1835* | 3/24 |
| Coconnes, Antoine | Nelson, Margaret | Jul 11 1848* | 8/315 |
| Codra, Beltran | Castoneil, Rosaline | Aug 20 1841* | 5/149B |
| Cody, Ellen | Brady, John | Aug 26 1841* | 5/150 |
| Cody, Patrick | Dwyer, Catherine | Apr 26 1843 | 5/264B |
| Coffee, Mary Jane | McGhie, Robert | Aug 10 1852 | 11/274 |
| Coffen, Anna | Pillerey, Bernard | Jun 1 1848* | 8/307 |
| Coffey, Edward | Rouan, Mary (Ronan) | Jul 24 1844 | 8/35B |
| Coffey, Sarah | Kenney, Lawrence R | Apr 23 1836* | 3/45 |
| Coffin, Mary Ann | North, Ralph | 1837* | OIB |

| BRIDE OR GROOM | SPOUSE | DATE | BOOK/PAGE |
|---|---|---|---|
| Cogburn, Martha E | Harwell, Barte S | May 20 1846 | 7/208 |
| Coger, Harry | McGravey, Bridget | Nov 19 1853 | 13/19 |
| Cohen, Augustine Lise | Bacceresse, Charles | Oct 19 1840* | 5/55B |
| Cohen, E R | Callaway, George | Oct 2 1838* | 3/142 |
| Cohen, Herman M | Tine, Caroline | Jan 10 1853 | 12/119 |
| Cohen, Joel | Adelheim, Adel | Jun 9 1853* | 12/312 |
| Cohen, Mary | Roney, Patrick | Jun 19 1843 | 5/283B |
| Cohen, Sabrina | Miller, Samuel (Hiller) | Dec 31 1845 | 8/134B |
| Cohen, Samuel | Hurlbutt, Hannah | May 17 1843* | 5/273B |
| Cohen, Sarah | Waldaner, Leon | May 3 1847 | 8/232 |
| Cohen, Sarah | Borrow, James | May 9 1848* | 8/303 |
| Coil, Catherine | Tracy, James | Jun 2 1836* | 3/49 |
| Coil, Catherine | Dunn, Michael | Feb 15 1841* | 5/103B |
| Coil, James | Dorgan, Catherine | Jul 31 1839* | 3/183 |
| Coin, Patrick (Cain) | Warner, Janette | Apr 13 1846 | 8/157B |
| Cokeley, Patrick | Killaher, Ellen | 1837* | OIB |
| Colbark, George (Coldlack) | Windham, Cynthia | Apr 15 1835 | 3/22 |
| Colbertson, Frances | Van Buren, Thomas W | May 24 1849 | 8/377 |
| Cole, Elizabeth | Mitcham, M | Jan 8 1818* | CM |
| Cole, Hannah | Turner, John Edward | Jan 27 1849* | 8/350 |
| Cole, Harriet | Cilbourne, James D | Jul 10 1818* | CM |
| Cole, Levera H | Banfield, John F | Mar 11 1840* | 5/15 |
| Cole, Margaret | DeMott, Michael | 1822* | OIB |
| Coleman, Alexander | Martin, Nancy W | May 20 1839* | 3/172 |
| Coleman, Alexander | Martin, Francesco | 1839* | OIB |
| Coleman, Henry F | Thompson, Margaret A | Jul 1 1846 | 8/176 |
| Coleman, Penny | Tate, David | Jun 26 1814* | WB 1/19 |
| Coles, Polly | Lyons, William | Mar 3 1813* | WB 1/6 |
| Colgin, Edward B | Courson, Amanda | Nov 18 1846 | 8/199 |
| Colin, Catherine | Durett, Vallere | May 20 1842 | 5/202B |
| Colin, Honore Jr | Finlay, Victoria | Oct 27 1841 | 5/154 |
| Colin, Jean | Lelande, Isabel | May 15 1832* | 2/1531 |
| Colin, Louise | Baudin, Celestin | May 13 1834* | 2/261 |
| Colin, Maximillian | Bernody, Hortense | Jul 11 1832* | 2/1411 |
| Colin, Victorie | Lalande, Adolphe | Mar 28 1842 | 5/189B |
| Colina, Louisa | Todd, John B | May 23 1845 | 8/97B |
| Collain, Peter | Durett, Isadore | Jun 20 1846 | 8/174 |
| Collaton, Martin | Tohal, Ann | Feb 27 1854 | 13/143 |
| Collier, Caroline | Jenkins, Thomas | Jan 21 1854 | 13/90 |
| Collier, John | Stone, Mary | Jul 1 1844 | 8/29B |
| Collin, Andrew | Black, Ann | Aug 14 1855 | 14/211 |
| Collin, Bridget Cecilia | Rushing, Charles E | Feb 4 1842 | 5/177B |
| Collin, Faustin | Huzont, Janne | Jul 9 1828 | 2/35 |
| Collin, Louisa | Hines, George | Jan 6 1842 | 6/45 |
| Collin, Margarite | Pinta, Jean Glode F | Oct 28 1828 | 2/49 |
| Collings, George | Brewster, Catherine | Nov 23 1837* | 3/101 |
| Collins, Andrew B | Sordin, Ellen | Jan 26 1836* | 3/38 |
| Collins, Artemus | Rouville, Sostine | 1827* | OIB |
| Collins, Bellmon | Edmonson, Humphrey | Aug 4 1841* | 5/146 |
| Collins, Benjamin | Cooper, Elizabeth | Dec 31 1831* | 2/1741 |
| Collins, Billinson | Edmonson, Humphrey | Aug 4 1841* | 4/3631 |
| Collins, Catherine | Hughes, Thomas | Jul 13 1850 | 11/73 |
| Collins, Celeste | Chastang, Edward | Aug 13 1841* | 5/148B |
| Collins, Charles L B | Gale, Maria R | Nov 28 1854 | 13/392 |
| Collins, Christopher B | Wheeler, Jane | Jun 3 1834* | 2/231 |
| Collins, Christopher B | Cooper, Bashaba | Sep 3 1828 | 2/39 |
| Collins, Christopher B | Wheeler, Elizabeth | Jul 4 1832 | 2/1421 |
| Collins, Christopher C Jr | Goff, Ellen | Apr 27 1840* | 5/21 |
| Collins, Christopher J | Baxter, Mary | Dec 9 1852 | 12/84 |
| Collins, Daniel | Ryan, Julia | Feb 3 1853 | 12/162 |
| Collins, Darling | Hewett, Maria B | Aug 5 1835* | 3/21 |
| Collins, Edward | Rabby, Josephine | Jun 28 1848* | 8/311 |
| Collins, Eliza | Parsons, Henry | Sep 15 1853 | 12/407 |
| Collins, Elizabeth | Halcum, John | Jan 15 1829 | 2/62 |

| BRIDE OR GROOM | SPOUSE | DATE | BOOK/PAGE |
|---|---|---|---|
| Collins, Elizabeth E | Meador, Benjamin | May 1 1845 | 8/90B |
| Collins, Ellen | Abernarthy, Thomas S | Apr 7 1851 | 11/135 |
| Collins, Eloisa | Laurendine, Benjamin | Aug 15 1821* | CM |
| Collins, Erosnnus W | Scarborough, Ann H | Jul 26 1852 | 11/271 |
| Collins, Euphosinia H | Pomeroy, Porter R | Jun 11 1846 | 8/171 |
| Collins, Hendrick H | Roberts, Billison | Apr 19 1828 | 2/12 |
| Collins, Isaac W | Rodgers, Margaret | Sep 14 1836* | 3/57 |
| Collins, Jacob | Baker, Batsey M | 1827* | OIB |
| Collins, Jane G | Lott, Benjamin | Mar 17 1854 | 13/160 |
| Collins, Johanna | Millerick, Thomas | Aug 2 1844 | 8/37B |
| Collins, John | Neil, Johanna | 1838* | OIB |
| Collins, John | Briody, Judy | Jun 15 1848* | 8/309 |
| Collins, John | Murphy, Joanna | Mar 13 1841* | 5/116B |
| Collins, John | O'Brien, Bridget | Jan 22 1845 | 8/67B |
| Collins, John | Durrett, Leonine | Oct 19 1853 | 12/420 |
| Collins, John K | Price, Teresa | Feb 10 1841* | 5/101B |
| Collins, Joseph | Wheeler, Seleter | Dec 3 1831* | 2/1791 |
| Collins, Joseph | Boda, Elizabeth (Bodet) | Sep 22 1842 | 5/220B |
| Collins, Joshua Jr | Baker, Sarah | Dec 5 1829* | 2/105 |
| Collins, Josiah | Benson, Maria L | Jan 15 1834* | 2/521 |
| Collins, Louisa | Hines, George | Jan 6 1842 | 5/168 |
| Collins, Margaret | Maples, Washington | Jul 15 1852 | 11/270 |
| Collins, Maria B | Eckford, William | May 24 1845 | 8/98B |
| Collins, Martha Ann | Littell, Thompson | Jul 16 1833* | 2/841 |
| Collins, Mary D | Lott, William | Dec 6 1852 | 12/83 |
| Collins, Mary Jane | Tosh, Peter | Sep 23 1846 | 8/190 |
| Collins, Michael | Ryan, Johanna | Jun 19 1852 | 11/263 |
| Collins, Nancy | Jones, Willis | Feb 24 1829 | 2/72 |
| Collins, Nancy | Rowe, Robb | May 20 1839* | 3/172 |
| Collins, Nancy Ann | Tarleton, John | Mar 24 1838 | 3/117 |
| Collins, Peter | Ward, Catherine | Dec 24 1841 | 5/164B |
| Collins, Peter | Rainwater, Miranda J | Dec 27 1853 | 13/54 |
| Collins, Rachel S | McGaughey, Daniel W | Dec 21 1854 | 13/416 |
| Collins, Robert | Stuart, Eliza | Nov 22 1848 | 8/333 |
| Collins, Sarah | Baker, William | Sep 18 1850 | 11/86 |
| Collins, Susan | Lacoste, Cyrus | Nov 6 1849 | 11/14 |
| Collins, Theodore | Andry, Jeane | Mar 15 1828 | 2/17 |
| Collins, Thomas | Herren, Catharine | Jan 30 1847 | 8/214 |
| Collins, Thomas | Sage, Catherine | Jan 8 1840* | 3/192 |
| Collins, William | Burke, Margaret | Jun 14 1854 | 13/255 |
| Coloin, Thomas | Riley, Mary Ann | Oct 22 1833* | 2/751 |
| Coloith, Margaret | Wright, John H | Jun 10 1842 | 5/205 |
| Colson, John | Fitzgerald, Catherine | May 24 1848 | 8/306 |
| Colthar, Sarah P | Bowen, Edward | Apr 17 1855 | 14/107 |
| Colthar, Virginia | Allen, William | Jun 4 1855 | 14/158 |
| Colthar, William | Attaway, Elsie A | Apr 10 1830 | 2/122 |
| Colthu, Elsy Amanda | Brown, Samuel | Mar 19 1839* | 3/161 |
| Colvilli, Margaret | Wright, John H | Jun 10 1842 | 6/159 |
| Colwell, Lewis | Mehen, Ellen | Dec 1 1844 | 8/55 |
| Coma, Noel Etienne | Vorsien, Cesarine | Mar 21 1851 | 11/130 |
| Comick, Robert | Donaldson, Mary | Apr 27 1854 | 13/208 |
| Commen, Elizabeth | Henke, Anthony | Apr 6 1840* | 5/17 |
| Commings, John | McCarthney, Ann | Aug 20 1839* | 3/184 |
| Conacke, Mary | Lewis, Peter | Apr 12 1853 | 12/236 |
| Conaty, Philip | Rudale, Nancy (Kadole) | Dec 8 1846* | 8/203 |
| Conce, Rose | Gobel, John | Apr 17 1841* | 5/124B |
| Condon, Alfred | West, Anna Helen | Jan 18 1855* | 14/19 |
| Condon, James | Means, Margaret (Mims) | Apr 29 1850 | 11/56 |
| Cone, Hannah | Isaacs, Marks J | Mar 5 1844* | 5/326B |
| Coneh, Alexander B | Wilkinson, Rebecca A | Jan 20 1836* | 3/37 |
| Coneham, James | Steers, Mary | Jun 11 1828* | 2/33 |
| Conell, Emily | Bell, Gamaliel | Dec 19 1819* | CM |
| Connell, Vincent | Catherine (NSL) | 1838* | OIB |
| Conely, Jane | Snelling, Ephnarin | Jul 20 1840 | 4/4011 |

| BRIDE OR GROOM | SPOUSE | DATE | BOOK/PAGE |
|---|---|---|---|
| Conerty, Catherine | McKeowen, Michael | May 11 1840* | 5/23 |
| Conick, Robert | Fullum, Catherine | Nov 22 1853* | 13/21 |
| Conklin, Anne | Buckley, Morris | Apr 13 1847 | 8/227 |
| Conley, Margarett | Talbot, James | Aug 28 1848* | 8/321 |
| Conley, Patrick C | Reese, Mary Jane | Dec 6 1854 | 13/403 |
| Conley, Thomas J | Dewitt, Margaret | Jan 3 1843 | 5/240B |
| Conlin, Catherine | Hill, John | Mar 18 1852 | 11/228 |
| Conlin, Peter | Keho, Catherine | Apr 27 1847* | 8/228 |
| Conlin, Thomas | Finlay, Henrietta | Mar 3 1852 | 11/224 |
| Conlon, Patrick | Caughlin, Ellen | Aug 29 1846 | 8/186 |
| Conly, Catherine | Scott, William | Apr 9 1845 | 7/629 |
| Connahen, Mary Jane | Parker, Ralph | May 27 1833* | 2/981 |
| Connaught, Ellen | Farley, John | Oct 20 1848* | 8/330 |
| Connell, John | Rainons, Catherine | Apr 26 1843* | 5/265B |
| Connelly, Michael | Coughlin, Rosannah | Aug 26 1834* | 2/191 |
| Connely, William | Jenkins, Ellen (Sinkin) | Oct 9 1843 | 5/298B |
| Conner, David S | Kennedy, Margaret E | Mar 2 1849 | 8/359 |
| Conner, Mary | Magee, James | Feb 5 1819* | CM |
| Conner, Patrick | Callahan, Joanna | Apr 26 1848* | 8/301 |
| Conners, Bridget | Hefferman, Dennis | Feb 11 1839* | 3/156 |
| Conners, Margaret | Spiver, Francis A | Dec 15 1842* | 5/234B |
| Connery, Tarrance H | Case, Bridget | Feb 11 1851* | 11/120 |
| Connolly, Ellen | Fowler, James | May 21 1850 | 11/62 |
| Connolly, Patrick | Mullen, Mary | Jul 17 1854 | 13/285 |
| Connoly, James | Smith, Helen | Jun 24 1845 | 8/106B |
| Connoly, Levi | Burks, Lucretia T | Oct 12 1852 | 12/28 |
| Connoly, Patrick | Gormon, Elizabeth | Dec 1 1849 | 11/20 |
| Connor, Ann | Dowd, Laurence | Jul 4 1853 | 12/347 |
| Connor, Catherine E | Roberts, Joseph M | Feb 21 1852* | 11/220 |
| Connor, Ephraim D | Robinson, Mary V | Dec 16 1844 | 8/59B |
| Connor, Margaret | Malone, John | Jan 30 1855 | 14/28 |
| Connor, Mary | Canovan, Anthony | Dec 15 1851 | 11/194 |
| Connor, Mary A | Durand, Manuel | May 26 1854 | 13/234 |
| Connor, Patrick O' (widr) | Burke, Johanna | Jul 14 1853 | 12/354 |
| Connor, Rose | Higgins, James | Jan 6 1832* | 2/1761 |
| Connors, Ann | Brown, Alexander | Jan 21 1853 | 12/139 |
| Connors, Mary | Scanlon, Patrick | Jan 7 1848* | 8/276 |
| Conroy, John | Fagan, Ann | Oct 29 1844 | 8/46B |
| Constantine, Francisco | Pettis, Rebecca (Pitts) | Jun 1 1833* | 2/961 |
| Constantine, Josephine | Essex, John S | Apr 21 1847 | 8/228 |
| Converse, Phebe | Bullard, Samuel P | Mar 21 1838* | 3/116 |
| Convin, Elizabeth | Hannon, Michael | May 14 1851 | 11/149 |
| Conway, Catherine | Scott, William | Apr 9 1845 | 8/85B |
| Conway, Corah F | Myers, Abram L | May 17 1848 | 8/304 |
| Conway, Delilah | Hindenberg, A | Dec 3 1819* | CM |
| Conway, Eliza F | Thompson, Drury | 1827* | OIB |
| Conway, Eliza F | Thompson, Drury | Dec 5 1829* | 2/106 |
| Conway, Elizabeth | Powers, James | Feb 6 1854 | 13/111 |
| Conway, Emma | Herbert, William | Nov 25 1850 | 11/99 |
| Conway, Emma (wid) | Castillo, Walter (wid) | Jul 20 1853 | 12/362 |
| Conway, James | Urquhart, Frances | Jan 19 1843 | 5/244B |
| Conway, Mary | Daily, D | Apr 15 1844 | 8/10B |
| Conway, Patsy | Plumly, William | Dec 19 1813* | WB 1/9 |
| Conway, Sarah | Davis, William H | Jun 10 1813* | WB 1/8 |
| Conway, Sarah | Starr, George D | 1826* | OIB |
| Conway, Sarah N | McDonald, John | Jan 17 1853 | 12/137 |
| Conway, Sarah N.H. | Gordon, Frederick | Jan 4 1846 | 8/136B |
| Conway, William (Conning) | O'Neil, Jane | May 11 1842 | 5/199B |
| Coogan, John | Fitzpatrick, Margt | Mar 7 1842* | 5/185B |
| Cook, Alexander | Andre, Modeste | Apr 26 1849 | 8/370 |
| Cook, Antonie | Forscheimer, Manuel | Feb 6 1854 | 13/113 |
| Cook, Charles D | Pinto, Odeal | Apr 23 1855 | 14/114 |
| Cook, Eliza Jane | Rutherford, James | Nov 9 1854 | 13/375 |
| Cook, Elizabeth | Mahler, William | Nov 25 1843* | 5/307B |

| BRIDE OR GROOM | SPOUSE | DATE | BOOK/PAGE |
|---|---|---|---|
| Cook, Henry | Stewart, Jane | Feb 29 1852 | 11/223 |
| Cook, Henry | Mark, Sarah (Monk) | May 6 1839* | 3/170 |
| Cook, John | Cook, Mary A | Jul 13 1839* | 3/182B |
| Cook, John | Weeks, Louisa | Mar 8 1831 | 2/153 |
| Cook, M Beal | Duffy, Susan | Jul 15 1841* | 5/143 |
| Cook, Martha P | Herbert, John | Sep 4 1850 | 11/84 |
| Cook, Mary | Moter, Jacob | Feb 12 1855 | 14/47 |
| Cook, Mary A | Cook, John | Jul 3 1839* | 3/182B |
| Cook, Robert | Porter, Elizabeth | May 17 1841* | 5/131B |
| Cook, Sophia J | Jenkins, Calvin L | Apr 13 1850 | 11/53 |
| Cook, Susan P | Shepherd, William | Apr 8 1846* | 8/155B |
| Cooke, Elizabeth A | Paine, Vierpyle | May 1 1851 | 11/143 |
| Cooke, Robert | Pasten, Elizabeth | May 17 1841 | 4/1281B |
| Cooly, Mary Ann | Suzor, Andri | Mar 16 1837* | 3/75 |
| Cooney, James | Burnett, Jane | Apr 24 1851 | 11/141 |
| Cooper, Bashaba | Collins, Christopher | Sep 3 1828 | 2/39 |
| Cooper, Caisin | Baker, Mary | Jan 9 1828* | 2/3 |
| Cooper, Caroline F | Curry, Edward | Nov 23 1846 | 8/200 |
| Cooper, Eliza S (wid) | Ellison, Thomas J (widr) | Feb 11 1853 | 12/170 |
| Cooper, Elizabeth | Collins, Benjamin | Dec 31 1831* | 2/1741 |
| Cooper, Ellen | Schilt, Joseph U | May 14 1841* | 5/130B |
| Cooper, Ferdenand | Wheeler, Judy E | Sep 4 1837* | 3/98 |
| Cooper, George | Mansken, Mary E (Mansker) | Jul 28 1846 | 8/182 |
| Cooper, Harriet | Scleske, Joseph | Nov 22 1847 | 8/266 |
| Cooper, Latham | Allaire, Jane | Mar 5 1831 | 2/152 |
| Cooper, Margaret | Johnson, William | Jan 3 1842 | 5/167B |
| Cooper, Margaret | Gavin, Francis | Jan 21 1854 | 13/100 |
| Cooper, Mary J | Atkins, David | Apr 26 1852 | 11/243 |
| Cooper, Samuel G | Walter, Elizabeth(Watley) | Aug 28 1851 | 11/174 |
| Cooper, Sitter J B | Juzan, Harriett | Oct 9 1838* | 3/143 |
| Cooper, Susan | White, Fisher A | Dec 26 1836* | 3/66 |
| Cooper, Thompson H | Stuart, Eliza S | May 14 1833* | 2/1011 |
| Copeland, Driscilla A | Parker, James M | Mar 28 1854 | 13/167 |
| Copeland, Elizabeth | Pax, James | Mar 10 1855 | 14/79 |
| Copeland, Henry | Watts, Martha | Jul 19 1847 | 8/246 |
| Copland, Robert | Luch, Sarah Ann | Jun 13 1839* | 3/179 |
| Copley, William | Stewart, Sarah | Apr 22 1853 | 12/250 |
| Corbatt, Dennis | Buckley, Catherine | Jan 28 1841* | 5/95B |
| Corbet, James | Lyons, Mary | 1851* | OIB |
| Corbett, Sarah | Black, John | May 19 1835 | 3/15 |
| Corbett, Mary | Littleton, James | Aug 24 1843 | 5/293B |
| Corbien, Marie A (Corbies) | Steiner, Henry | Jun 28 1841* | 5/140B |
| Corbit, Thomas | Leahy, Mary | Dec 14 1837* | 3/103B |
| Corbitt, Honora | Danneberg, Charles | Feb 25 1854 | 13/141 |
| Corbitt, Mary | Doyle, David | May 4 1855 | 14/129 |
| Cordier, Charles | Calon, Jane | Jul 18 1848 | 8/317 |
| Cordier, Ernest Eugene | Dudin, Victoria A | Jan 16 1852 | 11/204 |
| Cordier, Jeanne | Ignard, Philip | Apr 18 1854 | 13/190 |
| Cordis, William | Williams, Celina | Sep 2 1852 | 11/282 |
| Corey, Ann Eliza | Smith, Henry | Aug 5 1834* | 2/211 |
| Corkdale, Sarah | McIntyre, Patrick | Apr 30 1844 | 8/18B |
| Corkrin, John | McCormick, Catherine | Dec 26 1849 | 11/28 |
| Corlet, John | Gull, Biddy | May 21 1838* | 3/127 |
| Corley, Thompson | Turner, Polly | Feb 12 1844 | 5/321B |
| Corlis, Maria | McKenzie, Alexander | Mar 21 1844 | 5/329B |
| Cornhlion, Joanna | Donally, Daniel | Jul 3 1842* | 5/210 |
| Cornley, Jane | Snelling, Ephraim | Jul 20 1840* | 5/35 |
| Cornsky, Samuel | Levy, Caroline | Feb 18 1842* | 5/181 |
| Correjolles, Emily | Whitney, William L | Aug 9 1847* | 8/250 |
| Correll, John J | Graff, Margaret | Oct 13 1847 | 8/259 |
| Corrizilla, Rosalba | Daughin, Henry | Aug 14 1854 | 13/311 |
| Corry, Henry | Marvin, Louisa | Nov 2 1843 | 5/301 |
| Cosey, Harriett C (Cady) | Jewell, Robert G | Dec 3 1842 | 5/231B |
| Cosgrove, Richard | Lantree, Mary Ann ? | Nov 26 1842 | 5/229B |

| BRIDE OR GROOM | SPOUSE | DATE | BOOK/PAGE |
|---|---|---|---|
| Coslier, Alesandre | Detroyer, Marie A | May 24 1842 | 5/203B |
| Costa, Stephen | Botto, Rosa Sofia | Apr 19 1851 | 11/139 |
| Costa, Stephen | Glass, Mary Jane | Apr 19 1855 | 14/110 |
| Costanzi, Feliz Antoine | Deranco, Marie L | Nov 23 1846 | 8/200 |
| Costella, Mary Ann | Kelly, Thomas S | Apr 11 1842 | 6/116B |
| Costello, John | Alexander, Catherine | Feb 13 1844 | 7/133B |
| Coster, Hannah | Roman, Charles | May 1 1846 | 8/162B |
| Costigan, Mary Ann | Remy, John P | Mar 17 1831* | 2/155 |
| Costigin, Lewis A | Hobart, Delphine | Jun 6 1844 | 8/26B |
| Costillo, Walter | Culholy, Bridget | Nov 16 1837* | 3/101 |
| Coston, John W | Brannan, Nancy | Dec 17 1853 | 13/43 |
| Cotchett, John | Logan, Mary Ann | Dec 8 1840* | 5/73 |
| Cotter, Hanora | White, Abel | Jan 17 1849* | 8/348 |
| Cotter, Julia | Kurt, Pierce | Aug 21 1852 | 11/278 |
| Cotter, Mary | Lawler, Mathew C | Jan 23 1851 | 11/116 |
| Cotter, Maurice | Curtin, Julia | Jul 23 1849* | 8/382 |
| Cottez, Caroline | Guerin, Emile | Apr 2 1853 | 12/219 |
| Cottrill, William C | Weeks, Sarah | Aug 5 1847* | 8/249 |
| Couche, Mary Louisa | Rami, John (Hari) | Jul 15 1841* | 5/142 |
| Couell, Samuel S (Covell) | Auld, Miss Allison | Feb 21 1837* | 3/72 |
| Coughlen, Catherine | Faulkner, William | Jan 10 1851 | 11/110 |
| Coughlin, John K | McHugh, Sophia | Aug 25 1835* | 3/26 |
| Coughlin, Rosannah | Connelly, Michael | Aug 26 1834* | 2/191 |
| Coulin, Eliza | O'Conner, Timothy | Apr 10 1854 | 13/176 |
| Counahen, Mary Jane | Parker, Ralph | May 27 1833 | 2/981 |
| Coupland, Eliza | Martineau, Edward | Jun 8 1836* | 3/50 |
| Coupland, Julianna | Dorsey, Vernon | Dec 4 1837* | 3/102 |
| Cournell, Ann | Tonar, Patrick | Nov 6 1838* | 3/146 |
| Courson, Amanda | Colgin, Edward B | Nov 18 1846 | 8/199 |
| Courtney, John | Whitley, Nancy | Jun 3 1854 | 13/240 |
| Courton, Harriet | Barnes, James | Jul 3 1854 | 13/271 |
| Covell, Samuel S | Auld, Miss Allison | Feb 21 1837* | 3/72 |
| Covington, Mary Jane | Bramard, James M | Feb 22 1839* | 3/158 |
| Covington, Matilda | Burwell, John G | Mar 31 1855 | 14/94 |
| Covington, Thomas W | Longet, Jane E | Nov 16 1843 | 5/304B |
| Covins, James | Morris, Mary | Dec 19 1836* | 3/66 |
| Cowan, Juliett | Duncan, John | 1827* | OIB |
| Cowan, Sarah A | Cawthorn, Orville F | Feb 27 1855 | 14/71 |
| Coward, Elizabeth | Willis, David | Aug 7 1839* | 3/184 |
| Cowen, Louisa (Owen) | Garrett, C C | Jun 17 1841* | 5/139 |
| Cowhey, David | Griffin, Mary | Nov 7 1839* | 3/190 |
| Cowhey, David | O'Connor, Helen | Dec 10 1844 | 8/57B |
| Cowin, Esther | Pascoe, John | Jun 12 1837* | 3/88 |
| Cowles, John A | White, Lucy | Feb 16 1830* | 2/112 |
| Cowley, David | Leahy, Ellen | 1837* | OIB |
| Cowly, Timothy | Spillins, Ellen | Dec 9 1840* | 5/73 |
| Cox, Ann | Lockhart, David | Dec 22 1840* | 5/79B |
| Cox, Ann | Marshman, William | Jan 13 1855 | 14/15 |
| Cox, Benjamin B | McDonald, Ann | Mar 30 1843 | 5/256B |
| Cox, Eliza | Bunce, Thomas | Jan 29 1828 | 2/6 |
| Cox, Elizabeth Harriett | Steele, John D | Apr 23 1847 | 8/229 |
| Cox, George | Emmet, Elizabeth | Dec 9 1839* | 3/191 |
| Cox, George | Young, Susan | May 1 1835* | 3/23 |
| Cox, Henry T | Godfrey, Emily | Dec 8 1849 | 11/23 |
| Cox, Hetty | Preston, Simon S | Jul 29 1837* | 3/90 |
| Cox, Jane | Fields, Joseph W | Aug 31 1843 | 5/294B |
| Cox, Mary L | Allen, William B | Mar 25 1828 | 2/18 |
| Cox, Mary T | Lewis, Henry | May 28 1839* | 3/174 |
| Cox, Rose | Foley, Thomas | Mar 18 1854 | 13/158 |
| Cox, Thomas | Shields, Catherine | Jul 14 1851 | 11/164 |
| Coyle, Edward | Denny, Mary (Bennay) | Apr 16 1840* | 5/19 |
| Crabtree, Alfred | Sullivan, Matilda | Jul 27 1844 | 8/36B |
| Crabtree, Eliza | Patterson, Charles H | Mar 9 1847 | 8/221 |
| Crabtree, Emma | Padgett, John | Feb 9 1846 | 8/144B |

| BRIDE OR GROOM | SPOUSE | DATE | BOOK/PAGE |
|---|---|---|---|
| Crabtree, Ervin | Faggart, Sarah Ann | Jan 19 1834* | 2/541 |
| Crabtree, Haynes | Evans, Eliza | Aug 24 1853 | 12/395 |
| Crabtree, Jackson | Sullivan, Eliza | Mar 11 1843 | 5/253B |
| Crabtree, Louisa | Champenois, Isaac | Nov 3 1845 | 8/123B |
| Crabtree, Milley | Clark, Archibald | Mar 24 1853 | 12/205 |
| Cramer, Catherine | Stiller, William | Jun 9 1853 | 12/314 |
| Cramer, Charlotte (wid) | Weicke, Henry (wid) | Dec 23 1853 | 13/49 |
| Craig, Thomas L | Rutherford, Eliza A | Feb 20 1837* | 3/72 |
| Crane, A M (Mrs Ann) | Child, John V | Apr 26 1841* | 5/126B |
| Crane, Albert | Harris, Julia M | Nov 5 1853 | 13/35 |
| Crane, William Carey | Shepherd, Catherine | Apr 24 1845 | 8/88B |
| Crane, William R | Murphy, Catherine | Jun 23 1854 | 13/263 |
| Craney, Debora | Sims, Charles | Nov 15 1842* | 5/227B |
| Cranwell, Jane | Reid, David | Jun 12 1847 | 8/241 |
| Crawford, Emiline | Graham, Thomas | Aug 8 1841* | 5/146B |
| Crawford, Jonathan | Parish, Emeline | May 23 1835* | 3/15 |
| Crawford, Mary E | Groom, James W | Jun 21 1855 | 14/181 |
| Crawford, Robert L | Everitt, Martha | Feb 4 1835* | 3/6 |
| Crawford, Susan L | Sawyer, Julien E | Mar 13 1843 | 5/253B |
| Crawford, William | Morgan, Mary Ann | Aug 31 1844 | 8/40B |
| Crawford, William B | Gayle, Sarah | Dec 7 1842 | 5/233B |
| Crawley, Benjamin | Riles, Polly | Jul 5 1848 | 8/312 |
| Crawley, Catharine | Keef, John | Mar 25 1846 | 8/154B |
| Crawley, Ellen | Nixon, James L | Oct 19 1854 | 13/353 |
| Crawley, Rosa | Goodman, Peter | Apr 29 1842 | 5/195B |
| Creamer, John | Noland, Julia | Jul 10 1848* | 8/314 |
| Creighton, William | Campbell, Mary | Sep 24 1834* | 2/131 |
| Crenshaw, Jefferson | Turner, Malinda | Feb 5 1849 | 8/353 |
| Crenshaw, Samuel | Rayford, Isabella | Dec 6 1847 | 8/269 |
| Crevalleri, A G | Robinson, Margaret | Nov 28 1838* | 3/149 |
| Crickman, Elizabeth | Lyon, Samuel | Jun 29 1852* | 11/267 |
| Crippen, William Henry | Ashlock, Mary E | Feb 25 1851* | 11/124 |
| Criss, Mary | Dermar, Jose | Sep 30 1844 | 8/42B |
| Crissey, Elnathan F | Nunn, Alicia S | Mar 25 1854 | 13/166 |
| Crocker, Henry A | Kellogg, Mary Ellen | Jul 11 1840 | 5/35B |
| Crocker, Mary | Bosworth, William | Jan 21 1848 | 8/280 |
| Crocker, Sarah | Davis, William | Mar 24 1837* | 3/76 |
| Crockett, Lucy | McDonald, John | Dec 10 1855 | 14/301 |
| Crockett, William S | Flannary, Martha | Aug 17 1852 | 11/276 |
| Croley, John | Croley, Mary Ann | Mar 29 1842 | 5/190B |
| Croley, Mary Ann | Croley, John | Mar 29 1842 | 5/190B |
| Crone, George | Hines, Catharine | Jun 4 1851 | 11/155 |
| Cronin, Catherine | Kennedy, Bernard | Feb 22 1841* | 5/106B |
| Cronin, Hannah | Quest, John | Jul 27 1850 | 11/77 |
| Cronin, Veronica | Rutherford, Henry | Apr 24 1847* | 8/230 |
| Cronin, Mary | Lyons, Phelan B | Dec 11 1849 | 11/24 |
| Cronin, Timothy | Hendrix, Susannah | Sep 6 1843 | 5/295B |
| Crook, Henry V | Martin, Mourning | Apr 19 1839* | 3/167 |
| Crooker, Elenor | Fahey, Thomas | Mov 15 1837* | 3/100 |
| Crooks, Morning | Jones, Isaac | Dec 31 1846 | 8/207 |
| Croom, B F | Austin, Sarah V | Jan 27 1851* | 11/117 |
| Croom, Emily | Norris, Calvin | Jan 1 1835* | 3/2 |
| Croquir, Thomas | Rampon, Mary | Jul 2 1850 | 11/70 |
| Crosby, Ann (Mrs) | Hardy, Henry | Dec 13 1845 | 8/130B |
| Crosby, John | Gately, Bridget | Jul 28 1851 | 11/176 |
| Crosby, Margaret E | Leavett, Levi | Sep 12 1846* | 8/189 |
| Crosby, Margarett | Turner, Wright | Oct 13 1840* | 5/55B |
| Crosby, Mary | Wilson, William | Sep 22 1852* | 12/10 |
| Crosby, Rebecca | Cato, Alexander | Aug 7 1844 | 8/38B |
| Crosby, Thomas W | Johnston, Margaret | Apr 20 1829* | 2/81 |
| Croslent, Sarah | Sparanberg, William | Oct 1 1848* | 8/326 |
| Cross, Stephen | Jones, Lavinia | Sep 11 1829 | 2/95 |
| Crothers, Martha W | Fitler, Daniel | Jan 17 1855 | 14/18 |
| Crothers, Mary E | Westfeldt, Rienhold | Feb 22 1854 | 13/133 |

| BRIDE OR GROOM | SPOUSE | DATE | BOOK/PAGE |
|---|---|---|---|
| Crothers, William | Patterson, Mary | Dec 26 1845 | 8/133B |
| Crotty, Eliza | Fry, John | Feb 3 1842 | 5/177B |
| Crow, John F | Powell, Martha A (Mrs) | May 10 1853 | 12/276 |
| Crowell, William | Lambert, Rebecca | Jan 1 1819* | CM |
| Crowley, Ellen | McGane, James | Mar 27 1855 | 14/90 |
| Crowley, Mary | Murray, Thomas | Feb 7 1855 | 14/39 |
| Crump, Thomas M | Womack, Sarah Ann | Mar 22 1853 | 12/199 |
| Crut, Thomas | Pairu, Matilda (Paine) | Apr 22 1839* | 3/168 |
| Cruzat, Mary I | Cruzat, William | Apr 12 1849* | 8/368 |
| Cruzat, William | Cruzat, Mary I | Apr 12 1849* | 8/368 |
| Cruzat, Marie Modeste | Raymond, Henry H | Jun 5 1839* | 3/177 |
| Cuaudler, Sarah Ann | Wilson, L Madison | Dec 20 1837* | 3/104 |
| Cuensky, Samuel | Levy, Caroline | Feb 18 1842 | 6/82 |
| Cuete, Marchtalena | Vitman, Michael | Feb 14 1849 | 8/357 |
| Cuillin, George | Keeland, Sarah | Apr 15 1854 | 13/185 |
| Culbertson, John | Mervin, Elizabeth | Apr 29 1845 | 8/89B |
| Culholy, Bridget | Costillo, Walter | Nov 16 1837* | 3/101 |
| Cullen, Hannah | Johnston, Sandy | May 8 1852 | 11/246 |
| Cullian, Bridget | Balardo, G | 1852* | 0IB |
| Cullum, Catherine | Graham, William | Mar 24 1830 | 2/119 |
| Cullum, Charlotte | Jacques, Moses | May 30 1825 | 1/79 |
| Cullum, Eveline | Ryan, John C | Oct 19 1844 | 8/44B |
| Cullum, Mary B | Mooney, William S | Jan 6 1825 | 1/60 |
| Cumming, Jane | Sutherland, Alexander Jr | Sep 1 1854 | 13/327 |
| Cummings, David L | Wade, Caroline M | Sep 4 1851 | 11/176 |
| Cummings, George S | Barker, Ann | Jan 8 1844 | 5/314B |
| Cummings, Jesse J | Watson, Gavin G | Aug 23 1854 | 13/319 |
| Cummings, William | Durdon, Mary | Feb 7 1840* | 5/11 |
| Cummins, Elizabeth J | Wafford, James H | Apr 8 1848 | 8/297 |
| Cummins, Hannah | Brodie, William | Jan 7 1854 | 13/64 |
| Cummins, John | Gibson, Malinda | Jul 9 1846* | 8/177 |
| Cummins, John | Mullin, Ann | Jun 2 1854 | 13/239 |
| Cummins, Michael | Lehay, Ann | Nov 16 1852 | 12/63 |
| Cune, Sarah Cleveland | Boynton, Eli E | May 3 1847 | 8/232 |
| Cunningham, Bridgett | Billings, Samuel W | Sep 9 1846 | 8/188 |
| Cunningham, Caroline | Goodman, Thomas D | Nov 14 1848 | 8/332 |
| Cunningham, Catherine | Sanderford, John | Aug 14 1838* | 3/139 |
| Cunningham, Charlotte | Stratkins, Richard | Nov 5 1839* | 3/190 |
| Cunningham, Daniel | Dilon, Catharine | Jun 13 1839* | 3/179 |
| Cunningham, Ellen | Fields, George | Apr 1 1845 | 8/83B |
| Cunningham, Francis | Davis, Martha | Feb 5 1840* | 5/11 |
| Cunningham, James | Kelly, Mary | Aug 7 1823 | 1/10 |
| Cunningham, John | Cassanas, Josephine | Jan 30 1854* | 13/109 |
| Cunningham, Robert C | Gascoigne, Martha C | Jan 11 1848 | 8/277 |
| Cunningham, William | Dugan, Bridget | Apr 27 1843 | 5/265B |
| Cup, Mary | Davis, William | Feb 4 1833* | 2/1151 |
| Cuppum, Mary | Rodrigues, Joseph | Jul 9 1845 | 8/110B |
| Curity, Mary F | Kenny, James | Jan 8 1845 | 8/66 |
| Curlett, George | Adams, Lucy W | Apr 11 1848 | 8/298 |
| Curly, Patrick | Avey, Catherine | Apr 13 1844 | 8/12B |
| Curly, Patrick | Farren, Margaret | Sep 3 1851* | 11/176 |
| Curran, Charlotte | Hines, Michael | Jan 6 1843 | 5/168B |
| Curran, Elizabeth | Montigue, Edward | Feb 12 1855 | 14/49 |
| Curran, Joseph | O'Connor, Johanna | Feb 15 1831* | 2/151 |
| Currie, Edward | Linch, Mary | Sep 1 1851 | 11/175 |
| Currie, Roderick | Donelly, Catherine | Apr 16 1853 | 12/242 |
| Currie, Rose | Raffin, Joseph | Oct 20 1824 | 1/42 |
| Currier, Charles H | Kallinger, Mary | Jan 11 1851 | 11/111 |
| Curry, Edward | Cooper, Caroline P | Nov 23 1846 | 8/200 |
| Curry, Helen M | Goss, Henry A | Jun 25 1850 | 11/68 |
| Curry, Keren P | Winter, George | Nov 25 1851 | 11/189 |
| Curry, Mary Ann | Freeman, John W | Aug 17 1855 | 14/213 |
| Curry, Nancy | Maxwell, Benjamin | Jan 8 1855 | 14/3 |
| Curtain, Joanna | Donnovan, Dennis | Jun 7 1854 | 13/244 |

| BRIDE OR GROOM | SPOUSE | DATE | BOOK/PAGE |
|---|---|---|---|
| Curtain, Patrick | Sary, Mary (Kary) | Dec 23 1840 | 5/79B |
| Curtin, Ellen | Meade, Garrett | Mar 26 1842 | 5/188 |
| Curtin, Joanna | Lewis, William H | Aug 20 1850 | 11/81 |
| Curtin, John | Dunn, Ellen | Aug 24 1843 | 5/293 |
| Curtin, Julia | Cotter, Maurice | Jul 23 1849* | 8/382 |
| Curtin, Michael | Joice, Ann | Oct 18 1853 | 12/416 |
| Curtis, Harvey | Wilson, Mary | Mar 31 1831* | 2/160 |
| Curtis, Joseph | Garcier, Ramona | Sep 29 1853 | 12/411 |
| Curtis, Mary G | Blakester, George | Feb 22 1844 | 5/324B |
| Curtis, Susan | Newbold, Thomas D | Mar 8 1852 | 11/225 |
| Cusack, William | Burk, Mary | May 2 1852 | 11/245 |
| Cuslin, William | O'Brien, Hannah | Apr 20 1852 | 11/239 |
| Cussan, Ellen | Green, Thomas | Jan 28 1842 | 6/64B |
| Cuthbert, Cornelia M | Platt, William H | Apr 15 1848 | 8/299 |
| Cuthbert, Eloise | Goulding, Thomas B | Nov 23 1848* | 8/334 |
| Cuthbert, James | McLaughlin, Rose | Jan 5 1843* | 5/241B |
| Cuthbert, John C | Davis, Ada Eugenia | Dec 14 1848 | 8/339 |
| Cutler, Frances C | Baker, Albert W | May 15 1844 | 8/21B |
| Cypress, Rebecca | Ross, Andrew | Dec 23 1830* | 2/144 |

# D

| Dade, Agnes W | Tankersley, Frederick | Nov 20 1851 | 11/188 |
|---|---|---|---|
| Dade, Harriet E | Travis, Enoch | Mar 19 1839* | 3/160 |
| Dade, Mary E | Middleton, Lewis A | Feb 15 1844 | 5/322B |
| Dade, Mary S. | Lane, Robert C | May 13 1819* | CM |
| Dade, Robert R | Thomson, Mary | Jun 14 1820* | CM |
| Dade, Robert T | Mitchell, Mary E | Apr 13 1846* | 8/158B |
| Dade, Robert T. Jr | Ainsworth, Sarah | May 16 1844 | 8/21B |
| Dades, Virginia T | McKinstry, Alexander | Mar 20 1845 | 8/80B |
| Daffin, Rebecca | Dupertuis, George | Mar 8 1853 | 12/186 |
| Dailey, Bridget | Williams, Thomas | Mar 6 1852 | 11/225 |
| Dailey, Hanoughe | Kelly, Charles | Jun 4 1838* | 3/130 |

| BRIDE OR GROOM | SPOUSE | DATE | BOOK/PAGE |
|---|---|---|---|
| Dailey, Margaret | Fox, Felix | May 27 1851 | 11/153 |
| Dailey, Margarett | Byrne, James | Apr 23 1840 | 5/20 |
| Dailey, Matilda | Farrell, Edward | Oct 21 1850 | 11/90 |
| Dailey, Nathaniel | Langham, Mary | Sep 6 1832 | 2/1351 |
| Dailey, Norah | Wisdom, Patrick | May 27 1847* | 8/237 |
| Dailey, Thomas W | Weekes, Delphine | Oct 12 1815* | CM |
| Daily, Alexander | Alexander, Sarah | Jul 4 1851 | 11/161 |
| Daily, Ann | Quinn, Michael | Aug 25 1845 | 8/116B |
| Daily, Daniel | Conway, Mary | Apr 15 1844 | 8/10B |
| Dain, Nancy (Pain) | Hall, William M | Dec 12 1844 | 8/58B |
| Dakin, Charles B | Webb, Caroline | Mar 20 1837* | 3/76 |
| Dalbeare, Griswold H | Robbins, Ella | Jul 23 1839* | 3/182 |
| Dale, Thomas J | Wacker, Ann | Jan 9 1846* | 8/138B |
| Daley, Michael | Hagan, Rosa | Dec 19 1839* | 5/4 |
| Dally, Michael (Daily) | Callaghan, Julia | 1837* | OIB |
| Dalton, Ann | Smith, George | Jan 4 1854 | 13/61 |
| Dalton, Catharine | Dunoghue, John | May 25 1850 | 11/63 |
| Dalton, Eliza Ann | McGee, Robert | Apr 11 1850 | 11/52 |
| Dalton, Julia | Breadahbin, C.M. | Jun 5 1837* | 3/81 |
| Dalton, Margaret | Jones, William M | Nov 23 1833* | 2/691 |
| Daly, Ellen | Carson, Thomas | Apr 21 1843 | 5/263B |
| Damoan, Euphrosie (Demouy) | Blair, Thomas | Jun 12 1815* | CM |
| Dana, Caleb | Emmett, Ellen | Oct 10 1848 | 8/327 |
| Dana, Sarah Ann | Post, Ward | Dec 27 1849* | 11/29 |
| Danalen, Jane | Haley, Daniel | Jun 19 1855 | 14/178 |
| Danby, Dennis | Wells, Mary | Jul 31 1844 | 7/359 |
| Daniel, Abner | Jones, Elizabeth | 1837* | OIB |
| Daniel, Abner | Negus, Elizabeth | Sep 5 1833 | 2/791 |
| Daniel, Asa | Brasheirs, Rachael | Jun 12 1846 | 8/172 |
| Daniel, Ellen | Truwitt, Patrick | Jun 22 1853 | 12/328 |
| Daniels, Abner | Smith, Mary | Feb 22 1828* | 2/8 |
| Danley, Dennis | Wells, Mary | Jul 31 1844 | 8/37B |
| Dann, Stamath | Beielle, Catherine L | Dec 28 1850 | 11/106 |
| Danneberg, Charles | Corbitt, Henora | Feb 25 1854 | 13/141 |
| Dannhyser, Marks | David, Janete | Aug 4 1854* | 13/301 |
| Dantworth, David | Ford, Mary Ann | Mar 12 1846 | 7/680B |
| Darby, Ellen | Delanney, Michael | Apr 27 1839* | 3/169 |
| Darcy, Bridget | Bein, Patrick | Mar 31 1854 | 13/169 |
| Dargin, Edward | O'Neal, Selina | Feb 15 1855 | 14/52 |
| Dargin, John | Eastburn, Caroline A | Jun 29 1854 | 13/268 |
| Darling, Caroline | Flaut, Joseph H | 1827* | OIB |
| Darling, Eliza | Hammond, Charles | 1838* | OIB |
| Darling, Maria | Beaumont, William | Sep 2 1843 | 5/294B |
| Darlton, Valentine T | Edward, Rosena | Dec 28 1840* | 5/81B |
| Darrieux, John H | Pinta, Marie V (wid) | May 16 1853 | 12/285 |
| Darrington, Eliza C | Carter, John T | Dec 23 1854 | 13/419 |
| Daubert, Elizabeth Amanda | Vedrenne, Louis H N | May 27 1846 | 8/170 |
| Daughdrill, (NFN) | Vaughn, John B | Jul 9 1839* | 3/181 |
| Daugherty, Mary | McKibbon, Henry | Jan 25 1831* | 2/148 |
| Daugherty, Sarah | Hall, Edward L | Nov 4 1848 | 8/331 |
| Daughin, Henry | Corrizilla, Rosalba | Aug 14 1854 | 13/311 |
| Daughterty, Susan | Miller, Alex | Jul 22 1813* | WB1/7 |
| Daughtry, Turner | Davis, Susan | Jun 14 1844* | 8/28B |
| Daulworth, David | Ford, Mary Ann | Mar 12 1846 | 8/151B |
| Davenport, Charles | McFarren, Catherine | Mar 1 1836* | 3/41 |
| Davenport, Eliza M | McFarlen, Dugald | Mar 7 1825 | 1/66 |
| Davenport, Joanna ? | Blossman, Sampson | Mar 19 1838* | 3/115 |
| Davenport, Sarah Ann | Roper, James W | Jun 10 1830* | 2/130 |
| Daves, George Jr | Dunn, Roseanna | 1837* | OIB |
| David, Elizabeth | King, Alexander K | Jan 6 1834* | 2/571 |
| David, Francis | Lebaron, Mary Ellen | Jun 12 1850* | 11/66 |
| David, Janete | Dannhyser, Marks | Aug 4 1854* | 13/301 |
| David, Simon | Weathers, Elizabeth | 1826* | OIB |
| David, Tobias | Loeb, Schannet | Mar 3 1853* | 12/183 |

| BRIDE OR GROOM | SPOUSE | DATE | BOOK/PAGE |
|---|---|---|---|
| Davidson, Alley | Evans, Charles B | Aug 11 1818* | CM |
| Davidson, John | Bateman, Elizabeth | Nov 30 1844 | 8/55B |
| Davidson, John | McCune, Jane | May 10 1848 | 8/304 |
| Davidson, John C | Rodgers, Cynthia | Nov 7 1832* | 2/1301 |
| Davidson, John H | Morely, Clarissa A | Nov 8 1854 | 13/373 |
| Davidson, Joseph | Blackman, Sarah | May 4 1852* | 11/245 |
| Davidson, Julia | Turner, James | Jul 11 1833* | 2/851B |
| Davidson, Margaret | Traino, William | Dec 15 1851* | 11/194 |
| Davidson, Margaret | Brett, Michael | Mar 24 1852 | 11/230 |
| Davidson, Margaret Ann | Smith, William P | May 7 1855* | 14/133 |
| Davidson, Mary | Tucker, William | May 1 1824 | 1/29 |
| Davidson, Mary Ann | Childress, Samuel | Jun 29 1836* | 3/52 |
| Davidson, May | Veldaiser, Joseph | Apr 9 1840* | 5/18 |
| Davidson, Preston | Deakle, Louise | Sep 5 1854 | 13/330 |
| Davidson, Reana | Bozard, John | Apr 29 1844 | 8/17B |
| Davidson, Robert | Mott, Nancy M | May 23 1835* | 3/16 |
| Davidson, Robert J | Berg, Clara E | Jan 2 1855 | 13/430 |
| Davidson, Samuel | Twelves, Margaret | Dec 22 1843 | 5/310B |
| Davidson, William | Swift, Elizabeth | Dec 23 1845 | 8/132B |
| Davidson, William | Lamey, Severine | Jan 10 1855 | 14/12 |
| Davies, Sarah M | Edgerly, Daniel | Jun 25 1844 | 8/30B |
| Davis, Ada Eugenia | Cuthbert, John C | Dec 14 1848* | 8/339 |
| Davis, Adeline | Bixley, Edward J | Feb 5 1838* | 3/109 |
| Davis, Alvan P | Lappington, Mary Ann | Mar 4 1839* | 3/159 |
| Davis, Ann | Smith, George | Aug 13 1835* | 3/25 |
| Davis, Ann | Slavin, Edward | May 13 1836* | 3/47 |
| Davis, D R W | Norris, Mary | Dec 2 1840* | 5/71B |
| Davis, David | Howard, Axeth | Feb 15 1839* | 3/157 |
| Davis, Edward D | Flury, Nicy | Mar 19 1841* | 5/118B |
| Davis, Elizabeth | Smith, John R | 1827* | OIB |
| Davis, Elizabeth | Ressing, William | Jan 21 1851* | 11/116 |
| Davis, Elizabeth | Geyer, Peter | May 16 1832* | 2/1511 |
| Davis, Elizabeth | Saunders, Samuel | Jun 3 1828* | 2/30 |
| Davis, Elizabeth | Pearce, William | May 1 1829 | 2/83 |
| Davis, Elizabeth | Parsons, William | Jun 9 1830 | 2/128 |
| Davis, Elizabeth | Stafford, John F | Mar 3 1842* | 5/185B |
| Davis, Elizabeth A | Goff, Lewis T | Apr 11 1847 | 8/226 |
| Davis, Emma | Arguelles, Lewis D | Feb 3 1849 | 8/353 |
| Davis, George | Nouilin, Mary | Jun 9 1823* | 1/6 |
| Davis, George | Torbin, Alice | Apr 29 1854 | 13/210 |
| Davis, George Jr | O'Hara, Catherine | Dec 22 1849 | 11/27 |
| Davis, Hansford | Gilder, Sarah Ann E | Dec 22 1849 | 11/27 |
| Davis, Huldah | Charpin, Francis | Jul 22 1835* | 3/20 |
| Davis, Isaac S | Blakely, Matilda S | Apr 6 1841* | 5/121B |
| Davis, James | Tayler, Mary | Aug 5 1839* | 3/184 |
| Davis, James | Pierce, Nancy | Mar 20 1844 | 5/328B |
| Davis, Jane B | Malcomson, John | Sep 8 1845 | 8/117B |
| Davis, John | Strill, Elizabeth | May 9 1848* | 8/303 |
| Davis, John | Sallenant, Emiline ? | Aug 18 1840* | 5/43 |
| Davis, John | Lallemant, Emiline ? | Aug 18 1848* | 5/43 |
| Davis, John L | Thompson, Eliza | Apr 29 1850 | 11/56 |
| Davis, John W | Hall, Lucretia V | Mar 22 1853 | 12/198 |
| Davis, Julia Ann | Alexander, Jefferson | Jun 18 1836* | 3/51 |
| Davis, Julia Ann | Williams, Andrew J | Feb 23 1843 | 5/250B |
| Davis, Julia B | Lewis, Sanford | Sep 28 1848 | 8/326 |
| Davis, Lucy A | Ellis, Albert P | Dec 4 1850 | 11/101 |
| Davis, Margaret (wid) | Bousson, John A (widr) | Dec 30 1853 | 13/57 |
| Davis, Martha | Cunningham, Francis | Feb 5 1840* | 5/11 |
| Davis, Mary (wid) | Riley, Thomas (widr) | Feb 7 1853 | 12/167 |
| Davis, Mary | Jackson, William | Oct 20 1853 | 12/422 |
| Davis, Nicholas | Brown, Mary | 1837* | OIB |
| Davis, Sabrina C | Archer, John | Mar 11 1824 | 1/25 |
| Davis, Samuel | Weekley, Elizabeth | Dec 8 1819* | CM |
| Davis, Sarah | Robbins, Granberry | Jan 27 1853 | 12/149 |

| BRIDE OR GROOM | SPOUSE | DATE | BOOK/PAGE |
|---|---|---|---|
| Davis, Sarah | Hattenstein, Simon | Jan 1 1853 | 12/109 |
| Davis, Sarah M | Edgerly, Daniel | Jun 25 1844 | 8/30B |
| Davis, Susan | Daughtry, Turner | Jun 14 1844* | 8/28B |
| Davis, William | Cochran, Sarah | 1837* | OIB |
| Davis, William | Cup, Mary | Feb 4 1833* | 2/1151 |
| Davis, William | Lambert, Mary | Dec 4 1835* | 3/32 |
| Davis, William | Crocker, Sarah (Cochran) | Mar 24 1837* | 3/76 |
| Davis, William H | Conway, Sarah | Jun 10 1813* | WB1/8 |
| Davis, William H | Gaines, Helen T | Dec 29 1840* | 5/81B |
| Davis, William J | Overton, Matilda A | Sep 5 1849 | 11/2 |
| Davison, Betsy | Bosage, Victor | Mar 30 1837* | 3/77 |
| Davison, Samuel | Twelves, Margaret | Dec 22 1843 | 7/65B |
| Dawson, Bethia (wid ?) | Dinson, Matthew | May 6 1829 | 2/85 |
| Dawson, Elizabeth (wid) | Woolerd, Hugh | Feb 23 1819* | CM |
| Dawson, Elizabeth | Barry, Samuel D C | Dec 11 1855 | 14/302 |
| Dawson, Elizabeth Ann | Wells, John H | Jun 4 1828 | 2/31 |
| Dawson, John C | Harrison, Rose Earle | Apr 29 1846 | 8/161B |
| Dawson, Robert | Winship, Bathia | 1827* | OIB |
| Day, Ellen | Ivory, Edward | Jan 5 1844* | 5/313B |
| Day, Marie | Preour, Francois | Nov 15 1838* | 3/148 |
| Dea, John O (O'Day) | Sullivan, Bridget | Feb 11 1847* | 8/216 |
| Deakle, Elizabeth | Smith, Jesse C | Jun 11 1847* | 8/241 |
| Deakle, James A | Baker, Exer | Feb 27 1852 | 11/222 |
| Deakle, Louise | Davidson, Preston | Sep 5 1854 | 13/330 |
| Deakle, Mary | Bullard, James | Sep 2 1853* | 12/399 |
| Deakle, William | Childress, Elizabeth | Sep 22 1855 | 14/237 |
| Dealy, Richard | Dumouy, Marcelle | May 30 1814* | CM |
| Dean, Henry | Baptiste, Louisa | Sep 18 1848* | 8/322 |
| Dean, William | Mims, Sally | Jul 21 1842* | 5/212B |
| Deana, Anna F | Gage, Robert | Oct 2 1855 | 14/244 |
| Dearing, Michael | Wilson, Bridget (Mrs) | Apr 21 1851 | 11/140 |
| Dearmos, C Michel | Marchand, Martin A | Apr 25 1840 | 5/20 |
| Deas, Hopson | George, Emeline | Dec 21 1839* | 5/4 |
| Deas, John C | Auzi, A | Dec 22 1844 | 8/62B |
| Deas, Margaret | Anze, Charles A | May 24 1841* | 5/133 |
| Deas, Mary C | Brown, N Harleston | Dec 24 1850 | 11/105 |
| Deas, States G | Cluis, Emily A | Jan 5 1836* | 3/34 |
| Deas, Wiseman | Carpenter, Emily | Mar 29 1843 | 5/255B |
| Deaves, Edward F | Orr, Isabella | Mar 11 1854 | 13/154 |
| Debaker, Edward | Delaba, Delphine | Feb 13 1855 | 14/51 |
| Debell, Susan J | Leslie, Henry | May 5 1849* | 8/373 |
| Debeupart, Joanna    ? | Blossman, Sampson | Mar 19 1838* | 3/115 |
| Debore, Catherine | Parks, Augustus | Sep 25 1851 | 11/180 |
| Debose, Martha | McAm, John E (McCann) | Jan 24 1848* | 8/278 |
| Debose, Rebecca | Burwell, John G | Jan 1 1849 | 8/343 |
| Debosh, Fanny | Helverson, Godfrey | Aug 15 1823 | 1/11 |
| Deboure, John | Brown, Catharine | Mar 22 1849* | 8/363 |
| Deboutiere, Florida J | Cluis, Frederick V | Oct 27 1835* | 3/30 |
| Debrier(re), Antonie | Thary, Margaret N | Apr 27 1853 | 12/257 |
| Debriere, S T (St Anice) | Nicholas, Florentine | Jul 18 1853 | 12/359 |
| Debrierre, Antonio | Raffin, Rose | Aug 28 1835* | 3/26 |
| Debritton, Emma | Waggaman, Henry B | Jul 31 1849* | 8/385 |
| Debrow, George | Toulmin, Lucinda | Dec 30 1833 | 2/631 |
| Deburrows, Francis | Foreman, Cassandra | 1837* | OIB |
| Deburrows, Mary | Boyrus, Torrance | Feb 20 1852 | 11/219 |
| Decamp, Caroline  L M | Decamp, Vincent | May 7 1838* | 3/124 |
| Decamp, Caroline  M | Capus, Raymond | Sep 16 1841 | 4/921B |
| Decamp, Vincent | Decamp, Caroline L M | May 7 1838* | 3/124 |
| Decauss, Lucy Caroline M | Cassus, Ramond | Sep 15 1841* | 5/151 |
| Dechristain, Ellen | Lewis, Isaac | Jul 6 1831* | 2/178 |
| Decker, Catherine | Peter, Joseph | Sep 27 1851 | 11/180 |
| Deckmere, Louisa | Kibler, Christian | Jun 14 1841* | 5/135 |
| Decuy, Stanislaus | Sogey, Marie | Jul 17 1851 | 11/165 |
| Deebarco, John Baptiste | Sheils, Margarette | Feb 5 1840* | 5/11 |

41

| BRIDE OR GROOM | SPOUSE | DATE | BOOK/PAGE |
|---|---|---|---|
| Deeley, John H | Lee, Matilda C | Sep 4 1852 | 11/282 |
| Deene, Mary E | Starr, Richard T | May 18 1846 | 8/167B |
| Deering, Alexander W | Grant, Helen M | Nov 29 1845 | 7/852B |
| Dees, Elizabeth A | Easterling, William L | Dec 14 1855 | 14/305 |
| Dees, Sarah Ann | Brient, Adolphus | Aug 20 1845 | 8/115B |
| Dees, Willis | Brady, Mary | Feb 19 1851 | 11/123 |
| Deese, Creisey (wid) | Brown, George | Oct 19 1853 | 12/419 |
| Deflander, Rose | Saris, Cyprian | Mar 29 1847 | 8/223 |
| Dege, John A | Schamaker, Maria L | Feb 22 1854 | 13/131 |
| Degraces, Sophe Plena | Miland, Luc F | Mar 8 1828* | 2/13 |
| DeGuirmand, Morel I | Rauson, S Adele | Jun 25 1836* | 3/51 |
| Dehn, Andres | Hain, Barbara | Dec 26 1848* | 8/341 |
| Deidrick, Peter | Ellis, Joanna | Mar 18 1854 | 13/162 |
| Deiz, Joseph | Bozage, Matilda | Jun 27 1844 | 8/29B |
| Dejanvry, Pierre Pascal G | Vallat, Jeanne J (wid) | Jun 12 1848 | 8/308 |
| Dekle, William E (Dehle) | Roberts, Susan | May 21 1853 | 12/293 |
| Delaba, Delphine | Debaker, Edward | Feb 13 1855 | 14/51 |
| Delafore, Harriett | Gordon, John I | Dec 14 1835* | 3/33 |
| Delage, Charles Louis | Landry, Virgine G | May 17 1824 | 1/31 |
| Delage, Lucy A | Roulston, James T | Feb 4 1850 | 11/37 |
| Delamere, Edward J | Bird, Catharine | Jun 26 1849* | 8/393 |
| Delaney, Ann | Silver, Francis | Feb 10 1852 | 11/216 |
| Delaney, Patrick | Casey, Bridget | Jan 14 1854 | 13/78 |
| Delanney, Michael | Darby, Ellen | Apr 27 1839* | 3/169 |
| Delany, Jane | Gooden, James | Nov 4 1846 | 8/197 |
| Delany, William | Devine, Jane | Apr 3 1841* | 5/120B |
| Delarge, J B Charles | Peitcher, H C (Rettcher) | Dec 4 1838* | 3/151 |
| Delary, Henry | Farron, Mary | Jan 25 1838* | 3/109 |
| Delbarco, John Baptiste | Sheilds, Margarette | Feb 5 1840* | 5/11 |
| Del Barco, Joseph W | Dorman, Rosa Anna | Jun 23 1852 | 11/266 |
| Delbarco, Lewis | Lusse, Mary Louise | Mar 28 1842 | 5/189B |
| Delbecco, Margaret S | Stoude, Adolphe D | Apr 10 1855 | 14/101 |
| Delborce, Mary J | Hardaway, William A | Apr 7 1840* | 5/17 |
| Delchamps, John Julius | Bancroft, Sarah E | Nov 23 1844* | 8/54B |
| Dellmar, Maria (Dittmar) | McCoul, Thomas | Mar 1 1844 | 5/325 |
| Delmas, Carlos | Rabby, Sophia | Nov 5 1853 | 13/8 |
| Delmas, Mary H | Ellison, William P | Jan 2 1846 | 8/135B |
| Deloach, Thomas C | Perryman, Mary S | Nov 25 1845 | 8/126B |
| Delor, Simon | Igregoi, Epolite | Dec 9 1830* | 2/143 |
| Del Rosano, Chacine Maria | Ferino, Celso G | Feb 13 1841* | 5/104B |
| Demarest, John | Clawdes, Mary Ann C | Dec 29 1828 | 2/59 |
| Demath, James T ? | Gates, Adelia | Nov 2 1852 | 12/43 |
| Demerest, John B | Alexander, Eliza | Sep 20 1836* | 3/59 |
| Demeritt, J S | St Shackleford, Ruth | Jun 28 1838 | 3/134 |
| Demeritt, J S | Shackleford, Ruth | Jun 28 1838 | 3/134 |
| DeMiller, Sarah E | Perkins, William K | Dec 4 1852 | 12/82 |
| Demott, Margaret | Kibbe, Gaines | Sep 12 1844* | 8/40B |
| Demott, Michael | Cole, Margaret | 1822* | OIB |
| Demouy, Augustin | Fisher, Hypolite | Oct 25 1830* | 2/142 |
| Demouy, Catherine | Stephens, William | Apr 20 1840* | 3/198 |
| Demouy, Isabel | Bassford, Daniel C | Feb 10 1851 | 11/120 |
| Demouy, Joseph | Girard, Isabel | May 26 1851 | 11/152 |
| Demouy, Louis | Gerlot, Rosalie | Jun 6 1842 | 5/204B |
| Demouy, Margaret | Clements, Anderson | Dec 21 1831* | 2/1771 |
| Demouy, Merced | Antunez, Joaquim | Mar 3 1832* | 2/1691 |
| Demouy, Polite | Grelot, Maximillian | Jun 17 1851 | 11/158 |
| Dempsey, Caroline L | Labuze, John A | Apr 19 1828 | 2/11 |
| Dempsey, Susan | Boutin, Francis L L | 1827* | OIB |
| Demsey, Bridget | Johnson, George | Apr 13 1844 | 8/13B |
| Demten, C | Killy, Antonio S | Mar 14 1851 | 11/129 |
| Denhew, Daniel | Browhe, Margaret | Jan 22 1855 | 14/21 |
| Denice, Carmilla (Dennis) | Murdock, Thomas | Jun 15 1852 | 11/262 |
| Denin, More (Denison) | Moreland, Thomas | Dec 14 1827* | 2/185 |
| Denison, Elenah | Youman, John W | May 27 1847* | 8/237 |

| BRIDE OR GROOM | SPOUSE | DATE | BOOK/PAGE |
|---|---|---|---|
| Denison, More | Moreland, Thomas | Dec 14 1827* | 2/185 |
| Denley, Sarah Ann | McKenzie, Francis | Jan 3 1843 | 5/168 |
| Denmark, Bryant J | Lott, Elizabeth (Sott) | Sep 10 1842 | 5/219B |
| Dennett, William B | Haupt, Rebecca E | Feb 28 1853 | 12/181 |
| Denney, Bridget | Cameron, Roderick | Mar 10 1855 | 14/78 |
| Dennis, Duderick | Harris, Catherine | Aug 10 1842 | 6/184B |
| Dennis, Nora | Nowland, Thomas | Dec 14 1827 | 2/1 |
| Dennis, Peter H | Thompson, Betsy | Aug 10 1842 | 6/183B |
| Denny, Alec A | Drake, Ermeline | Dec 13 1819* | CM |
| Denny, Mary | Coyle, Edward | Apr 16 1840* | 5/19 |
| Denny, Mary Ann | McCauley, James | May 21 1831* | 2/171 |
| Dent, Maria | Rawls, John J | May 22 1851* | 11/151 |
| Dent, Robert K | Mason, Virginia A | Jun 10 1854 | 13/250 |
| Denton, Maria | Gezon, Louis | May 1 1850 | 11/58 |
| Denver, William | Skillman, Caroline A | Jan 25 1853* | 12/143 |
| Deolin, Catherine | Ayers, Andrew | Mar 21 1831* | 2/157 |
| Deolin, Mary | McIntyre, James | Feb 15 1855 | 14/54 |
| Deolin, Patrick (Devlin) | McCormick, Catherine | May 18 1854 | 13/228 |
| Depat, Jules ? | Dueros, M C Sophie | Apr 3 1837* | 3/78 |
| Depew, Ann E | Miley, John | Sep 12 1837* | 3/91 |
| DePre, James Henry | Jomaron, Mary L Z | 1826* | OIB |
| Deputron, Jacob | Nowlisa, Eliza (Noulin) | Apr 6 1839* | 3/164 |
| Deranco, Marie Louise T M | Costanzi, Felix A B | Nov 23 1846 | 8/200 |
| Dere, Columba (DeRe) | Capella, Francisco | Nov 10 1853 | 13/11 |
| Dere, Nicola | Botto, Columba | Mar 24 1851 | 11/131 |
| Derenbesher, Elizabeth | Wolfkul, Herman H | Jan 27 1855 | 14/23 |
| Derenek, Charles | Malone, Bridget | Jul 2 1842* | 5/210B |
| Dergus, Josephine | Fourment, Zepheren | May 31 1852 | 11/257 |
| Dermar, Jose (Dumas) | Criss, Mary (Creps) | Sep 30 1844 | 8/42B |
| Desage, Louisa A (DeLage) | Parker, Robert M | Jan 6 1842 | 5/169B |
| Descoges, Marie J L | Saint Guiron, Pierre P | Apr 26 1832* | 2/159 |
| Dese, William (Deas) | Rester, Eliza | Nov 12 1844 | 8/50B |
| Deshan, Phebe Ann | Smith, Murray F | May 30 1840* | 5/25 |
| Deshears, Elizabeth (wid) | Stevenson, Joseph (widr) | Jun 27 1853 | 12/331 |
| Deshee, Caroline | Barney, Hindrance | Mar 15 1847 | 8/221 |
| Deshon, Charles A | Smoot, Emma A | Aug 13 1850* | 11/79 |
| Deshon, Henry P | Henry, Martha W | Jul 26 1850 | 11/76 |
| Desloge, Augustus | Perier, Marie S | 1826* | OIB |
| Desmukes, Henry J | Boyles, Elizabeth S | Jul 12 1848* | 8/316 |
| Desmukes, Lucinda | Justis, Noah | May 28 1847 | 8/238 |
| Desmukes, Lydia A | Attwood, Malberry B | Feb 5 1852 | 11/212 |
| De St Cyr, Hyacinth | Batre, Zoe | Feb 11 1846 | 8/145B |
| Detroye, Marie Antoinette | Cosleir, Alexandre | May 24 1842 | 5/203B |
| Devanport, Joana | Blossman, Sampson | Mar 19 1838* | 3/115 |
| DeVaubercy, Isabella G | Lewis, Curtis | 1826* | OIB |
| Develin, Anna | Wallace, James | Jun 26 1820* | CM |
| DeVendel, Angele E | Hull, William H | Apr 20 1842 | 5/193B |
| DeVendel, Melanie Adelade | Nest, James Jr (West) | Oct 27 1841* | 5/155B |
| Devenen, Charles | Malene, Bridget | Jul 2 1842 | 6/170B |
| Devenie, Margaret (Devine) | Kelly, John | Jul 7 1855 | 14/191 |
| Devillers, Aimie J | Duprey, J B | Mar 9 1840* | 5/14 |
| Devin, Catherine | McDermott, Thomas | Jun 10 1839* | 3/177 |
| Devin, Margaret | Gyrell, William (Tyrrell) | Jul 21 1838* | 3/136 |
| Devin, William | O'Connor, Mary | Feb 11 1838* | 3/111 |
| Devine, Ann | Leonard, Martin | Dec 18 1852 | 12/98 |
| Devine, Colman | Welsh, Mary | Feb 20 1855 | 14/61 |
| Devine, James | Ward, Mary | Apr 7 1849* | 8/366 |
| Devine, Jane | Delany, William | Apr 3 1841* | 5/120B |
| Devine, John B | McGovern, Ann | Aug 30 1851* | 11/174 |
| Devine, Julia M E | Carey, Patrick M | Feb 9 1855 | 14/45 |
| Devine, Mary Ann | Ressijae, Louis S M | Jun 5 1843 | 5/278B |
| Devine, Patrick | Hesler, Mary | 1849* | OIB |
| Devine, Philip | Hilliard, Ann | Jun 10 1854 | 13/251 |
| Dewalt, Caroline | Barret, John W | Jul 19 1854 | 13/289 |

| BRIDE OR GROOM | SPOUSE | DATE | BOOK/PAGE |
|---|---|---|---|
| Dewier, Ellen (Dwyer) | Ross, Charles A | Apr 13 1840* | 5/19 |
| Dewitt, James | Irish, Margaret M | Apr 15 1841 | 5/123B |
| Dewitt, Margaret | Conley, Thomas L | Jan 3 1843 | 5/240B |
| Dewolff, Ellen D | Gayle, Andrew J | Jul 31 1845 | 8/113B |
| Di Andrea, Marquetta | Verdi, Luigi | Mar 13 1841 | 4/2831B |
| Di Andrea, Harietta | Verdi, Luigi | Mar 13 1841* | 5/119B |
| Dias, Barbary | Maure, Enacio | Sep 22 1852 | 12/11 |
| Dias, Jane | Robertson, James | Jun 8 1847 | 8/240 |
| Dias, John | Kline, Kitty | Apr 29 1814* | CM |
| Dias, Mary | Ganmon, William | Nov 25 1840 | 4/3271B |
| Dias, Serene C | Murphy, S. Jennings | May 25 1854 | 13/233 |
| Diaz, Joseph Lewis | Parra, Mary De Jesus | May 22 1847 | 8/236 |
| Dickeman, Cyrus  ? | Oliver, Susanna | 1823* | OIB |
| Dickens, Alonzo | Kellogg, Margaret | Jul 28 1825 | 1/87 |
| Dickey, William | Pierre, Catherine | Oct 16 1843 | 5/300B |
| Dickinson, Eli P | Powers, Caroline | Jan 27 1844 | 5/318B |
| Dickinson, Lois A | Haynie, John D | Feb 25 1836* | 3/41 |
| Dickinson, Louisa | Kiebler, Christian | Jun 4 1841 | 4/1861B |
| Dickinson, Rosanna | Love, Valentine | Jan 4 1840* | 5/7 |
| Dickson, Edward | Hamilton, Ann | Nov 21 1851 | 11/188 |
| Dickson, Edward | Flanegan, Mary Ann | Nov 30 1854* | 13/395 |
| Dickson, Mary T | Wetherwax, Jacob A | Jan 14 1847* | 8/212 |
| Diemer, Catherine | Peterson, Robert | Mar 4 1850 | 11/44 |
| Dies, Richard | Dorsey, Allice | Jul 11 1840 | 4/4021B |
| Dies, Sarah Ann | Brient, Adolphus | Aug 20 1845 | 8/215B |
| Diesher, Harman | Steinberg, Louisa | May 11 1842 | 5/199B |
| Dietrich, Barbara | Aubry, Michael | Jan 2 1846 | 8/135B |
| Diez, Joseph | Bossage, Matilda | Jun 27 1844 | 8/29B |
| DiGiovanna, Francois | Chevealleer, Marie | Apr 25 1854 | 13/205 |
| Dikeman, Burr | Kinneir, Georgiana B | Jan 25 1843 | 5/245B |
| Dikeman, Susan | Walker, Wilson | Nov 12 1834* | 2/11B |
| Dillard, William P | Pennington, Canzada Q | Oct 10 1853 | 12/413 |
| Dilleport, George | Campbell, Mary | Jan 25 1854 | 13/96 |
| Dilling, Philip | Lewis, Jane | Feb 25 1846* | 8/148B |
| Dillon, Elizabeth | Silk, William | Dec 29 1848* | 8/342 |
| Dillon, Louisa | Post, James B | Dec 26 1853 | 13/52 |
| Dillon, Margaret | Divine, James | Jan 8 1839* | 3/B152 |
| Dillon, Martin | Lawrence, Margaret | Aug 28 1834* | 2/181 |
| Dillon, Mary | McConnor, James | Apr 29 1838* | 3/121 |
| Dillon, Mary | Fenn, William (Ferm) | Dec 7 1842 | 5/232B |
| Dilon, Catharine | Cunningham, Daniel | Jun 13 1839* | 3/179 |
| Dinson, Matthew | Dawson, Bethia | May 6 1829 | 2/85 |
| Discher, Louisa | Frobos, Walter | Oct 23 1849 | 11/11 |
| Dismukes, Lucinda | Adams, Wyatt | Sep 13 1843 | 5/297B |
| Dismukes, Matilda | Richardson, William | Sep 29 1835* | 3/28 |
| Dismukes, Nancy M | Wainwright, Alexander | May 29 1843 | 5/276B |
| Disoney, Catherine | Stephens, William | Apr 20 1840* | 3/198 |
| Ditinar, Auguste | Amar, Mary | Aug 4 1835* | 3/21 |
| Ditman, Fanny | Markstein, David | Nov 24 1843 | 5/307B |
| Dittman, Marian (Dittmar) | McCoal, Thomas (McCoul) | Feb 6 1841 | 5/101B |
| Dittmar, Margaret L | Jackson, Stephen P | Dec 31 1853 | 13/58 |
| Dittmar, Maria | McCoul, Thomas | Mar 1 1844 | 5/325B |
| Dittmar, Maria | Horn, S H | May 30 1840* | 5/25 |
| Dittmar, Mary | Abels, Samuel W | Jan 4 1847 | 8/210 |
| Diveni, Michael (Devin) | Burke, Margaret | Aug 13 1853 | 12/381 |
| Divine, James | Dillon, Margaret | Jan 8 1839* | 3/152 |
| Dixey, Robert H | Minge, Jane O | Feb 3 1852 | 11/211 |
| Dixon, George | Nicholas, Florentine | May 31 1836* | 3/49 |
| Dixon, James | McDermott, Rosanna | Dec 8 1845 | 8/129B |
| Dobson, Elizabeth | Williams, Nathaniel F | 1827* | OIB |
| Dobson, Elizabeth | Nelson, John | Jun 21 1853* | 12/370 |
| Dobson, George | Toulmin, Lucinda | Dec 30 1833* | 2/631 |
| Dobson, Sarah Elizabeth | Hutchison, Alexander W | Aug 9 1853 | 12/378 |

| BRIDE OR GROOM | SPOUSE | DATE | BOOK/PAGE |
|---|---|---|---|
| Dodd, Mary | Dodge, Edmund | Feb 28 1844 | 5/325B |
| Dodds, Sarah | Sutten, John D | May 14 1845 | 8/95B |
| Dodge, Edmund | Dodd, Mary | Feb 28 1844 | 5/325B |
| Dodson, Wellington | Morgan, Theny | 1826* | OIB |
| Doggett, Thomas | Carman, Claire | Aug 4 1815* | CM |
| Dohn, Mary M | Wilkins, James | Sep 15 1841* | 5/151 |
| Dolan, Elizabeth | Graham, Thomas | May 29 1854 | 13/237 |
| Doland, Bridget | Struberg, Magmus P | Feb 26 1848 | 8/287 |
| Dolhende, Hry Alfred | Fourcard, Cauline | Apr 19 1852 | 11/239 |
| Dolin, Bridget | Cloonin, Michael | Jul 2 1850 | 11/71 |
| Doline, Mederick | Holley, Mary Ann | May 13 1835* | 3/14 |
| D'Olive, Catish | Vivare, Louis | Nov 2 1832* | 2/1321 |
| D'Olive, Mary D | Foster, Benjamin W | Jan 16 1854 | 13/80 |
| D'Olive, Mary M | Wilkins, James | Jan 15 1841 | 4/1791B |
| D'Olive, Mary | Wilkins, James | Sep 15 1841 | 5/151B |
| D'Olive, Mederick | Holley, Mary Ann | May 13 1835* | 3/14 |
| D'Olive, Modiste E | Weaver, James C | Nov 1 1848 | 8/331 |
| Dolman, Abraham H | Robinson, Mary Ann | Dec 12 1853 | 13/36 |
| Domingo, Joseph | Bonaville, Elizabeth | Aug 19 1854 | 13/315 |
| Dominique, Tujague | Prie, Francoise | Feb 17 1849* | 8/358 |
| Donaho, Ann | Rugan, Patrick | Jan 31 1853 | 12/157 |
| Donahoe, Patrick | Kennedy, Ellen | Feb 22 1854 | 13/132 |
| Donahue, Dennis | Keho, Catherine | Dec 20 1852 | 12/100 |
| Donako, Elizabeth | Higgins, Martin | Jan 5 1847 | 8/210 |
| Donald, Ann O | Stewart, James | Oct 15 1845 | 8/120B |
| Donald, Augustus H | Farley, Jane | Dec 14 1853 | 13/41 |
| Donald, Ellen | Flannery, John | Jul 11 1855 | 14/195 |
| Donald, Rosa O | Kainnary, John | Jan 24 1845⁻ | 8/68 |
| Donaldson, Helen | Benners, Edward G | Dec 16 1844 | 8/60B |
| Donaldson, Mary | Comick, Robert | Apr 27 1854 | 13/208 |
| Donally, Daniel | Cornhlion, Joanna | Jul 3 1842* | 5/210 |
| Donavan, Johanna | Lockman, Edward | Apr 26 1848* | 8/300 |
| Donavan, Michael | Doyle, Ellen | Jun 11 1855 | 14/167 |
| Donbach, Maria Louisa | Benhauser, Antoine | Dec 6 1836* | 3/63 |
| Donelly, Catherine | Currie, Roderick | Apr 16 1853 | 12/242 |
| Donn, William | Murray, Mary | Jan 14 1851 | 11/112 |
| Donnery, Tarrance H | Case, Bridget | Feb 11 1851* | 11/120 |
| Donnlly, Daniel | Carnhlion, Joanna | Jul 3 1842 | 6/172B |
| Donnolly, Eliza | McNulty, Patrick | Dec 2 1850 | 11/101 |
| Donnolly, Margaret | Feenny, Thomas | Mar 3 1851 | 11/127 |
| Donnoughouh, Ann (Mrs) | Foly, James | Nov 3 1851 | 11/186 |
| Donnovan, Dennis | Curtain, Joanna | Jun 7 1854 | 13/244 |
| Donoeff, Ellen D (Dewolff) | Gagle, Andrew I (Gayle) | Jul 31 1845 | 7/297B |
| Donoghoe, Jeremiah | Pendergast, Elizabeth wid | Jan 25 1853 | 12/144 |
| Donoghue, Jeremiah | Monaity, Margaret | Dec 29 1845 | 8/133B |
| Donohoe, Jeremiah | McMahon, Mary | Dec 4 1855 | 14/2982 |
| Donohoe, Mary | Egan, Mathew | Nov 11 1853 | 13/14 |
| Donohoe, Thomas | Martin, Ann | Jan 16 1854 | 13/83 |
| Donohue, Terry | Hogan, Elizabeth | Nov 24 1855* | 14/288 |
| Dooly, Thomas | Dowling, Mary | May 20 1852 | 11/253 |
| Doran, Catherine | Byrnes, Andrew | Dec 2 1854 | 13/396 |
| Doran, Hanora | Kelly, John | Jun 30 1852 | 11/268 |
| Doran, James | Taylor, Elizabeth | Nov 13 1843* | 5/303B |
| Doran, Mary | Bell, William | Jan 22 1850* | 11/35 |
| Doran, Mary | McGrath, Patrick | Oct 7 1852 | 12/25 |
| Dorathy, Sarah | McNaspy, James | Apr 12 1847* | 8/226 |
| Dore, Adrien | Judice, Marie Malvina | Apr 12 1853 | 12/237 |
| Dorey, Emily R | Rowell, Joseph | Oct 31 1838* | 3/145 |
| Dorgan, Andrew | Lappington, Mary A E | Jul 1 1851 | 11/161 |
| Dorgan, Catherine | Coil, James | Jul 31 1839* | 3/183 |
| Dorgan, Elizabeth | Geaudrean, John N | Sep 23 1852 | 12/13 |
| Dorherty, John | Boykin, June | Jan 8 1845* | 8/66B |
| Dorlan, Mulford | Lyons, Patsey | Jun 30 1845 | 8/108B |

| BRIDE OR GROOM | SPOUSE | DATE | BOOK/PAGE |
|---|---|---|---|
| Dorland, Carman | Hollinger, Maria | Oct 12 1841 | 5/153B |
| Dorman, Rosa Anna | Delbarco, Joseph W | Jun 23 1852 | 11/266 |
| Dorn, Lorni (Dorr) | Berral, Francoise (Benal) | Jun 7 1841 | 4/3241B |
| Dorphley, Lewis H | Mayland, Lucy A (Mrs) | Apr 10 1844 | 8/11B |
| Dorr, Louie (Dorn) | Benal, Francoin | Jun 7 1841* | 5/136 |
| Dorrance, Charles W | Mills, Mary A | May 18 1835* | 3/15 |
| Dorsey, Allice | Dies, Richard | Jul 11 1840 | 4/4021B |
| Dorsey, Vernon | Coupland, Julianna | Dec 4 1837* | 3/102 |
| Dortutor, Emily | Miller, John O | Apr 4 1851 | 11/134 |
| Dougherty, Barnard | McClelland, Margaret | Apr 21 1853 | 12/256 |
| Dougherty, Mary A | Honeywood, James | Jul 17 1854 | 13/284 |
| Dougherty, Michael | Caughlin, Joanna | Apr 13 1842 | 5/192B |
| Doughires, Anna Jane | Griffin, Saml B | Nov 12 1835* | 3/146 |
| Doughty, John | Fox, Anne C | Feb 8 1820* | CM |
| Douglass, Johannah | Ferguson, William F | Jul 13 1846 | 8/178 |
| Doulan, John | Finnery, Ellen | Apr 15 1846 | 8/157B |
| Doulon, Patrick | Higgins, Ellen | Jun 21 1853 | 12/323 |
| Dousley, John | Goodwyn, Elizabeth | Apr 27 1849* | 8/369 |
| Dowd, Laurence | Connor, Ann | Jul 4 1853 | 12/347 |
| Dowd, Maria | Stafford, Charles | Nov 6 1854 | 13/369 |
| Dowd, Winney | Kelly, Michael | Sep 13 1852 | 12/2 |
| Dowdell, Mary | Tighe, Philip | Dec 1 1843* | 5/308B |
| Dowdle, Rebecca | Watson, Charles | Jun 6 1833* | 2/951 |
| Dowlan, Maria | McDonald, Thomas | Sep 25 1834* | 2/111 |
| Dowling, Margaret | Runals, Benjamin P | Jan 18 1837* | 3/69 |
| Dowling, Mary | Dooly, Thomas | May 20 1852 | 11/253 |
| Downer, Louisa A | Brown, Josiah I | May 14 1842 | 5/200B |
| Downey, Anne | Murphy, Edward | Jan 28 1842 | 5/174B |
| Downey, Bridget | O'Brien, Owen | Jul 10 1847* | 8/244 |
| Downey, Ellen | Roberts, Edward | 1854* | OIB |
| Downing, Catherine | Moonan, James | Oct 27 1841 | 5/155B |
| Doyle, Alice | Rice, Hugh | Mar 14 1846* | 8/152B |
| Doyle, Andrew | Byrnes, Mary | Apr 15 1852 | 11/237 |
| Doyle, David | Corbitt, Mary | May 4 1855 | 14/129 |
| Doyle, Ellen | Kain, Daniel | May 17 1851 | 11/150 |
| Doyle, Ellen | Donavan, Michael | Jun 11 1855 | 14/167 |
| Doyle, George | McElroy, Margaret | Jan 30 1849* | 8/351 |
| Doyle, Lawrence | McQuillan, Catherine | Feb 12 1851 | 11/121 |
| Doyle, Mary | Kelly, Michael | Jul 14 1851 | 11/165 |
| Doyle, Mary Ann | Neville, John | Mar 30 1848* | 8/296 |
| Doyle, Mary Ann | Smith, John | Nov 9 1854 | 13/376 |
| Doyle, Patrick | Bird, Mary | May 10 1851 | 11/147 |
| Doyle, Rose Anna | Clancy, Michael | Nov 22 1852 | 12/70 |
| Dragis, Peter | Chestang, Gertrude | Nov 26 1846 | 8/202 |
| Drago, Antoinette | Horton, Peter | Jan 16 1851 | 11/113 |
| Drake, Ermeline | Denny, Alec A | Dec 13 1818* | CM |
| Draper, Christopher | Lawless, Bridget | Aug 16 1852* | 11/275 |
| Draper, Mary | Terry, James | Apr 30 1855 | 14/126 |
| Dras, Mgante | Ayer, Charles A | May 25 1841 | 4/3071B |
| Dresch, Francois H | Neiderberger, Madeline | Jul 22 1843* | 5/290B |
| Drew, Betsey Prior | Huntington, John | May 9 1838* | 3/124 |
| Drew, Julia J | Brewer, George | Sep 16 1851 | 11/179 |
| Drew, Levi | Webb, Patsey | Aug 11 1855 | 14/208 |
| Drew, Lucy | Boynton, Joseph W | May 9 1838* | 3/124 |
| Drew, Maria E | Allen, John B | Nov 12 1844* | 8/50B |
| Dricsoll, Mary | Martin, John | Jul 9 1839* | 3/181 |
| Drinkwater, Sewell | Chanceller, Mary A | May 24 1851 | 11/152 |
| Drinnan, Edward | Galliher, Bridget | 1840* | OIB |
| Driscall, Mary Ann | Buckman, John | May 16 1846 | 8/166B |
| Driscoll, Edward | Forgarty, Joana | Apr 9 1839* | 3/165 |
| Drool, Annette F | Chaudron, Julian | Dec 14 1832* | 2/1261 |
| Drosch, Francois Havier | Niedeslenger, Madeline | Jul 22 1843 | 6/400B |
| Droz, Louis | Robert, Eliza | Dec 13 1852 | 12/88 |
| Druger, Susan J | Massey, Joshua A | Apr 30 1846 | 8/161B |

| BRIDE OR GROOM | SPOUSE | DATE | BOOK/PAGE |
|---|---|---|---|
| Drummond, Thomas M | Cleveland, Mary A | Feb 20 1855 | 14/62 |
| Drury, Elizabeth | Stanton, Patrick | Apr 3 1839* | 3/164 |
| Drus, Jane (Dias) | Chesnut, William | Nov 12 1846 | 8/198 |
| Dubois, Edward | Farrell, Sarah L | Feb 5 1831* | 2/150 |
| Duboise, Rebecca | Hamond, Lewis | Aug 17 1844 | 8/39B |
| Dubose, James | Spence, Nancy | Oct 2 1852 | 12/16 |
| Dubose, Malachi | Kibbe, Margaret F | Jan 31 1837* | 3/71 |
| Dubracar, Josephine | Brigalie, Charles | Nov 29 1853 | 13/29 |
| Dubroca, Basile | Bernody, Catharine | Feb 18 1840* | 5/12 |
| Dubroca, Bazil | Chastang, Louise | Jun 27 1832* | 2/1441 |
| Dubroca, Catherine | Chavana, Vincent | Apr 17 1834* | 2/311 |
| Dubroca, Georgette | Moreno, Benino | Aug 26 1830* | 2/135 |
| Dubroca, Josephine | Brue, Lawrence | Aug 10 1824 | 1/36 |
| Dubroca, Maximilian | Bernody, Annettee | May 4 1831 | 2/166 |
| Dubroca, Metin | Bernody, Bretaigne | Apr 19 1834* | 2/291 |
| Dubroca, Sebastian | Goubill, Georgett | 1827* | OIB |
| Dubroca, Sylvestre | Alexander, Evelina | Apr 23 1835* | 3/22 |
| Dubroco, Virginia | Sarah, Adolphus | Sep 3 1850 | 11/83 |
| Ducarnean, Jules | Rhoda, Melissa | May 6 1852 | 11/246 |
| Ducarneau, Jules | Rodet, Melissa (Rhodet) | May 6 1852 | 11/246 |
| Duck, Lawrence | Robertson, Sarah | Feb 5 1835* | 3/8 |
| Duckett, Wylie J | Scroggins, Mary E | Jan 7 1854 | 13/63 |
| Duckworth, George | Patrick, Mary K | May 6 1829* | 2/84 |
| Duclos, Victor | Dumas, Marie J S | Jul 21 1847* | 8/246 |
| Dueros, M C Sophie | Depat, Jules | Apr 3 1837* | 3/78 |
| Duest, John (Quist) | Haines, Martha | Aug 2 1845* | 8/114B |
| Duff, John | Miller, Ellen | Jun 10 1839* | 3/178 |
| Duffie, Jane | Castilli, John | Feb 28 1840* | 3/195 |
| Duffie, Mary | Wilkinson, John | May 13 1842 | 5/200B |
| Duffin, William | Reynolds, Anne C | Jul 10 1849 | 8/387 |
| Duffy, Alice | McKenna, Michael | Apr 11 1843 | 5/260B |
| Duffy, Bridget | Golin, Patrick | Jan 22 1852 | 11/206 |
| Duffy, John | Wilson, Ansaline | Jan 4 1849* | 8/344 |
| Duffy, John | Jordan, Mary | May 11 1846 | 8/165B |
| Duffy, Nancy | Pullin, George F | Jan 31 1854 | 13/105 |
| Duffy, Susan | Cook, M Beal | Jul 15 1841* | 5/143B |
| Dufrenne, Ceoline | Andry, Felise | Feb 6 1824 | 1/20 |
| Dufur, Benjamin Franklin | Johnson, Harriett | Apr 14 1845 | 8/87B |
| Dugan, Bridget | Lucas, John | Jun 26 1850 | 11/68 |
| Dugan, Bridget | Cunningham, William | Apr 27 1843 | 5/265B |
| Dugan, Harriet B | Shed, William B | Oct 18 1842 | 5/224B |
| Dugan, Mary | Thomson, Walter | May 9 1849* | 8/375 |
| Duggan, Ann | Smith, Thomas | Feb 16 1855 | 14/55 |
| Duggan, Mary | McDonald, Thomas | Feb 24 1854 | 13/137 |
| Duggan, Michael | Shaw, Mary | Feb 8 1855 | 14/41 |
| Duignew, Bridget | Nicholas, Joakim | Jun 28 1853 | 12/333 |
| Dukes, Eliza | Aldredge, Green | Apr 4 1840* | 5/16 |
| Dukes, Sarah (Duval) | Witling, Daniel | 1849* | OIB |
| Dulff, Henry (Wulff) | Mullen, Martha | Jun 15 1842 | 5/206B |
| Dulton, William | Pasco, Hester | Jan 1 1837* | 3/106 |
| Dumas, Jose | Creps, Mary (Criss) | Sep 30 1844 | 8/42B |
| Dumas, Marie Julie S | Duclos, Victor | Jul 21 1847* | 8/246 |
| Dumei, Ernestine | Chantron, Pepin | Feb 28 1853* | 12/182 |
| Dumouy, Louis | Gurlotte, Irene | Feb 4 1817* | CM |
| Dumouy, Marcelle | Dealy, Richard | May 30 1814* | CM |
| Dunaho, Mary | Jarvis, Thomas | Mar 10 1843 | 5/252B |
| Dunaree, Jane | Casey, Michael | Feb 25 1851 | 11/124 |
| Duncan, Ann | McDevitt, Daniel | Nov 28 1855 | 14/291 |
| Duncan, John | Cowan, Juliett | 1827* | OIB |
| Duncan, John | Flinn, Margaret | Jul 28 1853 | 12/373 |
| Duncan, M H | Percy, Mary | Jun 20 1841 | 4/1851B |
| Duncan, Milton H | Pescom, Mary | Jun 2 1841* | 5/134 |
| Duncan, Robert M | Broduax, Sarah S | Jan 10 1854 | 13/69 |
| Dundon, Mary | Cummings, William | Feb 7 1840* | 5/11 |

| BRIDE OR GROOM | SPOUSE | DATE | BOOK/PAGE |
|---|---|---|---|
| Dunham, Daniel | Elliott, Francis | May 12 1825 | 1/76 |
| Dunlap, Eliza | Emmett, Joseph | Mar 20 1849* | 8/362 |
| Dunlap, Mary | Failey, Philip (Farley) | Sep 8 1849* | 11/3 |
| Dunlap, Sarah Jane | Canavillo, Charles F | Mar 18 1834* | 2/391 |
| Dunmore, Louison | Roney, James | Sep 15 1813* | CM |
| Dunn, Daniel | Fitzgerald, Ellen | Oct 17 1853 | 12/415 |
| Dunn, Eliza | Nolan, James | Jun 11 1853* | 12/315 |
| Dunn, Ellen | Curtin, John | Aug 24 1843 | 5/293B |
| Dunn, Lawrence William | Foy, Rosa Ann | Jun 12 1837* | 3/86 |
| Dunn, Mary | Fox, Thomas | Oct 26 1848* | 8/330 |
| Dunn, Michael | Coil, Catherine | Feb 15 1841* | 5/103B |
| Dunn, Roseanna | Daves, George Jr | 1837* | OIB |
| Dunn, Samuel J | Bagley, Elmira | Jan 1 1851 | 11/107 |
| Dunning, Edward | Hilliard, Elizabeth R | 1827* | OIB |
| Dunning, Edward | Turner, Martha W | 1834* | OIB |
| Dunning, Edward | Goodman, Emily R | Apr 27 1841* | 5/127B |
| Dunnington, Martha Jane | Buler, George W | May 12 1842 | 5/200B |
| Dunnison, Margaret | Smith, George F | Sep 17 1850* | 11/86 |
| Dunoghue, John | Dalton, Catharine | May 25 1850 | 11/63 |
| Dunwoody, Mary B | Frisby, William | Jun 14 1845 | 8/103B |
| Duod, Annette F | Chaudron, Julius | Dec 14 1832* | 2/1261 |
| Duperteus, H Louis | Quinn, Ellen | Jan 14 1852 | 11/203 |
| Dupertuis, George | Daffin, Rebecca | Mar 8 1853 | 12/186 |
| Duplessis, James | Withers, Margaret | May 29 1830 | 2/126 |
| Dupon, John | Leblanc, Anastasia | Mar 2 1848* | 8/288 |
| Dupont, Caterine | Krebs, Basile | Sep 8 1818* | CM |
| Dupree, Sterling | Parker, Abigail (Amelia) | Jan 25 1829 | 2/65 |
| Duprest, Susan | Hudson, William | Jan 16 1830 | 2/109 |
| Duprey, J B | Devillers, Aimie J | Mar 9 1840* | 5/14 |
| Durad, Annette | Goddard, Joseph | Feb 5 1853 | 12/163 |
| Durand, Aurora | Baiz, Desir | May 10 1834* | 2/271 |
| Durand, Manuel | Connor, Mary A | May 26 1854 | 13/234 |
| Durand, Martine | Rondeau, Marguerite A | 1825* | OIB |
| Durand, Stephania Lucy | Sands, James | Dec 6 1848* | 8/337 |
| Durant, Aurora | Baiz, Desir | May 10 1834* | 2/271 |
| Durant, Marie Aspassin | Peterd, Augustus | Mar 19 1829* | 2/77 |
| Durett, Elizabeth | Trenier, Ferron | Apr 23 1845 | 7/647B |
| Durett, Isadore | Collain, Peter | Jun 20 1846 | 8/174 |
| Durett, Vallere | Colin, Catharine | May 20 1842 | 5/202B |
| Durette, Constance | Durette, Rouse | Jan 14 1850 | 11/32 |
| Durette, Elizabeth | Trenier, Ferron | Apr 23 1845 | 8/88 |
| Durette, Isidore | St John, Claire | Mar 16 1831* | 2/154 |
| Durette, Joseph | Vivere, Catherine | Mar 26 1831* | 2/158 |
| Durette, Rouse | Durette, Constance | Jan 14 1850 | 11/32 |
| Durfey, Rebecca | Robinson, Thomas H | May 13 1839* | 3/171 |
| During, Alexander W | Grant, Helen M | Nov 29 1845 | 8/127 |
| Durn, Lucie | Favre, Abraham L | Jan 9 1837* | 3/69 |
| Duross, Charlotte | Leahy, William | Mar 22 1845 | 8/81B |
| Duroux, Michel | Remy, Adeline | Feb 22 1845 | 8/74B |
| Durrett, Leonine | Collins, John | Oct 19 1853 | 12/420 |
| Durud, Louis | Barry, Bridget | Oct 20 1852 | 12/32 |
| Duval, Philip | Caro, Matilda C | Dec 28 1844 | 8/63B |
| Duval, William J | Jeanerut, Helvirse | Jul 4 1845 | 8/108B |
| Duvas, Sarah (Duval) | Willing, Daniel | Nov 27 1849 | 11/19 |
| Dwinal, Henry (Devinal) | Mayal, Pheneley S | Mar 29 1844* | 8/7B |
| Dwyer, Catharine | Cody, Patrick | Apr 26 1843 | 5/264B |
| Dwyer, Edward | McCullough, Mary | Sep 13 1854 | 13/335 |
| Dwyer, James J | Holmes, Sophia | Jun 6 1843* | 5/278B |
| Dwyer, Michael | Neville, Eliza | Feb 17 1855 | 14/56 |
| Dwyer, Patrick | Williams, Mary Ann | Apr 23 1823 | 1/1 |
| Dwyer, Susan J | Massey, Joshua | Apr 30 1846* | 8/161B |
| Dwyne, John | Afannor, Ann (O'Connor) | Mar 7 1837* | 3/74 |
| Dyas, Ann | Brown, Peter L | Aug 27 1851 | 11/173 |
| Dyas, John | Byrde, Elizabeth | Sep 14 1847* | 8/256 |

| BRIDE OR GROOM | SPOUSE | DATE | BOOK/PAGE |
|---|---|---|---|
| Dyer, Gertrude F M | Belloc, Adolphe | Jun 21 1853 | 12/324 |
| Dyer, Malachi J | Hill, Barbara | Mar 25 1851 | 11/131 |
| Dyer, Watter G | Holmes, Harriett | May 10 1839* | 3/172 |
| Dyess, Elizabeth Ann | Williams, James E | Feb 27 1850 | 11/43 |
| Dyess, Thomas | Shelton, Nancy | Jan 12 1843* | 5/242B |

## E

| BRIDE OR GROOM | SPOUSE | DATE | BOOK/PAGE |
|---|---|---|---|
| Eadie, John | (Not Listed) | 1829* | OIB |
| Eagan, Bridget | Mooney, Mathew | Apr 27 1838* | 3/121 |
| Eagen, Mary | McGraw, John | Sep 13 1844 | 8/41B |
| Eakle, William B | Wright, Rachel | Nov 8 1854 | 13/372 |
| Earle, Peter C | Lawler, Julia | Dec 20 1844 | 8/61B |
| Easkin, Lucinda G | Ropell, William H | Nov 12 1846 | 8/198 |
| Eastburn, Caroline A | Dargin, John | Jun 29 1854 | 13/268 |
| Easterling, William L | Dees, Elizabeth A | Dec 14 1855 | 14/305 |
| Eastin, Mary Ann | Spotswood, William A | Nov 28 1842* | 5/230B |
| Eastin, Matilda E | Montgomery, Alexander | Sep 1 1843* | 5/294B |
| Eastment, Cecilia E | Heald, John | Jul 26 1854 | 13/294 |
| Easton, Sarah E | Ketchum, William H | Dec 5 1848* | 8/337 |
| Ebeltaft, Lucinda Ann | Gormond, Avry | Feb 23 1852 | 11/221 |
| Ebletoft, Gabriel William | Atwood, Lucinda | Mar 9 1846 | 8/150B |
| Ebbereck, Margaret R | Siegmund, John S | May 23 1855 | 14/148 |
| Eberlein, Anna | Osbahart, William | Jan 26 1853 | 12/148 |
| Eberlin, Babeth | Rediger, Hermann | Aug 8 1854* | 13/306 |
| Eberlin, Catherine | Eberlin, John | Jan 25 1854* | 13/99 |
| Eberlin, John | Eberlin, Catherine | Jan 25 1854 | 13/99 |
| Eberline, Mary | Hoppensits, John | Dec 20 1852 | 12/101 |
| Eck, Josephine | Goettinger, George | Jun 12 1854 | 13/254 |
| Eckford, William | Collins, Maria B | May 24 1845 | 8/98B |
| Eckstine, Jacob | Sylva, Mary Ann | Jun 20 1848* | 8/310 |
| Edduy, Elizabeth | Lewis, Gabriel | Dec 27 1819* | CM |
| Eder, David M | Levin, Fanny | Feb 5 1850* | 11/38 |
| Edgerly, Daniel | Davies, Sarah M | Jun 25 1844 | 8/30B |
| Edgerly, Eliza Jane | Smith, I Edwin | Apr 26 1842 | 5/194B |
| Edmond, Andrew G | Higgins, Sarah | Apr 26 1855 | 14/120 |
| Edmond, Cornelia | Bruse, William C | May 2 1838* | 3/122 |
| Edmond, Mary T | Bell, William A | Dec 3 1855 | 14/297 |
| Edmonds, Daniel | Perkins, Mary | Feb 23 1842 | 5/182B |
| Edmondson, Philip P | Smith, Elizabeth | Jun 16 1837* | 3/86 |
| Edmonson, Humphrey | Collins, Bellmon | Aug 4 1841* | 5/146B |
| Edstrom, Charles | Fratman, Mary | Feb 29 1840* | 5/13 |
| Edward, Rosena | Darlton, Valentine T | Dec 28 1840* | 5/81B |
| Edward, Senale | Monk, Martha | Jan 24 1839* | 3/154 |
| Edwards, Alex F | Hefferlin, Cassandra | Oct 5 1840* | 5/51B |
| Edwards, Cassandra G | Glisson, James S | Feb 17 1853 | 12/175 |
| Edwards, Elias M | Morrison, Henrietta | May 20 1848 | 8/305 |

| BRIDE OR GROOM | SPOUSE | DATE | BOOK/PAGE |
|---|---|---|---|
| Edwards, Eliza Jane | Posey, Felix | Jul 1 1841* | 5/141B |
| Edwards, George Mills | Ashley, Mary Ann | Mar 16 1850 | 11/46 |
| Edwards, James | Hightower, Eliza | Nov 3 1824 | 1/44 |
| Edwards, Jane Catharine | Morris, Samuel | Apr 29 1848 | 8/302 |
| Edwards, John H | Perry, Mary F | Nov 16 1848 | 8/333 |
| Edwards, Joseph R | Griffin, Adalide G D | Oct 7 1850 | 11/88 |
| Edwards, Mary Jane | Patton, Garrett L | Dec 29 1847 | 8/273 |
| Edwards, Rosilia | Datton, Valentine T | Dec 28 1840 | 5/81B |
| Edy, Elizabeth | Johnson, James | May 3 1824 | 1/30 |
| Egan, Mary | Hart, William | Nov 22 1855 | 14/285 |
| Egan, Mathew | Donohoe, Mary | Nov 11 1853 | 13/14 |
| Ege, John | Scheller, Barbara | Nov 7 1855 | 14/274 |
| Egenter, Alouise (wid) | Riese, Andrew (widr) | Apr 4 1853 | 12/220 |
| Eggart, Robert | White, Elizabeth | Aug 25 1855 | 14/216 |
| Egghart, Louisette | Windergast, Christoph | Nov 11 1852 | 12/61 |
| Ehlbert, Clara | Ehrman, Charles | Jul 27 1855* | 14/217 |
| Ehlers, Johana Louise | Schlon, John | Nov 8 1852 | 12/51 |
| Ehrman, Charles | Ehlbert, Clara | Jul 27 1855* | 14/217 |
| Eich, Jean | Henn, Margritte | Apr 9 1853 | 12/229 |
| Eich, Margretta | Huber, John H | Mar 19 1944 | 5/328B |
| Eichar, Peter | Tatem, Alabama | Nov 10 1853 | 13/12 |
| Eichner, William C | Michael, Eve | Oct 31 1832* | 2/1331 |
| Eifrat, Helen | Mendel, William | Dec 8 1845 | 7/798 |
| Eipat, Helen | Mendel, William | Dec 8 1845 | 8/129B |
| Ekston, Gustavers | Gibson, Sarah | Apr 17 1850 | 11/54 |
| Elder, James | Heard, Julia M | Aug 11 1841* | 5/147B |
| Elder, John | Husson, Elizabeth | Mar 26 1838* | 3/117 |
| Elder, Sarah J | Virger, Thomas J | 1850* | OIB |
| Elder, Sarah Jane | Koger, Thomas J | Feb 25 1850 | 11/42 |
| Elevell, Anna Maria | Pollard, George | Jan 6 1837* | 3/68 |
| Eley, Catherine | White, Charles | Feb 14 1833* | 2/1131 |
| Elfoord, Maria | Mulhorn, William | Jan 2 1855 | 14/2 |
| Elford, Eliza | Michold, Louis | Mar 10 1853 | 12/189 |
| Elgin, Armistead M | McCullough, Mary E | Nov 6 1854 | 13/370 |
| Elich, John | Hamilton, Huldoh | Jul 24 1847* | 8/247 |
| Elihlien, John A | Huber, Martaleny Eliz. | Jan 22 1853 | 12/141 |
| Elizabeth, Houston | McCoul, Thomas | Oct 10 1837* | 3/99 |
| Elizabeth, Betsey | Martinez, Manuel | Mar 6 1834* | 2/421 |
| Ellen, Mary | Rodgers, Joseph | Mar 5 1844 | 5/327B |
| Ellenbek, Maelena | Bingler, John | Mar 4 1852 | 11/224 |
| Elliott, Delouise | Osgood, Stephen | Apr 6 1837* | 3/79 |
| Elliott, Dempsey | Goodman, Elizabeth (Mrs) | Apr 20 1840* | 3/198 |
| Elliott, Elizabeth | Roberts, William | Apr 9 1821* | CM |
| Elliott, Elizabeth A | Vickery, Leander J | Apr 21 1854 | 13/200 |
| Elliott, Francis | Dunham, Daniel | May 12 1825 | 1/76 |
| Elliott, James G | Callaghan, Charlotte F | Jun 3 1840* | 5/26B |
| Elliott, John R | Chaudron, Emma | Feb 25 1830* | 2/115 |
| Elliott, Maria | Benson, Jesse W | Nov 10 1845 | 8/124B |
| Elliott, Maria | Lovell, John | Oct 30 1821* | CM |
| Elliott, Martha J | Wheeler, William F | Jun 4 1842 | 5/204B |
| Elliott, Nancy A | Campbell, Thomas S | Jun 23 1855 | 14/185 |
| Elliott, Robert | Merritt, Mary Ann | Mar 27 1848 | 8/295 |
| Elliott, Sophia | Johnston, Hamilton R | Feb 28 1842 | 5/184B |
| Elliott, Stephen | Russ, Mary | Mar 15 1852 | 11/227 |
| Elliott, Susan A | Kelsey, Edmund | Oct 5 1854 | 13/347 |
| Ellis, Albert P | Davis, Lucy A | Dec 4 1850 | 11/101 |
| Ellis, Arcissens | Hinkley, Alfred B | Feb 7 1843 | 5/248B |
| Ellis, Armississi | Windham, Jesse | Jul 18 1844 | 8/32B |
| Ellis, Daniel | Bethany, Elizabeth | May 13 1832* | 2/1471 |
| Ellis, Delano | Callahan, Lucinda | Jul 29 1854* | 13/297 |
| Ellis, Delano | Holly, Marinda | Dec 23 1854 | 13/420 |
| Ellis, James | Fannin, Mary | Oct 7 1846 | 8/193 |
| Ellis, Joanna | Deidrick, Peter | Mar 18 1854 | 13/162 |

| BRIDE OR GROOM | SPOUSE | DATE | BOOK/PAGE |
|---|---|---|---|
| Ellis, Joseph G | Goodman, Sarah | Nov 13 1844 | 8/50B |
| Ellis, Thomas L | Chisholm, Anne E | May 6 1851 | 11/146 |
| Ellison, Ainey | Archer, Benjamin | Sep 15 1829 | 2/97 |
| Ellison, Benjamin | Bigley, Bridget | Apr 10 1850 | 11/52 |
| Ellison, Berry | Johnson, Sophia | May 1 1847 | 8/231 |
| Ellison, Eliza | Vanness, Jacob | Sep 20 1824 | 1/38 |
| Ellison, Rebecca D | Murphy, Charles | Sep 8 1830* | 2/137 |
| Ellison, Rehamah | Blish, Samuel K | Jan 21 1832* | 2/1751 |
| Ellison, Robert C | Burgess, Ann E | Jan 4 1834* | 2/581 |
| Ellison, Thomas | Foster, Ellen | Jan 18 1834* | 2/511 |
| Ellison, Thomas | Krebs, Hippolite | May 10 1841* | 5/129B |
| Ellison, Thomas J (widr) | Cooper, Eliza S (wid) | Feb 11 1853 | 12/170 |
| Ellison, William Perrine | Delmas, Mary H | Jan 2 1846 | 8/135B |
| Elliston, Anna | Wildermain, Philip | May 3 1825 | 1/74 |
| Ellman, Sigismond | Baumblatt, Sabina | Jan 27 1853 | 12/151 |
| Elloitt, Dempsey ? | Goodwin, Elizabeth | Apr 20 1840* | 3/198 |
| Ellsworth, Martha | Adams, Jasper | May 13 1851 | 11/148 |
| Eloirt, Bridget | Welch, Michael | Sep 14 1850 | 11/85 |
| Elsworth, George L | Burke, Margaret | Feb 15 1847 | 8/218 |
| Elsworth, Isabelle | Sciple, George W | Apr 29 1852 | 11/243 |
| Elsworth, John L | Farley, Bridget | May 5 1846 | 8/164B |
| Elward, Ann | Mulhall, Martin | Aug 5 1854 | 13/303 |
| Elward, Daniel | Mealy, Ellen | Aug 5 1854 | 13/304 |
| Elward, Edmund | Lewis, Mary | Jul 26 1853 | 12/371 |
| Elwood, Amelia | Johnson, Ebeneza | Nov 10 1821* | CM |
| Elworth, Thomas | Powers, Ann | Sep 16 1850 | 11/85 |
| Ely, Margaret | Hamilton, Harris | Jul 23 1836* | 3/55 |
| Emanuel, Baruch M | Tannebaum, Dora | Nov 10 1852* | 12/57 |
| Emanuel, Eveline | Murrell, John W | Jun 7 1855 | 14/165 |
| Emanuel, Johnathan | King, Isabella | Mar 26 1832* | 2/1611 |
| Emanuel, Mary | Kennedy, Joshua | Mar 17 1853 | 12/195 |
| Emerson, Sinie | Evans, Young | Mar 6 1854 | 3/149 |
| Emily, Andre | Snyder, Risit | Mar 15 1825 | 1/67 |
| Emily, Frederica | Fisher, Dieterich | Feb 7 1829* | 2/70 |
| Emindoph, Louisa | Hudaff, Harm | Jul 28 1854 | 13/296 |
| Emley, Mary | Clauson, Peter | Oct 9 1843* | 5/299B |
| Emmet, Elizabeth | Cox, George | Dec 9 1839* | 3/191 |
| Emmett, Amelia Jane | Graham, Charles | Mar 18 1837* | 3/75 |
| Emmett, Ellen | Dana, Caleb | Oct 10 1848 | 8/327 |
| Emmett, Isabella Frances | Howard, John | Apr 2 1845 | 8/83B |
| Emmett, John D | McGill, Martha L | Feb 24 1853 | 12/180 |
| Emmett, Joseph | Dunlap, Eliza | Mar 20 1849* | 8/362 |
| Emslie, Margaret R | Wickes, Charles | Jun 21 1847 | 8/243 |
| Engel, Clara | Moore, Jonas | Aug 2 1854* | 13/299 |
| Engelson, Francis | Aggus, William B | Nov 28 1849 | 11/19 |
| Engleman, Margaret | O'Neil, Henry | Apr 24 1854 | 13/202 |
| Engleman, Margaret | Spindler, John | Sep 11 1855 | 14/228 |
| English, Eleanor | Carby, James | Jun 23 1838* | 3/133 |
| English, Jane | Case, Richard | Feb 1 1840* | 3/192 |
| English, John | O'Connell, Mary | Feb 4 1850 | 11/37 |
| English, John | McCoy, Mary | Dec 24 1851 | 11/198 |
| English, Mary | Pate, John | Nov 1 1855* | 14/268 |
| English, Thomas M | Toulmin, Susan | Nov 25 1833* | 2/681B |
| Engster, John | Maxwell, Elenor | Oct 6 1851 | 11/181 |
| Enholm, Avis E | Miller, William M | Dec 14 1853 | 13/40 |
| Ennis, Mary Ann | Gibson, John | Jun 29 1848* | 8/311 |
| Ensign, Henry P | Pollard, Phebe | Apr 2 1834* | 2/361 |
| Epstein, Isaac | Tanebaun, Amalia | Apr 29 1853* | 12/259 |
| Epstein, Joseph | Steirn, Tette (Steiner) | Feb 27 1854 | 13/144 |
| Epstein, Sophie | Frolickstein, William | Feb 17 1852 | 11/218 |
| Eqing, William (Ewing) | Treuathem, Elizabeth | Jul 9 1838* | 3/135 |
| Erd, Joseph | Smith, Margaret | Jan 15 1855 | 14/16 |
| Erety, Sarah Elizabeth | Heald, John | Nov 1 1847 | 8/263 |
| Erily, Lucy B | Heartwell, John | Jan 18 1840* | 5/8 |

| BRIDE OR GROOM | SPOUSE | DATE | BOOK/PAGE |
|---|---|---|---|
| Erst, William | Bates, Maria | Dec 16 1820* | CM |
| Erwin, Elizabeth | Kelso, George | May 9 1845* | 8/93B |
| Erwin, John | Young, Susan | Oct 3 1833* | 2/771 |
| Erwin, Mary J | Tait, Robert | Dec 2 1851 | 11/191 |
| Esins, Joseph (Esias) | Martin, Numnery (Memory) | Jan 24 1852 | 11/207 |
| Eslava, Constance Octavia | Girard, Emile | Oct 17 1849 | 11/10 |
| Eslava, Jerome | Mazange, Celistine | Feb 22 1827 | OIB/ADM |
| Eslava, Jerome | Caves, Mary E (Carey) | Jun 24 1851 | 11/159 |
| Eslava, Malvina G | Capell, Harvey S | Dec 11 1849* | 11/24 |
| Espaho, Catherine | Ingersoll, William I | Apr 25 1820* | CM |
| Espejo, Antonio | Sharpin, Mary | Apr 11 1825 | 1/72 |
| Espejo, Antonio | Gibson, Nancy Ann | Apr 24 1832* | 2/1581 |
| Espejo, Nancy | Fisher, John | Dec 24 1840* | 5/79B |
| Essex, John S | Constantine, Josephine | Apr 21 1847 | 8/228 |
| Estahooks, Mary J | Jones, William | Dec 22 1855 | 14/311 |
| Estapa, Mary S | High, Augustus | Nov 1 1854 | 13/367 |
| Estever, M Tacinte | Fourcarde, Clementine wid | Apr 5 1845 | 8/84B |
| Estil, Mary | Sebastian, Bocx | Apr 19 1854* | 13/193 |
| Estrezo, Nancy | Fisher, John | Jun 24 1841 | 4/271 |
| Esty, Bridget | Porter, Charles H | May 3 1848* | 8/303 |
| Esty, Charles H | O'Brien, Bridget | Oct 11 1847 | 8/258 |
| Etheridge, Ashbee W | Graves, Martha E | Mar 24 1835* | 3/12 |
| Etheridge, Ellen | King, Joseph G | Jan 11 1854 | 13/73 |
| Etheridge, John W | Typpenhowers, Mary A | Jun 7 1843 | 5/280B |
| Etheridge, Mary | Philips, Elam | 1827* | OIB |
| Etheridge, Mary E | Robbins, Frederick A | Mar 9 1850 | 11/45 |
| Etheridge, Susan | Skinner, Brelon W L | Dec 31 1839* | 5/6 |
| Etherige, Thomas | Shields, Margaret | Sep 13 1836* | 3/57 |
| Etienne, Julia | Soto, Raymond | Sep 12 1843 | 5/295 |
| Etter, Henry | Schneider, Johanna | Jun 10 1830* | 2/129 |
| Etts, Ann | Haney, Patrick | May 28 1830* | 2/125 |
| Euing, James | McFee, Jane | Dec 3 1844 | 8/56B |
| Eutis, Thaney | Blachenship, William | 1826* | OIB |
| Evans, Alfred | Brothers, Patience | Dec 26 1844* | 8/63B |
| Evans, Amelia | Patton, Robert | May 27 1845 | 8/99B |
| Evans, Carolina B | Troost, Lewis | Apr 15 1846 | 8/157B |
| Evans, Caroline | Lott, James | Jan 4 1845 | 8/65B |
| Evans, Charles B | Davidson, Alley | Aug 11 1818* | CM |
| Evans, Cyrus | Nicholson, Harriett | Aug 26 1829* | 2/93 |
| Evans, Eliza | Crabtree, Haynes | Aug 24 1853 | 12/395 |
| Evans, George | Blish, Cynthia R | Jul 17 1849* | 8/389 |
| Evans, James Guy | Pennington, Francis | Oct 15 1842 | 5/223B |
| Evans, James M | Page, Jennett | Jan 13 1846 | 8/140B |
| Evans, Jessee | Hopkins, Mahala Ann | May 23 1844* | 8/22B |
| Evans, Mary L | Roach, Jonathan | 1840* | OIB |
| Evans, Thomas R | Hughes, Catherine | Aug 12 1850* | 11/79 |
| Evans, William | Starke, Grace | Jan 30 1855 | 14/29 |
| Evans, Young | Emerson, Sinie | Mar 6 1854 | 13/149 |
| Evelly, James | Manning, Mary | Nov 2 1853 | 13/4 |
| Everett, Jane | Townsend, John W | 1827* | OIB |
| Everett, John F | Slade, Ann B | 1826* | OIB |
| Everett, Margaret | Byrne, Patrick | Jan 4 1851 | 11/109 |
| Everett, Margaret A | Jones, Simon | Apr 23 1847 | 8/229 |
| Everett, Marie | Beckley, Aaron | Nov 13 1839* | 3/191 |
| Everitt, Martha | Crawford, Robert L | Feb 4 1835* | 3/6 |
| Everitt, Mary | Brooks, Augustus | Feb 4 1835* | 3/7 |
| Eving, James (Ewing) | McFee, Jane | Dec 3 1844 | 7/457 |
| Ewers, Marcia H | Turner, Jarvis | Dec 11 1847 | 8/269 |
| Ewers, Susan | Bernbrock, Henry | Jun 9 1854 | 13/248 |
| Ewing, Andrew W | Hornbliss, Charlotte | May 7 1841* | 5/128B |
| Ewing, Cornelia J | Brown, P P | Feb 10 1840* | 3/193 |
| Ewing, Eliza A W | Ketchum, Charles T | Jul 5 1843 | 5/286B |
| Ewing, James | McFee, Jane | Dec 3 1844 | 8/56B |
| Ewing, James L (S) | Hunter, Martha Ann | Nov 22 1844 | 8/54B |

| BRIDE OR GROOM | SPOUSE | DATE | BOOK/PAGE |
|---|---|---|---|
| Ewing, William | Treuathem, Elizabeth | Jul 9 1838* | 3/135 |
| Exton, Ellenor C | Thompson, Thomas | Aug 7 1854* | 13/305 |
| Ezell, Eliza | Burke, John M | Apr 11 1838 | 3/118 |
| Ezell, Sarah | Windham, G W | Apr 9 1853 | 12/227 |

## F

| | | | |
|---|---|---|---|
| Fabel, Justin | Banere, John Emanuel | 1822* | OIB |
| Fagan, Ann | Conroy, John | Oct 29 1844 | 8/46B |
| Fagan, Anne | Arbery, George | Nov 4 1841* | 5/155 |
| Fagan, Bridget | Jones, William | 1838* | OIB |
| Fagan, John (widr) | Riley, Mary (wid) | Aug 24 1853 | 12/393 |
| Fagan, Peter | Casidy, Lydia | Dec 29 1853 | 13/56 |
| Faggar, D W | Bridgewood, B (Faggar) | Oct 2 1852 | 12/18 |
| Faggard, Catharine J | Kane, Thomas | May 30 1850 | 11/64 |
| Faggard, Jackson G | Williams, Elizabeth | Jan 19 1847 | 8/213 |
| Faggart, Sarah Ann | Crabtree, Ervin | Jan 19 1834* | 2/541 |
| Fagherty, Eliza | Pelitz, Augustus | Oct 21 1835* | 3/30 |
| Fahay, Michael | Clunin, Ann | Apr 21 1852 | 11/240 |
| Fahey, Thomas | Crooker, Ellenor | Nov 15 1837* | 3/100 |
| Fahl, Edward (widr) | Bean, Mary | Sep 17 1853 | 12/409 |
| Fail, Margaret (Fore) | Murry, James | Aug 1 1850* | 11/78 |
| Failey, Philip (Farley?) | Dunlap, Mary | Sep 8 1849* | 11/3 |
| Faines, William J | Morano, Sodriska C | Oct 13 1842* | 5/223 |
| Fair, Elisha H | Wyatt, Martha Ann | Apr 26 1849* | 8/370 |
| Fairley, Archibald G | Temple, Ann | Oct 17 1848 | 8/328 |
| Falk, Jeddah (Folk) | Songsfield, Jacob | Apr 19 1843* | 5/262B |
| Falker, Frank Martin | Grienbert, Virginia | Feb 21 1852 | 11/219 |
| Falkner, Catharine | Johnson, William | Feb 10 1844* | 5/321B |
| Falkner, Permealy | Phillips, Elijah R | Jul 19 1845 | 8/111B |
| Fallon, Bernard | Strawbridge, Susanna | Dec 12 1854 | 13/41 |
| Fallon, Mary F | Reynolds, George F | May 21 1855 | 14/147 |
| Fallond, James | Finnigan, Bridget | Oct 18 1847* | 8/260 |
| Falls, Bridget | Jones, John | Nov 4 1852 | 12/46 |
| Fanning, John | Hanlon, Mary | Jun 11 1853* | 12/316 |
| Fannin, Mary | Ellis, James | Oct 7 1846 | 8/193 |
| Fanning, Thomas | Hannogan, Mary | May 22 1852 | 11/254 |
| Fannon, John | Farle, Catherine | Feb 6 1855 | 14/37 |
| Farante, Catherine | Berger, Joseph | Jan 30 1843 | 5/247B |
| Farle, Catherine | Fannon, John | Feb 6 1855 | 14/37 |
| Farley, Bridget | Elsworth, John L | May 5 1846 | 8/164B |
| Farley, Catherine | Winterhalter, Thomas | Feb 12 1851 | 11/121 |
| Farley, Elizabeth | Flannagan, James | Nov 5 1853* | 13/7 |
| Farley, Jane | Donald, Augustus H | Dec 14 1853 | 13/41 |
| Farley, John | Connaught, Ellen | Oct 20 1848* | 8/330 |
| Farley, Julia | Gibbons, William | Apr 10 1852 | 11/234 |
| Farley, Margaret | Parker, Jonathan | May 25 1852 | 11/255 |
| Farley, Margaret | Gunn, Patrick | Nov 21 1854 | 13/388 |

| | | | |
|---|---|---|---|
| Farley, Patrick | Kelly, Bridget | Jun 9 1851 | 11/157 |
| Farley, Philip | Sullivan, Mary | Nov 25 1852* | 12/75 |
| Farley, Philip | Ponns, Mary A (Pound) wid | Sep 8 1853 | 12/403 |
| Farmer, John | Somer, Elizabeth | Sep 25 1834* | 2/121 |
| Farmer, Mary E | Greer, John T | Sep 20 1854 | 13/340 |
| Farrel, Martha E | Hugonin, M P | Apr 15 1853* | 12/241 |
| Farrell, Edward | Dailey, Matilda | Oct 21 1850 | 11/90 |
| Farrell, Julia | Stoddard, Gridley | May 4 1843 | 5/267B |
| Farrell, Mary | Turner, Noel | Feb 16 1833* | 2/1121 |
| Farrell, Mary | Scott, James | May 2 1832* | 2/1551 |
| Farrell, Sarah L | Dubois, Edward | Feb 5 1831* | 2/150 |
| Farren, Margaret | Curly, Patrick | Sep 3 1851* | 11/176 |
| Farris, William James | Morono, Sodriska (Morond) | Oct 13 1842 | 6/195B |
| Farrner, John | Somer, Elizabeth | Sep 25 1834* | 2/121 |
| Farron, Mary | Delary, Henry (Delaney) | Jan 25 1838* | 3/109 |
| Farrow, Henry | Stokes, Elizabeth J | Oct 27 1853 | 12/426 |
| Farrow, Mary A | Sheldon, E S | Apr 11 1853 | 12/232 |
| Faulkner, William | Coughlen, Catherine | Jan 10 1851 | 11/110 |
| Fath, Michael | Hooper, Eliza | Feb 24 1854* | 13/136 |
| Faure, Marie H (Favre) | Rouston, Honore | Oct 28 1847 | 8/262 |
| Favre, Abraham Lewis | Durn, Lucie | Jan 9 1837* | 3/69 |
| Fawley, Joanna | Lenguett, Benjamin | Apr 25 1850 | 11/56 |
| Featherstone, Catherine | McDonough, Joseph | Jun 28 1852 | 11/266 |
| Feely, William | Toole, Margaret | May 9 1855 | 14/135 |
| Feenny, Thomas | Donnolly, Margaret | Mar 3 1851 | 11/127 |
| Feeny, William H | McCavett, Mary A | Apr 1 1854 | 13/172 |
| Fegan, Thomas | Scale, Margaret | Jan 30 1843 | 5/246B |
| Feibelman, Marx | Feibelman, Therese | Mar 16 1855 | 14/85 |
| Feibelman, Therese | Feibelman, Marx | Mar 16 1855 | 14/85 |
| Feild, Hester (Field) | White, Hiram J | May 4 1842* | 5/61 |
| Feist, Rosina | Merchant, Louis | Jul 16 1855* | 14/190 |
| Felis, Sebastian | Butler, Mary | May 8 1850 | 11/60 |
| Felix, Jane (Felis?) | Chenault, William | Feb 5 1816* | CM |
| Fellonil, Louis | Sullivan, Mary | Nov 3 1843 | 5/302B |
| Fenkerhiel, Catherine | Arnold, Lewis | Feb 25 1843 | 6/288B |
| Fenn, William (Finn) | Dillon, Mary | Dec 7 1842 | 5/232B |
| Fennell, Elizabeth | Hall, Nathan | Mar 11 1854 | 13/155 |
| Fennely, Harriett E | Jackson, Samuel H | Jun 22 1825* | 1/81 |
| Fenner, Mary (Turner) | Shand, William | May 18 1842* | 5/201B |
| Fenouil, Francis | Tavernier, Elizabeth | Apr 17 1855 | 14/106 |
| Fenton, Julia | Ford, Thomas R | Dec 26 1846 | 8/207 |
| Fer, Constant | Simpson, Frances | Jan 20 1821* | CM |
| Ferguson, Anne | Wallace, George W | Jun 10 1851 | 11/157 |
| Ferguson, Edward | Kulan, Eliza Ann (Keelan) | Nov 11 1844 | 8/48B |
| Ferguson, William F | Douglas, Johannah | Jul 13 1846 | 8/178 |
| Ferino, Celso G | Chasene, Maria (Chachere) | Feb 13 1841* | 5/104B |
| Fernandez, Henry | Baldwin, Mary P | May 7 1850 | 11/59 |
| Feron, Joseph | McLaughlin, Catherine A | Oct 29 1852 | 12/39 |
| Ferray, Marie Antoinette | Gauvain, Michael A | 1823* | OIB |
| Ferrell, Ann (Farrell) | Carlin, John | Jan 31 1846 | 8/143B |
| Ferrell, William B | Hyde, Julia | Jan 31 1855 | 14/33 |
| Ferren, Elizabeth F ? | Landrum, James | Dec 11 1850 | 11/102 |
| Ferrill, Dilley | Rodgers, George | Dec 12 1848 | 8/338 |
| Fetters, John George | Williams, Catherine | Dec 27 1842* | 5/238B |
| Fettus, Catherine E | Pendarvis, William H | Jun 6 1854 | 13/243 |
| Fettyplace, Louisa D | Peabody, Herbert C | Feb 24 1846 | 8/147B |
| Few, Thomas | Slade, Elizabeth | Dec 21 1824 | 1/54 |
| Field, Frances, | Sherlock, Eliza D | Apr 5 1844 | 8/9B |
| Field, George | Williams, Louisa | Jun 3 1847 | 8/240 |
| Field, Hester | White, Hiram | May 4 1842 | 5/198B |
| Field, Hester | White, Hiram J | Nov 7 1840* | 4/3401B |
| Field, Joseph W (Fields) | Cox, Jane | Aug 31 1843 | 5/294B |
| Field, Mathew C (Will C) | Ludlow, Cornelia B | Feb 19 1841* | 5/105B |
| Field, Tabitha | Powell, Thomas | May 24 1816 | CM |

| BRIDE OR GROOM | SPOUSE | DATE | BOOK/PAGE |
|---|---|---|---|
| Fielding, Jacob | McConachie, Helen W | May 16 1855 | 14/142 |
| Fields, George | Cunningham, Ellen | Apr  1 1845 | 8/83B |
| Fields, John C | Maples, Herther | Apr 13 1835* | 3/13 |
| Fields, Joseph W | Cox, Jane | Aug 31 1843 | 5/294B |
| Fields, Mary Jane | Norbeck, John | Jan 18 1848 | 8/278 |
| Fife, Catherine | Poersheb, Edmond | Apr  4 1839* | 3/164 |
| Files, Catherine A | Cheseborough, Hiram | Jan 16 1833* | 2/1221 |
| Files, David | Childers, Mary E | Dec 21 1843 | 5/310B |
| Files, Emily F | White, Caleb E | Mar  9 1854* | 13/153 |
| Fillonil, Louis | Sullivan, Mary | Nov  3 1843 | 5/302B |
| Fillowell, Mary | Mahoney, James | Jan 24 1849* | 8/349 |
| Finch, John | Toulmy, Ann (Toomey) | Feb 21 1852 | 11/220 |
| Fincher, Fredrick | Baker, Sarah | Sep  4 1854 | 13/328 |
| Fincher, John | Tylee, Mary | Feb  4 1836* | 3/2 |
| Fink, George | Stauder, Magdalena | Feb 10 1847 | 8/215 |
| Finlay, Henrietta | Conlin, Thomas | Mar  3 1852 | 11/224 |
| Finlay, Joshua B | Scarbrough, Abigail | Nov 18 1843 | 5/305B |
| Finlay, Victoria | Colin, Honore, Jr | Oct 27 1841* | 5/154B |
| Finley, Mary | Kain, William | Jan 31 1849* | 8/352 |
| Finn, Davice (Daniel) | Reece, Therese | Feb 14 1852 | 11/217 |
| Finn, George (Venn) | Thomas, Norah | Apr  4 1843 | 5/258B |
| Finn, John | Barry, Mary | 1841* | OIB |
| Finnegan, James | Halland, Sarah | Sep 16 1854 | 13/337 |
| Finnegan, Thomas | Kearns, Elizabeth | Jan 11 1855 | 14/14 |
| Finnegin, Mary | Tracy, George | Aug 20 1849* | 8/398 |
| Finner, Patrick | Callaghan, Catherine | Jan  7 1837* | 3/68 |
| Finnery, Ellen | Doulan, John | Apr 15 1846 | 8/157B |
| Finnigan, Bridget | Fallond, James (Hallond) | Oct 18 1847 | 8/260B |
| Firhn, Jacob   ? | Hart, Charlotte | Apr 20 1843 | 6/323B |
| Fishe, William | Coan, Parnell | Jun 12 1837* | 3/88 |
| Fisher, Catherine | Harman, McGilbia | Apr 22 1852 | 11/241 |
| Fisher, Charles J B | Richardson, Bess | Jul 11 1845 | 8/110B |
| Fisher, Dieterich | Emily, Frederica | Feb  7 1829* | 2/70 |
| Fisher, Hypolite | Demouy, Augustin | Oct 25 1830* | 2/142 |
| Fisher, Jacob | Hart, Charlotte | Apr 20 1843 | 5/262B |
| Fisher, John | Espejo, Nancy | Dec 24 1840* | 5/79B |
| Fisher, John | Estrezo, Nancy | Jun 24 1841 | 4/271B |
| Fisher, John | Godshack, Margareta G | Nov 29 1851 | 11/198 |
| Fisher, John | Godshild, Margareta | Nov 29 1851 | 11/190 |
| Fisher, John E | Wiggins, Permelia E (wid) | Aug 17 1853 | 12/383 |
| Fisher, John H | Thomas, Louise S | Nov 17 1854 | 13/383 |
| Fisher, Josephine | Gurlote, William | Oct 18 1828 | 2/46 |
| Fisher, Lewis | Gray, Catharine (George) | Aug 18 1842 | 5/216B |
| Fisher, Marcellite | Trouillet, Peter L | Feb  6 1819* | CM |
| Fisher, Missle C | Bates, Joseph  Jr | Aug  7 1838* | 3/137 |
| Fisher, Rosina Mary | Clint, George | Oct 19 1846 | 8/194 |
| Fisher, William F | Greene, Catharine | 1853* | OIB |
| Fisher, William | Gurlotte, Catherine | Mar 16 1825 | 1/68 |
| Fisk, Ann Elizabeth | Greene, William | May 13 1849* | 8/375 |
| Fisk, Catherine | Mitchell, J J | Mar 24 1838* | 3/116 |
| Fiske, Thomas S | Walker, Mary I | Dec 24 1844* | 8/62B |
| Fitch, George W | Cleveland, Palestyne | Nov 29 1849 | 11/20 |
| Fitler, Daniel | Crothers, Martha W | Jan 17 1855 | 14/18 |
| Fitts, John | Rook, Mary | Apr 28 1851 | 11/142 |
| Fitz, Pattie A | Guild, LaFayette | Dec 14 1852 | 12/92 |
| Fitzgerald, Catherine | Sloman, Michael | Feb 23 1854 | 13/134 |
| Fitzgerald, Catherine A | Colson, John M | May 24 1848 | 8/306 |
| Fitzgerald, Daniel | McCarty, Ellen | Jun 27 1839* | 3/180 |
| Fitzgerald, Daniel | Buckley, Ellen | Jan 30 1841* | 5/97B |
| Fitzgerald, Daniel | Buckley, Ellen | Jan 20 1841* | 4/1621 |
| Fitzgerald, Eliza | Brown, Joshua | Oct 30 1849 | 11/12 |
| Fitzgerald, Ellen | Harold, Edward | May 27 1837* | 3/84 |
| Fitzgerald, Ellen | Dunn, Daniel | Oct 17 1853 | 12/415 |
| Fitzgerald, Harriett | Bell, Jackson | Mar 12 1832* | 2/1681 |

| BRIDE OR GROOM | SPOUSE | DATE | BOOK/PAGE |
|---|---|---|---|
| Fitzgerald, John | Strawbridge, Harriett | 1826* | OIB |
| Fitzgerald, John | Whitstone, Sarah | Jun 10 1841* | 5/136B |
| Fitzgerald, Maurice | Steck, Ellen | Feb 28 1854 | 13/146 |
| Fitzpatrick, Ann | Rodgers, Hugh | Apr 11 1851* | 11/136B |
| Fitzpatrick, Edward | McDonald, Mary | Jan 21 1854 | 13/93 |
| Fitzpatrick, Margaret | Coogan, John | Mar 7 1842* | 5/185B |
| Fitzpatrick, Michael | Johnson, Ann | Nov 24 1849 | 11/19 |
| Fitzpatrick, Timothy | McCarty, Ellen | Jul 8 1848* | 8/313 |
| Fitzsimmons, Adaliza | LeBaron, Charles L | Jan 23 1844 | 5/317B |
| Fitzsimmons, Clara | Quigley, Charles M | Jun 30 1840* | 5/30B |
| Fitzsimmons, Sarah Maria | Byrnes, John | Mar 5 1832* | 2/1661 |
| Fitzsimmons, Thomas | O'Keefe, Catherine | Jan 4 1855 | 13/435 |
| Fitzsimons, Philip | Niles, Mary Ann | Aug 7 1838* | 3/138 |
| Flanagan, James | Farley, Elizabeth | Nov 5 1853* | 13/7 |
| Flandray, Mary Ann | Line, John | Sep 14 1849* | 11/4 |
| Flanegan, Catherine | Bryant, John E | Apr 11 1853 | 12/234 |
| Flanegan, Mary Ann | Dickson, Edward | Nov 30 1854* | 13/395 |
| Flannary, Martha | Crockett, William S | Aug 17 1852 | 11/276 |
| Flannary, William | Fosch, Mary Ann (Tosh) | Feb 2 1844 | 5/319B |
| Flannegan, Bridget | Mulcahey, Thomas | Jul 13 1850 | 11/72 |
| Flannery, John | Donald, Ellen | Jul 11 1855 | 14/195 |
| Flannigan, Mary Ann | Sullivan, John | Jan 16 1849* | 8/347 |
| Flash, William | Wilkins, Georgette | May 20 1850 | 11/62 |
| Flaut, Caroline | Calvert, William | Jun 16 1831* | 2/176 |
| Flaut, Joseph H | Darling, Caroline | 1827* | OIB |
| Flecker, Marie Rose | Wagner, Louis | Jul 24 1844 | 8/35B |
| Fleming, Margaret | Lins, John | Apr 2 1853 | 12/214 |
| Flemming, James | Bachus, Elizabeth | Feb 5 1848 | 8/280 |
| Fletcher, George H | Morris, Martha | Jan 22 1852 | 11/206 |
| Fletcher, Sabrey Ann | Havens, John | Oct 18 1830* | 2/141 |
| Fletcher, Sarah Augusta | Beck, Richard M | Jan 20 1841* | 5/91B |
| Fleven, Ann Eliza | Carson, John P | Jul 28 1848* | 8/318 |
| Flin, Jane | Hogan, William | Nov 1 1839* | 3/189 |
| Flinn, Ann | Martin, John | Jan 11 1836* | 3/35 |
| Flinn, Ann | Petrinovich, Antonio | Dec 4 1854 | 13/399 |
| Flinn, Eliza | Richardson, Joseph M | Jan 10 1854 | 13/67 |
| Flinn, Lawrence | McHugh, Mary | Feb 4 1836* | 3/39 |
| Flinn, Margaret | Duncan, John | Jul 28 1853 | 12/373 |
| Flinn, Margaret | Quinn, James | Mar 10 1853 | 12/190 |
| Flinn, Mary | Robertson, James | Nov 5 1851 | 11/186 |
| Flinn, Mary | Sherry, Frank | May 23 1855 | 14/150 |
| Flinn, Mary Ann | Thomason, James H | Jun 23 1842 | 5/207B |
| Flinn, Maurice | Smith, Bridget | Nov 7 1850* | 11/95 |
| Flinn, Morris | Hall, Mary A | May 12 1853 | 12/279 |
| Flock, James B | Kienle, Wilhelmiene | May 18 1853 | 12/289 |
| Floherty, Mary (Flaherty ) | Welch, David | Sep 25 1849 | 11/7 |
| Floid, Catherine A | Weekley, Joseph P | Jan 2 1855 | 13/431 |
| Flood, Hugh | Broderick, Margaret | Apr 29 1854 | 13/209 |
| Flood, James | Magn, Sophia Mrs (Magee) | Jun 24 1841* | 5/139 |
| Flowers, Mary | Chapman, Hiram | Nov 8 1851 | 11/186 |
| Flowers, Rachael | Huffman, Lopon ? | Jul 22 1847 | 8/247 |
| Floyd, James | Myers, Mary | Jun 24 1841 | 4/891B |
| Flury, Nicy (Fluny)? | Davis, Edward D | Mar 19 1841* | 5/118B |
| Flyn, Rose | Robertson, William R | Dec 11 1850 | 11/102 |
| Flynn, Ann | Myers, John | Jun 4 1845 | 8/101B |
| Flynn, Ann (wid) | Case, John | Oct 1 1846* | 8/192 |
| Flynn, Margaret | Acker, James | Aug 4 1851 | 11/171 |
| Flynn, Maria | Kinfield, Nicholas | Jun 18 1847 | 8/242 |
| Flynn, Mary | Mundy, Thomas | Oct 19 1842* | 5/225 |
| Flynn, Mary | Brewer, Charles | Apr 1 1843 | 5/257 |
| Foarte, Elizabeth | Summerlin, David | Jul 3 1849* | 8/395 |
| Fogerty, Margaret | Preston, William (widr) | Dec 22 1853 | 13/46 |
| Fogerty, Thomas | Welsh, Margaret | Jun 17 1852 | 11/264 |
| Fogger, D W | Bridgewood, B (Mrs) | Oct 2 1852 | 12/18 |

| BRIDE OR GROOM | SPOUSE | DATE | BOOK/PAGE |
|---|---|---|---|
| Foley, David | Brookey, Ann (Brooker) | Jan 8 1842 | 5/170B |
| Foley, Elizabeth | Tobin, Thomas | Apr 22 1854 | 13/201 |
| Foley, Julia | Keily, Jeremiah | Jul 10 1852 | 11/269 |
| Foley, Mary | O'Neal, Owen | Feb 27 1854 | 13/142 |
| Foley, Peter | McDonald, Mary J | Feb 7 1855 | 14/40 |
| Foley, Thomas | Cox, Rose | Mar 18 1854 | 13/158 |
| Folin, Thomas | Joyce, Mary | Apr 14 1845 | 8/86B |
| Folk, George | High, Christiana | Feb 18 1841* | 5/105B |
| Folk, James | Wylie, Mary Jane | May 9 1843 | 5/269B |
| Folk, Jedith (Judith?) | Langsfield, Jacob H | Apr 19 1843 | 5/262B |
| Folke, Christian | Sweetser, Henry C | May 8 1852 | 11/247 |
| Foly, James (Foley) | Donnoughouh, Ann (Mrs) | Nov 3 1851 | 11/186 |
| Fonde, Charles H | McLester, Elizabeth | Jun 5 1851* | 11/156 |
| Fonerent, Rosalie | Seifert, Jossue | Apr 24 1821* | CM |
| Fontaine, Mary E | Stewart, Charles H | Dec 12 1844 | 8/58B |
| Fontaine, Millicent C | McQueen, Lewis | Jan 12 1847 | 8/212 |
| Fonville, Stevenson S | Shackelford, Charlotte G | 1839* | OIB |
| Foolkes, John | Bergh, Honorine | May 23 1835* | 3/16 |
| Foote, Charles K | Lyon, Sarah B (wid) | Jul 11 1843 | 5/287B |
| Foote, Lydia E | Seward, George W | Feb 12 1844 | 5/321B |
| Foote, Lydia E | Keenan, Michael J | Nov 2 1848 | 8/331 |
| Forbes, Gifford | Smith, Sarah | May 5 1846 | 8/164B |
| Forbes, Margaret | Powell, James | Jan 9 1847 | 8/211 |
| Forbes, Thomas | Smith, Elizabeth | Apr 16 1850 | 11/54 |
| Forcheimer, Manuel | Cook, Antonie | Feb 6 1854 | 13/113 |
| Ford, Clinton | Laurendine, Marcelite | Sep 29 1831* | 2/182 |
| Ford, Ellen | Laurence, Christopher | Jan 13 1851 | 11/112 |
| Ford, Louisa | Johnson, Nicholas | Jan 29 1835* | 3/6 |
| Ford, Mary Ann | Daulworth, David | Mar 12 1846 | 8/151B |
| Ford, Thomas (Fox) | Fenton, Julia | Dec 26 1846 | 8/207 |
| Fore, Emily S | Maples, Simeon | Sep 17 1851 | 11/180 |
| Foreman, Cassandra | Deburrows, Francis | 1837* | OIB |
| Forest, Aglae | Jeunelot, Charles | Feb 10 1825* | 1/62 |
| Forest, Alexander | Brown, Barbara (Broom) | Jan 1 1838* | 3/106 |
| Forgarty, Joana | Driscoll, Edward | Apr 9 1839* | 3/165 |
| Forlay, Ellen (Farley) | Swiney, Thomas (Sweeney) | Jun 12 1852 | 11/261 |
| Forley, Edwin (Farley) | Butler, Mary | May 16 1851 | 11/150 |
| Forley, Terrence | McDonoughouh, Ann (Mrs) | 1851* | OIB |
| Formerville, Charles W | Beard, Margaret | Feb 8 1841* | 5/101 |
| Forney, Mary E | Smith, Melancthon | Mar 8 1853 | 12/187 |
| Forrest, George | Ware, Loretta E | Dec 23 1839* | 5/5 |
| Forster, James | Forster, Susan E | Jan 24 1843* | 5/172B |
| Forster, John | Williams, Eleanor | May 12 1823 | 1/3 |
| Forster, Susan Ellen | Forster, James | Jan 24 1843* | 5/172B |
| Forsyth, F.D. | Kelly, Delice (Delia) | Apr 10 1852* | 11/234 |
| Forsyth, Mary | Merritt, Charles | Sep 3 1820* | CM |
| Forsyth, Robert C (Richard) | Hull, Julia | Jun 27 1850 | 11/70 |
| Forsyth, Robert T | Wilkins, Mary I | Dec 3 1845 | 8/128B |
| Forte, Margaret Ann | Palliser, John | May 14 1847* | 8/235 |
| Fortner, Alonzo | Sergo, Emelie | Mar 6 1850 | 11/48 |
| Fosch, Mary Ann (Tosch) | Flannary, William | Feb 2 1844 | 5/319B |
| Foster, Benjamin W | D'Olive, Mary D | Jan 16 1854 | 13/80 |
| Foster, Bridget | Osborne, George | Jun 15 1852 | 11/263 |
| Foster, Elizabeth | Suarez, Joseph | Jul 15 1819* | CM |
| Foster, Elizabeth | Waits, Esaias | Jan 11 1836* | 3/34 |
| Foster, Ellen | Ellison, Thomas | Jan 19 1834* | 2/511 |
| Foster, George | Rodgers, Bridget | Aug 23 1849* | 8/399 |
| Foster, George | Thompson, Pholley | Apr 10 1846 | 8/156B |
| Foster, John | Baker, Martha Ann | Nov 29 1854 | 13/394 |
| Foster, John | Heher, Catherine | May 10 1854 | 13/221 |
| Foster, John M | Ryals, Lila | Jun 14 1852 | 11/262 |
| Foster, Levi | Wright, Ellen A | May 30 1851 | 11/153 |
| Foster, Nancy | Havens, John S | May 31 1828* | 2/29 |
| Foster, Sarah Ann | Knapp, Chester P | Jun 24 1842* | 5/208B |

| BRIDE OR GROOM | SPOUSE | DATE | BOOK/PAGE |
|---|---|---|---|
| Foster, William | Lyons, Elizabeth | Jun 15 1846* | 8/173 |
| Fountain, David | Burns, Mary | Jul 13 1846* | 8/178 |
| Fountain, Polly | Buzhart, Thomas | Jul 11 1825 | 1/86 |
| Fountain, Susan | Helverson, Richard | Sep 21 1824 | 1/39 |
| Fountain, Thomas | Rasher, Sarah | Nov 13 1824 | 1/47 |
| Fountaine, Sarah | Malone, Ivy | Oct 16 1823* | 1/8 |
| Fouqust, Minselle Rose | Record, Hippolite | Aug 13 1838* | 3/138 |
| Fourcade, John Baptist | Rondeau, Maria C | Jul 25 1828 | 2/37 |
| Fourcard, Cauline | Dolhende, H E Alfred | Apr 19 1852 | 11/239 |
| Fourcard, Clara | Sossaman, William | Jan 8 1855 | 14/4 |
| Fourment, Zepheren | Dergus, Josephine | May 31 1852 | 11/257 |
| Fournier, Hemelie | Bozage, Sidoine | Feb 27 1829* | 2/73 |
| Fourvett, Lewis N | Pate, Margaret | 1827* | OIB |
| Fowel, Ardel | Grelot, Sefroy | Mar 24 1853* | 12/203 |
| Fowler, Daniel Jr | Coan, Mary Ann | 1826* | OIB |
| Fowler, Ellen | Hines, John | Apr 10 1852 | 11/235 |
| Fowler, James | Connolly, Ellen | May 21 1850 | 11/62 |
| Fowler, John | Pollard, Harriett | Aug 28 1830* | 2/136 |
| Fowler, John D | Russell, Virginia A | May 23 1853 | 12/296 |
| Fowler, Mary C | Cleveland, Henderson K | Nov 29 1855 | 14/293 |
| Fowler, Russell | Ridgeway, Sarah | Jan 28 1836* | 3/38 |
| Fox, Ann | Badget, James | Jan 3 1852 | 11/201 |
| Fox, Anne S | Doughty, John | Feb 8 1820* | CM |
| Fox, Avia | Henson, John | Sep 5 1851 | 11/176 |
| Fox, Catherine | Keho, James | 1827* | OIB |
| Fox, Catharine | Horsefield, Andrew | May 29 1845 | 8/99B |
| Fox, Catharine | Larkin, James | Jan 6 1846 | 8/137B |
| Fox, Felix | Dailey, Margaret | May 27 1851 | 11/153 |
| Fox, Felix | Churchill, Sarah | Nov 29 1854 | 13/393 |
| Fox, Maria | Wallace, William | Aug 22 1846 | 8/185 |
| Fox, Peter | Cassady, Catharine | Aug 30 1852 | 11/280 |
| Fox, Sarah | Bradley, Andrew | Oct 21 1843 | 5/300B |
| Fox, Sarah | Parker, Levi J | Apr 19 1851 | 11/139 |
| Fox, Thomas | Dunn, Mary | Oct 26 1848* | 8/330 |
| Fox, Thomas R | Fenton, Julia | 1846* | OIB |
| Foy, Ann | Moore, Edward | Mar 13 1848* | 8/295 |
| Foy, Daniel | Jones, Amelia | Mar 26 1847 | 8/222 |
| Foy, Eliza | Kelly, James | Jun 17 1853 | 12/321 |
| Foy, Rosa Ann | Dunn, Lawrence W | Jun 12 1837* | 3/86 |
| Foy, Rosanna | Freher, John | 1838* | OIB |
| Franceville, Charles W | Beard, Margaret | Feb 8 1841 | 4/2991 |
| Francis, Manuel | Leavens, Elizabeth | Jun 17 1854 | 13/260 |
| Francis, Rebecca | Smith, Douglas | Mar 15 1848 | 8/293 |
| Franelich, Thomas | Weinheimer, Otilia | Jul 26 1851 | 11/169 |
| Frank, Benedict | Allarnst, Ada ? | Apr 28 1842* | 5/194B |
| Frank, Lawrence | Bitzer, Margaret | Oct 29 1844 | 8/46B |
| Frank, Lewis | Kahn, Bertha | Jun 8 1852* | 11/260 |
| Frank, Louisa | Hartel, Frederic | May 9 1855 | 14/135 |
| Frank, Mary Matilda (Funk) | Spurre, Gastaf (Sparre) | Jun 12 1843 | 5/281B |
| Frank, Mena | Smith, Christian | Nov 13 1849 | 11/15 |
| Frank, Rosa | Baumblatt, Aaron | Nov 24 1854 | 13/390 |
| Franklin, Benjamin | Shagn, Catherine ? | Jul 1 1843* | 5/285B |
| Franklin, Benjamin T | Hobart, May M | May 28 1840* | 5/24 |
| Franklin, Helena | Noahe, Meyer | Mar 12 1851* | 11/126 |
| Franklin, Irene | Sidney, John | Jul 5 1853 | 12/348 |
| Fraser, William M | Tanner, Elizabeth A | Mar 17 1853* | 12/196 |
| Frasier, George | Stewart, Mahala | Nov 5 1831 | 2/183 |
| Fratman, Mary | Edstrom, Charles | Feb 29 1840* | 5/13 |
| Fratus, William | Richards, Elizabeth | Jun 22 1853 | 12/327 |
| Frayer, Rudina A | Ross, John McD | Dec 15 1840* | 5/75 |
| Frazier, John | Brown, Susanna | Oct 19 1846 | 8/195 |
| Frederick, George | Hill, Marti | Mar 3 1841* | 5/112B |
| Freeman, John W | Curry, Mary Ann | Aug 17 1855 | 14/213 |
| Freeman, Mary R | Nettles, John M  (widr) | Sep 12 1853 | 12/404 |

| BRIDE OR GROOM | SPOUSE | DATE | BOOK/PAGE |
|---|---|---|---|
| Freeman, Pewninah ? | Cawfield, William A | Mar 25 1835 | 3/12 |
| Freeman, Rueben H | Andrews, Martha J | Jan 27 1852 | 11/209 |
| Freeman, Samuel T | Kelly, Martha J | Dec 13 1853 | 13/39 |
| Freeman, William A | Smith, Mary | Feb 13 1851 | 11/122 |
| Freher, John | Foy, Rosanna | 1838* | OIB |
| Frelekstein, Matilda | Goldsmith, Isaac | Apr 18 1846 | 8/158B |
| French, Jane | Trask, Frederick | Sep 27 1843* | 5/298B |
| French, Zerubabel | Clark, Elizabeth | Oct 4 1849 | 11/8 |
| French, Zorobabel ? | Roberts, Celia | Feb 10 1852 | 11/215 |
| Frink, Eliza | Bolman, John | Aug 9 1848 | 8/319 |
| Frink, William | Rowland, Clara | Oct 25 1849 | 11/11 |
| Frisbie, Jane | Jenkins, Henry J | Aug 19 1850 | 11/81 |
| Frisby, William | Julian, Drusilla | Sep 11 1848 | 8/324 |
| Frisby, William | Dunwoody, Mary B | Jun 14 1845 | 8/103 |
| Frisk, Charles | Harty, Frances ? | Nov 3 1851 | 11/185 |
| Frobos, Walter | Discher, Louisa | Oct 23 1849 | 11/11 |
| Frolichstein, Henry | Leib, Sarah | 1847* | OIB |
| Frolichstein, Henry | Maas, Babet | Jun 24 1853* | 12/330 |
| Frolichstein, Matilda | Goldsmith, Isaac | Apr 18 1846 | 8/158B |
| Frolickstein, Henry | Weinberg, Mina | Feb 10 1854 | 13/117 |
| Frolickstein, William | Epstein, Sophie | Feb 17 1852 | 11/218 |
| Froliekstein, Jesse | Froliekstein, Matilda | Nov 6 1852* | 12/48 |
| Froliekstein, Matilda | Frohliekstein, Jesse | Nov 6 1852* | 12/48 |
| Frost, Eben H | Wyman, Nancy A | Nov 16 1854 | 13/381 |
| Frowner, James | Acre, Mary A | May 3 1839* | 3/176 |
| Fry, Budd H | Waters, Frances E | Jan 3 1842 | 5/167B |
| Fry, John | Crotty, Eliza | Feb 3 1842 | 5/177B |
| Fry, Rosana | Burke, Thomas | Oct 20 1842 | 5/225B |
| Fukner, Elizabeth ? | McCreay, Isaiah (Isoar) | Oct 23 1838* | 3/144 |
| Fulham, Patrick | Brown, Mary | May 22 1854 | 13/231 |
| Fullam, Safford Eddy | Seymour, Jane Eliza | Feb 17 1848 | 8/284 |
| Fuller, George | Sills, Elizabeth (Mrs) | Oct 6 1846* | 8/193 |
| Fuller, Lewis | Burgett, Barbara | Feb 8 1848 | 8/281 |
| Fullum, Catherine | Conick, Robert (wid) | Nov 22 1853 | 13/21 |
| Funk, Mary Matilda (Frank) | Sparre, Gastaf ? | Jun 12 1843 | 6/377B |
| Furlong, James | Gates, Elizabeth | Sep 12 1842 | 5/219B |
| Furness, Orlando | Magee, Caroline V | Oct 13 1847 | 8/262 |
| Futch, Isaac | Lott, Elizabeth | Oct 27 1841* | 5/155B |
| Futz, Bridget | Besanceny, Christostime | Apr 18 1854 | 13/189 |
| Fyffe, John | Williams, Catherine | May 28 1821* | CM |

## G

| | | | |
|---|---|---|---|
| Gabel, Johanna B | Raue, Julius A | Jun 12 1854* | 13/253 |
| Gabert, Maria | Snyder, J. Otto | Oct 14 1852 | 12/29 |
| Gabriel, Thomas | Boyls, Euphame | Jul 25 1853 | 12/368 |
| Gaddes, Ann | Sixsmith, Joseph | Sep 18 1855 | 14/232 |
| Gaffney, Ann | Thompson, Lawrence | Jun 8 1846 | 8/171 |
| Gaffney, Michael | Clinton, Alice | Sep 30 1842* | 5/221B |
| Gage, Mariana | Bock, Moretz | Jun 27 1853* | 12/332 |
| Gage, Robert | Deana, Anna F | Oct 2 1855 | 14/244 |
| Gage, Rosanna | Williams, John | May 2 1851 | 11/144 |
| Gager, Aretusa ? | Carmelich, George | Jan 3 1852 | 11/200 |
| Gager, John | Gellott, Louisa (Grelot) | Apr 27 1852 | 11/242 |

| BRIDE OR GROOM | SPOUSE | DATE | BOOK/PAGE |
|---|---|---|---|
| Gager, Roxana (Hoxana?) | Arti, George | Sep 6 1845 | 8/117B |
| Gagle, Andrew I (Gayle) | Dondeff, Ellen (Dewolff) | Jul 31 1845 | 8/113B |
| Gaham, John | Hoven, Sarah | Jun 29 1843* | 5/284B |
| Gaham, John | Lehey, Eliza (Lahey) | Jul 18 1844 | 8/33B |
| Gahan, John | Mamie, Mary A ? | Apr 1 1839 | 3/163 |
| Gaillard, Lydia H | Alderson, William S | Dec 5 1854 | 13/400 |
| Gaillard, Mary Ann | Willison, Edward F | Apr 19 1853 | 12/245 |
| Gaines, Edmund P | Toulmin, May (Mary) | Feb 12 1847 | 8/216 |
| Gaines, Ellen Frances | St John, Thomas | Dec 20 1843 | 5/310B |
| Gaines, Helen T | Davis, William | Dec 29 1840* | 5/81B |
| Gaines, Henry T | Waugh, Joana | Nov 12 1850 | 11/96 |
| Gaines, James J | Hails, Harriet E | Aug 22 1849* | 8/399 |
| Gaines, Mary H | Morris, John Jr | May 2 1825 | 1/73 |
| Galaway, Rita | Bozage, Eugene | Jul 27 1852* | 11/272 |
| Gale, Maria R | Collins, Charles LeB | Nov 28 1854 | 13/392 |
| Gales, Emeline | Carver, Thomas J | Nov 15 1838* | 3/147 |
| Galindo, Richard M | Hall, Catharine L | Jan 6 1849* | 8/346 |
| Gallager, Mahala | Andrews, John M | Aug 17 1850 | 11/80 |
| Gallaghen, Thomas Michael | Mabhullen, Mary ? | Jun 15 1842 | 6/162B |
| Gallagher, Amelia | Valero, Francisco | Feb 28 1854 | 13/145 |
| Gallagher, Ann | Rone, James | 1840* | OIB |
| Gallagher, Con | Smith, Maria | Dec 13 1852 | 12/87 |
| Gallagher, Elizabeth | Kemper, Robert | Jan 22 1844 | 5/316B |
| Gallagher, Henry | McLaughlin, Margt | May 4 1852 | 11/245 |
| Gallagher, James | Sullivan, Priscilla | Feb 20 1846 | 8/146B |
| Gallagher, Jane | Mackin, Patrick (Markin) | Jan 14 1844* | 5/314B |
| Gallagher, Thomas M | Malholm, Mary ? | Jun 15 1842* | 5/206B |
| Gallaway, Martha | Lucas, Beasley | Feb 12 1848* | 8/283 |
| Galle, Louis | Bozarge, Artimese | Dec 8 1845 | 8/128B |
| Galle, Louis | Machien, Martha | Jan 5 1853 | 12/115 |
| Galle, Marie Virginia | LeMoin, Victor | Apr 25 1829* | 2/82 |
| Gallegher, Bridget | Auzy, George | Jul 24 1851 | 11/169 |
| Gallert, Benjamin C ? | Richards, Francis E | Apr 29 1845 | 7/655B |
| Galligan, Margaret | Mangal, Michael | Oct 1 1855 | 14/242 |
| Galligar, Alfoy | Serra, Louis | Apr 15 1854 | 13/182 |
| Galligher, Martin | Welsh, Levina | Aug 29 1850 | 11/83 |
| Gallihar, Mary | Ivis, Richard | May 6 1854 | 13/218 |
| Galliher, Bridget | Drinnan, Edward | 1840* | OIB |
| Galliher, Samuel C | McEvoy, Mary E | Nov 1 1853 | 13/3 |
| Gallowa(y), Maria | Bozarge, Seadwin | Nov 8 1852* | 12/49 |
| Galloway, Alexander | McLean, Catharine | Sep 28 1840* | 5/47B |
| Galloway, John | Ballard, Louisa | Feb 13 1815* | CM |
| Galloway, Martha | Barron, John W | Jul 13 1843 | 5/288B |
| Gallup, Benjamin C | Richards, Francis E | Apr 29 1845 | 8/89B |
| Gallup, George | Cannon, Elizabeth T | Aug 28 1854 | 13/324 |
| Galvery, Louisa | Nicholas, Varius | Nov 12 1834* | 2/186B |
| Galway, Louisa | Nicholas, Varius | Nov 12 1834* | 2/186 |
| Gamber, Jane (Gamble) | Jiles, Robert | Sep 25 1838* | 3/141 |
| Gamble, Jane | O'Brien, James | Apr 1 1845 | 8/82B |
| Gamble, Margaret | Swear, Peter (Saurez) | Aug 31 1818* | CM |
| Gamble, Philip | Harvey, Kyle | Dec 24 1844 | 8/62B |
| Gamble, Thomas | McKey, Letitice | Dec 17 1852 | 12/96 |
| Gambling, Nancy | Morris, George W | Dec 22 1852 | 12/104 |
| Gamel, Samuel | O'Donnel, Rosanna | Feb 21 1851 | 11/123 |
| Gammon, William (Gorman) | Martin, Mary | Nov 25 1840* | 5/67 |
| Gamora, Jose Manuel M | Hericourt, Anna M J | May 12 1853 | 12/278 |
| Gandin, John (Gaudin) | Shields, Elizabeth | Sep 29 1845 | 8/119B |
| Gange, Numa (Gauge)? | Provost, Cecilia | Aug 20 1852* | 11/277 |
| Ganmon, William | Dias, Mary | Nov 25 1840 | 4/3271B |
| Gannan, Elizabeth | Irwin, Joseph | Apr 30 1841* | 5/127B |
| Gannard, Fercol Victor | Perault, Elizabeth (wid) | Jun 25 1819* | CM |
| Gannard, Victor | Sands, Susan M | 1826* | OIB |
| Gannaway, James | Magee, Mary A | Jan 19 1844 | 5/315B |
| Ganson, Angeline (Gannon) | Graham, Thomas | Sep 18 1841 | 5/152 |

| BRIDE OR GROOM | SPOUSE | DATE | BOOK/PAGE |
|---|---|---|---|
| Garcia, Joseph | Bazer, Martha | Jan 19 1829* | 2/64 |
| Garcia, Mary Ann | Gonzales, Joseph | Apr 1 1848 | 8/296 |
| Garcier, Ramona | Curtis, Joseph | Sep 29 1853 | 12/411 |
| Gardim, Emma B ? | Brodaux, Henry W | Nov 7 1849 | 11/15 |
| Gardner, David B | Spalding, Martha M | Mar 12 1851 | 11/129 |
| Gardner, Jesse Jr | Motsack, Philena ? | Oct 8 1840* | 5/53B |
| Gardner, John R | Henry, Clarissa | 1837* | OIB |
| Gardner, William A | Wilkerson, Nancy | Jul 4 1845 | 8/108B |
| Garland, James | Woods, Mary | Feb 8 1842 | 5/178B |
| Garner, Burgess | Sanders, Mary J | Feb 20 1855 | 14/66 |
| Garner, Julia Ann | Bell, Samuel | Dec 14 1852 | 12/89 |
| Garner, June | Lawson, Lewis | Oct 26 1844* | 8/46B |
| Garner, Matilda | Woods, Charles | Jan 11 1848* | 8/276 |
| Garner, Matilda | Walker, Charles | Dec 6 1845 | 8/135B |
| Garner, Thomas | Quiner, Mary | Nov 12 1835* | 3/28 |
| Garoen, Willy (Garvin) | Pomeroy, Elizabeth | May 6 1835* | 3/24 |
| Garoty, Bridget | McMahon, Thomas | Apr 6 1854 | 13/174 |
| Garrahan, Ann B (Mrs) | Stringer, Thomas | Jul 17 1843 | 5/289B |
| Garraway, Elizabeth | Sunter, Joseph | Nov 12 1855 | 14/280 |
| Garrett, Charles C | Owens, Louise C | Jun 17 1840* | 4/1611B |
| Garrett, Charles C | Cowen, Louisa | Jun 17 1841* | 5/139B |
| Garrett, Joyce | Gilbert, Allen R | May 25 1831 | 2/172 |
| Garrett, Lydia | Anderson, Samuel | Dec 23 1837* | 3/105 |
| Garrett, Mary S | Peebles, James A | Jun 11 1855 | 14/166 |
| Garrett, Richard W | Taylor, Charlotte M | Mar 24 1847* | 8/222 |
| Garrett, William | Henry, Julia B | Apr 22 1843 | 5/264B |
| Garrow, William M | Walker, Virginia L | 1838* | OIB |
| Gartling, Mary Ann | Martin, Patrick | Jun 29 1846 | 8/175 |
| Gartman, Alabama | Pond, William O | Jul 2 1853 | 12/340 |
| Gartman, George | Miller, Emily Ann | Dec 20 1847* | 8/272 |
| Gartman, Henry A | Taylor, Loisa (wid) | Jan 29 1853 | 12/154 |
| Gartman, Mary | Grug, Robert ? | May 23 1838* | 3/128 |
| Gartman, Philip | Campbell, Mary | Jun 2 1855 | 14/157 |
| Garvey, George | Shannon, Mary | Mar 24 1852 | 11/229 |
| Garvey, Margaret | Cahill, James | Sep 12 1843* | 5/296B |
| Garvey, Sarah Louisa | Pease, Alvin | Mar 17 1852 | 11/227 |
| Garvin, Mills | Pomeroy, Elizabeth | May 6 1835* | 3/24 |
| Gascoigne, Charles W | Chapman, Antoinette E | Feb 19 1855 | 14/58 |
| Gascoigne, Elmira D | Wright, Charles | Nov 16 1846 | 8/199 |
| Gascoigne, Maria S | Walker, Robert S | Dec 7 1842 | 5/232B |
| Gascoigne, Martha C | Cunningham, Robert | Jan 11 1848 | 8/277 |
| Gasin, Benjamin ? | Maura, Florestin | Dec 25 1843 | 5/311B |
| Gaston, Matthew A | Soren, Caroline (Loren) | Feb 18 1843* | 5/249B |
| Gasulle, Lawrence (Gassill) | Sussusant, Sophie ? | May 10 1838* | 3/125 |
| Gasz, Catherine | Rieke, Dederich | Oct 20 1847* | 8/260 |
| Gately, Ann | Newman, Dorman | Jan 10 1842 | 5/170B |
| Gately, Bridget | Crosby, John | Jul 28 1851 | 11/170 |
| Gately, Bridget | Geoghegan, Miachael | Jun 23 1852 | 11/265 |
| Gately, Winney | Gormon, Patrick | Jun 20 1850 | 11/67 |
| Gates, Adelia | Demath, James T | Nov 2 1852 | 12/43 |
| Gates, Elizabeth | Furlong, James | Sep 12 1842 | 5/219B |
| Gates, Emeline | Carver, Thomas J | 1838* | OIB |
| Gates, Hezekiah | McKinsey, Adelle | Oct 13 1834* | 3/5 |
| Gates, Joseph R | Pritchett, Marian E | Aug 12 1848* | 8/320 |
| Gates, Rose | Young, John | May 7 1849* | 8/373 |
| Gatting, Sarah Ann | Alexander, Jefferson | Mar 9 1846 | 8/150B |
| Gauge, Numa | Provost, Cecelia | Aug 20 1852* | 11/277 |
| Gause, Austin B | Waters, Elizabeth | Dec 3 1845 | 8/128B |
| Gautreaus, Joseph | Lenorman, Charlotte | Dec 4 1854 | 13/397 |
| Gauvain, Michael A | Ferray, Marie Antoinette | 1823* | OIB |
| Gavin, Francis | Cooper, Margaret | Jan 21 1854 | 13/100 |
| Gavin, John | McMahon, Mary | Jan 10 1854 | 13/70 |
| Gavin, Mary | McMahon, Patrick | Feb 4 1854 | 13/110 |
| Gay, George W | Rainwater, Elizabeth S | Jul 22 1843 | 5/290B |

| BRIDE OR GROOM | SPOUSE | DATE | BOOK/PAGE |
|---|---|---|---|
| Gay, Sissly Ann | Herring, Caleb F | Mar 20 1852* | 11/229 |
| Gayer, Ledyard D (Gager) | Clark, Sarah Ann | Apr 15 1844 | 8/219B |
| Gayle, A. J. (Gagle) | George, Malinda E (Gage) | Apr 8 1852 | 11/233 |
| Gayle, Amelia R | Gorgas, Josiah | Dec 28 1853 | 13/55 |
| Gayle, Andrew J | DeWolff, Ellen D | Jul 31 1845 | 8/113 |
| Gayle, Anna | Owen, Richard B | Jun 26 1850 | 11/69 |
| Gayle, Anne M | Bayne, Thomas L | Dec 21 1853 | 13/44 |
| Gayle, Mary | Aikin, Hugh K | Dec 15 1852 | 12/94 |
| Gayle, Sarah | Crawford, William B | Dec 7 1842 | 5/233B |
| Gayle, William L | Norman, Emily | Jul 18 1849* | 8/388 |
| Gaylord, Mary E | Holt, George W | Jun 2 1845 | 3/100B |
| Gays, Frances Eliza | Griffin, James L | May 8 1839* | 3/170 |
| Gaz, Fredricka | La Pre, Peter | Mar 24 1849* | 8/364 |
| Gazzam, Catherine S | Hitchcock, John A | Feb 21 1850 | 11/41 |
| Gazzam, Mary A | Butler, Sage O | Jun 10 1833* | 2/941 |
| Geandreau, John | Lioni, Margaret | Dec 12 1828* | 2/55 |
| Geandreau, Mary M | Baas, Joseph W | May 8 1855 | 14/134 |
| Geandreau, William A | Lassabe, Mary E | Apr 28 1853 | 12/258 |
| Geary, Daniel | Parker, Louisa A | Oct 4 1852 | 12/21 |
| Geaudrean, John H ? | Dorgan, Elizabeth | Sep 23 1852 | 12/13 |
| Gedder, Carolina | Steele, Michael | Jun 3 1852 | 11/260 |
| Gee, Gideon | Singletary, Harriet | Nov 24 1841* | 5/159B |
| Geelin, Patrick | Baker, Louisa | Mar 27 1855 | 14/91 |
| Geher, Joseph W | Harriss, Sarah E | Dec 14 1855 | 14/304 |
| Gehr, Joseph W | Wemberly, Elizabeth J | May 13 1853 | 12/281 |
| Geiler, Catherine | Williams, George | Nov 23 1848 | 8/334 |
| Gelbk, Caroline | Schoeman, Anthony | Aug 27 1852 | 11/279 |
| Gellek, Jean Marie | Brown, Ann Marie | Feb 5 1839* | 3/155 |
| Gellott, Louisa (Gerlott) | Gager, John | Apr 27 1852 | 11/242 |
| Gelvan, Patrick | Barret, Catherine | May 18 1852 | 11/250 |
| Gentry, Robert | O'Donald, Mary | Jun 2 1845 | 8/100B |
| Geoghegan, Michael | Gately, Bridget | Jun 23 1852 | 11/265 |
| George, Adele | Bright, Michael Jr | Nov 28 1851 | 11/190 |
| George, Caroline | Byrd, Berry | 1837* | OIB |
| George, Catherine | Kelly, John | May 12 1845 | 8/94B |
| George, Claiborne R | Malone, Janey | Apr 15 1834* | 2/321 |
| George, Edward V | Campbell, Hellen E | Mar 16 1853 | 12/193 |
| George, Elizabeth | Sims, Berry | Oct 9 1847* | 8/258 |
| George, Emeline | Deas, Hopson | Dec 21 1839* | 5/4 |
| George, Harriet | Malone, Griffin | Jun 3 1839* | 3/176 |
| George, Harriett | Monk, Thomas | Jul 1 1834* | 2/251 |
| George, Henrietta E. | Van Hook, Marcus A | Jun 22 1852 | 11/264 |
| George, Isaac | Sims, Elizabeth | Oct 6 1851 | 11/181 |
| George, Joseph | Byrd, Sarah | Aug 6 1831 | 2/179 |
| George, Joseph | Herkins, Easter ? | Jan 15 1836* | 3/36 |
| George, Malinda E | Gayle, A J | Apr 8 1852 | 11/233 |
| George, Margaret Ann | Moore, William V | Dec 9 1845 | 8/130B |
| George, Mary | Boch, Sebastien | Apr 11 1853 | 12/231 |
| George, Mary E (Mrs) | Kendall, Lyman R | Jun 24 1842 | 5/208B |
| George, Mary F | Jude, Alexander J | Apr 6 1842* | 5/191B |
| George, Mary S | Johns, Zephaniah | Apr 13 1852 | 11/236 |
| George, Mikile (Michael) | Harvey, Alfred | Feb 24 1842 | 5/183B |
| George, Mildred | Oliver, Henry H | Jun 3 1853 | 12/308 |
| George, Nancy | Kinney, Henderson | Nov 12 1833* | 2/721 |
| George, Sarah | Little, George | Jul 8 1833 | 2/861 |
| George, Sophie | Smith, Pevico ? | Feb 10 1848 | 8/282 |
| George, Susan | Lewis, Seaborn | Mar 28 1829* | 2/78 |
| George, Travis | Ulricke, Melissa P | Mar 4 1852 | 11/224 |
| George, William | Watkins, Elizabeth | Aug 8 1840* | 5/39B |
| George, William H | Beam, Jane Augusta | Dec 30 1848 | 8/342 |
| Gerald, Julia Ann | Pitts, Washington | Mar 28 1833* | 2/1061 |
| Gerald, Francis Lazarus | Rabby, Susan | Dec 7 1844* | 8/57B |
| Gerard, Francis | Grelote, Isabel | 1824* | OIB |
| Gercke, Hannah H | Oelrich, Geroge A | Sep 20 1855 | 14/234 |

| BRIDE OR GROOM | SPOUSE | DATE | BOOK/PAGE |
|---|---|---|---|
| Gerles, Ardomisa | Pickering, John | Aug 31 1854 | 13/326 |
| Gerlot, Rosalie | Demouy, Louis | Jun  6 1842* | 5/204B |
| Gerlott, John | Carter, Mary | Oct 18 1852* | 12/30 |
| German, Robert | Allen, Isabella | Mar 11 1820* | CM |
| Gero, Mary Ann (Gerow) | Key, David S | Jul 21 1852* | 11/271 |
| Gerom, Mary    (Gerow) | Murphy, Thomas | Dec  6 1847 | 8/269 |
| Gerow, Warren D | Linnell, Charlotte | Nov 19 1844 | 8/52B |
| Gets, Henry | Mitchell, Ann | Nov 20 1849* | 11/17 |
| Gevey, Stephen (Geary) | Knowland, Honore | Sep  9 1828* | 2/40 |
| Geyer, Peter | Davis, Elizabeth | May 16 1832* | 2/1511 |
| Gezon, Louis (Gegon) | Denton, Maria | May  1 1850 | 11/58 |
| Gibb, Helen | Sciple, John | Nov  6 1855 | 14/273 |
| Gibbons, Catherine | Smith, Michael | Jan 19 1854 | 13/89 |
| Gibbons, John | Quin, Mary | May 10 1852* | 11/248 |
| Gibbons, Minerva | Lyon, Charles | Jul  2 1849 | 8/395 |
| Gibbons, William | Farley, Julia | Apr 10 1852 | 11/234 |
| Gibbs, James | Miles, Ann | Apr 25 1838* | 3/121 |
| Gibbs, John H | Wilkinson, Catherine E | May  4 1854 | 13/214 |
| Gibbs, Mary | Waters, Leaven | Jan 21 1850 | 11/34 |
| Gibbson, Emeline | Miller, Thomas | 1840* | OIB |
| Giblin, Daniel | Gowin, Ellen (McGowan) | Apr  1 1839* | 3/163 |
| Gibson, Caroline | Gonzales, Dominique | Jun  9 1854 | 13/247 |
| Gibson, Gilbert | Moore, Elnora | Feb 18 1845* | 8/73B |
| Gibson, John | Ennis, Mary Ann | Jun 29 1848* | 8/311 |
| Gibson, John | Chamberlain, Reubanna L | Dec 18 1845 | 8/131B |
| Gibson, Malinda | Cummings, John | Jul  9 1846* | 8/177 |
| Gibson, Nancy Ann | Espejo, Antonio | Apr 24 1832* | 2/1581 |
| Gibson, Sarah | Ekston, Gustavus | Apr 17 1850 | 11/54 |
| Gibson, Silas | Hammond, Martha N | Jun 29 1853 | 12/336 |
| Gibson, Stephen | Stokes, Jane A | Mar 11 1854 | 13/156 |
| Giddens, James W | Holland, Leona A | Apr 18 1850 | 11/54 |
| Giffon, Mary | Anderson, John | Nov  4 1829* | 2/101 |
| Gilbert, Allen R | Garrett, Joyce | May 25 1831 | 2/172 |
| Gilbert, Camilla | Gough, Jonathan B | Sep 26 1850 | 11/87 |
| Gilbert, Charles | Manson, Mary Jane | Jun 21 1842 | 5/207B |
| Gilbert, Elizabeth M | Snyder, Theobold | Feb 19 1844 | 5/323B |
| Gilbertson, Charles F | McGuire, Ellen | Apr  5 1853 | 12/221 |
| Gilbraith, John (Gilreath) | Reavidine, Catherine | Oct 14 1843 | 5/300B |
| Gilchrist, Anna B | Morris, John | May 19 1838* | 3/127 |
| Gilchrist, Elizabeth | Smith, Edward G | Apr 15 1850* | 11/53 |
| Gilchrist, Isabella | Nooten, Alexander ?? | Jan 20 1851* | 11/115 |
| Gilchrist, John | Brabner, Judith | Jan  5 1853 | 12/112 |
| Gilchrist, Mary A | Holly, William DeForest | 1827* | OIB |
| Gilchrist, Mary L | Lacoste, Benjamin | Feb 23 1830* | 2/114 |
| Gilchrist, Philip | Hays, Mary | Jul  1 1839* | 3/180 |
| Gilchrist, Philomena | Henescey, Thomas H | Feb  4 1835* | 3/7 |
| Gildemaster, Hugo C | Allard, Marie I | Apr 25 1836* | 3/45 |
| Gilder, Sarah Ann E | Davis, Hansford | Dec 22 1849 | 11/27 |
| Giles, William Lion | Brady, Roseanna | Nov 18 1844 | 8/51B |
| Gilgan, Martin | Begley, Ellen | Nov 17 1855 | 14/283 |
| Gilgen, Christiane | Held, Joseph | Jun 28 1852 | 11/267 |
| Gilhooly, Patrick | McGirl, Alice | Feb 23 1850 | 11/42 |
| Gill, Barney | Michael, Mary | Apr 13 1842 | 5/195B |
| Gill, James | McCormick, Julia | Jan 30 1855 | 14/31 |
| Gill, Mary | Bryne, Benny   (Boyne) | Mar 18 1844 | 5/328B |
| Gill, Mary Ann | Ruhuley, Fredric | Mar  6 1846 | 8/149B |
| Gillan, Andrew | Minor, Bridget | Apr 28 1855 | 14/122 |
| Gilleland, Emilier | Skaates, B.S. | Feb 10 1838* | 3/111 |
| Gillen, Isaac | Bandler, Elizabeth | Feb 17 1849 | 8/354 |
| Gillespie, Anna Ann | Malone, Barney | Jan 10 1846 | 8/138B |
| Gillespie, Clayton C | Stuart, Caroline E | Nov 17 1847* | 8/265 |
| Gillespie, Ellen | Baxter, John | Apr 14 1853 | 12/240 |
| Gillespie, George W C | Turner, Virtue | May  5 1845 | 8/91B |
| Gillick, Hugh | Masterson, Elizabeth | Nov 23 1855 | 14/286 |

| BRIDE OR GROOM | SPOUSE | DATE | BOOK/PAGE |
|---|---|---|---|
| Gillin, James (Gillise) | Hogan, Jane (June) | Nov 3 1845 | 8/123B |
| Gilmor, Robert | Morgan, Jennett (Magee) | May 24 1841* | 5/132B |
| Gilmore, William | Riley, Elizabeth | Oct 31 1845 | 8/122B |
| Gilpin, Ann | Stav, Ola | Jan 5 1848 | 8/275 |
| Gilroy, Ann | McMinn, Thomas | Feb 23 1852 | 11/221 |
| Ginn, J S | O'Reilly, Sarah | 1840* | OIB |
| Ginochi, Mary | Blossini, Francisco | May 8 1852 | 11/247 |
| Girard, Edward | Jacob, Julie | Nov 22 1829* | 2/103 |
| Girard, Elvina | Iveland, John J (Ireland) | Dec 12 1851 | 11/193 |
| Girard, Emile | Eslava, Constance O | Oct 17 1849 | 11/10 |
| Girard, Hermine | Herpin, Felix | Aug 5 1828 | 2/38 |
| Girard, Isabel | Demouy, Joseph | May 26 1851 | 11/152 |
| Girard, Isabella | Noel, Theodore | Dec 2 1835* | 3/32 |
| Girard, Joanna (Julia) | Spullen, Stephen | Jan 25 1842* | 5/174B |
| Girard, Joseph | Purdy, Wineford | Dec 20 1833* | 2/651 |
| Girard, Laura L | Green, Andrew | Jan 16 1855 | 14/17 |
| Girard, Margaret Clair | Lioni, Joseph C | Jun 22 1819* | CM |
| Girard, Mary | Antunes, Joaquim | Aug 27 1823 | 1/12 |
| Girard, Sarah | Benetes, Manuel | Oct 19 1854 | 13/354 |
| Girard, Severine | Hurtel, Firmin | Dec 22 1835* | 3/34 |
| Given, Alexander | Barker, Elizabeth | May 17 1847 | 8/235 |
| Gladsman, Josephine | Haberle, Jacob | May 25 1852 | 11/255 |
| Glaize, Rebecca | Baston, Joseph O | Jan 22 1846 | 7/756B |
| Glargon, Sarah | Stoppin, Loopold | Jul 21 1838* | 3/137 |
| Glase, Rebecca | Pendavis, Henry | Mar 3 1825 | 1/65 |
| Glasgow, Stephen | Summer, Sarah | Nov 26 1834 | 2/1851 |
| Glass, Mary Jane | Costa, Stephen | Apr 19 1855 | 14/110 |
| Gleason, James S | Harris, Louisa | Apr 17 1839* | 3/167 |
| Gleason, John | Brown, Easter | Jun 18 1853 | 12/322 |
| Gleason, Margaret M | Hammond, John | Jun 18 1840* | 5/28B |
| Gleason, Thomas | Barry, Ellen | Apr 21 1855 | 14/113 |
| Gleeson, Michael | St John, Eliza | Feb 17 1852 | 11/218 |
| Glenholme, Anna M | Overall, John W | Mar 12 1855 | 14/82 |
| Glennen, Catherine | Kelly, John | May 19 1853 | 12/291 |
| Glennin, Michael | Ryan, Mary | Jul 24 1854 | 13/293 |
| Glennon, Catherine | McTiernan, Patrick | Sep 6 1854 | 13/332 |
| Glennon, Michael | McDemott, Catherine | Apr 10 1841* | 5/122B |
| Glenson, Angline (Ganson) | Graham, Thomas | Sep 18 1841 | 5/152B |
| Gliddon, John S | Ballinger, Charlotte | Jan 30 1840* | 5/10 |
| Gliddon, Sarah E | Riley, Thomas | Jun 4 1850 | 11/64 |
| Gliddon, Susannah | Hearin, William J | Apr 9 1846 | 8/156B |
| Glisson, James S (wid) | Edwards, Cassandra (wid) | Feb 17 1853 | 12/175 |
| Gloom, Caroline A | Prudert, James A | Sep 10 1841 | 4/3311 |
| Glorinny, Mary Ann Jane | Broderick, James | Mar 28 1851 | 11/132 |
| Glover, Caroline A | Prudat, Louis Ernest | Sep 15 1841* | 5/152B |
| Glover, Henry W | Green, Mary A | Aug 26 1854 | 13/321 |
| Glover, John | Clarke, Mary A | Nov 21 1854 | 13/386 |
| Glover, John A | Sanders, Isabella | Feb 10 1853 | 12/168 |
| Glyce, Martin | Powers, Johanna | Aug 25 1838* | 3/141 |
| Glynn, Joanna | Maguire, Patrick | Jul 18 1848* | 8/317 |
| Gobal, John Adam | Roh, Joana Barbary | Jan 6 1853 | 12/117 |
| Gobel, John | Conce, Rose | Apr 17 1841* | 5/124B |
| Godard, Cesarine (wid) | Lestrade, Taegues | Apr 3 1843 | 5/257B |
| Godard, Eleanor | Mathien, Claudious ? | Jan 10 1848* | 8/276 |
| Godbold, George | Wilson, Ann E | Jul 19 1836* | 3/54 |
| Godbold, Martha Caroline | Van Dorn, Earl | Dec 23 1843* | 5/311 |
| Goddard, Joseph | Durad, Annette | Feb 5 1853 | 12/163 |
| Godefroy, Emily | Cox, Henry T | Dec 8 1849 | 11/23 |
| Godet, Leda Marie | Armstrong, John | Aug 5 1849* | 8/390B |
| Godley, Harriet E (wid) | Miller, Robert W | Aug 15 1853 | 12/382 |
| Godshild, Margareta C | Fisher, John | Nov 29 1851 | 11/190 |
| Goettinger, George | Eck, Josephine | Jun 12 1854 | 13/254 |
| Goff, Aaron | Rechie, Mary Ann ? | Mar 27 1847* | 8/223 |
| Goff, Arnal | Wheeler, Nancy | Mar 20 1849* | 8/362 |

| BRIDE OR GROOM | SPOUSE | DATE | BOOK/PAGE |
|---|---|---|---|
| Goff, Ellen | Collins,Christopher C Jr | Apr 27 1840* | 5/21 |
| Goff, George W | Helveston, Nancy | Jun 14 1844 | 8/28B |
| Goff, Harmen (Harrison) | Heard, Sarah E. A. | Nov 22 1849 | 11/18 |
| Goff, Henry | (Not Listed) | 1841* | OIB |
| Goff, James | Powell, Euseiabee | Oct 16 1850 | 11/89 |
| Goff, James | Tanner, Sally M | Feb 28 1834* | 2/451B |
| Goff, James | Hoaket, Sarah E  ? | Mar 22 1852 | 11/229 |
| Goff, John S | Jordan, Mary I | Nov 22 1842 | 5/228B |
| Goff, Justin | Harris, Susannah | Feb 15 1855 | 14/53 |
| Goff, Lewis T | Davis, Elizabeth A | Apr 11 1847 | 8/226 |
| Goff, Lorenzo D | Clark, Mary J | Jan  7 1851 | 11/110 |
| Goff, Lorrena | Wainwright, Charles C | Sep 12 1855 | 14/229 |
| Goff, Paulina | Gomes, Joseph | Feb  9 1852 | 11/213 |
| Goff, Sally Ann | Roberts, Aaron | Apr  7 1840* | 5/17 |
| Goff, Saraphiney | Lacoste, Nicholas | Feb 16 1848 | 8/283 |
| Goff, William | Raeford, Mary Jane | Apr 21 1840* | 5/19 |
| Goff, William P | Turner, Martha (Tanner) | Jun  6 1851 | 11/156 |
| Goffe, Elizabeth G | Nance, Rutherford | Jan  5 1853 | 12/116 |
| Gogare, C F | Lesseman, Amelina | Apr 27 1840 | 5/21 |
| Golbien, Michael (Gaulbien) | Hover, Mary | Nov 13 1849 | 11/16 |
| Golden, Catherine | Williams, George | Mar 24 1842 | 5/188B |
| Golden, Ellen | Bachelor, John | Jun  3 1837* | 3/87 |
| Goldridge, Ann | Judge, William | Dec 28 1850 | 11/107 |
| Goldsby, Thomas J | Winston, Mary A | Apr 24 1855 | 14/117 |
| Goldschmidt, Babet | Schuster, Joseph B | Mar  7 1854 | 13/150 |
| Goldslig, William | Teschemacker, Julia | Feb  2 1850 | 11/37 |
| Goldsmith, Esther | Goldsmith, Leopold | Nov 11 1852* | 12/60 |
| Goldsmith, Isaac | Freleksten, Matilda | Apr 18 1846 | 8/158B |
| Goldsmith, Leopold | Goldsmith, Esther | Nov 11 1852 | 12/60 |
| Goldsmith, Mayer | Siegel, Sarah | Dec 12 1849* | 11/25 |
| Goldsmith, Mingo H | Rothan, Rosa | Jun 14 1841* | 5/138B |
| Goldsmith, Philip | Lipman, Sophia (Lisman) | Apr 21 1841* | 5/125B |
| Goldsteiker, Babes | Weiss, Abraham J | May  4 1847 | 8/232 |
| Goldstein, Ricke | Hufter, Lewis | Feb  3 1854 | 13/108 |
| Goldsticker, Abram | Bloch, Jeanette | Apr 29 1850* | 11/57 |
| Goldstricker, Therese | Jacoby, Henry | Apr  1 1850* | 11/49 |
| Goldstryker, Hamryhen | Bloch, Joseph | Sep  7 1849 | 11/3 |
| Goleman, Lucinda | Bozage, Edward | Jul 13 1846 | 8/177 |
| Goleman, Mary Ann | Rester, Frederick | Dec 15 1841 | 5/161B |
| Goleman, Matilda Emaline | Lardner, Alphonse | Jun 10 1846 | 8/171 |
| Goleman, Wilson C | Stringfellow, Susan | Dec 15 1841 | 5/161B |
| Golin, Patrick | Duffy, Bridget | Jan 22 1852 | 11/206 |
| Golphe, Helene C | Prados, Francis | 1837* | OIB |
| Gomes, Joseph | Goff, Paulina | Feb  9 1852 | 11/213 |
| Gomez, Francis | Stuart, Rosalie | Aug  5 1847 | 8/250 |
| Gomez, Laurence | Burbe, Anne | Aug  3 1847* | 8/249 |
| Gomez, Lorenzo | Miedenez, Margaret | Aug  7 1849* | 8/391 |
| Gomez, Lorenzo | Burk, Jane | Jun 19 1847 | 8/242 |
| Gono, John  (Goud) | Mulligan, Catherine | Jun 24 1843 | 5/283B |
| Gonzalas, Francis | Kelley, Catherine | Aug 12 1847* | 8/251 |
| Gonzales, Joseph | Garcia, Mary Ann | Apr  1 1848 | 8/296 |
| Gonzalez, Dominique | Gibson, Caroline | Jun  9 1854 | 13/247 |
| Gonzalez, James | McClelland, Frances | Jul 20 1853 | 12/364 |
| Goode, Garland | Burns, Frances | Nov 26 1846* | 8/202 |
| Goode, Mary Ann | Stallworth, Benjamin J | Apr 23 1850* | 11/55 |
| Gooden, James | Delaney, Jane | Nov  4 1846 | 8/197 |
| Goodgame, Lucretia | Madden, John | Apr  9 1852 | 11/233 |
| Goodman, Alex W | Caunahan, Jane  ? | May 22 1838* | 3/128 |
| Goodman, Ellen | McCormick, Martin | Sep 12 1843 | 5/296B |
| Goodman, Emily R | Dunning, Edward | Apr 27 1841* | 5/127B |
| Goodman, Emma Frances | Test, Edward F | May 24 1841* | 5/132B |
| Goodman, James M | Brown, Louisa A | Oct 30 1850 | 11/93 |
| Goodman, James M | Woods, Sarah | May 10 1850 | 11/60 |
| Goodman, James W | Sossaman, Caroline | Dec 20 1837* | 3/103 |

| BRIDE OR GROOM | SPOUSE | DATE | BOOK/PAGE |
|---|---|---|---|
| Goodman, John A | Roane, Ellen | Jan 15 1847 | 8/212 |
| Goodman, Julia A M | Layden, James | Aug 7 1843 | 5/291B |
| Goodman, Martha Bennett | Turner, Samuel C | Jan 28 1847 | 8/213 |
| Goodman, Mary D | Hemphill, Felix T | Jun 30 1842* | 5/209B |
| Goodman, Peter | Crawley, Rose | Apr 29 1842 | 5/195B |
| Goodman, Sarah | Thomas, Mark | Feb 21 1844 | 5/324B |
| Goodman, Sarah | Ellis, Joseph G | Nov 13 1844 | 8/50B |
| Goodman, Thomas D | Cunningham, Caroline | Nov 14 1848 | 8/332 |
| Goodrich, Elizabeth A | Wentworth, William Jr | Dec 4 1844 | 8/56B |
| Goodrich, Margaret V | Julian, Charles A | Nov 9 1852 | 12/55 |
| Goodrich, Matthew J | Porter, Sarah | Jul 8 1836* | 3/52 |
| Goodrich, Orlando Allen | Robertson, Nancy A | Jan 30 1849 | 8/350 |
| Goodsil, Jesse | Johnstone, Mary | Oct 16 1821* | CM |
| Goodson, John A | Carter, Phebe | May 1 1828* | 2/24 |
| Goodson, Phoebe | Chadick, Asa | Aug 23 1854 | 13/318 |
| Goodwin, Amelia | McGonigal, James | Aug 7 1852 | 11/274 |
| Goodwin, Catharine | Paine, William S | Feb 14 1837* | 3/71 |
| Goodwin, Elizabeth (Mrs) | Elliott, Dempsey | Apr 20 1840* | 3/198 |
| Goodwin, James | Bliss, Catherine H | Feb 23 1832* | 2/1671 |
| Goodwin, John | Callahan, Amanda | Dec 27 1837* | 3/106 |
| Goodwin, Minerva E | Akridge, Daniel | Dec 24 1853 | 13/51 |
| Goodwin, Sarah | Chailan, James ? | Sep 29 1846 | 8/190 |
| Goodwin, William Henry | Young, Elizabeth | Dec 11 1852 | 12/86 |
| Goodwyn, Elizabeth | Dousley, John | Apr 27 1849* | 8/369 |
| Goodwynn, Harriett W | Warner, Moses C | Dec 23 1850 | 11/105 |
| Gopan, Mary Claudine ? | Holcomb, A. D | Sep 27 1845 | 8/118B |
| Gordon, Ann | Mitchell, John | May 31 1853* | 12/304 |
| Gordon, Frederick E | Conway, Sarah N | Jan 4 1846 | 8/136B |
| Gordon, John I | Delafore, Harriett | Dec 14 1835* | 3/33 |
| Gordon, Maria | Wilkinson, Isaac | May 12 1838* | 3/125 |
| Gordon, Mark | Babe, Rosalie (Beebe) | Dec 10 1846 | 8/204 |
| Gordon, Theodore | Jones, Fanny | Dec 17 1851 | 11/195 |
| Gordon, Willie B | Herriott, Mary R | Jan 13 1846* | 8/139B |
| Gorgas, Josiah | Gayle, Amelia R | Dec 28 1853 | 13/55 |
| Gorlott, Nancy | Miller, Andrew | 1825* | OIB |
| Gorman, Bridget | Lyles, Richard | Jul 21 1838* | 3/136 |
| Gorman, Jane Sarah | Violette, Louis A | Jun 11 1844 | 8/27B |
| Gorman, John | McMahon, Catherine | Jan 14 1853 | 12/132 |
| Gorman, Thomas | Manahan, Margaret | Apr 4 1847 | 8/223 |
| Gormon, Elizabeth | Connoly, Patrick | Dec 1 1849 | 11/20 |
| Gormon, Mary | McDonald, Eugene | Jan 2 1851 | 11/108 |
| Gormon, Patrick | Gately, Winney | Jun 20 1850 | 11/67 |
| Gormond, Avry | Ebeltaft, Lucinda | Feb 23 1852 | 11/221 |
| Gorsuch, Elizabeth J | Ostrander, James M | Nov 27 1848* | 8/335 |
| Goscoigne, Elmira D | Wright, Charles | Nov 16 1846 | 8/199 |
| Goss, Adam | Beckler, Louisa | Oct 21 1850 | 11/90 |
| Goss, Hensby A | Curry, Helen M | Jun 25 1850 | 11/68 |
| Goss, Margarette | Leaduff, John ? | May 2 1850 | 11/58 |
| Gosson, Mary Claudine | Holcomb, A D | Sep 27 1845 | 8/118B |
| Gosson, Mary E | Borden, William J | Aug 17 1855 | 14/212 |
| Gostenhofes, Lewis H | Band, Eleanor J (Bind) | Mar 1 1841* | 5/109B |
| Gottscholk, Jacob | Mooring, Margaret | Jun 2 1838 | 3/130 |
| Gottseelig, F.J.Wilhelm | Hammon, Louise (Harmon) | Jan 21 1850* | 11/35 |
| Goubill, Georgette | DuBroca, Sebastian | 1827* | OIB |
| Goud, John (Gono) | Mulligan, Catharine | Jun 24 1843 | 5/283B |
| Gough, Jonathan B | Gilbert, Camilla A | Sep 26 1850 | 11/87 |
| Gould, Edwin B | Morris, Martha | 1837* | OIB |
| Gould, Horatio N | Morris, Barbara J | Dec 28 1843* | 5/312B |
| Goulding, Ellen | Snider, John | Jan 30 1842* | 5/176B |
| Goulding, Thomas B | Cuthbert, Eloise | Nov 23 1848* | 8/334 |
| Goule, Aimee Barbara | Oliver, Henry | Apr 27 1844 | 8/17B |
| Gourlote, William (Gurlot) | Fisher, Josephine | Oct 18 1828 | 2/46 |
| Goush, Mary | Nelson, Henry G | Feb 7 1849 | 8/355 |
| Govnn, Eliza Mack | Ruiz, Joseph | Oct 31 1853 | 13/1 |

| BRIDE OR GROOM | SPOUSE | DATE | BOOK/PAGE |
|---|---|---|---|
| Gowen, Elizah O (McGowin) | Christain, Amelia | Sep  8 1840 | 5/45B |
| Gowin, Ellen M | Giblin, Daniel | Apr  1 1839* | 3/163 |
| Gowrner, Josephine | Buscail, Francis | Aug 13 1840 | 4/2401B |
| Grabold, Martha Caroline | Vern Dorn, Earl | Dec 23 1843 | 7/67B |
| Grady, Ann | Perry, Edward C | Aug 17 1850 | 11/80 |
| Grady, Catharine | Casal, Joseph | Jul 24 1849* | 8/382 |
| Graff, Margaret | Correll, John J | Oct 13 1847 | 8/259 |
| Graff, Mary | Hines, Jacob | Jul 10 1850 | 11/71 |
| Graft, John | Meyers, Augustine | Feb 10 1845 | 8/72B |
| Graham, Amelia | Hutchison, James H | May 15 1838* | 3/126 |
| Graham, Charles | Emmett, Amelia J | Mar 18 1837* | 3/75 |
| Graham, Charles W | Vose, Scottana R | Mar  8 1828* | 2/16 |
| Graham, Ellen Jane | McDonald, Alexander | Mar 20 1838* | 3/117 |
| Graham, Francis E | Samini, Joseph | Jan 25 1854 | 13/97 |
| Graham, James R | Mulholland, Ann | Sep 17 1855 | 14/232 |
| Graham, Louisa | Riley, Richard | Jan  7 1852 | 11/201 |
| Graham, Melissa | Saunders, Henry | Dec 31 1843* | 5/313B |
| Graham, Moses | Johnson, Martha | Apr 19 1855 | 14/111 |
| Graham, Thomas | Crawford, Emiline | Aug  8 1841* | 5/146B |
| Graham, Thomas | Ganson, Angeline(Glenson) | Sep 18 1841 | 5/152B |
| Graham, Thomas | Dolan, Elizabeth | May 29 1854 | 13/237 |
| Graham, Walter  (widr) | Anderson, Martha | May  5 1853 | 12/271 |
| Graham, William | Cullum, Catherine | Mar 24 1830 | 2/119 |
| Graham, William | Springer, Francis E | Sep 14 1853 | 12/405 |
| Grandpre, Alexander | Kyle, Catherine A | Jun 11 1851* | 11/157 |
| Granger, Luther B | Hall, Amanda | Nov  4 1840* | 5/59B |
| Grant, Eliza | Laurence John | 1838* | OIB |
| Grant, Helen M | Deering, Alexander W | Nov 29 1845 | 8/127B |
| Grant, Isabella | Willis, Julius | Apr  2 1850 | 11/49 |
| Grant, John | Casey, Ellen | Jan 28 1841* | 5/95B |
| Grant, John | Monk, Martha | Feb 22 1842 | 5/181B |
| Grant, Rachael R | Borum, James C | Feb 12 1846 | 8/145B |
| Grantham, Caroline | Mahany, Michael | May 22 1837* | 3/83 |
| Gras, Margaret | Alsferssen, Jacob | May 13 1845 | 8/100B |
| Grasham, Penine | Kedwell, Robert C | Jul  5 1824 | 1/35 |
| Grassman, John | Marchell, Barbara | May  7 1855 | 14/132 |
| Gratrex, Elizabeth | Young, Charles T | May 17 1845 | 8/95B |
| Gratrix, Martha | Williams, Lewis | Feb  3 1844* | 5/320B |
| Graves, Benjamin H | Spencer, Ann | Dec 24 1830 | 2/145 |
| Graves, Charity | Taylor, William | Jun 30 1842* | 5/209B |
| Graves, Eliza | Adkins, George B | Jan 17 1833* | 2/1211 |
| Graves, Martha E | Etheridge, Ashbee W | Mar 24 1835* | 3/12 |
| Graves, Rebecca | Wilson, James D | 1827* | OIB |
| Graves, Samuel D | Rawls, Minerva | May 24 1843 | 5/275B |
| Gray, Caroline | Marx, Lyman | Aug 21 1855 | 14/215 |
| Gray, Catherine | Fisher, Lewis | Aug 18 1842 | 5/216B |
| Gray, Charles E | Murray, Cecelia | Jul 23 1850 | 11/75 |
| Gray, Rosaline | Rodriguez, J M | Jul  6 1842 | 5/210B |
| Gray, Virginia | Alexander, James P | May 27 1837* | 3/84 |
| Gredoh, Rosalie (Grelot) | Demouy, Louis | Jun  6 1842 | 5/204B |
| Greely, Bridget | Miley, John | May 22 1846 | 8/169B |
| Green, Aaron | Read, Unity Richards | Dec 15 1852 | 12/95 |
| Green, Agnes C | Weed, Edward H | Sep  4 1855 | 14/225 |
| Green, Andrew | Girard, Laura L | Jan 16 1855 | 14/17 |
| Green, Anna M | Barvoe, Theodore | Jul 22 1854 | 13/292 |
| Green, Elizabeth | Steele, Samuel A | Jun 16 1842 | 5/207B |
| Green, Ellen | Roberts, George | Jan 22 1851 | 11/115 |
| Green, Frances Ann (Greer) | Richardson, Robert J | Mar 31 1846 | 7/462 |
| Green, John | Nixon, Anna | Jul  3 1833* | 2/871 |
| Green, John A | Simpson, Isabella | Jan 26 1843 | 5/245B |
| Green, Margaret | Townsend, George | Jun 15 1843 | 5/282B |
| Green, Mary A | Glover, Henry W | Aug 26 1854 | 13/321 |
| Green, Thomas | Cussan, Ellen | Jan 28 1842 | 6/64B |
| Green, William | Mitchell, Elmira | Nov 24 1845 | 8/126B |

| BRIDE OR GROOM | SPOUSE | DATE | BOOK/PAGE |
|---|---|---|---|
| Greene, Catharine | Fisher, William F | 1853* | OIB |
| Greene, Elizabeth | Miller, John | May 4 1843 | 5/268B |
| Greene, William, | Fisk, Ann E | May 13 1849* | 8/375 |
| Greening, Mary | Solle, William R | Jul 1 1852 | 11/268 |
| Greer, Frances Ann (Green) | Richardson, Robert J | Mar 21 1846 | 8/154B |
| Greer, Jane | Patterson, Nicholas | Sep 19 1832* | 2/1341 |
| Greer, John T | Farmer, Mary E | Sep 20 1854 | 13/340 |
| Greger, Robert Fulton | Morgan, Elizabeth | Oct 8 1851 | 11/182 |
| Gregory, George W | Moreno, Antoinette | May 15 1849* | 8/375 |
| Gregory, Louisa | Chandler, Charles G | Mar 12 1855 | 14/80 |
| Gregory, Mary | Laurendine, Pierre | Mar 17 1836* | 3/43 |
| Greig, Robert | Howard, Isabella F | Oct 22 1855 | 14/258 |
| Grelot, Cecile | Bozage, John B | Aug 20 1851 | 11/173 |
| Grelot, Maximillian | Demouy, Polite | Jun 17 1851 | 11/158 |
| Grelot, Sefroy | Fowel, Ardel | Mar 24 1853* | 12/203 |
| Grelote, Isabel | Gerard, Frances | 1824* | OIB |
| Grelote, Jean Batiste | Lodenere, Virgine | 1836* | OIB |
| Grelott, Louise | Bosarge, Calvin | Dec 21 1854 | 13/417 |
| Gremer, Isaac ? | Stein, Henrietta | Jun 12 1850 | 11/66 |
| Greoi, Caroline ? | Riebe, Frederick ? | May 11 1852 | 11/249 |
| Gretopull, Thomas | Case, Elizabeth | Mar 29 1851 | 11/132 |
| Gretzner, Julius | Kern, Amelia | May 3 1855 | 14/128 |
| Greve, Fredrick | Sagehorn, Anna | May 3 1854 | 13/213 |
| Greyer, Frances N | Humphrey, James | Mar 24 1852* | 11/230 |
| Grica, Jane | Walton, Ginyo ? | Jun 22 1838* | 3/132 |
| Grienbert, Virginia | Falker, Frank M | Feb 21 1852 | 11/219 |
| Griffin, Adalide G | Edwards, Joseph R | Oct 7 1850 | 11/88 |
| Griffin, Catherine | McGlow, Patrick | Jan 27 1852 | 11/209 |
| Griffin, Edmund | Sidgreaves, Cordelia | Nov 20 1846 | 8/200 |
| Griffin, Eliza (wid) | Kernan, Edward (widr) | Nov 24 1853 | 13/27 |
| Griffin, James L | Gays, Frances E (Hays) | May 8 1839* | 3/170 |
| Griffin, Jane | McCarty, John | Sep 23 1840* | 5/47B |
| Griffin, John | Pierce, Tempe | Nov 14 1849 | 11/16 |
| Griffin, Margaret | Walton, Richard | Feb 24 1845 | 8/75 |
| Griffin, Mary | Cowhey, David | Nov 7 1839* | 3/190 |
| Griffin, Mary | Leonard, Patrick | May 30 1841* | 5/133B |
| Griffin, Mary | Barrett, Robert | May 4 1849* | 8/372 |
| Griffin, Nancy J | Holland, Jacob F | Dec 20 1851 | 11/196 |
| Griffin, Riley | Woolard, Milly | 1826* | OIB |
| Griffin, Samuel B | Doughries, Anna J | Nov 12 1835* | 3/146 |
| Griffin, Sarah Ann | Williams, Daniel W | Nov 18 1850 | 11/98 |
| Griffin, Susanna | Murray, Edwin | Feb 26 1845 | 8/76B |
| Griffin, William | Brown, Eliza | Nov 13 1852 | 12/62 |
| Griffing, Mary E | Payne, Albert A | Dec 3 1849 | 11/21 |
| Grigsly, Margaret Ann | Seel, William | Jul 8 1850 | 11/71 |
| Grimes, Phoebe | Busby, William | Jun 2 1851 | 11/153 |
| Grimes, Rebecca | Andrews, John M | Oct 30 1852 | 12/41 |
| Grimlar, Samuel H ? | Stevens, Mary O | May 14 1852 | 11/249 |
| Grimsley, William D | Alexander, Lucretia | Feb 26 1845 | 8/76B |
| Grinnell, Bridget | Callan, James | May 2 1835* | 3/23 |
| Grinnell, Michael (McGrinel) | Morgan, Bridget | Apr 22 1828 | 2/21 |
| Gripon, Sarah M (Grissom) | Hardy, Isham B | Aug 10 1846 | 8/184 |
| Grissom, Frances H | Newman, John J | Mar 12 1852 | 11/225 |
| Grlotzengel, Christian | Kruse, Anna | Sep 1 1855 | 14/223 |
| Groom, James W | Crawford, Mary E | Jun 21 1855 | 14/181 |
| Groom, Mary E | Lude, Lewis S | Sep 7 1853 | 12/402 |
| Groseman, Anna | Vonars, John | May 29 1852 | 11/256 |
| Grove, John | Julian, Josephine C | Nov 29 1842* | 5/230B |
| Grove, Sylvester C | Cannon, Caroline | Dec 28 1839* | 5/6 |
| Grug, Robert | Gartman, Mary | May 23 1838* | 3/128 |
| Gseller, Julius (Geller) | Kiende, Marie | Apr 23 1853 | 12/252 |
| Gueruard, Amelia T (Gerard) | McVoy, Martin | May 7 1835* | 3/13 |
| Guerin, Emil | Cottez, Caroline | Apr 2 1853 | 12/219 |
| Gues, Maria A | Boudinet, Sebastian | May 31 1852 | 11/258 |

| BRIDE OR GROOM | SPOUSE | DATE | BOOK/PAGE |
|---|---|---|---|
| Guesnard, Athalie | Michaeloffesky, John G | Jan 23 1840* | 5/9 |
| Guesnard, Emma | Ramel, Felix | Jul 9 1852* | 11/268 |
| Guesnard, Heroine | Jacquelin, Henri E | Mar 26 1850 | 11/47 |
| Guesnard, Theodore Jr | Hurtell, Lea M | Feb 16 1841* | 5/105B |
| Guild, Harvey | Lee, Evelina B | Aug 18 1851 | 11/173 |
| Guild, Lafayette | Fitz, Pattie A | Dec 14 1852 | 12/92 |
| Gull, Biddy | Corlet, John | May 21 1838* | 3/127 |
| Gully, William | Rines, Elizabeth | Aug 27 1839* | 3/185 |
| Gunn, Julia | Hanson, Peter | Jan 27 1855 | 14/25 |
| Gunn, Patrick | Farley, Margaret | Nov 21 1854 | 13/388 |
| Gunnison, Clementine F | Taylor, John M | Dec 4 1850 | 11/101 |
| Gunnison, Henry | Juzan, Louisa (Ingram) | May 14 1825 | 1/77 |
| Gunnison, Louisa | Ripley, Fitz Henry | Aug 15 1849* | 8/398 |
| Gunnon, Elizabeth (Gannon) | James, Joseph (Irwin) | Apr 30 1841 | 5/127B |
| Gurley, Leonard | Thompson, Catherine | Jan 1 1842* | 5/166B |
| Gurlie, Artemisia | Nicholas, Ebenezer A | Aug 3 1854 | 13/300 |
| Gurlot, Melissa | Bosage, Alfred | Dec 14 1847 | 8/270 |
| Gurlote, Joseph | Ladnear, Caroline | Feb 17 1824 | 1/21 |
| Gurlott, Sifroy | Ladneres, Baptiste ? | Aug 23 1830* | 2/134 |
| Gurlott, Victor | Westbrook, Adaline | Sep 21 1855 | 14/236 |
| Gurlotte, Catharine | Fisher, William | Mar 16 1825 | 1/68 |
| Gurlotte, Irene | Dumouy, Louis | Feb 4 1817* | CM |
| Gusset, Peter | Habinson, Eve | May 5 1853 | 12/272 |
| Gusterer, Catherine | Roe, Jacob | Dec 7 1849 | 11/22 |
| Gustus, Henry | Kavannah, Julia | Jan 20 1844 | 7/97B |
| Guton, Jean Batiste | Todenere, Virgine | Nov 23 1836* | 3/63 |
| Gutus, Henry ? | Rossanah, Julia | Jan 21 1844 | 5/316B |
| Gwin, Thomas | Callem, Ellen | Jan 28 1842 | 5/175 |
| Gyrell, William (Tyrell) | Devin, Margaret | Jul 21 1838* | 3/136 |

## H

| | | | |
|---|---|---|---|
| Haas, Catharine | Hemley, John | Dec 16 1847* | 8/271 |
| Haas, George | Haei, Catherine ? | Nov 24 1838* | 3/148 |
| Haberle, Jacob | Gladsman, Josephine | May 25 1852 | 11/255 |
| Habinson, Eve | Gusset, Peter | May 5 1853 | 12/272 |
| Hackmier, Wilhelmina | Binzer, William E | May 28 1847 | 8/239 |
| Hadaway, Ann | Wickham, James | Apr 5 1848 | 8/297 |
| Hade, Henry A (Slade) | Martin, Eliza A | Mar 27 1832* | 2/1601 |
| Hadger, Maria ? | Rewer, Donnie ? | Oct 31 1842* | 5/226B |
| Haei, Catherine ? | Haas, George | Nov 24 1838* | 3/148 |
| Haff, John (Happ) | O'Connor, Bridget | May 16 1846 | 8/166B |
| Haffler, Caroline | Wittman, Jacob | Oct 29 1855 | 14/267 |
| Hag, Sarah | Wendham, Joseph W | Apr 10 1839* | 3/166 |
| Hagan, Anne (Fagan) | Arberry, George | Nov 4 1841* | 5/155B |
| Hagan, James | Oliver, Bettie D | Mar 8 1854 | 13/152 |
| Hagan, Rosa | Daley, Michael | Dec 19 1839* | 5/4 |
| Hagan, Rosannah | Brown, Edward | May 30 1836* | 3/48 |
| Hagan, Sarah A | Mullen, William | May 13 1836* | 3/47 |
| Hagerty, Mary | Preans, Julian ? | Apr 10 1848 | 8/297 |
| Hagerty, Mary | Nevin, William | Jul 1 1848* | 8/311 |
| Haggerty, Patrick | Burke, Anne | Sep 10 1842* | 5/219B |
| Hagnes, Claresa | Byrne, Peter C | Feb 24 1841* | 5/109 |
| Hags, Daniel | Pearce, Elizabeth | Apr 18 1836* | 3/44 |
| Hahill, Harriet W | Jean, Peter | Nov 13 1854 | 13/377 |
| Haibeha, Korlina | Hosfelt, John | Mar 6 1854 | 13/148 |
| Haifleigh, William F | Churpantien, Azilie | Jul 12 1843* | 5/287B |
| Haig, John | McKeen, Virginia H | Sep 11 1851 | 11/178 |

| BRIDE OR GROOM | SPOUSE | DATE | BOOK/PAGE |
|---|---|---|---|
| Haigal, Jacob | Kral, Catharine | Feb 25 1848 | 8/286 |
| Hails, Harriet E | Gaines, James J | Aug 22 1849* | 8/399 |
| Hails, Mary A | Marshall, William T | Jun 12 1841* | 5/137 |
| Hain, Barbara | Dehn, Andres | Dec 26 1848* | 8/341 |
| Haines, Martha | Duest, John (Quist?) | Aug 2 1845* | 8/114B |
| Haines, William W | Harben, Frances M | Jan 8 1840* | 5/7 |
| Hainsworth, Martha | Tachoir, Francois | Jul 15 1846* | 8/179 |
| Hair, Isadore | Rice, Elizabeth J | Jun 22 1847 | 8/243 |
| Haitz, Mary A | Marshall, Wm. T | Jun 12 1841 | 4/801B |
| Halcum, John (Holcomb) | Collins, Elizabeth | Jan 15 1829 | 2/62 |
| Haley, Catharine | McSwinney, Miles | Jan 14 1853 | 12/133 |
| Haley, Daniel | Danalen, Jane | Jun 19 1855 | 14/178 |
| Haley, Maria E | Murphy, John | Sep 20 1852 | 12/9 |
| Hall, Amanda | Granger, Luther B | Nov 4 1840* | 5/59B |
| Hall, Catharine L | Galindo, Richard M | Jan 6 1849* | 8/346 |
| Hall, Daniel E | Kennedy, Delphine E | Jan 13 1840* | 5/7 |
| Hall, Daniel E | Brien, Emily | May 23 1851 | 11/151 |
| Hall, Daniel E, Jr | Trotter, Ann | Feb 5 1845 | 8/71B |
| Hall, Delphine G | Leadbetter, Daniel | May 21 1855 | 14/144 |
| Hall, Edward L | Daugherty, Sarah | Nov 4 1848* | 8/331 |
| Hall, Elizabeth | Jewitt, John F | Apr 19 1843 | 5/261 |
| Hall, Ephraim L | Starks, Eliza | Feb 8 1842 | 5/178B |
| Hall, Henry | Smoot, Anna Mary | Apr 19 1853 | 12/244 |
| Hall, Howard | Stramler, Frances A | Jan 27 1852 | 11/210 |
| Hall, John S | Townsend, Margaret | Jul 23 1855 | 14/197 |
| Hall, Leonora | McKenney, Patrick | May 4 1842 | 5/198B |
| Hall, Lucretia V | Davis, John W | Mar 22 1853 | 12/198 |
| Hall, Maria | Ludlow, William W | Jun 25 1851 | 11/160 |
| Hall, Mary | Rodgers, William V | May 31 1852 | 11/257 |
| Hall, Mary | Micklin, James Jr | Oct 3 1837 | 3/92 |
| Hall, Mary A | Flinn, Morris | May 12 1853 | 12/279 |
| Hall, Mary Jane | Wallace, Thomas S | Jul 17 1842* | 5/211B |
| Hall, Missouri | Tibble, John L | May 28 1842 | 5/204B |
| Hall, Namon | Tribble, Mary | Aug 7 1844 | 8/38B |
| Hall, Nathan | Fennell, Elizabeth | Mar 11 1854 | 13/155 |
| Hall, Patience | Bartlett, James R | Nov 8 1824 | 1/45 |
| Hall, Patience | Quinn, William | 1826* | 01B |
| Hall, Sarah | King, James | Nov 13 1832* | 2/1311 |
| Hall, Sarah Ann | Thierriat, Ambrose | Apr 8 1837* | 3/80 |
| Hall, William | Mervin, Laura | Sep 14 1820* | CM |
| Hall, William A | Larkins, Eliza F | Jun 22 1852* | 11/265 |
| Hall, William M | Pain, Nancy | Dec 12 1844 | 8/58B |
| Halland, Sarah | Finnegan, James | Sep 16 1854 | 13/337 |
| Hallett, William H | Murrell, Virginia A | Dec 18 1855 | 14/307 |
| Hallett, William R | Judson, Catherine S | Nov 11 1824 | 1/46 |
| Hallick, Anna | Lassinger, Charles | Jun 8 1853 | 12/311 |
| Hallohan, Catharine | McCluskey, Edward T | May 22 1852 | 11/254 |
| Hallond, James (Fallond) | Finnigan, Bridget | Oct 18 1847* | 8/268 |
| Halpan, Mathew | Burke, Catherine | Dec 3 1852 | 12/81 |
| Hamberry, Julia (Heneberry) | Hanlin, Martin | May 17 1852 | 11/250 |
| Hambleton, Jemimah | Stringfellow, Harmon | Sep 8 1834* | 2/171 |
| Hamblett, Martha | Knaggs, Thomas | Nov 5 1840* | 5/61B |
| Hamblin, Charlotte ? | Ewing, Andrew W | May 7 1841* | 5/128B |
| Hamby, Susannah | Shepard, Thomas | Feb 6 1830* | 2/110 |
| Hamet, Francis (wid) | Philips, Willis H | Dec 24 1853 | 13/50 |
| Hamilton, Andrew | Cilburn, Harriett ? | Feb 2 1832* | 2/1711 |
| Hamilton, Ann | Dickson, Edward | Nov 21 1851 | 11/188 |
| Hamilton, Benjamin | Baker, Irene | Mar 23 1853 | 12/201 |
| Hamilton, Eliza | Lyons, John | Apr 20 1844 | 8/16B |
| Hamilton, Elizabeth | Liebert, Frederick C | Sep 28 1854 | 13/344 |
| Hamilton, Fredrick | Wells, Emeline | May 21 1852 | 11/253 |
| Hamilton, George M | Taylor, Cynthia Ann | Jul 4 1855 | 14/187 |
| Hamilton, Harris | Ely, Margaret | Jul 23 1836* | 3/55 |
| Hamilton, Huldah | Elich, John ? | Jul 24 1847* | 8/247 |

| Hamilton, James L | Case, Kate C | Sep 5 1855 | 14/226 |
| Hamilton, Peter | Beers, Anna M W (Burns) | Dec 26 1840* | 5/81B |
| Hamilton, Sarah Jane | Laguire, Francis | Apr 14 1845 | 8/86B |
| Hamilton, Thomas A | Hogan, Lucy B | Nov 24 1847 | 8/268 |
| Hammett, Jackson H | Phillips, Francis | Jun 8 1850 | 11/65 |
| Hammon, Louise (Harmon) | Gottseelig, F.J. Wilhelm | Jan 21 1850* | 11/35 |
| Hammond, Alexander T | Ross, Drucilla | Nov 20 1851 | 11/188 |
| Hammond, Charles | Darling, Eliza | 1838* | 0IB |
| Hammond, John | Gleason, Margaret M | Jun 18 1840* | 5/28B |
| Hammond, Lewis | Duboise, Rebecca | Aug 17 1844 | 8/39B |
| Hammond, Lewis C | Pool, Sarah E | Dec 8 1848* | 8/338 |
| Hammond, Mary | New, Gray B | Feb 19 1842 | 5/181B |
| Hammond, Martha N | Gibson, Silas | Jun 29 1853 | 12/336 |
| Hammond, William P | Stickney, Caroline | Jul 9 1842* | 5/211B |
| Hampshire, Richard | Ware, Mary | Jun 15 1854 | 13/259 |
| Hancock, Martha | Orr, Joseph | Apr 12 1851 | 11/138 |
| Hanberry, Michael | Hanlan, Mary | Apr 19 1854 | 13/194 |
| Hanbery, Mary | Mullen, Peter | Jul 28 1853 | 12/372 |
| Hand, Anthony | McCarle, Ann | Apr 10 1855 | 14/104 |
| Hand, Patrick | Roach, Mary | Apr 11 1853 | 12/233 |
| Hand, Thomas | O'Brien, Ann | Jul 3 1849* | 8/396B |
| Haneman, William | Bellougnet, Louise | May 30 1843 | 5/276B |
| Hanes, Adelheid | Richter, Tobias | Jan 29 1850 | 11/36 |
| Haney, Alice | Bridge, Henry (wid) | Jan 29 1853 | 12/156 |
| Haney, Ellen | Reese, Robert | Apr 8 1853 | 12/224 |
| Haney, Patrick (Henry) | Etts, Ann | May 28 1830* | 2/125 |
| Hanford, Charles | Wilson, Jane | May 16 1840* | 5/22 |
| Hanley, Thomas | Hayes, Mary | Apr 18 1844 | 8/15B |
| Hanlan, Mary | Hanberry, Michael | Apr 19 1854 | 13/194 |
| Hanlin, Martin | Hamberry, Julia | May 17 1852 | 11/250 |
| Hanlon, Mary | Fanning, John | Jun 11 1853* | 12/316 |
| Hanna, James J | Schilt, Ellen (Mrs) | Sep 22 1845 | 8/118B |
| Hannan, Catherine | Mulvany, Christopher | Jun 13 1853 | 12/317 |
| Hannevig, John | Burke, Louise | Mar 30 1854 | 13/168 |
| Hannis, Julia | Phillips, Charles | Feb 20 1855 | 14/65 |
| Hannogan, Mary | Fanning, Thomas | May 22 1852 | 11/254 |
| Hannon, Michael | Agin, Rosa (Ayin) | Dec 24 1838* | 3/A153 |
| Hannon, Michael | Convin, Elizabeth | May 14 1851 | 11/149 |
| Hanol, Elizabeth | Miles, Benjamin | Mar 30 1850 | 11/48 |
| Hansbery, Joseph | Tracy, Mary A | Nov 22 1853 | 13/23 |
| Hanschelt, Peter | Hoffman, Margrette | Sep 9 1848* | 8/323 |
| Hanscom, Frank D | Thompson, Martha E | Apr 12 1854* | 13/179 |
| Hansey, Mary | Silva, Daniel M | Jul 27 1850 | 11/77 |
| Hanson, Hans Jacob | Peterson, Johanna | Dec 6 1854 | 13/404 |
| Hanson, Peter | Gunn, Julia | Jan 27 1855 | 14/25 |
| Harben, Frances M | Haines, William W | Jan 8 1840* | 5/7 |
| Harben, Margarette C | Holland, Jacob | Sep 2 1848 | 8/323 |
| Harbin, Sarah Ann | Richey, James | Jan 23 1844 | 5/317B |
| Hardaway, William A | DelBarco, Mary J | Apr 7 1840* | 5/17 |
| Hardie, Charles L | LaBarthe, Louisa D | Dec 12 1849 | 11/25 |
| Hardy, Henry | Crosby, Ann (Mrs) | Dec 13 1845 | 8/130B |
| Hardy, Isham B | Gripon, Sarah M (Grisson) | Aug 10 1846 | 8/184 |
| Hardy, William H | McConnell, Elizabeth | Jul 23 1853 | 12/365 |
| Hare, William | Michon, Rebecca | Apr 4 1855 | 14/98 |
| Haregal, Henrietta (Mrs) | Kull, William | Oct 18 1855* | 14/254 |
| Harenarr, Michael (Hannon) | Ayin, Rosa (Agin) | Dec 24 1838* | 3/A153 |
| Harford, Ellen | Leonard, Christopher J | Nov 22 1853 | 13/22 |
| Hargar, John B | Anderson, Clara L | Jul 9 1838* | 3/53 |
| Hargrove, Lucy | Loftin, Albert G | Jun 23 1847* | 8/243 |
| Harigan, Bridget | Maloney, John | Apr 28 1855 | 14/124 |
| Harkey, David M | Jones, Emily L | Mar 7 1855 | 14/77 |
| Harkins, Emily | Simmons, Henry | Dec 17 1842* | 5/235B |
| Harkins, James | Williams, Elizabeth | Dec 14 1840* | 5/75 |
| Harman, McGilbia D | Fisher, Catherine | Apr 22 1852 | 11/241 |

| BRIDE OR GROOM | SPOUSE | DATE | BOOK/PAGE |
|---|---|---|---|
| Harmeyer, Mary Catherine | Kruse, John H | Sep 8 1846 | 8/187 |
| Harmon, Anthony | Rice, Mary | Nov 3 1846 | 8/197 |
| Harmon, Louise | Gottseelig, F.J.W. | Jan 21 1850 | 11/35 |
| Harmon, Rachael (Haverman) | Brasheun, Alexander | Jan 14 1846 | 8/140B |
| Harmon, Sarah J | Kemble, Aaron A | Dec 28 1836* | 3/67 |
| Harmsmire, Hannah ? | Miller, Andrew | Jan 11 1849 | 8/347 |
| Harold, Edward | Fitzgerald, Ellen | May 27 1837* | 3/84 |
| Harper, Samuel | Wortherington, Mariah | Jul 5 1851 | 11/162 |
| Harrell, Ann | Murray, James | Dec 25 1847 | 8/273 |
| Harrell, Arnett W | Ross, Hannah L | Nov 3 1828* | 2/50 |
| Harrell, Edy | Howard, Daniel | Oct 28 1829 | 2/99 |
| Harrell, Jacob | Howard, Eunice | 1825* | OIB |
| Harrell, Lucy Ann | Mizell, Josiah | Sep 12 1846 | 8/189 |
| Harrelson, Elizabeth M | Montgomery, James | Jan 21 1847 | 8/213 |
| Harrelson, Martha | Leech, Charles | Dec 30 1848* | 8/342 |
| Harri, John (Rami) | Couche, Mary Louise | Jul 15 1841 | 5/142B |
| Harrilson, Mary Jane | Simpson, John C | Mar 2 1846 | 7/650 |
| Harrington, Ann | Healy, John (widr) | May 12 1853 | 12/280 |
| Harrington, Cornelius | Sullivan, Julia | Nov 11 1851 | 11/187 |
| Harrington, Cornelius J | Sullivan, Mary | Sep 28 1854 | 13/345 |
| Harrington, Elizabeth | McGinnis, John | Mar 29 1842 | 5/189B |
| Harrington, Hannah | Clay, William H | Jun 20 1854 | 13/261 |
| Harrington, Mary E | Smith, Robert | Apr 19 1855 | 14/109 |
| Harris, Benjamin F | Russell, Jeannett | Jul 11 1854 | 13/279 |
| Harris, Catherine | Dennis, Duderick | Aug 10 1842 | 6/184B |
| Harris, Charles E | Sager, E A (Mrs) | Oct 31 1839* | 3/189 |
| Harris, Charles, M | Leath, Sarah | Jun 30 1840* | 5/30B |
| Harris, Cyrus L | Sibley, Caroline F | Mar 9 1853 | 12/188 |
| Harris, Dan | James, Ann | Mar 29 1844 | 8/8B |
| Harris, Edwin B | Sheppard, Sarah E | Jul 24 1848 | 8/318 |
| Harris, Elizabeth | Burney, James D | May 18 1852 | 11/251 |
| Harris, Elizabeth | Bryan, Martin H | Dec 15 1851 | 11/194 |
| Harris, Frederick | Zertehel, Barbara ? | Jul 7 1851 | 11/163 |
| Harris, George W | Barney, Susan M | Nov 6 1854 | 13/368 |
| Harris, James W | Carlysle, Mary | May 27 1848 | 8/306 |
| Harris, John | Wileford, Mary A | 1827* | OIB |
| Harris, John M | Watts, Sarah J | Dec 13 1853 | 13/38 |
| Harris, Joseph | Miles, Helen | Apr 5 1850 | 11/51 |
| Harris, Julia Ann | Byrd, James | Aug 6 1845 | 8/115B |
| Harris, Julia M | Crane, Albert | Nov 5 1853 | 13/35 |
| Harris, Louisa | Gleason, James S | Apr 17 1839* | 3/167 |
| Harris, Lud W | Bates, Mary Ann | 1827* | OIB |
| Harris, Mary | Moore, Michael | Feb 10 1847 | 8/215 |
| Harris, Mary | Thomas, Henry | Jan 6 1843* | 5/241B |
| Harris, Richmond B (widr) | Smith, Margaret | Nov 22 1853 | 13/24 |
| Harris, Sarah | Smith, Nicolas | May 7 1845 | 8/93 |
| Harris, Susannah | Goff, Justin | Feb 15 1855 | 14/53 |
| Harris, William | Saxon, Elizabeth | Sep 4 1850 | 11/83 |
| Harrison, Adolph | Stewart, Columbus | Jun 28 1842 | 5/208B |
| Harrison, Catherine | Simson, Sampson J | Mar 27 1839* | 3/162 |
| Harrison, Cecelia | Bowen, Daniel E | Feb 4 1854 | 13/109 |
| Harrison, Edward | Roberts, Missouri | Mar 3 1845 | 8/77B |
| Harrison, Edward | O'Heirn, Mary | Feb 18 1854 | 13/126 |
| Harrison, J W | Michael, Barbary | Mar 2 1852* | 11/223 |
| Harrison, Jane V | Bibb, Joseph D | Apr 2 1845 | 8/83B |
| Harrison, Kirkland | Smith, Margaret | Apr 5 1845 | 8/84B |
| Harrison, Mary Jane | Simpson, John C | Mar 2 1846 | 8/149B |
| Harrison, Rose Earle | Dawson, John C | Apr 29 1846 | 8/161B |
| Harrison, Sarah | Smith, Nicholas | May 7 1845 | 7/675B |
| Harrison, William | Baglin, Rosales | Apr 14 1847 | 8/227 |
| Harriss, Richmond B | Carlin, Mary | Nov 1 1850 | 11/94 |
| Harriss, Sarah E | Geher, Joseph W | Dec 14 1855 | 14/304 |
| Harrub, Thomas | Ashburn, Mary | Feb 23 1854 | 13/135 |
| Hart, Bridget Ann | Billings, Samuel W | Jun 9 1840* | 5/27B |

| BRIDE OR GROOM | SPOUSE | DATE | BOOK/PAGE |
|---|---|---|---|
| Hart, Charlotte | Fisher, Jacob (Firhn) | Apr 20 1843 | 5/262B |
| Hart, Charlotte | Firhn, Jacob | Apr 20 1843 | 5/262B |
| Hart, Elizabeth | Bradford, King | Aug 4 1849* | 8/390 |
| Hart, Ellen | Tully, John | Mar 7 1846 | 8/150B |
| Hart, Hannah | Allen, James W | Dec 31 1846 | 8/206 |
| Hart, Isabella | King, Richard J | Jan 15 1848* | 8/278 |
| Hart, Margaret | Ross, William | Dec 3 1844 | 8/55B |
| Hart, Rosalie | Priour, Jean Marie | Oct 24 1844 | 8/45B |
| Hart, Sopha | Millick, Antoine | Apr 16 1849* | 8/368 |
| Hart, Thomas | Lannigan, Margaret | May 3 1841* | 5/128B |
| Hart, William | Egan, Mary | Nov 22 1855 | 14/285 |
| Hartel, Frederic | Frank, Louisa | May 9 1855 | 14/135 |
| Hartley, Alexander | Rawls, Mary | Mar 30 1843* | 5/257B |
| Hartley, Daniel | Simms, Sally | Nov 1 1824 | 1/43 |
| Hartley, Elizabeth | Lacoste, Augustine | Jul 19 1818* | CM |
| Hartley, Frederick | Broughton, Peggy | Dec 24 1814* | CM |
| Hartley, Irene | Alvarez, William Henry | Oct 12 1847 | 8/258 |
| Hartley, Mary | Hicklin, William C | May 21 1842 | 5/203B |
| Hartley, Michael | Tompkins, Caroline | May 17 1840* | 5/28B |
| Hartley, Sarah (wid) | Bonner, William | Aug 20 1853 | 12/388 |
| Hartley, Sarah | Alvarez, Henry | Nov 9 1852 | 12/54 |
| Hartley, Susan M | Baldwyn, Henry C | Jul 2 1844 | 8/31B |
| Hartman, Caroline | McKnight, William | Aug 29 1842* | 5/217B |
| Hartmann, William | Sanders, Reiena | Dec 21 1855 | 14/309 |
| Hartmeyer, Anna M | Marsanary, Joseph (widr) | Sep 1 1853 | 12/401 |
| Hartwell, John | Erily, Lucy B (Earty) | Jan 18 1840* | 5/8 |
| Harty, Frances | Frisk, Charles | Nov 3 1851 | 11/185 |
| Harvey, Alfred | George, Mikile | Feb 24 1842 | 5/183B |
| Harvey, Joseph H | Richardson, Margaret | May 4 1842 | 5/198B |
| Harvey, Kyle | Gamble, Philip | Dec 24 1844 | 8/62B |
| Harwell, Barte S | Cogburn, Martha E | May 21 1846 | 8/168B |
| Harwell, Jesse G | Noel, Cecile | Feb 18 1854 | 13/125 |
| Harwell, Martha J | Verneuille, Joseph | Jan 17 1854 | 13/85 |
| Harwell, Warren J | Palmer, Eliza A | Mar 12 1850 | 11/45 |
| Harwell, Wilbur F | Goff, Almanza | Jan 17 1854 | 13/84 |
| Haskin, Isabella | Rogers, John | Jun 24 1841* | 5/140B |
| Hastie, J. Hamilton | Kennedy, Secluza | Jun 10 1839* | 3/178 |
| Hatcher, John | Killcrease, Patsey | Oct 1 1813* | WB1/19 |
| Hatchett, Charlotte C | Pierson, Abram B | May 12 1843 | 5/270B |
| Hatfield, Eliza Ann | Keeling, William H | Jun 14 1845 | 8/103B |
| Hattenstein, Simon | Davis, Sarah Ann | Jan 1 1853 | 12/109 |
| Hau, Ferdinand | Seyfreiden, Catherine | May 14 1855 | 14/140 |
| Haupt, Mary S | Shaffer, Edward A | Dec 12 1849 | 11/25 |
| Haupt, Rebecca | Dennett, William B | Feb 28 1853 | 12/181 |
| Hausler, Charles | Kauch, Catherine | Dec 9 1854 | 13/408 |
| Havard, John | Havard, Sarah | Dec 22 1853 | 13/48 |
| Havard, Sarah | Havard, John | Dec 22 1853 | 13/48 |
| Havens, Ann | Brunsled, Henry | Oct 20 1839* | 3/189 |
| Havens, Curtis | Laurie, Ann | May 14 1846 | 8/165B |
| Havens, Eliza | Johnson, Elijah | Apr 26 1855 | 14/119 |
| Havens, John | Fletcher, Sabrey Ann | Oct 18 1830* | 2/141 |
| Havens, John S | Foster, Nancy | May 31 1828* | 2/29 |
| Havens, Joseph | Burns, Catherine | Apr 10 1847 | 8/225 |
| Haverman, Rachel W | Brushears, Alexander | Jan 14 1846 | 8/140B |
| Hawkin, Jordie | Myre, Ann E | Jan 20 1844 | 5/315B |
| Hawkins, Henry J | Hodge, Mary Ann | Feb 2 1843* | 5/247B |
| Hawks, William | Keitty, Mary (Keilty) | Mar 28 1851 | 11/131 |
| Hawthorn, Joseph R | Herbert, Harriett | Apr 19 1852* | 11/239 |
| Hay, Anna | Henry, LeClair | Oct 31 1854* | 13/366 |
| Hayden, Isabella | Reach, Peter ? | Dec 19 1838* | 3/A152 |
| Hayes, Catherine | Fisher, William F | May 23 1853 | 12/297 |
| Hayes, Mary | Hanley, Thomas | Apr 18 1844 | 8/15B |
| Haynes, Clara S | Byran, Patrick C | Feb 24 1841 | 4/3001B |
| Haynes, Priscilla H | Semans, Thomas | May 5 1851* | 11/145 |

| BRIDE OR GROOM | SPOUSE | DATE | BOOK/PAGE |
|---|---|---|---|
| Haynes, Sarah Ann | Clark, Moses | Mar 20 1830* | 2/118 |
| Haynie, John D | Dickinson, Lois A | Feb 25 1836* | 3/41 |
| Haynie, John D | Brown, Ann | Jun 12 1837* | 3/88 |
| Hays, Ann | Shaughnasy, Edward | Sep 13 1843 | 5/296B |
| Hays, Catherine | Smith, Frederick | Sep 5 1845* | 8/191B |
| Hays, Charles | Stafford, Ann | Jan 23 1832* | 2/1731 |
| Hays, Charles | McKibbon, Caroline | Feb 24 1854 | 13/138 |
| Hays, George | Steers, Susan | Dec 16 1823* | 1/16 |
| Hays, Honorough (Honora) | Kennedy, Michael | Nov 16 1844 | 8/51B |
| Hays, James | Alphen, Catherine | Jun 5 1852 | 11/260 |
| Hays, Jemima | Lebow, Frances | Jan 4 1847 | 8/210 |
| Hays, Mary | Gilchrist, Philip | Jul 1 1839* | 3/180 |
| Hays, Michael | Hines, Katharine | Apr 19 1852 | 11/238 |
| Hays, Nancy | Benjamin, Joseph | Apr 22 1845 | 8/88B |
| Hays, Rebecca | Ashley, John S | May 2 1844 | 8/18B |
| Hays, Sarah | Windham, Joseph W | 1839* | OIB |
| Haywood, William | Hollaran, Bridget | Feb 2 1849* | 8/353 |
| Hazard, Charles C | Livingston, Cornelia | 1827* | OIB |
| Hazard, Mary | Whittaker, Benj. A | Apr 25 1848* | 8/301 |
| Heafy, Mary ? | Moore, John | Jun 3 1823 | 1/5 |
| Heald, John | Erety, Sarah E ? | Nov 1 1847 | 8/263 |
| Heald, John | Eastment, Cecelia E | Jul 26 1854 | 13/294 |
| Healey, Ellen | Shaw, Patrick | Oct 20 1855 | 14/256 |
| Healy, Daniel (widr) | Murray, Mary (wid) | Jul 11 1853 | 12/349 |
| Healy, John | Morgan, Bridget | Sep 24 1849 | 11/6 |
| Healy, John | McKnight, Mary | May 24 1845 | 8/98B |
| Healy, John | Roberts, Eliza | Jul 21 1854 | 13/290 |
| Healy, John (widr) | Harrington, Ann | May 12 1853 | 12/280 |
| Healy, Margaret | Sullivan, Richard | Dec 27 1852 | 12/105 |
| Healy, Patrick | Lorrigan, Ann | Aug 24 1847* | 8/253 |
| Heaney, Margaret | Arnold, William | Oct 1 1855 | 14/243 |
| Heard, Ann B | Butt, Cary W | Aug 22 1849* | 8/399 |
| Heard, Cornelia H | Reader, William C | Apr 18 1844 | 8/15B |
| Heard, Franklin C | Woolsey, Emily | Oct 16 1839* | 3/188 |
| Heard, John B | Powers, Sarah | Dec 15 1836* | 3/64 |
| Heard, Julia M | Elder, James | Aug 11 1841* | 5/147B |
| Heard, Robert A | Awtry, Sarah R | Apr 2 1847 | 8/229 |
| Heard, Sarah E A | Goff, Harmen | Nov 22 1849 | 11/18 |
| Hearin, William J | Gliddon, Susannah | Apr 9 1846 | 8/156B |
| Heaythorow, Elizabeth | Rose, Benjamin | Mar 30 1840* | 3/197 |
| Heckmier, Lizzitta | Shoemaker, Henry | May 1 1845 | 8/90 |
| Heely, Hugh (Healy) | McDonald, Bridget | Dec 13 1841 | 5/165B |
| Hefferlin, Cassandra | Edwards, Alexander | Oct 5 1840* | 5/51B |
| Hefferman, Dennis | Conners, Bridget | Feb 11 1839* | 3/156 |
| Heher, Catherine | Foster, John | May 10 1854 | 13/221 |
| Heibacher, Louisa | Hosfelt, John | May 20 1852 | 11/252 |
| Heidelberg, Rebecca | Benustein, Nathan ? | Mar 16 1850 | 11/46 |
| Heidrick, Catherine | Nunagasser, Henry | May 4 1854 | 13/215 |
| Heiser, John (Imheisen) | Bouch, Rachael | Jan 13 1846 | 8/140B |
| Heit, Lewis | Ramsfieldt, Margaret | Feb 20 1855 | 14/20 |
| Held, Joseph | Gilgen, Christiane | Jun 28 1852 | 11/267 |
| Heldenberg, Carmelite | Henry, Charles A | 1825* | OIB |
| Hellen, Abby | Wier, William W | Dec 9 1851 | 11/193 |
| Hellen, Susan L | Hellen, Wright | May 28 1844 | 8/23B |
| Hellen, Wright | Hellen, Susan | May 28 1844 | 8/23B |
| Helson, Joseph | Shanahan, Anastasia | Dec 7 1854 | 13/405 |
| Helverson, Ellenear | Lewis, Howell | May 7 1844 | 8/19B |
| Helverson, Godfrey | DeBosh, Fanny | Aug 15 1823 | 1/11 |
| Helverson, Harriet | Watts, David | Sep 10 1849 | 11/3 |
| Helverson, Nancy | Goff, George W | Jun 14 1844 | 8/28B |
| Helverson, Richard | Fountain, Susan | Sep 21 1824 | 1/39 |
| Helverson, Sarah | Kidd, Oliver J | Aug 7 1855 | 14/205 |
| Helverson, Susanna | McNeil, Thomas L | Aug 30 1855 | 14/221 |
| Helverston, Caroline | Richardson, Henry B | Sep 1 1855 | 14/222 |

| BRIDE OR GROOM | SPOUSE | DATE | BOOK/PAGE |
|---|---|---|---|
| Hemly, John | Haas, Catherine | Dec 16 1847* | 8/271 |
| Hemmingway, Ann | Burke, Edward | Aug 1 1838* | 3/137 |
| Hemphill, Burburn | Jones, Catherine | May 28 1852 | 11/256 |
| Hemphill, Felix B | Goodman, Mary V | Jun 30 1842* | 5/209 |
| Hendeaberry, Jane | Aycock, A.S. (L) | Apr 15 1841* | 5/123B |
| Henderson, Ann | Morrison, William G | Apr 18 1839* | 3/167 |
| Henderson, Eliza | King, Cyrus | Mar 17 1838* | 3/116 |
| Henderson, Jane | Reese, Joseph | Sep 29 1836* | 3/60 |
| Henderson, Martha M | Wright, William W | Nov 26 1846 | 8/201 |
| Henderson, Rebecca | Roach, Richard | Apr 29 1846 | 8/161B |
| Hendinburg, Eleanor (wid) | Krebs, Joseph | Jan 12 1816* | CM |
| Hendover, Simeon D | Horress, Mary | Jul 5 1843 | 5/286 |
| Hendrick, Martha | Long, John | Apr 26 1848 | 8/302 |
| Hendrisce, Sarah | Perkins, William C | Aug 29 1846 | 8/186 |
| Hendrix, Ellen | Jackson, Samuel W | Jan 8 1855 | 14/5 |
| Hendrix, Joel | Taylor, Martha Ann | Oct 16 1840* | 5/49B |
| Hendrix, Lydia | Vallance, Jeremiah | May 21 1853 | 12/294 |
| Hendrix, Neomi | Taylor, James H | Aug 14 1850 | 11/80 |
| Hendrix, Susannah | Cronin, Timothy | Sep 6 1843 | 5/295B |
| Henescey, Thomas H | Gilchrist, Philomena | Feb 4 1835* | 3/7 |
| Henessy, Margaret | Anderson, John | May 26 1847 | 8/237 |
| Henke, Anthony | Commen, Elizabeth | Apr 6 1840* | 5/17 |
| Henley, Julian | Ross, George | Apr 24 1840* | 5/20 |
| Henn, Margritte | Eich, Jean | Apr 9 1853 | 12/229 |
| Henn, Sarah | Sloan, John | Jan 22 1844 | 7/103 |
| Hennerberry, John | McGraw, Hannah | Aug 7 1849* | 8/391 |
| Hennemuth, Henry | Holmes, Hannah | Feb 21 1853 | 12/178 |
| Hennesee, Bridget | Chapman, Patrick | Jan 24 1854* | 13/94 |
| Hennesy, Bridget | Scott, Matthew | Jun 16 1843 | 5/282B |
| Hennisegen, Christin | Roth, Joseph | Nov 25 1823 | 1/14 |
| Henry, Alexandrine | Andry, Sylvester | Apr 8 1830* | 2/121 |
| Henry, Charles A | Heldenberg, Carmelite | 1825* | OIB |
| Henry, Clarissa | Gardner, John R | 1837* | OIB |
| Henry, Ellen | Vignroe, Francois | Dec 21 1824 | 1/55 |
| Henry, Francis | Batre, Coralie | Apr 8 1845 | 8/85B |
| Henry, John | McNamara, Mary | Dec 1 1840* | 5/83B |
| Henry, Josephine E | Ballantyne, Hamilton | Mar 31 1851 | 11/133 |
| Henry, Julia B | Garrett, William | Apr 22 1843 | 5/264B |
| Henry, Leclair | Hay, Anna | Oct 31 1854* | 13/366 |
| Henry, Martha N | Junelot, Julius | Oct 10 1855 | 14/251 |
| Henry, Martha N (wid) | Williams, John | Oct 29 1853 | 12/427 |
| Henry, Martha W | Deshon, Henry P | Jul 26 1850 | 11/76 |
| Henry, Mary | Trenier, John | 1826* | OIB |
| Henry, Mary | Trenier, John | 1827* | OIB |
| Henry, Nancy | Smith, Matthew B | 1826* | OIB |
| Henry, Sarah J | Mintzer, William H | Jun 14 1851* | 11/158 |
| Henry, Susan | Petit, Theodore | Feb 20 1850 | 11/41 |
| Henry, Thomas | Kane, Margaret | Feb 10 1842 | 5/179B |
| Henry, Thomas | Nugent, Mary | Oct 6 1849* | 11/8 |
| Hensaling, Lewis | Brainnan, Betsey | 1826* | OIB |
| Hensel, Anna | Partsh, Charles | Dec 4 1854 | 13/398 |
| Henserling, Lewis | Mott, Emeline | Oct 14 1828* | 2/45 |
| Henson, John | Fox, Avia | Sep 5 1851 | 11/176 |
| Henson, Sarah L | Smith, William A | Oct 5 1837* | 3/93 |
| Henvey, Susan | Cassas, Ramon | Feb 10 1842 | 6/80 |
| Heohleihstein, Hirsh ? | Leib, Sarah | Jul 24 1847 | 8/247 |
| Heple, Conrad | Schickner, Malinda | Oct 18 1855 | 14/255 |
| Hepp, Cora G | Shields, Thomas | Mar 18 1847 | 8/221 |
| Hepp, Sarah A | Tuttle, Charles S | Oct 19 1838* | 3/144 |
| Heppler, Charles | Racklus, Caroline | Nov 14 1840* | 5/61B |
| Heppler, Charles | Buckley, Caroline | Nov 14 1840* | 5/61B |
| Herberson, Bridget | Holligan, Thomas | Apr 23 1843 | 5/264 |
| Herbert, Ellen | Hesser, Julius | Mar 22 1848 | 8/294 |
| Herbert, Harriett | Hawthorn, Joseph R | Apr 19 1852* | 11/239 |

| BRIDE OR GROOM | SPOUSE | DATE | BOOK/PAGE |
|---|---|---|---|
| Herbert, John | Cook, Martha P | Sep 4 1850 | 11/84 |
| Herbert, William | Conway, Emma | Nov 25 1850 | 11/99 |
| Herbison, Ave | Rodrigus, Joseph | Sep 21 1849 | 11/6 |
| Herbison, Bridget | Horrigan, Thomas | 1843* | OIB |
| Herhey, Thomas | Smullur, Mary | Jan 15 1837* | 3/97 |
| Hericourt, Anna M J | Gamora, Jose Manuel M | May 12 1853 | 12/278 |
| Herkins, Easter | George, Joseph | Jan 15 1836* | 3/36 |
| Herkins, Patience | Malone, William | Dec 17 1831* | 2/1781 |
| Herley, Mary | Jordan, William E | Aug 27 1855 | 14/218 |
| Herlinger, Catherine | Stutz, George | Nov 14 1855 | 14/281 |
| Herman, Henry | Kank, Emiline | Mar 30 1840* | 3/196 |
| Hermann, Francois J A | Peirrot, Elois | Dec 16 1850 | 11/103 |
| Hermann, Moses | Tim, Esther | Jan 6 1855* | 14/1 |
| Hermason, Mary | Luke, Christian | Jun 14 1848 | 8/309 |
| Hermerberry, John ? | McGran, Hannah (McGraw) | Aug 7 1849* | 8/391 |
| Hern, Mary | Sloan, John | Jan 22 1844* | 5/317 |
| Herpin, Edward P | Lopez, Mary T | Nov 23 1853 | 13/25 |
| Herpin, Eliza | Partridge, Charles S | Oct 26 1854 | 13/363 |
| Herpin, Felix | Girard, Hermine | Aug 5 1828 | 2/38 |
| Herpin, Natale | Salles, Dominique | Jan 31 1821* | CM |
| Herpin, Urania M | Townsend, Lemuel R | May 1 1850 | 11/57 |
| Herren, Catharine | Collins, Thomas | Jan 30 1847 | 8/214 |
| Herring, Caleb F | Gay, Sissley Ann | Mar 20 1852* | 11/229 |
| Herring, Elizabeth | Putts, William | Apr 15 1831 | 2/162 |
| Herriott, Mary R | Gordon, Willie B | Jan 13 1846 | 8/139B |
| Herterick, Amelia | Krohnut, John F | Feb 28 1839* | 3/159 |
| Hertz, Rachel | Marks, Jacob | Jun 1 1855 | 14/155 |
| Herv, M | Bernstein, C | Jan 3 1851* | 11/108 |
| Hervey, Eliza | Andre, Claiborne | Aug 2 1849* | 8/386 |
| Hervey, Susan | Capas, Ramon (Cassas) | Feb 10 1842* | 5/180B |
| Hesler, Mary (Hester) | Devine, Patrick | 1849* | OIB |
| Hesley, Hannah | Burge, John | Aug 14 1851 | 11/172 |
| Heslin, Bridget | See, Francis | Apr 30 1838* | 3/122 |
| Hesser, Julius (Hassee) | Herbert, Ellen | Mar 22 1848 | 8/294 |
| Hester, Joseph W | Moore, Mary | Mar 20 1846 | 8/153B |
| Heuer, Sophei Wilhelmeni | Nelson, Peter | Feb 6 1845 | 8/71B |
| Hewett, Frederick | LeBrouche, Angelina | Apr 8 1840* | 5/18 |
| Hewett, Maria B | Collins, Darling | Aug 5 1835* | 3/21 |
| Heyder, Catherine | Ball, Joseph | May 21 1855 | 14/145 |
| Heyer, Cornelius | Kelly, Sophia | Oct 22 1850 | 11/92 |
| Heyl, Morris | Rie, Therese | Dec 9 1832* | 2/1281 |
| Hian, Sophia Catherine | LaCroise, John Batiste | 1822* | OIB |
| Hibbits, Bridgett | Maguire, William | Jun 24 1846 | 8/175 |
| Hibbitts, Margaret | Sinclair, John | Jun 5 1848* | 8/308 |
| Hibbits, Michael | MacAvoy, Ann | Jun 9 1854 | 13/249 |
| Hickes, Frances F | McLaughlin, Catherine | Apr 12 1853 | 12/235 |
| Hickey, Bridget | Turner, James | Feb 23 1846 | 8/146B |
| Hickey, Thomas | Troy, Margaret | Feb 19 1855 | 14/60 |
| Hicklin, William C | Hartley, Mary S (Hanley) | May 21 1842 | 5/203B |
| Hickman, Frances V | Matthys, John A | Sep 16 1851 | 11/179 |
| Hickman, Joseph M | Strike, Francis | Apr 2 1840* | 3/197 |
| Hicks, John W | Lacoste, Louisa | Feb 1 1837* | 3/71 |
| Hiestand, Asa | Scott, Mary | Nov 15 1855 | 14/282 |
| Hieton, Eva | Nicolas, Meisius | Mar 1 1852 | 11/223 |
| Higgin, Robert | Williams, Susan K | Mar 20 1832* | 2/1641 |
| Higgins, Ellen | Killigan, Thomas | Jul 23 1850 | 11/74 |
| Higgins, Ellen | McMahon, Patrick | Jan 11 1855 | 14/13 |
| Higgins, Ellen | Doulon, Patrick | Jun 21 1853 | 12/323 |
| Higgins, James | Connor, Rose | Jan 6 1832* | 2/1761 |
| Higgins, Martin | Donaho, Elizabeth | Jan 5 1847 | 8/210 |
| Higgins, Mary Ann | Travers, Patrick | Apr 13 1852 | 11/236 |
| Higgins, Noah | Quinn, Ann | Jul 30 1842* | 5/213B |
| Higgins, Sarah | Edmond, Andrew G | Apr 26 1855 | 14/120 |
| High, Augustus | Estapa, Mary S (Escatapa) | Nov 1 1854 | 13/367 |

| BRIDE OR GROOM | SPOUSE | DATE | BOOK/PAGE |
|---|---|---|---|
| High, Christiana | Folk, George | Feb 18 1841* | 5/105B |
| Highland, John | Reed, Ellen | May 15 1839* | 3/171 |
| Hightower, Eliza | Edwards, James | Nov 3 1824 | 1/44 |
| Hightower, Emeline | Wright, John | 1827* | OIB |
| Higinbotham, O | Bellas, Terese | 1833* | OIB |
| Hildebrand, Charles | Luckhaupt, Catherine S | Feb 8 1855 | 14/42 |
| Hildebrande, Charles | Peters, Sophia | Feb 16 1848 | 8/284 |
| Hildreth, Elizabeth L | Roberts, Evan | 1848* | OIB |
| Hiles, Sarah | McMorris, Morgan | Nov 28 1838* | 3/150 |
| Hill, Barbara | Schellong, Henry | Feb 25 1846 | 8/148B |
| Hill, Barbara | Dyer, Malachi J | Mar 25 1851 | 11/131 |
| Hill, Bridget | Burk, Farley | Feb 7 1852 | 11/213 |
| Hill, Eliza | Jeffery, William | Aug 10 1840 | 5/41B |
| Hill, Elizabeth Caroline | Stincen, Samuel | Dec 22 1842 | 5/237B |
| Hill, John | Conlin, Catherine | Mar 18 1852 | 11/228 |
| Hill, Marti | Frederick, George | Mar 3 1841* | 5/112B |
| Hill, Nancy | Woods, William | Jan 22 1844* | 5/316B |
| Hill, Thomas | Riley, Sarah | Jun 3 1851 | 11/155 |
| Hillard, Mary | Morgan, James | Nov 25 1852 | 12/73 |
| Hiller, Samuel | Cohen, Sabrina | Dec 31 1845 | 8/134 |
| Hilliard, Ann | Devine, Philip | Jun 10 1854 | 13/251 |
| Hilliard, Elizabeth R | Dunning, Edward | 1827* | OIB |
| Hillion, Thomas (Hilton) | Lewis, Lavina | Sep 12 1836* | 3/57 |
| Hills, Wingate F | McDermott, Jane | Oct 30 1843* | 5/301B |
| Hillyer, Giles M | Rolston, Elizabeth | Jan 4 1843 | 5/240B |
| Hind, Joseph | Murphy, Ellen | May 31 1853 | 12/301 |
| Hindemberg, A (Antonio) | Conway, Delilah | Dec 3 1819* | CM |
| Hindemberg, Antonio | Kreps, Genevieve | May 23 1815* | CM |
| Hines, Bridget | Lyons, Cornelius | Mar 8 1844 | 5/327B |
| Hines, Catharine | Crone, George | Jun 4 1851 | 11/155 |
| Hines, Elizabeth | Badgenstos, George W | Dec 6 1851 | 11/192 |
| Hines, George | Collins, Louisa | Jan 6 1842 | 5/168B |
| Hines, Jacob | Graff, Mary | Jul 10 1850 | 11/71 |
| Hines, John | Fowler, Ellen | Apr 10 1852 | 11/235 |
| Hines, Katharine | Hays, Michael | Apr 19 1852 | 11/238 |
| Hines, Mary | Butler, Martin | Jul 2 1842 | 5/209B |
| Hines, Michael | Currun, Charlotte | Jan 6 1842 | 5/168B |
| Hingel, Friedericka | Schilling, Franz (widr) | Mar 21 1853 | 12/211 |
| Hinkley, Alfred B | Ellis, Arcissens | Feb 7 1843 | 5/248B |
| Hinsay, Anna | Reader, Alfred | 1850* | OIB |
| Hinson, Lucinda C | Rhodes, Anderson K | Dec 14 1850 | 11/103 |
| Hinson, May | Sturtevant, Thomas | Aug 3 1825 | 1/88 |
| Hintze, Ernest | Smith, Anne | Dec 18 1843* | 5/309B |
| Hippler, Frank | Willrich, Christina | Nov 9 1854 | 13/374 |
| Hirchy, Benjamin | Schneider, Johanna H | May 14 1828* | 2/26 |
| Hire, Nancy ? | Woods, William | Jan 22 1844 | 7/99 |
| Hiren, Catherine A | Tereice, William J | Jan 10 1855 | 14/11 |
| Hirley, Mary | McGuire, John | Oct 6 1852 | 12/23 |
| Hirsch, Milco | Citron, Jacob | Apr 1 1854* | 13/170 |
| Hitchcock, John A | Gazzam, Catherine S | Feb 21 1850 | 11/41 |
| Hoaket, Sarah E | Goff, James | Mar 22 1852 | 11/229 |
| Hoay, William | Kary, Ann S (Skary) | Dec 29 1842 | 5/239B |
| Hobart, Calvin G N | Bancroft, Elmira | Feb 18 1852 | 11/219 |
| Hobart, Caroline M | Tompkins, Thomas G | Apr 24 1828 | 2/23 |
| Hobart, Delphine M A | Costigin, Lewis A | Jun 6 1844 | 8/26B |
| Hobart, Euphrosyne P | Steele, Joseph | 1826* | OIB |
| Hobart, Hannah Annetta | Stillman, John F | Jul 20 1841* | 5/143B |
| Hobart, May M | Franklin, Benjamin T | May 28 1840* | 5/24 |
| Hobby, Uriah | Weiswall, Catherine | 1826* | OIB |
| Hodge, Mary Ann | Hawkins, Henry J | Feb 2 1843* | 5/247B |
| Hodge, Mary L | Barnes, Reuben | Sep 10 1839* | 3/186 |
| Hodges, Ann Maria | Whitney, John S | Aug 21 1847 | 8/252 |
| Hodges, Frances A | Sherman, Jesse T | Sep 8 1855 | 14/227 |
| Hodges, Virginia A | Tuttle, George R | May 29 1849* | 8/378 |

| BRIDE OR GROOM | SPOUSE | DATE | BOOK/PAGE |
|---|---|---|---|
| Hodgson, John | Nevin, Anne | Nov 16 1847 | 8/265 |
| Hoey, John | Casey, Bridget | Feb 11 1854 | 13/118 |
| Hofer, August | Stiehl, Mary | Aug 8 1855 | 14/206 |
| Hoffman, Catherine | Mulder, Antoine | Oct 28 1852 | 12/38 |
| Hoffman, Margrette | Hanschelt, Peter | Sep 9 1848* | 8/323 |
| Hofhaines, Charles F | Leonard, Mary Ann | Apr 20 1841* | 5/124B |
| Hogan, Amelia E | Burns, Oliver S | Feb 23 1842* | 5/182B |
| Hogan, Ann M | Byard, Garrett H | May 31 1837* | 3/85 |
| Hogan, Bridget | Richardson, George W | Apr 22 1852 | 11/241 |
| Hogan, Bridget | Hogan, James | Jan 22 1838* | 3/108 |
| Hogan, Catherine | Tiarney, Paul | May 24 1843* | 5/275B |
| Hogan, Daniel | Tyler, Rosa | Apr 1 1850 | 11/49 |
| Hogan, Elizabeth | Donohue, Terry | Nov 24 1855* | 14/288 |
| Hogan, James | Hogan, Bridget | Jan 22 1838* | 3/108 |
| Hogan, James G | Simmons, Susan | Sep 13 1849 | 11/4 |
| Hogan, Jane (June) | Gillin, James | Nov 3 1845 | 8/123B |
| Hogan, John | Luced, Mary | Jun 15 1855 | 14/174 |
| Hogan, John B | Owen, Georgianna V | Feb 20 1850 | 11/41 |
| Hogan, Julia | Lee, David | Nov 22 1843* | 5/306B |
| Hogan, June | Gillin, James | Nov 3 1845 | 7/855 |
| Hogan, Lucy B | Hamilton, Thomas A | Nov 24 1847 | 8/268 |
| Hogan, Sarah B | Meikle, William | Jun 4 1855 | 14/161 |
| Hogan, William | Flin, Jane | Nov 1 1839* | 3/189 |
| Hokett, Martha (wid) | Skinner, John W (wid) | Aug 18 1853* | 12/387 |
| Holborne, Mary | Stiver, Peter | Jan 3 1846 | 8/136B |
| Holcomb, A D | Gopan, Mary C (Gosson) | Sep 27 1845 | 8/118B |
| Holcomb, Maria L | Tanner, Franklin | Jan 24 1849 | 8/349 |
| Holcombe, Bettie L | Keevan, A H | May 29 1850 | 11/63 |
| Holcombe, Cornelia A | Slough, Robert H | Oct 29 1846 | 8/196 |
| Holcombe, E Antonette | Sayne, Milborne | Apr 11 1841* | 5/130B |
| Holcombe, E P | Johnson, Mary E | Jun 21 1853 | 12/326 |
| Holcombe, John C | Pattison, Mary | Jul 24 1850 | 11/76 |
| Holcombe, Lydia M | Pope, Joseph Henry | Nov 5 1845 | 8/123B |
| Holcombe, Virginia A | Taylor, William S | Apr 20 1841* | 5/125B |
| Holden, Ann | McDonald, Patrick | Feb 18 1854 | 13/124 |
| Holden, Bridget | Belton, Edmund L | Jan 18 1850 | 11/34 |
| Holder, Ann M | Kimball, Franklin G | Feb 22 1830* | 2/113 |
| Holdinberg, Maria L | Truker, Engelberg | Jul 22 1844 | 8/34B |
| Holland, Elizabeth Ann | Roberts, Morris | Jul 5 1847 | 8/244 |
| Holland, H M | Lanock, Rosanna M | Apr 1 1841* | 5/120B |
| Holland, Jacob | Harben, Margarette C | Sep 2 1848 | 8/323 |
| Holland, Jacob F | Griffin, Nancy J | Dec 20 1851 | 11/196 |
| Holland, Leona A | Giddens, James W | Apr 18 1850 | 11/54 |
| Holland, Robert | Sumrall, Susanna | Jul 15 1844 | 8/32B |
| Hollaran, Bridget | Haywood, William | Feb 2 1849* | 8/353 |
| Holley, Mary Ann | Doline, Medrick (D'Olive) | May 13 1835* | 3/14 |
| Holley, Richard | Ryan, Margaret | May 10 1825 | 1/75 |
| Holligan, Thomas | Herberson, Bridget | Apr 23 1843 | 5/264 |
| Holligin, Maria | Dorlon, Cornum | Oct 12 1841 | 5/153B |
| Holliman, Aeson B | Beasley, Amanda W | May 2 1843 | 5/266B |
| Hollinger, Cecelia R | Cleveland, John G Jr | Jun 15 1849* | 8/379 |
| Hollinger, Cornelia E | Hunter, Harry | Jun 14 1854 | 13/257 |
| Hollinger, Elizabeth B | Russell, Gilbert C. Jr | Dec 10 1849* | 11/23 |
| Hollinger, Elizabeth B | Rupell, Gilbert C Jr | Dec 10 1849* | 11/23 |
| Hollinger, Louisa O | Malone, Thomas Jr | Dec 8 1849* | 11/23 |
| Hollinger, Margaret Jane | Campbell, Edward | Jul 30 1847 | 8/248 |
| Hollinger, Margarett | Tortes, James | Apr 8 1839* | 3/165 |
| Hollinger, Maria | Dorland, Carman | Oct 12 1841 | 5/153B |
| Hollinger, Mary J | Wickwin, Charles W | Oct 17 1849 | 11/10 |
| Hollinger, Mary L | Senac, Felix | Apr 16 1843 | 5/261B |
| Hollinger, Mary M | O'Neal, James W M | Jan 9 1850 | 11/31 |
| Hollinger, Octavia | Tilghman, John H | Dec 20 1849 | 11/26 |
| Hollinger, Sarah C | Roach, Jonathan | Nov 22 1849 | 11/18 |
| Hollinger, Swepson H | Russell, George W | Apr 18 1855 | 14/108 |

| BRIDE OR GROOM | SPOUSE | DATE | BOOK/PAGE |
|---|---|---|---|
| Hollingsworth, Zenty | Reid, Joseph P | Jun 19 1855 | 14/176 |
| Hollomon, Thomas | Hyde, Elizabeth | Feb 6 1854 | 13/112 |
| Holloway, James W | Bomheart, Elizabeth | Jun 27 1835* | 3/18 |
| Holloway, James W | Breen, Briszy | Jun 8 1843 | 5/272B |
| Hollowell, Elizabeth | Brown, Thomas H | May 4 1847 | 8/233 |
| Holly, Hilleary C | Thomas, Miranda C | Mar 10 1849* | 8/361 |
| Holly, Marinda | Ellis, Delano | Dec 23 1854 | 13/420 |
| Holly, William DeForest | Gilchrist, Mary A | 1827* | OIB |
| Holly, William DeForest | Slatter, Ann Parrish | Jul 5 1851* | 11/162 |
| Holly, Winney | Atkison, Raymond | Aug 25 1814* | WB1/25 |
| Holman, William H | Palmer, Martha | Jul 17 1849* | 8/388 |
| Holmes, Angus D | Perry, Hannah M | Aug 20 1853 | 12/389 |
| Holmes, Elizabeth | Alexander, Joseph | Sep 18 1852 | 12/8 |
| Holmes, Hannah | Hennemuth, Henry | Feb 21 1853 | 12/178 |
| Holmes, Harriett | Dyer, Watter G | May 10 1839* | 3/172 |
| Holmes, Sophia | Dyer, James J | Jun 6 1843* | 5/278B |
| Holoman, Thomas | Chatham, Rebecca | Mar 26 1836* | 3/54 |
| Holt, Caroline E | Kirby, Jared E | Dec 6 1854 | 13/402 |
| Holt, George W | Gaylord, Mary E | Jun 2 1845 | 8/100B |
| Holt, Mary A | Murray, Alfred R | Nov 14 1853 | 13/15 |
| Holthoff, Frank | Mason, Sarah | Jun 20 1855 | 14/180 |
| Homal, Henry | Hurtan, Lodusky (wid) | Apr 20 1853 | 12/247 |
| Homer, James B (Horner) | Nichols, Adaline | Apr 1 1833* | 2/1041B |
| Homer, William H (Horner) | Ward, Harriett R | Dec 27 1843* | 5/311B |
| Homer, William | Sheppard, Agnes | Nov 12 1850 | 11/97 |
| Homith, Stevenson L | Shuckleford, Charlotte G | Aug 3 1839* | 3/183 |
| Honan, William | McCantiff, Catharine | May 28 1847 | 8/239 |
| Honey, Elias F | Jayne, Emma Q | May 13 1845 | 8/95B |
| Honeywood, James | Dougherty, Mary A | Jul 17 1854 | 13/284 |
| Hooker, Frances | Wood, Edward | May 21 1844 | 8/22B |
| Hooks, Samuel W D | Smith, Catharine | Jul 23 1849* | 8/383 |
| Hooper, Eliza | Fath, Michael | Feb 24 1854* | 13/136 |
| Hoot, Stephen | Isaaus, Rebecca | Jul 2 1839* | 3/180 |
| Hopkins, Ann | Bissell, Elijah | Dec 28 1850 | 11/106 |
| Hopkins, Augusta | Rice, John W | May 22 1851 | 11/151 |
| Hopkins, Louisa G | Blevins, George P | May 4 1846 | 8/163B |
| Hopkins, Mahala Ann | Evans, Jessee | May 23 1844* | 8/22B |
| Hopkins, Samuel | Percay, Anfelica | Sep 13 1844 | 8/41B |
| Hoppensits, John | Eberline, Mary | Dec 20 1852 | 12/101 |
| Horan, Sarah | Charpentier, Stephen | May 24 1847* | 8/236 |
| Horlock, John | Biley, Lucetta | Mar 6 1848 | 8/291 |
| Horlock, John | Bloomendele, Anna | Jun 11 1840* | 4/4161B |
| Horn, Eliza | Thompson, William | Aug 17 1854 | 13/313 |
| Horn, John | Loftus, Mary | Apr 25 1855 | 14/118 |
| Horn, S H | Dittmar, Maria | May 30 1840* | 5/25 |
| Hornberg, Joseph | Newberg, Margarett | Apr 9 1840* | 5/18 |
| Hornbliss, Charlotte L | Ewing, Andrew W | May 7 1841* | 5/128B |
| Horner, James B | Nichols, Adaline | Apr 1 1833 | 2/1041 |
| Horner, William H | Ward, Harriett R | Dec 27 1843 | 7/71 |
| Horoman, Louisa | Kuhna, John | Feb 25 1850 | 11/43 |
| Horress, Mary | Hendover, Simeon D | Jul 5 1843 | 5/286B |
| Horress, Mary | Wendover, Simeon D | Jul 5 1843 | 5/286B |
| Horrigan, Thomas | Herbison, Bridget | 1843* | OIB |
| Horsefield, Andrew | Fox, Catharine | May 29 1845* | 8/99B |
| Horst, Martin | Berg, Apolonia | Dec 28 1854 | 13/421 |
| Horton, Elizabeth M | Allen, Isaac L | Mar 30 1850 | 11/48 |
| Horton, Peter | Drago, Antoinette | Jan 16 1851 | 11/113 |
| Hosey, Ellen | Shermann, John V | Sep 15 1852 | 12/5 |
| Hosfelt, John | Haibeha, Korlina | Mar 6 1854 | 13/148 |
| Hosfett, John | Heibacher, Louisa | May 20 1852 | 11/252 |
| Hoskins, Isabella (Haskins) | Rodgers, John | Jun 24 1841* | 5/140B |
| Hough, Alston | Ogbourn, Sarah A | Oct 31 1850 | 11/94 |
| Houpt, Lewis | McEwen, Mary W | Dec 29 1845 | 8/134B |
| Hourcarde, Clementine (wid) | Estever, M Tacinto | Apr 5 1845 | 8/84B |

| BRIDE OR GROOM | SPOUSE | DATE | BOOK/PAGE |
|---|---|---|---|
| Hourley, William ? | Moore, Elizabeth | Feb 11 1852 | 11/217 |
| Hourre, Louise | Steiner, Henry | Aug 28 1848* | 8/322 |
| House, Reubin | Webb, Hetty | Sep 15 1836* | 3/58 |
| Houson, Daniel (Hanson) | Lucas, Bridget | Jan 3 1838* | 3/107 |
| Houston, Elizabeth | McCoul, Thomas | Oct 10 1837* | 3/99 |
| Houston, Jesse | Clark, Nancy | Aug 19 1852 | 11/277 |
| Houston, Martha A | Mulder, Thomas J | Jan 6 1848 | 8/275 |
| Houston, Moses W | Vail, Ann E | Dec 30 1854 | 13/425 |
| Hoven, Sarah | Gahan, John | Jun 29 1843* | 5/284B |
| Hover, John B | Murphy, Mary Louisa | Jan 7 1852 | 11/201 |
| Hover, Mary | Golbien, Michael | Nov 13 1849 | 11/16 |
| How, Mary | Schuiermann, John V | Jan 26 1853 | 12/146 |
| Howard, Axeth | Davis, David | Feb 15 1839* | 3/157 |
| Howard, Daniel | Harrell, Edy | Oct 28 1829 | 2/99 |
| Howard, Eli | Reston, Serinne | Nov 16 1854 | 13/382 |
| Howard, Elizabeth | Landrum, Solomon | Apr 23 1848 | 8/300 |
| Howard, Eunice | Harrell, Jacob | 1825* | OIB |
| Howard, Isabella F | Greig, Robert | Oct 22 1855 | 14/258 |
| Howard, Isabella Holmes | Young, Joseph H | Dec 14 1842 | 5/234B |
| Howard, James | Sweeney, Elisabeth | Nov 8 1852 | 12/52 |
| Howard, John | Emmett, Isabella F | Apr 2 1845 | 8/83B |
| Howard, Joshua | Spriggs, Harriet | Mar 10 1843 | 5/253B |
| Howard, Loammi | Prine, Delilah Ann | Jan 1 1833 | 2/1241 |
| Howard, Martha | Peters, Nathaniel | Oct 9 1828* | 2/44 |
| Howard, Martha | Perkins, Silas | Mar 30 1853 | 12/210 |
| Howard, Mary Ann | Baxter, Noble W | Oct 19 1854 | 13/352 |
| Howard, Mima Jane | Powell, Richmond | Dec 29 1854* | 13/424 |
| Howard, Nancy | Powell, William | May 28 1852 | 11/255 |
| Howard, Nancy | Lambert, Nathaniel | Sep 22 1848 | 8/325 |
| Howard, Thomas | Allen, Mary Ann | Dec 22 1842 | 5/237B |
| Howe, Bridget | Kelly, Patrick | Jul 13 1852 | 11/269 |
| Howe, Charles F | McKea, Bridget | Feb 19 1853 | 12/177 |
| Howell, Benjamin | Stringfellow, Ellenor | Jun 5 1829* | 2/88 |
| Howell, Benjamin | Williams, Tamsen | Apr 4 1844 | 8/9B |
| Howell, Charles F | Williams, Mary E | Mar 6 1851 | 11/128 |
| Howell, Civility | Allen, William | Mar 20 1851 | 11/130 |
| Howell, Emily H | Turner, Samuel M | Apr 10 1849* | 8/367 |
| Howell, Henrietta M | Massee, James | Mar 4 1834* | 2/431B |
| Howell, James | Allen, Mary E | Jun 3 1851 | 11/155 |
| Howell, Sarah | Allen, John E | Nov 29 1849 | 11/20 |
| Howes, Malchus R | Baldwin, Sarah | 1825* | OIB |
| Howland, Jeremy | Starr, Sarah | Aug 12 1835* | 3/24 |
| Hoy, Margaret | Yost, Frederick | Jun 8 1850 | 11/65 |
| Hoyle, Alexander M | Wooster, Olive A (wid) | May 27 1854* | 13/236 |
| Hoyle, William | Perry, Mary Ann | Mar 29 1838* | 3/118 |
| Hoyt, John C | Salter, Susanna | Mar 24 1846 | 8/153B |
| Hubbard, Emily | Ramierez, John B | Apr 7 1834* | 2/341 |
| Hubbell, Julius | Ingersoll, Mary (spinster) | 1826* | OIB |
| Hubbert, Francisca | Mehnerd, Frederick E | Aug 29 1853* | 12/397 |
| Huber, John H | Eich, Margretta | Mar 19 1844 | 5/328B |
| Huber, Martaleny | Elihlien, John A | Jan 22 1853 | 12/141 |
| Huber, Martin | Smith, Elizabeth | Jan 22 1853 | 12/140 |
| Huber, Mary | Kraus, George | Mar 9 1841 | 5/114B |
| Hubert, Maria | Soobert, Stephens | Oct 18 1847* | 8/259 |
| Huchberger, Lehman | Tim, Sarah | Dec 3 1855 | 14/298 |
| Hudaff, Harm | Emindoph, Louisa | Jul 28 1854 | 13/296 |
| Huddleston, Emily A | Long, John H | Jul 19 1849* | 8/383 |
| Hudgins, Amanda | Rich, James | Mar 9 1840* | 5/14 |
| Hudson, Ataline | Smith, William | Sep 27 1854 | 13/342 |
| Hudson, Deril | Clark, Milbry | Aug 18 1838* | 3/140 |
| Hudson, Ellen | Rasberry, William G (wid) | May 5 1855* | 14/130 |
| Hudson, William | Duprest, Susan | Jan 16 1830 | 2/109 |
| Huff, James G | Mercy, Sarah Ann (Marlow) | Apr 23 1853 | 12/251 |
| Huffman, Alvina | Taylor, William | Mar 3 1848* | 8/289 |

| BRIDE OR GROOM | SPOUSE | DATE | BOOK/PAGE |
|---|---|---|---|
| Huffman, Lopon | Flowers, Rachael | Jul 22 1847 | 8/247 |
| Hufter, Lewis | Goldstein, Ricke | Feb 3 1854 | 13/108 |
| Huggins, Charles W | Medlock, Martha A | Jun 1 1844 | 8/24B |
| Huggins, George | Pollard, Louisa | Apr 20 1831* | 2/163 |
| Huggins, Louisa (wid) | Wright, William C | Apr 9 1853 | 12/228 |
| Huggins, Phoebe E | Black, William | Feb 28 1855 | 14/72 |
| Hughes, Asa | New, Martha Ann | Feb 23 1855 | 14/67 |
| Hughes, Catherine | Evans, Thomas R | Aug 12 1850* | 11/79 |
| Hughes, Catherine | McKinsie, William | Jun 4 1853 | 12/309 |
| Hughes, Edward | Brown, Jane | Dec 21 1842 | 5/237B |
| Hughes, Elizabeth | Lovly, James | Feb 2 1844* | 5/319B |
| Hughes, Mary | Wilson, William | Sep 26 1849 | 11/7 |
| Hughes, Mary | Ross, Andrew | Jul 23 1851 | 11/168 |
| Hughes, Sarah (wid) | Welsh, Michael | Feb 27 1855* | 14/69 |
| Hughes, Thomas | Collins, Catherine | Jul 13 1850 | 11/73 |
| Hughes, William | Wattes, Ann | Dec 18 1837* | 3/93 |
| Hughs, Areline | Brooks, James P | Mar 24 1845 | 8/81B |
| Hughs, Hannah | Patterson, William | Mar 29 1853 | 12/208 |
| Hughs, John M (wid) | Anderson, Mary Ann (wid) | Jul 2 1853 | 12/339 |
| Hughs, Martha Ann | Thompson, B W | Oct 21 1845 | 8/121B |
| Hugo, Simeon | Slute, Eusophrine (State) | Mar 15 1850 | 11/46 |
| Hugonin, M P | Farrel, Martha E | Apr 15 1853* | 12/241 |
| Hulen, Samuel | Williams, Mary E | Apr 30 1839* | 3/170 |
| Huler, Mary | Platt, Peter (widr) | Oct 29 1853 | 12/429 |
| Hull, Angela | Brewer, Henry O | Jan 7 1843 | 5/242B |
| Hull, Elizabeth (Hall) | Jewett, John T | Apr 19 1843 | 5/261B |
| Hull, Hannah | Cambron, Levi | Jun 13 1833* | 2/931 |
| Hull, Julia | Forsyth, Robert C | Jun 27 1850 | 11/70 |
| Hull, Latham | Shea, Mary | Feb 10 1848* | 8/283 |
| Hull, Susan | Ogden, Samuel M | Feb 24 1848* | 8/286 |
| Hull, William H ? | DeVendel, Angele E | Apr 20 1842 | 5/193B |
| Hulyr, Thomas (Huyle) | Walker, Mary | Sep 19 1842 | 5/220B |
| Humphell, Felix T(Hemphill) | Goodman, Mary D | Jun 30 1842 | 5/209B |
| Humphrey, James | Greyer, Frances N | Mar 24 1852* | 11/230 |
| Humphrey, Martha A | Wright, Achilles E A | Jan 21 1841* | 5/93B |
| Humphrey, William D | Tally, Sarah Jane | Aug 22 1845 | 8/116B |
| Humphries, Henry G | Krebs, Corrienne | Jul 15 1850* | 11/73 |
| Hunt, Harriett E | Pierce, Ezekiel W | Nov 2 1852 | 12/44 |
| Hunt, Saphronia A | Van Bibber, Flabins J | Mar 7 1853 | 12/185 |
| Hunt, Thomas | Wheeler, Emily | Nov 30 1848 | 8/335 |
| Hunter, Charles | Turner, Rebecca (Terisis) | Oct 14 1840* | 5/55B |
| Hunter, Harry | Hollinger, Cornelia E | Jun 14 1854 | 13/257 |
| Hunter, Helen Gains | Ross, Francis A | Dec 21 1844 | 8/61B |
| Hunter, Martha Ann | Ewing, James L | Nov 22 1844 | 8/54B |
| Hunter, W H | Ryninger, Annie F | Feb 22 1851 | 11/123 |
| Huntington, John | Drew, Betsey Prior | May 9 1838* | 3/124 |
| Hurdle, Caroline | Wilson, Seymour S | May 30 1843* | 5/277B |
| Hurlbutt, Hannah | Cohen, Samuel | May 17 1843* | 5/273B |
| Hurley, Ann | Rogers, John | Jan 6 1849* | 8/346 |
| Hurley, Catherine | Brown, Peter | Jan 2 1854* | 13/75 |
| Hurley, Charles | Cating, Mary Ann | Jan 11 1842 | 5/171B |
| Hursey, Anna | Rinder, Alfred A | Jun 29 1850 | 11/70 |
| Hursted, Ann | Williams, Charles | Jun 10 1841* | 5/137 |
| Hurtan, Lodusky (wid) | Homal, Henry | Apr 20 1853 | 12/247 |
| Hurtel, Felecia | Robinson, Murray | Dec 2 1839* | 5/2 |
| Hurtel, Finnan | Noel, Deolice | Jan 21 1843 | 5/244B |
| Hurtel, Firmin | Girard, Severine | Dec 22 1835* | 3/34 |
| Hurtel, Odalie Ann | Parham, John | Jul 13 1840* | 5/35 |
| Hurtell, Lea M | Guesnard, Theodore Jr | Feb 16 1841* | 5/105B |
| Hurter, Mary Ann | Barnes, John | Sep 12 1829 | 2/96 |
| Hury, George | Rabman, Madelina | Apr 15 1854 | 13/184 |
| Husson, Elizabeth | Elder, John | Mar 26 1838* | 3/117 |
| Huston, Bernard | Clarke, Bridget | Feb 17 1844 | 5/323B |
| Huston, Louisa J | Taylor, John W | Dec 10 1838* | 3/151 |

| BRIDE OR GROOM | SPOUSE | DATE | BOOK/PAGE |
|---|---|---|---|
| Huston, J W | Roberts, Elizabeth (wid) | May  2 1853 | 12/268 |
| Hutchinson, John | Ryan, Maria | Jul 20 1853 | 12/363 |
| Hutchison, Alexander W | Dobson, Sarah E | Aug  9 1853 | 12/378 |
| Hutchison, Boliver | Keely, Elizabeth | Jul 17 1851 | 11/166 |
| Hutchison, James H | Graham, Amelia | May 15 1838* | 3/126 |
| Hutchison, Mary | Adams, William S | Jun 22 1839* | 3/179 |
| Hutchison, Peter | Miller, Mary Craig | Mar 29 1844 | 8/7B |
| Hutchisson, James F | Spencer, Ann B | Sep 19 1836* | 3/59 |
| Hutchisson, James H | Steele, Martha M | Jan 31 1855 | 14/34 |
| Hutton, Catherine A | Luterage, Marke | 1838* | OIB |
| Hutton, Charlotte Anna | Vienne, Honore T | Feb 24 1846 | 8/147B |
| Huxham, Mary | Burnes, William S | Jul 12 1848* | 8/316 |
| Huyle, Thomas | Walker, Mary | Sep 19 1842 | 5/220B |
| Huzont, Janne | Collin, Faustin | Jul  9 1828 | 2/35 |
| Hyams, Hamilton | Jones, Adelaide | Oct 15 1855 | 14/251 |
| Hyde, Elizabeth | Hollomon, Thomas | Feb  6 1854 | 13/112 |
| Hyde, James | Toomey, Mary | Dec 31 1844 | 8/64B |
| Hyde, Julia | Ferrell, William B | Jan 31 1855 | 14/33 |
| Hyems, Nathaniel | Bant, Maria H | May  9 1836* | 3/46 |

# I

| | | | |
|---|---|---|---|
| Ibach, Nimpha | Chimps, Andrew | Dec 26 1851 | 11/199 |
| Ibert, Thomas | Loughry, Catharine | Dec 26 1848* | 8/341 |
| Igg, Nannette | Chastang, John | Jul  5 1831* | 2/177 |
| Ignard, Philip | Cordier, Jeanne | Apr 18 1854 | 13/190 |
| Igregoi, Epolite | Delor, Simon | Dec  9 1830* | 2/143 |
| Illingworth, Thomas M | McMahon, Bridget | Jan 20 1851 | 11/114 |
| Imeaub, Eugenia | Antuney, Joseph | Aug 10 1854 | 13/309 |
| Imheisen, John (Heiser) | Bouch, Rachael | Jan 13 1846 | 8/140B |
| Inez, Edward | Sylvester, Mary | Sep 16 1841 | 5/152 |
| Ingerman, Conrardina L | Bille, Peter | Aug 31 1847 | 8/254 |
| Ingerman, Valentine | Kohler, Mary E | Aug  9 1842* | 5/219B |
| Ingersoll, Andrew J | Simms, Mary M | Nov 12 1846 | 8/198 |
| Ingersoll, Helen | Barnwell, William Jr | Nov 17 1848* | 8/333 |
| Ingersoll, Mary (spinster) | Hubbell, Julius | 1826* | OIB |
| Ingersoll, William I | Espaho, Catherine | Apr 25 1820* | CM |
| Inglemen, Denah | McDonald, Andrew | Jul 14 1847* | 8/245 |
| Ingleson, Christina | Myers, Joseph | Dec 21 1849 | 11/26 |
| Ingraham, James G | Maguire, Ellen R | May 19 1838* | 3/127 |
| Ingram, Thomas | Chastang, Julia | Jun 29 1843 | 6/386 |
| Innerarity, Francis | Markham, Eliza | May 24 1855 | 14/151 |
| Inson, William B (Juzan) | Rogers, Rebecca | Feb 23 1832* | 2/1701 |
| Instant, Robert | Pete, Eliza | Oct 14 1846 | 8/193 |
| Inzan, Mary M  (Juzan) | Chastang, Sidione J | Jan 15 1846 | 7/750 |
| Inzcan, Thomas  (Juzan) | Chastang, Salia | Jun 29 1843 | 5/284 |
| Ipstine, Calini (Justine) | Roundik, Joseph (Roundel) | Jan 25 1844 | 5/318B |
| Ireland, John J | Girard, Elvina | Dec 12 1851 | 11/193 |
| Irish, Margaret | Dewitt, James | Apr 15 1841* | 5/123B |
| Irvain, Henry | Jones, Mary E | May 27 1839* | 3/174 |
| Irvin, Alexander | Parks, Caroline | Jan 28 1854 | 13/101 |
| Irvin, Ann (Irwin) | Lambert, Thomas | Oct 24 1843 | 5/301B |
| Irvin, Ramson P | Warner, Harriett W | Sep 15 1854 | 13/336 |
| Irwin, John | Woodall, Eliza E | Sep 26 1843 | 5/297B |
| Irwin, John I | Robinson, Jane | Feb 11 1834* | 2/461 |
| Irwin, Joseph | McBamay, Jane | Mar 12 1839* | 3/160 |

| BRIDE OR GROOM | SPOUSE | DATE | BOOK/PAGE |
|---|---|---|---|
| Irwin, Joseph | Gannan, Elizabeth | Apr 30 1841* | 5/127 |
| Irwin, Richard | Weldin, Elizabeth | Nov 5 1842* | 5/226B |
| Isaacs, Marks I | Cone, Hannah | Mar 5 1844* | 5/326B |
| Isaaus, Rebecca | Hoot, Stephen | Jul 2 1839* | 3/180 |
| Iveland, John J (Ireland) | Girard, Elvina | Dec 12 1851 | 11/193 |
| Ivers, Mary A | Jones, William | Sep 16 1851 | 11/179 |
| Ivers, Bridget | Cload, James Joseph | Mar 12 1840* | 5/15 |
| Ives, John (Ivis) | Buckley, Johannah | Apr 9 1853 | 12/225 |
| Ivey, Jane (Ivis) | Quinn, Patrick | Mar 21 1850 | 11/47 |
| Ivis, Catherine | Scarpa, Julius | May 13 1854 | 13/222 |
| Ivis, Elizabeth | McGuire, Matthew | Jun 22 1855 | 14/184 |
| Ivis, Richard | Gallihar, Mary | May 6 1854 | 13/218 |
| Ivory, Edward | Day, Ellen | Jan 5 1844* | 5/313B |

## J

| BRIDE OR GROOM | SPOUSE | DATE | BOOK/PAGE |
|---|---|---|---|
| Jackson, Catherine | Nelson, Admeral | 1840* | OIB |
| Jackson, Catherine | Brown, Edward | Nov 18 1850 | 11/98 |
| Jackson, Harriet E | Ogden, Wyal | May 28 1828* | 2/28 |
| Jackson, James | Shultes, Eunice | Dec 24 1820* | CM |
| Jackson, James | Martin, Terrilla | Dec 5 1848* | 8/337 |
| Jackson, John L | Roan, Mary | Aug 19 1852 | 11/277 |
| Jackson, Mary Ann | Wells, Richard | Feb 24 1849* | 8/359 |
| Jackson, Samuel H | Fennely, Harriett E | Jun 22 1825* | 1/81 |
| Jackson, Samuel W | Hendrix, Ellen | Jan 8 1855 | 14/5 |
| Jackson, Stephen P | Dittmar, Margaret L | Dec 31 1853 | 13/58 |
| Jackson, William | Davis, Mary | Oct 20 1853 | 12/422 |
| Jacob, Catherine | Toca, Joseph A | Dec 3 1833* | 2/661 |
| Jacob, Julie | Girard, Edward | Nov 22 1829* | 2/103 |
| Jacobs, Elizabeth | Pocheler, Arnauld | Oct 8 1852 | 12/26 |
| Jacobson, Matilda | Phillipe, Antonio | Oct 28 1850 | 11/93 |
| Jacoby, Henry | Goldstricker, Therese | Apr 1 1850* | 11/49 |
| Jacquelin, Henri Eugene | Guenard, Heroine | Mar 26 1850 | 11/47 |
| James, Ann | Harris, Dan | Mar 29 1844 | 8/8B |
| James, Elizabeth | Titus, Joseph | Jun 5 1837* | 3/85 |
| James, Emily | Blount, Frederick S | Dec 10 1835* | 3/33 |
| James, Joel C | Tappler, Lydia | Jan 15 1853 | 12/134 |
| James, Joseph (Irwin) | Gunnun, Elizabeth | Apr 30 1841 | 4/3781 |
| James, Madison | Johnson, Harriet (Mrs) | Aug 22 1850 | 11/82 |
| James, Rositta | Lyon, William A | 1838* | OIB |
| James, Sarah | Peterson, William | Jan 17 1845 | 8/67B |
| James, Thomas S | Bell, Laura | Jan 16 1836* | 3/36 |
| James, William F | Powers, Nancy M | Dec 7 1855 | 14/300 |
| Jameson, Narcissa | Taylor, Henry A | 1838* | OIB |
| Jameson, Robert | Scribner, Mary E | Mar 22 1855 | 14/87 |
| Jane (NSL) | Bonhagan, Frederick | Nov 16 1843* | 5/305B |
| Jantan, Mary | Perrine, George W | Dec 5 1851 | 11/192 |
| Jaques, Moses | Cullum, Charlotte | May 30 1825 | 1/79 |
| Jarvis, Francis R (James) | Willan, Julia | Dec 29 1852 | 12/106 |
| Jarvis, Margaret | Bell, William | Mar 19 1850 | 11/47 |
| Jarvis, Margaret | Keenan, Francis | Feb 11 1854 | 13/120 |
| Jarvis, Mary Ann | Wilson, George | Jan 29 1841* | 5/139B |
| Jarvis, Thomas | Dunaho, Mary | Mar 10 1843 | 5/252B |

| BRIDE OR GROOM | SPOUSE | DATE | BOOK/PAGE |
|---|---|---|---|
| Jarvis, Thomas | Burns, Margaret | Apr 10 1844 | 8/11B |
| Jasmein, Caroline | Petit, Valerie | Jul 18 1854 | 13/288 |
| Jaymes, Elizabeth J | Birch, William H | Aug 19 1854 | 13/316 |
| Jayne, Almira | Randall, William D | May 17 1832* | 2/1501 |
| Jayne, Ann Augusta | Robbins, Martin | May 9 1845 | 8/93B |
| Jayne, Emma O | Honey, Elias F | May 13 1845 | 8/95B |
| Jayne, Harriett A | Sturtevant, Francis | May 18 1833* | 2/1001 |
| Jean, Eshrazeh | Boudin, Alexander H | Oct 10 1838* | 3/143 |
| Jean, Peter | Hahill, Harriet W | Nov 13 1854 | 13/377 |
| Jeanenert, Helverse | Duval, William J | Jul -4 1845 | 8/108B |
| Jeantin, Pierre William | Benite, Mary | Feb 17 1840* | 3/194 |
| Jeffery, Eliza | Ross, Amost | Apr 5 1843 | 5/259B |
| Jeffery, William | Hill, Eliza | Aug 10 1840 | 5/41B |
| Jemison, Eliza Ann | Roper, James W | Nov 22 1838* | 3/148 |
| Jenical, Amabb (Senical) | Mathews, Heloise F H | Jan 25 1845 | 8/68B |
| Jenkin, Ellen | Connely, William | Oct 9 1843* | 5/298B |
| Jenkins, Calvin L | Cook, Sophia J | Apr 13 1850 | 11/53 |
| Jenkins, Henry J | Frisbie, Jane | Aug 19 1850 | 11/81 |
| Jenkins, Sarah Hane | Kohl, Charles | Mar 17 1835* | 3/11 |
| Jenkins, Thomas | Collier, Caroline | Jan 21 1854 | 13/90 |
| Jennett, Albert H | Russell, Mary S | Sep 6 1842 | 5/218B |
| Jennings, Melissa | Leavens, Benjamin F | Oct 1 1844 | 8/42B |
| Jennings, Sebeastian S | Smoot, Margaret | Dec 27 1836 | 3/66 |
| Jennings, William E | Brown, Martha P | Jan 26 1833* | 2/1191 |
| Jepay, John (Jessay) | Wilson, Ellen | 1839* | 0IB |
| Jester, Hugh T | Randall, Jane | Jan 25 1842 | 5/173B |
| Jeunelot, Charles | Forest, Aglae | Feb 10 1825* | 1/62 |
| Jeuswift, Charles A | Overstreet, Melissa | Oct 13 1835* | 3/29 |
| Jewell, Robert G W | Cosey, Harriet C (Cady) | Dec 3 1842 | 5/231B |
| Jewett, Adams | Smith, Mary P P | Jul 1 1841* | 5/141 |
| Jewett, John T | Hull, Elizabeth (Hall) | Apr 19 1843 | 5/261B |
| Jewett, Mary Elizabeth | McCullough, Charles | May 26 1843 | 5/271B |
| Jiles, Robert | Gamber, Jane | Sep 25 1838* | 3/141 |
| John, David | Adler, Jeannette | Oct 29 1847 | 8/262 |
| John, Genetta | Nordlinger, Solomon | Jun 26 1848* | 8/310 |
| Johns, Zephaniah | George, Mary S | Apr 13 1852 | 11/236 |
| Johnson, Amanda M | Uneiland,Jonas (Vreeland) | Dec 9 1846 | 8/204 |
| Johnson, Amelia | Peabody, Oren | Mar 12 1828 | 2/15 |
| Johnson, Ameline | Williams, James | Jul 5 1854 | 13/274 |
| Johnson, Ann | Fitzpatrick, Michael | Nov 24 1849 | 11/19 |
| Johnson, Bridget | Bodelson, Andrew | Apr 26 1848* | 8/301 |
| Johnson, Catherine | Sholts, Fredrick | Mar 19 1834* | 2/381 |
| Johnson, Charles | Jointer, Mary Julie | Jan 8 1851 | 11/110 |
| Johnson, Charles H | Tease, Nancy | Mar 1 1842 | 5/185B |
| Johnson, Charlott | Shelton, James | Oct 11 1841 | 5/153B |
| Johnson, Christopher | Sheppard, Sarah Jane | Jun 18 1846 | 8/174 |
| Johnson, Christopher | Phelps, Lylie | Sep 24 1855 | 14/239 |
| Johnson, Ebenezer | Elwood, Amelia | Nov 10 1821* | CM |
| Johnson, Elijah | Havens, Eliza | Apr 26 1855 | 14/119 |
| Johnson, Eliza | Smith, Daniel | May 3 1851 | 11/145 |
| Johnson, Elizabeth | Chambers, George A | May 22 1841* | 5/131B |
| Johnson, Francis A | Paden, George | Jul 18 1854 | 13/287 |
| Johnson, George | MacKay, Elizabeth | Dec 23 1833* | 2/641 |
| Johnson, George | Demsey, Bridget | Apr 13 1844 | 8/13B |
| Johnson, George W | Rice, Rebecca | Feb 17 1836* | 3/40 |
| Johnson, Harriet (Mrs) | James, Madison | Aug 22 1850 | 11/82 |
| Johnson, Harriett | Dufur, Benjamin, F | Apr 14 1845 | 8/87B |
| Johnson, Hepsay | Beardsley, Cyrus | Jan 11 1820* | CM |
| Johnson, Jacob | Johnson, Mary | Apr 24 1855 | 14/116 |
| Johnson, J James Jr | Boudett, Harriett ? | Apr 26 1852 | 11/242 |
| Johnson, J James Jr | Roudett, Harriett ? | Apr 26 1852 | 11/242 |
| Johnson, James | Edy, Elizabeth | May 3 1824 | 1/30 |
| Johnson, James | Allen, Elizabeth | Jan 20 1820* | CM |
| Johnson, John | Bruce, Mary Ann | Jul 6 1839* | 3/181 |

| BRIDE OR GROOM | SPOUSE | DATE | BOOK/PAGE |
|---|---|---|---|
| Johnson, John | Parisine, Josephine | Oct 20 1845 | 8/195 |
| Johnson, John L | McGee, Eliza | May 20 1824* | 1/32 |
| Johnson, Lavinia | Wilson, Thomas | Jan 25 1848 | 8/279 |
| Johnson, Lavinia | Tompkins, William Q | May 31 1855 | 14/154 |
| Johnson, Lucy | Stephens, William | Feb 4 1837* | 3/96 |
| Johnson, Lucy | Purcell, Isaac | Apr 21 1853 | 12/249 |
| Johnson, Maria | Joseph, Casene | Nov 1 1849 | 11/12 |
| Johnson, Maria | Nichols, Charles | Feb 23 1841* | 5/108B |
| Johnson, Martha | Graham, Moses | Apr 19 1855 | 14/111 |
| Johnson, Mary | Murphy, Albert J | Feb 18 1851 | 11/122 |
| Johnson, Mary | Johnson, Jacob | Apr 24 1855 | 14/116 |
| Johnson, Mary E | Holcombe, E P | Jun 21 1853 | 12/326 |
| Johnson, Mary Jane | Seale, William | Dec 27 1841* | 5/165B |
| Johnson, Mena | Sherman, Philip | Dec 27 1855 | 14/318 |
| Johnson, Nicholas | Ford, Louisa | Jan 29 1835* | 3/6 |
| Johnson, Oscar | Sheean, Bridget | Apr 3 1855 | 14/97 |
| Johnson, Peter I | Thompson, Mary | May 12 1841* | 5/130B |
| Johnson, Peyton | Volik, Susannah | Feb 24 1844 | 5/324B |
| Johnson, Robert C (widr) | Rascup, Jane (wid) | Mar 4 1853 | 12/184 |
| Johnson, Samuel | Bouvier, Mariah | Jun 30 1838* | 3/135 |
| Johnson, Samuel | Myrick, Emelia | Oct 20 1848* | 8/329 |
| Johnson, Sarah | Welsh, William | Apr 20 1850* | 11/55 |
| Johnson, Sarah | Cashin, Denis | Jan 31 1852 | 11/210 |
| Johnson, Sarah J | Walker, George | Oct 23 1852 | 12/33 |
| Johnson, Sophia | Ellison, Berry | May 1 1847 | 8/231 |
| Johnson, Thomas | Pattison, Mary A (wid) | Dec 22 1853 | 13/47 |
| Johnson, Virgil A | Beckler, Margaret | Mar 6 1855 | 14/76 |
| Johnson, William | Cooper, Margaret | Jan 3 1842 | 5/167B |
| Johnson, William | Falkner, Catharine | Feb 10 1844* | 5/321B |
| Johnson, William | Allen, Mary | Jun 19 1851 | 11/159 |
| Johnson, William | Baptiste, Isabella | Nov 4 1853 | 13/6 |
| Johnson, William D | Pipkin, Mary E | Jun 19 1850 | 11/67 |
| Johnson, William H | McDaniel, Mary L | Jan 4 1849 | 8/345 |
| Johnson, William J | Bridges, Elizabeth H | Dec 18 1844 | 8/60B |
| Johnston, Daniel L | Linder, Harriett | 1827* | OIB |
| Johnston, George | Ward, Eliza | 1823* | OIB |
| Johnston, Glorvina E | Rush, John G | Jan 24 1852 | 11/207 |
| Johnston, Hamilton R | Elliott, Sophia M (W) | Feb 28 1842 | 5/184B |
| Johnston, Hamilton R | Owen, Catharine C | Jun 21 1849* | 8/392 |
| Johnston, John | Rasher, Mary | 1827* | OIB |
| Johnston, Margaret | Vandalson, James H | May 22 1852 | 11/254 |
| Johnston, Margaret E | Crosby, Thomas W | Apr 20 1829* | 2/81 |
| Johnston, Martha | Rea, Jeremiah | 1829* | OIB |
| Johnston, Mary | O'Carroll, John | Jul 23 1850 | 11/75 |
| Johnston, Nancy | Ware, John | 1825* | OIB |
| Johnston, Nancy | Lamphier, William | Jan 30 1829* | 2/68 |
| Johnston, Robert | Mahab, Mary Ann (Nahob) | May 18 1829* | 2/87 |
| Johnston, Sandy | Cullen, Hannah | May 8 1852 | 11/246 |
| Johnston, William | Slaton, Amanda Jane | Nov 9 1852 | 12/53 |
| Johnstone, Mary | Goodsil, Jesse | Oct 16 1821* | CM |
| Joice, Ann | Curtin, Michael | Oct 18 1853 | 12/416 |
| Joiner, Delia A | Rester, Narvil | Jan 1 1855 | 13/427 |
| Joiner, Mary | Jones, Richard H | Aug 10 1854 | 13/310 |
| Jointer, Mary Julie | Johnson, Charles | Jan 8 1851 | 11/110 |
| Jomaron, Mary L | DePre, James Henry | 1826* | OIB |
| Jones, Adelaide | Hyams, Hamilton | Oct 15 1855 | 14/251 |
| Jones, Adelle | Soto, Zero | Oct 19 1850 | 11/90 |
| Jones, Amelia | Foy, Daniel D | Mar 26 1847 | 8/222 |
| Jones, Ann | Kelsey, George | May 11 1844 | 8/20B |
| Jones, Anna H | West, Louis | Dec 22 1851 | 11/197 |
| Jones, Bridget | McHugh, John | Apr 6 1847 | 8/225 |
| Jones, Calvin J | Sedam, Laura B | Mar 13 1854 | 13/157 |
| Jones, Carmelite | Laurendine, Edmond | Jul 15 1843 | 5/288B |
| Jones, Caroline V | Ruport, James C | Mar 2 1840* | 3/195 |

| BRIDE OR GROOM | SPOUSE | DATE | BOOK/PAGE |
|---|---|---|---|
| Jones, Catharine | Hemphill, Burborn | May 28 1852 | 11/256 |
| Jones, Delilah | Nicholas, Dennis | Mar 14 1836* | 3/43 |
| Jones, Edward | Sylvester, Mary | Sep 16 1841 | 5/152B |
| Jones, Edward A | Wilson, Amelia | Jun 6 1846* | 8/173 |
| Jones, Edward S | Biles, Eunice A | Jan 18 1840* | 5/9 |
| Jones, Eliza | Malone, John | Dec 19 1828* | 2/56 |
| Jones, Eliza Jane | McNeill, Daniel | Aug 26 1847 | 8/253 |
| Jones, Elizabeth | Daniel, Abner | 1837* | OIB |
| Jones, Elizabeth | Ryder, Richard G | Mar 2 1830* | 2/116 |
| Jones, Elizabeth | Beaudreaux, Zeferan | Aug 3 1842* | 5/214B |
| Jones, Ellen | Tolle, Charles H | Jan 15 1852* | 11/204 |
| Jones, Emanuel | Stickney, Hannah J | Nov 28 1842 | 5/230B |
| Jones, Emily A | Harkey, David M | Mar 7 1855 | 14/77 |
| Jones, Fanny | Gordon, Theodore | Dec 17 1851 | 11/195 |
| Jones, Henry (Corry) | Marvin, Louisa | Nov 2 1843 | 7/11 |
| Jones, Herbert | Shaw, Elizabeth | Dec 15 1819* | CM |
| Jones, Isaac | Crooks, Morning | Dec 31 1846 | 8/207 |
| Jones, James C | Lee, Martha E | Mar 18 1843 | 5/254B |
| Jones, John | Levings, Nancy | Aug 19 1813* | CM |
| Jones, John | Adams, Ann | Jan 17 1841* | 5/89B |
| Jones, John | Carter, Mary | Jun 26 1851* | 11/160 |
| Jones, John | Falls, Bridget | Nov 4 1852 | 12/46 |
| Jones, John W | Bolton, Lucinda | Jul 19 1848 | 8/317 |
| Jones, Lavina | Cross, Stephen | Sep 11 1829 | 2/95 |
| Jones, Margaret | Bowman, William | Apr 14 1838 | 3/119 |
| Jones, Martha | Ranagar, Jackson | Dec 8 1846 | 8/203 |
| Jones, Martha E | Try, William W | Jun 30 1838* | 3/134 |
| Jones, Mary | Scarboro, Peter | Mar 24 1845 | 8/81B |
| Jones, Mary E | Irvain, Henry | May 27 1839* | 3/174 |
| Jones, Mary E | Capps, Bassett | Jan 23 1855 | 14/22 |
| Jones, Nancy | Parmenter, William | Aug 29 1831* | 2/165B |
| Jones, Nathan | Burns, Jane | Jul 7 1845 | 8/109B |
| Jones, Richard | Joiner, Mary | Aug 10 1854 | 13/310 |
| Jones, Rositta | Lyon, William | Jan 1 1838 | 3/108 |
| Jones, Sarah | Walker, Benjamin F | Apr 3 1837* | 3/77 |
| Jones, Sarah | Morrison, Joseph | Dec 14 1852* | 12/90 |
| Jones, Sarah A E | Simmons, Henry A | Jan 27 1852 | 11/209 |
| Jones, Sarah Ann | Stackhouse, William D | Jul 10 1848* | 8/314 |
| Jones, Simon | Everett, Margaret A | Apr 23 1847 | 8/229 |
| Jones, Willei | Baxter, Levine | May 19 1823* | 1/4 |
| Jones, William | Fagan, Bridget | 1837* | OIB |
| Jones, William | Baxter, Harriette | May 28 1839* | 3/174 |
| Jones, William | White, Rebecca | Jan 13 1836* | 3/35 |
| Jones, William | Carr, Bridget | May 5 1838* | 3/123 |
| Jones, William | Ivers, Mary A | Sep 16 1851 | 11/179 |
| Jones, William | Scarborough, Julia A | Nov 24 1851 | 11/189 |
| Jones, William | McElroy, Catharine | Nov 13 1847 | 8/264 |
| Jones, William | Estahooks, Mary J | Dec 22 1855 | 14/311 |
| Jones, William B | Bryan, Mary Louisa | May 21 1853 | 12/270 |
| Jones, William H | Dalton, Margaret | Nov 23 1833* | 2/691 |
| Jones, Willis | Collins, Nancy | Feb 24 1829 | 2/72 |
| Jordan, Elizabeth | Pelham, Jepthy V | Mar 22 1847 | 8/222 |
| Jordan, Isaac S | Cavendish, Rebecca | Jul 5 1836* | 3/52 |
| Jordan, Mary | Cain, Thomas | Mar 17 1845 | 8/79B |
| Jordan, Mary | Duffy, John | May 11 1846 | 8/165B |
| Jordan, Mary I | Goff, John S | Nov 22 1842 | 5/228B |
| Jordan, Thomas G | Lewis, Eliza | Nov 17 1836* | 3/62 |
| Jordan, William | Leach, Catharine | May 3 1843 | 5/267B |
| Jordan, William E | Herley, Mary | Aug 27 1855 | 14/218 |
| Jordon, Samuel T | Summerland, Matilda | Jul 16 1842 | 5/211B |
| Jorette, John | Thompson, Margarett | Sep 22 1840* | 5/47 |
| Joseph, Anthony | Thompson, Elizabeth | Mar 29 1844 | 8/8B |
| Joseph, Casene | Johnson, Maria | Nov 1 1849 | 11/12 |
| Joseph, Clomint B | Roby, Elodir | May 29 1839* | 3/175 |

| BRIDE OR GROOM | SPOUSE | DATE | BOOK/PAGE |
|---|---|---|---|
| Joseph, Felicianna | Vis, Bornard | Mar 31 1829* | 2/80 |
| Joseph, Thomas | Riley, Sarah Ann | Feb 8 1844 | 5/320B |
| Josh, Lewis Prosper | Anderson, Mary Jane | Mar 22 1843 | 5/255 |
| Joullain, Louise | Sossaman, Augustus A | Jan 26 1848 | 8/279 |
| Jourdan, Cassy A | O'Neal, Little B | Apr 1 1833* | 2/1051 |
| Jourdan, Edward | Pendegrast, Sophie | Dec 29 1836* | 3/67 |
| Journie, Josephine | Rusearl, Francois | Aug 13 1840 | 5/41 |
| Journy, Marie | Metrand, Pierre | Dec 3 1841* | 5/159B |
| Joyce, Mary | Folin, Thomas | Apr 14 1845 | 8/86B |
| Joyet, Venor | Nicholas, John P | Jun 27 1829 | 2/89 |
| Joyne, Henry L (Jayne) | Newbold, Mary I | May 5 1840* | 5/22 |
| Judah, Eugenia | Young, Thomas H | Dec 2 1845 | 8/127B |
| Jude, Alexander J | George, Mary F | Apr 6 1842* | 5/191B |
| Jude, Mary Frances | Provost, William J | Feb 13 1845 | 8/73B |
| Juden, Eliza Susan | Bastock, James B | Apr 2 1846 | 8/154B |
| Judice, Marie M | Dore, Adrien | Apr 12 1853 | 12/237 |
| Judge, Anthony | Sullivan, Julia | Oct 22 1850 | 11/91 |
| Judge, William | Goldridge, Ann | Dec 28 1850 | 11/107 |
| Judson, Catherine Susan | Hallett, William R | Nov 11 1824 | 1/46 |
| Judson, Lewis | Thorn, Mary | 1826* | OIB |
| Jujean, Romane (Juzan) | Andry, Alexandrine | Aug 10 1852 | 11/275 |
| Jule, Josephine | Lefort, Louis | Oct 16 1844 | 8/43B |
| Julian, Charles A | Goodrich, Margaret V | Nov 9 1852 | 12/55 |
| Julian, Drusilla | Frisby, William | Sep 11 1848 | 8/324 |
| Julian, Josephine C | Grove, John | Nov 29 1842* | 5/230B |
| Julien, Caroline C | Sossaman, Blount | Dec 9 1851* | 11/193 |
| Junelot, Julius | Henry, Martha N | Oct 10 1855 | 14/251 |
| Jungfermann, Clara | Scheppen, August H | Aug 18 1853 | 12/386 |
| Jusan, Mary M | Chastang, Sidoine J | Jan 15 1846 | 8/141B |
| Justice, Ann | Brown, Patrick | Dec 6 1844 | 8/56B |
| Justine, Calmi | Roundell, Joseph | Jan 25 1844* | 5/318B |
| Justis, Noah | Desmukes, Lucinda | May 28 1847 | 8/238 |
| Juzan, Adele | Opeinheimer, C | Jan 19 1831* | 2/147 |
| Juzan, Arminth | Toulmin, Theoph L | May 13 1821* | CM |
| Juzan, Daniel | Chastang, Margarete | May 20 1813* | WB 1/7 |
| Juzan, Delphine | Chastang, Fostin | Aug 14 1848* | 8/320 |
| Juzan, Elizabeth | Chouifse, Ellis | May 4 1854 | 13/216 |
| Juzan, Harriett | Cooper, Sitter J B | Oct 9 1838* | 3/143 |
| Juzan, John Baptiste | Chastang, Gertrude | May 18 1829 | 2/86 |
| Juzan, Louisa | Gunnison, Henry | May 14 1825 | 1/77 |
| Juzan, Mary M | Chastang, Sidione J | Jan 15 1846 | 8/141B |
| Juzan, Romane | Andry, Alexandrine | Aug 10 1852 | 11/275 |
| Juzan, Thomas | Chastang, Salia (Julia) | Jun 29 1843 | 5/284 |
| Juzan, William B (Inson) | Rogers, Rebecca | Feb 23 1832* | 2/1701 |

## K

| | | | |
|---|---|---|---|
| Kahn, Bertha | Frank, Lewis | Jun 8 1852* | 11/260 |
| Kaho, James (Kehoe) | Simmons, Mary | Jun 12 1823* | 1/7 |
| Kaigler, Eliza | Slappey, John G | Nov 13 1850 | 11/97 |
| Kail, Sarah | Lambert, William | Dec 11 1854 | 13/410 |

| BRIDE OR GROOM | SPOUSE | DATE | BOOK/PAGE |
|---|---|---|---|
| Kain, Daniel | Doyle, Ellen | May 17 1851 | 11/150 |
| Kain, Julia, | Kain, Patrick | Apr 30 1851 | 11/142 |
| Kain, Patrick | Kain, Julia | Apr 30 1851 | 11/142 |
| Kain, William | Finley, Mary | Jan 31 1849* | 8/352 |
| Kaine, Mary | Burke, John | Apr 2 1853 | 12/215 |
| Kainnary, John | O'Donald, Rosa | Jan 24 1845 | 8/68B |
| Kallinger, Mary | Currier, Charles H | Jan 11 1851 | 11/111 |
| Kanada, Judy | McNamara, Stephen | Nov 20 1851 | 11/187 |
| Kane, Margaret | Henry, Thomas | Feb 10 1842 | 5/179B |
| Kane, Patrick | McCormick, Mary | Jan 28 1843* | 5/245B |
| Kane, Thomas | Faggard, Catharine J | May 30 1850 | 11/64 |
| Kane, William | Reid, Jane (June) | Jul 1 1843 | 5/285B |
| Kanedy, William (Kennedy) | Alexander, Frosine | May 29 1841* | 5/133B |
| Kank, Emiline ? | Herman, Henry | Mar 30 1840* | 3/196 |
| Karnar, Mary | Capmann, Stephen | Mar 18 1852 | 11/227 |
| Karney, Mary | Kastler, Antonio | Dec 1 1855 | 14/294 |
| Kary, Ann S (Skary) | Hoay, William ? | Dec 29 1842 | 5/239B |
| Kastler, Antonio | Karney, Mary | Dec 1 1855 | 14/294 |
| Katon, Ellen | Moriaty, Donald | Jan 18 1853 | 12/138 |
| Kauch, Catherine | Hausler, Charles | Dec 9 1854 | 13/408 |
| Kaufman, Elizabeth | Peres, Stephen | Feb 3 1855 | 14/35 |
| Kaufman, Joseph | Britling, Magdelina | Jul 29 1847 | 8/248 |
| Kavanagh, Margaret | Malone, John | Feb 5 1855 | 14/36 |
| Kavanagh, Thomas | McDonald, Mary | Feb 19 1851 | 11/122 |
| Kavannah, Julia (Rosanah) | Gustus, Henry (Gutus) | Jan 20 1844 | 5316B |
| Kavauagh, Thomas (Kavanagh) | McDonald, Mary | Feb 19 1851 | 11/122 |
| Kayser, Henry | Bernstein, Caroline | Jan 31 1853* | 12/158 |
| Kean, Martin | Martin, Margaret | Apr 1 1839 | 3/163 |
| Keane, William | O'Brien, Catharine | Aug 18 1848* | 8/321 |
| Kearns, Elizabeth | Finnegan, Thomas | Jan 11 1855 | 14/14 |
| Kearns, John | Leonard, Ellen | Jun 19 1855 | 14/175 |
| Kearns, Mary | O'Neal, Christopher | Jan 27 1851 | 11/117 |
| Kearns, Owen | O'Connor, Ellen | Feb 24 1851 | 11/124 |
| Keates, Mary Jane | King, Franklin W | May 15 1849 | 8/376 |
| Keates, Thomas S | Song, Mary Jane | Jul 11 1846 | 8/177 |
| Keating, Nicholas | McCormick, Bridget | Feb 8 1842 | 5/178B |
| Kedwell, Robert C | Grasham, Penine | Jul 5 1824 | 1/35 |
| Keef, John | Crawley, Catherine | Mar 25 1846 | 8/154B |
| Keefe, William | Kelly, Catharine | Feb 26 1848* | 8/287 |
| Keeland, Ellen | McKinna, James | May 4 1838* | 3/123 |
| Keeland, Sarah | Cuillin, George (Quillen) | Apr 15 1854 | 13/185 |
| Keeland, William | Roman, Mary S | Oct 21 1851 | 11/183 |
| Keeley, Nancy | Allen, William | Jun 21 1855 | 14/183 |
| Keeling, William H | Hatfield, Eliza Ann | Jun 14 1845 | 8/103B |
| Keely, Elizabeth | Hutchison, Boliver | Jul 17 1851 | 11/166 |
| Keen, Catherine | Byrnes, Michael | Dec 2 1835* | 3/32 |
| Keenan, Francis | Jarvis, Margaret | Feb 11 1854 | 13/120 |
| Keenan, Michael J | Foote, Lydia E | Nov 2 1848 | 8/331 |
| Keevan, A. H. | Holcombe, Bettie L | May 29 1850 | 11/63 |
| Keevan, John | Noland, Mary Ann | Jul 26 1851 | 11/170 |
| Kehler, Helena | Soger, John | Mar 9 1848* | 8/291 |
| Kehler, Terresa | Adolph, Henry | Feb 15 1849* | 8/357 |
| Keho, Catharine | Conlin, Peter | Apr 20 1847* | 8/228 |
| Keho, Catherine | Donahue, Dennis | Dec 20 1852 | 12/100 |
| Keho, James | Fox, Catherine | 1827* | OIB |
| Keho, John | Williams, Mary Ann | Jan 25 1825 | 1/61 |
| Keho, Mary Ann | Rumsay, Joseph | 1826* | OIB |
| Keily, Jeremiah | Foley, Julia | Jul 10 1852 | 11/269 |
| Keith, Henry C L | LaPorte, Sarah E | Mar 29 1852 | 11/231 |
| Keith, Mary (Krish) | Clair, John | Nov 2 1849* | 11/13 |
| Keitty, Mary (Keilty) | Hawks, William | Mar 28 1851 | 11/131 |
| Kelley, Amanda | Witpen, Dederick (Withen) | May 19 1846 | 8/167B |
| Kelley, Catherine | Gonzalas, Francis | Aug 12 1847* | 8/251 |
| Kellog, Theron | Beeber, Eliza (Beebe) | Dec 25 1815* | CM |

| BRIDE OR GROOM | SPOUSE | DATE | BOOK/PAGE |
|---|---|---|---|
| Kellog, Theron | Killiher, Margaret | Feb 17 1819* | CM |
| Kellogg, Margaret | Dickens, Alonzo | Jul 28 1825 | 1/87 |
| Kellogg, Mary Ellen | Crocker, Henry A. | Jul 11 1840* | 5/35B |
| Kelly, Ann | Barry, John | Jan 20 1844* | 5/318B |
| Kelly, Ann | McGlinn, John | Jun 9 1844 | 8/27B |
| Kelly, Anne | Reid, John | Feb 21 1837* | 3/73 |
| Kelly, Bridget | Farley, Patrick | Jun 9 1851 | 11/157 |
| Kelly, Bridget | McDermott, Joseph | May 29 1843 | 5/276B |
| Kelly, Catharine | Keefe, William | Feb 26 1848* | 8/287 |
| Kelly, Catherine | Platt, Peter | Jun 1 1852 | 11/258 |
| Kelly, Charles | Daley, Hanoughe | Jun 4 1838* | 3/130 |
| Kelly, Christopher | Brennan, Ann | Feb 1 1854 | 13/106 |
| Kelly, Daniel | Smith, Ann | Jun 3 1844 | 8/24B |
| Kelly, Delice | Forsyth, F. D. | Apr 10 1852* | 11/234 |
| Kelly, Eliza | Burh, Patrick (Burk) | May 23 1855 | 14/149 |
| Kelly, Ellen | Myrick, James H | Dec 2 1845 | 8/127B |
| Kelly, Ellen C | O'Hara, John | Apr 28 1855 | 14/123 |
| Kelly, Jane | Maynes, James (Magnes) | Dec 3 1842 | 5/231B |
| Kelly, James | Foye, Eliza | Jun 17 1853 | 12/321 |
| Kelly, James | Martin, Margaret | Jun 22 1854 | 13/242 |
| Kelly, John | Myrick, Ellen | Nov 2 1850 | 11/94 |
| Kelly, John | Doran, Hanora | Jun 30 1852 | 11/268 |
| Kelly, John | George, Catherine | May 12 1845 | 8/94B |
| Kelly, John | Devenie, Margaret | Jul 7 1855 | 14/191 |
| Kelly, John | Glennen, Catherine | May 19 1853 | 12/291 |
| Kelly, Joseph | Burns, Alice | Jan 19 1850 | 11/34 |
| Kelly, Margaret | Phelan, Jeremiah | Feb 5 1853 | 12/165 |
| Kelly, Martha J | Freeman, Samuel T | Dec 13 1853 | 13/39 |
| Kelly, Mary | Cunningham, James | Aug 7 1823 | 1/10 |
| Kelly, Mary | Artegus, Valentine | Mar 25 1845 | 8/82B |
| Kelly, Michael | Doyle, Mary | Jul 14 1851 | 11/165 |
| Kelly, Michael | Dowd, Winney | Sep 13 1852 | 12/2 |
| Kelly, Nancy | Stringer, Larry | Jan 14 1853 | 12/131 |
| Kelly, Patrick | Howe, Bridget | Jul 13 1852 | 11/269 |
| Kelly, Patrick | Swift, Mary | Apr 15 1854 | 13/183 |
| Kelly, Peter | Caffie, Alice ? | Feb 24 1846 | 8/147B |
| Kelly, Sophia | Heyer, Cornelius | Oct 22 1850 | 11/92 |
| Kelly, Thomas | Swift, Ann | Aug 18 1853 | 12/384 |
| Kelly, Thomas S | Costella, Mary Ann | Apr 11 1842 | 5/191B |
| Kelsen, Mathew | Roh, Frederika | Jan 4 1853 | 12/111 |
| Kelsen, Mathias | Roh, Pauline | Mar 19 1855 | 14/86 |
| Kelsey, Edmund | Elliott, Susan A | Oct 5 1854 | 13/347 |
| Kelsey, George | Jones, Ann | May 11 1844 | 8/20B |
| Kelso, George | Erwin, Elizabeth | May 9 1845* | 8/93B |
| Kelson, Elizabeth | Pierce, Charles L | Apr 10 1855 | 14/102 |
| Kemble, Aaron A | Harmon, Sarah J | Dec 28 1836* | 3/67 |
| Kemmer, Johanna C H | Trachy, Edward | Apr 5 1852 | 11/232 |
| Kemmer, Rebecca A. C. | Peters, John C | May 2 1846 | 8/162B |
| Kempe, Thomas B | Bowen, Margaret P | Apr 9 1849* | 8/366 |
| Kemper, Robert | Gallagher, Elizabeth | Jan 22 1844 | 5/316B |
| Kenann, M | Quinn, Ann | Apr 19 1838* | 3/120 |
| Kendall, Elizabeth (Mrs) | Bennett, James H | Aug 12 1843 | 5/292B |
| Kendall, Lyman R | George, Mary E (Mrs) | Jun 24 1842 | 5/208B |
| Kener, Fransna (Kiener) | Britton, Harriett E | Oct 11 1843* | 5/299B |
| Kenley, Eureka | Phifer, John | May 22 1850 | 11/63 |
| Kennedy, Alfred B | Malone, Susanna E | Jul 26 1853 | 12/369 |
| Kennedy, Augusta | Bloodgood, M Hildreth | Feb 15 1853 | 12/172 |
| Kennedy, Bernard | Cronin, Catherine | Feb 22 1841* | 5/106B |
| Kennedy, Catherine | Morgan, Charles | Feb 11 1850 | 11/39 |
| Kennedy, Catherine | Malone, Thomas A | Dec 11 1854 | 13/409 |
| Kennedy, Clarissa A | Aikin, John G | Jun 4 1844* | 8/25B |
| Kennedy, Delphine E | Hall, Daniel E | Jan 13 1840* | 5/7 |
| Kennedy, Ellen | Donahoe, Patrick | Feb 22 1854 | 13/132 |
| Kennedy, Euphrozine | Chastang, Augustus | Jan 12 1854 | 13/762 |

| BRIDE OR GROOM | SPOUSE | DATE | BOOK/PAGE |
|---|---|---|---|
| Kennedy, Glorvina A | Walker, Robert L | Nov 10 1833* | 2/731 |
| Kennedy, James | Soto, Merced | Mar 3 1851 | 11/127 |
| Kennedy, John | Seymour, Sarah | Apr 13 1850 | 11/53 |
| Kennedy, John | Barker, Edy | Apr 20 1839* | 3/168 |
| Kennedy, John | Lambert, Nancy | Dec 29 1840* | 5/83B |
| Kennedy, John | Roberts, S. A. | Sep 10 1838* | 3/141 |
| Kennedy, John | Turnbit, Nancy (Lambert) | Dec 29 1841 | 4/1181 |
| Kennedy, Joshua | Kitchens, Susan | Dec 15 1818* | CM |
| Kennedy, Joshua | Emanuel, Mary | Mar 17 1853 | 12/195 |
| Kennedy, Margaret | Peterson, Nicholas | Nov 26 1844 | 8/54B |
| Kennedy, Margaret E | Conner, David S | Mar 2 1849 | 8/359 |
| Kennedy, Martha M | Mather, Francis W | Jan 3 1855 | 13/434 |
| Kennedy, Mary E | Meslier, Augustus R | Apr 23 1842 | 5/193 |
| Kennedy, Mary Louisa | Carter, Jesse | May 28 1835 | 3/16 |
| Kennedy, Michael | Hays, Honorough | Nov 16 1844 | 8/51B |
| Kennedy, Michael | Welsh, Joanna | Jan 29 1853 | 12/155 |
| Kennedy, Patrick | Barford, Belinda | May 21 1852 | 11/253 |
| Kennedy, Secluza | Hastie, Hamilton | Jun 10 1839* | 3/178 |
| Kenney, Lawrence R | Coffey, Sarah | Apr 23 1836* | 3/45 |
| Kenny, James | Curity, Mary F (Flarity) | Jan 8 1845 | 8/66B |
| Kensella, Rosanna | Masterson, James | Dec 26 1837* | 3/105 |
| Kenzie, Roderick (McKenzie) | Mooney, Catherine | Jun 25 1838* | 3/133 |
| Keohl, Franz | Kienle, Sophia | Jan 13 1854 | 13/77 |
| Kepliager, Samuel | Parsmon, Elizabeth | Apr 24 1838* | 3/120 |
| Kepner, Daniel | Paul, Alafare | Dec 16 1851 | 11/195 |
| Kerger, Frederick | Mugel, Epher | May 3 1850 | 11/59 |
| Kern, Amelia | Gretzner, Julius | May 3 1855 | 14/128 |
| Kern, Christian | Schule, Albertina | May 31 1853 | 12/305 |
| Kernan, Edward (widr) | Griffin, Eliza (wid) | Nov 24 1853 | 13/27 |
| Kerns, David | Armstrong, Mary | Aug 31 1849 | 11/1 |
| Kerns, John | McNulty, Catherine | May 31 1852* | 11/257 |
| Kerr, Henry M | Lee, Rebecca E | Feb 25 1849* | 3/10 |
| Kerr, Victor | Mitchell, Felecia | Jan 1 1849 | 8/343 |
| Kerry, Helena S | Smith, William T | Jul 25 1848* | 8/318 |
| Kestlen, Madaline | Chevalier, Julien | Nov 24 1849 | 11/18 |
| Ketchum, Charles T | Ewing, Eliza A W | Jul 5 1843 | 5/286B |
| Ketchum, William H | Easton, Sarah E | Dec 5 1848* | 8/337 |
| Key, David S | Gero, Mary Ann (Gerow) | Jul 21 1852* | 11/271 |
| Keyland, Mary Jane | Porter, James | Nov 2 1849 | 11/13 |
| Keys, J R | Thompson, Elizabeth H | Jan 15 1841* | 5/89B |
| Keyser, Louisa K | Cato, Philip H | Mar 21 1854 | 13/165 |
| Kianezler, Catherine | Martin, Francis | May 19 1855 | 14/143 |
| Kibbe, Gaines | Demott, Margaret | Sep 12 1844* | 8/40B |
| Kibbe, Margaret F | Dubose, Malachi | Jan 31 1837* | 3/71 |
| Kibler, Christian | Deckmere, Louisa | Jun 14 1841* | 5/135 |
| Kidd, Charity | Miller, Louis | Aug 22 1853 | 12/391 |
| Kidd, James N | Lonton, Julia A | Dec 19 1854 | 13/415 |
| Kidd, Martha J | Cauley, Purtsman | Apr 11 1853 | 12/243 |
| Kidd, Oliver J | Helverson, Sarah | Aug 7 1855 | 14/205 |
| Kidney, John | Wilson, Margaret | Jul 31 1832 | 2/1381 |
| Kiebler, Christian | Dickinson, Louisa | Jun 4 1841 | 4/1861B |
| Kiegan, Catharien | Morgan, John S | Jul 6 1849* | 8/386 |
| Kiencke, Earnest C | Ramseger, Julia A | Nov 6 1849* | 11/13 |
| Kiende, Marie | Gseller, Julius (Geller) | Apr 23 1853 | 12/252 |
| Kienle, Charlotte | Mayer, John | Dec 24 1849 | 11/28 |
| Kienle, Sophia | Keohl, Franz | Jan 13 1854 | 13/77 |
| Kienle, Wilhelmiene | Flock, James B | May 18 1853 | 12/289 |
| Kifer, Mary A | Wilson, George F | Oct 17 1855 | 14/253 |
| Kilaher, Ellen | Cokeley, Patrick | 1837* | OIB |
| Kilbery, Peter A ? | Kurr, Louisa | Jan 2 1834* | 2/591 |
| Kilduff, Hannah D | Mulvee, Anthony | Jan 17 1853 | 12/136 |
| Kilduff, Mary | Norton, Hubert | Sep 7 1854 | 13/333 |
| Kilfir, Sarah ? | Smith, N. Henry | Oct 21 1850 | 11/91 |
| Killcrease, Patsey | Hatcher, John | Oct 1 1813* | WB 1/9 |

| BRIDE OR GROOM | SPOUSE | DATE | BOOK/PAGE |
|---|---|---|---|
| Killigan, Thomas | Higgins, Ellen | Jul 23 1850 | 11/74 |
| Killiher, Margaret | Kellog, Theron | Feb 17 1819* | CM |
| Killy, Antonio S | Demten, C | Mar 14 1851 | 11/129 |
| Kimball, Cornelia A | Boullemet, Augustus | Dec 18 1854 | 13/413 |
| Kimball, Emma Pauline | Stute, Benjamin (Steele) | Sep 15 1851 | 11/178 |
| Kimball, Franklin | Riley, Mary C | Apr 10 1855 | 14/100 |
| Kimball, Franklin G | Holder, Ann M | Feb 22 1830* | 2/113 |
| Kimball, Martha Ann | St John, Richard Jr | May 4 1840 | 5/21 |
| Kimberly, Ophelia G | Sayne, E Sanford | Apr 18 1844 | 8/15 |
| Kimbert, Elizabeth ? | Shafer, Jacob | Sep 1 1842* | 5/218B |
| Kincey, Hardy G | Lambert, Sarah O | Oct 13 1849 | 11/9 |
| Kindall, Lyman R | George, Mary E (Mrs) | Jun 24 1842 | 5/208 |
| Kindall, Elizabeth (Mrs) | Bennett, James W | Aug 12 1843 | 5/292 |
| Kinfield, Nicholas | Flynn, Maria | Jun 18 1847 | 8/242 |
| King, Alexander K | David, Elizabeth | Jan 6 1834* | 2/571 |
| King, Cyrus | Henderson, Eliza | Mar 17 1838* | 3/116 |
| King, Daniel | Rouse, Mary E | May 23 1843 | 5/275B |
| King, Ellen | Bermen, Christian (Buman) | Jan 3 1843 | 5/240B |
| King, Franklin W | Keates, Mary Jane | May 15 1849 | 8/376 |
| King, George F | Bowen, Aribella | Dec 1 1853 | 13/32 |
| King, Isabella | Emanuel, Jonathan | Mar 26 1832* | 2/1611 |
| King, James | Hall, Sarah | Nov 13 1832* | 2/1311 |
| King, James M | Quinn, Mary | Aug 31 1852 | 11/281 |
| King, Joseph G | Ethridge, Ellen | Jan 11 1854 | 13/73 |
| King, Martha | Rider, Charles | Nov 9 1850 | 11/96 |
| King, Mary | Parker, George | Sep 4 1835 | 3/27 |
| King, Mary Ann | Young, Charles | Jan 16 1849* | 8/347 |
| King, Poet | McClarey, Lucy | Dec 14 1847* | 8/270 |
| King, Richard J | Hart, Isabella E | Jan 15 1848* | 8/278 |
| King, Rosannah | Cato, Phillip | Nov 22 1821* | CM |
| King, Sarah A | McGuire, John | Apr 4 1840* | 5/16 |
| King, Thomas | Welsh, Jane | May 26 1848* | 8/306 |
| King, Thomas | Malone, Eliza T | Jul 30 1845 | 8/113B |
| Kinneir, Georgiana B | Dikeman, Burr | Jan 25 1843 | 5/245B |
| Kinners, Charlotte A W | Bacon, John D | Jul 2 1841* | 5/141 |
| Kinney, Ann | McGinnis, Daniel | Feb 17 1855 | 14/57 |
| Kinney, Ellen | Caldwell, Cyrus | Jun 4 1836* | 3/49 |
| Kinney, Hanora | Molloy, John | Apr 11 1855 | 14/105 |
| Kinney, Henderson | George, Nancy | Nov 12 1833* | 2/721 |
| Kinney, Richard | Casey, Mary | Aug 6 1853 | 12/376 |
| Kinsey, Mary | Wilson, John | Apr 8 1851 | 11/135 |
| Kinsler, Catharine | Neill, James | May 24 1849* | 8/378 |
| Kirby, David R | Maryhour, Adrina (Mangham) | Feb 15 1853 | 12/173 |
| Kirby, Jared E | Holt, Caroline E | Dec 6 1854 | 13/402 |
| Kirby, Mary (Kelly) | Artegus, Valentine | Mar 25 1845* | 8/82B |
| Kirby, Richard | Turnstall, Phoebe | May 11 1843 | 5/270B |
| Kirk, Adelia Maria | Blissfellows, James | Dec 31 1851* | 11/200 |
| Kirk, George S | Backus, Eliza E | Sep 24 1855 | 14/240 |
| Kirkbride, Jonathan | Baptist, Elizabeth | Dec 18 1844 | 8/60B |
| Kirkland, Isaac W | Roulston, Rebecca | Oct 23 1848* | 8/329 |
| Kirkland, Sarah | McShapick, James | Jan 25 1838* | 3/109 |
| Kirkwood, Margaret | Philibert, Tolisfon | Oct 18 1845 | 8/120B |
| Kistler, Magdalina | Breinkenin, Charles | Apr 29 1848 | 8/302 |
| Kitchen, Susan | Kennedy, Joshua | Dec 15 1818* | CM |
| Klamon, Barbary | Allenback, Jacob | Apr 1 1852 | 11/232 |
| Kleinschrodt, George | Lattimer, Elizabeth | Aug 25 1849 | 11/1 |
| Klien, Louisa | Urtman, Philip | Feb 12 1852 | 11/217 |
| Kline, Francis | Schidal, Helena | Nov 30 1850 | 11/100 |
| Kline, Kitty | Dias, John | Apr 29 1814* | CM |
| Knaggs, Martha | McDonald, John | Mar 8 1845 | 8/78B |
| Knaggs, Martha C | Anderson, Isaac A | Sep 3 1847 | 8/254 |
| Knaggs, Thomas | Hamblett, Martha | Nov 5 1840* | 5/61B |
| Knapp, Chester P | Foster, Sarah Ann | Jun 24 1842* | 5/208B |
| Knapp, Jacob Jr (Kapp) | Kuhner, Margaret | Nov 7 1836* | 3/61 |

| BRIDE OR GROOM | SPOUSE | DATE | BOOK/PAGE |
|---|---|---|---|
| Knauf, Katarina | Schreiber, Frederick | Feb 20 1855* | 14/63 |
| Knauf, Sophia | Poetz, Andrew | Nov 22 1852 | 12/68 |
| Knight, Hugh | Peters, Caroline | Apr 20 1846 | 8/159B |
| Knight, Reuben H | Locke, Mary A | Nov 23 1855 | 14/287 |
| Knight, William | Stringer, Frances | Jan 19 1837* | 3/70 |
| Knoblock, Frederick | Winterhalter, Perpetua | May 2 1837* | 3/82 |
| Knowland, Honore | Gevey, Stephen (Geary) | Sep 9 1828* | 2/40 |
| Knox, Eliza | Wright, William | Jan 16 1850* | 11/33 |
| Kobeloth, Marie M | Morasini, Napoleon | Dec 19 1846 | 8/206 |
| Kockler, Phillip | Weber, Mary | Feb 12 1851 | 11/120 |
| Koger, Thomas J | Elder, Sarah Jane | Feb 25 1850 | 11/42 |
| Kohl, Charles | Jenkins, Sarah Jane | Mar 17 1835* | 3/11 |
| Kohler, George | Mugel, Margareta | Dec 12 1832* | 2/1271 |
| Kohler, Mary E | Ingermon, Valentine | Aug 9 1842* | 5/214B |
| Kokler, Teresa | Adolph, Henry | Feb 15 1849* | 8/357 |
| Kornegan, Hester | Carmichael, Daniel | Dec 12 1855 | 14/303 |
| Korner, Margaretta | Tobler, Paul | Dec 18 1832* | 2/1251 |
| Kortjohn, John | Pullen, Calrine E | May 5 1838* | 3/123 |
| Kosmensky, Abraham | Stein, Catherine | Jul 26 1855 | 14/199 |
| Koster, Regina | Neef, John | Jan 4 1851 | 11/109 |
| Kraiger, Gustavies | Waggoner, Doras | Feb 18 1850 | 11/40 |
| Kral, Catharine | Haigal, Jacob | Feb 25 1848 | 8/286 |
| Kraus, George | Huber, Mary | Mar 9 1841* | 5/114B |
| Krebs, Bazile | Dupont, Caterine | Sep 8 1818* | CM |
| Krebs, Corrienne | Humphries, Henry G | Jul 15 1850* | 11/73 |
| Krebs, Hippolite | Ellison, Thomas | May 10 1841* | 5/129B |
| Krebs, Joseph | Hendinburg,Eleanor (wid) | Jan 12 1816* | CM |
| Krebs, Joseph | Trouilet, Marceline | 1826* | OIB |
| Kreps, Genevieve | Hindemberg, Antonio | May 23 1815* | CM |
| Krohnut, John Frederick | Herterick, Amelia | Feb 28 1839* | 3/159 |
| Kroner, Margaretta | Tobler, Paul | Dec 18 1832* | 2/1251 |
| Krums, Catherine | Nelson, Charles | Dec 8 1846 | 8/203 |
| Kruse, Anna | Glotzengel, Christian | Sep 1 1855 | 14/223 |
| Kruse, John Henry | Harmeyer, Mary C | Sep 8 1846 | 8/187 |
| Kuhna, John | Horoman, Louisa | Feb 25 1850 | 11/43 |
| Kuhner, Margaret (Kincher) | Knapp, Jacob Jr | Nov 7 1836* | 3/61 |
| Kuhns, August Wilhelm | Steinbeck, Sophie | Jul 28 1851 | 11/170 |
| Kulan, Eliza Ann | Ferguson, Edward | Nov 11 1844 | 8/48B |
| Kull, William | Haregal, Henrietta | Oct 18 1855* | 14/254 |
| Kumpfmiller, August | Weinscheuk, Cath. | Jul 31 1846 | 8/182 |
| Kurr, Louisa | Kilberry, Peter A | Jan 2 1834* | 2/591 |
| Kurt, Pierce | Cotter, Julia | Aug 21 1852 | 11/278 |
| Kuth, Patience | O'Connor, Michael | May 14 1839* | 3/171 |
| Kyle, Catherine Ann | Grandpre, Alexander | Jun 11 1851* | 11/157 |
| Kylie, Lewis | Lebenstein, Lische | Mar 13 1852* | 11/226 |

L

| | | | |
|---|---|---|---|
| Labarthe, Louisa D | Hardie, Charles L | Dec 12 1849 | 11/25 |
| Labatt, Mirriam H | Smith, John B | Sep 1 1846 | 8/187 |
| Labernadie, John (Widr) | Traicy, Anne (wid) | Nov 17 1853 | 13/16 |
| Labidir, Marlezette | Brown, Watler C | May 29 1839* | 3/175 |

| BRIDE OR GROOM | SPOUSE | DATE | BOOK/PAGE |
|---|---|---|---|
| Labonnell, Charles | Carter, Jane | Dec 11 1843 | 5/309 |
| Labove, Rosa | Landry, Alexandre D | Jun 28 1854 | 13/267 |
| Labryan, Sarah M (Labuzan) | MacLean, Andrew C | Sep 23 1850* | 22/87 |
| Labuzan, Sarah M | MacLean, Andrew C | Dec 23 1850 | 11/87 |
| Labuzan, Louisa V | MacLean, Robert | Dec 15 1847 | 8/271 |
| Labuze, John A | Dempsey, Caroline L | Apr 19 1828 | 2/11 |
| Lacane, Leontine | Montiel, John Emile | May 8 1841* | 5/129B |
| Lacost, Mathilda (Saroste) | Mechon, Peter T | Oct 3 1840 | 5/51B |
| Lacoste, A | Simmons, Elijah | Jan 11 1844 | 5/314B |
| Lacoste, Augustin | Hartley, Elizabeth | Jul 19 1818* | CM |
| Lacoste, Benjamin | Gilchrist, Mary L | Feb 23 1830* | 2/114 |
| Lacoste, Claudine | Roberts, Seth W | May 10 1847 | 8/234 |
| Lacoste, Corinne | Barlow, Robert Z | Jul 21 1851 | 11/168 |
| Lacoste, Cyrus | Collins, Susan | Nov 6 1849 | 11/14 |
| Lacoste, Elizabeth | Bailey, John | Jun 17 1845 | 8/104B |
| Lacoste, Eulalu Hortense | Rance, Henry Gaspard | Feb 3 1841* | 5/99B |
| Lacoste, Irene C | Tipton, William B | Nov 19 1853 | 13/17 |
| Lacoste, John | Morris, Ann | Jun 14 1843* | 5/28B |
| Lacoste, Louisa | Hicks, John W | Feb 1 1837* | 3/71 |
| Lacoste, Nicholas | Goff, Saraphiney | Feb 16 1848 | 8/283 |
| Lacroise, John Batiste | Hian, Sophia Catherine | 1822* | OIB |
| Lacy, Martha E | Shockley, Theodore W | Jul 20 1855 | 14/196 |
| Ladanair, Clarisa (Clara) | Bozans, Lamas (Bosarge) | Aug 12 1841 | 5/147B |
| Ladanar, John B (Ladnier) | Lome, Dolarate (Lami) | Oct 20 1828* | 2/47 |
| Ladel, Amelia | Zaph, Charles | Feb 12 1849* | 8/355 |
| Ladenere, Virgine | Grelote, Jean Batiste | 1836* | OIB |
| Ladenier, Adele | Ladenier, John | Apr 27 1854 | 13/207 |
| Ladenier, John | Ladenier, Adele | Apr 27 1854 | 13/207 |
| Ladenres, Teatist (Baptist) | Gurlott, Sifroy | Aug 23 1830* | 2/134 |
| Ladinier, Emanuel | Bozage, Louise | Jan 24 1853* | 12/142 |
| Ladnear, Caroline | Gurlote, Joseph | Feb 17 1824 | 1/21 |
| Ladner, Melissaine | Lamy, Gierre (Pierre) | Dec 19 1824 | 1/53 |
| Ladner, Valery | Roney, Mary | Jun 13 1834* | 2/221 |
| Ladnier, Baptiste | Gurlott, Sifroy | Aug 23 1830* | 2/134 |
| Ladnier, Carmilite | Wallace, Charles | Nov 15 1847 | 8/265 |
| Ladnier, Constant | Lame, Alexander | 1827* | OIB |
| Lafargue, Alexander | Rabby, Mary | Jul 18 1844 | 8/33B |
| Lagomaggiore, Anna E | Winslow, Giovanni | Nov 28 1850 | 11/100 |
| Laguire, Francis | Hamilton, Sarah Jane | Apr 14 1845 | 8/86B |
| Lahie, Mary (Leahy) | McArdle, James | Oct 10 1855 | 14/250 |
| Lahy, Mary (Leahy) | Mulrick, Richard | Feb 4 1852 | 11/213 |
| Laighe, Mary | Sandres, Bat | Jun 13 1853 | 12/318 |
| Laingos, Maria (Launger) | Mohnsamen, Frederick | Feb 23 1843* | 5/250 |
| Lalande, Adolphe | Colin, Victorie | Mar 28 1842 | 5/189B |
| Lalande, Charles Jr | Baudain, Cecile B | Jan 8 1842 | 5/169B |
| Lalande, Mary Ann | Laurendine, Gregoire | Nov 15 1843 | 5/304B |
| Lallemant, Anthony | Stauter, Catherine | Aug 12 1841 | 5/147 |
| Lallhamon, Christ | White, Elizabeth | 1839* | OIB |
| Laluse, Merceill | Bermoody, Babaltite | May 15 1851 | 11/149 |
| Lamar, Teresa | Pericone, Francis | Jul 4 1855 | 14/188 |
| Lamas, Alice Frances | Tappia, Manuel Jose | Mar 2 1848* | 8/288 |
| Lambert, Henry | Reichel, Elizabeth | Jul 8 1854 | 13/277 |
| Lambert, James | Moore, Ellen B | Jan 12 1852* | 11/203 |
| Lambert, James | Moore, Hellen | Jan 26 1853 | 12/145 |
| Lambert, Mary | Davis, William | Dec 4 1835* | 3/32 |
| Lambert, Nancy | Kennedy, John | Dec 29 1840* | 5/83 |
| Lambert, Nancy Ann | Reel, John M | Mar 22 1848 | 8/294 |
| Lambert, Nathaniel | Howard, Nancy | Sep 22 1848 | 8/325 |
| Lambert, Rebecca | Crowell, William | Jan 1 1819* | CM |
| Lambert, Sarah | Reed, John S (L) | Jun 9 1845 | 8/102B |
| Lambert, Sarah C | Kincey, Hardy G | Oct 13 1849 | 11/9 |
| Lambert, Thomas | Irvin, Ann (Irwin) | Oct 24 1843* | 5/301B |
| Lambert, William | Padgett, Nancy | Jan 5 1849* | 8/345 |
| Lambert, William | Kail, Sarah | Dec 11 1854 | 13/410 |

| BRIDE OR GROOM | SPOUSE | DATE | BOOK/PAGE |
|---|---|---|---|
| Lame, Alexander | Ladnier, Constant | 1827* | OIB |
| Lame, Ellen | Sibley, Matthew | 1823* | OIB |
| Lamey, Severine | Davidson, William | Jan 10 1855 | 14/12 |
| Lamock, Rosanna M (Lanock) | Holland, H M | Apr 1 1841 | 5/120B |
| Lamoule, Marie | Portier, Louis | Apr 29 1839* | 3/169 |
| Lamp, John | Schroeder, Mary | Nov 30 1847* | 8/268 |
| La(u)mpford, Rebecca | Walker, John | May 27 1844* | 8/23B |
| Lamphier, William | Johnston, Nancy | Jan 30 1829* | 2/68 |
| Lamy, Gierre (Pierre) | Ladner, Melissaine | Dec 19 1824 | 1/53 |
| Landoz, Mary Ann (Sandoz) | Lopez, Bartoloma | May 8 1832* | 2/1541 |
| Landras, Bartholemew ? | Mussina, Mary ? | May 10 1852* | 11/248 |
| Landrum, James | Ferren, Elizabeth F | Dec 11 1850 | 11/102 |
| Landrum, Solomon | Howard, Elizabeth | Apr 23 1848 | 8/300 |
| Landry, Alexandre D | LaBove, Rosa | Jun 28 1854 | 13/267 |
| Landry, Dorcilly | Broussard, Celie ? | Jan 22 1851 | 11/115 |
| Landry, Felicia | Neperaux, Auguste | Jan 29 1851* | 11/118 |
| Landry, Virgine Gabriel | DeLage, Charles L | May 17 1824 | 1/31 |
| Lane, George | Wheeler, Nancy | Apr 21 1853 | 12/248 |
| Lane, Robert Carr | Dade, Mary S | Apr 8 1819* | CM |
| Lang, Angelina | Boone, George T | Dec 3 1851* | 11/191 |
| Lang, James W | Roux, Emma C | Apr 9 1844* | 8/10B |
| Langdon, Margaret | Buck, William A | Oct 28 1852 | 12/37 |
| Langford, Jane | Pierce, Lewis | Apr 29 1844 | 8/18B |
| Langford, Mary Ann | McInis, Philip | Jan 15 1828* | 2/4 |
| Langford, Stephen | Bird, Polly | 1822* | OIB |
| Langforth, Judith | Byrd, Jesse | 1823* | OIB |
| Langham, Mary | Dailey, Nathaniel | Sep 6 1832 | 2/1351B |
| Langloir, Louise (Langlois) | Abbadie, Bertrand | Oct 29 1853 | 12/428 |
| Langlois, Victor | Lestrade, Cesarine | Dec 22 1855 | 14/312 |
| Langsfield, Jacob H | Folk, Jeddth (Falk) | Apr 19 1843 | 5/262B |
| Laniers, Michael | Stanford, Eliza | Feb 14 1843 | 5/249B |
| Lankforth, Daniel ? | Lott, Vice | Apr 4 1825 | 1/71 |
| Lannigan, Margaret ? | Hart, Thomas | May 3 1841* | 5/128B |
| Lanock, Rosanna M | Holland, H.M. | Apr 1 1841* | 5/120 |
| Lanquet, Elizabeth | Bozage, Denny | Jul 30 1853* | 12/374 |
| Lansdale, Abigail | Van Houten, Cornelius P | Oct 28 1834* | 2/41 |
| Lantree, Mary Ann (Santree) | Cosgrove, Richard | Nov 26 1842 | 5/229B |
| LaPorte, Sarah E | Keith, Henry C | Mar 29 1852 | 11/231 |
| Lappington, Mary A E | Dorgan, Andrew | Jul 1 1851* | 11/161 |
| Lappington, Mary Ann | Davis, Alvan P | Mar 4 1839* | 3/159 |
| LaPre, Peter (Laffre) | Gaz, Fredericka ? | Mar 24 1849* | 8/364 |
| LaQuaite, Jean Baptiste | Ballos, Eugenia (Battes) | Apr 6 1850 | 11/51 |
| Laran, Susan | Robertson, Willis | Feb 23 1835* | 3/9 |
| Lardner, Alphonse | Goleman, Matilda E | Jun 10 1846 | 8/171 |
| Lardiner, Clara | Bozans, Lamas (Bosarge) | Aug 12 1841 | 4/1821 |
| Larkin, Catherine | Mahoney, Patrick | Mar 5 1845 | 8/77B |
| Larkin, James | Fox, Catharine | Jan 6 1846 | 8/137B |
| Larkins, Ann | Butler, William | Jun 1 1855 | 14/156 |
| Larkins, Eliza F | Hall, William | Jun 22 1852* | 11/265B |
| Larkins, Mary C | Rice, James H | Feb 15 1849 | 8/357 |
| Larnard, Samuel ? | Sanford, Julia H | Nov 23 1850* | 11/99 |
| LaRoch, John | Mullin, Mary Ann | Dec 2 1828* | 2/52 |
| LaRoux, Augustus | Schenck, Caroline | Mar 12 1846 | 8/151 |
| Larrey, Malies | Sylas, Joseph (Salas) | Aug 24 1853* | 12/394 |
| LaRue, John C | Mintzer, Margueretta A | May 14 1853 | 12/283 |
| Larx, John B (Lax) | McMillan, Mary C | May 19 1842 | 5/202B |
| LaSalle, Victoria S | LaValle, Philip | Jan 10 1852 | 11/202 |
| Lassabe, Emma | Cain, Jesse T | Dec 2 1841 | 5/160B |
| Lassabe, John R | Caro, Adelia A (Andrea) | Nov 10 1852 | 12/59 |
| Lassabe, Justin | Lassabe, Zoe | Jul 8 1848 | 8/313 |
| Lassabe, Mary Euphemia | Geandreau, William A | Apr 28 1853 | 12/258 |
| Lassabe, Remy (Renny) | Socier, Bazelia (Saucier) | Feb 14 1838* | 3/113 |
| Lassabe, Zoe | Lassabe, Justin | Jul 8 1848 | 8/313 |
| Lassase, Louisa (Lassabe) | Myer, Charles A | Apr 6 1854 | 13/173 |

| BRIDE OR GROOM | SPOUSE | DATE | BOOK/PAGE |
|---|---|---|---|
| Lassinger, Charles | Hallick, Anna | Jun 8 1853 | 12/311 |
| Lasso, John J | McGraw, Anna | Feb 2 1852 | 11/211 |
| LaTorre, Alvarez | Bousses, Camille ? | Jan 2 1850 | 11/30 |
| LaTour, John | Brandein, Margt. N | Feb 7 1848* | 8/281 |
| LaTourelle, Charles | Carter, Jane | Dec 11 1843 | 5/309B |
| Latson, Winifred | Stanmire, William | Feb 20 1820* | CM |
| Lattimer, Elizabeth | Kleinschrodt, George | Aug 25 1849 | 11/1 |
| Laughlin, Ann (wid) | McManus, Patrick | Jul 1 1853 | 12/337 |
| Launger, Maria (Laingos) | Mohnsamen, Frederick | Feb 23 1843 | 5/250B |
| Launrigurez, Margaret | Hart, Thomas | May 3 1841 | 5/128B |
| Laurence, Christopher | Ford, Ellen | Jan 13 1851 | 11/112 |
| Laurence, John | Grant, Eliza | 1838* | OIB |
| Laurendine, Benjamin | Collins, Eloisa | Aug 15 1821* | CM |
| Laurendine, Caroline | Roulston, George M | May 7 1849* | 8/374 |
| Laurendine, Edward (Edmond) | Jones, Carmelite | Jul 15 1843 | 5/288B |
| Laurendine, Gregoire | Lalande, Mary Ann | Nov 15 1843 | 5/304B |
| Laurendine, Jacob | Sauvage, Marie T.C. | Jul 23 1846 | 8/181 |
| Laurendine, Joseph | Bozars, Virginia | Feb 10 1840* | 3/193 |
| Laurendine, Josephine | Barriel, Joseph | Apr 9 1828 | 2/10 |
| Laurendine, Marcelite | Ford, Clinton | Sep 29 1831* | 2/182 |
| Laurendine, Mary | Carey, William H | Apr 24 1828 | 2/22 |
| Laurendine, Matilda | Rondeau, John,Jr | Jun 15 1835* | 3/17 |
| Laurendine, Peter | Burrows, Elizabeth | Feb 22 1814* | WB 1/17 |
| Laurendine, Pierre | Gregory, Mary | Mar 17 1836* | 3/43 |
| Laurent, Michael | Bimane, Pauline D ? | Feb 19 1850 | 11/40 |
| Laurie, Ann (Saurie) | Havens, Curtis | May 14 1846 | 8/165 |
| Laurine, Adler | Cashell, Thursby H | Nov 11 1841 | 5/158B |
| Lavalle, Mary | Arrego, John | Jan 13 1853 | 12/129 |
| LaValle, Philip | LaSalle, Victoria S | Jan 10 1852 | 11/202 |
| Lavens, Edward ? | Berry, Laura | Jan 2 1841 | 4/1441 |
| Laverty, Catherine | Brazille, Francisco Jr | Mar 12 1842* | 5/186B |
| Law, Sarah | White, Joseph | May 26 1854 | 13/235 |
| Lawler, Jane | Burns, James | Mar 18 1854 | 13/161 |
| Lawler, Julia | Earle, Peter C | Dec 20 1844 | 8/61B |
| Lawler, Mathew C | Cotter, Mary | Jan 23 1851 | 11/116 |
| Lawless, Bridget | Draper, Christopher | Aug 16 1852* | 11/275 |
| Lawrence, Margaret | Dillon, Martin | Aug 28 1834* | 2/181 |
| Lawrence, Margaret | MacMillan, William | Jun 29 1833* | 2/881 |
| Lawrence, Robert J | Ledyard, Mary L | May 11 1853* | 12/277 |
| Laws, Catherine | Winter, Charles | Apr 12 1854 | 13/180 |
| Laws, David (Lewis) | Reeks, Mary E ? | May 6 1846 | 8/164B |
| Laws, Jeremiah N or W | Long, Eliza | Aug 10 1845 | 5/216B |
| Lawson, Lewis | Garner, June | Oct 26 1844* | 8/46B |
| Lax, John B (Larx | McMillan, Mary C | May 19 1842 | 5/202B |
| Layden, James | Goodman, Julia A.M. | Aug 7 1843 | 5/291B |
| Laynick, Caroline (Saynick) | Stikes, John | May 20 1845* | 8/96B |
| Layton, David | Phillips, Rebecca | Dec 16 1841 | 5/162B |
| LBorne, Pierre | Baptiste, Catherine | Oct 7 1854 | 13/346 |
| LBorns, Pierre | Baptiste, Catherine | Sep 29 1854 | 13/346B |
| Lea, Emily L (Sea) | Peabody, Herbert C | Jan 5 1841* | 5/85B |
| Lea, Frosina (Lee) | Moorehouse, Joseph | Aug 18 1841* | 5/149B |
| Leach, Catharine | Jordan, William | May 3 1843 | 5/267B |
| Leadbetter, Daniel | Hall, Delphine G | May 21 1855 | 14/144 |
| Leadon, Mary Ann ? | Wright, Samuel L | Mar 3 1841* | 5/112B |
| Leadoff, John | Goss, Margarette | May 2 1850 | 11/58 |
| Leahy, Bridget | Cahill, Patrick | Jul 3 1854 | 13/272 |
| Leahy, Ellen | Cowley, David | 1837* | OIB |
| Leahy, Mary | Corbit, Thomas | Dec 14 1837 | 3/103B |
| Leahy, Patrick | Percy, Mary | Jul 13 1853 | 12/353 |
| Leahy, William | Duross, Charlotte | Mar 22 1845 | 8/81B |
| Leanders, Batt | Nolan, Sarah | May 15 1854 | 13/224 |
| Leary, Hannah | Ricker, Georgew | Apr 8 1852 | 11/233 |
| Leath, Sarah | Harris, Charles M | Jun 30 1840* | 5/30B |
| Leathe, Thelitha (Seathe) | O'Connor, Michael | Mar 29 1842 | 5/190B |

| BRIDE OR GROOM | SPOUSE | DATE | BOOK/PAGE |
|---|---|---|---|
| Leaven, John F | Barnes, Adalaide | Nov 1 1855 | 14/269 |
| Leavens, Benjamin F | Jennings, Melissa | Oct 1 1844 | 8/42B |
| Leavens, Elizabeth | Francis, Manuel | Jun 17 1854 | 13/260 |
| Leavitt, Levi | Crosby, Margaret | Sep 12 1846* | 8/189B |
| LeBaron, Charles S (or L) | Fitzsimmons, Adaliza | Jan 23 1844 | 5/317B |
| LeBaron, Mary Ellen | David, Francis | Jun 12 1850* | 11/66 |
| LeBaron, Mary Josephine | Sands, Robert M | Oct 15 1848 | 8/327 |
| LeBaron, William A | Robb, Eliza J | Jul 11 1848 | 8/315 |
| Lebenstein, Lische | Kylie, Lewis | Mar 13 1852* | 11/226 |
| LeBlanc, Anastasia | Dupon, John | Mar 2 1848* | 8/288 |
| LeBlanc, Annie | Rul, John | Oct 23 1841* | 5/154 |
| LeBourgeris, Emma | Chenet, Louis | May 2 1853 | 12/264 |
| LeBow, Frances | Hays, Jemima | Jan 4 1847 | 8/210 |
| LeBrouche, Angelina E.F. | Hewett, Frederick | Apr 8 1840* | 5/18 |
| LeCatt, Littleton | Surtell, Ann | Jul 19 1813* | WB 1/8 |
| Ledyard, Elizabeth D | Morrison, James J | Jan 14 1853 | 12/130 |
| Ledyard, Mary L | Lawrence, Robert J | May 11 1853* | 12/277 |
| Ledyard, Sarah F | Rice, James A | May 13 1850 | 11/61 |
| Lee, David | Hogan, Julia | Nov 22 1843* | 5/306B |
| Lee, Elizabeth | Sewel, James | Aug 25 1846 | 8/185 |
| Lee, Ellen | Prescott, James E | Apr 4 1846 | 8/155 |
| Lee, Evelina B | Guild, Harvey | Aug 18 1851 | 11/173 |
| Lee, Frank (wid) | MacNiff, Ann (wid) | Apr 9 1855* | 14/99 |
| Lee, George | Campbell, Jane | Jul 19 1851 | 11/167 |
| Lee, Hannah V | Rounvill, Artemus ? | Jun 2 1840* | 5/26 |
| Lee, Josiah B | Street, Martha | Jul 11 1837* | 3/89 |
| Lee, Margaret | Tulee, Thomas | 1827* | OIB |
| Lee, Martha Elizabeth | Jones, James C | Mar 18 1843 | 5/254B |
| Lee, Mary | Murphy, Edmund | Dec 31 1845 | 7/778B |
| Lee, Mary Ann | Sylvia, John | Aug 17 1841* | 5/148B |
| Lee, Mary C | Van Vleek, G.W. (Kleek) | Oct 31 1838* | 3/145 |
| Lee, Matilda C | Deeley, John H | Sep 4 1852 | 11/282 |
| Lee, Rebecca | Anderson, Solomon | Jan 1 1852 | 11/200 |
| Lee, Rebecca E | Kerr, Henry M | Feb 25 1835* | 3/10 |
| Lee, William | Burns, Susan | Feb 18 1847 | 8/218 |
| Lee, William | Newberry, Mary Ann | Jun 14 1855 | 14/173 |
| Leech, Charles | Harrelson, Martha | Dec 30 1848* | 8/342 |
| Leeds, Richard (Seeds) | Lyons, Mary Ann | May 7 1831 | 2/169 |
| Leeman, Elizabeth F | Bunnell, William H | Mar 19 1842* | 5/187B |
| Lees, Peter | Priford, Elizabeth ? | Dec 23 1842* | 5/238B |
| LeFebre, Isaac (Lefefere) | Tucker, Polly | Jul 20 1837* | 3/98 |
| LeFevre, Francis A | Carter, Julia A | 1838* | OIB |
| LeFevre, Martha | Page, James | Nov 4 1837* | 3/100 |
| Lefort, Louis ? | Jule, Josephine | Oct 16 1844 | 8/43B |
| LeFort, Louis | Silvi, Josephine J | Oct 16 1844 | 8/43B |
| Lehay, Ann | Cummins, Michael | Nov 16 1852 | 12/63 |
| Lehey, Eliza | Gahan, John | Jul 18 1844 | 8/33B |
| Leib, Sarah | Heohleihstein, Hirsh | Jul 24 1847 | 8/247 |
| Leich, Emma C | Waterman, Thomas | Oct 25 1849 | 11/11 |
| Leinkauf, William H | Block, Caroline | Mar 21 1854 | 13/164 |
| Leipt, Adam | Schonmeier, Ernstina | Dec 3 1853 | 13/34 |
| Leister, Mary L | Bass, Henry | Jun 1 1852 | 11/259 |
| Leland, Lewis Jr | Beal, Louisa P | Feb 8 1829* | 2/71 |
| Leland, Stephen | Watkins, Maria | Jun 28 1833* | 2/901 |
| Lelande, Isabel | Colin, Jean | May 15 1832* | 2/1531 |
| Lelande, Lewis | Rafael, Martha | Jul 21 1832* | 2/1391 |
| Lemerson, Boyd D | Barante, Martha T | Oct 21 1840* | 5/57 |
| LeMoin, Victor | Galle, Marie V | Apr 25 1829* | 2/82 |
| LeMoine, Henrietta F | Armstrong, William | Jun 17 1841* | 5/138B |
| LeMoine, Victorini L | Robert, John | Jan 2 1849 | 8/344 |
| Lenguett, Benjamin ? | Fawley, Joanna | Apr 25 1850 | 11/56 |
| Lennehan, Jeremiah | McGuire, Ann | Oct 18 1854 | 13/349 |
| Lennon, Mary Ann | McLeod, David | Jan 27 1845 | 8/69B |
| Lenoir, Julius | Charpenter, Mary D | Jan 4 1845 | 8/65B |

| BRIDE OR GROOM | SPOUSE | DATE | BOOK/PAGE |
|---|---|---|---|
| Lenoir, Louisiana | Rea, Peletiah P | Oct 2 1830* | 2/138 |
| Lenorman, Charlotte | Gautreaux, Joseph | Dec 4 1854 | 13/397 |
| Lenox, Margaret | Pomeroy, James M | Jul 28 1835 | 3/20 |
| Leo, David | Hogan, Julia | Nov 22 1843 | 7/41 |
| Leon, Caroline | Lippman, Leon | Oct 16 1846 | 8/194 |
| Leon, Florence | Cazeaux, Ulysses | Jan 30 1851 | 11/119 |
| Leonard, Ann | Matthews, Thomas | Jun 29 1849* | 8/394 |
| Leonard, Ann | Rouse, William | Jun 26 1841 | 5/140B |
| Leonard, Barbary | Roberts, Joseph | Apr 22 1850 | 11/55 |
| Leonard, Bridget | O'Brien, Thomas | Nov 16 1833* | 2/711 |
| Leonard, Christopher J | Harford, Ellen | Nov 22 1853 | 13/22 |
| Leonard, Ellen | Kearns, John | Jun 19 1855 | 14/175 |
| Leonard, James | Mulligan, Catherine | Dec 6 1842 | 5/232B |
| Leonard, Martin | Devine, Ann | Dec 18 1852 | 12/98 |
| Leonard, Mary | Natali, Batiste | May 14 1855 | 14/139 |
| Leonard, Mary Ann | Hofhaines, Chas F | Apr 20 1841* | 5/124B |
| Leonard, Patrick | Griffin, Mary | May 30 1841* | 5/133B |
| Leslie, Albert J | Ruynal, Emma | May 1 1849* | 8/372 |
| Leslie, Caroline F | VanNess, James | Jan 27 1836* | 3/38 |
| Leslie, Henry | Debell, Susan J | May 5 1849* | 8/373 |
| Lesseman, Amelina | Gogare, C F  ? | Apr 27 1840 | 5/21 |
| Lestrade, Cesarine | Langlois, Victor | Dec 22 1855 | 14/312 |
| Lestrade, Jane | Robinson, Charles | Apr 21 1841* | 5/127B |
| Lestrade, Taegues (Jacques) | Godard, Cesarine  (wid) | Apr 3 1843 | 5/257B |
| Levelle, Patrick (Lavelle) | Smith, Rose | Feb 2 1854 | 13/107 |
| Leverona, Rosa | Simetovitch, F S | Nov 7 1852 | 12/47 |
| Levert, Henry S | Walton, Octavia C | Feb 6 1836* | 3/40 |
| Levi, Soloman | Matzar, Betsey | Feb 12 1850* | 11/39 |
| Levi, Terese | Threefoot, Abraham | Nov 13 1850* | 11/97 |
| Levin, Fanny | Eder, David M | Feb 5 1858* | 11/38 |
| Levings, Nancy | Jones, John | Aug 19 1813* | CM |
| Levitt, Mary | Rego, George (Rejo) | Nov 10 1845 | 8/124B |
| Levy, Caroline | Cornsky, Samuel | Feb 18 1842* | 5/181B |
| Levy, Michael | Lyons, Marla (Maria) | Mar 14 1846 | 8/151B |
| Lewis, Angus | Murrell, Zilpah | Jun 5 1850 | 11/65 |
| Lewis, Barbour | Wolcott, Francis J | Jan 2 1849* | 8/344 |
| Lewis, Curtis | DeVaubercy, Isabella | 1826* | OIB |
| Lewis, David  (Laws) | Reeks, Mary Eliza | May 6 1846 | 8/164B |
| Lewis, Delia | Rabby, John | Aug 10 1846 | 8/184 |
| Lewis, Eliza | Jordan, Thomas G | Nov 17 1836* | 3/62 |
| Lewis, Eliza | Oraner, Franklin ? | Oct 26 1848 | 8/330 |
| Lewis, Gabriel | Edduy, Elizabeth ? | Dec 27 1819* | CM |
| Lewis, Henry G | Cox, Mary T | May 28 1839* | 3/174 |
| Lewis, Howell | Helverson, Ellenear | May 7 1844 | 8/19B |
| Lewis, Isaac | De Christain, Ellen | Jul 6 1831* | 2/178 |
| Lewis, James | Smith, Maraetta | May 7 1855 | 14/131 |
| Lewis, Jane M | Muher, Isaac (Maher) | 1825* | OIB |
| Lewis, Jane | Dilling, Philip | Feb 25 1846* | 8/148B |
| Lewis, Javind ? | Hillion, Thomas  ? | Sep 12 1836* | 3/57 |
| Lewis, John | Randolph, Lucretia | Oct 8 1835* | 3/29 |
| Lewis, John | Blackmore, Jane | Dec 31 1849 | 11/30 |
| Lewis, John B | Quigley, Margaret E | Jun 30 1846 | 8/176 |
| Lewis, Jordan | Malone, Margaret | Mar 16 1853 | 12/192 |
| Lewis, Julia A | Sutton, John S | May 6 1845* | 8/92B |
| Lewis, Lavina | Hilton, Thomas | 1836* | OIB |
| Lewis, Loren R | Lord, Mary Ann | Oct 7 1824 | 1/41 |
| Lewis, Martha | Brown, William L | Aug 10 1842 | 5/215B |
| Lewis, Mary | Lord, John | Oct 6 1851 | 11/181 |
| Lewis, Mary | Elward, Edmund | Jul 26 1853 | 12/371 |
| Lewis, Mary E | Todd, William L | Mar 30 1843 | 5/256B |
| Lewis, Peter | Conake, Mary | Apr 12 1853 | 12/236 |
| Lewis, Rupel (Russel) | Steele, Mary L | 1822* | OIB |
| Lewis, Samuel (Lyons) | Beebe, Leshey ? | Jan 25 1841* | 5/93B |
| Lewis, Sanford | Davis, Julia B | Sep 28 1848 | 8/326 |

| --- | --- | --- | --- |
| Lewis, Sarah | Wheeler, Ausman | Jan 27 1846 | 8/141B |
| Lewis, Seaborn | George, Susan | Mar 28 1829* | 2/78 |
| Lewis, Susannah | Bankston, Thomas | 1826* | OIB |
| Lewis, Thomas F | Alleyn, Rosanna | Apr 29 1820* | CM |
| Lewis, William | Rabby, Hermina | Apr 20 1846* | 8/168B |
| Lewis, William H | Curtin, Joanna | Aug 20 1850 | 11/81 |
| L'Hommedieu, Ann Amelia | McGinnis, Edward W | Jan 26 1853* | 12/147 |
| Liblenjohns, John | Taylor, Betsey | 1826* | OIB |
| Liebert, Frederick C | Hamilton, Elizabeth | Sep 28 1854 | 13/344 |
| Liehen, Margaret ? | Twelves, Robert | Jul  9 1841* | 5/142 |
| Light, Catherine E | Turcher, James | Oct 28 1835* | 3/31 |
| Light, William | Ryder, Catherine | Mar 27 1828* | 2/20 |
| Ligons, Ramaha | Mason, John | Dec 29 1842 | 5/239 |
| Linder, Harriett | Johnston, Daniel L | 1827* | OIB |
| Lindsay, David | Carragun, Mary | Mar 20 1845 | 8/80B |
| Line, John | Flandray, Mary Ann | Sep 14 1849* | 11/4 |
| Linehan, Fanny | Byrnes, Dennis | Jan 30 1849* | 8/351 |
| Linn, Cranford | Mullin, Mary | Dec 27 1849 | 11/29 |
| Linnell, Charlotte Ann | Gerow, Warren D | Nov 19 1844 | 8/52B |
| Lins, John | Fleming, Margaret | Apr  2 1853 | 12/214 |
| Linskey, Thomas | Murphy, Ann | Mar 16 1855 | 14/84 |
| Lintch, Mary (Linch) | Currie, Edward | Sep  1 1851 | 11/175 |
| Lioni, Joseph Charles | Girard, Margaret C | Jun 22 1819* | CM |
| Lioni, Margaret | Geandreau, John | Dec 12 1828* | 2/55 |
| Lipman, Sophia    ? | Goldsmith, Philip | Apr 21 1841* | 5/125B |
| Lippman, Leon | Leon, Caroline | Oct 16 1846 | 8/194 |
| Lipps, Jacob | Schieman, Julian | Dec 27 1854 | 13/420 |
| Lips, Nicholas | Shutz, Barbara | Jan  8 1853 | 12/118 |
| Lips, Terese | Bower, John | Mar 22 1851 | 11/130 |
| Lipscomb, Ellen | Walker, Percy | Dec 27 1836* | 3/67 |
| Lish, Philip A | Rodeman, Cresent | Feb 27 1851 | 11/125 |
| Litchfield, Martha A | Masters, Enoch G | Oct 11 1853 | 12/414 |
| Littell, Thompson | Collins, Martha Ann | Jul 16 1833* | 2/841 |
| Little, Florah Ann | Boyd, James P | Apr 30 1852 | 11/244 |
| Little, George | George, Sarah | Jul  8 1833* | 2/861 |
| Littleton, James | Corbett, Mary | Aug 24 1843 | 5/293B |
| Livingston, Cornelia | Hazard, Chas C | 1827* | OIB |
| Livingston, Imogine C | Montigue, Edward F | May  3 1850* | 11/58 |
| Livingston, Mary J | Long, John | Jan 10 1853 | 12/120 |
| Lloyd, Joseph C | Winter, Harriet | Sep  8 1854 | 13/334 |
| Lockard, Mary | Martin, Joseph | Dec  6 1828* | 2/54 |
| Locke, Mary A | Knight, Reuben H | Nov 23 1855 | 14/287 |
| Locke, Richard H | Ballinger, Susannah | Oct  1 1833* | 2/781 |
| Lockhart, David | Cox, Ann | Dec 22 1840* | 5/79B |
| Lockhart, John | Peck, Mary | Apr 10 1854 | 13/175 |
| Lockhart, John A | Palmer, Margaret | Dec  6 1849* | 11/22 |
| Lockman, Edward | Donavan, Johanna | Apr 26 1848* | 8/300 |
| Lodenere, Virgine | Grelote, Jean Batiste | 1836* | OIB |
| Lodge, Jane | Brien, William | Jul  7 1825* | 1/84 |
| Loeb, Schannet | David, Tobias | Mar  3 1853* | 12/183 |
| Loften, Van | Cockran, Mary | Jun 29 1833* | 2/891 |
| Loftin, Albert G | Hargrove, Lucy | Jun 23 1847* | 8/243 |
| Loftin, Susan | Steger, Henry | Dec 21 1840* | 5/77 |
| Lofton, Elizabeth | Morgan, William R | Dec 22 1855 | 14/310 |
| Loftus, Mary | Horn, John | Apr 25 1855 | 14/118 |
| Loftus, Thomas | Rafferty, Ann | May 17 1853 | 12/286 |
| Logan, Benjamin B | Caldwell, Ariann A | Aug 18 1853 | 12/385 |
| Logan, Elizabeth J | Nicholson, Charles D | Nov 12 1855 | 14/208 |
| Logan, Maria E | Stinson, Joseph | Jun  1 1848 | 8/307 |
| Logan, Mary Ann | Catchett, John | Dec  8 1840* | 5/73B |
| Logan, Selina C | O'Carroll, John | Jul 23 1850* | 11/75 |
| Loh, Elizabeth | Futch, Isaac | Oct 27 1841 | 5/155B |
| Lohan, Mary | McCowan, Michael | Jul 18 1853 | 12/360 |
| Lohman, Jacob | Oppenheimer, Augusta | Dec  7 1844 | 8/57B |

| BRIDE OR GROOM | SPOUSE | DATE | BOOK/PAGE |
|---|---|---|---|
| Loht, Caroline | Pefferle, John B | Jan 1 1855 | 13/426 |
| Loker, Martin | Rothe, Ann Maria C | Jan 1 1829* | 2/61 |
| Loker, Mary | Vielli, Joseph V | Mar 7 1838* | 3/114 |
| Lollins, Martin | Mahoney, Catharine | May 20 1852 | 11/252 |
| Lome, Dolarate (Lami) | Ladanar, John B | Oct 20 1828* | 2/47 |
| Londano, Giebbe (Sondano) | Nugent, Mary | Dec 31 1841 | 5/166B |
| Lonergene, Ellen (Lonegren) | Barry, Joseph | Aug 15 1840* | 5/41B |
| Long, Eliza | Laws, Jeremiah | Aug 10 1842 | 5/216B |
| Long, Harriet | Lyons, Charles | Oct 22 1845 | 8/121B |
| Long, John | Barnard, Deliede | Jun 6 1855 | 14/163 |
| Long, John | Livingston, Mary J | Jan 10 1853 | 12/120 |
| Long, John H | Hendrick, Martha | Apr 26 1848 | 8/302 |
| Long, John H | Huddleston, Emily A | Jul 19 1849* | 8/383 |
| Long, Nancy | Rogers, William V | Sep 3 1835* | 3/27 |
| Long, Richard H | Norton, Imogine | Dec 31 1846 | 8/208 |
| Long, William H | Nicholas, Frances | Jul 19 1851 | 11/167 |
| Longe, Numa | Provost, Cecilia | Aug 30 1852 | 11/280 |
| Longet, Jane Elizabeth | Covington, Thomas W | Nov 16 1843 | 5/304B |
| Longfield, J Alabama | Wilson, Newton J | Aug 18 1849* | 8/391 |
| Longfield, Margaret | Sheffield, Frederick | Mar 17 1835* | 3/11 |
| Longhurst, George | Callahan, Bridget | Jan 23 1851* | 11/116 |
| Lonnon, Mary Ann ? | McLeod, David | Jan 27 1845 | 8/69 |
| Lonony, John (Lowary) | Sossaman, Adeline | Nov 25 1842 | 5/229B |
| Lonsdale, Horatio B ? | Cheyse, Mary (Cheyn) | Mar 8 1841 | 5/114B |
| Lonton, Julia A | Kidd, James N | Dec 19 1854 | 13/415 |
| Looby, James (Lovly) | Hughes, Elizabeth | Feb 2 1844* | 5/319B |
| Lopez, Bartoloma | Sandoz, Mary A (Landoz) | May 8 1832* | 2/1541 |
| Lopez, Mary T | Herpin, Edward P | Nov 23 1853 | 13/25 |
| Loprester, Salvador | Cavallara, Sarah | Feb 18 1853 | 12/176 |
| Lorant, Matilda | Brue, Benoy | Jun 19 1855 | 14/177 |
| Lord, John | Mott, Matilda | 1825* | OIB |
| Lord, John | Wilson, Rebecca | Apr 21 1832 | 2/1591 |
| Lord, John | Lewis, Mary | Oct 6 1851 | 11/181 |
| Lord, Mary Ann | Lewis, Loren R | Oct 7 1824 | 1/41 |
| Lord, Rebecca | Brown, John M | Feb 11 1835* | 3/8 |
| Lorent, Joseph | Chastang, Isabelle | Jul 14 1830* | 2/131 |
| Lorey, Susan | Watson, Augustus F | Dec 29 1854 | 13/423 |
| Loring, Ann | Williams, Henry | Jul 20 1841* | 5/143 |
| Lorrigan, Ann | Healy, Patrick | Aug 24 1847* | 8/253 |
| Lorydale, Horatio B | Cheyn, Mary (Cheyse) | Mar 8 1841* | 5/114B |
| Lose, Jacob | Armor, Elizabeth | Apr 12 1844 | 8/12B |
| Lott, Benjamin | Collins, Jane G | Mar 17 1854 | 13/160 |
| Lott, Berry | McLeod, Margaret | Jan 15 1834* | 2/531B |
| Lott, Dorcas | Sumrall, Moses | Apr 3 1834* | 2/401B |
| Lott, Elisha B | Swain, Mary E | Jan 21 1845 | 8/67B |
| Lott, Elizabeth (Loh) | Futch, Isaac | Oct 27 1841 | 5/155B |
| Lott, Elizabeth (Sott) | Denmark, Bryant | Sep 10 1842 | 5/219B |
| Lott, James | Evans, Caroline | Jan 4 1845 | 8/65B |
| Lott, Marion | Byrd, Robert | Jul 15 1835* | 3/20 |
| Lott, Sally | Mason, Calderwood | Dec 24 1821* | CM |
| Lott, Vice | Lankforth, Daniel | Apr 4 1825 | 1/71 |
| Lott, William | Collins, Mary D | Dec 6 1852 | 12/83 |
| Lough, Owen | Manney, Mary | Jul 15 1853 | 12/357 |
| Loughry, Catharine | Ibert, Thomas | Dec 26 1848* | 8/341 |
| Loughry, Catherine | Norton, William | Jul 16 1855 | 14/189 |
| Loughy, Patrick (Longhy) | Walker, Jane | Dec 17 1841 | 5/162B |
| Louton, Frederick J | Morse, Julia A | May 5 1851* | 11/146 |
| Love, Valentine | Dickinson, Rosanna | Jan 4 1840* | 5/7 |
| Lovell, John | Elliott, Maria | Oct 30 1821* | CM |
| Loveridge, Charles E | Thompson, Ann | May 28 1844 | 8/23B |
| Lovly, James (Looby) | Hughes, Elizabeth | Feb 2 1844* | 5/319B |
| Lowary, John (Lonon) | Sossaman, Adeline | Nov 25 1842 | 5/229B |
| Lowary, John | Malone, Louisa O | Aug 13 1855 | 14/209 |
| Lowell, Marlin | Thompson, Clarinda | Jun 1 1846 | 8/170 |

| BRIDE OR GROOM | SPOUSE | DATE | BOOK/PAGE |
|---|---|---|---|
| Loyd, Emiline | Robinson, David | Mar 18 1841* | 5/118B |
| Lucas, Beasley | Gallaway, Martha | Feb 12 1848* | 8/283 |
| Lucas, Bridget | Houson, Daniel (Hanson) | Jan  3 1838* | 3/107 |
| Lucas, John | Dugan, Bridget | Jun 26 1850 | 11/68 |
| Lucas, John | Rester, Naoma | Sep  6 1850 | 11/84 |
| Lucas, William | Webb, Sarah | Jul  7 1825 | 1/83 |
| Luced, Mary | Hogan, John | Jun 15 1855 | 14/174 |
| Lucey, Elmira R | Smith, Robert | Jan 11 1848 | 8/277 |
| Luch, Sarah Ann | Copland, Robert | Jun 13 1839* | 3/179 |
| Lucid, John | Brasnolran, Joanna | Nov 27 1855 | 14/290 |
| Luckhaupt, Catherine S | Hildebrand, Charles | Feb  8 1855 | 14/42 |
| Lude, Lewis S | Groom, Mary E | Sep  7 1853 | 12/402 |
| Ludley, William  ? | Bias, Elizabeth | Apr 28 1846 | 8/160B |
| Ludlow, Cornelia B | Field, Mathew C (Will C) | Feb 19 1841* | 5/105B |
| Ludlow, Mary D | Arnold, William A | Feb 14 1853 | 12/171 |
| Ludlow, William W | Hall, Maria | Jun 25 1851 | 11/160 |
| Luke, Christian | Hermason, Mary | Jun 14 1848 | 8/309 |
| Lumpford, Rebecca | Walker, John | May 27 1844 | 8/23B |
| Lundy, Charles P | Smith, Nancy A | Aug 28 1855 | 14/219 |
| Lunney, John | Murphy, Margaret | Oct 22 1847* | 8/261B |
| Lusher, Bernard | Bottleman, Fredrika | Jan 21 1854* | 13/91 |
| Lusser, Mary Louise | Delbarco, Lewis | Mar 28 1842 | 5/189B |
| Luterage, Marke ? | Hutton, Catherine A | 1838* | OIB |
| Lutz, John | Baumann, Elizabeth | Jul  6 1854* | 13/275 |
| Lyle, Sarah | Wattey, Reuben | Sep  2 1852 | 11/281 |
| Lyles, Mary | Cerbut, James ? | Sep 10 1851 | 11/177 |
| Lyles, Richard | Gorman, Bridget | Jul 21 1838* | 3/136 |
| Lynch, Andrew | McGinnis, Ellen | Jan 12 1852 | 11/202 |
| Lynch, Caroline (wid) | Osborn, George  (wid) | Oct 18 1853* | 12/418 |
| Lynch, Elizabeth | Malone, Patrick | Apr  2 1853 | 12/218 |
| Lynch, Joanna | Carlin, James | Dec 15 1841 | 5/162B |
| Lynch, John  ? | Smith, Bridget | Oct 13 1848* | 8/327 |
| Lynch, John | Timmons, Jane | Oct 15 1839* | 3/188 |
| Lynch, Mary | Riley, Thomas | Apr  5 1843 | 5/258B |
| Lynch, Michael | Ryan, Ellen | Jun 25 1851 | 11/160 |
| Lynch, Thomas | Spillard, Catharine | Apr 13 1842 | 5/196B |
| Lynes, Mary | Thornton, Thomas | Sep  6 1852 | 11/283 |
| Lynnott, John Carrol | Tice, Eliza | Jan 28 1845* | 8/69B |
| Lynsh, Cullen  (Lynch) | Watkins, Martha | May 13 1847 | 8/234 |
| Lyon, Charles | Gibbons, Minerva | Jul  2 1849 | 8/395 |
| Lyon, Daniel | Callahan, Margaret (wid) | Jul 23 1853 | 12/366 |
| Lyon, Eliza | Roane, William A | Mar  4 1850 | 11/44 |
| Lyon, James G  (Wid) | Smoot, Lavinia C (Wid) | Feb  9 1833* | 2/1141 |
| Lyon, Samuel | Crickman, Elizabeth | Jun 29 1852* | 11/267 |
| Lyon, Sarah B | Foote, Charles K | Jul 11 1843 | 5/287B |
| Lyon, Thomas | Newberry, Susanna | Apr  5 1852 | 11/232 |
| Lyon, William | Jones, Rositta | Jan 23 1838 | 3/108B |
| Lyon, William A | James, Rositta | 1838* | OIB |
| Lyons, Abbe | Vigo, Raymond | Jul 12 1849* | 8/389 |
| Lyons, Ann | Quarles, Benjamin | Feb  8 1848 | 8/282 |
| Lyons, Catharine | Marshall, Frances | Aug 16 1846* | 8/183 |
| Lyons, Charles | Long, Harriet | Oct 22 1845 | 8/121B |
| Lyons, Cornelius | Hines, Bridget | Mar  8 1844 | 5/327B |
| Lyons, Elizabeth, | Mills, David | Jan 28 1833* | 2/1181 |
| Lyons, Elizabeth | Foster, William | Jun 15 1846* | 8/173 |
| Lyons, John | Hamilton, Eliza | Apr 20 1844 | 8/16B |
| Lyons, John | Wadley, Nancy | Jun 15 1853 | 12/320 |
| Lyons, Margaret | McDonald, James | Feb 24 1845 | 8/75B |
| Lyons, Marla (Maria) | Levy, Michael | Mar 14 1846 | 8/151B |
| Lyons, Martha | Woody, Rublarc ? | Apr  4 1837* | 3/96 |
| Lyons, Martha | Moody, Richard | 1837* | OIB |
| Lyons, Mary | Stone, Edward | May  1 1837* | 3/82 |
| Lyons, Mary | Corbet, James | 1851* | OIB |
| Lyons, Mary Ann | Seeds, Richard  (Leeds) | May  7 1831 | 2/169 |

| BRIDE OR GROOM | SPOUSE | DATE | BOOK/PAGE |
|---|---|---|---|
| Lyons, Patsey | Dorlon, Mulford | Jun 13 1845 | 8/108B |
| Lyons, Phelan B | Cronin, Mary | Dec 11 1849 | 11/24 |
| Lyons, Ramaha | Mason, John | Dec 29 1842 | 5/239B |
| Lyons, Samuel | Beebe, Lishey | Jan 25 1841 | 5/239B |
| Lyons, Thomas B | McCoy, Susan Ann | Jun 15 1853 | 12/319 |
| Lyons, William | Coles, Polly | Mar  3 1813* | WB 1/6 |

## M

| | | | |
|---|---|---|---|
| Maas, Babet | Frolichstein, Henry | Jun 24 1853* | 12/330 |
| Mabhullen, Mary (Malholm) | Gallagher, Thomas | Jun 15 1842* | 5/206B |
| Mables, Tisher | Newman, Henry | Oct 22 1844 | 8/45B |
| MacAvoy, Ann | Hibbits, Michael | Jun  9 1854 | 13/249 |
| Machien, Martha | Galle, Louis | Jan  5 1853 | 12/115 |
| Machune, Jerry | Smith, Catherine | Oct 23 1852 | 12/34 |
| Mack, Elizabeth (Monk) | Bogue, Terrance | Jul 25 1844 | 8/35B |
| Mack, Thomas | Welch, Anna  (Mrs) | Jan 17 1850 | 11/33 |
| Mack, William | Blundell, Sarah | May 18 1852 | 11/251 |
| MacKay, Elizabeth | Johnson, George | Dec 23 1833* | 2/641B |
| MacKay, Robert | Tarlton, Caroline | May 10 1852* | 11/248 |
| Mackay, Robert W | Mitchell, Lucy | Jul 18 1846 | 8/180 |
| Macken, Mary | O'Neil, Francis | Jul  3 1837* | 3/93 |
| Mackin, Patrick | Martin, Catherine | Aug 24 1852* | 11/279 |
| Macklin, John | Riley, Catherine | Apr 20 1854 | 13/199 |
| MacLary, Edward W | Barton, Fanny | Jun  5 1854 | 13/241 |
| MacLean, Andrew C | Labuzan, Sarah M | Sep 23 1850* | 11/87 |
| MacLean, Robert | Labuzan, Louisa V | Dec 15 1847 | 8/271 |
| MacMillan, William | Lawrence, Margaret | Jun 29 1833* | 2/881 |
| MacNamara, Mary A | Austin, Hiram B | May 13 1840* | 5/23 |
| MacNiff, Ann  (wid) | Lee, Frank  (wid) | Apr  9 1855* | 14/99 |
| Macon, Thomas W | Moore, Margaret Ann | Dec 24 1851 | 11/197 |
| MacRe, Adele | Batre, Charles | Dec 25 1824* | 1/59 |
| MacRe, Eugenia Louisa | Austin, Charles H | Dec 21 1829* | 2/107 |
| Macy, Robert C | Mills, Julia A | Nov 24 1845 | 8/125B |
| Madden, John | Goodgame, Lucretia | Apr  9 1852 | 11/233 |
| Madigan, Mary | White, William J | Aug 26 1843* | 5/293B |
| Madot, Catherine | Valle, Joseph E | Oct 23 1838* | 3/144 |
| Maedor, Benjamin | Collins, Elizabeth | May  1 1845 | 8/90 |
| Magee, Ann | Springer, John C | Feb 22 1854 | 13/129 |
| Magee, Caroline V | Furness, Orlando | Oct 13 1847 | 8/262 |
| Magee, Hariett | Woodall, Tarlton | Jun 13 1832 | 2/1521 |
| Magee, Jacob | Tisdale, Mary E | Dec  4 1834* | 2/1841 |
| Magee, James | Conner, Mary | Feb  5 1819* | CM |
| Magee, James P | Stocking, Maria H | Feb 14 1842 | 5/180B |
| Magee, Jennett (Morgan) | Gilmore, Robert | May 24 1841 | 5/132B |
| Magee, Mary A | Gannaway, James | Jan 19 1844 | 5/315B |

| --- | --- | --- | --- |
| Magee, Sophia (Mrs) | Flood, James | Jun 24 1841 | 5/139B |
| Magee, William | Bass, Margaret M | Nov 3 1828* | 2/51 |
| Magestra, Caroline | Boe, Paul | Apr 27 1849 | 8/371 |
| Magn, Sophia, Mrs | Flood, James | Jun 24 1841* | 5/139 |
| Magner, James (Maynes) | Kelly, Jane | Dec 3 1842 | 5/231B |
| Magooran, John (McGorman) | Smith, Elizabeth | Feb 5 1850* | 11/38 |
| Maguire, Catherine C | Swift, Samuel G | Aug 30 1833* | 2/811 |
| Maguire, Ellen R | Ingraham, James G | May 19 1838* | 3/127 |
| Maguire, Mary | Pettis, David | Oct 29 1840* | 5/57B |
| Maguire, Patrick | Glynn, Joanna | Jul 18 1848* | 8/317 |
| Maguire, William | Hibbits, Bridget | Jun 24 1846 | 8/175 |
| Mahab, Mary Ann | Johnston, Robert | May 18 1829* | 2/87 |
| Maham, Susan (Mahon) | Maneny, Jeremiah (Mahony) | Nov 28 1840* | 5/69 |
| Mahany, Michael | Grantham, Caroline | May 22 1837* | 3/83 |
| Maheny, Jeremiah (Mahony) | Maham, Susan (Mahon) | Nov 28 1840* | 5/69B |
| Mahlen, John | Scheoffer, Amelia | Feb 20 1839* | 3/157 |
| Mahler, Evrad | Allen, Mary A | Jul 1 1854 | 13/270 |
| Mahler, William | Cook, Elizabeth | Nov 25 1843* | 5/307B |
| Mahon, Mary Ann | Ray, Hiram | Jul 3 1840* | 5/33B |
| Mahon, Susan | Mahony, Jeremiah | Nov 28 1840* | 5/69B |
| Mahoney, Catharine | Lollins, Martin (Collins) | May 20 1852 | 11/252 |
| Mahoney, James | Fillowell, Mary | Jan 24 1849* | 8/349 |
| Mahoney, Michael | Clark, Catherine | Jun 5 1843 | 5/278B |
| Mahoney, Patrick | Larkin, Catharine | Mar 5 1845 | 8/77B |
| Mahony, Mary Jane | Barnard, James R | Dec 29 1843* | 5/312B |
| Mailfer, Peter Constant | Sabriyer, Juliette ? | Aug 24 1848 | 8/321 |
| Malcomson, John | Davis, Jane B (David) | Sep 8 1845 | 8/117B |
| Malene, Bridget | Devenen, Charles | Jul 2 1842 | 6/170 |
| Maley, Ellen | Williams, Thomas | Apr 10 1852 | 11/235 |
| Maley, Mary | Sheridan, Richard | Jan 17 1851 | 11/114 |
| Malloney, John | O'Connor, Bridget | Jan 3 1851 | 11/108 |
| Mallory, Henry | Alexander, Mary | Sep 19 1854 | 13/338 |
| Mallory, Urial | Marshall, Sarah Jane | Jan 21 1854 | 13/92 |
| Malone, Ann | McInroa, Lawrence ? | Jun 5 1855 | 14/162 |
| Malone, Anna | Branning, William | Aug 13 1825 | 1/89 |
| Malone, Barney | Gillespie, Anna | Jan 10 1846 | 8/138B |
| Malone, Bridget | Derenek, Charles ? | Jul 2 1842* | 5/210B |
| Malone, Bridget | Devenen, Charles ? | Jul 2 1842* | 5/210B |
| Malone, Edward | Russell, Ann M | Dec 20 1852 | 12/99 |
| Malone, Eliza T | King, Thomas | Jul 30 1845 | 8/113B |
| Malone, Emily W | Tuttle, Stephen | Mar 5 1829* | 2/74 |
| Malone, Griffin | George, Harriet | Jun 3 1839* | 3/176 |
| Malone, Ivy | Fountaine, Sarah | Oct 16 1823* | 1/8 |
| Malone, Janey | George, Claiborn R | Apr 15 1834* | 2/321 |
| Malone, John | Jones, Eliza | Dec 19 1828* | 2/56 |
| Malone, John | Connor, Margaret | Jan 30 1855 | 14/28 |
| Malone, John | Kavanagh, Margaret | Feb 5 1855 | 14/36 |
| Malone, Louisa H | Bingham, Charles | Sep 7 1829* | 2/94 |
| Malone, Louisa O | Lowary, John | Aug 13 1855 | 14/209 |
| Malone, Lucy | Risher, James Jr | May 12 1828* | 2/25 |
| Malone, Margaret | Lewis, Jordan | Mar 16 1853 | 12/192 |
| Malone, Martin | Boyla, Margaret | 1836* | 0IB |
| Malone, Mary | Miatovick, Spiro | Jun 1 1852 | 11/258 |
| Malone, Mary M | Willcox, William W | Feb 25 1852 | 11/221 |
| Malone, Parnecia E | Boice, George L | May 30 1854 | 13/238 |
| Malone, Patrick | Lynch, Elizabeth | Apr 2 1853 | 12/218 |
| Malone, Richard | Martin, Elizabeth | Feb 5 1853 | 12/166 |
| Malone, Susanna E | Kennedy, Alfred B | Jul 26 1853 | 12/369 |
| Malone, Thomas A | Kennedy, Catherine | Dec 11 1854 | 13/409 |
| Malone, Thomas Jr | Hollinger, Louisa O | Dec 8 1849 | 11/23 |
| Malone, Virginia | Shelton, William B | Oct 15 1851 | 11/182 |
| Malone, William | Herkins, Patience | Dec 17 1831* | 2/1781 |
| Maloney, John | Harigan, Bridget | Apr 28 1855 | 14/124 |
| Maloney, William (Mahoney) | Brady, Ellen | Apr 27 1849* | 8/371 |

| BRIDE OR GROOM | SPOUSE | DATE | BOOK/PAGE |
|---|---|---|---|
| Maloy, Julia | Sheriden, James | Nov 19 1852 | 12/66 |
| Mamie, Mary Ann | Gahan, John | Apr 1 1839 | 3/163 |
| Mamse, Pierre (Marnse) | Chastang, Louise | May 19 1842 | 5/201B |
| Manahan, Margaret | Gorman, Thomas | Apr 4 1847 | 8/223 |
| Manasco, Rhoda C | Moore, Augustus G | Nov 22 1842 | 5/228B |
| Mann, Benito (Mon) | Bozars, Mary | May 21 1842* | 5/202B |
| Mann, John | Brown, May | Apr 28 1823 | 1/2 |
| Mann, John H (Marsh) | Adams, Ann | Feb 11 1842 | 5/179B |
| Mann, Joseph (Menne) | Peckler, Elizabeth | Nov 27 1840* | 5/67B |
| Mann, Marianna | Stephenson, John H | Feb 12 1845 | 8/73B |
| Mann, Thomas N | Beam, Jemima C | Jan 25 1851 | 11/117 |
| Manney, James | Patterson, Nancy | Jul 2 1835* | 3/19 |
| Manney, Mary | Lough, Owen | Jul 15 1853 | 12/357 |
| Manning, Leonard | Smith, Elizabeth | Apr 4 1844 | 8/9B |
| Manning, Mary | Evelly, James | Nov 2 1853 | 13/4 |
| Manny, Caroline | Clark, William | Feb 10 1847 | 8/215 |
| Manogin, Ellen | Wilson, Henry | Jan 27 1853 | 12/152 |
| Mansa, Florestin (Maura) | Gasin, Benjamin | Dec 25 1843 | 5/311B |
| Mansen, Augustus | McQuilen, Mary Jane | Dec 5 1849 | 11/21 |
| Mansfield, Catharine | Neilen, William | Apr 5 1847 | 8/224 |
| Mansfield, Margaret | McCarthy, John | Nov 24 1851 | 11/189 |
| Mansfield, Michael | Beadan, Bridget | Apr 19 1853 | 12/246 |
| Mansken, Mary Ellen | Cooper, George | Jul 28 1846 | 8/182 |
| Mansker, James E | Thomas, Amazon C | Apr 11 1854 | 13/178 |
| Mansker, Margaret | Clemmons, George C | Oct 23 1855 | 14/262 |
| Mansker, Sarah J (Mausker) | Wilhelm, Jacob S | Feb 27 1846 | 8/149B |
| Manson, Mary Jane | Gilbert, Charles A | Jun 21 1842 | 5/207B |
| Mansony, Charles G | Soto, Merced | May 22 1824 | 1/33 |
| Maple, James (Massee) | Howell, Henrietta M | Mar 4 1834* | 2/431 |
| Maples, Elijah | Murphy, Mary | Feb 16 1848 | 8/284 |
| Maples, Herther | Fields, John C | Apr 13 1835* | 3/13 |
| Maples, Rebecca | Wheeler, Simeon | Jul 16 1850 | 11/74 |
| Maples, Simeon | Fore, Emily S | Sep 17 1851 | 11/180 |
| Maples, Washington | Collins, Margaret | Jul 15 1852 | 11/270 |
| March, Andrew | Violette, Sarah J | Aug 8 1854 | 13/307 |
| March, Edward | Bacchos, Mary | Oct 13 1836* | 3/60 |
| March, John | Baron, Elizabeth J | Nov 13 1838* | 3/146 |
| Marchand, Louis (Merchant) | Barnes, Mary (Wid) | Jan 2 1855* | 13/432 |
| Marchand, Martin A | Dearmos, C Michel | Apr 25 1840 | 5/20 |
| Marchell, Barbara | Grassman, John | May 7 1855 | 14/132 |
| Marcus, August | Stern, Eva | May 1 1843* | 5/266B |
| Margaret (NSL) | Chastang, John J | Mar 13 1832* | 2/1651 |
| Mark, Sarah | Cook, Henry | May 6 1839* | 3/170 |
| Markan, Mary | Roasch, Francisco | Dec 27 1838* | 3/B152 |
| Markey, Elizabeth | Randolph, Phineas B | Apr 14 1851 | 11/138 |
| Markham, Eliza | Innerarity, Francis | May 24 1855 | 14/151 |
| Markham, William H | Williams, Libby E | Jun 26 1854 | 13/264 |
| Markin, Patrick (Mackin) | Gallagher, Jane | Jan 14 1844* | 5/314B |
| Marks, Jacob | Hertz, Rachel | Jun 1 1855 | 14/155 |
| Marks, James B | Marmillion, Adelaide ? | May 30 1838 | 3/129 |
| Markstein, A | Burnstein, Bevert | Feb 26 1850* | 11/43 |
| Markstein, David | Ditman, Fanny (Ditmar) | Nov 24 1843* | 5/307B |
| Markstein, Henrietta (Mrs) | Picard, Isaac | Nov 9 1855* | 14/275 |
| Marlen, Madame | Cawpano, Felix | Oct 1 1833* | 3/142 |
| Marlow, George F | Thompson, Cornelia J | Oct 16 1839* | 3/188 |
| Marmillion, Adelaide B ? | Marks, James B | May 30 1838 | 3/129 |
| Marnische, Emilius William | Perriliat, Adelaide U | Jun 22 1840 | 5/29B |
| Marnse, Pierre (Mamse) | Chastang, Louise | May 19 1842* | 5/201B |
| Marone, Louisa | Ponis, Henry | 1843* | 0IB |
| Marques, Sarah (Mrs) | Revas, Leonardo | Jan 22 1839* | 3/B153 |
| Marques, Simon | Sencholl, Elizabeth | Oct 23 1855 | 14/260 |
| Marr, Ann | Randal, William C | Aug 26 1836* | 3/56 |
| Marrow, Eliza | Streach, David | Jul 29 1848* | 8/319 |
| Marsanary, Joseph (widr) | Hartmeyer, Anna M | Sep 1 1853 | 12/401 |

| BRIDE OR GROOM | SPOUSE | DATE | BOOK/PAGE |
|---|---|---|---|
| Marsenat, Edward | Sanlima, Henrietta ? | Jun 4 1839* | 3/176 |
| Marsh, John H (Mann) | Adams, Ann | Feb 11 1842 | 5/179B |
| Marsh, Mary | Acker, Herbert F | Jul 10 1855 | 14/194 |
| Marshall, Frances | Lyons, Catharine | Aug 16 1846* | 8/183 |
| Marshall, Harriet L | Swainey, George | Feb 26 1844 | 5/325B |
| Marshall, Jacob | Berg, Louisa | Apr 8 1844 | 8/10B |
| Marshall, James | Steele, Parmelia (Slute) | Jan 29 1842* | 5/175B |
| Marshall, Parmela E H | Byers, James M | May 30 1836* | 3/48 |
| Marshall, Sarah | Robert, William | Jul 30 1855 | 14/201 |
| Marshall, Sarah Jane | Mallory, Urial | Jan 21 1854 | 13/92 |
| Marshall, Thomas | Steal, Barbara (Steele) | Dec 15 1842 | 5/234B |
| Marshall, William T | Hails, Mary A (Haitz) | Jun 12 1841* | 5/137 |
| Marshman, William | Cox, Ann | Jan 13 1855 | 14/15 |
| Marston, Elizabeth G | Moore, William P | May 7 1849* | 8/374 |
| Marthet, Leshem | Mormier, Mary Roe ? | Jul 22 1844 | 8/34B |
| Martin, Amelia Ann | Verneuille, Jacinth | Apr 15 1851 | 11/138 |
| Martin, Ann | Donohoe, Thomas | Jan 16 1854 | 13/83 |
| Martin, Ann Jane | Baker, William G | Nov 10 1847 | 8/263 |
| Martin, Ann Matilda | Whitten, Asberry | Oct 24 1850 | 11/93 |
| Martin, Anna | Michely, Andreas | Oct 15 1833* | 2/761 |
| Martin, Bernard | West, Dorothy | Oct 28 1835* | 3/31 |
| Martin, Caroline | McQuoid, James | Nov 18 1847 | 8/266 |
| Martin, Catherine | Mackin, Patrick | Aug 24 1852* | 11/279 |
| Martin, Dominique | Miensseny, Jean M | Jun 6 1843 | 5/279B |
| Martin, Eliza A | Slade, Henry A (Hade) | Mar 27 1832* | 2/1601 |
| Martin, Elizabeth | Malone, Richard | Feb 5 1853 | 12/166 |
| Martin, Elizabeth L | Buckley, Horrace | Nov 26 1842 | 5/229B |
| Martin, Felix | Burns, Mary | Jan 22 1842 | 5/172B |
| Martin, Felix | Butler, Bridget | Nov 12 1842 | 5/227B |
| Martin, Felix | Brown, Ann | Nov 22 1843* | 5/306B |
| Martin, Frances H | Scollick, Joseph M | Jan 17 1849* | 8/348 |
| Martin, Francis | Kianezler, Catherine | May 19 1855 | 14/143 |
| Martin, Frank | Stafford, Mary | Sep 24 1849 | 11/6 |
| Martin, Fredrick | Stone, Caroline E | Oct 18 1853 | 12/417 |
| Martin, James | Robinson, Elizabeth | Apr 6 1843 | 5/259B |
| Martin, James | McGarvey, Margaret | Jun 2 1847 | 8/240 |
| Martin, John | Rigoge, Martell E ? | 1826* | OIB |
| Martin, John | Driscoll, Mary | Jul 9 1839* | 3/181 |
| Martin, John | Flinn, Ann | Jan 11 1836* | 3/35 |
| Martin, John | Thompson, Mary Ann | Sep 18 1852* | 12/7 |
| Martin, Joseph | Lockard, Mary | Dec 6 1828* | 2/54 |
| Martin, Lorris | Cochran, Louisa | Feb 25 1840* | 3/194 |
| Martin, Louisa D | Peters, Wyatt M | Jul 17 1843* | OIB/AMC |
| Martin, Margaret | Kean, Martin | Apr 1 1839* | 3/163 |
| Martin, Margaret | Kelly, James | Jun 22 1854 | 13/242 |
| Martin, Marins (Marius) | Carthy, Susannah | Feb 2 1839 | 3/154 |
| Martin, Mary | Bassford, Griffith | Apr 27 1835* | 3/23 |
| Martin, Mary | Gammon, William | Nov 25 1840* | 5/67 |
| Martin, Mary | Phillip, Angelo | Jul 29 1843 | 5/290B |
| Martin, Mary Josephine | Bassett, Andrew K | Jul 23 1849* | 8/379 |
| Martin, Mathew | McGowan, Ann | Feb 17 1844* | 5/323B |
| Martin, Merthi (Martha) | Cassagne, Francois | Nov 24 1845 | 8/125B |
| Martin, Mourning | Crook, Henry V | Apr 19 1839* | 3/167 |
| Martin, Nancy W | Coleman, Alexander | May 20 1839* | 3/172 |
| Martin, Noel F | Michell, Victoire | May 28 1831* | 2/174 |
| Martin, Nunnery (Memory) | Esins, Joseph (Esias) | Jan 24 1852 | 11/207 |
| Martin, Patrick | Gartling, Mary Ann | Jun 29 1846 | 8/175 |
| Martin, Sarah | Basley, John | Feb 28 1850 | 11/88 |
| Martin, Susan | Maura, Philomen | Feb 7 1849* | 8/355 |
| Martin, Terissa | Jackson, James | Dec 5 1848* | 8/337 |
| Martin, William | Parmly, Martha J | Oct 27 1845 | 7/849B |
| Martin, William | McArthur, Margaret | Mar 24 1855 | 14/88 |
| Martineau, Edward | Coupland, Eliza | Jun 8 1836* | 3/50 |
| Martinez, Manuel | Elizabeth, Betsey ? | Mar 6 1834* | 2/421 |

| BRIDE OR GROOM | SPOUSE | DATE | BOOK/PAGE |
|---|---|---|---|
| Martino, Peter | Run, Susanna | Dec 23 1824 | 1/56 |
| Marvin, Louisa | Corry, Henry | Nov 2 1843 | 5/301B |
| Marx, Ester | Strouse, Simon | Jan 30 1855 | 14/30 |
| Marx, Jette | Remach, Joseph | Mar 7 1854 | 13/151 |
| Marx, Lyman | Gray, Caroline | Aug 21 1855 | 14/215 |
| Maryhour, Adrina F | Kirby, David F | Feb 15 1853 | 12/173 |
| Maryland, Lucy A (Mrs) | Dorphley, Lewis H | Apr 10 1844 | 8/11B |
| Mason, Calderwood | Lott, Sally | Dec 24 1821* | CM |
| Mason, Calderwood | Sumrall, Sarah | May 3 1832 | 2/1571 |
| Mason, Charlotte | McNulty, Terrence | Dec 20 1851 | 11/196 |
| Mason, Cely | Brannan, Samuel | 1822* | OIB |
| Mason, Eliza | Stewart, James | Aug 20 1850 | 11/81 |
| Mason, Fannie V | Bedell, John | Aug 1 1855 | 14/203 |
| Mason, Frances | Brannan, James | Sep 12 1834* | 2/161 |
| Mason, John | Lyons, Ramaha | Dec 29 1842 | 5/239B |
| Mason, John | Brannan, Sarah | Sep 3 1846 | 8/187 |
| Mason, Lucretia | Williams, Jonathan C | Aug 15 1833* | 2/831 |
| Mason, Powell | Blackledge, Martha C | Nov 1 1852 | 12/32 |
| Mason, Rufus | Bray, Sophia | May 24 1855 | 14/152 |
| Mason, Sarah | Holthoff, Frank | Jun 20 1855 | 14/180 |
| Mason, Virginia A | Dent, Robert K | Jun 10 1854 | 13/250 |
| Massee, James (Maple) | Howell, Henrietta M | Mar 4 1834 | 2/431 |
| Massey, Joshua A | Dwyer, Susan J | Apr 30 1846* | 8/161B |
| Massey, Mary A | Caille, Adolphus | 1837* | OIB |
| Masters, Enoch G | Litchfield, Martha A | Oct 11 1853 | 12/414 |
| Masters, John | Rabano, Tarasa | Dec 21 1853 | 13/45 |
| Masters, Martha | Carter, William S | Aug 23 1838* | 3/140 |
| Masterson, Edward | McHugh, Bridget | Nov 28 1855 | 14/292 |
| Masterson, Elizabeth | Gillick, Hugh | Nov 23 1855 | 14/286 |
| Masterson, Hugh | Morrison, Margaret | May 28 1847 | 8/238 |
| Masterson, Hugh | Ayers, Jane A | Aug 9 1853 | 12/377 |
| Masterson, James | Kensella, Rosanna | Dec 26 1837* | 3/105 |
| Mather, Francis W | Kennedy, Martha M | Jan 3 1855 | 13/434 |
| Mather, Olivia (Mathews) | McKinstry, E | May 1 1841* | 5/128B |
| Mather, Thomas | Taylor, Olivia A | 1827* | OIB |
| Mathews, Heloise F | Senical, Amable (Jenical) | Jan 25 1845 | 8/68B |
| Mathien, Claudious    ? | Godard, Eleanor | Jan 10 1848* | 8/276 |
| Matlock, William C | Ramirez, Caroline | Jun 9 1836* | 3/50 |
| Matsinger, Mary | Siefert, Charles | Feb 21 1852 | 11/220 |
| Matthews, Benjamin F | Basford, Margaret | Jan 13 1853 | 12/128 |
| Matthews, Thomas | Leonard, Ann | Jun 29 1849* | 8/394 |
| Matthys, John A    ? | Hickman, Frances W | Sep 16 1851 | 11/179 |
| Matzar, Betsey | Levi, Solomon | Feb 12 1850* | 11/39 |
| Maura, Florestin (Mansa) | Gasin, Benjamin | Dec 25 1843 | 5/311B |
| Maura, Josephine | Palmes, Emanuel (Palmer) | Jul 5 1845 | 8/109B |
| Maura, Josephine | Castillo, Joseph | Mar 18 1848 | 8/293 |
| Maura, Philomen | Martin, Susan | Feb 7 1849* | 8/355 |
| Maura, Susan | Weaver, George | Dec 12 1846 | 8/204 |
| Maure, Enacio | Dias, Barbary | Sep 22 1852 | 12/11 |
| Mauro, Joseph | Buss, Mary Eliz. (Bass) | Sep 11 1846 | 8/188 |
| Maximillian, Adelaide B | Marks, James B | May 30 1838 | 3/129 |
| Maxsim, Elizabeth | Sills, James | Mar 7 1838* | 3/115 |
| Maxwell, Benjamin | Curry, Nancy | Jan 8 1855 | 14/3 |
| Maxwell, Catharine | Vincent, Joseph | Jun 11 1840* | 5/27B |
| Maxwell, Elenor | Engster, John | Oct 6 1851 | 11/181 |
| Maxwell, George | Moore, Susan | Oct 25 1855 | 14/265 |
| Maxwell, Henry | Porter, Mary | Sep 5 1854 | 13/329 |
| Maxwell, John | Snyder, Christine | Dec 31 1846 | 8/208 |
| May, George | Miller, Jane | Nov 23 1847 | 8/266 |
| May, George | Clark, Mary | Mar 22 1853* | 12/200 |
| Mayal, Pheneley S  ? | Dwinal, Henry (Devinal) | Mar 29 1844* | 8/7B |
| Mayberry, Thomas | Moffit, Jane, Mrs | Nov 6 1849* | 11/14 |
| Mayer, John | Kienle, Charlotte | Dec 24 1849 | 11/28 |
| Mayland, Daniel | Spear, Lucy T  ? | 1838* | OIB |

| BRIDE OR GROOM | SPOUSE | DATE | BOOK/PAGE |
|---|---|---|---|
| Mayland, Lucy A (Maryland) | Dorphley, Lewis H | Apr 10 1844 | 8/11B |
| Maynes, James (Magner) | Kelly, Jane | Dec 3 1842 | 5/231B |
| Mayrant, Mary M | Smith, William R | Nov 19 1835* | 3/31 |
| Maysin, Elizabeth | Sills, James | Mar 7 1835 | 3/115 |
| Mazange, Celistine | Eslava, Jerome | Jun 22 1827 | OIB/ADM |
| Mazange, Helene | Aubert, Mark Thomas | Feb 13 1830* | 2/111 |
| McAdams, Harvey | Bowzer, Caroline | Nov 8 1849 | 11/15 |
| McAfee, Eliza | Byrnes, Thomas | Feb 27 1843 | 5/251B |
| McAlpin, Martha C | McCan, Augustus S (McCoy) | Oct 20 1841 | 5/154B |
| McAm, John E (McCarn) | Debose, Martha | Jan 24 1848* | 8/278 |
| McArdle, James | Lahie, Mary | Oct 10 1855 | 14/250 |
| McArdle, James | McArdle, Margaret | Mar 28 1853 | 12/207 |
| McArdle, Margaret | McArdle, James | Mar 28 1853 | 12/207 |
| McArthur, Margaret | Martin, William | Mar 24 1855 | 14/88 |
| McAuley, John C | Smith, Mary J | Dec 5 1854 | 13/401 |
| McBamay, Jane ? | Irwin, Joseph | Mar 12 1839* | 3/160 |
| McBoy, Euphosyne | Pagles, John F | May 1 1832* | 2/1561 |
| McBoy, Philippa | Payne, Augustus (Payen) | Jul 28 1827 | OIB/ADM |
| McBride, Alice | Smith, John | Nov 3 1838* | 3/145 |
| McBride, James F | Moore, Margaret | Oct 5 1830* | 2/139 |
| McBride, Tabitha S | Pope, William O | Apr 14 1847 | 8/227 |
| McBrior, Alice (McBride) | Smith, John | Nov 3 1838* | 3/145 |
| McCabe, Catherine | Byrnes, James | May 25 1846 | 8/169B |
| McCabe, Mary | Bellew, James | Jan 29 1855 | 14/26 |
| McCabe, Susan | Ternan, Thomas M | Apr 19 1855 | 14/112 |
| McCafferty, Patrick | McDonald, Fanny | Oct 17 1844 | 8/43B |
| McCallis, Ann | McNicholas, John | Feb 3 1844* | 5/320B |
| McCallum, Jane | Bruce, James | Feb 28 1840* | 5/13 |
| McCalmoil, James ? | Whelm, Mary ? | Oct 24 1851 | 11/184 |
| McCan, Augustus (McCoy) | McAlpin, Martha C | Oct 20 1841 | 5/154B |
| McCan, Hugh (Carr) | Morris, Ann Eliza | Jun 22 1840 | 5/29B |
| McCann, Catherine D | Torrans, William P | Apr 5 1851 | 11/135 |
| McCann, Florence | Moore, Sampson L | Dec 20 1855 | 14/308 |
| McCann, John E | Dubose, Martha | Jan 24 1848* | 8/278 |
| McCanner, Ellen (McCannen) | Case, Henry (Care) | Dec 21 1842* | 5/236B |
| McCantiff, Catharine ? | Honan, William ? | May 28 1847 | 8/239 |
| McCarle, Ann | Hand, Anthony | Apr 10 1855 | 14/104 |
| McCarley, Michael | Barry, Helena | Nov 20 1840* | 5/65B |
| McCarthney, Ann (McCarthey) | Commings, John | Aug 20 1839* | 3/184 |
| McCarthy, Jeremiah | Audrahen, Ellen(Andrahen) | May 20 1838* | 3/129 |
| McCarthy, John | Mansfield, Margaret | Nov 24 1851 | 11/189 |
| McCarthy, Michael J | Shehan, Winny | Aug 27 1852 | 11/279 |
| McCartney, Mary Ann | McFloyd, Charley | May 6 1851 | 11/147 |
| McCartney, Nancy Jane | Nevill, William G | Apr 12 1851 | 11/137 |
| McCartney, Patrick | Terle, Maria | Mar 31 1855 | 14/93 |
| McCarty, Catharine | Alexander, Obediah | Aug 25 1841* | 5/149B |
| McCarty, Ellen | Fitzpatrick, Timothy | Jul 8 1848* | 8/313 |
| McCarty, Ellen | Fitzgerald, Daniel | Jun 27 1839* | 3/180 |
| McCarty, Ellen | Smith, George | Jul 15 1854 | 13/282 |
| McCarty, Hannah | McMahon, George | Dec 20 1850 | 11/100 |
| McCarty, Hannah (McCurty) | McDonald, Dennis | Feb 8 1842 | 5/179B |
| McCarty, Joanna | Ryan, Patrick H | Apr 21 1843 | 5/263B |
| McCarty, John | Griffin, Jane | Sep 23 1840* | 5/47B |
| McCarty, Julutte A ? | Coates, Esborn (Cooly) | Aug 26 1837 | 3/98 |
| McCarty, Mary | McMahon, Michael | Jan 29 1843 | 5/246 |
| McCarty, Mary | Moore, Robert G | Dec 14 1852 | 12/93 |
| McCarty, Mitchell | Simmons, Elizabeth A | Apr 20 1844 | 8/16B |
| McCary, Frances S | Motes, Green A | Dec 25 1851 | 11/198 |
| McCaskill, Allen | Smith, Maria | Sep 30 1840* | 5/49B |
| McCaskill, Maria | Turner, Henry | Apr 22 1846 | 8/160B |
| McCaughan, John J | Regnault, Maria H | Oct 4 1852 | 12/19 |
| McCauley, Catherine (wid) | Richards, John | Jun 2 1853 | 12/307 |
| McCauley, James | Denny, Mary Ann (Demouy) | May 21 1831* | 2/171 |
| McCavett, Mary A | Feeny, William H | Apr 1 1854 | 13/172 |

| BRIDE OR GROOM | SPOUSE | DATE | BOOK/PAGE |
|---|---|---|---|
| McClarey, Lucy | King, Poet | Dec 14 1847* | 8/270 |
| McClay, David (McKay) | White, Mary | Nov 30 1842 | 5/231 |
| McClellan, Margaret | Smith, John O' (O'Smith) | Oct 20 1845 | 8/121B |
| McClelland, Frances | Gonzalez, James | Jul 20 1853 | 12/364 |
| McClelland, Margaret | Dougherty, Barnard | Apr 21 1853 | 12/256 |
| McClelland, Mary | Wolf, John | May 24 1853* | 12/298 |
| McClenachan, James | Callahan, Catherine | Jul 16 1845 | 8/111B |
| McCleskey, George J | Meeker, Harriet C | Dec 25 1846 | 8/207 |
| McClester, Elizabeth R ? | Fonde, Charles H | Jun  5 1851* | 11/156 |
| McCloud, Elizabeth | Negus, Thomas | 1826* | OIB |
| McCloud, Joseph | Sears, Elizabeth | Mar  9 1824 | 1/24 |
| McClure, John | Murray, Catherine | Aug  3 1841 | 5/150 |
| McCluskey, Edward T | Hallohan, Catharine | May 22 1852 | 11/254 |
| McCoal, Thomas | Dittman, Marion | Feb  6 1841 | 5/101B |
| McCoint, William | McMenemy, Maria ? | Jul 11 1848 | 8/315 |
| McCollum, Elizabeth | Randall, Bryant B | 1820* | OIB |
| McConachie, Helen W | Fielding, Jacob | May 16 1855 | 14/142 |
| McConnell, Elizabeth | Hardy, William H | Jul 23 1853 | 12/365 |
| McConnor, James | Dillon, Mary | Apr 29 1838* | 3/121 |
| McCordy, Michael (McCarley) | Barry, Catherine | Nov 20 1840* | 5/65B |
| McCormick, Benjamin | Turner, Susan | Sep 10 1847* | 8/255 |
| McCormick, Bridget | Keating, Nicholas | Feb  8 1842 | 5/178B |
| McCormick, Catherine | Deolin, Patrick | May 18 1854 | 13/228 |
| McCormick, John | McKeon, Mary | Mar 28 1853 | 12/206 |
| McCormick, Julia | Gill, James | Jan 30 1855 | 14/31 |
| McCormick, Martin | Goodman, Ellen | Sep 12 1843 | 5/296B |
| McCormick, Mary | Kane, Patrick | Jan 28 1843* | 5/245B |
| McCort, William | Morecroft, Mary | Aug 21 1852* | 11/278 |
| McCoul, Ann  (McCowl) | Cappick, James | Jul  1 1843 | 5/285B |
| McCoul, Thomas | Dittmar, Maria | Feb  6 1841* | 5/101 |
| McCoul, Thomas | Dellmar, Maria (Dittman) | Mar  1 1844 | 5/325B |
| McCoul, Thomas | Houston, Elizabeth | Oct 10 1837* | 3/99 |
| McCourt, William | McMenemy, Maria | Jul 11 1848 | 8/315 |
| McCowan, Michael | Lohan, Mary | Jul 18 1853 | 12/360 |
| McCowen, Alexander | McKibbon, Jane | Jun  3 1851 | 11/154 |
| McCowen, Robert | Tool, Bridget (O'Toole) | Jun  2 1851 | 11/154 |
| McCoy, Augustus (McCan) | McAlpin, Martha C | Oct 20 1841 | 5/145B |
| McCoy, Julia | Allen, George | Jan 26 1852 | 11/208 |
| McCoy, Mary | English, John | Dec 24 1851 | 11/198 |
| McCoy, Susan Ann | Lyons, Thomas B | Jun 15 1853 | 12/319 |
| McCoy, Thomas W | Poe, Anna M | May 19 1831* | 2/170 |
| McCrae, Maria Louisa | Tisdale, Nathan O I | Sep 29 1838* | 3/142 |
| McCrarey, Elizabeth (wid) | Morris, George W (wid) | Feb  6 1855* | 14/38 |
| McCreay, Isoar (Isaiah) | Fukner, Elizabeth | Oct 23 1838* | 3/144 |
| McCullough, Charles | Jewett, Mary Elizabeth | May 26 1843 | 5/271B |
| McCullough, George | Williams, Nancy J | Jul  4 1853 | 12/346 |
| McCullough, Mary | Dwyer, Edward | Sep 13 1854 | 13/335 |
| McCullough, Mary E | Elgin, Armistead | Nov  6 1854 | 13/370 |
| McCune, Catharine | Briedy, Michael | May 19 1848* | 8/305 |
| McCune, Jane | Davidson, John | May 10 1848 | 8/304 |
| McCurty, Hannah | McDonald, Dennis | Feb  8 1842 | 5/179B |
| McDaniel, Mary Louisa | Johnson, William H | Jan  4 1849 | 8/345 |
| McDemeott, Catharine ? | Glennen, Michael | Apr 10 1841* | 5/122B |
| McDermott, Jane (Mrs) | Baker, Charles | Dec  8 1845 | 8/129B |
| McDermott, Jane | Hills, Wingate F | Oct 30 1843* | 5/301B |
| McDermott, Joseph | Kelly, Bridget | May 29 1843 | 5/276B |
| McDermott, Julia M | O'Connor, Dennis | Mar 24 1840* | 5/15 |
| McDermott, Mary | Sheerin, James ? | Feb  8 1850 | 11/38 |
| McDermott, P H M | Bateman, Cecelia Ann | May 10 1845 | 8/94B |
| McDermott, Rosanna | Dixon, James | Dec  8 1845 | 8/129B |
| McDermott, Thomas | Devin, Catherine | Jun 10 1839* | 3/177 |
| McDermott, Winford | Powers, William | Mar 21 1844 | 5/329B |
| McDevitt, Bridget | McDevitt, James | Aug  9 1843 | 5/292B |
| McDevitt, Daniel | Duncan, Ann | Nov 28 1855 | 14/291 |

| BRIDE OR GROOM | SPOUSE | DATE | BOOK/PAGE |
|---|---|---|---|
| McDevitt, Hannah | Baker, George | Jan 31 1842* | 5/176B |
| McDevitt, James | McDevitt, Bridget | Aug 9 1843 | 5/292 |
| McDevitt, James | Mulligan, Bridget | Aug 9 1843 | 6/406 |
| McDieauerette, Thomas ? | Trouillet, Louise | Jul 1 1835* | 3/18 |
| McDonald, Alexander | Graham, Ellen J | Mar 20 1838* | 3/117 |
| McDonald, Andrew | Inglemen, Denah | Jul 14 1847* | 8/245 |
| McDonald, Andrew | Burke, Ann | Aug 4 1847 | 8/249 |
| McDonald, Ann | Sonergain, John | Aug 25 1846 | 8/185 |
| McDonald, Ann | Lonergain, John | Aug 25 1846 | 8/185 |
| McDonald, Ann | Cox, Benjamin B | Mar 30 1843 | 5/256B |
| McDonald, Ann | Neill, George | Oct 20 1854 | 13/355 |
| McDonald, Bridget | Heely, Hugh | Dec 13 1841 | 5/165B |
| McDonald, Bridget | Ring, William | Jan 27 1851 | 11/118 |
| McDonald, Catharine | Burns, Robert | Aug 4 1846 | 8/183 |
| McDonald, Catharine | McGrath, John | Apr 28 1851 | 11/141 |
| McDonald, Catherine | Slalters, James | Feb 28 1840* | 3/195 |
| McDonald, Catharine | Slattery, James ? | Feb 8 1841 | 5/87 |
| McDonald, Catharine | Thompson, John | Jun 2 1841* | 5/134B |
| McDonald, Daniel | Butler, Mary | Feb 20 1845 | 8/70 |
| McDonald, Dennis | McCurty, Hannah | Feb 8 1842 | 5/179B |
| McDonald, Edward | Rooney, Mary Ann | Apr 26 1853 | 12/254 |
| McDonald, Ellen | Stubbs, Matthew | Jan 18 1852 | 11/205 |
| McDonald, Eugene | Gormon, Mary | Jan 2 1851 | 11/108 |
| McDonald, Fanny | McCafferty, Patrick | Oct 17 1844 | 8/43B |
| McDonald, James | Lyons, Margaret | Feb 24 1845 | 8/75B |
| McDonald, John | Knaggs, Martha | Mar 8 1845 | 8/78B |
| McDonald, John | Crockett, Lucy | Dec 10 1855 | 14/301 |
| McDonald, John | Conway, Sarah N | Jan 17 1853 | 12/137 |
| McDonald, Margaret | Anderson, Claes | Jan 25 1852 | 11/206 |
| McDonald, Mary | Kavanaugh, Thomas | Feb 19 1851 | 11/122 |
| McDonald, Mary | Clary, P F | Nov 12 1850 | 11/96 |
| McDonald, Mary | Fitzpatrick, Edward | Jan 21 1854 | 13/93 |
| McDonald, Mary Ann | Risher, Andrew B | Sep 13 1847* | 8/256 |
| McDonald, Mary J | Foley, Peter | Feb 7 1855 | 14/40 |
| McDonald, Owen | Riley, Catharine A | Apr 12 1852 | 11/236 |
| McDonald, Patrick | Holden, Ann | Feb 18 1854 | 13/124 |
| McDonald, Peter | Murphy, Mary Jane | Jul 18 1844 | 8/33B |
| McDonald, Philip H | Urquhart, Polly | Feb 3 1829* | 2/69 |
| McDonald, Thomas | Dowlan, Maria | Sep 25 1834* | 2/111 |
| McDonald, Thomas | Michael, Sophia | Aug 5 1833* | 2/821 |
| McDonald, Thomas | Callaghan, Margarette | Jun 12 1837* | 3/87 |
| McDonald, Thomas | Duggan, Mary | Feb 24 1854 | 13/137 |
| McDonald, Thomas | O'Brien, Bridget | Sep 15 1852 | 12/4 |
| McDonough, Ann | McNally, Bernard | Apr 30 1850 | 11/57 |
| McDonough, Joseph | Featherstone, Catherine | Jun 28 1852 | 11/266 |
| McDougall, William | Venier, Ann ? | Jan 3 1848 | 8/274 |
| McDury, Catharine ? | Roberts, Edward | Sep 20 1848* | 8/324 |
| McDury, James | O'Brien, Ann | Feb 10 1842* | 5/180B |
| McElroy, Catharine | Jones, William | Nov 13 1847 | 8/264 |
| McElroy, Margaret | Doyle, George | Jan 30 1849* | 8/351 |
| McEvoy, Mary E | Galliher, Samuel C | Nov 1 1853 | 13/3 |
| McEwen, Mary W | Houpt, Lewis | Dec 29 1845 | 8/134B |
| McFadden, Mary | Walley, Thomas | Mar 13 1844 | 5/327B |
| McFall, Catharine | Smith, Patrick | Sep 20 1848 | 8/324 |
| McFarlen, Dugald ? | Davenport, Eliza M | Mar 7 1825 | 1/66 |
| McFarren, Catherine ? | Davenport, Charles | Mar 1 1836* | 3/41 |
| McFee, Jane | Eving, James (Ewing) | Dec 3 1844 | 8/56B |
| McFloyd, Charley | McCartney, Mary Ann | May 6 1851 | 11/147 |
| McGahee, Martha Ann | Sutter, William | Mar 1 1851 | 11/126 |
| McGahee, Nancyh D | Williams, Seaborn | Jun 25 1846 | 8/175 |
| McGane, James | Crowley, Ellen | Mar 27 1855 | 14/90 |
| McGarahay, Jane | Ardogno, Bartolome | Oct 30 1854 | 13/364 |
| McGarr, Peter | Tisley, Henrietta | Jun 7 1844 | 8/26B |
| McGarvey, Margaret | Martin, James | Jun 2 1847 | 8/240 |

| BRIDE OR GROOM | SPOUSE | DATE | BOOK/PAGE |
|---|---|---|---|
| McGary, Ann | Terril, William | Apr 5 1845 | 8/84B |
| McGaughey, Daniel W | Collins, Rachel S | Dec 21 1854 | 13/416 |
| McGee, Eliza | Johnson, John L | May 20 1824* | 1/32 |
| McGee, Johanna | Thompson, George | Jun 18 1845 | 8/104B |
| McGee, Robert | Dalton, Eliza Ann | Apr 11 1850 | 11/52 |
| McGhie, Robert | Coffee, Mary Jane | Aug 10 1852 | 11/274 |
| McGibney, Ellen (McGilbrey) | Noyes, David | Nov 1 1845 | 8/122B |
| McGill, Harriet | Turner, David | Mar 29 1842* | 5/190 |
| McGill, John | Carroll, Ann | Nov 30 1843* | 5/308B |
| McGill, Margaret | McKeon, Patrick (McKern) | Jan 14 1843 | 5/243B |
| McGill, Margaret | Snow, Harvey | Feb 16 1852 | 11/218 |
| McGill, Martha L | Emmett, John D | Feb 24 1853 | 12/180 |
| McGinnis, Daniel | Kinney, Ann | Feb 17 1855 | 14/57 |
| McGinnis, Edward W | L'Hommedieu, Ann Amelia | Jan 26 1853* | 12/147 |
| McGinnis, Ellen | Lynch, Andrew | Jan 12 1852 | 11/202 |
| McGinnis, John | Harrington, Eliz. | Mar 29 1842 | 5/189B |
| McGinnis, Rosanna | Slater, John | Sep 16 1843 | 5/297B |
| McGirl, Alice | Gilhooly, Patrick | Feb 23 1850 | 11/42 |
| McGlinn, John | Kelly, Ann | Jun 9 1844 | 8/27B |
| McGlow, Patrick | Griffin, Catherine | Jan 27 1852* | 11/209 |
| McGonighal, Rosanna | Rokert, Henry (Rickert) | Jun 3 1844 | 8/24 |
| McGonigal, James | Goodwin, Amelia | Aug 7 1852 | 11/274 |
| McGonigal, Rosanna | Perkins, Henry | Jun 3 1844 | 7/279 |
| McGovern, Ann | Devine, John | Aug 30 1851* | 11/174 |
| McGovern, Margaret | Campbell, Michael | Jul 19 1854 | 11/167 |
| McGowan, Ann | Martin, Mathew | Feb 17 1844* | 5/323B |
| McGowan, Ellen M | Giblin, Daniel | Apr 1 1839 | 3/163 |
| McGowin, Cynthia | Taylor, Champe | Sep 26 1839* | 3/187 |
| McGowin, Elijah O | Christain, Amelia (Mrs) | Sep 8 1840* | 5/45B |
| McGrain, Ann | Callan, James | Feb 21 1848* | 8/285 |
| McGraine, Thomas | Byrnes, Catharine | May 2 1843* | 5/205B |
| McGrath, Ann | Byrnes, Denis | May 16 1843 | 5/273B |
| McGrath, Bridget | O'Connor, John | Jan 1 1842 | 5/167 |
| McGrath, John | McDonald, Catharine | Apr 28 1851 | 11/141 |
| McGrath, Mary | Bannon, James | Feb 5 1853 | 12/164 |
| McGrath, Patrick | Murphy, Catherine | Jun 22 1850* | 11/68 |
| McGrath, Patrick | Omahie, Mary ? | Apr 2 1853 | 12/216 |
| McGrath, Patrick | Doran, Mary | Oct 7 1852 | 12/25 |
| McGravey, Bridget | Coger, Harry | Nov 19 1853 | 13/19 |
| McGraw, Anna | Lasso, John J. | Feb 2 1852 | 11/211 |
| McGraw, Hannah | Hennerberry, John | Aug 7 1849* | 8/391 |
| McGraw, John | Eagen, Mary | Sep 13 1844 | 8/41B |
| McGraw, Thomas | Verneuille, Marie P | Apr 5 1853 | 12/222 |
| McGrime, Thomas | Brynes, Catherine | May 2 1843 | 5/267 |
| McGrinell, Dennis (Grinnel) | Morgan, Bridget | Apr 22 1828 | 2/21 |
| McGrow, James (McGrew) | Catherine (NSL) | Jun 8 1842 | 6/157B |
| McGuiness, George | Moore, Hetty | Jun 12 1855 | 14/168 |
| McGuire, Ann | Lennehan, Jeremiah | Oct 18 1854 | 13/349 |
| McGuire, Ellen | Gilbertson, Charles F | Apr 5 1853 | 12/221 |
| McGuire, John | Roane, Annette | Aug 3 1841* | 5/145B |
| McGuire, John | King, Sarah A. | Apr 4 1840* | 5/16 |
| McGuire, John | Hirley, Mary (Hurley) | Oct 6 1852 | 12/23 |
| McGuire, Matthew | Ivis, Elizabeth | Jun 22 1855 | 14/184 |
| McGuire, Patrick G. | McVoy, Louise | Dec 5 1839* | 5/3 |
| McGullion, Henry J. | Miller, Isabella Jane | May 6 1843 | 5/268B |
| McGurr, Peter (McGarr) | Titley, Henrietta | Jun 7 1844 | 8/26B |
| McHugh, Bridget | Masterson, Edward | Nov 28 1855 | 14/292 |
| McHugh, Catharine | McManus, John | Feb 6 1849* | 8/354 |
| McHugh, Jane | Barfoot, Robert L. | May 15 1835* | 3/14 |
| McHugh, John | Jones, Bridget (Toner) | Apr 6 1847 | 8/225 |
| McHugh, Mary | Flinn, Lawrence | Feb 4 1836* | 3/39 |
| McHugh, Mary Ann | Wilson, James H | Sep 3 1855 | 14/224 |
| McHugh, Sophia | Coughlin, John K | Aug 25 1835* | 3/26 |
| McIlvain, Andrew | Tatum, Sarah E | Jul 25 1844 | 8/34B |

| BRIDE OR GROOM | SPOUSE | DATE | BOOK/PAGE |
|---|---|---|---|
| McInnis, Philip | Langford, Mary Ann | Jan 15 1828* | 2/4 |
| McInroa, Lawrence | Malone, Ann | Jun 5 1855 | 14/162 |
| McIntire, Peter | Wilkinson, Zelphia | Jan 26 1835* | 3/6 |
| McIntire, Thomas | Cannon, Eliza | May 5 1842 | 5/199B |
| McIntyre, Helen | Parnel, Moses | Apr 23 1842 | 5/193B |
| McIntyre, James | Deolin, Mary | Feb 15 1855 | 14/54 |
| McIntyre, Patrick | Corkdale, Sarah | Apr 30 1844 | 8/18B |
| McIntyre, William | McLaurin, Sarah | Jan 6 1855 | 13/436 |
| McKain, Catharine | Quinn, Matthew | Aug 15 1848* | 8/320 |
| McKay, Charles | Brown, Lucinda | Jul 8 1854 | 13/278 |
| McKay, David (McClay) | White, Mary | Nov 30 1842 | 5/231B |
| McKay, John | Titter, Margaret (Titler) | Jan 3 1848 | 8/274 |
| McKay, Nancy | White, Alexander H | May 5 1836* | 3/46 |
| McKay, Rosanna | Lawless, William | Feb 11 1838* | 3/112 |
| McKay, William | Toomy, Julia Ann | Jan 7 1846 | 8/137B |
| McKea, Bridget | Howe, Charles F | Feb 19 1853 | 12/177 |
| McKearn, Joseph | Gallagher, Catherine | 1849* | OIB |
| McKee, Ann | Wickwire, Moses | Dec 5 1828* | 2/53 |
| McKee, Ann (wid) | Clifford, John (widr) | May 2 1853 | 12/266 |
| McKeen, Martha Ann | Browning, Joseph S | Oct 19 1846 | 8/194 |
| McKeen, Virginia H | Haig, John | Sep 11 1851 | 11/178 |
| McKeever, Hugh | Williamson, Sarah | Oct 18 1854 | 13/351 |
| McKenna, Michael | Duffy, Alice | Apr 11 1843 | 5/260B |
| McKenneth, Sarah | McMullin, William | Feb 7 1814* | WB 1/16 |
| McKenney, Patrick | Hall, Leonora | May 4 1842 | 5/198B |
| McKensey, Caroline | Wood, George | Oct 14 1834* | 3/4 |
| McKenzie, Alexander | Corlis, Maria | Mar 21 1844 | 5/329B |
| McKenzie, Amelia Jane | Wyatt, W.R.R. | Apr 7 1843 | 5/259B |
| McKenzie, Francis | Denley, Sarah Ann | Jan 3 1842* | 5/168B |
| McKenzie, Roderick W | Mooney, Catherine | Jun 25 1838 | 3/133 |
| McKeon, Mary | McCormick, John | Mar 28 1853 | 12/206 |
| McKeon, Patrick | McGill, Margaret | Jan 14 1843 | 5/243B |
| McKeowen, Michael | Conerty, Catherine | May 11 1840* | 5/23 |
| McKern, Carolina A | Moffitt, F. A. | Oct 24 1850* | 11/92 |
| McKern, Georgia B | Brown, Perino | Oct 24 1850* | 11/92 |
| McKever, Alexander | O'Connor, Mary A | Jun 8 1854 | 13/246 |
| McKevitt, James | Regan, Margaret | Jul 20 1846 | 8/180 |
| McKey, Letitice | Gamble, Thomas | Dec 17 1852 | 12/96 |
| McKibbon, Caroline | Hays, Charles | Feb 24 1854 | 13/138 |
| McKibbon, Henry | Daugherty, Mary | Jan 25 1831* | 2/148 |
| McKibbon, James | Nelligan, Mary | Feb 10 1855 | 14/46 |
| McKibbon, Jane | McCowen, Alexander | Jun 3 1851 | 11/154 |
| McKiernan, Mary | Smith, Wilson A | Nov 27 1850 | 11/99 |
| McKinna, James | Keeland, Ellen | May 4 1838* | 3/123 |
| McKinna, Peter | Miller, Jane A | Mar 10 1838* | 3/115 |
| McKinney, Hugh | O'Brien, Ann | 1841* | OIB |
| McKinsey, Adeline | Pierce, Thomas | Feb 5 1833* | 2/1161 |
| McKinsey, Adelle | Gates, Hezekiah | Oct 13 1834* | 3/5 |
| McKinsey, Benjamin | Ratcliff, Ann | Mar 27 1839* | 3/161 |
| McKinsey, Caroline | Wood, George | 1834* | OIB |
| McKinsey, Margueretta | Williams, William | Jul 31 1855 | 14/202 |
| McKinsie, William | Hughes, Catherine | Jun 4 1853 | 12/309 |
| McKinstry, Alexander | Dade, Virginia T | Mar 20 1845 | 8/80B |
| McKinstry, E | Mather, Olivia (Mathews) | May 1 1841* | 5/128B |
| McKinstry, Thomas | Child, Susan | Dec 1 1841* | 5/160B |
| McKnight, Margaret | Clark, Robert C | Nov 11 1839* | 3/191 |
| McKnight, Mary | Healy, John | May 24 1845 | 8/98B |
| McKnight, William | Hartman, Caroline | Aug 29 1842* | 5/217B |
| McLacklin, Mary Ann | Shafer, Charles | Sep 18 1849 | 11/5 |
| McLain, William | Small, Catherine | Jan 23 1843 | 5/172B |
| McLaren, Duncan | Munroe, Sarah | Feb 19 1845 | 8/74B |
| McLaughlin, Ann | Smith, George | Nov 19 1839* | 5/1 |
| McLaughlin, Anne | Casey, Richard T. | Jun 18 1845 | 8/105B |
| McLaughlin, Bridget | Castillo, Walter | Mar 21 1843 | 5/255B |

| BRIDE OR GROOM | SPOUSE | DATE | BOOK/PAGE |
|---|---|---|---|
| McLaughlin, Catharine | Stevens, John | Jun 11 1845 | 8/102B |
| McLaughlin, Catherine | Hickes, Frances F | Apr 12 1853 | 12/235 |
| McLaughlin, Catherine A | Feron, Joseph | Oct 29 1852 | 12/39 |
| McLaughlin, Eliza G | Ogden, Morgan S. | Jul 7 1841* | 5/85B |
| McLaughlin, John | Nugent, Mary Ann | Jan 16 1851 | 11/113 |
| McLaughlin, John (wid) | O'Rouke, Maria (wid) | Aug 22 1853 | 12/392 |
| McLaughlin, Margaret | Gallagher, Henry | May 4 1852 | 11/245 |
| McLaughlin, Rose | Cuthbert, James | Jan 5 1843* | 5/241B |
| McLaughlin, Thomas | Brady, Mary | Jun 5 1841* | 5/135B |
| McLaughlin, Thomas | Murphy, Mary | Sep 29 1841* | 5/153B |
| McLaughton, Ellen | Moon, Henry | May 24 1839* | 3/173 |
| McLaurin, Sarah | McIntyre, William | Jan 6 1855 | 13/436 |
| McLean, Ann | Means, Robert | Nov 9 1846 | 8/197 |
| McLean, Catharine | Galloway, Alexander | Sep 28 1840* | 5/47B |
| McLean, Daniel | Turner, Martha | Feb 3 1845 | 8/70B |
| McLean, John | Allen, Elizabeth | Feb 26 1842 | 5/183B |
| McLean, Susan C | Rowe, Benjamin F | Oct 21 1854 | 13/358 |
| McLean, William B. | Smoot, Susan | Aug 14 1840* | 5/43B |
| McLelland, Robert John | Anderson, Ann | Aug 16 1851 | 11/172 |
| McLeod, David | Lennon, Mary Ann (Lorman) | Jan 27 1845 | 8/69B |
| McLeod, Margaret | Lott, Berry | Jan 15 1834* | 2/531 |
| McLeod, Mary | Mordough, James H. | May 20 1852 | 11/252 |
| McLester, Elizabeth R | Fonde, Charles H | Jun 5 1851 | 11/186 |
| McLoud, Charles | Campbell, Frances | Mar 5 1849* | 8/360 |
| McMahan, Bridget | Rodgers, Edward | Sep 17 1853 | 12/408 |
| McMahon, Bridget | Illingworth, Thomas | Jan 20 1851 | 11/114 |
| McMahon, Catherine | Gorman, John | Jan 14 1853 | 12/132 |
| McMahon, Catherine | Ahern, John | Jul 28 1855 | 14/200 |
| McMahon, George | McCarty, Hannah | Dec 20 1850 | 11/104 |
| McMahon, James | Byrne, Mary | Nov 28 1848* | 8/335 |
| McMahon, Mary | Donohoe, Jeremiah | Dec 4 1855 | 14/2982 |
| McMahon, Mary Ann | Oldmixon, George A. | May 3 1850* | 11/59 |
| McMahon, Michael | McCarty, Mary | Jan 29 1843 | 5/246 |
| McMahon, Michael | Camody, Catherine | Apr 1 1854 | 13/171 |
| McMahon, Patrick | Higgins, Ellen | Jan 11 1855 | 14/13 |
| McMahon, Patrick | Gavin, Mary | Feb 4 1854 | 13/110 |
| McMahon, Thomas | Garoty, Bridget | Apr 6 1854 | 13/174 |
| McManus, Ann | Brown, James | Apr 20 1854 | 13/197 |
| McManus, John | McHugh, Catharine | Feb 6 1849* | 8/354 |
| McManus, Patrick | Laughlin, Ann | Jul 1 1853 | 12/337 |
| McManus, William | Roper, Sarah | Jun 1 1853 | 12/306 |
| McMenemy, Maria | McCoint, William | Jul 11 1848* | 8/315 |
| McMillan, Mary C. | Larx, John B (Lax) | May 19 1842 | 5/202B |
| McMillan, Mary E. | Bridges, Charles E. | May 5 1852 | 11/246 |
| McMillan, William | O'Neil, Massey | Mar 3 1834* | 2/441 |
| McMinn, Thomas | Gilroy, Ann | Feb 23 1852 | 11/221 |
| McMorris, Morgan | Files, Sarah (Hiles) | Nov 28 1838* | 3/150 |
| McMullen, Sarah | Roberts, William | 1826* | OIB |
| McMullin, William | McKenneth, Sarah | Feb 7 1814* | WB 1/16 |
| McNally, Bernard | McDonough, Ann | Apr 30 1850 | 11/57 |
| McNally, Bridget | Stanley, Edward | Jan 16 1854 | 13/81 |
| McNamara, Daniel | Spilleoon, Mary | Apr 12 1849* | 8/368 |
| McNamara, Ellen | Anderson, John N. | Feb 29 1840* | 5/13 |
| McNamara, Margarette | Quinn, P. | Jun 13 1838* | 3/132 |
| McNamara, Mary | Henry, John | Dec 1 1840* | 5/83B |
| McNamara, Michael | Saucier, Hipolite | Dec 10 1820* | CM |
| McNamara, Stephen | Kanada, Judy | Nov 20 1851 | 11/187 |
| McNamee, Ann | Quinn, Michael | Feb 22 1854 | 13/130 |
| McNaspy, James | Dorathy, Sarah | Apr 12 1847* | 8/226 |
| McNaughton, Florian | Turner, John | Jan 15 1834* | 2/551 |
| McNaughton, Francis | Shidell, Emeline | Nov 21 1848* | 8/332 |
| McNeil, Archibald | Parmer, Margaret | Nov 10 1852 | 12/58 |
| McNeil, Thomas L | Helverson, Susanna | Aug 30 1855 | 14/221 |
| McNeill, Daniel | Jones, Eliza Jane | Aug 26 1847 | 8/253 |

| BRIDE OR GROOM | SPOUSE | DATE | BOOK/PAGE |
|---|---|---|---|
| McNeill, Jane | Stevens, Andrew | Mar 21 1843 | 5/254B |
| McNellage, Jane Matilda | Baptiste, John P. | Oct 8 1842 | 5/222B |
| McNellage, John J. | Miller, Mary | Dec 28 1848 | 8/341 |
| McNespey, James | Myers, Mahala | Nov 9 1852 | 12/56 |
| McNicholas, John | McCallis, Ann | Feb 3 1844* | 5/320B |
| McNiff, Catherine | Murray, John | Dec 3 1855 | 14/295 |
| McNulty, Patrick | Donnolly, Eliza | Dec 2 1850 | 11/101 |
| McNulty, Terrence | Mason, Charlotte | Dec 20 1851 | 11/196 |
| McNutty, Catherine ? | Kerns, John | May 31 1852* | 11/257 |
| McPherson, John | Smith, Eliza J. | Jun 1 1840* | 5/26B |
| McPhillips, Ann | Church, James | May 4 1844 | 8/19B |
| McQuaid, John | O'Donnell, Margaret | Sep 1 1851 | 11/175 |
| McQueen, Lewis | Fontaine, Millicent | Jan 12 1847 | 8/212 |
| McQuillan, Catherine | Doyle, Lawrence | Feb 12 1851 | 11/121 |
| McQulen, Mary Jane | Mansen, Augustus | Dec 5 1849 | 11/21 |
| McQuoid, James | Martin, Caroline | Nov 18 1847 | 8/266 |
| McRae, Catherine | Stall, Frederick | Sep 3 1853 | 12/400 |
| McRae, Colman | Bass, Mary | 1827* | OIB |
| McRae, Malcolm I. | Taylor, Mary A. | Aug 24 1842 | 5/217B |
| McRoberts, Benjamin | Parmeler, Eliza | Dec 25 1834* | 3/5 |
| McShapick, James | Kiruland, Sarah (Keeland) | Jan 25 1838* | 3/109 |
| McSweeney, Ellen | Ryan, Robert | Jul 11 1841* | 5/87B |
| McSwinney, Miles | Haley, Catherine | Jan 14 1853 | 12/133 |
| McTeirnan, Patrick K | Toemey, Bridget | Oct 25 1855 | 14/264 |
| McTiernan, Patrick | Glennon, Catherine | Sep 6 1854 | 13/332 |
| McTernan, Catherine | O'Brien, Thomas | Jan 27 1855 | 14/24 |
| McTyeire, Holland N. | Townsend, Amelia | Nov 8 1847 | 8/264 |
| McVarmara, Mary (McNamara) | Henry, John | Dec 1 1840* | 5/83B |
| McVay, Martin | Gueruard, Amelia T. | May 7 1835* | 3/13 |
| McVoy, Isabella | Stickney, Daniel H. | Feb 1 1841* | 5/99B |
| McVoy, Louise | McGuire, Patrick G. | Dec 5 1839* | 5/3 |
| McWaine, Margaret | Belknap, William | Jun 2 1823* | 1/9 |
| McWhister, Robert | Sims, Messieir | Aug 17 1847* | 8/252 |
| McWilliams, Hugh | Runnells, Susan | Oct 29 1846 | 8/196 |
| Mead, Eliza H. | Taylor, William | May 27 1828 | 2/27 |
| Mead, Hannah | O'Brien, John | Apr 10 1841* | 5/121B |
| Meade, Garrett | Curtin, Ellen | Mar 26 1842 | 5/188B |
| Meader, William E. | Switt, Carolina B. | Sep 18 1839* | 3/187 |
| Meador, Benjamin | Collins, Elizabeth | May 1 1845 | 8/90B |
| Mealue, Ann | Reed, George I. | Sep 11 1849* | 11/4 |
| Mealy, Cecile O | Neville, Thomas | Jul 13 1853 | 12/350 |
| Mealy, Ellen | Elward, Daniel | Aug 5 1854 | 13/304 |
| Means, Margaret | Condon, James | Apr 29 1850 | 11/56 |
| Means, Robert | McLean, Ann | Nov 9 1846 | 8/197 |
| Measles, Reubin | Clark, Lucinda | Aug 24 1847* | 8/252 |
| Meazles, Mary Jane | Stroud, William | Aug 27 1850 | 11/82 |
| Mechon, Peter | Saroste, Mathilde ? | Oct 3 1840* | 5/51B |
| Mechon, Peter | Lacost, Mathilde | Oct 3 1840* | 5/51B |
| Medlock, Martha A. | Huggins, Charles W. | Jun 1 1844 | 8/24B |
| Meek, John | Penton, Mary | Jun 27 1814* | WB 1/19 |
| Meeker, Barbary R | Wright, Reuben T | Nov 17 1855 | 14/284 |
| Meeker, Harriet C. | McCleskey, George J. | Dec 25 1846 | 8/207 |
| Meeker, Louisa | Taylor, John W. | May 4 1847 | 8/233 |
| Meeker, Nathan | Ballisette, Francis | Nov 20 1844 | 8/52B |
| Mehen, Ellen | Colwell, Lewis | Dec 1 1844 | 8/55 |
| Mehnerd, Frederick E | Hubbert, Francisca | Aug 29 1853* | 12/397 |
| Mehrtens, George H. | Beckman, Dorethea | Mar 11 1848 | 8/292 |
| Meigs, Louisa (Mugs) | Trenier, John B | Jan 5 1841* | 5/85B |
| Meikle, William | Hogan, Sarah V | Jun 4 1855 | 14/161 |
| Meiners, Diedrich | Stoll, Nancy | Apr 5 1850 | 11/51 |
| Meinhin, Catherine | Sullivan, Jeremiah | Mar 13 1837* | 3/74 |
| Meley, Elisabeth | Sweeny, John | Jul 26 1850 | 11/272 |
| Mellen, Charles | York, Eliza A. | Jan 23 1849* | 8/349 |
| Mellon, Eliza | Thompson, William | Aug 13 1847 | 8/253 |

| BRIDE OR GROOM | SPOUSE | DATE | BOOK/PAGE |
|---|---|---|---|
| Melrose, John G. | Robinson, Miss A.E. | May 1 1838* | 3/122 |
| Menasco, Andrew J. | Saxon, Matilda C.R. | Aug 14 1845 | 8/115B |
| Menasco, Jacob | Saxon, Elmira | Aug 23 1845 | 8/116B |
| Mendel, William | Steil, Christine | Apr 9 1842* | 5/191B |
| Mendel, William | Eipat, Helen (Eifrat) | Dec 8 1845 | 8/129B |
| Mengie, John (Menzie) | Scott, Sarah E. | Nov 4 1840* | 5/59 |
| Menne, Joseph (Mann) | Peckler, Elizabeth | Nov 27 1840* | 5/67B |
| Mercer, Jane A | Shoemaker, Samuel | May 2 1853 | 12/267 |
| Mercer, Peter (Meslier) | Schroebel, Margaret | Jul 17 1850 | 11/74 |
| Merchant, Louis (Marchand) | Barnes, Mary (wid) | Jan 2 1855* | 13/432 |
| Merchant, Louis ? | Feist, Rosina | Jul 6 1855* | 14/190 |
| Mercy, Sarah Ann | Huff, James G | Apr 23 1853 | 12/251 |
| Merlin, Augustus R. | Kennedy, Mary E. | Apr 23 1842 | 5/193 |
| Merlin, Thomas P (Miller) | Williams, Eliza E. | May 20 1843* | 5/274B |
| Merrill, Daniel F. | Bell, Luella B. | May 21 1845 | 8/96B |
| Merrina, Louis (Mersina) | Smullen, Mairy | Jan 21 1842 | 5/171B |
| Merrit, Charles | Forsyth, Mary | Sep 3 1820* | CM |
| Merritt, Alabama W. | Smith, Sidney | Mar 28 1835 | 3/13 |
| Merritt, Mary Ann | Elliott, Robert | Mar 27 1848 | 8/295 |
| Merritt, Randolph | Skinner, Sarah | Jan 31 1849* | 8/351 |
| Mersina, Lewis (Merrina) | Smullin, Mary | Jan 21 1842 | 5/171B |
| Mervin, Elizabeth A. | Culbertson, John | Apr 29 1845 | 8/89B |
| Mervin, Laura | Hall, William | Sep 14 1820* | CM |
| Mervin, William | Bateman, Mary Cath. | Jan 7 1846 | 8/137B |
| Merz, Charles | Assing, Elizabeth | Oct 22 1855 | 14/259 |
| Merz, William R | Remetsh, Maria C | Nov 19 1853 | 13/18 |
| Mesa, Francisca | Ring, Simon | Aug 1 1850* | 11/78 |
| Meslier, Ann | Quarmby, John | May 1 1854 | 13/211 |
| Meslier, Basilia A. | Silor, Joshua S. | Oct 11 1834* | 2/91 |
| Metrand, Pierre | Journy, Marie | Dec 3 1841* | 5/159B |
| Metzger, Adam | Straus, Babeth | May 13 1850* | 11/61 |
| Meyers, Augustine | Graft, John | Feb 10 1845 | 8/72B |
| Miatovick, Spiro | Malone, Mary | Jun 1 1852 | 11/258 |
| Michael, Barbary | Harrison, J.W. | Mar 2 1852* | 11/223 |
| Michael, Eve | Eichner, William | Oct 31 1832* | 2/1331 |
| Michael, George | Braitlinger, Maria | Oct 31 1833* | 2/611 |
| Michael, Mary | Gill, Barney | Apr 13 1842 | 5/195B |
| Michael, Sophia | McDonald, Thomas | Aug 5 1833* | 2/821 |
| Michaeloffesky, John | Guesnard, Athalie | Jan 23 1840* | 5/9 |
| Michell, Victoire | Martin, Noel F | May 28 1831* | 2/174 |
| Michely, Andreas | Martin, Anna | Oct 15 1833* | 2/761 |
| Michold, Louis | Elford, Eliza | Mar 10 1853 | 12/189 |
| Michon, Rebecca | Hare, William | Apr 4 1855 | 14/98 |
| Micklin, James, Jr. | Hall, Mary | Oct 3 1837* | 3/92 |
| Middleton, Eadie | Barker, William | May 18 1836* | 3/48 |
| Middleton, Lewis A. | Dade, Mary E. | Feb 15 1844 | 5/322B |
| Miedenez, Margaret | Gomez, Lorenzo | Aug 7 1849* | 8/391 |
| Mienssem, Jeanne Marie | Martin, Dominique | Jun 6 1843 | 5/279B |
| Mifflin, David | Barnett, Fanny | Apr 20 1854 | 13/198 |
| Mighall, Joseph | Storer, Mary Ann L. | Jul 5 1848* | 8/312 |
| Mignon, I. | Pradien, Josephine | May 23 1838* | 3/129 |
| Miland, Luc F | De Graces, Sophe Plena | Mar 8 1828* | 2/13 |
| Miles, Ann | Gibbs, James | Apr 25 1838* | 3/121 |
| Miles, Benjamin | Hanol, Elizabeth | Mar 30 1850 | 11/48 |
| Miles, Helen | Harris, Joseph | Apr 5 1850 | 11/51 |
| Miles, Lucy T (Niles) | Ryland, Allen H. | Nov 19 1840* | 5/65B |
| Miles, Margaret | Baptiste, Adolphe | Sep 29 1852* | 12/14 |
| Miles, Margaret | Overstreet, Stephen | May 16 1854 | 13/225 |
| Miles, Martha E | Russell, John N | Feb 27 1851 | 11/25 |
| Miles, Mary J | Roberts, Daniel | Jan 18 1854 | 13/87 |
| Miley, Dennis (Milry) | Pollard, Dorthea | May 6 1843 | 5/269B |
| Miley, John | Greely, Bridget | May 22 1846 | 8/169B |
| Miley, John | Depew, Ann E. | Sep 12 1837* | 3/91 |
| Miley, John B. | O'Donald, Ellen | Feb 16 1841* | 5/104B |

| BRIDE OR GROOM | SPOUSE | DATE | BOOK/PAGE |
|---|---|---|---|
| Miller, Alex | Daughterty, Susan | Jul 22 1813* | WB 1/7 |
| Miller, Amanda | Thompson, Charles J | Jul 2 1853 | 12/344 |
| Miller, Andrew | Gorlott, Nancy | 1825* | OIB |
| Miller, Andrew | Harmshire, Hannah | Jan 11 1849 | 8/347 |
| Miller, Ann | Ridley, James | Dec 1 1821* | CM |
| Miller, Catherine (Milton) | Cesaneny, Chrisostome | Apr 21 1843 | 5/262B |
| Miller, Catherine A | Baldwin, William J | Jun 9 1853 | 12/313 |
| Miller, Charles | Baker, Margaret | Oct 6 1847 | 8/257 |
| Miller, Christinna | Rarford, Dudley | Jan 14 1839* | 3/B152B |
| Miller, Dorice | Untrener, Peter | Jan 17 1852 | 11/204 |
| Miller, Eliza | Bindge, John M (Burge) | Apr 6 1842* | 5/190B |
| Miller, Eliza | Bosarge, Maximillian | Mar 26 1855 | 14/89 |
| Miller, Eliza Ann | Boullemils, Millon | Oct 1 1839* | 3/187 |
| Miller, Ellen | Duff, John | Jun 10 1839* | 3/178 |
| Miller, Emily Ann | Gartman, George | Dec 20 1847* | 8/272 |
| Miller, Emma Eliza | Morris, William | Jul 15 1845 | 8/110B |
| Miller, Francis W. | Thompson, Jane | Jul 26 1845 | 8/112B |
| Miller, George | Bozard, Mary | Aug 25 1838* | 3/140 |
| Miller, George | Simeon, Ann | Sep 22 1846 | 8/189 |
| Miller, Isabella Jane | McGullion, Henry I. | May 6 1843 | 5/268B |
| Miller, James | Chivers, Jane | Nov 6 1843* | 5/302B |
| Miller, Jane | O'Brien, William | Jan 21 1839* | 3/B153 |
| Miller, Jane | May, George | Nov 23 1847 | 8/266 |
| Miller, Jane A. | McKinna, Peter | Mar 10 1838* | 3/115 |
| Miller, Janet Elliot | Brent, R. Carrere | Jul 19 1851 | 11/166 |
| Miller, John | Greene, Elizabeth | May 4 1843 | 5/268B |
| Miller, John | Sullivant, Emiline | Aug 18 1840 | 4/3961B |
| Miller, John O. | Dortutor, Emily | Apr 4 1851 | 11/134 |
| Miller, Louis | Kidd, Charity | Aug 22 1853 | 12/391 |
| Miller, Margaret | Tagart, Jacob A | Mar 12 1853 | 12/191 |
| Miller, Margaret M. | Tyner, Benjamin | Aug 16 1842 | 5/217B |
| Miller, Mary | McNellage, John J. | Dec 28 1848 | 8/341 |
| Miller, Mary | Bell, John J | Aug 28 1854 | 13/322 |
| Miller, Mary (wid) | Chisolm, Jonathan (widr) | Dec 31 1853 | 13/59 |
| Miller, Mary Ann | Morehouse, Avnan | Mar 13 1839* | 3/160 |
| Miller, Mary Craig | Hutchison, Peter | Mar 29 1844 | 8/7B |
| Miller, Mary M | Blount, Felix E | Sep 13 1855 | 14/230 |
| Miller, Nathan W. | Roach, Eliz. Ann | Feb 1 1849 | 8/352 |
| Miller, Peter I. | Butler, Cinderilla | Feb 10 1834* | 2/471 |
| Miller, Presteline (wid) | Thomas, Young (wid) | Mar 13 1855* | 14/83 |
| Miller, Robert W | Godley, Harriet E (wid) | Aug 15 1853 | 12/382 |
| Miller, Robinson | Tankersly, Gertrude | Dec 5 1848 | 8/336 |
| Miller, Samuel | Cohen, Sabrina | Dec 31 1845 | 8/134B |
| Miller, Sarah | Rabie, Pier | 1825* | OIB |
| Miller, Sarah (Milton) | Wilkie, James | Dec 17 1842 | 5/235B |
| Miller, Susana | Roberts, William | Jan 27 1839* | 3/B153 |
| Miller, Therese | Pound, Godfrey | Mar 2 1836* | 3/41 |
| Miller, Thomas | Gibbson, Emeline | 1840* | OIB |
| Miller, Thomas P (Merlin) | Williams, Eliza E. | May 20 1843 | 5/274B |
| Miller, William M | Enholm, Avis E | Dec 14 1853 | 13/40 |
| Millerick, Thomas | Collins, Johanna | Aug 2 1844 | 8/37B |
| Millick, Antoine | Hart, Sopha | Apr 16 1849* | 8/368 |
| Milligan, Ellen | Bride, James | Nov 27 1850 | 11/100 |
| Millise, Elizabeth | Tally, Horace | Apr 18 1838* | 3/119 |
| Mills, Catharine | Sprinkles, Peter | Nov 7 1850 | 11/95 |
| Mills, David (Miller) | Lyons, Elizabeth | Jan 28 1833* | 2/1181 |
| Mills, Jane E. | Parker, Gideon M. | Nov 11 1843* | 5/303B |
| Mills, Julia A. | Macy, Robert C. | Nov 24 1845* | 8/125B |
| Mills, Mary A. | Dorrance, Chas. W. | May 18 1835* | 3/15 |
| Milry, Dennis (Miley) | Pollard, Dorothea | May 6 1843 | 5/269B |
| Milton, Catherine (Miller) | Cesanceney, Chrisostome | Apr 21 1843 | 5/262B |
| Milton, Sarah (Miller) | Wilkie, James | Dec 17 1842 | 5/235B |
| Mimms, Nancy Jane | Cleveland, John M. | Jun 10 1852 | 11/261 |
| Mims, Sally (Minn) | Dean, William | Jul 21 1842 | 5/212B |

| BRIDE OR GROOM | SPOUSE | DATE | BOOK/PAGE |
|---|---|---|---|
| Minge, Jane O. | Dixey, Robert H. | Feb 3 1852 | 11/211 |
| Mink, Peter | Shwenk, Mary | Dec 3 1855 | 14/296 |
| Minn, Sally | Dean, William | Jul 21 1842* | 5/212B |
| Minor, Bridget | Gillan, Andrew | Apr 28 1855 | 14/122 |
| Mintzer, Margueretta A | Larue, John C | May 14 1853 | 12/283 |
| Mintzer, William H | Henry, Sarah J. | Jun 14 1851* | 11/158 |
| Mitaine, Madelene | Christian, Joseph | Mar 17 1842* | 5/186B |
| Mitcham, M. | Cole, Elizabeth | Jan 8 1818* | CM |
| Mitchell, Amanda | Roach, John | Jan 12 1848 | 8/277 |
| Mitchell, Ann | Gets, Henry | Nov 20 1849* | 11/17 |
| Mitchell, Bernard D. | Smith, Almira C. | Mar 8 1841* | 5/114B |
| Mitchell, Caroline | Nimocks, Walter S. | May 7 1849* | 8/373 |
| Mitchell, Ellis | Reeves, Nancy | May 10 1851 | 11/147 |
| Mitchell, Elmira | Green, William | Nov 24 1845 | 8/126B |
| Mitchell, Felecia | Kerr, Victor | Jan 1 1849 | 8/343 |
| Mitchell, Frank | Andrews, Lavinia | Mar 9 1850 | 11/44 |
| Mitchell, J.J. | Fisk, Catherine | Mar 24 1838* | 3/116 |
| Mitchell, John | Gordon, Ann | May 31 1853* | 12/304 |
| Mitchell, John I. | Reynolds, Elizabeth | Jul 1 1829 | 2/90 |
| Mitchell, Julia A. | Strong, William A. | Apr 11 1844 | 8/12B |
| Mitchell, Lucy | Mackay, Robert W. | Jul 18 1846 | 8/180 |
| Mitchell, Lydia B. | Preis, John J. | Feb 10 1847 | 8/216 |
| Mitchell, Mary E. | Dade, Robert T. | Apr 13 1846* | 8/158B |
| Mitchell, Rosanna | Byrne, Patrick T. | Dec 17 1841 | 5/163B |
| Mitchell, Sarah | Monk, Menan (wid) | Nov 10 1853 | 13/13 |
| Mitchell, Sarah A. | Chappell, Lewis W. | Dec 19 1846 | 8/206 |
| Mitchell, Sarah Ellenor | Tingman, John | Apr 1 1844 | 8/8B |
| Mitchell, William M | Childers, Amanda M (wid) | Dec 13 1853 | 13/37 |
| Mizell, James | Tillman, Martha | Feb 11 1845 | 8/72B |
| Mizell, Josiah | Harrell, Lucy Ann | Sep 12 1846 | 8/189 |
| Mobley, John | Parker, Charlotte | Dec 25 1828 | 2/58 |
| Mock, Peter | Myers, Elizabeth | Feb 3 1853* | 12/161 |
| Moffat, Matilda Ann | Shelby, Louie | Feb 10 1852 | 11/215 |
| Moffatt, Thomas T. | Ashley, Jane Harriet | Jun 16 1846 | 8/173 |
| Moffet, Henry | Smith, Jane E. | Jun 29 1838* | 3/134 |
| Moffett, Gabriel | Williams, Rebecca M. | Sep 6 1841 | 5/150B |
| Moffett, John M. | Murrell, Mary F. | Nov 17 1840* | 5/63B |
| Moffit, Margaret | Barrenos, Joakin | Apr 12 1841* | 5/122B |
| Moffitt, F.A. | McKern, Carolina A. | Oct 24 1850* | 11/92 |
| Moffitt, Jane Mrs. | Mayberry, Thomas | Nov 6 1849* | 11/14 |
| Moffitt, Margarett | Barvilli, Joachim | Apr 12 1841* | 5/122B |
| Mohnsamen, Frederick | Laingos, Maria (Launger) | Feb 23 1843* | 5/250B |
| Mohon, Mary Ann (Mahon) | Ray, Hiram | Jul 3 1840* | 5/33 |
| Molden, Nelson | Barnes, Philipe Margte. | Mar 17 1837* | 3/75 |
| Molliere, Augustus | Cialos, Bienna | Apr 3 1855 | 14/96 |
| Molloy, John | Kinney, Hanora | Apr 11 1855 | 14/105 |
| Mompert, Mary | Schriener, Conrad | Nov 15 1851 | 11/187 |
| Mon, Benito (Mann) | Bozars, Mary | May 21 1842* | 5/202B |
| Monaity, Margaret | Donoghue, Jeremiah | Dec 29 1845 | 8/133B |
| Monarty, Margaret | Silva, Francisco | Feb 23 1842 | 5/182B |
| Mondon, Jean Mari | Prieau, Jeane Marie | Oct 3 1842 | 5/221B |
| Mondrano, Paul | Tendral, Amanda (Tindal) | Feb 17 1849 | 8/358 |
| Moneagle, Edward | Walker, Mary | Feb 21 1854 | 13/128 |
| Monk, Elizabeth (Mack) | Bogue, Terrance | Jul 25 1844 | 8/35B |
| Monk, Elizabeth A | Stanton, Zachariah A | Jan 9 1855 | 14/7 |
| Monk, Francis M. | Thomas, John | Oct 26 1847 | 8/261 |
| Monk, Harriet C. | Champanois, Simon P. | Dec 19 1848 | 8/339 |
| Monk, John | Rogers, Isabella B. | Mar 2 1848* | 8/289 |
| Monk, Martha | Grant, John | Feb 22 1842 | 5/181B |
| Monk, Martha | Edward, Senale | Jan 24 1839* | 3/154 |
| Monk, Martha | Baptiste, Edward | Dec 19 1839* | 5/4 |
| Monk, Mary | Williams, Henry | 1825* | OIB |
| Monk, Menan (widr) | Mitchell, Sarah | Nov 10 1853 | 13/13 |
| Monk, Menon | Zurban, Phedora | Sep 29 1849 | 11/8 |

| BRIDE OR GROOM | SPOUSE | DATE | BOOK/PAGE |
|---|---|---|---|
| Monk, Nancy | Ryals, Perry | Feb 10 1851 | 11/119 |
| Monk, Noah | Smart, Mary | Mar 11 1841* | 5/116B |
| Monk, Patience | Roach, John | Feb 1 1836* | 3/39 |
| Monk, Rebecca | Todd, William | Apr 19 1823 | 1/0 |
| Monk, Rhody | Staylor, William | Sep 19 1825 | 1/91 |
| Monk, Thomas | George, Harriett | Jul 1 1834* | 2/251 |
| Monk, Wiley | Anderson, Laura Ann | Mar 21 1834* | 2/371 |
| Monnahan, Alice | Casbrey, James | Jul 27 1851 | 11/169 |
| Monnin, Louis | Chighizola, Marie | Sep 9 1848 | 8/323 |
| Monore, Fanny | Story, Abraham | May 22 1854 | 13/232 |
| Monrghin, Mary (Mourghin) | O'Brien, Patrick | May 18 1843 | 5/274B |
| Monroe, Abby | Mryan, William ? | Apr 8 1839* | 3/165 |
| Monroe, Abby | Ryan, Willliam M | Apr 8 1839* | 3/165B |
| Monroe, Alexander | Nelins, Tracey | Aug 31 1839* | 3/185 |
| Monroe, Margaret | Baptiste, John P. | Mar 18 1848 | 8/294 |
| Montague, Joseph H. | Wilkins, Henrietta | May 17 1832* | 2/1491 |
| Montgomery, Adeline | Woodwik, Abraham S. | Dec 11 1834* | 2/184 |
| Montgomery, Adeline | Woodcock, Abraham S | Dec 11 1834 | 2/184B |
| Montgomery, Alexander | Eastin, Matilda E. | Sep 1 1843* | 5/294B |
| Montgomery, Elijah | Smoot, Adeline | Dec 28 1827* | 2/2 |
| Montgomery, Eliza F. | Wiswall, Joseph | Mar 14 1829* | 2/76 |
| Montgomery, James | Harrelson, Elizabeth M | Jan 21 1847 | 8/213 |
| Montgomery, Jeannett (wid) | Reid, Mury (widr) | May 14 1853 | 12/282 |
| Montgomery, John A. | Blocker, Julia M. | Nov 15 1849 | 11/17 |
| Montgomery, Mary E. | Owen, Robert B. | Jan 13 1836* | 3/35 |
| Montgomery, William S. | Thompson, Janet | Jun 2 1849 | 8/379 |
| Montiel, John Emile | Lacone, Leontine ? | May 8 1841* | 5/129B |
| Montigue, Edward | Curran, Elizabeth | Feb 12 1855 | 14/49 |
| Montigue, Edward F. | Livingston, Imogine | May 3 1850* | 11/58 |
| Moody, Arbin C | Scarbrough, Emeline | Jul 6 1854 | 13/276 |
| Moody, Martha | Smith, John L. | Apr 13 1841* | 5/123B |
| Moody, Richard | Lyons, Martha | 1837* | OIB |
| Moon, Henry (Moor) | McLaughton, Ellen | May 24 1839* | 3/173 |
| Moonan, James | Downing, Catherine | Oct 27 1841 | 5/155B |
| Mooney, Catherine | Kenzie, Roderick W. | Jun 25 1838* | 3/133 |
| Mooney, Ellis | Sicet, William | Aug 3 1839* | 3/183 |
| Mooney, Hugh | O'Meara, Elizabeth | Oct 5 1854 | 13/348 |
| Mooney, Jane | Birch, Joseph | Jun 26 1852 | 11/266 |
| Mooney, Margaret Jane | Roycroft, John | Oct 7 1852 | 12/24 |
| Mooney, Mathew | Eagan, Bridget | Apr 27 1838* | 3/121 |
| Mooney, William Smith | Cullum, Mary B | Jan 6 1825 | 1/60 |
| Moonhouse, Joseph | Lea, Frosina | Aug 18 1841 | 5/149B |
| Moor, William | Benedict, Rachel | 1826* | OIB |
| Moore, Alza C | Olston, Henrietta | Oct 4 1852 | 12/20 |
| Moore, Augustus G | Manasco, Rhoda C. | Nov 22 1842 | 5/228B |
| Moore, Catherine A | Moore, John P | Jan 10 1855 | 14/8 |
| Moore, Edward | Foy, Ann | Mar 13 1848* | 8/295 |
| Moore, Edward W. | Tew, Caroline M. | Mar 15 1848 | 8/292 |
| Moore, Elizabeth | Hourley, William | Feb 11 1852 | 11/217 |
| Moore, Ellen B. | Lambert, James | Jan 12 1852* | 11/203 |
| Moore, Elnora | Thomas, Lewis A. | Apr 8 1846 | 8/156B |
| Moore, Elnora | Gibson, Gilbert | Feb 18 1845* | 8/73B |
| Moore, Finton | Nolan, Mary | Apr 1 1853 | 12/213 |
| Moore, Hellen | Lambert, James | Jan 26 1853 | 12/145 |
| Moore, Hetty | McGuiness, George | Jun 12 1855 | 14/168 |
| Moore, Jane | Plunkett, John | Oct 6 1855 | 14/246 |
| Moore, John | Heafy, Mary (Healy) | Jun 3 1823 | 1/5 |
| Moore, John P | Moore, Catherine A | Jan 10 1855 | 14/8 |
| Moore, John P | Brereton, Elisabeth Ann | Dec 11 1852 | 12/85 |
| Moore, John W. | Roberts, Mahala | Oct 23 1847 | 8/261 |
| Moore, Jonas | Engel, Clara | Aug 2 1854* | 13/299 |
| Moore, Joseph | Wingate, Caroline | Mar 21 1845 | 8/82B |
| Moore, June S | Cochran, William L | May 9 1835 | 3/14 |
| Moore, Margaret | St Clair, Willis | Oct 22 1850 | 11/91 |

| BRIDE OR GROOM | SPOUSE | DATE | BOOK/PAGE |
|---|---|---|---|
| Moore, Margaret | McBride, James F. | Oct 5 1830* | 2/139 |
| Moore, Margaret Ann | Macon, Thomas W. | Dec 24 1851 | 11/197 |
| Moore, Martha | Wroten, William H. | Mar 22 1849 | 8/363 |
| Moore, Martha | Newman, Charles L. | Jul 9 1840 | 5/33B |
| Moore, Martha E | Moore, William K | Dec 17 1851 | 11/195 |
| Moore, Martha J | Alexander, Francis Jr | Jul 3 1855 | 14/186 |
| Moore, Mary | Hester, Joseph W. | Mar 20 1846 | 8/153B |
| Moore, Mary | Stewart, Alexander | Jan 1 1848 | 8/274 |
| Moore, Mary W. | Tew, Thomas R. | Mar 14 1848 | 8/292 |
| Moore, Michael | Harris, Mary | Feb 10 1847 | 8/215 |
| Moore, Nancy (Mrs) | Newman, Henry | Sep 7 1847 | 8/255 |
| Moore, Parmelia | Carter, Thomas | Jul 16 1851* | 11/165 |
| Moore, Preston | Muller, Jane (Miller) | May 21 1839* | 3/173 |
| Moore, Robert | Wilson, Margaret M. | Oct 23 1844 | 8/45B |
| Moore, Robert G (Moon) | McCarty, Mary | Dec 14 1852 | 12/93 |
| Moore, Sampson L | McCann, Florence | Dec 20 1855 | 14/308 |
| Moore, Susan | Maxwell, George | Oct 25 1855 | 14/265 |
| Moore, Thomas J (wid) | Smith, Sarah (wid) | Oct 8 1853* | 12/412 |
| Moore, William K. | Moore, Martha E. | Dec 17 1851 | 11/195 |
| Moore, William P. | Marston, Elizabeth | May 7 1849* | 8/374 |
| Moore, William V. | George, Margaret Ann | Dec 9 1845 | 8/130B |
| Moorehouse, Joseph | Smith, Jane | Apr 9 1845 | 8/86B |
| Mooring, Margarett | Gottschlok, Jacob | Jun 2 1838 | 3/130 |
| Moose, Charles | Moreland, Martha A. | Jul 13 1852 | 11/270 |
| Morand, Sodriska C | Faines, William J | Oct 13 1842* | 5/223B |
| Morasini, Napoleon | Kobeloth, Marie M. | Dec 19 1846 | 8/206 |
| Mordecai, Mary E | Brown, Charles D | Jan 18 1854 | 13/86 |
| Mordough, James H. | McLeod, Mary | May 20 1852 | 11/252 |
| Morecroft, Mary Ann | McCort, William | Aug 21 1852 | 11/278 |
| Morehouse, Avnan | Miller, Mary Ann | Mar 13 1839* | 3/160 |
| Morehouse, Cornelia H | Riley, James | Apr 24 1855 | 14/115 |
| Morehouse, Joseph | Lee, Frosina | Aug 18 1841 | 5/149B |
| Moreland, James | O'Connor, Alice W | Jul 10 1834* | 2/212 |
| Moreland, Margaret | Robert, George | Apr 4 1850* | 11/50 |
| Moreland, Martha A. | Moose, Charles | Jul 13 1852 | 11/270 |
| Moreland, Mary O | Murray, Daniel | Jan 24 1854 | 13/95 |
| Moreland, Thomas | Denin, More | Dec 14 1827* | 2/185 |
| Morely, Clarissa A | Davidson, John H | Nov 8 1854 | 13/373 |
| Moreno, Antoinette Clara | Gregory, George W. | May 15 1849* | 8/375 |
| Moreno, Benino | Dubroca, Georgette | Aug 26 1830* | 2/135 |
| Moreno, Cecelia M | Alvarez, Alexander E | Dec 16 1853 | 13/42 |
| Moreno, Genevive | Barclay, Henry A. | Mar 17 1831* | 2/156 |
| Morgan, Bridget | Healy, John | Sep 24 1849 | 11/6 |
| Morgan, Bridget | McGrinnill, Dennis | Apr 22 1828 | 2/21 |
| Morgan, Charles | Kennedy, Catherine | Feb 11 1850 | 11/39 |
| Morgan, Elizabeth | Stevens, Rasberry | 1826* | OIB |
| Morgan, Elizabeth | Greger, Robert F. | Oct 8 1851 | 11/182 |
| Morgan, Ellen | Murphy, James | Apr 13 1842 | 5/196B |
| Morgan, James | Hillard, Mary | Nov 25 1852 | 12/73 |
| Morgan, Jennett (Magee) | Gilmor, Robert | May 24 1841* | 5/132B |
| Morgan, John | Campbell, Roseanna | Sep 23 1852 | 12/12 |
| Morgan, John S. | Kiejan, Catharien | Jul 6 1849* | 8/386 |
| Morgan, Mary | Burkhardt, Charlie B | May 8 1841* | 5/129B |
| Morgan, Mary Ann | Crawford, William | Aug 31 1844 | 8/40B |
| Morgan, Ransom | Phillips, Fanny | Mar 7 1841* | 5/119B |
| Morgan, Resse | Philips, Elizabeth | Dec 11 1834* | 2/184 |
| Morgan, Seley | Weekes, Samuel K | 1826* | OIB |
| Morgan, Theny | Dodson, Wellington | 1826* | OIB |
| Morgan, William | Muker, Deby Elizabeth | Apr 19 1844 | 8/16B |
| Morgan, William M (Mryan) | Monroe, Abby | Apr 8 1839* | 3/165 |
| Morgan, William R | Lofton, Elizabeth | Dec 22 1855 | 14/310 |
| Moriarty, Ellen | Bock, Sebastian | Mar 2 1855 | 14/73 |
| Moriaty, Donald (Daniel) | Katon, Ellen (Keating) | Jan 18 1853 | 12/138 |
| Morley, George | O'Meara, Mary Ann | May 14 1855 | 14/138 |

| | | | |
|---|---|---|---|
| Morley, William F | Rafferty, Ann | Nov  4 1852 | 12/45 |
| Mormier, Mary Roe | Marthet, Leshem | Jul 22 1844 | 8/34B |
| Morow, Camillo | Brados, Charles | Mar 29 1849 | 8/364 |
| Morrell, Rebecca | Ratcliff, Frederick | Feb 28 1852 | 11/222 |
| Morrill, Mary F (Murrell) | Moffett, John M. | Nov 17 1840* | 5/63B |
| Morris, Ann | LaCoste, John | Jun 14 1843* | 5/28B |
| Morris, Ann Eliza | McCan, Hugh (Carr) | Jun 22 1840 | 5/29B |
| Morris, Barbara J. | Gould, Horatio N. | Dec 28 1843* | 5/312B |
| Morris, Emma Matilda | Rice, Joseph P | Feb 17 1853 | 12/174 |
| Morris, George W (wid) | McCrarey, Elizabeth (wid) | Feb  6 1855* | 14/38 |
| Morris, George W | Gambling, Nancy | Dec 22 1852 | 12/104 |
| Morris, J P | Reeder, Mary A | May 31 1853* | 12/302 |
| Morris, Jane | Alvarez, Vincent | Jul 28 1841* | 5/144B |
| Morris, John | Gilchrist, Anna B. | May 19 1838* | 3/127 |
| Morris, John Jr. | Gaines, Mary H. | May  2 1825 | 1/73 |
| Morris, Martha | Gould, Edwin B | 1837* | OIB |
| Morris, Martha L. | Fletcher, George H. | Jan 22 1852 | 11/206 |
| Morris, Mary | Burke, John | Jun 19 1845* | 8/105B |
| Morris, Mary | Covins, James | Dec 19 1836* | 3/66 |
| Morris, Mary Jane | Thompson, Alexander | Sep 19 1845 | 8/118B |
| Morris, Mathew | Campbell, Mary | Jul  8 1851 | 11/163 |
| Morris, Michael | Byrnes, Bridget | Aug 14 1843 | 5/292B |
| Morris, Samuel | Edwards, Jane C. | Apr 29 1848 | 8/302 |
| Morris, William | Miller, Emma Eliza | Jul 15 1845 | 8/110B |
| Morrison, Henrietta M. | Edwards, Elias M. | May 20 1848 | 8/305 |
| Morrison, James J | Ledyard, Elizabeth D | Jan 14 1853 | 12/130 |
| Morrison, John | Spillard, Mary | Feb 24 1840* | 3/194 |
| Morrison, John | Webb, Isabella | Jan 15 1853 | 12/135 |
| Morrison, Joseph | Jones, Sarah | Dec 14 1852* | 12/90 |
| Morrison, Margaret | Masterson, Hugh | May 28 1847 | 8/238 |
| Morrison, William G. | Henderson, Ann | Apr 18 1839* | 3/167B |
| Morse, Julia | Turner, Amasa | 1826* | OIB |
| Morse, Julia A C | Louton, Fredrick J | May  5 1851* | 11/146 |
| Mortimer, Thomas V | White, Mary | 1838* | OIB |
| Morton, Cornelia S | Sanford, Thadeus | 1827* | OIB |
| Morton, John C. | Turner, Sarah L. | Jan  7 1851 | 11/109 |
| Morton, William S | Campbell, Caledonia | Nov 20 1852 | 12/65 |
| Morw, John F (Moor)(Moon) | Polhomus, Ann L. | Jan 28 1839* | 3/154 |
| Mosely, Lucy A | Chamberlain, Barlett S | Dec 13 1854 | 13/412 |
| Moser, Samuel | Caufman, Sarah | Jul 26 1844* | 8/36B |
| Moses, Elmira | Swasey, Henry R | Aug  4 1845 | 8/114B |
| Moss, Sarah Boardman | Selfridge, Christ. G | Nov 24 1847* | 8/267 |
| Motania, Regarter | Nieles, Charles Silvaus | Nov  8 1834* | 3/4 |
| Motch, Theresa | Bareso, George | May 24 1837 | 3/84 |
| Moter, Jacob | Cook, Mary | Feb 12 1855 | 14/47 |
| Motes, Green A | McCary, Frances S | Dec 25 1851 | 11/198 |
| Motley, Mary Ann | Scaver, Lewis | 1826* | OIB |
| Motsack, Phelina ? | Gardner, Jessie Jr | Oct  8 1840* | 5/53B |
| Mott, Emeline | Henserling, Lewis | Oct 14 1828* | 2/45 |
| Mott, Henry | Pickens, Elizabeth | Nov 15 1854 | 13/380 |
| Mott, James S | Tucker, Margaret | Jan 24 1845 | 8/68B |
| Mott, Matilda | Lord, John | 1825* | OIB |
| Mott, Nancy M | Davidson, Robert | May 23 1835* | 3/16 |
| Mott, Thomas L | Barker, Mary | 1826* | OIB |
| Mottus, Gertrude | Tankersley, Richard | Apr  3 1818* | CM |
| Mountain, Mary Jane | Quigley, Stephen B | Sep 13 1855 | 14/231 |
| Mourghin, Mary | O'Brien, Patrick | May 18 1843 | 5/274B |
| Mouroux, Adolphe | Rousselot, Rosine | Mar 25 1835* | 3/12 |
| Moxton, Elizabeth | Bettisworth, James | May 10 1836* | 3/47 |
| Mryan, William (Morgan) | Monroe, Abby | Apr  8 1839* | 3/165 |
| Muckin, Patrick (Macken) | O'Neal, Susan | Dec 23 1848 | 8/340 |
| Mudge, A | Springstale, Mary ? | Apr 19 1842* | 5/192B |
| Mugel, Epher | Kerger, Frederick | May  3 1850 | 11/59 |
| Mugel, Jacob | Raer, Margaret | Nov  6 1835* | 3/27 |

| BRIDE OR GROOM | SPOUSE | DATE | BOOK/PAGE |
|---|---|---|---|
| Mugel, Margaretta | Kohler, George | Dec 12 1832* | 2/1271 |
| Mugs, Louisa (Meigs) | Trenier, John B (Tremier) | Jan 5 1841* | 5/85B |
| Muker, Deby Elizabeth | Morgan, William | Apr 19 1844 | 8/16B |
| Mulaugh, Ellen | Butler, Edward | Jul 15 1853 | 12/358 |
| Mulcahey, Thomas | Flannegan, Bridget | Jul 13 1850 | 11/72 |
| Mulder, Antoine | Hoffman, Catherine | Oct 28 1852 | 12/38 |
| Mulder, Thomas J | Houston, Martha A | Jan 6 1848 | 8/275 |
| Muldron, Margaret | Murphy, Moses P | Aug 12 1846 | 8/184 |
| Mulhall, Martin | Elward, Ann | Aug 5 1854 | 13/303 |
| Mulholland, Ann | Graham, James R | Sep 17 1855 | 14/232 |
| Mulholland, James | Toomey, Margaret | Jan 12 1854 | 13/74 |
| Mulholland, John | Sooney, Margaret ? | Jul 27 1850 | 11/77 |
| Mulhorn, William | Elfoord, Maria | Jan 6 1855 | 14/2 |
| Mulhym, Elizabeth | Roberts, Issaul | 1840* | OIB |
| Mulinelle, Angelina | Oneto, John | Dec 21 1842 | 5/236B |
| Mullen, Catherine | Webster, James | Jul 7 1849* | 8/387 |
| Mullen, Martha | Wulff, Henry (Dulff) | Jun 15 1842 | 5/206B |
| Mullen, Mary | Connolly, Patrick | Jul 17 1854 | 13/285 |
| Mullen, Peter | Hanbery, Mary | Jul 28 1853 | 12/372 |
| Mullen, William | Hagan, Sarah A | May 13 1836* | 3/47 |
| Mullen, Winney | O'Hare, Patrick | Mar 12 1855 | 14/81 |
| Muller, Frederick W. | Bowers, Laura M | Jun 23 1845 | 8/106B |
| Muller, Jane | Moore, Preston | May 21 1839* | 3/173 |
| Mulligan, Bridget | McDevitt, James | Aug 9 1843 | 5/292B |
| Mulligan, Catharine | Goud, John ? | Jun 24 1843 | 5/283B |
| Mulligan, Catherine | Leonard, James | Dec 6 1842 | 5/232B |
| Mulligan, Cecilia | Swaglich, Joseph | Jul 28 1849* | 8/384 |
| Mulligan, Elizabeth | Roberts, Israel | Mar 7 1840* | 5/196 |
| Mulligan, Elizabeth | Babbit, Charles | Jun 2 1852 | 11/259 |
| Mulligan, Felix | Smith, Bridget Ann | Feb 17 1846 | 8/145B |
| Mulligan, Grace | Bayle, Dennis (Boyle) | Jan 24 1843 | 5/244B |
| Mulligan, John | Cayetanos, Miran | Apr 7 1840* | 3/198 |
| Mullikin, Benjamin | Ayres, Catherine | Jan 16 1840* | 5/8 |
| Mullin, Ann | Cummins, John | Jun 2 1854 | 13/239 |
| Mullin, Mary | Linn, Cranford | Dec 27 1849 | 11/29 |
| Mullin, Mary Ann | Laroch, John | Dec 2 1828* | 2/52 |
| Mullins, Catherine | Prout, John | Apr 19 1854 | 13/195 |
| Mulrick, Richard | Lahy, Mary | Feb 4 1852 | 11/213 |
| Mulvany, Christopher | Hannan, Catherine | Jun 13 1853 | 12/317 |
| Mulvee, Anthony | Kilduff, Hannah D | Jan 17 1853 | 12/136 |
| Mumbert, Elizabeth ? | Shafer, Jacob | Sep 1 1842* | 5/218B |
| Mundy, Thomas | Flynn, Mary | Oct 19 1842* | 5/225B |
| Munnerlyn, Benjamin C | Spence, Mary | Dec 14 1852 | 12/91 |
| Munroe, Sarah | McLaren, Duncan | Feb 19 1845 | 8/74B |
| Murdock, Thomas | DeNice, Carmilla | Jun 15 1852 | 11/262 |
| Murfree, Sarah | Thompson, John | Jun 22 1852* | 11/265 |
| Murlin, Aulden | Baiz, Sea | Jun 4 1838* | 3/130 |
| Murphey, Bridget (wid) | O'Rourke, Daniel | Jun 22 1854 | 13/262 |
| Murphey, John D | Slate, Catherine | Apr 10 1855 | 14/103 |
| Murphr, Ellen ? | Tazhf, Napoleon (Quebeuf) | Jan 30 1841* | 5/97B |
| Murphy, Albert J | Johnson, Mary | Feb 18 1851 | 11/122 |
| Murphy, Ann | Strein, John ? | May 20 1840* | 5/23 |
| Murphy, Ann | Linskey, Thomas | Mar 16 1855 | 14/84 |
| Murphy, B.H. (F) | O'Reilly, John | Dec 25 1839* | 5/5 |
| Murphy, Bridget | Anderson, John | Oct 12 1850 | 11/89 |
| Murphy, Bridget | Biihler, Frank J | May 31 1855 | 14/153 |
| Murphy, Catherine | McGrath, Patrick | Jun 22 1850* | 11/68 |
| Murphy, Catherine | Crane, William R | Jun 23 1854 | 13/263 |
| Murphy, Charles | Ellison, Rebecca D | Sep 8 1830* | 2/137 |
| Murphy, Edmund | Lee, Mary | Dec 31 1845 | 7/778B |
| Murphy, Edward | Downey, Anne | Jan 28 1842 | 5/174B |
| Murphy, Eliza | Clark, John E | Feb 10 1853 | 12/169 |
| Murphy, Elizabeth | Ruby, John | May 29 1840* | 5/25 |
| Murphy, Ellen | Hind, Joseph | May 31 1853 | 12/301 |

| BRIDE OR GROOM | SPOUSE | DATE | BOOK/PAGE |
|---|---|---|---|
| Murphy, James | Morgan, Ellen | Apr 13 1842 | 5/196B |
| Murphy, James | O'Keith, Ellen | Oct 27 1851 | 11/184 |
| Murphy, Jane | Anderson, John | May 20 1854 | 13/230 |
| Murphy, Joanna | Collins, John | Mar 13 1841* | 5/116B |
| Murphy, John | Cain, Anna | Apr 14 1853 | 12/239 |
| Murphy, John | Haley, Maria E | Sep 20 1852 | 12/9 |
| Murphy, Margaret | Raley, Jeremiah | Mar 1 1842 | 5/184B |
| Murphy, Margaret | Lunney, John | Oct 10 1847* | 8/261 |
| Murphy, Margaret | O'Donnell, Phillip | Apr 22 1851 | 11/140 |
| Murphy, Margarett Ann | Tylee, Horace | Sep 3 1851 | 11/175 |
| Murphy, Mary | McLaughlin, Thomas | Sep 29 1841* | 5/153B |
| Murphy, Mary | Maples, Elijah | Feb 16 1848 | 8/284 |
| Murphy, Mary | Tallent, Patrick | Apr 17 1854 | 13/186 |
| Murphy, Mary Jane | McDonald, Peter | Jul 18 1844 | 8/33B |
| Murphy, Mary Louisa | Hover, John B | Jan 7 1852 | 11/201 |
| Murphy, Michael (widr) | O'Brien, Mary | May 3 1853 | 12/269 |
| Murphy, Moses P | Muldron, Margaret | Aug 12 1846 | 8/184 |
| Murphy, S. J. | Reynolds, C.C. | Aug 4 1841* | 5/145B |
| Murphy, S. Jennings | Dias, Serene C | May 25 1854 | 13/233 |
| Murphy, Samuel J | Batteaste, Mary E | Apr 19 1849* | 8/369 |
| Murphy, Thomas | Gerom, Mary (Gerow) | Dec 6 1847 | 8/269 |
| Murphy, William | Waters, Charlotte ? | Mar 23 1842 | 5/187B |
| Murphy, William E | Alvarez, Citye Rose | May 15 1843* | 5/271B |
| Murray, Alfred R | Holt, Mary A | Nov 14 1853 | 13/15 |
| Murray, Catherine | McClure, John | Aug 3 1841 | 5/150 |
| Murray, Catherine | Stirling, Daniel | Oct 20 1854 | 13/357 |
| Murray, Cecelia | Gray, Charles E | Jul 23 1850* | 11/75 |
| Murray, Daniel | Moreland, Mary O | Jan 24 1854 | 13/95 |
| Murray, David K | Albritton, Polly A | Mar 20 1854 | 13/163 |
| Murray, Edwin | Rounde, Eliza | 1827* | OIB |
| Murray, Edwin | Griffin, Susanna | Feb 26 1845 | 8/76B |
| Murray, Edwin Jr | Simpson, Jane Eliz. | Feb 6 1849* | 8/354 |
| Murray, James | Tomley, Susannah (Tomby) | Mar 7 1843 | 5/252B |
| Murray, James | Sloan, Eliza | Aug 7 1851 | 11/171 |
| Murray, James | Harrell, Ann (Farrell) | Dec 25 1847 | 8/273 |
| Murray, John | Thornton, Rosanna | Oct 13 1847* | 8/259 |
| Murray, John | McNiff, Catherine | Dec 3 1855 | 14/295 |
| Murray, Mary | Donn, William | Jan 14 1851 | 11/112 |
| Murray, Mary (wid) | Healy, Daniel (widr) | Jul 11 1853 | 12/349 |
| Murray, Thomas | Crowley, Mary | Feb 7 1855 | 14/39 |
| Murrell, John W | Emanuel, Eveline | Jun 7 1855 | 14/165 |
| Murrell, Mary F (Morrill) | Moffett, John M | Nov 17 1840* | 5/63B |
| Murrell, Virginia A | Hallet, William H | Dec 18 1855 | 14/307 |
| Murrell, Zilpah | Lewis, Angus | Jun 5 1850 | 11/65 |
| Murry, James | Fail, Margaret (Fore) | Aug 1 1850* | 11/78 |
| Murtough, John | Armstrong, Mary Ann | Jul 27 1852 | 11/273 |
| Mussina, Mary | Landras, Bartholemew | May 10 1852* | 11/248 |
| Muxon, Mary | Butler, Francis | Jan 9 1850 | 11/32 |
| Myer, Charles A | Lassase, Louise (Lassabe) | Apr 6 1854 | 13/173 |
| Myer, John H | Thomas, Ann Eliz | Mar 28 1840* | 3/196 |
| Myers, Abram L | Conway, Corah F | May 17 1848 | 8/304 |
| Myers, Daniel Porter | Simmons, Mary Ann | May 2 1843 | 5/266B |
| Myers, Elizabeth | Mock, Peter | Feb 3 1853* | 12/161 |
| Myers, George W | Windham, Patience | Mar 9 1840* | 5/14 |
| Myers, John | Flynn, Ann | Jun 4 1845 | 8/101B |
| Myers, John E | Powers, Elizabeth | Aug 12 1851 | 11/172 |
| Myers, Joseph | Ingleson, Christina | Dec 21 1849 | 11/26 |
| Myers, Mahala | McNespey, James | Nov 9 1852 | 12/56 |
| Myers, Mary | Floyd, James | Jun 24 1841 | 4/891B |
| Myers, Nancy | Spaulding, Stephen | Sep 16 1813* | WB1/8 |
| Myre, Ann E | Hawkin, Jordie | Jan 20 1844 | 5/315B |
| Myrick, Ellen | Kelly, John | Nov 2 1850 | 11/94 |
| Myrick, Emelia | Johnson, Samuel | Oct 20 1848* | 8/329 |
| Myrick, George W | Bradley, Martha A | Sep 25 1855 | 14/241 |

| BRIDE OR GROOM | SPOUSE | DATE | BOOK/PAGE |
|---|---|---|---|
| Myrick, James H | Kelly, Ellen | Dec 2 1845 | 8/127B |

**N**

| BRIDE OR GROOM | SPOUSE | DATE | BOOK/PAGE |
|---|---|---|---|
| Nager, T S | Baker, John H. | Feb 23 1850 | 11/142 |
| Namond, H.N. | Chastang, Clare | Jun 25 1839* | 3/133 |
| Nance, H. Amelia | Shepherd, Thomas M. | Jun 26 1850 | 11/69 |
| Nance, Rutherford | Goffe, Elizabeth G | Jan 5 1853 | 12/116 |
| Nancy (NSL) | Andre, Felix | Jul 28 1849* | 8/384 |
| Nangal, Michael | Galligan, Margaret | Oct 1 1855 | 14/242 |
| Nash, Minerva Eliza | Robinson, Edward | Apr 1 1839* | 3/162 |
| Natali, Batiste | Leonard, Mary | May 14 1855 | 14/139 |
| Nau, Mary | Scheuneman, John | May 9 1854 | 13/220 |
| Naugel, Michael | Reed, Maria | May 22 1845 | 8/97B |
| Navarro, Emanuel | Smith, Caroline | Mar 3 1848 | 8/289 |
| Neagle, Bridget | White, Peter | Mar 30 1855 | 14/92 |
| Neal, Mary | Ballaron, Joseph | Feb 15 1847 | 8/217 |
| Neal, West | Williams, Sarah | Nov 7 1829* | 2/102 |
| Neeff, John | Koster, Regina | Jan 4 1851 | 11/109 |
| Negus, Elizabeth | Daniel, Abner | Sep 5 1833* | 2/791 |
| Negus, Elizabeth A. | Rone, Samuel W (Roue) | Jan 12 1846 | 8/139B |
| Negus, Thomas | McCloud, Elizabeth | 1826* | OIB |
| Neiderberger, Madeline | Dresch, Francois H. | Jul 22 1843* | 5/290 |
| Neil, Henry S | Shay, Margaret | Feb 18 1819* | CM |
| Neil, Johanna | Collins, John | 1838* | OIB |
| Neil, John | Smith, Sarah | Sep 20 1836* | 3/59 |
| Neilen, William | Mansfield, Catharine | Apr 5 1847 | 8/224 |
| Neill, Eliza | Sherwood, Robert | Jan 31 1855 | 14/32 |
| Neill, George | McDonald, Ann | Oct 20 1854 | 13/355 |
| Neill, James | Kinsler, Catharine | May 24 1849* | 8/378 |
| Neisins, Nicholas | Schenkilberg, Caroline | Nov 23 1852 | 12/71 |
| Nelins, Tracey | Monroe, Alexander | Aug 31 1839* | 3/185 |
| Nelios, Catharine Ann | Soost, Andrew Daniel | Oct 9 1844 | 8/43B |
| Nelius, Jasper | Witsman, Catharine | Dec 20 1851 | 11/196 |
| Nelius, Mary Margaret | Tuttle, William H. | Mar 18 1852 | 11/228 |
| Nelligan, Mary | McKibbon, James | Feb 10 1855 | 14/46 |
| Nellus, Gasper | Rhan, Esther | Dec 27 1841* | 5/165B |
| Nelson, Admeral | Jackson, Catherine M | 1840* | OIB |
| Nelson, Charles | Krums, Caterina (Kraus) | Dec 8 1846 | 8/203 |
| Nelson, Elizabeth A. | Underwood, Nimrod | Apr 12 1851 | 11/137 |
| Nelson, Henry G. | Goush, Mary (Quirt) | Feb 7 1849 | 8/355 |
| Nelson, Henry J (widr) | Smith, Isabella (wid) | Mar 18 1853 | 12/197 |
| Nelson, John | Dobson, Elizabeth | Jun 21 1853* | 12/370 |
| Nelson, Margaret | Coconnes, Antoine | Jul 11 1848* | 8/315 |
| Nelson, Mary A. | Roane, John | Jan 9 1847 | 8/211 |
| Nelson, Mary Ann | Richard, Jacob | Dec 30 1843 | 5/313B |
| Nelson, Mary J | Peters, Cornelius | Nov 12 1855 | 14/279 |
| Nelson, Peter | Heuer, Sophia W. | Feb 6 1845 | 8/71B |
| Nelson, Sarah A. | Carver, William J. | Apr 12 1851 | 11/137 |
| Nelson, Washington | Ward, Nancy J. | Mar 26 1852 | 11/231 |
| Neperaux, Auguste | Landry, Felicia | Jan 29 1851* | 11/118 |
| Nest, James Jr. (West) | De Vendel, Milanie A | Oct 27 1841 | 5/155B |
| Nethercott, Edward H. | Walton, Mary | May 3 1844 | 8/19B |

| BRIDE OR GROOM | SPOUSE | DATE | BOOK/PAGE |
|---|---|---|---|
| Netius, Albert | Noetrnell, Anna | Dec 27 1838* | 3/A153 |
| Nettles, John M (widr) | Freeman, Mary R | Sep 12 1853 | 12/404 |
| Nevill, Samuel L. | Bowers, Eudora C | Jun 6 1848* | 8/308 |
| Nevill, William G. | McCartney, Nancy J. | Apr 12 1851 | 11/137 |
| Neville, Eliza | Dwyer, Michael | Feb 17 1835 | 14/56 |
| Neville, Hannah | Brown, William | Feb 2 1841* | 5/99B |
| Neville, John | Doyle, Mary Ann | Mar 30 1848* | 8/296 |
| Neville, Thomas | Mealy, Cecile O (O'Mealy) | Jul 13 1853 | 12/350 |
| Nevin, Anne | Hodgson, John | Nov 16 1847 | 8/265 |
| Nevin, William | Hagerty, Mary | Jul 1 1848* | 8/311 |
| Nevins, Mary | Woods, Charles P. | Sep 10 1850 | 11/84 |
| New, Gray B. | Hammond, Mary | Feb 19 1842 | 5/181B |
| New, Martha Ann | Hughes, Asa | Feb 23 1855 | 14/67 |
| Newberg, Margarett | Hornberg, Joseph | Apr 9 1840* | 5/18 |
| Newberry, Charles Maxwell | Sharpe, Emily | Feb 8 1843* | 5/248B |
| Newberry, Eliza | Stewart, James | Jan 30 1835* | 3/4 |
| Newberry, Mary Ann | Lee, William | Jun 14 1855 | 14/173 |
| Newberry, Susanna | Lyon, Thomas | Apr 5 1852 | 11/232 |
| Newbold, Mary T. | Joyne, Henry L. | May 5 1840* | 5/22 |
| Newbold, Sarah Louisa | Stanton, William Jr. | Apr 9 1845 | 8/85B |
| Newbold, Thomas D. | Curtis, Susan | Mar 8 1852 | 11/225 |
| Newbold, Thomas G. | Cadet, Barbara | May 22 1815* | CM |
| Newman, Bridgit | Sabernadie, John | Jun 7 1843 | 5/280B |
| Newman, Charles L. | Moore, Martha | Jul 9 1840* | 5/33B |
| Newman, Dorman | Gately, Ann | Jan 10 1842 | 5/170B |
| Newman, Henry | Mables, Tisher | Oct 22 1844 | 8/45B |
| Newman, Henry | Moore, Nancy (Mrs) | Sep 7 1847 | 8/255 |
| Newman, John J. | Grissom, Frances H. | Mar 12 1852 | 11/225 |
| Nichalson, Charles | Callaghan, Mary | Jul 13 1850 | 11/72 |
| Nicholas, Augustus | Trenier, Sabine | Feb 4 1834* | 2/481 |
| Nicholas, Dennis | Jones, Delilah | Mar 14 1836* | 3/43 |
| Nicholas, Ebenezer A | Gurlie, Artemisia | Aug 3 1854 | 13/300 |
| Nicholas, Florentine | Dixon, George | May 31 1836* | 3/49 |
| Nicholas, Florentine | Debriere, St | Jul 18 1853 | 12/359 |
| Nicholas, Frances | Long, William H. | Jul 19 1851 | 11/167 |
| Nicholas, Joakim | Duignew, Bridget | Jun 28 1853 | 12/333 |
| Nicholas, John Pierre | Joyet, Venor | Jun 27 1829 | 2/89 |
| Nicholas, Josephine | Whitley, James J | Jun 26 1854 | 13/266 |
| Nicholas, Matilda | Raffee, Thomas | Nov 22 1854 | 13/389 |
| Nicholas, Seraphine T. | Veque, John B.G. | Jan 27 1829* | 2/66 |
| Nicholas, Varius | Galway, Louisa (Galvery) | Nov 12 1834* | 2/11 |
| Nicholas, William | Varie, Rosalie V. | Oct 3 1848 | 8/326 |
| Nicholes, Michael | Underman, Mary (Anderman) | Nov 15 1841 | 5/157B |
| Nichols, Adaline | Homer, James B (Horner) | Apr 1 1833* | 2/1041 |
| Nichols, Ann | Powers, William L | Dec 9 1854 | 13/407 |
| Nichols, Charles | Johnson, Maria | Feb 23 1841* | 5/108B |
| Nicholson, Catherine | Robishow, Alvan | 1815* | 0IB |
| Nicholson, Charles D | Logan, Elizabeth J | Nov 12 1855 | 14/278 |
| Nicholson, Eunice | Rochon, John | Jun 3 1830 | 2/127 |
| Nicholson, Harriet | Evans, Cyrus | Aug 26 1829* | 2/93 |
| Nicholson, Sarah | Chrelien, Tony | Jun 21 1853 | 12/325 |
| Nicholson, William R. | Shard, Jane (Shaw) | Nov 26 1845 | 8/126B |
| Nicolas, Meisius | Hieton, Eva | Mar 1 1852 | 11/223 |
| Niedeslenger, Madeline | Drosch, Francois H | Jul 22 1843* | 5/290B |
| Nieles, Charles Silvaus | Motania, Regarter | Nov 8 1834* | 3/4 |
| Nieth, Jacob H | Tyler, Elizabeth R | Aug 5 1854 | 13/302 |
| Nile, Sarah | Pelham, William | Dec 21 1829 | 2/108 |
| Nilegas, Abbot | Aldan, Mary | Dec 8 1840* | 5/71 |
| Niles, Lucy T (Miles) | Ryland, Allen H. | Nov 19 1840* | 5/65B |
| Niles, Mary Ann | Fitzsimons, Philip | Aug 7 1838* | 3/138 |
| Niles, Rosanna | Baker, William | Oct 3 1835* | 3/29 |
| Nimocks, Walter S. | Mitchell, Caroline | May 7 1849* | 8/373 |
| Nixon, Anna | Green, John | Jul 3 1833* | 2/871 |
| Nixon, James L | Crawley, Ellen | Oct 19 1854 | 13/353 |

| BRIDE OR GROOM | SPOUSE | DATE | BOOK/PAGE |
|---|---|---|---|
| Nixon, Maria Louisa | Buchanan, Henry | Apr 6 1841* | 5/121B |
| Nixon, Martha | Spencer, Richard | Oct 6 1849 | 11/9 |
| Noahe, Meyer | Franklin, Helena | Mar 12 1851* | 11/126 |
| Noel, Cecile | Harwell, Jesse G | Feb 18 1854 | 13/125 |
| Noel, Deolice | Hurtel, Finnan | Jan 21 1843 | 5/244B |
| Noel, Theodore | Girard, Isabella | Dec 2 1835* | 3/32 |
| Noetrnell, Anna | Netius, Albert | Dec 27 1838* | 3/A153 |
| Nolan, James | Dunn, Eliza (Quinn) | Jun 11 1853* | 12/315 |
| Nolan, James | Quinn, Eliza (Dunn) | Jun 11 1853* | 12/315 |
| Nolan, Mary | Moore, Finton | Apr 1 1853 | 12/213 |
| Nolan, Sarah | Leanders, Batt | May 15 1854 | 13/224 |
| Noland, Julia | Creamer, John | Jul 10 1848* | 8/314 |
| Noland, Mary Ann | Keevan, John | Jul 26 1851 | 11/170 |
| Nongeson, Henry | Shoemaker, Dory | Nov 1 1844 | 8/47B |
| Noonan, Ann | O'Neal, Cornelius | Apr 29 1852 | 11/243 |
| Noonan, Margaret | Wisdom, William | May 26 1849* | 8/378 |
| Noonder, Edward (Noonan) | Casey, Margaret | Apr 5 1847 | 8/224 |
| Nooten, Alexander | Gilchrist, Isabella | Jan 20 1851* | 11/115 |
| Norbeck, John | Fields, Mary Jane | Jan 18 1848 | 8/278 |
| Nordlinger, Solomon | John, Genetta | Jun 26 1848* | 8/310 |
| Norman, Emily | Gayle, William L. | Jul 18 1849* | 8/388 |
| Norman, Joanna F. | Chambers, Augustus | Nov 14 1843 | 5/304B |
| Norman, John Moore | Talcott, Emma | Nov 21 1843 | 5/306B |
| Normon, Emeline | Chisolm, Jonathan | Jun 5 1828* | 2/32 |
| Norris, Calvin | Croom, Emily | Jan 1 1835 | 3/2 |
| Norris, Mary W. | David, D.R.W. | Dec 2 1840* | 5/71B |
| Norris, Thomas (VOID) | Shiel, Rose | Dec 20 1852* | 12/103 |
| North, Stephen B. | Smith, Emma Matilda | Sep 12 1837* | 3/91 |
| North, Ralph | Coffin, Mary Ann | 1837* | OIB |
| Northrop, Eliza R | Riley, William B | Jun 14 1854 | 13/256 |
| Norton, Edward L. | Payne, Sarah Ann | Apr 3 1843 | 5/258B |
| Norton, Ellen | O'Grady, Dominick | Dec 1 1853 | 13/30 |
| Norton, Hiram | Sager, Elizabeth (Sayer) | Mar 2 1844 | 5/326B |
| Norton, Hubert | Killduff, Mary | Sep 7 1854 | 13/333 |
| Norton, Imogine | Long, Richard H. | Dec 31 1846 | 8/208 |
| Norton, Martha S. | Shelton, Alexander | Jul 26 1852 | 11/271 |
| Norton, Thomas | Cain, Margaret | Jan 14 1843* | 5/243 |
| Norton, Thomas | O'Connor, Maurica | Jan 14 1843 | 6/267 |
| Norton, William | Loughry, Catherine | Jul 6 1855 | 14/189 |
| Norvitt, William (Norville) | O'Connor, Ann | Oct 20 1851 | 11/183 |
| Nouilin, Mary | Davis, George | Jun 9 1823* | 1/6 |
| Novack, William | Shul, Mary C (wid) | Sep 28 1853 | 12/410 |
| Nowland, Thomas | Dennis, Nora | Dec 14 1827 | 2/1 |
| Nowlin, Mary E. | Roberts, Marlin R. | Jan 2 1847 | 8/209 |
| Nowlin, Silvanas | Reniger, Catherine | Jun 2 1852 | 11/259 |
| Nowlisa, Eliza | Deputron, Jacob | Apr 6 1839* | 3/164 |
| Noyes, David | McGibney, Ellen | Nov 1 1845 | 8/122B |
| Noyes, Enoch | Oliver, Margaret | Mar 8 1836* | 3/42 |
| Nubert, Marie Therese | Rudren, Joseph | Aug 14 1849* | 8/390 |
| Nugent, Charles | Overton, Catherine | Jan 5 1850 | 11/31 |
| Nugent, Mary | Henry, Thomas | Oct 6 1849* | 11/8 |
| Nugent, Mary | Sondana, Giebbe (Londano) | Dec 31 1841 | 5/166B |
| Nugent, Mary Ann | McLaughlin, John | Jan 16 1851 | 11/113 |
| Nunagasser, Henry | Heidrick, Catherine | May 4 1854 | 3/215 |
| Nunn, Alicia S | Crissey, Elnathan F | Mar 25 1854 | 13/166 |
| Nye, Henry | Sutherland, Eliza | Jun 19 1843 | 5/283B |

O

| Bride or Groom | Spouse | Date | Book/Page |
|---|---|---|---|
| Oakes, Frederick | Raritan, Eliza | Jun 12 1843 | 5/281B |
| O'Bear, Eliza | Pollard, George | Dec 3 1853* | 13/33 |
| Obering, Frederick W. | Aberich, Margaret | Apr 12 1852 | 11/235 |
| O'Birrim, William | Welsh, Rebecca | May 10 1855 | 14/137 |
| O'Brien, Abby | Bailey, Thomas | Feb 13 1847 | 8/217 |
| O'Brien, Ann | McKinney, Hugh | 1841* | OIB |
| O'Brien, Ann | Rogers, Mathew M. | Jun 6 1839* | 3/177 |
| O'Brien, Ann | Hand, Thomas | Jul 3 1849* | 8/396 |
| O'Brien, Anne | McDury, James | Feb 10 1842* | 5/180B |
| O'Brien, Bridget | Esty, Charles H. | Oct 11 1847 | 8/258 |
| O'Brien, Bridget | Collins, John | Jan 22 1845 | 8/67B |
| O'Brien, Bridget | McDonald, Thomas | Sep 15 1852 | 12/4 |
| O'Brien, Catharine | Keane, William | Aug 18 1848* | 8/321 |
| O'Brien, Catherine | Burke, Michael | Nov 25 1852 | 12/74 |
| O'Brien, Dennis | Powers, Mary (Sowers) | Oct 6 1840* | 5/53B |
| O'Brien, Ellen | Barcelonio, Antonio | Oct 1 1852 | 12/15 |
| O'Brien, Hannah | Cuslin, William | Apr 20 1852 | 11/239 |
| O'Brien, Hanora | Reed, John | Apr 26 1852 | 11/242 |
| O'Brien, James | Gamble, Jane | Apr 1 1845 | 8/82B |
| O'Brien, Joanna | Welsh, Michael | Jan 25 1842 | 5/173B |
| O'Brien, John | Mead, Hannah | Apr 10 1841* | 5/21B |
| O'Brien, Julia | Sloan, John | May 28 1847* | 8/239 |
| O'Brien, Mary | Murphy, Michael (widr) | May 3 1853 | 12/269 |
| O'Brien, Mary E. | Roulston, Richard B. | Apr 28 1851 | 11/143 |
| O'Brien, Owen | Downey, Bridget | Jul 10 1847* | 8/244 |
| O'Brien, Patrick | Monrghin, Mary (Mourghin | May 18 1843 | 5/274B |
| O'Brien, Patrick | Baker, Roseanna | May 30 1853 | 12/300 |
| O'Brien, Thomas | Leonard, Bridget | Nov 16 1833* | 2/711 |
| O'Brien, Thomas | Carrigin, Ann | May 13 1844 | 8/20B |
| O'Brien, Thomas | McTernan, Catherine | Jan 27 1855 | 14/24 |
| O'Brien, Timothy | Baker, Mary | Jan 7 1843 | 5/241B |
| O'Brien, William | Miller, Jane | Jan 21 1839* | 3/B153 |
| O'Callahan, Charlotte | Elliott, James G | Jun 3 1840* | 5/26B |
| O'Carroll, John | Johnston, Mary | Jul 23 1850 | 11/75 |
| O'Carroll, John | Logan, Selina C. | Jul 23 1850* | 11/75 |
| O'Connell, Mary | English, John | Feb 4 1850 | 11/37 |
| O'Conner, Bridget | Malloney, John | Jan 3 1851 | 11/108 |
| O'Conner, Ellen | Kearns, Owen | Feb 24 1851 | 11/124 |
| O'Conner, Mary | Devin, William | Feb 11 1838* | 3/111 |
| O'Conner, Mary A | McKever, Alexander | Jun 8 1854 | 13/246 |
| O'Conner, Timothy | Coulin, Eliza (Conlin) | Apr 10 1854 | 13/176 |
| O'Connor, Alice M. | Moreland, James | Jul 10 1834* | 2/212 |
| O'Connor, Ann | Dwyne, John | Mar 7 1837* | 3/74 |
| O'Connor, Ann | Norvitt, William | Oct 20 1851 | 11/183 |
| O'Connor, Ann | Anderson, Elias | Jan 6 1849* | 8/346 |
| O'Connor, Bridget | Haff, John | May 16 1846 | 8/166B |
| O'Connor, Cecilia F. | Stuart, William (Stewart) | May 8 1843 | 5/252B |
| O'Connor, Dennis | Barry, Honora | Apr 23 1851 | 11/141 |
| O'Connor, Dennis | McDermott, Julia M. | Mar 24 1840* | 5/15 |
| O'Connor, Edward | Tardy, Cecilia F. | Sep 24 1834* | 2/141 |
| O'Connor, Helen | Cowhey, David | Dec 10 1844 | 8/57B |
| O'Connor, Johanna | Curran, Joseph | Feb 15 1831* | 2/151 |
| O'Connor, John | McGrath, Bridget | Jan 1 1842 | 5/167 |

| BRIDE OR GROOM | SPOUSE | DATE | BOOK/PAGE |
|---|---|---|---|
| O'Connor, Margaret A | Caufield, John C | 1838* | OIB |
| O'Connor, Mary | Smith, George | Feb  8 1854 | 13/115 |
| O'Connor, Maurica | Norton, Thomas | Jan 14 1843 | 6/267B |
| O'Connor, Michael | Kuth, Patience | May 14 1839* | 3/171 |
| O'Connor, Michael | Seathe, Thelitha (Leath) | Mar 29 1842 | 5/190B |
| O'Connor, Morris | Tracy, Ellen | Nov 29 1840* | 5/69B |
| O'Connor, Patrick  (wid) | Burke, Johanna | Jul 14 1853 | 12/354 |
| O'Connor, Timothy | Canoven, Anastasia | May  1 1845 | 8/90B |
| O'Day, John (Dea) | Sullivan, Bridget | Feb 11 1847* | 8/216 |
| Odoin, Christian | Bosech, Geshine | Aug  8 1850 | 11/78 |
| Odom, Isabella | Clark, Heyskiah | Aug 17 1852 | 11/276 |
| Odom, Vincent | Sweat, Martha | Feb 22 1853 | 12/179 |
| O'Donaghue, Timothy | Canivin, Mary | Mar 18 1851 | 11/129 |
| O'Donald, Ann | Stewart, James | Oct 15 1845 | 8/120B |
| O'Donald, Ellen | Miley, John B. | Feb 16 1841* | 5/104B |
| O'Donald, Mary | Gentry, Robert | Jun  2 1845 | 8/100B |
| O'Donald, Rosa | Kainnary, John | Jan 24 1845 | 8/68B |
| O'Donald, Sarah | Silvi, Jule | Mar 31 1841* | 5/120B |
| O'Donnel, Bridget | Smith, George | May  3 1851 | 11/145 |
| O'Donnel, Rosanna | Gamel, Samuel | Feb 21 1851 | 11/123 |
| O'Donnell, Ann | Parker, Charles H. | Jun 15 1843 | 5/282B |
| O'Donnell, Margaret | McQuaid, John | Sep  1 1851 | 11/175 |
| O'Donnell, Phillip | Murphy, Margaret | Apr 22 1851 | 11/140 |
| O'Drescol, Cornelius | Cocklin, Mary | Dec 24 1837 | 3/104 |
| Oelrich, George A | Gercke, Hannah H | Sep 20 1855 | 14/234 |
| Offin, Cecelia J  (wid) | Burgess, Joshua P (widr) | Apr 30 1853 | 12/261 |
| Ogbourn, Sarah A. | Hough, Alston | Oct 31 1850 | 11/94 |
| Ogden, Cornelius A. | Tuttle, Emily W. | May  6 1845 | 8/92B |
| Ogden, Morgan S. | McLaughlin, Eliza G. | Jul  7 1841* | 5/85B |
| Ogden, Samuel M. | Hull, Susan | Feb 24 1848* | 8/286 |
| Ogden, Wyal  ? | Jackson, Harriet E. | May 28 1828* | 2/28 |
| O'Grady, Ann | Rhill, James | Aug  9 1854 | 13/308 |
| O'Grady, Dominick | Norton, Ellen | Dec  1 1853 | 13/30 |
| O'Hara, Catherine | Davis, George Jr. | Dec 22 1849 | 11/27 |
| O'Hara, Charles K | Carney, Ann | Dec 18 1854 | 13/414 |
| O'Hara, John | Kelly, Ellen C | Apr 28 1855 | 14/123 |
| O'Hare, Patrick | Mullen, Winney | Mar 12 1855 | 14/81 |
| O'Harra, Sarah | Tachoir, Francis | Jul 28 1846 | 8/182 |
| O'Heirn, Mary | Harrison, Edward | Feb 18 1854 | 13/126 |
| O'Keefe, Catherine | Fitzsimmons, Thomas | Jan  4 1855 | 13/435 |
| O'Keith, Ellen | Murphy, James | Oct 27 1851 | 11/184 |
| Oldmixon, George A | McMahon, Mary Ann | May  3 1850* | 11/59 |
| Oleva, Barbara | Peter, John | Oct 27 1828* | 2/48 |
| Oliphant, William | Wright, Ann | Feb  3 1852* | 11/212 |
| Olive, Young B. | Child, Beulah M. | Dec 18 1850 | 11/103 |
| Oliver, Bettie D | Hagan, James | Mar  8 1854 | 13/152 |
| Oliver, Frances H. | Armor, Angeline | Oct 14 1842 | 5/223B |
| Oliver, Henry | Goule, Aimee Barbara | Apr 27 1844 | 8/17B |
| Oliver, Henry H | George, Mildred | Jun  3 1853 | 12/308 |
| Oliver, Jane | Carr, Thomas A. | Mar 22 1836* | 3/43 |
| Oliver, Margaret | Noyes, Enoch | Mar  8 1836* | 3/42 |
| Oliver, Martha Ann | Rhodes, John R | 1827* | OIB |
| Oliver, Mary V. | Ravesies, Paul T. | Mar  1 1848 | 8/287 |
| Oliver, Susanna | Dickeman, Cyrus | 1823* | OIB |
| Oliver, William Jackson | White, Mary | Dec  9 1843* | 5/309B |
| Olston, Henrietta | Moore, Alza C | Oct  4 1852 | 12/20 |
| Omahie, Mary (wid) | McGrath, Patrick | Apr  2 1853 | 12/216 |
| O'Mealey, Cicily | Cain, John | Apr 10 1854 | 13/177 |
| O'Meara, Elizabeth | Mooney, Hugh | Oct  5 1854 | 13/348 |
| O'Meara, Mary Ann | Morley, George | May 14 1855 | 14/138 |
| O'Neal, Ann M | Rotheray, Daniel | Aug 26 1835* | 3/26 |
| O'Neal, Christopher | Kearns, Mary | Jan 27 1851 | 11/117 |
| O'Neal, Cornelius | Noonan, Ann | Apr 29 1852 | 11/243 |
| O'Neal, Eliza | Scanlon, Robert | Aug  2 1836* | 3/55 |

| BRIDE OR GROOM | SPOUSE | DATE | BOOK/PAGE |
|---|---|---|---|
| O'Neal, George | Pickett, Elizabeth | Apr 17 1854 | 13/187 |
| O'Neal, James W M | Hollinger, Mary M | Jan 9 1850 | 11/31 |
| O'Neal, Little B. | Jourdan, Cassy A. | Apr 1 1833* | 2/1051 |
| O'Neal, Owen | Foley, Mary | Feb 27 1854 | 13/142 |
| O'Neal, Patrick G. | Tierney, Ellen | Jun 7 1838* | 3/131 |
| O'Neal, Rose | Rosett, Peter (wid) | Nov 21 1853 | 13/20 |
| O'Neal, Selina | Dargin, Edward | Feb 15 1855 | 14/52 |
| O'Neal, Susan | Muckin, Patrick (Mackin) | Dec 23 1848 | 8/340 |
| O'Neall, Bridget | O'Neall, John | May 23 1842 | 5/203B |
| O'Neall, John | O'Neall, Bridget | May 23 1842 | 5/203B |
| O'Neil, Francis | Macken, Mary | Jul 3 1837* | 3/93 |
| O'Neil, Henry | Engleman, Margaret | Apr 24 1854 | 13/202 |
| O'Neil, Jane | Conway, William | May 11 1842 | 5/199B |
| O'Neil, Margaret | Beroujon, Claude | Feb 22 1837 | OIB/ADM |
| O'Neil, Massey | McMillan, William | Mar 3 1834* | 2/441 |
| Oneto, John | Mulinelle, Angelina | Dec 21 1842 | 5/236B |
| Openheimer, Cauffman | Juzan, Adele | Jan 19 1831* | 2/147 |
| Oppenheimer, Auguste | Lohman, Jacob | Dec 7 1844 | 8/57B |
| O'Rain, Gregory | Winter, Julia Agloe | May 23 1838* | 3/128 |
| Oraner, Franklin | Lewis, Eliza | Oct 26 1848 | 8/330 |
| Orange, Anna | Tarnaker, John (Tumaker) | Apr 20 1846 | 8/159B |
| O'Reilly, John | Murphy, B H | Dec 25 1839* | 5/5 |
| O'Reilly, Sarah | Ginn, J S | 1840* | OIB |
| O'Riley, Mary Ann (Ryan) | Pietri, Rocco | Mar 22 1841* | 5/119B |
| Orkerk, Elizabeth | Thompson, Charles | 1849* | OIB |
| Orme, Charlott | Canovan, Anthony | Jun 19 1849* | 8/392 |
| Ormond, James M. | Pope, Elizabeth S. | Jan 29 1850* | 11/36 |
| O'Rouke, Daniel | Murphey, Bridget (wid) | Jun 22 1854* | 13/262 |
| O'Rouke, Maria (wid) | McLaughlin, John (widr) | Aug 22 1853 | 12/392 |
| O'Rourke, Catherine | Ryan, John | Jun 20 1855 | 14/179 |
| Orr, Isabella | Deaves, Edward F | Mar 11 1854 | 13/154 |
| Orr, Joseph | Hancock, Martha | Apr 12 1851 | 11/138 |
| Orr, Joseph | Burke, Charlotte | Oct 23 1846 | 8/195 |
| Orsina, Cornelia | Petty, John F | Oct 23 1855 | 14/261 |
| Ortsched, Andrew | Seip, Margaret (Leip) | Jul 31 1848* | 8/319 |
| Osbahart, William | Eberlein, Anna | Jan 26 1853 | 12/148 |
| Osborne, George | Foster, Bridget | Jun 15 1852 | 11/263 |
| Osborne, George (wid) | Lynch, Caroline (wid) | Oct 18 1853* | 12/418 |
| Osgood, Stephen | Elliott, Deloise | Apr 6 1837* | 3/79 |
| O'Smith, John | McClellan, Margaret | Oct 20 1845 | 8/121 |
| Ostrander, James M | Gorsuch, Elizabeth J | Nov 27 1848* | 8/335 |
| Otis, William | Bancroft, Anna Margaret | Dec 18 1850 | 11/104 |
| Otte, Christina | Vengertsman, Conrad | Aug 12 1850 | 11/79 |
| Oudin, Victoria Amelia | Cordier, Ernest E. | Jan 16 1852 | 11/204 |
| Overall, John W | Glenholme, Anna M | Mar 12 1855 | 14/82 |
| Overstreet, Melissa | Jeuswift, Charles | Oct 13 1835* | 3/29 |
| Overstreet, Nathaniel D | Rister, Mary Jane | Jan 5 1853 | 12/113 |
| Overstreet, Stephen | Miles, Margaret | May 16 1854 | 13/225 |
| Overton, Catherine | Nugent, Charles | Jan 5 1850 | 11/31 |
| Overton, Matilda A. | Davis, William J | Sep 5 1849 | 11/2 |
| Overton, Olive Ann | Worrister, Samuel ? | Jun 6 1843 | 5/279B |
| Overton, Thomas | Smith, Julia | Oct 31 1854 | 13/365 |
| Owen, Ann O. | Rowan, Byron C. | Aug 13 1845 | 8/117B |
| Owen, Catharine C. | Johnston, Hamilton | Jun 21 1849* | 8/392 |
| Owen, Georgianna V. | Hogan, John B. | Feb 20 1850 | 11/41 |
| Owen, Mary E. | Cleveland, George A. | Jun 14 1845 | 8/103B |
| Owen, Richard B. | Gayle, Anna | Jun 26 1850 | 11/69 |
| Owen, Robert B. | Montgomery, Mary E. | Jan 13 1836* | 3/35 |
| Owen, Susan M. | Barney, Josiah M. | Jun 4 1845 | 8/101B |
| Owens, Louise (Cowen) | Garrett, Charles C. | Jun 17 1840 | 5/139B |
| Oxendale, Rebecca | Clark, John | Apr 13 1844 | 8/13B |
| Oxenham, Mary Ann | Sysuan, Edward B. | Dec 18 1835* | 3/33 |

P

| Bride or Groom | Spouse | Date | Book/Page |
|---|---|---|---|
| Paasch, Henry | Zahn, Sophia | Mar 10 1845 | 8/78B |
| Pace, William J. | Wells, Parmelia | Jan 16 1851 | 11/114 |
| Paden, George | Johnson, Francis A | Jul 18 1854 | 13/287 |
| Padgett, John | Crabtree, Emma | Feb 9 1846 | 8/144B |
| Padgett, Nancy | Lambert, William | Jan 5 1849* | 8/345 |
| Page, Annony | Barstow, Nathaniel | Mar 4 1843 | 5/251B |
| Page, James | Lefevre, Martha | Nov 4 1837* | 3/100 |
| Page, James | Risher, Eliza | Dec 5 1833* | 2/671 |
| Page, Jennett | Evans, James M. | Jan 13 1846 | 8/140B |
| Page, Sarah | Stewart, Charles A | 1827* | OIB |
| Page, Willis | Pierce, Betsey Ann | Jan 10 1833* | 2/1231 |
| Pages, Martha (Mrs) | Bush, Marshall | Jun 12 1850 | 11/66 |
| Pagles, John F. | McBoy, Euphosyne | May 1 1832* | 2/1561 |
| Pain, Nancy | Hall, William M. | Dec 12 1844 | 8/58B |
| Paine, Vierpyle Jr. | Cooke, Elizabeth A. | May 1 1851 | 11/143 |
| Paine, William S. | Goodwin, Catharine | Feb 14 1837* | 3/71 |
| Pairu, Matilda | Crut, Thomas | Apr 22 1839* | 3/168 |
| Pake, Sigfried | Unger, Rebecca | Mar 19 1852* | 11/228 |
| Pallise, Diego (Palliser) | Stafort, Susan | Jul 27 1854* | 13/295 |
| Palliser, John | Pretus, Margaret | Nov 16 1849 | 11/17 |
| Palliser, John | Forte, Margaret Ann | May 14 1847* | 8/235 |
| Palmer, Delphia | Wheeler, William | Jul 11 1843 | 5/287B |
| Palmer, Eliza A. | Harwell, Warren J. | Mar 12 1850 | 11/45 |
| Palmer, Emanuel (Palmes) | Maura, Josephine | Jul 5 1845 | 8/109B |
| Palmer, Margaret | Lockhart, John A. | Dec 6 1849* | 11/22 |
| Palmer, Martha | Holman, William H. | Jul 17 1849* | 8/388 |
| Palmes, Emanuel | Maura, Josephine | Jul 5 1845 | 8/109B |
| Parcell, Charles J. | Stork, Sara | Nov 4 1837* | 3/100 |
| Parham, John | Hurtel, Odalie Ann | Jul 13 1840* | 5/35 |
| Paris, Laurentine | Rochon, Wilson | Jun 11 1852 | 11/262 |
| Paris, Sarah | Butler, Joseph | Aug 15 1836* | 3/56 |
| Parish, Emeline | Crawford, Jonathan | May 23 1835* | 3/15 |
| Parish, Walter A. | Brown, Catharine E (Mrs) | Dec 19 1845 | 8/131B |
| Parisine, Josephine | Johnson, John | Oct 20 1846 | 8/195 |
| Parker, Abigail | Dupree, Sterling | Jan 25 1829 | 2/65 |
| Parker, Albert G. | Pattison, Ann | Dec 20 1848 | 8/339 |
| Parker, Ann | Snediku, Samul | Nov 29 1838* | 3/150 |
| Parker, Caroline C. | Tautchton, Sandsley | Oct 8 1836* | 3/60 |
| Parker, Charles H. | O'Donnell, Ann | Jun 15 1843 | 5/282B |
| Parker, Charlotte | Mobley, John | Dec 25 1828 | 2/58 |
| Parker, Chrispe | Barnes, Thomas | 1826* | OIB |
| Parker, George | King, Mary | Sep 4 1835 | 3/27 |
| Parker, Gideon Marsena | Mills, Jane E. | Nov 11 1843* | 5/303B |
| Parker, James M | Copeland, Driscilla A | Mar 28 1854 | 13/167 |
| Parker, Jane | Andry, Seymour | Sep 28 1854 | 13/343 |
| Parker, Jonathan | Farley, Margaret | May 25 1852 | 11/255 |
| Parker, Levi J. | Fox, Sarah | Apr 19 1851 | 11/139 |
| Parker, Louisa A | Geary, Daniel | Oct 4 1852 | 12/21 |
| Parker, Mary | Banesse, George | May 17 1841* | 5/131B |
| Parker, Ralph | Connahen, Mary Jane | May 27 1833* | 2/981 |
| Parker, Robert M. | Desage, Louisa A. | Jan 6 1842 | 5/169B |
| Parkhurst, John | Ronan, Mary | Sep 13 1852* | 12/3 |

| --- | --- | --- | --- |
| Parkhurst, John | Welch, Ellen | Jan 3 1853 | 12/110 |
| Parks, Augustus | Debore, Catherine(DeBose) | Sep 25 1851 | 11/180 |
| Parks, Caroline | Irvin, Alexander | Jan 28 1854 | 13/101 |
| Parmeler, Eliza | McRoberts, Benjamin | Dec 25 1834* | 3/5 |
| Parmenter, Nancy | Porter, John | Oct 27 1851 | 11/184 |
| Parmenter, William | Jones, Nancy | Aug 29 1831* | 2/165 |
| Parmentier, Amelia | Waljamott, Thomas | Oct 22 1851 | 11/183 |
| Parmer, Margaret | McNeil, Archibald | Nov 10 1852 | 12/58 |
| Parmly, Ludolph | Sandford, Maria L. | Nov 20 1840* | 5/65B |
| Parmly, Martha J. | Martin, William | Oct 27 1845 | 5/122 |
| Parnel, Moses | McIntyre, Helen | Apr 23 1842 | 5/193 |
| Parnell, Margaret | Bayte, James | 1826* | OIB |
| Parra, Mary DeJesus | Diaz, Joseph Lewis | May 22 1847 | 8/236 |
| Parsmon, Elizabeth M. | Kepliager, Samuel | Apr 24 1838* | 3/120 |
| Parsons, Henry | Collins, Eliza | Sep 15 1853 | 12/407 |
| Parsons, William | Davis, Elizabeth | Jun 9 1830 | 2/128 |
| Partridge, Charles S | Herpin, Eliza | Oct 26 1854 | 13/363 |
| Partridge, Daniel | Steele, Martha J | 1823* | OIB |
| Partridge, Mary Ann | Seymour, Alva | Apr 12 1848 | 8/298 |
| Partsch, Charles | Hensel, Anna | Dec 4 1854 | 13/398 |
| Pasco, Hester | Dulton, William | Jan 1 1837* | 3/106 |
| Pascoe, John (Pascol) | Cowin, Esther | Jun 12 1837* | 3/88 |
| Pasqual, Demon (Simon) | Besanceney, Rose    ? | Jun 12 1843 | 5/281B |
| Pasqual, Dumont | Betbeze, Jeane | Sep 27 1848 | 8/325 |
| Pate, John | English, Mary | Nov 1 1855* | 14/268 |
| Pate, Margaret | Fourvett, Lewis N P | 1827* | OIB |
| Patrick, Mary K. | Duckworth, George | May 6 1829* | 2/84 |
| Patterson, Charles | Seabrooke, Holland | May 19 1852 | 11/251 |
| Patterson, Charles H W | Crabtree, Eliza | Mar 9 1847 | 8/221 |
| Patterson, Elizabeth | Walton, John M. | Oct 18 1847 | 8/260 |
| Patterson, George M C | Alexander, Mary Ann | May 22 1837* | 3/83 |
| Patterson, James | Shaw, Catherine | Oct 27 1855 | 14/266 |
| Patterson, Mary Anna | Crothers, William | Dec 26 1845 | 8/133B |
| Patterson, Nancy | Manney, James | Jul 2 1835* | 3/19 |
| Patterson, Nicholas G S | Greer, Jane | Sep 19 1832* | 2/1341 |
| Patterson, William | Safley, Frances Ann | Jun 3 1844 | 8/25B |
| Patterson, William | Scypes, Mary Eliz. | May 6 1845 | 8/92B |
| Patterson, William | Roan, Nancy | Oct 24 1854 | 13/362 |
| Patterson, William | Hughs, Hannah | Mar 29 1853 | 12/208 |
| Patterson, William E. | Barnes, Frances L. | Mar 4 1848* | 8/291 |
| Pattison, Ann | Parker, Albert G. | Dec 20 1848 | 8/339 |
| Pattison, Mary | Holcombe, John C. | Jul 24 1850 | 11/76 |
| Pattison, Mary A (wid) | Johnson, Thomas | Dec 22 1853 | 13/47 |
| Patton, Emily | Bonne, Arthur | May 1 1849* | 8/372 |
| Patton, Garrett L. | Edwards, Mary Jane | Dec 29 1847 | 8/273 |
| Patton, Joseph | Robeshaw, Catherine | Jan 17 1829 | 2/63 |
| Patton, Margaret B. | Anderson, James H. | Apr 16 1844 | 8/14B |
| Patton, Margarett | Carroll, William B. | Feb 3 1840* | 3/192 |
| Patton, Robert | Evans, Amelia | May 27 1845 | 8/99B |
| Paudely, Helena | Cana, Demetry (Caua) | Oct 11 1834* | 2/101 |
| Paul, Alafare | Kepner, Daniel | Dec 16 1851 | 11/195 |
| Pax, James | Copeland, Elizabeth | Mar 10 1855 | 14/79 |
| Payen, Auguste | McBoy, Phillipa | Jul 28 1827 | OIB/ADM |
| Payne, Albert A. | Griffing, Mary E. | Dec 3 1849 | 11/21 |
| Payne, Augustus (Payen) | McBoy, Philippa | Jul 28 1827 | OIB/ADM |
| Payne, John | Busbee, Marande | Jan 21 1852 | 11/205 |
| Payne, John H | Permentier, Minerva | Jul 3 1854 | 13/273 |
| Payne, Sarah Ann | Norton, Edward L. | Apr 3 1843 | 5/258B |
| Payson, Lewis | Smith, Mary | Apr 30 1852 | 11/244 |
| Payton, Charles | Brakes, Milly E.J. | Mar 30 1852 | 11/231 |
| Peabody, Herbert Cheever | Fettyplace, Louisa | Feb 24 1846 | 8/147B |
| Peabody, Herbert C. | Lea, Emily S (Lea) | Jan 5 1841* | 5/85B |
| Peabody, Oren | Johnson, Amelia | Mar 12 1828 | 2/15 |
| Peach, Mary L. | Caster, Holsworth | Nov 27 1838* | 3/149 |

| BRIDE OR GROOM | SPOUSE | DATE | BOOK/PAGE |
|---|---|---|---|
| Pearce, Elizabeth | Hags, Daniel | Apr 18 1836* | 3/44 |
| Pearce, Rebecca | Bailey, William | Jun 16 1832* | 2/1451 |
| Pearce, Silas | Stringfellow, Mary | Jul 10 1839* | 3/182 |
| Pearce, William | Davis, Elizabeth | May 1 1829* | 2/83 |
| Pearl, Elizabeth J | Yoist, Francis M (Yost) | Nov 10 1855 | 14/277 |
| Pease, Alvin | Garvey, Sarah Louisa | Mar 17 1852 | 11/227 |
| Peck, Mary | Lockhart, John | Apr 10 1854 | 13/175 |
| Peckler, Elizabeth | Mann, Joseph (Menne) | Nov 27 1840* | 5/67B |
| Peden, John W. | Caldwell, Mary Ann (Mrs) | Aug 5 1841* | 5/146B |
| Peebles, James A | Garrett, Mary S | Jun 11 1855 | 14/166 |
| Pefferle, John B | Loht, Caroline | Jan 1 1855 | 13/426 |
| Pegin, Lucinda | Brown, Noah | Nov 6 1844 | 8/48B |
| Peirrot, Elois | Hermann, Francois | Dec 16 1850 | 11/103 |
| Peitcher, H.C. | DeLarge, I.B Chas. | Dec 4 1838* | 3/151 |
| Pelerron, William | Barton, Julia | Dec 15 1837* | 3/103 |
| Pelez, Barbary | Stoyer, Mitchell | Dec 3 1836* | 3/63 |
| Pelham, Jepthy V. | Jordan, Elizabeth | Mar 22 1847 | 8/222 |
| Pelham, Sarah | Wood, Jesse S. | Oct 20 1848 | 8/328 |
| Pelham, William | Nile, Sarah | Dec 21 1829 | 2/108 |
| Pelitz, Augustus | Fagherty, Eliza | Oct 21 1835* | 3/30 |
| Pellet, Mary Ann | Cerulalon, Pierre I. | May 25 1847* | 8/236 |
| Pendarvis, William H | Fettus, Catherine E | Jun 6 1854 | 13/243 |
| Pendavis, Henry | Glase, Rebecca | Mar 3 1825 | 1/65 |
| Pendergast, Elizabeth (wid) | Donoghoe, Jeremiah | Jan 25 1853 | 12/144 |
| Pendergrast, Sophie | Jourdan, Edward | Dec 29 1836* | 3/67 |
| Pene, Amelia | Pene, John | Sep 3 1849 | 11/1 |
| Pene, John | Pene, Amelia | Sep 3 1849 | 11/1 |
| Pennington, Bennet L | Rogers, Sarah | Jan 29 1855 | 14/27 |
| Pennington, Canzada Q (wid) | Dillard, William P (wid) | Oct 10 1853 | 12/413 |
| Pennington, Francis | Evans, James Guy | Oct 15 1842 | 5/223B |
| Pennington, James | Bryson, Frances | Dec 19 1836* | 3/65 |
| Penny, Samuel | Bruce, Elizabeth Welch | May 21 1845 | 8/96B |
| Peno, Felix | Walker, Laura | May 31 1853* | 12/303 |
| Pensill, Charles J | Sparks, Lora | 1837* | OIB |
| Penton, Mary | Meek, John | Jun 27 1814* | WB1/19 |
| Perault, Eliz. (Wid) | Gannard, Fercol V. | Jun 25 1819* | CM |
| Percay, Anfelica | Hopkins, Samuel | Sep 13 1844 | 8/41B |
| Percay, Sophia A. | Badger, Charles H | Apr 16 1844 | 8/14B |
| Percy, Mary (Pescom) | Duncan, Milton H | Jun 20 1841 | 4/1851 |
| Percy, Mary | Leahy, Patrick | Jul 13 1853 | 12/353 |
| Peres, Stephen | Kaufmann, Elizabeth | Feb 3 1855 | 14/35 |
| Pericone, Francis | Lamar, Teresa | Jul 4 1855 | 14/188 |
| Perier, Marie S | Desloge, Augustus | 1826* | OIB |
| Perkins, David | Bell, Laura J. | Dec 29 1847 | 8/273 |
| Perkins, Henry | McGonigal, Rosanna | Jun 3 1844 | 7/279B |
| Perkins, Henry H | Aymard, Rosalie | Nov 8 1852 | 12/50 |
| Perkins, Lucretia | Pitman, Joseph | Dec 25 1824 | 1/58 |
| Perkins, Mary | Edmonds, Daniel | Feb 23 1842 | 5/182B |
| Perkins, Rebecca | Turner, Joel L. | Jan 28 1841* | 5/95B |
| Perkins, Rufus L. | Smith, Abbie L. | Jun 18 1851 | 11/159 |
| Perkins, Silas | Howard, Martha | Mar 30 1853 | 12/210 |
| Perkins, William | Spillings, Jane L. | Apr 2 1849* | 8/365 |
| Perkins, William C. | Hendrisce, Sarah | Aug 29 1846 | 8/186 |
| Perkins, William K | DeMiller, Sarah E | Dec 4 1852 | 12/82 |
| Perley, George H | Whiting, Caroline | Mar 6 1855 | 14/75 |
| Permentier, Minerva | Payne, John H | Jul 3 1854 | 13/273 |
| Pernall, John | Cannon, Mary | Jul 20 1836* | 3/54 |
| Perrault, Michael | Chastang, Elizabeth | Jul 5 1813* | WB1/7 |
| Perriliat, Adelaide | Marnische, Emilius Wm | Jun 22 1840 | 5/29B |
| Perrillent, Hormosande J ? | Salle, Pierre Arsene | Aug 27 1840 | 5/45B |
| Perrine, George W. | Jantan, Mary | Dec 5 1851 | 11/192 |
| Perry, Catherine | Carl, Thomas H | May 22 1833* | 2/971 |
| Perry, Edward C. | Grady, Ann | Aug 17 1850 | 11/80 |
| Perry, Hannah | Holmes, Angus D | Aug 20 1853 | 12/389 |

| BRIDE OR GROOM | SPOUSE | DATE | BOOK/PAGE |
|---|---|---|---|
| Perry, Mary Ann | Hoyle, William | Mar 29 1838* | 3/118 |
| Perry, Mary F. | Edwards, John H. | Nov 16 1848 | 8/333 |
| Perry, Morgan B | Ragsdale, Narcissa | Mar 12 1851 | 11/128 |
| Perryman, E S | Bondurant, E A | May 17 1853* | 12/287 |
| Perryman, Martha E. | Thomas, Edgar | Feb 4 1852 | 11/212 |
| Perryman, Mary S. | Deloach, Thomas C. | Nov 25 1845 | 8/126B |
| Pervis, Adelaide Ursula | Williams, Emilins | Jun 18 1840* | 5/29 |
| Pescay, Sophia A. | Badger, Charles H. | Apr 16 1844 | 8/14B |
| Pescom, Mary (Percy) | Duncan, Milton H | Jun 2 1841* | 5/265B |
| Pete, Eliza | Instant, Robert | Oct 14 1846 | 8/193 |
| Peter, Elizabeth | Young, John | Apr 22 1839* | 3/169 |
| Peter, John | Oleva, Barbara | Oct 27 1828* | 2/48 |
| Peter, Joseph | Decker, Catherine | Sep 27 1851 | 11/180 |
| Peterd, Augustus | Durand, Marie A | Mar 19 1829* | 2/77 |
| Petern, Julien | Schuble, Frederick | Apr 26 1843 | 5/265B |
| Peters, Caroline | Knight, Hugh | Apr 20 1846 | 8/159B |
| Peters, Cornelius | Nelson, Mary J | Nov 12 1855 | 14/279 |
| Peters, John | Borguare, Madelaine | 1827* | OIB |
| Peters, John C. | Kemmer, Rebecca A C | May 2 1846 | 8/162B |
| Peters, Mary E | Thomas, William | 1822* | OIB |
| Peters, Michael | Sollinger, Catherine | Aug 4 1853 | 12/375 |
| Peters, Nathaniel | Howard, Martha | Oct 9 1828* | 2/44 |
| Peters, Sophia | Hilderbrande, Chas. | Feb 16 1848 | 8/284 |
| Peters, Wyatt M. | Martin, Louisa D. | Jul 17 1843 | OIB/AMC |
| Peterson, Frederick | Boyles, Jane E. | Jan 21 1836* | 3/37 |
| Peterson, Johanna | Hanson, Hans J | Dec 6 1854 | 13/404 |
| Peterson, John R. | Bray, Anna Mary (Brown) | Mar 16 1846 | 8/152B |
| Peterson, Nicholas | Kennedy, Margaret | Nov 26 1844 | 8/54B |
| Peterson, Robert | Diemer, Catherine | Mar 4 1850 | 11/44 |
| Peterson, William | James, Sarah (Jones) | Jan 17 1845 | 8/67B |
| Petit, Theodore | Henry, Susan | Feb 20 1850 | 11/41 |
| Petit, Valerie | Jasmein, Caroline | Jul 18 1854 | 13/288 |
| Petite, Mary | Chastang, Edward | Sep 11 1843 | 5/295B |
| Petrice, Eliza H. | Place, Robert S. | Oct 22 1849 | 11/10 |
| Petrinovich, Antonio | Flinn, Ann | Dec 4 1854 | 13/399 |
| Pettes, Mary | Alford, William C. | Apr 30 1852 | 11/244 |
| Pettis, David | Maguire, Mary (Meayrin) | Mar 29 1840* | 5/57B |
| Pettis, Rebecca | Constantine, Francisco | Jun 1 1833* | 2/961 |
| Pettroff, Conrad | Tosch, Margaret | Feb 25 1854* | 13/139 |
| Petty, George | Pledger, Ann | Mar 7 1833* | 2/1081 |
| Petty, John F | Orsina, Cornelia | Oct 23 1855 | 14/261 |
| Petzer, John | Betz, Margaret | Apr 3 1834* | 2/351 |
| Pewett, Mary Elizabeth | McCullough, Charles | May 16 1843 | 5/271 |
| Pfeiffer, Margaret | Spanagel, George | Oct 18 1854 | 13/350 |
| Pfeiffer, Sarah | Turne, Charles | Apr 26 1854 | 13/206 |
| Pfeninger, Risalin | Benedict, Joseph | Feb 11 1839* | 3/156 |
| Pfister, Amantene R. | Allen, Samuel W. | Aug 12 1834* | 2/201 |
| Phelan, Jeremiah | Kelly, Margaret | Feb 5 1853 | 12/165 |
| Phelps, Jefferson | Casey, Mary Ann | Dec 8 1836* | 3/64 |
| Phelps, Lylie | Johnson, Christopher | Sep 24 1855 | 14/239 |
| Phifer, John | Kenley, Eureka | May 22 1850 | 11/63 |
| Philan, Edward | Toomey, Bridget | Nov 2 1839* | 3/190 |
| Philibert, Francis | Privat, Sophia | May 2 1842 | 5/197B |
| Philibert, Josephine | Barclay, Henry W | Dec 29 1842 | 8/120B |
| Philibert, Tolisfon | Kirkwood, Margaret | Oct 18 1845 | 8/120B |
| Philippi, C | Baird, Adele | Aug 6 1844 | 8/38 |
| Philips, Elam | Etheridge,, Mary | 1827* | OIB |
| Philips, Elizabeth | Morgan, Risse | Dec 11 1834* | 2/184 |
| Philips, Mary | Bullard, Samuel P. | Oct 22 1834* | 3/5 |
| Philips, Missouri Ann | Urquhart, Henry | Jun 13 1855 | 14/172 |
| Philips, Willis H | Hamet, Francis | Dec 24 1853 | 13/50 |
| Phillebent, Cecille M. | Prados, Joseph Jr. | Aug 15 1836* | 3/55 |
| Phillip, Angelo | Martin, Mary | Jul 29 1843 | 5/290B |
| Phillipe, Antonio | Jacobson, Matilda | Oct 28 1850 | 11/93 |

| BRIDE OR GROOM | SPOUSE | DATE | BK/PAGE |
|---|---|---|---|
| Phillipp, Elizabeth | Callahan, John | Dec 9 1839* | 5/3 |
| Phillips, Ann | Richmon, Francis | May 9 1853 | 12/273 |
| Phillips, C | Baird, Adele | Aug 6 1844 | 8/38B |
| Phillips, Charles | Hannis, Julia | Feb 20 1855 | 14/65 |
| Phillips, Delphine | Archer, Thomas F | Jun 3 1837* | 3/97 |
| Phillips, Elizjah R | Falkner, Permealy | Jul 19 1845 | 8/111B |
| Phillips, Fanny | Morgan, Ransom | Mar 7 1841* | 5/119B |
| Phillips, Francis | Hammett, Jackson H | Jun 8 1850 | 11/65 |
| Phillips, Martha | Baker, Jefferson | Nov 7 1849* | 11/14 |
| Phillips, Martha Ann | Spensler, John B | Aug 3 1844 | 7/363B |
| Phillips, Rebecca | Layton, David | Dec 16 1841 | 5/162B |
| Phillips, Virginia | Bell, Charles | Dec 29 1844 | 8/63B |
| Phillips, William | Andrews, Sarah A E | Jul 10 1850* | 11/72 |
| Phillips, William | Andrews, Sarah E | Jul 2 1852* | 11/273 |
| Picard, Isaac (Pecard) | Markstein, Henrietta Mrs | Nov 9 1855 | 14/275 |
| Pickens, Elizabeth | Mott, Henry | Nov 15 1854 | 13/380 |
| Pickering, John | Gerles, Ardomisa | Aug 31 1854 | 13/326 |
| Pickett, Elizabeth | O'Neal, George | Apr 17 1854 | 13/187 |
| Pie, Mary Ann | Young, Daniel | Jan 13 1852 | 11/203 |
| Piechowski, Rose A | Pillard, Eugene | Dec 24 1855 | 14/314 |
| Pierce, Betsey Ann | Page, Willis | Jan 10 1833* | 2/1231 |
| Pierce, Charles L | Kelson, Elizabeth | Apr 10 1855 | 14/102 |
| Pierce, Ezekiel W | Hunt, Harriett E | Nov 2 1852 | 12/44 |
| Pierce, George | Stringfellow, Tomzil | Oct 9 1843 | 5/298B |
| Pierce, Jeremiah | Williams, Susanna | Jun 17 1845 | 8/104B |
| Pierce, Jeremiah | Chapman, Mary | Nov 2 1855 | 14/270 |
| Pierce, Larkin | Pierce, Martha | Dec 20 1852 | 12/102 |
| Pierce, Lewis | Langford, Jane | Apr 29 1844 | 8/18B |
| Pierce, Lewis | Stringfeller, Sarah | Dec 22 1849 | 11/26 |
| Pierce, Martha | Pierce, Larkin | Dec 20 1852 | 12/102 |
| Pierce, Matilda | Brown, Brinkley | 1827* | 0IB |
| Pierce, Nancy | Davis, James | Mar 20 1844 | 5/328B |
| Pierce, Patrick | Brusenhaur, Ellen ? | Jan 22 1852 | 11/207 |
| Pierce, Rebecca | Seyfer, John | 1825* | 0IB |
| Pierce, Tempe | Griffin, John | Nov 14 1849 | 11/16 |
| Pierce, Thomas | McKinsey, Adeline | Feb 5 1833* | 2/1161 |
| Pierce, William | Riels, Lucinda J | Apr 1 1853 | 12/212 |
| Pierce, Z Davis | Arnold, Rebecca | Jun 6 1844 | 8/25B |
| Piere, Elizabeth (Piero) | Scott, Samuel E | Sep 16 1840* | 5/45B |
| Pierre, Catherine | Dickey, William | Oct 16 1843 | 5/300B |
| Pierre, Catherine | Rives, James M | Mar 12 1850 | 11/45 |
| Pierre, John H | Reeves, Ellen | Jul 13 1846 | 8/178 |
| Pierre, Mary Barbary H | Alexander, Henry | Aug 2 1842 | 5/213B |
| Pierre, Nicholas H | Rasher, Sarah Ann Eliz. | Jun 21 1844 | 8/28B |
| Pierry, John B ? | Boissint, Magdalen ? | Jan 30 1829* | 2/67 |
| Pierson, Abram B | Hatchett, Charlotte C | May 12 1843 | 5/270B |
| Pietre, Rocco | Ryan, Mary Ann (O'Riley) | Mar 22 1841* | 5/119B |
| Pillans, Palmer J | Roberts, Laura M | Feb 1 1845 | 8/70B |
| Pillard, Eugene | Piechowski, Rose A | Dec 24 1855 | 14/314 |
| Pillerey, Bernard | Coffen, Anna | Jun 1 1848* | 8/307 |
| Pillet, Mary Josephine | Vantrot, Gustavus E.S. | Jul 21 1851 | 11/168 |
| Pindolf, Jacob | Selhsh, Bridget Ann ? | May 9 1852 | 11/247 |
| Pinkham, Eliza | Center, Henry | 1822* | 0IB |
| Pinkham, George R | Bleeker, Eliza M | May 26 1819* | CM |
| Pinkham, Hannah | Williams, Charles | Jul 10 1851 | 11/163 |
| Pinney, Emeline M | Bright, Henry | Feb 10 1835 | 3/8 |
| Pinta, Ellen | Ball, John | Apr 2 1855 | 14/95 |
| Pinta, Jean F (T) | Rabbie, Victoire | Nov 15 1833* | 2/712 |
| Pinta, Jean Glode Folde | Collin, Margarite | Oct 28 1828 | 2/49 |
| Pinta, Joseph | Rabbie, Julie | Jan 4 1837* | 3/68 |
| Pinta, Marie V (wid) | Darrieux, John H | May 16 1853 | 12/285 |
| Pinto, Antonio | Canaville, Marie C | 1826* | 0IB |
| Pinto, Cara (Tuite) | Torrance, George W | Jul 6 1848* | 8/313 |
| Pinto, Odeal | Cook, Charles D | Apr 23 1855 | 14/114 |

131

| BRIDE OR GROOM | SPOUSE | DATE | BK/PAGE |
|---|---|---|---|
| Pipkin, Mary E | Johnson, William D | Jun 19 1850 | 11/67 |
| Pitch, Sarah | Brown, Alexander G | Jan 26 1850 | 11/35 |
| Pitman, Joseph | Perkins, Lucretia | Dec 25 1824 | 1/58 |
| Pitt, William | Adams, Mary I | Oct 10 1840* | 5/53B |
| Pittman, Emily | Sossomon, John F | Feb 16 1837* | 3/72 |
| Pittman, Lucretia | Smith, James | Nov 24 1831* | 2/1831 |
| Pitts, John G W | Williams, Sarah Ann | May 26 1845 | 8/98B |
| Pitts, Washington | Gerald, Julia Ann | Mar 28 1833* | 2/1061 |
| Pitts, William | Adams, Josephine | Oct 10 1840 | 4/1381B |
| Pizzini, Domonique | Starck, Margaret | Aug 16 1852 | 11/276 |
| Place, Robert S | Petrice, Eliza H | Oct 22 1849 | 11/10 |
| Platt, Peter | Kelly, Catherine | Jun 1 1852 | 11/258 |
| Platt, Peter (widr) | Sims, Marcella | Apr 19 1849* | 8/369 |
| Platt, Peter | Huler, Mary | Oct 29 1853 | 12/429 |
| Platt, William H | Cuthbert, Cornelia M | Apr 15 1848 | 8/299 |
| Pledger, Abel K | Carter, Margaret Ann | Feb 14 1843 | 5/249B |
| Pledger, Ann | Petty, George | Mar 7 1833* | 2/1081 |
| Plum, Mary A | Caldwell, John F | Jul 6 1844 | 8/32B |
| Plumb, Mary | Bass, Ebenezer A | Feb 25 1848 | 8/286 |
| Plumley, William | Conway, Patsy | Dec 19 1813* | WB1/9 |
| Plunkett, John | Moore, Jane | Oct 6 1855 | 14/246 |
| Poalk, Joseph | Welch, Shady Ann | May 23 1853 | 12/295 |
| Pocheler, Arnauld | Jacobs, Elizabeth | Oct 8 1852 | 12/26 |
| Poe, Anna M | McCoy, Thomas W | May 19 1831* | 2/170 |
| Poe, Catherine | Robinson, William S | Apr 1 1838* | 3/118 |
| Poe, George Jr | Toulmin, Emma M | 1827* | OIB |
| Poe, George W | Toulmin, Frances E | Feb 1 1833* | 2/1171 |
| Poersheb, Edmond | Fife, Catherine E | Apr 4 1839* | 3/164 |
| Poetz, Andrew | Knauf, Sophia | Nov 22 1852 | 12/68 |
| Points, George W | Stuart, Delphine | Nov 8 1853 | 13/9 |
| Poitevin, Eugene | Stuardi, Amanda | Aug 13 1855 | 14/210 |
| Polhomus, Ann L | Morw, John H | Jan 28 1839* | 3/154 |
| Pollard, Dorthea | Miley, Dennis (Milry) | May 6 1843 | 5/269B |
| Pollard, Eliza | Case, Joseph (Cade?) | Oct 30 1833* | 2/741 |
| Pollard, George | Elevell, Anna Maria | Jan 6 1837* | 3/68 |
| Pollard, George | O'Bear, Eliza | Dec 3 1853* | 13/33 |
| Pollard, Harriett | Fowler, John | Aug 28 1830* | 2/136 |
| Pollard, James | Bolton, Matilda A | Jun 3 1848 | 8/307 |
| Pollard, John | Stanton, Alice | Jan 27 1834* | 2/501 |
| Pollard, Louisa | Huggins, George | Apr 20 1831* | 2/163 |
| Pollard, Mary L | Bancroft, Charles Jr | Jan 2 1850 | 11/30 |
| Pollard, Phoebe | Ensign, Henry P | Apr 2 1834* | 2/361 |
| Pollard, Robert P | Anderson, Lydia | Nov 5 1844 | 8/47B |
| Pollard, William | Calahan, Polly | Jun 2 1834* | 2/241 |
| Pollard, William | Barlow, Joice | Mar 1 1820* | CM |
| Pollard, William | Callahan, Mary | Jan 20 1836 | 3/37 |
| Pollard, William | Calahan, Polly | Jun 2 1834* | 2/241 |
| Pollard, William A | Bolton, Mary E | Apr 2 1853 | 12/217 |
| Poller, Julie | Chaix, Pierre Germueil | May 20 1839* | 3/173 |
| Pomeroy, Elizabeth | Garden, Willy | May 6 1835* | 3/24 |
| Pomeroy, Elizabeth | Garvin, Mills | May 7 1835* | 3/24 |
| Pomeroy, James M | Lenox, Margaret | Jul 28 1835 | 3/20 |
| Pomeroy, James M | Robinson, Charlotte P | Feb 1 1844 | 5/319B |
| Pomeroy, Mary | Barrow, Oliver | 1837* | OIB |
| Pomeroy, Porter R | Collins, Euphosinia H | Jun 11 1846 | 8/171 |
| Pond, William O | Gartman, Alabama | Jul 2 1853 | 12/340 |
| Ponis, Henry | Marone, Louisa | 1843* | OIB |
| Ponns, Mary A (wid) | Farley, Philip | Sep 8 1853 | 12/403 |
| Pons, Megile M (Miguel) | Betbeze, Justina | Oct 20 1854 | 13/356 |
| Pontappidan, George | Snyder, Margaret | Apr 30 1842* | 5/196B |
| Pool, Jechonias P | Clark, Alafal | May 18 1854 | 13/229 |
| Pool, Sarah E | Hammond, Lewis C | Dec 8 1848* | 8/338 |
| Poor, Mary | Alverez, William | Feb 5 1838* | 3/110 |
| Pope, Elizabeth S | Ormond, James M | Jan 29 1850* | 11/36 |

| BRIDE OR GROOM | SPOUSE | DATE | BK/PAGE |
|---|---|---|---|
| Pope, Joseph Henry | Holcombe, Lydia M | Nov 5 1845 | 8/123B |
| Pope, Maria Jane | St John, Newton | Feb 24 1835 | 3/10 |
| Pope, William | Berry, Margaret A | Jun 28 1853 | 12/334 |
| Pope, William B | Adams, Mary E | Dec 18 1846 | 8/205 |
| Pope, William D | McBride, Tabitha S | Apr 14 1847 | 8/227 |
| Pope, William L | Williams, M Susan | Jan 28 1853 | 12/153 |
| Porter, Arnold W | Carr, Henrietta | Jul 31 1854 | 13/298 |
| Porter, Charles | Esty, Bridget | May 3 1848* | 8/303 |
| Porter, Elizabeth | Cook, Robert | May 17 1841* | 5/131B |
| Porter, George | Robertson, Elenor | Apr 17 1841* | 5/124B |
| Porter, James | Keyland, Mary Jane | Nov 2 1849 | 11/13 |
| Porter, John | Parmenter, Nancy | Oct 27 1851 | 11/184 |
| Porter, Mary | Maxwell, Henry | Sep 5 1854 | 13/329 |
| Porter, Sarah | Goodrich, Matthew J | Jul 8 1836* | 3/52 |
| Porter, Sidney D (widr) | Rouse, Nancy S | Jul 14 1853 | 12/356 |
| Porter, William | Veira, Louisa | Jul 14 1847 | 8/245 |
| Portier, Honori | Reggio, Irene | Oct 30 1845 | 8/119B |
| Portier, Louis | Lamoule, Marie | Apr 29 1839* | 3/169 |
| Posey, Felix | Edwards, Eliza Jane | Jul 1 1841* | 5/141B |
| Posey, Yancy | Selause, Battitte | Jul 14 1838* | 3/136 |
| Poso, Frances | Toutchstone, Mary | Mar 30 1829* | 2/79 |
| Post, Anna Catherina | Thormerhlen, Claus | Jun 6 1844 | 8/26B |
| Post, James B | Dillon, Louisa | Dec 26 1853 | 13/52 |
| Post, Ward | Dana, Sarah Ann | Dec 27 1849* | 11/29 |
| Potter, Frances E | Alvirez, Emanuel | Jan 12 1837* | 3/69 |
| Pottier, Honori | Reggio, Irene | Oct 30 1845 | 8/119B |
| Poulet, Marie L | Chatard, John | Jun 14 1854 | 13/258 |
| Poulnot, Jacob W (Toulnot) | Wylie, Mary Jane | Dec 22 1845 | 8/131 |
| Pound, Godfrey | Miller, Therese | Mar 2 1836* | 3/41 |
| Powell, Caroline E | Roach, Shadrach D | Nov 3 1855 | 14/271 |
| Powell, Elijah | Bates, Caroline | Nov 30 1829 | 2/104 |
| Powell, Elisha | Williams, Camerene | Oct 4 1837* | 3/92 |
| Powell, Eliza | Rabby, Zephariah | Oct 8 1855 | 14/247 |
| Powell, Euseiabee | Goff, James | Oct 16 1850 | 11/89 |
| Powell, Hiram | Scarbrough, Mary | Sep 26 1849 | 11/7 |
| Powell, Isaiah | Scarbrough, Nancy | Jul 10 1838* | 3/135 |
| Powell, James | Forbes, Margaret | Jan 9 1847 | 8/211 |
| Powell, Martha A (Mrs) | Crow, John F | May 10 1853 | 12/276 |
| Powell, Mary | Waggoner, Coleman | Apr 25 1852 | 11/241 |
| Powell, Richmond | Howard, Mima Jane | Dec 29 1854* | 13/424 |
| Powell, Thomas | Field, Tabitha | May 24 1816* | CM |
| Powell, William | Howard, Nancy | May 28 1852 | 11/255 |
| Powers, Abbey M | Stringer, William W | Feb 26 1846 | 8/148B |
| Powers, Ann | Elworth, Thomas | Sep 16 1850 | 11/85 |
| Powers, Caroline | Dickinson, Eli P | Jan 27 1844 | 5/318B |
| Powers, Elizabeth | Myers, John E | Aug 12 1851 | 11/172 |
| Powers, James | Conway, Elizabeth | Feb 6 1854 | 13/111 |
| Powers, Johanna | Glyce, Martin | Aug 25 1838* | 3/141 |
| Powers, Julia Ann | Robinson, Henry A | Nov 7 1845 | 8/124B |
| Powers, Mary | Bull, Alfred | Feb 5 1838* | 3/110 |
| Powers, Mary | O'Brien, Dennis | Oct 6 1840* | 5/53B |
| Powers, Nancy M | James, William F | Dec 7 1855 | 14/300 |
| Powers, Paul | Wilson, Susan A | Nov 25 1839* | 5/2 |
| Powers, Sarah | Heard, John B | Dec 15 1836* | 3/64 |
| Powers, William | McDermott, Winford | Mar 21 1844 | 5/329B |
| Powers, William L | Nichols, Ann | Dec 9 1854 | 13/407 |
| Pradien, Josephine | Mignon, I | May 23 1838* | 3/129 |
| Prados, Antoine | Ramel, Celestine | Apr 1 1837* | 3/77 |
| Prados, Francis | Golphe, Helene C | 1837* | OIB |
| Prados, Joseph Jr | Phillebert, Cecille M | Aug 15 1836* | 3/55 |
| Pratt, George | Anderson, Emeline | Jul 13 1853 | 12/352 |
| Preans, Julian | Hagerty, Mary | Apr 10 1848 | 8/297 |
| Preis, John J | Mitchell, Lydia B | Feb 10 1847 | 8/216 |
| Prentice, Mary | Talbot, John | Feb 18 1825 | 1/64 |

133

| BRIDE OR GROOM | SPOUSE | DATE | BK/PAGE |
|---|---|---|---|
| Preour, Francois | Day, Marie | Nov 15 1838* | 3/148 |
| Prepell, Thomas (Pressell) | Wilde, Christina | May 1 1845 | 8/91B |
| Prescott, James E | Tucker, Mary | Aug 20 1835* | 3/25 |
| Prescott, James E | Lee, Ellen | Apr 4 1846 | 8/155B |
| Prescott, Nancy Ann | Swain, Stephen | Mar 24 1825* | 1/70 |
| Preston, Royal | Chandler, Philinda B | Jun 5 1851 | 11/156 |
| Preston, Sarah | Smith, Thomas Brown | May 15 1848* | 8/304 |
| Preston, Simon S | Cox, Hetty M | Jul 29 1837* | 3/90 |
| Preston, William | Fogerty, Margaret | Dec 22 1853 | 13/46 |
| Pretlove, John | Carroll, Rosaline | Sep 28 1847* | 8/257 |
| Pretus, Margaret | Palliser, John | Nov 16 1849 | 11/17 |
| Price, Phedre Matilda | Williams, Lewis | Jan 1 1847 | 8/209 |
| Price, Teresa | Collins, John K | Feb 10 1841* | 5/101B |
| Prie, Francoise | Dominique, Tujague | Feb 17 1849* | 8/358 |
| Prieau, Jeane Marie | Mondon, Jean Mari | Oct 3 1842 | 5/221B |
| Priester, Rudolph | Thompson, Elizabeth | Mar 12 1841* | 5/116B |
| Priford, Elizabeth | Lees, Peter (Sees) | Dec 23 1843* | 5/238B |
| Priford, Elizabeth | Sees, Peter (Lees) | Dec 23 1842* | 5/238B |
| Prine, Delilah Ann | Howard, Loammi | Jan 1 1833 | 2/1241 |
| Pringle, Virginia | Still, Charles | Oct 23 1854 | 13/360 |
| Priour, Jean Marie | Hart, Rosalie | Oct 24 1844 | 8/45B |
| Prison, Eliza (Brison) | Callahan, William | Apr 28 1842 | 5/195B |
| Prister, Rudolph (Priester) | Thompson, Elizabeth | Mar 12 1841* | 5/116B |
| Pritchard, Daniel M | Alvarez, Mary | Jan 14 1836* | 3/36 |
| Pritchett, Marian E | Gates, Joseph R | Aug 12 1848* | 8/320 |
| Pritchett, Robert | Alexander, Ann Eliza | Feb 10 1845* | 8/71B |
| Privat, Sophia | Philibert, Francis | May 2 1842 | 5/197B |
| Proctin, Thomas S | Cavin, Charlotte | Nov 20 1842 | 5/228B |
| Pron, Mary (Prou) | Reinheart, Christopher | Jan 15 1850 | 11/33 |
| Propell, Thomas | Wilde, Christina | May 1 1845 | 8/91B |
| Prou, Mary (Pron) | Reinheart, Christopher | Jan 15 1850 | 11/33 |
| Prout, John | Mullins, Catherine | Apr 19 1854 | 13/195 |
| Provincial, E Paul | Tayler, Catharine | Jan 13 1851 | 11/111 |
| Provost, Cecilia | Gange, Numa | Aug 20 1852* | 11/277 |
| Provost, Ecilia | Longe, Numa | Aug 30 1852 | 11/280 |
| Provost, William J | Jude, Mary Frances | Feb 13 1845 | 8/73B |
| Prudat, Louis Ernest | Glover, Caroline A | Sep 15 1841* | 5/152B |
| Prudert, James Ames | Gloom, Caroline Augustmer | Sep 10 1841 | 4/3311B |
| Prudhomme, Josephine A | Charpentier, Raymond | Jun 7 1843 | 5/280B |
| Prudhomme, Mary L | Avril, Martial | Apr 21 1843 | 5/263B |
| Pruitt, Thomas L | Wyatt, Elizabeth | Dec 30 1851 | 11/199 |
| Puckett, James | Ballinger, Mary Jane | Jun 25 1833* | 2/911 |
| Pullen, Calrine Elizabeth | Kortjohn, John | May 5 1838* | 3/123 |
| Pullin, George F | Duffy, Nancy | Jan 31 1854 | 13/105 |
| Purcell, Charles Jones ? | Starkes, Sarah ? | 1839* | OIB |
| Purcell, Hellen Louisa | Bartlett, John Jr | Feb 6 1839* | 3/155 |
| Purcell, Isaac | Johnson, Lucy | Apr 21 1853 | 12/249 |
| Purdy, Alexander M (widr) | Ringgold, Harriet C | Dec 1 1853 | 13/31 |
| Purdy, Wineford | Girard, Joseph | Dec 20 1833* | 2/651 |
| Purtell, Mary | Byrne, John | Jan 10 1854 | 13/66 |
| Putcher, Fanny | Tobias, Theodore | Mar 15 1852* | 11/226 |
| Putts, William | Herring, Elizabeth | Apr 15 1831 | 2/162 |
| Pyers, William J | Ryan, Johanna | Jul 31 1845 | 8/114B |
| Pyor, Christopher J Jr | Walker, Allice B | Sep 15 1853 | 12/406 |

| BRIDE OR GROOM | SPOUSE | DATE | BK/PAGE |
|---|---|---|---|

Q

| BRIDE OR GROOM | SPOUSE | DATE | BK/PAGE |
|---|---|---|---|
| Quarles, Benjamin | Lyons, Ann | Feb 8 1848 | 8/282 |
| Quarles, Julia Ann | Bryan, Isaac | Jul 15 1830 | 2/132 |
| Quarmby, John | Meslier, Ann | May 1 1854 | 13/211 |
| Quest, John | Cronin, Hannah | Jul 27 1850 | 11/77 |
| Quebeuf, Napoleon | Cashmier, Ellen | Jan 30 1841* | 5/97B |
| Quigley, Charles M | Fitzsimmons, Clara | Jun 30 1840* | 5/30B |
| Quigley, Cordelia A | Shackleford, Robert | Aug 26 1846 | 8/186 |
| Quigley, Margaret E | Lewis, John B | Jun 30 1846 | 8/176 |
| Quigley, Margaretta A | Roberts, William H | Jun 16 1851 | 11/158 |
| Quigley, Martina T | Roberts, Reuben H | Mar 4 1851 | 11/128 |
| Quigley, Nathan C | Somers, Deborah Ann | May 5 1831* | 2/167 |
| Quigley, Stephen B | Mountain, Mary Jane | Sep 13 1855 | 14/231 |
| Quigly, Ann | Ayheir, Dave | May 19 1838* | 3/126 |
| Quin, Ann | Rooney, Martin | Nov 18 1841* | 5/157B |
| Quin, John W (McGuire) | Roane, Annette | Aug 3 1841* | 5/145B |
| Quin, Mary | Gibbons, John | May 10 1852* | 11/248 |
| Quin, Nicholas | Turney, Lucy | Jan 2 1847 | 8/209 |
| Quina, Margaret | Touart, Louis | Nov 18 1833* | 2/701 |
| Quiner, Mary | Garner, Thomas | Nov 12 1835* | 3/28 |
| Quinlan, James | Barrett, Abigail | Mar 3 1851 | 11/127 |
| Quinlan, P | Ward, Margaret Ann | Sep 4 1849 | 11/2 |
| Quinland, Andrew | Thompson, Mary | May 16 1854 | 13/226 |
| Quinn, Ann | Higgins, Noah | Jul 30 1842* | 5/213B |
| Quinn, Ann | Kenann, M | Apr 19 1838* | 3/120 |
| Quinn, Ann | Whiting, Oscar | May 6 1854 | 13/217 |
| Quinn, Ellen | Duperteus, H Louis | Jan 14 1852 | 11/203 |
| Quinn, James | Flinn, Margaret | Mar 10 1853 | 12/190 |
| Quinn, John | Aegan, Rosana | Feb 13 1849* | 8/356 |
| Quinn, Mary | King, James M | Aug 31 1852 | 11/281 |
| Quinn, Mary | Smith, John | Jun 10 1844 | 8/27B |
| Quinn, Matthew | Boyce, Gacy | Aug 17 1836* | 3/56 |
| Quinn, Matthew | McKain, Catharine | Aug 15 1848* | 8/320 |
| Quinn, Michael | Dailey, Anne | Aug 25 1845 | 8/116B |
| Quinn, Michael | McNamee, Ann | Feb 22 1854 | 13/130 |
| Quinn, P | McNamara, Margarette | Jun 13 1838* | 3/132 |
| Quinn, Patience | Burnham, Alonzo H | Mar 12 1830* | 2/117 |
| Quinn, Patrick | Ivey, Jane | Mar 21 1850 | 11/47 |
| Quinn, William | Hall, Patience | 1826* | OIB |
| Quirk, J D G | Alexander, Roselia | Nov 8 1843 | 5/302B |
| Quist, John (Duest) | Haines, Martha | Aug 2 1845* | 8/114B |

R

| Bride or Groom | Spouse | Date | BK/Page |
|---|---|---|---|
| Rabano, Tarasa | Masters, John | Dec 21 1853 | 13/45 |
| Rabbie, Anatol | Bang, Desire | Apr 9 1834* | 2/331 |
| Rabbie, Julie | Pinta, Joseph | Jan 4 1837* | 3/68 |
| Rabbie, Victoire | Pinta, Jean F | Nov 15 1833* | 2/712 |
| Rabby, Elizabeth A | Cain, Joseph S | May 15 1855 | 14/141 |
| Rabby, Hermina | Lewis, William | Apr 20 1846* | 8/168B |
| Rabby, Jacob M | Vidmer, Adele | Aug 30 1855 | 14/220 |
| Rabby, John | Lewis, Delia | Aug 10 1846 | 8/184 |
| Rabby, Josephine | Collins, Edward | Jun 28 1848* | 8/311 |
| Rabby, Mary | Lafargue, Alexander | Jul 18 1844 | 8/33B |
| Rabby, Mary | Clayton, Charles A | Jun 28 1852 | 11/266 |
| Rabby, Sophia | Delmas, Carlos | Nov 5 1853 | 13/8 |
| Rabby, Susan | Gerard, Francis Lazarus | Dec 7 1844* | 8/57B |
| Rabby, Zephariah | Powell, Eliza | Oct 8 1855 | 14/247 |
| Rabec, Annita (Rabie) | Riva, Antonio | May 7 1849 | 8/374 |
| Rabie, Pier | Miller, Sarah | 1825* | 0IB |
| Rabman, Madelina | Hury, George | Apr 15 1854 | 13/184 |
| Racklus, Caroline (Buckley) | Heppler, Charles | Nov 14 1840* | 5/61B |
| Radomich, Stephen | Cazelos, Mary | Dec 22 1849 | 11/27 |
| Raeford, Mary Jane | Goff, William | Apr 21 1840* | 5/19 |
| Raer, Margaret | Mugel, Jacob | Nov 6 1835* | 3/27 |
| Rafael, Martha | Lelande, Lewis | Jul 21 1832* | 2/1391 |
| Raffee, Thomas | Nicholas, Matilda | Nov 22 1854 | 13/389 |
| Rafferty, Ann | Loftus, Thomas | May 17 1853 | 12/286 |
| Rafferty, Ann | Morley, William F | Nov 4 1852 | 12/45 |
| Raffin, Delphine | Calcina, Joseph | Nov 18 1844 | 8/51B |
| Raffin, Joseph | Currie, Rose | Oct 20 1824 | 1/42 |
| Raffin, Rose | Debrierre, Antonio | Aug 28 1835* | 3/26 |
| Ragsdale, Narcissa B | Perry, Morgan B | Mar 12 1851 | 11/128 |
| Ragusin, Antonio | Smith, Anne | May 22 1845 | 8/97B |
| Rahilly, Thomas H | Burke, Mary | Feb 20 1855 | 14/64 |
| Raiford, Susannah | Clark, Micajah | Apr 12 1847 | 8/226 |
| Rainons, Catharine | Connell, John | Apr 26 1843* | 5/265B |
| Rainwater, Elizabeth C | Bryran, George (Bryson) | Dec 13 1845* | 8/130B |
| Rainwater, Elizabeth S | Gay, George W | Jul 22 1843 | 5/290B |
| Rainwater, Miranda J | Collins, Peter | Dec 27 1853 | 13/54 |
| Rainwater, William James | Bolton, Martha | Sep 21 1848 | 8/325 |
| Raley, Jeremiah | Murphy, Margaret | Mar 1 1842 | 5/184B |
| Ramel, Celestine | Prados, Antoine | Apr 1 1837* | 3/77 |
| Ramel, Felix | Guesnard, Emma | Jul 9 1852* | 11/268 |
| Rameras, Seraphine | Verde, Franciso Benito | Feb 21 1848 | 8/285 |
| Rami, John | Couche, Mary Louisa | Jul 15 1841* | 5/142B |
| Ramierez, John B | Hubbard, Emily | Apr 7 1834* | 2/341 |
| Ramirez, Caroline | Matlock, William C | Jun 9 1836* | 3/50 |
| Ramirez, Emily | Romero, John B | Jan 19 1844 | 5/315B |
| Rampon, Mary | Croquir, Thomas | Jul 2 1850 | 11/70 |
| Ramseger, Julia A | Kiencke, Earnest C | Nov 6 1849* | 11/13 |
| Ramsey, Thomas M | Bancroft, Elizabeth | Feb 4 1846 | 8/144B |
| Ramsfieldt, Margaret | Heit, Lewis | Feb 20 1855 | 14/20 |
| Ramstein, Agatha | Burgmiere, Simon · | Nov 14 1836* | 3/62 |
| Ranagar, Jackson | Jones, Martha | Dec 8 1846 | 8/203 |
| Rance, Henry Gaspard | Lacoste, Eulalu H | Feb 3 1841* | 5/99B |
| Randal, William C | Marr, Ann | Aug 26 1836* | 3/56 |
| Randall, Bryant B | McCollum, Elizabeth | 1820* | 0IB |

| BRIDE OR GROOM | SPOUSE | DATE | BK/PAGE |
|---|---|---|---|
| Randall, Jane | Jester, Hugh T | Jan 25 1842 | 5/173B |
| Randall, Malvina | Celburn, James L | Aug 10 1847 | 8/251 |
| Randall, Marcus Tullus C | Blackwell, Dorcas | Jun 28 1845 | 8/107B |
| Randall, Margaret Ann | Wilson, James B | Sep 10 1825* | 1/90 |
| Randall, Unito Minerva | Williams, Jeremiah | Jun 26 1850 | 11/69 |
| Randall, William D | Jayne, Almira | May 17 1832* | 2/1501 |
| Randolph, Lucretia | Lewis, John | Oct 8 1835* | 3/29 |
| Randolph, Phineas B | Markey, Elizabeth | Apr 14 1851 | 11/138 |
| Rane, Edward (widr) | Ringler, Marie (wid) | Nov 24 1853 | 13/26 |
| Raney, Catherine | Sitzler, William W | Dec 1 1831* | 2/182 |
| Ranger, Theresa J | Chandler, John B | Sep 6 1847 | 8/254 |
| Rankin, Ann | Armstrong, Michael | Jan 3 1855 | 13/433 |
| Ransifer, Ira E | Brannan, Elizabeth | Jan 28 1837* | 3/70 |
| Raoul, Nicholas | Sinibaldi, Theresa A | Nov 29 1824 | 1/51 |
| Rapier, Thomas G | Senac, Evelina | Dec 21 1837* | 3/104 |
| Rarford, Dudley | Miller, Cristinna | Jan 14 1839* | 3/B152 |
| Raridon, Eliza | Adrian, Thomas W | Feb 22 1847 | 8/219 |
| Raritan, Eliza | Oakes, Frederick | Jun 12 1843 | 5/281B |
| Rasberry, William G (widr) | Hudson, Ellen | May 5 1855* | 14/130 |
| Rasberry, William G | Ship, Mary | ND (1854)* | 13/761 |
| Rascup, Jane (wid) | Johnson, Robert E (widr) | Mar 4 1853 | 12/184 |
| Rasher, Elizabeth | Pierre, Nicholas H | Jun 19 1844 | 7/305B |
| Rasher, Jacob | Anderson, Lydia Lucinda | Jul 2 1840* | 5/33 |
| Rasher, Mary | Johnston, John | 1827* | OIB |
| Rasher, Redding | Brown, Jane | Jul 9 1828* | 2/36 |
| Rasher, Sarah | Fountain, Thomas | Nov 13 1824 | 1/47 |
| Rasher, Sarah Ann Elizabeth | Pierre, Nicholas H | Jun 21 1844 | 8/28B |
| Ratcliff, Ann | McKinsey, Benjamin | Mar 27 1839* | 3/161 |
| Ratcliff, Frederick | Morrell, Rebecca | Feb 28 1852 | 11/222 |
| Rathbone, Charles D | Rogers, Bridget | Dec 23 1854 | 13/418 |
| Raue, Julius | Gabel, Johanna B | Jun 12 1854* | 13/253 |
| Rauson, S Adele | Deguiramand, Morel I | Jun 25 1836* | 3/51 |
| Ravesies, Paul T | Oliver, Mary V | Mar 1 1848 | 8/287 |
| Rawlins, Thomas | Wrey, Julia A | Feb 14 1850 | 11/39 |
| Rawls, Antoinette A | Redus, Leonard H | Jan 1 1855 | 13/429 |
| Rawls, Francis | Brown, Willie B | Dec 22 1841 | 5/164B |
| Rawls, John J | Dent, Maria | May 22 1851* | 11/151 |
| Rawls, Mary | Hartley, Alexander | Mar 30 1843* | 5/257B |
| Rawls, Minerva | Graves, Samuel D | May 24 1843 | 5/275B |
| Rawls, Thomas H | Brown, Sarah G | Oct 27 1853 | 12/425 |
| Ray, Hiram | Mahon, Mary Ann | Jul 3 1840* | 5/33B |
| Ray, James | Soger, Helena | Sep 2 1848 | 8/322 |
| Ray, Patrick | Silvey, Mary | Jan 26 1852 | 11/208 |
| Rayford, Isabella | Crenshaw, Samuel | Dec 6 1847 | 8/269 |
| Rayford, William | Tucker, Elizabeth | May 27 1845 | 8/99B |
| Rayman, John | Weatherall, Emma | Apr 21 1846 | 8/159B |
| Raymond, Henry H | Cruzat, Marie Modeste | Jun 5 1839* | 3/177 |
| Raymond, Hurbert N | Bowers, Catherine A | May 27 1833* | 2/991 |
| Raymond, Serie | Bellanger, Anastasie P | Dec 31 1833* | 2/261 |
| Raynalds, Emma | Leslie, Albert J | May 1 1849 | 8/372 |
| Rea, Jeremiah | Johnston, Martha | 1829* | OIB |
| Rea, Peletiah P | Lenoir, Louisiana | Oct 2 1830* | 2/138 |
| Reach, Abegail | Cannon, William D | Jan 20 1840* | 5/9 |
| Reach, Peter | Hayden, Isabella | Dec 19 1838* | 3/A152 |
| Read, Alvin A | Budlong, Rebecca A | Jan 14 1854 | 13/79 |
| Read, Joshua H | Vankleek, Virginia M | Mar 16 1843 | 5/254B |
| Read, Quartus M | Caille, Augusta | Jan 9 1855 | 14/6 |
| Read, Unity Richards | Green, Aaron | Dec 15 1852 | 12/95 |
| Read, Virginia M | Tisdale, John B | Feb 15 1849* | 8/358 |
| Reader, Alfred A | Hinsay, Anna | 1850* | OIB |
| Reader, William C | Heard, Cornelia H | Apr 18 1844 | 8/15B |
| Reardon, Eliza T | Viney, Charles | Jan 7 1854 | 13/65 |
| Reardon, Joanna | Baron, Francis | Oct 9 1852 | 12/27 |
| Reardon, Patrick | Carlin, Ann | Sep 6 1851 | 11/177 |

| BRIDE OR GROOM | SPOUSE | DATE | BK/PAGE |
|---|---|---|---|
| Reavidine, Catherine | Gillraeth, John | Oct 14 1843 | 5/300B |
| Reavidine, Catherine | Gilbraith, John | Oct 14 1843 | 5/300B |
| Rechie, Mary Ann | Goff, Aaron | Mar 27 1847* | 8/223 |
| Record, Hippolite | Fouqust, Minselle Rose | Aug 13 1838* | 3/138 |
| Reddin, Eliza | Rodgers, Joseph | Dec 4 1847 | 8/268 |
| Rediger, Herman | Eberlin, Babeth | Aug 8 1854* | 13/306 |
| Redus, Augustus F | Cocke, Ann E | Dec 12 1844 | 8/58B |
| Redus, Leonard H | Rawls, Antoinette A | Jan 1 1855 | 13/429 |
| Redwood, Martha C | Bidgood, Thomas S | Dec 21 1847 | 8/272 |
| Reece, Therese | Finn, Davice | Feb 14 1852 | 11/217 |
| Reed, Ellen | Highland, John | May 15 1839* | 3/171 |
| Reed, George I | Mealue, Ann | Sep 11 1849* | 11/4 |
| Reed, Jeanett T | Wulff, Richard | Aug 20 1855 | 14/213 |
| Reed, John | O'Brien, Hanora | Apr 26 1852 | 11/242 |
| Reed, John L | Lambert, Sarah | Jun 9 1845 | 8/102B |
| Reed, Joseph | Simmons, Henriette | May 20 1850 | 11/62 |
| Reed, Maria | Naugel, Michael | May 22 1845 | 8/97B |
| Reed, Nancy | Stinnitt, George W | Jun 30 1844 | 8/29B |
| Reeder, Mary A | Morris, J P | May 31 1853* | 12/302 |
| Reeks, Mary Eliza | Lewis, David (Laws) | May 6 1846 | 8/164B |
| Reel, Catharine | Schmidt, Frederick | Apr 5 1849* | 8/366 |
| Reel, John M | Lambert, Nancy Ann | Mar 22 1848 | 8/294 |
| Reel, John M | LeBlanc, Victorin | Oct 23 1841 | 6/2B |
| Reese, Ellen | Carver, John S | May 8 1854 | 13/219 |
| Reese, Jacob | Taylor, Mary Jane | Mar 10 1849 | 8/361 |
| Reese, Joseph | Henderson, Jane | Sep 29 1836* | 3/60 |
| Reese, Mary Jane | Conley, Patrick C | Dec 6 1854 | 13/403 |
| Reese, Robert | Haney, Ellen | Apr 8 1853 | 12/224 |
| Reeves, Ellen | Pierre, John H | Jul 13 1846 | 8/178 |
| Reeves, James M (widr) | Ross, Emeline | Mar 30 1853 | 12/209 |
| Reeves, Nancy | Stinnett, George W | Jun 30 1849 | 8/394 |
| Reeves, Nancy | Mitchell, Ellis | May 10 1851 | 11/147 |
| Regan, Margaret | McKevitt, James | Jul 20 1846 | 8/180 |
| Reggio, Irene | Portier, Honori | Oct 30 1845 | 8/119B |
| Regnauld, Mary Isabel | Robbins, Elliott | May 11 1843 | 5/271B |
| Regnault, Maria H | McCaughan, John J | Oct 4 1852 | 12/19 |
| Rego, George | Levitt, Mary | Nov 10 1845 | 8/124B |
| Reichel, Elizabeth | Lambert, Henry | Jul 8 1854 | 13/277 |
| Reid, David | Cranwell, Jane | Jun 12 1847 | 8/241 |
| Reid, Jane (June) | Kane, William | Jul 1 1843 | 5/285B |
| Reid, John | Kelly, Anne | Feb 21 1837* | 3/73 |
| Reid, John Jr | Sherwood, Julia Louisa | Nov 14 1842* | 5/227B |
| Reid, John R | Smith, Maria Louisa | Jan 27 1837* | 3/70 |
| Reid, Joseph P | Hollinsworth, Zenity | Jun 19 1855 | 14/176 |
| Reid, Mury (widr) | Montgomery, Jeanett (wid) | May 14 1853 | 12/282 |
| Reid, Mary E | Robinson, Levi | May 1 1851 | 11/143 |
| Reid, Nancy | Stinnett, George W | Jun 27 1844 | 8/29B |
| Reid, Robert | Welman, Catharine J | Apr 17 1854 | 13/188 |
| Reid, Sarah | Silliman, Alexander P | Oct 20 1851 | 11/182 |
| Reilly, James | Tegan, Margaret | Mar 29 1851 | 11/132 |
| Reilly, James W | Cherry, Cornelia | Jul 26 1841* | 5/93B |
| Reinach, Frederick M | Beer, Jetty | Apr 9 1847 | 8/225 |
| Reiners, Mathias | Span, Anna | Feb 9 1852 | 11/214 |
| Reinheart, Christoper | Prou, Mary | Jan 15 1850 | 11/33 |
| Rejo, George | Levere, Mary | Nov 10 1845 | 8/124B |
| Remach, Joseph | Marx, Jette | Mar 7 1854 | 13/151 |
| Remacle, Joseph | Tormey, Marie L | Aug 9 1853 | 12/379 |
| Remetsh, Maria C | Merz, William R | Nov 19 1853 | 13/18 |
| Remy, Adeline | Duroux, Michel | Feb 22 1845 | 8/74B |
| Remy, John P | Costigan, Mary Ann B | Mar 17 1831* | 2/155 |
| Reneaud, Adolph | Soto, Camilla | Feb 20 1841* | 5/106B |
| Reniga, Margaret | Adams, Livin | Dec 23 1841 | 5/164B |
| Reniger, Catherine | Nowlin, Silvanas | Jun 2 1852 | 11/259 |
| Renova, Francis | Antonio, Betsy | Apr 28 1820* | CM |

138

| BRIDE OR GROOM | SPOUSE | DATE | BK/PAGE |
|---|---|---|---|
| Renstin, Sophia (Restin) | Rotham, Joseph | Jun 12 1841 | 5/138B |
| Restin, Sophia | Rotham, Joseph | Jun 12 1841 | 5/138B |
| Ressijae, Louis Simon M | Devine, Mary Ann | Jun 5 1843 | 5/278B |
| Ressing, William | Davis, Elizabeth | Jan 21 1851* | 11/116 |
| Rester, Anna | Alexander, Francis | Jun 15 1835* | 3/17 |
| Rester, Eliza | Dese, William | Nov 12 1844 | 8/50B |
| Rester, Frederick | Golemon, Mary Ann | Dec 15 1841 | 5/161B |
| Rester, Naoma | Lucas, John | Sep 6 1850 | 11/84 |
| Rester, Narvil | Joiner, Delia A | Jan 1 1855 | 13/427 |
| Reston, Serinne | Howard, Eli | Nov 16 1854 | 13/382 |
| Revas, Sionardo (Leonardo) | Marques, Sarah (Mrs) | Jan 22 1839* | 3/B153 |
| Reven, Henry L | Rossiter, Sarah C | Oct 12 1842 | 5/222B |
| Reveno, Artimis | Andre, Louis | Jun 10 1841* | 5/137B |
| Revere, John W | Barclay, Josephine | Apr 29 1844 | 8/17B |
| Revoult, Josephine | Cherry, C L | Feb 14 1838* | 3/112 |
| Rewer, Dannie | Hadgn, Maria (Hadger) | Oct 31 1842* | 5/226B |
| Reynals, Emma | Leslie, Albert J | May 1 1849 | 8/372 |
| Reynolds, Anna Carolin | Williams, Andrew J | Oct 25 1849 | 11/12 |
| Reynolds, Anne C | Duffin, William | Jul 10 1849 | 8/387 |
| Reynolds, Annette | Smoot, Edward M | Aug 2 1841* | 5/145B |
| Reynolds, Catherine | Reynolds, John | 1839* | OIB |
| Reynolds, C C | Murphy, S J | Aug 4 1841* | 5/145B |
| Reynolds, Elizabeth | Mitchell, John I | Jul 1 1829 | 2/90 |
| Reynolds, George F | Fallon, Mary F | May 21 1855 | 14/147 |
| Reynolds, John | Reynolds, Catherine | 1839* | OIB |
| Reynolds, John | Cary, Ellen | Nov 22 1845 | 8/125B |
| Reynolds, Jonathan | Cleveland, Mary E | Mar 10 1835* | 3/11 |
| Reynolds, Mary Ann | Broderick, Thomas | May 15 1851 | 11/149 |
| Reynolds, Sarah B | Spears, Isaac D | Dec 18 1838* | 3/A152 |
| Rhan, Esther | Nellus, Gasper | Dec 27 1841* | 5/165B |
| Rhan, Margaret | Thompson, Samuel J | Jun 29 1840* | 5/30B |
| Rhill, James | O'Grady, Ann | Aug 9 1854 | 13/308 |
| Rhoda, Melissa | Ducarnean, Jules | May 6 1852 | 11/246 |
| Rhodes, Anderson K | Hinson, Lucinda C | Dec 14 1850 | 11/103 |
| Rhodes, Elizabeth | Cash, Silas W | Sep 12 1834* | 2/151 |
| Rhodes, John | Wotten, Elizabeth | Aug 20 1839* | 3/185 |
| Rhodes, John R | Oliver, Martha Ann | 1827* | OIB |
| Rhodes, Sophia | Wernoth, Morton | May 6 1850 | 11/60 |
| Rials, Adela | Smith, George W | Dec 24 1845 | 8/132B |
| Rice, Elizabeth Jane | Hair, Isadore | Jun 22 1847 | 8/243 |
| Rice, Hugh | Doyle, Alice | Mar 14 1846* | 8/152B |
| Rice, James A | Ledyard, Sarah F | May 13 1850 | 11/61 |
| Rice, James H | Larkins, Mary C | Feb 15 1849 | 8/357 |
| Rice, John | Carson, Eliza J | Jul 23 1855 | 14/198 |
| Rice, John W | Hopkins, Augusta | May 22 1851 | 11/151 |
| Rice, Joseph P | Morris, Emma Matilda | Feb 17 1853 | 12/174 |
| Rice, Mary | Harmon, Anthony | Nov 3 1846 | 8/197 |
| Rice, Rebecca | Johnson, George W | Feb 17 1836* | 3/40 |
| Rich, James | Hudgins, Amanda | Mar 9 1840* | 5/14 |
| Richard, Jacob | Nelson, Mary Ann | Dec 30 1843 | 5/313B |
| Richard, Samuel | Seigel, Elisa | Oct 1 1850* | 11/88 |
| Richards, Elizabeth | Fratus, William | Jun 22 1853 | 12/327 |
| Richards, Eugenia E | Brown, Robert | Apr 3 1846 | 8/155B |
| Richards, Frances E | Gallup, Benjamin C ? | Apr 29 1845 | 8/89B |
| Richards, John | McCauley, Catherine (wid) | Jun 2 1853 | 12/307 |
| Richards, Mary | Brooks, John R | Nov 16 1852* | 12/64 |
| Richardson, Bess | Fisher, Charles J B | Jul 11 1845 | 8/110B |
| Richardson, George W | Hogan, Bridget | Apr 22 1852 | 11/241 |
| Richardson, Harriet C | Truwit, William L | Jan 31 1843 | 5/247B |
| Richardson, Henry B | Helverston, Caroline | Sep 1 1855 | 14/222 |
| Richardson, John E | Tuttle, Mary L | Nov 27 1852 | 12/77 |
| Richardson, John W | Clegg, Susan | Apr 12 1841* | 5/122B |
| Richardson, Joseph M | Flinn, Eliza | Jan 10 1854 | 13/67 |
| Richardson, Lucinda | Bonique, Germaine | Jan 27 1842 | 5/174B |

| BRIDE OR GROOM | SPOUSE | DATE | BK/PAGE |
|---|---|---|---|
| Richardson, Margaret | Harvey, Joseph | May 4 1842 | 5/198B |
| Richardson, Richard C | Spam, Eleanor N | Nov 16 1838* | 3/147 |
| Richardson, Robert J | Greer, Frances Ann | Mar 21 1846 | 8/154B |
| Richardson, William | Dismukes, Matilda | Sep 29 1835* | 3/28 |
| Richeford, Catherine | Shannon, Michael | Dec 28 1854 | 13/422 |
| Richey, James | Harbin, Sarah Ann | Jan 23 1844 | 5/317B |
| Richmon, Francis | Phillips, Ann | May 9 1853 | 12/273 |
| Richmond, Francis | Riley, Ann | Feb 27 1855 | 14/70 |
| Richter, Tobias | Hanes, Adelheid | Jan 29 1850 | 11/36 |
| Rickard, Joseph | Capuck, Ellen | May 18 1849* | 8/376 |
| Ricker, George | Leary, Hannah | Apr 8 1852 | 11/233 |
| Rider, Charles | King, Martha | Nov 9 1850 | 11/96 |
| Ridgeway, Sarah | Fowler, Russell | Jan 28 1836* | 3/38 |
| Ridley, James | Miller, Ann | Dec 1 1821* | CM |
| Rie, Therese | Heyl, Morris | Dec 9 1832* | 2/1281 |
| Riebe, Frederick | Greoi, Caroline (Greer) | May 11 1852 | 11/249 |
| Rieke, Dederich | Gasz, Catherine | Oct 20 1847* | 8/260 |
| Riels, Lucinda J | Pierce, William | Apr 1 1853 | 12/212 |
| Riese, Andrew (widr) | Egenter, Alouise (wid) | Apr 4 1853 | 12/220 |
| Riggle, Henry A | Smith, Sarah A | Feb 20 1854 | 13/127 |
| Riggs, Martha A | Tartt, Thomas E | Jun 20 1840* | 5/29B |
| Rigoge, Martell E | Martin, John | 1826* | OIB |
| Rigtsby, Francis | Roper, Elizabeth | Oct 21 1818* | CM |
| Rikert, Henry | McGonighal, Rosanna | Jun 3 1844 | 8/24 |
| Riles, Elizabeth | Woodline, Peter | Dec 24 1850 | 11/105 |
| Riles, Polly | Crawley, Benjamin | Jul 5 1848 | 8/312 |
| Riley, Ann | Richmond, Francis | Feb 27 1855 | 14/70 |
| Riley, Arthur W | Clark, Elizabeth | Apr 1 1851 | 11/133 |
| Riley, Catherine | Macklin, John | Apr 20 1854 | 13/199 |
| Riley, Catharine A | McDonald, Owen | Apr 12 1852 | 11/236 |
| Riley, Elizabeth | Gilmore, William | Oct 31 1845 | 8/122B |
| Riley, James | Morehouse, Cornelia H | Apr 24 1855 | 14/115 |
| Riley, Jane | Semoud, Robert | Oct 6 1846 | 8/192 |
| Riley, John G | Scrivener, Mary V | Apr 22 1846 | 8/160B |
| Riley, Mary (wid) | Fagan, John (wid) | Aug 24 1853 | 12/393 |
| Riley, Mary | Wilkerson, James | Dec 29 1852 | 12/107 |
| Riley, Mary Ann | Calvin, Thomas (Coloin) | Oct 22 1833* | 2/751 |
| Riley, Mary C | Kimball, Franklin | Apr 10 1855 | 14/100 |
| Riley, Owen | Winecore, Lavinia | Dec 30 1842* | 5/236B |
| Riley, Richard | Graham, Louisa | Jan 7 1852 | 11/201 |
| Riley, Sarah | Hill, Thomas | Jun 3 1851 | 11/155 |
| Riley, Sarah Ann | Joseph, Thomas | Feb 8 1844 | 5/320B |
| Riley, Thomas | Lynch, Mary | Apr 5 1843 | 5/258B |
| Riley, Thomas | Davis, Mary | Feb 7 1853 | 12/167 |
| Riley, Thomas J | Gliddon, Sarah E | Jun 4 1850 | 11/64 |
| Riley, William B | Northrop, Eliza R | Jun 14 1854 | 13/256 |
| Rinder, Alfred A | Hursey, Anna | Jun 29 1850 | 11/70 |
| Rines, Elizabeth | Gully, William | Aug 27 1839* | 3/185 |
| Ring, Simon | Mesa, Francisca | Aug 1 1850* | 11/78 |
| Ring, William | McDonald, Bridget | Jan 27 1851 | 11/118 |
| Ringgold, Harriet C | Purdy, Alexander M (widr) | Dec 1 1853 | 13/31 |
| Ringler, Marie (wid) | Rane, Edward (widr) | Nov 24 1853 | 13/26 |
| Ripley, Fitz Henry | Gunnison, Louisa | Aug 15 1849* | 8/398 |
| Risher, Andrew B | McDonald, Mary Ann | Sep 13 1847* | 8/256 |
| Risher, Eliza | Page, James | Dec 5 1833* | 2/671 |
| Risher, Jacob | Anderson, Amanda Malvina | Mar 24 1832* | 2/1621 |
| Risher, James Jr | Malone, Lucy | May 12 1828* | 2/25 |
| Rister, Mary Jane | Overstreet, Nathaniel D | Jan 5 1853 | 12/113 |
| Rittan, Salley | Bower, John | Apr 11 1837* | 3/80 |
| Ritten, William | Ruhland, Harriette | Apr 19 1837* | 3/80 |
| Ritter, Henrietta | Brown, John | Jan 4 1840* | 5/6 |
| Riva, Antonio | Rabec, Annita (Rabie) | May 7 1849 | 8/374 |
| Rives, James M | Pierre, Catherine | Mar 12 1850 | 11/45 |
| Roach, Abigail (Reach) | Cannon, William D | Jan 20 1840* | 5/9 |

| BRIDE OR GROOM | SPOUSE | DATE | BK/PAGE |
|---|---|---|---|
| Roach, Elizabeth Ann | Miller, Nathan W | Feb 1 1849 | 8/352 |
| Roach, Joanna (Roads) | Barry, Edmond | Feb 22 1841* | 5/106B |
| Roach, John | Monk, Patience | Feb 1 1836* | 3/39 |
| Roach, John | Adams, Mary | Oct 17 1844 | 8/44B |
| Roach, John | Mitchell, Amanda | Jan 12 1848 | 8/277 |
| Roach, Jonathan | Evans, Mary L | 1840* | OIB |
| Roach, Jonathan | Hollinger, Sarah C | Nov 22 1849 | 11/18 |
| Roach, Joshua H | Attaway, Lucinda | Feb 16 1836* | 3/40 |
| Roach, Lucinda | Brown, Thomas | Jun 26 1843* | 5/284B |
| Roach, Mary | Hand, Patrick | Apr 11 1853 | 12/233 |
| Roach, Richard | Henderson, Rebecca | Apr 29 1846 | 8/161B |
| Roach, Shadrach D | Powell, Caroline E | Nov 3 1855 | 14/271 |
| Roan, Mary | Jackson, John L | Aug 19 1852 | 11/277 |
| Roan, Mary A | Chaney, William P | Jun 22 1852 | 11/264 |
| Roan, Nancy | Patterson, William | Oct 24 1854 | 13/362 |
| Roane, Annette | McGuire, John (Quin) | Aug 3 1841* | 5/145B |
| Roane, Ellen | Goodman, John A | Jan 15 1847 | 8/212 |
| Roane, John | Nelson, Mary A | Jan 9 1847 | 8/211 |
| Roane, Sarah A | Wright, Benjamin H | Jan 15 1840* | 5/8 |
| Roane, William A | Lyon, Eliza | Mar 4 1850 | 11/44 |
| Roasch, Franisco | Markan, Mary | Dec 27 1838* | 3/B152 |
| Robb, Eliza Josephine | Lebaron, William A | Jul 11 1848 | 8/315 |
| Robb, Jane G | Wheeler, Charles J | Dec 12 1837* | 3/102 |
| Robbins, Eliza | Dalbeare, Griswold H | Jul 23 1839* | 3/182 |
| Robbins, Elliott | Regnauld, Mary Isabel | May 11 1843 | 5/271B |
| Robbins, Frederick A | Etheridge, Mary E | Mar 9 1850 | 11/45 |
| Robbins, Granberry | Davis, Sarah | Jan 27 1853 | 12/149 |
| Robbins, Martin | Jayne, Ann Augusta | May 9 1845 | 8/93B |
| Robbs, William | Carlin, Joanna (Mrs) | Apr 20 1854 | 13/196 |
| Roberson, Dones (Robinson) | Barboda (NSL) | Feb 5 1842 | 5/177B |
| Robert, Eliza | Droz, Louis | Dec 13 1852 | 12/88 |
| Robert, George | Moreland, Margaret | Apr 4 1850* | 11/50 |
| Robert, John | Lemoine, Victorini L | Jan 2 1849 | 8/344 |
| Robert, William | Marshall, Sarah | Jul 30 1855 | 14/201 |
| Roberts, Aaron | Goff, Sally Ann | Apr 7 1840* | 5/17 |
| Roberts, Billison | Collins, Hendrick H | Apr 19 1828 | 2/12 |
| Roberts, Celia | French, Zorobabel | Feb 10 1852 | 11/215 |
| Roberts, Daniel | Miles, Mary J | Jan 18 1854 | 13/87 |
| Roberts, Edward | Downey, Ellen | 1854* | OIB |
| Roberts, Edward | McDury, Catharine | Sep 20 1848* | 8/324 |
| Roberts, Eliza | Healy, John | Jul 21 1854 | 13/290 |
| Roberts, Elizabeth (wid) | Huston, J W | May 2 1853 | 12/268 |
| Roberts, Evan | Hildreth, Elizabeth L | 1848* | OIB |
| Roberts, Exis | Carter, Matthew | Sep 17 1839* | 3/186 |
| Roberts, George | Green, Ellen | Jan 22 1851 | 11/115 |
| Roberts, Henry J | Anderson, Ann J | May 18 1853 | 12/290 |
| Roberts, Issaul | Mulhym, Elizabeth | 1840* | OIB |
| Roberts, Israel | Mulligan, Elizabeth | Mar 7 1840* | 3/196 |
| Roberts, Joel A | Bolles, Mary T | Feb 17 1840* | 5/12 |
| Roberts, Joseph | Leonard, Barbary | Apr 22 1850 | 11/55 |
| Roberts, Joseph M | Connor, Catherine E | Feb 21 1852* | 11/220 |
| Roberts, Laura M | Pillans, Palmer J | Feb 1 1845 | 8/70B |
| Roberts, Mahala | Moore, John W | Oct 23 1847 | 8/261 |
| Roberts, Marlin R | Nowlin, Mary E | Jan 2 1847 | 8/209 |
| Roberts, Minerva | Aycock, Augustus S | Sep 28 1835* | 3/28 |
| Roberts, Missouri | Harrison, Edward | Mar 3 1845 | 8/77B |
| Roberts, Morris | Holland, Elizabeth Ann | Jul 5 1847 | 8/244 |
| Roberts, R W | Spencer, Martha | Mar 23 1839* | 3/161 |
| Roberts, Reuben H | Quigley, Martina T | Mar 4 1851 | 11/128 |
| Roberts, S A | Kennedy, John | Sep 10 1838* | 3/141 |
| Roberts, Seth W | Lacoste, Claudine | May 10 1847 | 8/234 |
| Roberts, Susan | Dekle, William E | May 21 1853 | 12/293 |
| Roberts, William | McMullen, Sarah | 1826* | OIB |
| Roberts, William | Miller, Susana | Jan 27 1839* | 3/B153 |

| BRIDE OR GROOM | SPOUSE | DATE | BK/PAGE |
|---|---|---|---|
| Roberts, William | Elliott, Elizabeth (wid) | Apr 9 1821* | CM |
| Roberts, William H | Quigley, Margaretta A | Jun 16 1851 | 11/158 |
| Roberts, William H | Bull, Sarah C | Apr 25 1854 | 13/203 |
| Robertson, Anna | Sims, Daniel | Jun 5 1845* | 8/101B |
| Robertson, Daniel | Wilkinson, Mary Jane | Nov 27 1838* | 3/149 |
| Robertson, Douglas | Armburn, Marie Carmetite | Feb 8 1840 | 3/193 |
| Robertson, Elenor | Porter, George | Apr 17 1841* | 5/124B |
| Robertson, Elizabeth A | Sherwood, John J | May 9 1843 | 5/269B |
| Robertson, Frederick | Angier, Samuella M R | May 31 1843 | 5/277B |
| Robertson, James | Flinn, Mary | Nov 5 1851 | 11/186 |
| Robertson, James | Smith, Janet | May 15 1852 | 11/250 |
| Robertson, James | Dias, Jane | Jun 8 1847 | 8/240 |
| Robertson, Jzett | Brabman, Ann | Oct 8 1855 | 14/249 |
| Robertson, Maria L | Butler, Laird M H | May 16 1850 | 11/61 |
| Robertson, Nancy A | Goodrich, Orlando Allen | Jan 30 1849 | 8/350 |
| Robertson, Rachael | Bowers, Samuel | Mar 12 1836* | 3/42 |
| Robertson, Richard B | Allaire, Maria L  (B) | Dec 4 1841* | 5/160B |
| Robertson, S J | Brown, Joseph | Nov 3 1836* | 3/61 |
| Robertson, Sarah | Duck, Lawrence | Feb 5 1835* | 3/8 |
| Robertson, William | Sims, Lavinia | May 7 1821* | CM |
| Robertson, William H | Toulmin, Jane | Jan 1 1821* | CM |
| Robertson, William R | Flyn, Rose | Dec 11 1850 | 11/102 |
| Robertson, Willis | Laran, Susan | Feb 23 1835* | 3/9 |
| Robeshaw, Catherine | Patton, Joseph | Jan 17 1829 | 2/63 |
| Robins, Stuart | Blansford, Eliza Jane | Feb 27 1837* | 3/73 |
| Robinson, Charles | Lestrade, Jane | Apr 21 1841* | 5/127B |
| Robinson, Charlotte P | Pomeroy, James M | Feb 1 1844 | 5/319B |
| Robinson, David | Loyd, Emiline | Mar 18 1841* | 5/118B |
| Robinson, Davis (Dones) | Barboda  (NSL) | Feb 5 1842 | 5/177B |
| Robinson, Edward | Nash, Minerva Eliza | Apr 1 1839* | 3/162 |
| Robinson, Elenor | Porter, George | Apr 17 1841 | 5/124B |
| Robinson, Elizabeth A | Martin, James | Apr 6 1843 | 5/259B |
| Robinson, Henry A | Powers, Julia Ann | Nov 7 1845 | 8/124B |
| Robinson, Jane | Irwin, John I | Feb 11 1834* | 2/461 |
| Robinson, Levi | Reid, Mary E | May 1 1851 | 11/143 |
| Robinson, Margaret | Crevalleri, A G | Nov 28 1838* | 3/149 |
| Robinson, Mary Ann | Dolman, Abraham H | Dec 12 1853 | 13/36 |
| Robinson, Mary V | Connor, Ephraim D | Dec 16 1844 | 8/59B |
| Robinson, Miss A E | Melrose, John G | May 1 1838* | 3/122 |
| Robinson, Murray | Hurtel, Felecia | Dec 2 1839* | 5/2 |
| Robinson, Patrick | Byrns, Margaret | Oct 2 1852 | 12/17 |
| Robinson, Samuel | Allen, Bridget | Jul 12 1851 | 11/164 |
| Robinson, Thomas H | Durfey, Rebecca | May 13 1839* | 3/171 |
| Robinson, William | Cannon, Levina | 1840* | OIB |
| Robinson, William S | Poe, Catherine | Apr 1 1838* | 3/118 |
| Robishaw, Alvan | Nicholson, Catherine | 1815* | OIB |
| Robshow, Louisa I | Saltonstall, Seneca A | Mar 9 1836* | 3/42 |
| Roby, Elodir | Joseph, Clomint B | May 29 1839* | 3/175 |
| Rochon, John | Nicholson, Eunice | Jun 3 1830 | 2/127 |
| Rochon, Wilson | Paris, Laurentine | Jun 11 1852 | 11/262 |
| Rockwell, Julia | Smith, George S | Jan 1 1838* | 3/107 |
| Rockwell, Nathan F | Scarver, Amanda | Dec 8 1854 | 13/406 |
| Rodeman, Cresent | Lish, Philip A | Feb 27 1851 | 11/125 |
| Rodgers, Bridget | Foster, George | Aug 23 1849* | 8/399 |
| Rodgers, Cynthia | Davidson, John C | Nov 7 1832* | 2/1301 |
| Rodgers, Ellen | Bertrand, Isaac | Feb 17 1846 | 8/146B |
| Rodgers, George | Ferrill, Dilley | Dec 12 1848 | 8/338 |
| Rodgers, Hugh | Fitzpatrick, Ann | Apr 11 1851* | 11/136B |
| Rodgers, John | Hoskins, Isabella | Jun 24 1841* | 5/140B |
| Rodgers, Joseph | Ellen, Mary | Mar 5 1844 | 5/327B |
| Rodgers, Joseph | Reddin, Eliza | Dec 4 1847 | 8/268 |
| Rodgers, Margaret | Collins, Isaac W | Sep 14 1836* | 3/57 |
| Rodgers, Mary | Shed, John | Apr 3 1837* | 3/78 |
| Rodgers, William V P | Hall, Mary | May 31 1852 | 11/257 |

| BRIDE OR GROOM | SPOUSE | DATE | BK/PAGE |
|---|---|---|---|
| Rodregues, Manuel | Bokey, Margaret | Feb 20 1849 | 8/359 |
| Rodrigues, Joaquim | Tarditto, Isabella H | Oct 23 1837* | 3/93 |
| Rodrigues, Joseph | Cuppum, Mary | Jul 9 1845 | 8/110B |
| Rodriguez, J M (Josi) | Gray, Roseline | Jul 6 1842 | 5/210B |
| Rodrigus, Joseph | Herbison, Ave | Sep 21 1849 | 11/6 |
| Roe, Jacob | Gusterer, Catherine | Dec 7 1849 | 11/22 |
| Roff, Henry I | Roper, Mary J | Jun 4 1838* | 3/132 |
| Rogers, Bethel T | Tew, Elenor H | Jan 3 1848 | 8/275 |
| Rogers, Bridget | Birch, Joseph | Jan 25 1854 | 13/98 |
| Rogers, Bridget | Rathbone, Charles D | Dec 23 1854 | 13/148 |
| Rogers, Catherine | Williamson, John | Jul 30 1844 | 8/37B |
| Rogers, Edward | McMahan, Bridget | Sep 17 1853 | 12/408 |
| Rogers, Elizabeth | Broadhurst, Moses | Oct 5 1820* | CM |
| Rogers, Hugh | Fitzpatrick, Ann | May 3 1851 | 11/144 |
| Rogers, Isabella B | Monk, John | Mar 2 1848* | 8/289 |
| Rogers, John | Hoskins, Isabella | Jun 24 1841* | 5/140B |
| Rogers, John | Hurley, Ann | Jan 6 1849* | 8/346 |
| Rogers, Martha | Snell, Samuel | Oct 4 1824* | 1/40 |
| Rogers, Mathew M | O'Brien, Ann | Jun 6 1839* | 3/177 |
| Rogers, Rebecca | Inson, William B | Feb 23 1832* | 2/1701 |
| Rogers, Sarah | Pennington, Bennet L | Jan 29 1855 | 14/27 |
| Rogers, Thomas | Church, Margaret | Apr 9 1853 | 12/226 |
| Rogers, William V P | Long, Nancy | Sep 3 1835* | 3/27 |
| Roh, Frederika | Kelsen, Mathew | Jan 4 1853 | 12/111 |
| Roh, Joana Barbary | Gobal, John Adam | Jan 6 1853 | 12/117 |
| Roh, Pauline | Kelsen, Mathias | Apr 19 1855 | 14/86 |
| Rokert, Henry (Rikert) | McGonigal, Rosanna | Jun 3 1844 | 8/24 |
| Roland, Martin | Shelean, Ellen (Shehan) | Apr 17 1852 | 11/238 |
| Roland, Peter | Schneider, Barbara | May 14 1841* | 5/89B |
| Rolefron, John | Schwartzback, Maria M | Nov 4 1838* | 3/150 |
| Rolls, James A | Wheeler, Sarah | Jul 21 1845 | 8/112B |
| Rolls, William H | Turner, Sarah | Nov 13 1846 | 8/199 |
| Rolston, Elizabeth | Hillyer, Giles M | Jan 4 1843 | 5/240B |
| Rolston, John | Smoot, Virginia A | Sep 23 1846 | 8/190 |
| Roman, Charles | Coster, Hannah | May 1 1846 | 8/162B |
| Roman, Mary S | Keeland, William | Oct 21 1851 | 11/183 |
| Romero, John B | Ramirez, Emily | Jan 19 1844 | 5/315B |
| Ronan, James | Bailey, Mary | Nov 24 1854 | 13/391 |
| Ronan, Mary | Parkhurst, John | Sep 13 1852* | 12/3 |
| Rondeau, Constance | Soto, John | 1827* | OIB |
| Rondeau, John Jr | Laurendine, Matilda | Jun 15 1835* | 3/17 |
| Rondeau, Marguerite A | Durand, Martine | 1825* | OIB |
| Rondeau, Maria Clementine | Fourcade, John Baptist | Jul 25 1828 | 2/37 |
| Rondeau, Mary L | Chamberlain, Robert T | Jan 27 1853 | 12/150 |
| Rone, Eliza A | Wainwright, Luck | Dec 7 1846 | 8/202 |
| Rone, James | Gallagher, Ann | 1840* | OIB |
| Rone, Samuel W | Negus, Elizabeth A | Jan 12 1846 | 8/139B |
| Roney, James | Dunmore, Louison | Sep 15 1813* | CM |
| Roney, Mary | Ladner, Valery | Jun 13 1834* | 2/221 |
| Roney, Patrick | Cohen, Mary | Jun 19 1843* | 5/283B |
| Ronlufts, John | Cochran, P Malinda | Oct 1 1842* | 5/221B |
| Rood, John S | Wolfe, Jane | Dec 27 1849* | 11/29 |
| Rook, Mary | Fitts, John | Apr 28 1851 | 11/142 |
| Roonen, Ann | Smith, Patrick I | May 2 1845 | 8/91B |
| Rooney, John | Clark, Mary | May 16 1853 | 12/284 |
| Rooney, Martin | Quin, Ann | Nov 18 1841* | 5/157B |
| Rooney, Mary Ann | McDonald, Edward | Apr 26 1853 | 12/254 |
| Root, Margaret Ann | Spencer, Richard | Oct 2 1855 | 14/245 |
| Rop, John B (Ross) | Strong, Hannah L | May 30 1825 | 1/80 |
| Ropell, William H (Rossell) | Eastin, Lucinda G | Nov 12 1846 | 8/198 |
| Roper, Elizabeth | Rigtsby, Francis | Oct 21 1818* | CM |
| Roper, James W | Jemison, Eliza Ann | Nov 22 1838* | 3/148 |
| Roper, James W | Davenport, Sarah Ann | Jun 10 1830* | 2/130* |
| Roper, Mary J | Roff, Henry I | Jun 4 1838* | 3/132 |

| BRIDE OR GROOM | SPOUSE | DATE | BK/PAGE |
|---|---|---|---|
| Roper, Sarah | McManus, William | Jun  1 1853 | 12/306 |
| Rose, Benjamin | Heaythorow, Elizabeth | Mar 30 1840* | 3/197 |
| Rose, John | Wilkey, Catherine | Jan 20 1852 | 11/205 |
| Rosenberg, Marcus | Wiehelhansen, Regine | Oct 30 1852* | 12/40 |
| Rosett, Peter (widr) | O'Neal, Rose | Nov 21 1853 | 13/20 |
| Ross, Amos | Jeffery, Eliza | Apr  5 1843 | 5/259B |
| Ross, Andrew | Cypress, Rebecca | Dec 23 1830* | 2/144 |
| Ross, Andrew | Hughes, Mary | Jul 23 1851 | 11/168 |
| Ross, Charles A | Dewier, Ellen | Apr 13 1840* | 5/19 |
| Ross, Daniel | Wren, Maria | Dec 29 1855 | 14/320 |
| Ross, Drucilla | Hammond, Alexander T | Nov 20 1851 | 11/188 |
| Ross, Elizabeth | Centener, George Adam | Dec 24 1849 | 11/28 |
| Ross, Emeline | Reeves, James M (widr) | Mar 30 1853 | 12/209 |
| Ross, Francis A | Hunter, Helen Gains | Dec 21 1844 | 8/61B |
| Ross, George | Henley, Julian | Apr 24 1840* | 5/20 |
| Ross, Hannah Louisa | Harrell, Arnett W | Nov  3 1828* | 2/50 |
| Ross, Jane | Cleveland, Isaac M | Jun  7 1855 | 14/164 |
| Ross, John B | Strong, Hannah L | May 30 1825 | 1/80 |
| Ross, John McD | Frayer, Rudina A | Dec 15 1840* | 5/75 |
| Ross, Martha E | Rutter, William | May  4 1843 | 5/268B |
| Ross, Mary Ann | Casser, Laveria | Dec 17 1840* | 5/75B |
| Ross, William | Hart, Margaret | Dec  3 1844 | 8/55B |
| Rossannah, Julia (Kavanagh) | Gutus, Henry | Jan 20 1844* | 5/316B |
| Rossell, William H | Eastin, Lucinda G | Nov 12 1846 | 8/198 |
| Rossett, Pier | Washington, Celeste | Jul  5 1845* | 8/109B |
| Rossett, Peter | Taylor, Catherine | Mar 31 1842* | 5/190B |
| Rossiter, John | Scott, Rebecca | Aug 17 1841* | 5/148B |
| Rossiter, Sarah C | Reven, Henry L | Oct 12 1842 | 5/222B |
| Roth, Joseph | Hennisegen, Christin | Nov 25 1823 | 1/14 |
| Rotham, Joseph | Renstin, Sophia | Jun 12 1841* | 5/138B |
| Rothe, Ann Maria Catherine | Loker, Martin | Jan  1 1829* | 2/61 |
| Rotheray, Daniel | O'Neal, Ann M | Aug 26 1835* | 3/26 |
| Rothhan, Rosa | Goldsmith, Mingo H | Jun 14 1841 | 5/138B |
| Rouan, Mary | Coffey, Edward | Jul 24 1844 | 8/35B |
| Rouch, Andres | Shiremann, Rosalie | Mar 17 1848 | 8/293 |
| Roudett, Harriett | Johnson, J James Jr | Apr 26 1852 | 11/242 |
| Roue, Eliza A (Rone) | Wainwright, Luck | Dec  7 1846 | 8/202 |
| Roue, Samuel W (Rone) | Negus, Elizabeth A | Jan 12 1846 | 8/139B |
| Roulston, George McC | Laurendine, Caroline | May  7 1849* | 8/374 |
| Roulston, James T | Delage, Lucy A | Feb  4 1850 | 11/37 |
| Roulston, Rebecca | Kirkland, Isaac W | Oct 23 1848* | 8/329 |
| Roulston, Richard B | O'Brien, Mary E | Apr 28 1851 | 11/143 |
| Roulufs, John | Clevelend, Martha Ellen | Jul 27 1852 | 11/272 |
| Roulutz, John | Cocknane, Pricilla M | Oct  1 1842 | 5/221B |
| Round, George | Brotherson, Mary | Feb 22 1838* | 3/113 |
| Roundell, Joseph (Roundek) | Justine, Calmi (Ipstine) | Jan 25 1844* | 5/318B |
| Roundo, Eliza (Rondeau) | Murray, Edwin | 1827* | OIB |
| Rounsavel, William | Clark, Elizabeth | 1825* | OIB |
| Rounvill, Artemus | Lee, Hannah V | Jun  2 1840* | 5/26 |
| Rouse, Layfield | Waltz, Martha E | Jan 10 1853 | 12/121 |
| Rouse, Louise F (Roux) | Southworth, Edward C | Feb 24 1842 | 5/183B |
| Rouse, Mary E | King, Daniel | May 23 1843 | 5/275B |
| Rouse, Nancy S | Porter, Sidney D (widr) | Jul 14 1853 | 12/356 |
| Rouse, William | Leonard, Ann | Jun 26 1841 | 5/140B |
| Roussell, Edward | Spikes, Angeline | Oct 26 1852 | 12/36 |
| Rousselot, Rosine | Mouroux, Adolphe | Mar 25 1835* | 3/12 |
| Rouston, Honore | Faure, Marie Henriette | Oct 28 1847 | 8/262 |
| Rouville, Lucy | Baptiste, John | May 19 1846 | 8/167B |
| Rouville, Sostine | Collins, Artemus | 1827* | OIB |
| Roux, Emma C | Lang, James W | Apr  9 1844* | 8/10B |
| Roux, Louisa F (Rouse) | Southworth, Edward A | Feb 24 1842 | 5/183B |
| Rovira, Josephine | Baldo, Leon M | Apr 18 1854 | 13/191 |
| Rowan, Byron C | Owen, Ann O | Aug 13 1845 | 8/117B |
| Rowe, Benjamin F | McLean, Susan C | Oct 21 1854 | 13/358 |

| BRIDE OR GROOM | SPOUSE | DATE | BK/PAGE |
|---|---|---|---|
| Rowe, Catherine | Broades, Mathew (Brody) | Sep 19 1854 | 13/339 |
| Rowe, Robb | Collins, Nancy | May 20 1839* | 3/172 |
| Rowell, Franklin | White, Elizabeth | Feb 12 1851* | 11/121 |
| Rowell, James A | Salter, Sarah Jane | Jun 2 1851 | 11/154 |
| Rowell, Joseph | Dorey, Emily R (Dorsey) | Oct 31 1838* | 3/145 |
| Rowell, Tilman T | Barrow, Jane A | Jul 19 1853 | 12/361 |
| Rowland, Clara | Frink, William E | Oct 25 1849 | 11/11 |
| Rowland, Eveline | Serville, Jeremiah I | Jul 23 1842 | 5/212B |
| Rowland, Eveline | Saville, Jermiah I | Jul 23 1842 | 5/212B |
| Roycroft, John | Mooney, Margaret J | Oct 7 1852 | 12/24 |
| Royster, Ajax | Bell, Josephine F | Feb 25 1847 | 8/220 |
| Rozeist, Pier (Rossett) | Washington, Celest | Jul 5 1845* | 8/109B |
| Ruby, John | Murphy, Elizabeth | May 29 1840* | 5/25 |
| Rudale, Nancy | Conaty, Philip | Dec 8 1846* | 8/203 |
| Ruder, Alfred A | Snow, Emily | Apr 9 1839* | 3/166 |
| Rudren, Joseph | Nubert, Marie Therese | Aug 14 1849* | 8/390 |
| Rue, Marie (Mormier) | Marthet, Leshen | Jul 22 1844 | 8/34B |
| Rue, Rebecca | Baptiste, John P. | Dec 22 1844 | 8/61B |
| Rugan, Patrick | Donaho, Ann | Jan 31 1853 | 12/157 |
| Rugeley, Alphonse J | Blair, Ellen C | Dec 28 1855 | 14/319 |
| Ruggles, Sumner S | Schroebel, Laura S | Nov 20 1852 | 12/67 |
| Ruhland, Harriette | Ritten, William | Apr 19 1837* | 3/80 |
| Ruhuley, Frederick | Gill, Mary Ann | Mar 6 1846 | 8/149B |
| Ruiz, Joseph | Govnn, Eliza Mack | Oct 31 1853 | 13/1 |
| Ruiz, Joseph | McGowin, Eliza (McGovern) | Oct 31 1853 | 13/1 |
| Ruiz, Maria D | Smith, Ralph S | May 26 1853 | 12/299 |
| Rul, John | Leblanc, Annie | Oct 23 1841* | 5/154 |
| Rumsay, Joseph | Keho, Mary Ann | 1826* | OIB |
| Run, Susanna | Martino, Peter | Dec 23 1824 | 1/56 |
| Runals, Benjamin P | Dowling, Margaret | Jan 18 1837* | 3/69 |
| Runnells, Susan | McWilliams, Hugh | Oct 29 1846 | 8/196 |
| Rupall, John G ? | Burch, Julia Ann | Apr 15 1842 | 6/118B |
| Rupell, Gilbert C Jr ? | Hollinger, Elizabeth B | Dec 10 1849* | 11/23 |
| Rupell, Matilda ? | Caranegh, James ? | Feb 9 1847* | 8/214 |
| Rupell, Matilda | Cavanegh, James | Feb 9 1847* | 8/214 |
| Ruport, James C | Jones, Caroline V | Mar 2 1840* | 3/195 |
| Ruse, Jane | Cloudis, George W | Oct 31 1840* | 5/59B |
| Ruse, Maria Louisa | Brown, Alexander | Jul 28 1847* | 8/248 |
| Rusearl, Francois | Journie, Josephine | Aug 13 1840 | 5/41 |
| Rush, Eliza | Brown, Herman H | Sep 27 1854 | 13/341 |
| Rush, John G | Johnston, Glorvina E | Jan 24 1852 | 11/207 |
| Rusher, Eliza | Springer, Isaac B | Dec 31 1845* | 8/134B |
| Rushing, Charles E | Collin, Bridget Cecelia | Feb 4 1842 | 5/177B |
| Russ, Mary | Elliott, Stephen | Mar 15 1852 | 11/227 |
| Russall, John G ? | Buch, Julia Ann (Burk) | Apr 15 1842 | 6/118B |
| Russell, Adolphus | Burke, Mary A | Jul 17 1854 | 13/286 |
| Russell, Albert R | Buchannan, Betsey Ann | Dec 31 1852 | 12/108 |
| Russell, Ann M | Malone, Edward | Dec 20 1852 | 12/99 |
| Russell, Edward | Wilcox, Jane | Mar 23 1849* | 8/363 |
| Russell, Eliza J | Brooks, Robert | Jan 9 1850 | 11/32 |
| Russell, Ellen | Thompson, Edward | Jan 29 1840* | 5/10 |
| Russell, George W | Hollinger, Swepson (wid) | Apr 18 1855 | 14/108 |
| Russell, Henry C | Smith, Sarah Jane | Dec 7 1848* | 8/338 |
| Russell, James H | Young, Emma | Jun 23 1853 | 12/329 |
| Russell, Jeanett | Harris, Benjamin F | Jul 11 1854 | 13/279 |
| Russell, John N | Miles, Martha E | Feb 27 1851 | 11/125 |
| Russell, John Y ? | Birch, Julia Ann ? | Apr 12 1842* | 5/192B |
| Russell, Mary | Scameron, Solomon | Dec 24 1855 | 4/315 |
| Russell, Mary S | Jennett, Albert H | Sep 6 1842 | 5/218B |
| Russell, Matilda | Caranegh, James ? | Feb 9 1847* | 8/214 |
| Russell, Virginia A | Fowler, John D | May 23 1853 | 12/296 |
| Rutherford, Eliza A | Craig, Thomas L | Feb 20 1837* | 3/72 |
| Rutherford, Henry | Cronin, Veronica | Apr 24 1847* | 8/230 |
| Rutherford, James | Cook, Eliza Jane | Nov 9 1854 | 13/375 |

| BRIDE OR GROOM | SPOUSE | DATE | BK/PAGE |
|---|---|---|---|
| Rutherford, Walter | Blair, Rosina | Sep 15 1849 | 11/5 |
| Rutter, William | Ross, Martha E | May 4 1843 | 5/268B |
| Ruynal, Emma | Leslie, Albert J | May 1 1849* | 8/372 |
| Ryals, Henry | Burnes, Eliza | Apr 6 1837* | 3/79 |
| Ryals, Lila | Foster, John M | Jun 14 1852 | 11/262 |
| Ryals, Perry | Monk, Nancy | Feb 10 1851 | 11/119 |
| Ryan, Ellen | Lynch, Michael | Jun 25 1851 | 11/160 |
| Ryan, Johanna | Pyers, William J | Jul 31 1845 | 8/114B |
| Ryan, John | Cullum, Eveline | Oct 19 1844 | 8/44B |
| Ryan, John | O'Rourke, Catherine | Jun 20 1855 | 14/179 |
| Ryan, Julia | Collins, Daniel | Feb 3 1853 | 12/162 |
| Ryan, Margaret | Holley, Richard | May 10 1825 | 1/75 |
| Ryan, Maria | Hutchinson, John | Jul 20 1853 | 12/363 |
| Ryan, Mary | Glennin, Michael | Jul 24 1854 | 13/293 |
| Ryan, Mary Ann (O'Riley) | Pietre, Rocco | Mar 22 1841 | 5/119B |
| Ryan, Michael | Summers, Mary Ann | Apr 30 1853 | 12/263 |
| Ryan, Morris | Shea, Mary | Mar 21 1842 | 5/190B |
| Ryan, Moses | Buckley, Martha C | Apr 16 1844* | 8/14B |
| Ryan, Patrick H | McCarty, Joanna | Apr 21 1843 | 5/263B |
| Ryan, Robert | McSweeney, Ellen | Jul 11 1841* | 5/87B |
| Ryan, William M | Monroe, Abby | Apr 8 1839* | 3/165B |
| Ryder, Catharine | Light, William | Mar 27 1828* | 2/20 |
| Ryder, Jane | Wilkins, Benjamin | Mar 26 1828* | 2/19 |
| Ryder, Richard G | Jones, Elizabeth | Mar 2 1830* | 2/116 |
| Ryland, Allen H | Miles, Lucy T (Niles) | Nov 19 1840* | 5/65B |
| Ryninger, Annie F | Hunter, W H | Feb 22 1851 | 11/123 |

S

| | | | |
|---|---|---|---|
| Sabernadie, John ? | Newman, Bridgit | Jun 7 1843 | 5/280B |
| Sabriyer, Juliette | Mailfer, Peter Constant | Aug 24 1848 | 8/321 |
| Saely, James (Sorley) ? | Steve, Mary J (Sterie) | Mar 4 1847* | 8/220 |
| Safley, Frances Ann | Patterson, William | Jun 3 1844 | 8/25B |
| Sage, Catherine | Collins, Thomas | Jan 8 1840* | 3/192 |
| Sagehorn, Anna | Greve, Frederick | May 3 1854 | 13/213 |
| Sagehorn, Anna | Sexaure, Edward | May 2 1853 | 12/265 |
| Sager, E A     Mrs | Harris, Charles E | Oct 31 1839* | 3/189 |
| Sager, Edmund M | Talcott, Virginia | Aug 24 1841* | 5/132B |
| Sager, Edmund M | Brooks, Louisa M | Sep 18 1852 | 12/6 |
| Sager, Elizabeth (Sayer) | Norton, Hiram | Mar 2 1844 | 5/326B |
| Sagnaile, Jean Baptiste | Battes, Eugenie | 1850* | OIB |
| Sagomagiore, Chiora | Chichyola, Giacoma | Apr 3 1837* | 3/78 |
| Saink, Spencer | Violet, Matilda | Apr 17 1834* | 2/301 |
| Saint Guirons, Pierre P | Descoges, Marie Josephe L | Apr 26 1832* | 2/159 |
| Salle, Pierre A | Perrilent, F Josephine | Aug 27 1840* | 5/45B |
| Sallenant, Emiline ? | Davis, John | Aug 18 1840* | 5/43 |
| Salles, Dominique | Herpin, Natale | Jan 31 1821* | CM |
| Sallhamus, Chust | Veit, Seef | Feb 25 1839* | 3/158 |
| Salter, Sarah Jane | Rowell, James A | Jun 2 1851 | 11/154 |

| BRIDE OR GROOM | SPOUSE | DATE | BK/PAGE |
|---|---|---|---|
| Salter, Susanna | Hoyt, John C | Mar 24 1846 | 8/153B |
| Saltonstall, Seneca A | Robshow, Louisa I | Mar 9 1836* | 3/42 |
| Samini, Joseph | Graham, Francis E | Jan 25 1854 | 13/97 |
| Sanderford, John | Cunningham, Catherine | Aug 14 1838* | 3/139 |
| Sanders, Isabella | Glover, John A | Feb 10 1853 | 12/168 |
| Sanders, Mary J | Garner, Burgess | Feb 20 1855 | 14/66 |
| Sanders, Mary M (Mrs) | Wackernah, Christopher | Jul 2 1853 | 12/341 |
| Sanders, Reina | Hartmann, William | Dec 21 1855 | 14/309 |
| Sanders, William C | Bartlett, Helen L | May 15 1849* | 8/376 |
| Sanderson, Amanda U | Barrath, John H | Feb 15 1847 | 8/217 |
| Sandiford, John B | Taylor, Martha M | Jun 15 1848* | 8/309 |
| Sandoz, Christine A | Sauviac, Pierre | Jul 11 1854 | 13/280 |
| Sandoz, Mary Ann (Landoz) | Lopez, Bartoloma | May 8 1832* | 2/1541 |
| Sandres, Bat (Landres) | Laighe, Mary (wid) | Jun 13 1853 | 12/318 |
| Sands, Abra L Capt | Tabele, Maria A | Aug 16 1820* | CM |
| Sands, James | Durand, Stephania Lucy | Dec 6 1848* | 8/337 |
| Sands, Robert M | Lebaron, Mary Josephine | Oct 15 1848 | 8/327 |
| Sands, Susan M | Gannard, Victor | 1826* | OIB |
| Sanford, Frances | Barrett, B T | May 1 1846 | 8/162B |
| Sanford, Julia H | Larnard, Samuel | Nov 23 1850* | 11/99 |
| Sanford, Maria Louisa | Parmly, Ludolph | Nov 20 1840* | 5/65B |
| Sanford, Mary A | Brown, Thomas G | Aug 5 1840* | 5/39 |
| Sanford, Mary F | Ward, Rian | Dec 25 1851 | 11/198 |
| Sanford, Thadeus | Morton, Cornelia S | 1827* | OIB |
| Sangrouber, Albertine | Baarcke, Charles | Jun 9 1846* | 8/176 |
| Sanlima, Henrietta Eliz | Marsenat, Edward | Jun 4 1839* | 3/176 |
| Santern, William | Ashton, Lydia J | May 14 1847 | 8/235 |
| Santree, Mary Ann (Lantree) | Cosgrove, Richard | Nov 26 1842 | 5/229B |
| Sarah, Adolphus | Dubroco, Virginia | Sep 3 1850 | 11/83 |
| Sardner, Alphonse (Lardner) | Goleman, Matilda Emaline | Jun 10 1846 | 8/171 |
| Saris, Cyprian | DeFlander, Rose | Mar 29 1847 | 8/223 |
| Sarneck, Arabella | Simon, Andrew | Apr 10 1839* | 3/166 |
| Saroste, Mathilde (Lacost) | Mechon, Peter T | Oct 3 1840* | 5/51B |
| Sarradait, John | Turpen, Rosealie A | Mar 11 1854 | 13/159 |
| Sarrouil, Pascal | Buquiet, Elizabeth | Nov 24 1846 | 8/201 |
| Sary, Mary | Curtain, Patrick | Dec 23 1840 | 5/79B |
| Saucier, Hipolite | McNamara, Michael S | Dec 10 1820* | CM |
| Sauers, Edward | Barry, Leonore | Jan 21 1841* | 5/91 |
| Saulnier, Joseph | Brannan, Caroline E | Feb 10 1854 | 13/116 |
| Saunders, Henry | Graham, Melissa M | Dec 31 1843* | 5/313B |
| Saunders, Mary L | Blair, Henry D | Feb 25 1852* | 11/222 |
| Saunders, Samuel | Davis, Elizabeth | Jun 3 1828* | 2/30 |
| Saurie, Ann | Havens, Curtis | May 14 1846 | 8/165 |
| Sauvage, Antoine | Andry, Juli | Sep 18 1850 | 11/85 |
| Sauvage, Maria Thesese C | Laurendine, Jacob | Jul 23 1846 | 8/181 |
| Sauviac, Pierre | Sandoz, Christine A | Jul 11 1854 | 13/280 |
| Savage, George P | Stuart, Rose E | Nov 21 1854 | 13/387 |
| Savage, Obed W | Baldwin, Emma W | Nov 6 1848* | 8/332 |
| Saville, Jeremiah J | Rowland, Eveline | Jul 23 1842 | 5/212B |
| Sawlop, William (Lawless) | McKay, Rosanna | Feb 11 1838* | 3/112 |
| Sawyer, Enoch | Barclay, Sophie E | May 12 1852 | 11/249 |
| Sawyer, Julian E | Crawford, Susan L V | Mar 13 1843 | 5/253B |
| Sawyer, Mary | Singleton, William | Jun 23 1846 | 8/174 |
| Saxon, Elizabeth | Harris, William | Sep 4 1850 | 11/83 |
| Saxon, Elmira | Menasco, Jacob | Aug 23 1845 | 8/116B |
| Saxon, Jacob J | Thomas, Martha Ann | Jul 30 1845 | 8/113B |
| Saxon, Matilda C R | Menasco, Andrew J | Aug 14 1845 | 8/115B |
| Sayne, E Sanford (Sayre) | Kimberly, Ophelia G | Apr 18 1844 | 8/15 |
| Sayne, Milborne (Sayre) | Holcombe, E Antoinette | Apr 11 1841* | 5/130B |
| Saynick, Caroline ? | Stikes, John | May 20 1845* | 8/96B |
| Sayre, Fanny A | Schroeder, Charles H | Apr 25 1854 | 13/204 |
| Scale, Margaret | Fegan, Thomas | Jan 13 1843 | 5/246B |
| Scameron, Solomon | Russell, Mary | Dec 24 1855 | 14/315 |
| Scamerorn, Solomon | Waters, Mary | Jan 13 1843 | 5/243B |

| BRIDE OR GROOM | SPOUSE | DATE | BK/PAGE |
|---|---|---|---|
| Scanlin, Mary | Smith, Lorens | Apr 17 1845 | 8/87B |
| Scanlon, Catharine | Wilson, William | Apr 13 1843 | 5/260B |
| Scanlon, Patrick | Connors, Mary | Jan 7 1848* | 8/276 |
| Scanlon, Robert | O'Neal, Eliza | Aug 2 1836* | 3/55 |
| Scarboro, Peter | Jones, Mary | Mar 24 1845 | 8/81B |
| Scarborough, Ann H | Collins, Erosnnus W | Jul 26 1852 | 11/271 |
| Scarborough, Julia Ann | Jones, William | Nov 24 1851 | 11/189 |
| Scarbrough, Abigil | Finlay, Joshua B | Nov 18 1843 | 5/305B |
| Scarbrough, Emeline | Moody, Arbin C | Jul 6 1854 | 13/276 |
| Scarbrough, Mary | Powell, Hiram | Sep 26 1849 | 11/7 |
| Scarbrough, Nancy | Powell, Isaiah | Jul 10 1838* | 3/135 |
| Scarpa, Julius | Ivis, Catherine | May 13 1854 | 13/222 |
| Scartergoods, Benjamin F | Tatum, Mary G | Oct 12 1842* | 5/222B |
| Scarver, Amanda | Rockwell, Nathan F | Dec 8 1854 | 13/406 |
| Scaver, Lewis | Motley, Mary Ann | 1826* | 0IB |
| Schamaker, Maria L | Dege, John A | Feb 22 1854 | 13/131 |
| Scharden, Mary (Scherman) | Strike, John (Stuke) | Oct 24 1840* | 5/57B |
| Scheller, Barbara | Ege, John | Nov 7 1855 | 14/274 |
| Schellong, Henry | Hill, Barbara | Feb 25 1846 | 8/148B |
| Schenck, Caroline | Laroux, Augustus | Mar 12 1846 | 8/151B |
| Schenkilberg, Caroline | Neisins, Nicholas | Nov 23 1852 | 12/71 |
| Scheoffer, Amelia | Mahlen, John | Feb 20 1839* | 3/157 |
| Scheppen, August H | Jungfermann, Clara | Aug 18 1853 | 12/386 |
| Schickner, Malinda | Heple, Conrad | Oct 18 1855 | 14/255 |
| Schidal, Helena | Kline, Francis | Nov 30 1850 | 11/100 |
| Schieman, Julian | Lipps, Jacob | Dec 27 1854 | 13/420 |
| Schilling, Franz (widr) | Hingel, Friedericka | Mar 21 1853 | 12/211 |
| Schilt, Ellen (Mrs) | Hanna, James J | Sep 22 1845 | 8/118B |
| Schilt, Joseph U | Cooper, Ellen | May 14 1841* | 5/130B |
| Schirtterle, John | Stanter, Margrethee | Oct 17 1836* | 3/61 |
| Schlon, John | Ehlers, Johanna Louise | Nov 8 1852 | 12/51 |
| Schmidt, Frederick | Reel, Catharine | Apr 5 1849* | 8/366 |
| Schneider, Barbara | Roland, Peter | May 14 1841* | 5/89B |
| Schneider, Johanna H R | Hirchy, Benjamin | May 14 1828* | 2/26 |
| Schneider, Johanna | Etter, Henry | Jun 10 1830* | 2/129 |
| Schnekelberger, Carolina | Wagner, John | Oct 28 1841* | 5/155B |
| Schock, Philip | Bennett, Ellen (wid) | Aug 10 1853 | 12/380 |
| Schoeman, Anthony | Gelbk, Caroline | Aug 27 1852 | 11/279 |
| Schonmeier, Ernstina | Leipt, Adam | Dec 3 1853 | 13/34 |
| Schreiber, Frederick | Knauf, Katarina | Feb 20 1855* | 14/63 |
| Schriener, Conrad | Mompert, Mary | Nov 15 1851 | 11/187 |
| Schrobel, Juliana A | Battelle, John A | Feb 7 1843 | 0IB/AMC |
| Schroebel, Henry Alfred ? | Schuyler, Martha V | Jun 30 1845 | 8/107B |
| Schroebel, Laura S | Ruggles, Samner (Sumner) | Nov 20 1852 | 12/67 |
| Schroebel, Louisa A | Thomison, Mathew D | Mar 22 1848* | 8/295 |
| Schroebel, Margaret P | Mercer, Peter | Jul 17 1850 | 11/74 |
| Schroeder, Charles H | Sayre, Fanny A | Apr 25 1854 | 13/204 |
| Schroeder, Henry A | Schuyler, Martha V | Jun 30 1845 | 8/107B |
| Schroeder, Mary | Lamp, John | Nov 30 1847* | 8/268 |
| Schuble, Frederick ? | Petern, Julien | Apr 26 1843 | 5/265B |
| Schuiermann, John V | How, Mary | Jan 26 1853 | 12/146 |
| Schule, Albertina | Kern, Christian | May 31 1853 | 12/305 |
| Schulz, Deiterick | Stockman, Rebecca | Mar 24 1853 | 12/204 |
| Schuster, Joseph B | Goldschmidt, Babet | Mar 7 1854 | 13/150 |
| Schuyler, Martha V | Schroebel, Henry Alfred | Jun 30 1845 | 8/107B |
| Schwartzback, Maria M | Rolefron, John | Nov 4 1838* | 3/150 |
| Schwors, Elizabeth | Berkhardt, John Henry | Oct 5 1852 | 12/22 |
| Scipes, Ann Thomas | Barclay, Stephen | May 3 1842* | 5/197B |
| Sciple, George W | Elsworth, Isabelle | Apr 29 1852 | 11/243 |
| Sciple, John | Gibb, Helen | Nov 6 1855 | 14/273 |
| Scleske, Joseph | Cooper, Harriet | Nov 22 1847 | 8/266 |
| Scollick, Joseph M | Martin, Frances H | Jan 17 1849* | 8/348 |
| Scopinich, Antonia | Tarobocchia, Thomas | Aug 25 1854 | 13/320 |
| Scott, Ann Eliza | Shiltito, Henry A | Aug 29 1853 | 12/396 |

| BRIDE OR GROOM | SPOUSE | DATE | BK/PAGE |
|---|---|---|---|
| Scott, Henry H | Toman, Mary | Jun 17 1836* | 3/51 |
| Scott, James | Farrell, Mary | May  2 1832* | 2/1551 |
| Scott, John | Battle, Annie E | Dec 24 1855 | 14/313 |
| Scott, Mary | Hiestand, Asa | Nov 15 1855 | 14/282 |
| Scott, Mathew | Blythe, Rachel | May  1 1854 | 13/212 |
| Scott, Matthew | Hennesy, Bridgit | Jun 16 1843 | 5/282B |
| Scott, Rebecca | Rossiter, John | Aug 17 1841* | 5/148B |
| Scott, Samuel E | Piere, Elizabeth (Piero) | Sep 16 1840* | 5/45B |
| Scott, Sarah E | Mengie, John (Menzie) | Nov  4 1840* | 5/59B |
| Scott, Thomas | Wells, Elizabeth | Apr 26 1837* | 3/96 |
| Scott, William | Tracy, Ann | Apr 17 1851 | 11/139 |
| Scott, William | Conway, Catherine (Conly) | Apr  9 1845 | 8/85B |
| Scott, William | Tracey, Ann | Sep 12 1839* | 3/186 |
| Scribner, Mary E | Jameson, Robert | Mar 22 1855 | 14/87 |
| Scrivener, Christopher C | Skinner, Martha G | Apr 24 1847 | 8/230 |
| Scrivener, Mary V | Riley, John G | Apr 22 1846 | 8/160B |
| Scroggins, Mary E | Duckett, Wylie J | Jan  7 1854 | 13/63 |
| Scully, Mary | Swain, Isaac | Jul 14 1847 | 8/245 |
| Scypes, Mary Elizabeth | Patterson, William | May  6 1845 | 8/92B |
| Sea, Emily S (Lea) | Peabody, Herbert C | Jan  5 1841* | 5/85B |
| Sea, Margarette | Tachois, Francois | May 14 1838* | 3/125 |
| Seaberry, James H | Williams, Mary E | Jul 26 1850 | 11/76 |
| Seabrooke, Holland Ann | Patterson, Charles | May 19 1852 | 11/251 |
| Seahy, Mary | Corbit, Thomas | Dec 14 1837* | 3/103B |
| Seale, William | Johnson, Mary Jane | Dec 27 1841* | 5/165B |
| Seaman, John | Byrnes, Ann | Jul 14 1854 | 13/281 |
| Sears, Elizabeth | McCloud, Joseph | Mar  9 1824 | 1/24 |
| Sears, George H | Wade, Sarah Ann | Jul  5 1848 | 8/312 |
| Seathe, Thelitha (Leathe) | O'Connor, Michael | Mar 29 1842 | 5/190B |
| Seawell, Elizabeth A | Wetherby, Alvan | Apr  7 1836* | 3/44 |
| Seawell, Elizabeth G (Mrs) | Bowen, Silas | 1837* | OIB |
| Seawell, Joseph | Camphete, Eliza C  ? | Jun 24 1837* | 3/87 |
| Seawell, Mary | Carnfield, Josphe S | Jun  8 1835* | 3/17 |
| Seawell, William B | Butt, Martha A | Nov 29 1852 | 12/78 |
| Sebastian, Bocx | Estil, Mary | Apr 19 1854* | 13/193 |
| Sebon, Josephine | Adrughan, Benjamin F | Jun 10 1839* | 3/178 |
| Sebon, Josephine | Adrington, Benjamin F | Jun 10 1839* | 3/178 |
| Sedam, Laura B | Jones, Calvin J | Mar 13 1854 | 13/157 |
| See, Ellen (Lee) | Prescott, James E | Apr  4 1846 | 8/155B |
| See, Francis | Heslin, Bridget | Apr 30 1838* | 3/122 |
| Seed, John | Sheredan, Mary | Feb  4 1840* | 5/10 |
| Seeds, Richard | Lyons, Mary Ann | May  7 1831 | 2/169 |
| Seek, Susan | Armindinger, George | Oct 28 1835* | 3/30 |
| Seel, William | Grigsly, Margaret Ann | Jul  8 1850 | 11/71 |
| Sefeore, Francis A | Alareer, Julia | Apr 19 1838 | 3/119 |
| Seger, Maria Agatha | Cocauape, Anthony | Jul 24 1846 | 8/181 |
| Seifert, Jossue | Fonerant, Rosalie | Apr 24 1821* | CM |
| Seigel, Elisa | Richard, Samuel | Oct  1 1850* | 11/88 |
| Seip, Margaret | Ortsched, Andrew | Jul 31 1848* | 8/319 |
| Selause, Battitte | Posey, Yancy | Jul 14 1838* | 3/136 |
| Selfridge, Christopher Gore | Moss, Sarah Boardman | Nov 24 1847* | 8/267 |
| Selhsh, Bridget Ann | Pindolf, Jacob | May  9 1852 | 11/247 |
| Sellers, Artemesia L | Whitehead, John | Jan  6 1854 | 13/62 |
| Semans, Thomas | Haynes, Priscilla H | May  5 1851* | 11/145 |
| Semerni, Henrietta F  ? | Armstrong, William | Jun 17 1841* | 5/138B |
| Semon, Hans | Wright, Jane | Sep 12 1846 | 8/188 |
| Semoud, Robert | Riley, Jane | Oct  6 1846 | 8/192 |
| Senac, Evelina | Rapier, Thomas G | Dec 21 1837* | 3/104 |
| Senac, Felix | Hollinger, Mary L | Apr 16 1843 | 5/261B |
| Sencholl, Elizabeth | Marquez, Simon | Oct 23 1855 | 14/260 |
| Sendfludt, Johanna | Ahrens, August William | May  5 1851 | 11/146 |
| Senical, Amable (Jenical) | Mathews, Heloise F | Jan 25 1845 | 8/68B |
| Sercy, Eliza | Bumhaur, Alonzo H | Apr 21 1838* | 3/120 |
| Serda, Catharine | Carles, Peter | Jun 12 1846 | 8/172 |

| BRIDE OR GROOM | SPOUSE | DATE | BK/PAGE |
|---|---|---|---|
| Sergo, Emelie | Fortner, Alonzo | Mar 6 1850 | 11/48 |
| Serra, Angelina J | Trull, D C | May 9 1853 | 12/274 |
| Serra, Louis | Galligher, Alfoy | Apr 15 1854 | 13/182 |
| Serra, Vincent | Vivaret, Mannette | Jan 5 1846* | 8/136B |
| Serrill, George L | Wilkins, Martha J | May 10 1845 | 8/94B |
| Serville, Jeremiah I ? | Rowland, Eveline | Jul 23 1842 | 5/212B |
| Seward, George W | Foote, Lydia E | Feb 12 1844 | 5/321B |
| Sewel, James | Lee, Elizabeth | Aug 25 1846 | 8/185 |
| Sexaure, Edward | Sagehorn, Anna | May 2 1853 | 12/265 |
| Seyfer, John ? | Pierce, Rebecca | 1825* | OIB |
| Seyfreiden, Catherine | Hau, Ferdinand | May 14 1855 | 14/140 |
| Seymour, Alva | Partridge, Mary Ann | Apr 12 1848 | 8/298 |
| Seymour, Emerant | Chieusse, Joseph E | Mar 19 1849 | 8/362 |
| Seymour, Jane Eliza | Fullam, Safford Eddy | Feb 17 1848 | 8/284 |
| Seymour, Sarah | Kennedy, John | Apr 13 1850 | 11/53 |
| Shackleford, Charlotte G | Fonville, Stevenson | 1839* | OIB |
| Shackleford, Robert | Quigley, Cordelia A | Aug 26 1846 | 8/186 |
| Shackleford, Ruth H | Demeritt, J S | Jun 28 1838 | 3/134 |
| Shafer, Charles | McLacklin, Mary Ann | Sep 18 1849 | 11/5 |
| Shafer, Jacob | Kimbert, Elizabeth ? | Sep 1 1842* | 5/218B |
| Shafer, Jacob | Mumbert, Elizabeth ? | Sep 1 1842* | 5/218B |
| Shaffer, Edward A | Haupt, Mary S | Dec 12 1849 | 11/25 |
| Shagn, Catharine | Franklin, Benjamin | Jul 1 1843* | 5/285B |
| Shanahan, Anastasia | Helson, Joseph | Dec 7 1854 | 13/405 |
| Shand, William | Turner, Mary (Fenner) | May 18 1842* | 5/201B |
| Shanghnasy, Edward | Hays, Ann | Sep 13 1843 | 5/296B |
| Shannon, Mary | Garvey, George | Mar 24 1852 | 11/229 |
| Shannon, Michael | Richeford, Catherine | Dec 28 1854 | 13/422 |
| Sharp, Missouri A | Voorhis, Peter | Apr 21 1852 | 11/240 |
| Sharpe, Emily | Newberry, Charles Maxwell | Feb 8 1843* | 5/248B |
| Sharpin, Mary | Espejo, Antoine | Apr 11 1825 | 1/72 |
| Shaughnessy, Margaret O | Barnes, David | Jul 9 1855 | 14/193 |
| Shaw, Catherine | Patterson, James | Oct 27 1855 | 14/266 |
| Shaw, Elizabeth | Jones, Herbert | Dec 15 1819* | CM |
| Shaw, Jane (Shard) | Nicholson, William R | Nov 26 1845 | 8/126B |
| Shaw, Jepthah | Baley, Elizabeth | Jun 18 1819* | CM |
| Shaw, Mary | Duggan, Michael | Feb 8 1855 | 14/41 |
| Shaw, Narcissa T | Wilson, Davis | Dec 18 1850 | 11/104 |
| Shaw, Patrick | Healey, Ellen | Oct 20 1855 | 14/256 |
| Shay, Julia Ann | Story, Abraham | Dec 11 1849 | 11/24 |
| Shay, Margaret | Neil, Henry S | Feb 18 1819* | CM |
| Shay, Mary (wid) | Castello, William (widr) | Jan 30 1854* | 13/104 |
| Shea, Bridget | Shields, Nicholas | Aug 17 1838* | 3/139 |
| Shea, Margaret | Wainwright, Isaac | Jun 10 1854 | 13/252 |
| Shea, Mary | Ryan, Morris | Mar 21 1842 | 5/190B |
| Shea, Mary | Hull, Latham | Feb 10 1848* | 8/283 |
| Shea, Thomas | Verneuille, Eliza | Dec 26 1853 | 13/53 |
| Shed, John (Shea) | Rodgers, Mary | Apr 3 1837* | 3/78 |
| Shed, William B | Dugan, Harriet B | Oct 18 1842 | 5/224B |
| Shedal, Charles H | Shemfield, Emma | Feb 22 1847 | 8/219 |
| Sheean, Bridget | Johnson, Oscar | Apr 3 1855 | 14/97 |
| Sheehan, Elizabeth | Sheehan, Patrick | Feb 10 1841* | 5/103B |
| Sheehan, Patrick | Sheehan, Elizabeth | Feb 10 1841* | 5/103B |
| Sheelby, Eunice | Benjamin, Joseph | Nov 20 1837* | 3/101 |
| Sheelby, Eunice | Martin, Joseph | 1837* | OIB |
| Sheerin, James | McDermott, Mary | Feb 8 1850 | 11/38 |
| Sheet, Alexander M | Bowers, Helen M | Apr 9 1849* | 8/367 |
| Sheffield, Frederick | Longfield, Margaret | Mar 17 1835* | 3/11 |
| Shehan, Winny | McCarthy, Michael J | Aug 27 1852 | 11/279 |
| Sheils, Margarette | Deebarco, John Baptiste | Feb 5 1840* | 5/11 |
| Sheirmann, Theresa | Straub, Godfred | Oct 21 1854* | 13/359 |
| Shelby, Louie | Moffatt, Matilda Ann | Feb 10 1852 | 11/215 |
| Sheldon, E S | Farrow, Mary A | Apr 11 1853 | 12/232 |
| Shelean, Ellen | Roland, Martin | Apr 17 1852 | 11/238 |

| BRIDE OR GROOM | SPOUSE | DATE | BK/PAGE |
|---|---|---|---|
| Shelton, Alexander | Norton, Martha S | Jul 26 1852 | 11/271 |
| Shelton, Emeline | Ahlgren, John | May 2 1851 | 11/144 |
| Shelton, James | Johnson, Charlotte | Oct 11 1841 | 5/153B |
| Shelton, John Jefferson | Stokes, Caroline A | Mar 15 1845 | 8/78B |
| Shelton, Louisa | Williams, Levi | Nov 10 1841 | 5/155B |
| Shelton, Nancy | Dyess, Thomas | Jan 12 1843 | 5/242B |
| Shelton, William B | Malone, Virginia | Oct 15 1851 | 11/182 |
| Shemfield, Emma | Shedal, Charles H | Feb 22 1847 | 8/219 |
| Shepard, Rebecca | Cleveland, John G | Sep 16 1824 | 1/37 |
| Shepard, Thomas | Hamby, Susannah | Feb 6 1830* | 2/110 |
| Shepherd, Catharine | Crane, William Carey | Apr 24 1845 | 8/88B |
| Shepherd, Charles J | Brack, Roxie | Mar 16 1853 | 12/194 |
| Shepherd, Helen M | Clark, Francis B | Jun 9 1845 | 8/102B |
| Shepherd, James | Steele, Hellen | 1840* | 0IB |
| Shepherd, Sarah D | Anderson, Moses S | Jun 30 1845 | 8/107B |
| Shepherd, Thomas M | Nance, H Amelia | Jun 26 1850 | 11/69 |
| Shepherd, William S | Cook, Susan P | Apr 8 1846* | 8/155B |
| Sheppard, Agnes | Homer, William H | Nov 12 1850 | 11/97 |
| Sheppard, Christopher | Campbell, Agnes | Oct 15 1845 | 8/120B |
| Sheppard, Sarah Eliza | Harris, Edwin B | Jul 24 1848 | 8/318 |
| Sheppard, Sarah Jane | Johnson, Christopher | Jun 18 1846 | 8/174 |
| Sheredan, Mary | Seed, John | Feb 4 1840* | 5/10 |
| Sheridan, Ellen | Walsh, Michael | Mar 11 1839* | 3/159 |
| Sheridan, Richard | Maley, Mary | Jan 17 1851 | 11/114 |
| Sheriden, James | Maloy, Julia | Nov 19 1852 | 12/66 |
| Sherlock, Eliza D | Field, Frances | Apr 5 1844 | 8/9B |
| Sherman, Jesse T | Hodges, Frances A | Sep 8 1855 | 14/227 |
| Sherman, Philip | Johnson, Mena | Dec 27 1855 | 14/318 |
| Shermann, John Valentine | Hosey, Ellen | Sep 15 1852 | 12/5 |
| Sherry, Frank | Flinn, Mary | May 23 1855 | 14/150 |
| Sherwood, Emily | Wilkins, Richard R | Apr 28 1830* | 2/124 |
| Sherwood, John J | Robertson, Elizabeth A | May 9 1843 | 5/269B |
| Sherwood, Julia Louisa | Reid, John Jr | Nov 14 1842* | 5/227B |
| Sherwood, Robert | Neill, Eliza | Jan 31 1855 | 14/32 |
| Sheuneman, John | Nau, Mary | May 9 1854 | 13/220 |
| Shidell, Emeline | McNaughton, Francis | Nov 21 1848* | 8/332 |
| Shiel, Rose    (VOID) | Norris, Thomas | Dec 20 1852* | 12/103 |
| Shield, Cornelius | Burns, Ellen | Jul 25 1840* | 5/37B |
| Shields, Bridget | Sloan, John | Dec 30 1844 | 8/64B |
| Shields, Catherine | Cox, Thomas | Jul 14 1851 | 11/164 |
| Shields, Elizabeth | Burns, James | Dec 30 1840* | 5/71B |
| Shields, Elizabeth | Gandin, John | Sep 29 1845 | 8/119B |
| Shields, Margaret | Etherige, Thomas | Sep 13 1836* | 3/57 |
| Shields, Nicholas | Shea, Bridget | Aug 17 1838* | 3/139 |
| Shields, Thomas | Hepp, Cora G | Mar 18 1847 | 8/221 |
| Shiltito, Henry A | Scott, Ann Eliza | Aug 29 1853 | 12/396 |
| Ship, Mary | Rasberry, William G | (ND) (1854)* | 13/761 |
| Shipley, Josephine | Chamberlain, Henry | Jan 28 1842* | 5/175B |
| Shiremann, Rosalie | Rouch, Andres | Mar 17 1848 | 8/293 |
| Shockley, Theodore W | Lacy, Martha E | Jul 20 1855 | 14/196 |
| Shoemaker, Dory | Nongeson, Henry | Nov 1 1844 | 8/47B |
| Shoemaker, Henry | Heckmier, Lizzita | May 1 1845 | 8/90B |
| Shoemaker, Samuel | Mercer, Jane A | May 2 1853 | 12/267 |
| Sholts, Frederick | Johnson, Catherine | Mar 19 1834* | 2/381 |
| Short, John  (Thomas) | Whitney, Catharine | Mar 1 1837* | 3/73 |
| Shuckleford, Charlotte G | Homith, Stevenson L | Aug 3 1839* | 3/183 |
| Shul, Mary C   (wid) | Novack, William | Sep 28 1853 | 12/410 |
| Shultes, Eunice | Jackson, James | Dec 24 1820* | CM |
| Shumacher, Henry | Brannes, Dorothea | Jan 16 1838* | 3/107 |
| Shutz, Barbara | Lips, Nicholas | Jan 8 1853 | 12/118 |
| Shwenk, Mary | Mink, Peter | Dec 3 1855 | 14/296 |
| Sibley, Caroline | Harris, Cyrus L | Mar 9 1853 | 12/188 |
| Sibley, Ellen | Warder, Henry | May 28 1831* | 2/173 |
| Sibley, Matthew | Lame, Ellen | 1823* | 0IB |

| BRIDE OR GROOM | SPOUSE | DATE | BK/PAGE |
|---|---|---|---|
| Sicet, William | Mooney, Ellis | Aug 3 1839* | 3/183 |
| Sidgreaves, Cordelia M | Griffin, Edmund | Nov 20 1846 | 8/200 |
| Sidney, John | Franklin, Irene | Jul 5 1853 | 12/348 |
| Siefert, Charles | Matsinger, Mary | Feb 21 1852 | 11/220 |
| Siegel, Sarah | Goldsmith, Mayer | Dec 12 1849* | 11/25 |
| Siegmund, John S | Ebbereck, Margaret R | May 23 1855 | 14/148 |
| Silburn, James | Thomas, Susan | Apr 28 1855 | 14/121 |
| Siler, Theresa | Aufleger, Albert | Feb 9 1855 | 14/43 |
| Silk, William | Dillon, Elizabeth | Dec 29 1848* | 8/342 |
| Silliman, Alexander P | Reid, Sarah | Oct 20 1851 | 11/182 |
| Sills, Elizabeth | Fuller, George | Oct 6 1846* | 8/193 |
| Sills, James | Mrxsim, Elizabeth (Maxim) | Mar 7 1838* | 3/115 |
| Silor, Joshua S | Meslier, Basilia A | Oct 11 1834* | 2/91 |
| Silva, Daniel M | Hansey, Mary | Jul 27 1850 | 11/77 |
| Silva, Francisco | Monarty, Margaret | Feb 23 1842 | 5/182B |
| Silver, Francis | Delaney, Ann | Feb 10 1852 | 11/216 |
| Silvey, Mary | Ray, Patrick | Jan 26 1852 | 11/208 |
| Silvi, Jule | O'Donald, Sarah | Mar 31 1841* | 5/120B |
| Silvin, Ann | Sturken, John Henry | Sep 14 1849 | 11/5 |
| Simeon, Ann | Miller, George | Sep 22 1846 | 8/189 |
| Simerson, Eliza Ann | Walker, Francis | Jun 4 1855 | 14/159 |
| Simetovich, F S | Leverona, Rosa | Nov 7 1852 | 12/47 |
| Simison, B D | Barrett, Martha T | Oct 20 1840 | 5/57B |
| Simmons, Butler | Brown, Eliza | Apr 14 1843* | 5/261B |
| Simmons, Elijah | Lacoste, A | Jan 11 1844 | 5/314B |
| Simmons, Elizabeth A | McCarty, Mitchell | Apr 20 1844 | 8/16B |
| Simmons, Francis R E | Taylor, Stephen B | Dec 1 1840* | 5/69B |
| Simmons, Henriette | Reed, Joseph | May 20 1850 | 11/62 |
| Simmons, Henry | Harkins, Emily | Dec 17 1842* | 5/235B |
| Simmons, Henry A | Jones, Sarah A E | Jan 27 1852 | 11/209 |
| Simmons, James E | Cates, Cynthia | Apr 10 1851 | 11/136 |
| Simmons, John | Cates, Elizabeth | Nov 29 1852 | 12/79 |
| Simmons, Malachi | Billing, Mary | Apr 25 1818* | CM |
| Simmons, Mary | Kaho, James | Jun 12 1823* | 1/7 |
| Simmons, Mary Ann | Myers, Daniel Porter | May 2 1843 | 5/266B |
| Simmons, Susan | Hogan, James G | Sep 13 1849 | 11/4 |
| Simms, Mary M | Ingersoll, Andrew Jackson | Nov 12 1846 | 8/198 |
| Simms, Sally | Hartley, Daniel | Nov 1 1824 | 1/43 |
| Simon, Andrew | Sarneck, Arabella | Apr 10 1839* | 3/166 |
| Simonds, James | Woods, Malinda | Mar 31 1851 | 11/133 |
| Simpson, Ellen | Baird, James | Jun 15 1840* | 5/27 |
| Simpson, Frances | Fer, Constant | Jan 20 1821* | CM |
| Simpson, Frederick | Taylor, Margaret | Feb 1 1853 | 12/159 |
| Simpson, Isabella A | Green, John A | Jan 26 1843 | 5/245B |
| Simpson, Jane Elizabeth | Murray, Edwin Jr | Feb 6 1849* | 8/354 |
| Simpson, John C | Harrison, Mary Jane | Mar 2 1846 | 8/149B |
| Simpson, Lavina | Bidwell, Solomon S | Jan 10 1854 | 13/72 |
| Simpson, Thomas | Turner, Harriett | 1822* | OIB |
| Sims, Berry | George, Elizabeth | Oct 9 1847* | 8/258 |
| Sims, Charles | Craney, Debora | Nov 15 1842* | 5/227B |
| Sims, Daniel | Robertson, Anna | Jun 5 1845* | 8/101B |
| Sims, Elizabeth | Booth, Noah | Nov 19 1840* | 5/63B |
| Sims, Elizabeth | George, Isaac | Oct 6 1851 | 11/181 |
| Sims, Lavinia | Robertson, William | May 7 1821* | CM |
| Sims, Marcella | Platt, Peter | Apr 19 1849* | 8/369 |
| Sims, Mary J | Thompson, Andrew | Oct 21 1853 | 12/424 |
| Sims, Messieir | McWhister, Robert | Aug 17 1847* | 8/252 |
| Simson, Sampson J | Harrison, Catherine | Mar 27 1839* | 3/162 |
| Sinclair, John | Hibbitts, Margaret | Jun 5 1849* | 8/308 |
| Singletary, Harriet | Gee, Gideon | Nov 24 1841* | 5/159B |
| Singleton, William | Sawyer, Mary | Jun 23 1846 | 8/174 |
| Sinibaldi, Theresa Albora | Raoul, Nicholas | Nov 29 1824 | 1/51 |
| Sinnot, John A | Chester, Caroline E | Feb 13 1855 | 14/50 |
| Sitzler, William W | Raney, Catherine | Dec 1 1831* | 2/1821 |

| BRIDE OR GROOM | SPOUSE | DATE | BK/PAGE |
|---|---|---|---|
| Sixsmith, Joseph | Gaddes, Ann | Sep 18 1855 | 14/233 |
| Skaates, B S | Gilleland, Emilier | Feb 10 1838* | 3/111 |
| Skary, Ann (Kary) | Hoay, William | Dec 29 1842 | 5/239B |
| Skillman, Caroline A | Denver, William | Jan 25 1853* | 12/143 |
| Skinner, Anna H | Bates, James F | Nov 15 1854* | 13/379 |
| Skinner, Brelon W L | Etheridge, Susan | Dec 31 1839* | 5/6 |
| Skinner, John W (wid) | Hokett, Martha (wid) | Aug 18 1853* | 12/387 |
| Skinner, Martha G | Scrivener, Christopher C | Apr 24 1847 | 8/230 |
| Skinner, Sarah | Merritt, Randolph | Jan 31 1849* | 8/351 |
| Skinner, Sarah E | Bennett, Robert F | Dec 16 1844 | 8/59B |
| Slade, Ann B | Everett, John F | 1826* | 01B |
| Slade, Elizabeth (Hade) | Few, Thomas | Dec 21 1824 | 1/54 |
| Slade, Henry A | Martin, Eliza A | Mar 27 1832* | 2/1601 |
| Slade, Joseph | Charbonnet, Amelia | Jul 25 1845 | 8/112B |
| Slalters, James | McDonald, Catherine | Feb 28 1840* | 3/195 |
| Slappey, John G | Kaigler, Eliza C | Nov 13 1850 | 11/97 |
| Slate, Catherine | Murphey, John D | Apr 10 1855* | 14/103 |
| Slater, John | McGinnis, Rosanna | Sep 16 1843 | 5/297B |
| Slaton, Amanda Jane | Johnston, William | Nov 9 1852 | 12/53 |
| Slaton, William | Baker, Arina | Nov 5 1844 | 8/47B |
| Slatter, Ann Parrish | Holly, William Deforest | Jul 5 1851* | 11/162 |
| Slattery, James | McDonald, Catharine | Feb 8 1841 | 5/87 |
| Slavin, Edward | Davis, Ann | May 13 1836* | 3/47 |
| Sloan, Eliza | Murray, James | Aug 7 1851 | 11/171 |
| Sloan, John | Shields, Bridget | Dec 30 1844 | 8/64B |
| Sloan, John | O'Brien, Julia | May 28 1847* | 8/239 |
| Sloan, John | Hern, Mary (Henn) | Jan 22 1844* | 5/317B |
| Sloan, John | Henn, Sarah (Hern) | Jan 22 1844* | 5/317B |
| Sloan, Thomas | Waters, Eunice | Feb 11 1838* | 3/111 |
| Slocum, John | Browning, Matilda | Dec 4 1838* | 3/151 |
| Sloman, Michael | Fitzgerald, Catherine | Feb 23 1854 | 13/134 |
| Slough, Robert H | Holcombe, Cornelia A | Oct 29 1846 | 8/196 |
| Slute, Eusophrine S | Hugo, Simeon | Mar 15 1850 | 11/46 |
| Sly, Eliza | Wilkinson, William L | Aug 7 1847 | 8/250 |
| Small, Catherine | McLane, William | Jan 22 1842 | 5/172B |
| Smallhf, William (Smullhy) | Andrews, Catherine | Jan 1 1841* | 5/83 |
| Smart, Elizabeth | Smith, Jason | Dec 13 1850 | 11/102 |
| Smart, Mary | Monk, Noah | Mar 11 1841* | 5/116B |
| Smith, Abbie L | Perkins, Rufus L | Jun 18 1851 | 11/159 |
| Smith, Almeda | Swis, John | Apr 1 1840* | 3/197 |
| Smith, Almira C | Mitchell, Bernard D | Mar 8 1841* | 5/114B |
| Smith, Ann | Kelly, Daniel | Jun 3 1844 | 8/24B |
| Smith, Anna | Whitehall, Joseph | Jul 7 1851 | 11/162 |
| Smith, Anna E | Vail, Lovick B | Dec 2 1839* | 5/2 |
| Smith, Anne | Hintze, Ernest | Dec 18 1843* | 5/309B |
| Smith, Anne | Ragusin, Antonio | May 22 1845 | 8/97B |
| Smith, Barbara | Smith, Samuel | Jun 29 1853 | 12/335 |
| Smith, Bridget | Lynch, John | Oct 13 1848* | 8/327 |
| Smith, Bridget | Flinn, Maurice | Nov 7 1850* | 11/95 |
| Smith, Bridgett Ann | Mulligan, Felix | Feb 17 1846 | 8/145B |
| Smith, Caroline | Navarro, Emanuel | Mar 3 1848 | 8/289 |
| Smith, Caroline | Bicknell, John | Aug 6 1852 | 11/274 |
| Smith, Catherin | Smith, Henry H | Aug 15 1829* | 2/92 |
| Smith, Catharine | Underwood, Thomas | Jun 28 1832* | 2/1431 |
| Smith, Catharine | Hooks, Samuel W D | Jul 23 1849* | 8/383 |
| Smith, Catherine | Townsley, Francis | Jun 12 1855 | 14/170 |
| Smith, Catherine | Machune, Jerry | Oct 23 1852 | 12/34 |
| Smith, Catharine Ann | Bryant, Joseph | Oct 17 1842* | 5/224B |
| Smith, Charity | Woodruff, H N (T) | Nov 2 1842* | 5/226B |
| Smith, Charles | Todd, Martha B | Aug 6 1840* | 5/39B |
| Smith, Charles | Boykin, Mary Ann | Dec 8 1843 | 5/308B |
| Smith, Christian | Frank, Mena | Nov 13 1849 | 11/15 |
| Smith, Clarissa | Wilson, Benjamin | May 9 1833* | 2/1021 |
| Smith, Daniel | Johnson, Eliza | May 3 1851 | 11/145 |

| BRIDE OR GROOM | SPOUSE | DATE | BK/PAGE |
|---|---|---|---|
| Smith, David | Bayzon, Caroline | Sep 23 1847 | 8/256 |
| Smith, Douglas | Francis, Rebecca W | Mar 15 1848 | 8/293 |
| Smith, Edward | Smith, Jane | Mar 10 1837* | 3/74 |
| Smith, Edward G | Gilchrist, Elizabeth | Apr 15 1850* | 11/53 |
| Smith, Eliza | Snedicor, Platt | Mar 7 1838* | 3/114 |
| Smith, Eliza | Carroll, John | Dec 18 1852 | 12/97 |
| Smith, Eliza J | McPherson, John | Jun 1 1840* | 5/26B |
| Smith, Elizabeth | Manning, Leonard | Apr 4 1844 | 8/9B |
| Smith, Elizabeth | Magooran, John | Feb 5 1850* | 11/38 |
| Smith, Elizabeth | Yeend, John F | Apr 2 1850 | 11/50 |
| Smith, Elizabeth | Forbes, Thomas | Apr 16 1850 | 11/54 |
| Smith, Elizabeth | Edmondson, Philip P | Jun 16 1837* | 3/86 |
| Smith, Elizabeth | Thompson, Aaron | Aug 30 1851 | 11/174 |
| Smith, Elizabeth | Huber, Martin | Jan 22 1853 | 12/140 |
| Smith, Emma Matilda | North, Kluplum B | Sep 12 1837* | 3/91 |
| Smith, Epsey C | Thomas, Benjamin T | Dec 26 1855 | 14/317 |
| Smith, Frederick | Hays, Catharine | Sep 5 1845* | 8/191B |
| Smith, George | McLaughlin, Ann | Nov 19 1839* | 5/1 |
| Smith, George | O'Donnel, Bridget | May 3 1851 | 11/145 |
| Smith, George | Davis, Ann | Aug 13 1835* | 3/25 |
| Smith, George | Wemberly, Jane | Apr 26 1853* | 12/255 |
| Smith, George | Dalton, Ann | Jan 4 1854 | 13/61 |
| Smith, George | O'Connor, Mary | Feb 8 1854 | 13/115 |
| Smith, George | McCarty, Ellen | Jul 15 1854 | 13/282 |
| Smith, George F | Dunnison, Margaret | Sep 17 1850* | 11/86 |
| Smith, George S | Rockwell, Julia | Jan 1 1838* | 3/107 |
| Smith, George W | Rials, Adela | Dec 24 1845 | 8/132B |
| Smith, Helen | Connoly, James | Jun 24 1845 | 8/106B |
| Smith, Henry | Corey, Ann Eliza | Aug 5 1834* | 2/211 |
| Smith, Henry H | Smith, Catherin | Aug 15 1829* | 2/92 |
| Smith, I Edwin | Edgerly, Eliza Jane | Apr 26 1842 | 5/194B |
| Smith, Ira B | Brashears, Emeline | Dec 24 1850 | 11/106 |
| Smith, Isaac | Brathard, Ruthy | Feb 27 1824* | 1/23 |
| Smith, Isabella | Clancy, Jeremiah | Nov 22 1841 | 5/158B |
| Smith, Isabella (wid) | Nelson, Henry J (widr) | Mar 18 1853 | 12/197 |
| Smith, James | Pittman, Lucretia | Nov 24 1831* | 2/1831 |
| Smith, James M | Tisdale, Hannah C | Apr 12 1836* | 3/44 |
| Smith, Jane | Bracy, Samuel | Dec 10 1836* | 3/64 |
| Smith, Jane | Smith, Edward | Mar 10 1837* | 3/74 |
| Smith, Jane | Moorhouse, Joseph | Apr 9 1845 | 8/86B |
| Smith, Jane E | Moffett, Henry | 1835* | OIB |
| Smith, Jane E | Moffet, Henry | Jun 29 1838* | 3/134 |
| Smith, Janet | Robertson, James | May 15 1852 | 11/250 |
| Smith, Jason | Smart, Elizabeth | Dec 13 1850 | 11/102 |
| Smith, Jesse C | Deakle, Elizabeth | Jun 11 1847* | 8/241 |
| Smith, John | McBrior, Alice | Nov 3 1838* | 3/145 |
| Smith, John | Carson, Sarah | Nov 16 1824 | 1/49 |
| Smith, John | Quinn, Mary | Jun 10 1844 | 8/27B |
| Smith, John | Doyle, Mary Ann | Nov 9 1854 | 13/376 |
| Smith, John | Whatley, Lucy | Feb 24 1855 | 14/68 |
| Smith, John B | Labatt, Mirriam H | Sep 1 1846 | 8/187 |
| Smith, John L | Moody, Martha | Apr 13 1841* | 5/123B |
| Smith, John O | McClellan, Margaret | Oct 20 1845 | 8/121B |
| Smith, John R | Davis, Elizabeth | 1827* | OIB |
| Smith, Josiah L | Chesnut, Jane | Jan 5 1853 | 12/114 |
| Smith, Julia | Overton, Thomas | Oct 31 1854 | 13/365 |
| Smith, Lorens | Scanlin, Mary | Apr 17 1845 | 8/87B |
| Smith, Maraetta | Lewis, James | May 7 1855 | 14/131 |
| Smith, Margaret | Bunch, Richard L | Jul 21 1846 | 8/180 |
| Smith, Margaret | Erd, Joseph | Jan 15 1855 | 14/16 |
| Smith, Margaret | Harris, Richmond B (widr) | Nov 22 1853 | 13/24 |
| Smith, Margaret Ann | Harrison, Kirkland | Apr 5 1845 | 8/84B |
| Smith, Maria | McCaskill, Allen | Sep 30 1840* | 5/49B |
| Smith, Maria | Gallagher, Con | Dec 13 1852 | 12/87 |

| BRIDE OR GROOM | SPOUSE | DATE | BK/PAGE |
|---|---|---|---|
| Smith, Maria Louisa | Reid, John R | Jan 27 1837* | 3/70 |
| Smith, Martha E | Bullock, William F | Apr 18 1848 | 8/299 |
| Smith, Mary | Bryars, Laz I | Oct 4 1816* | CM |
| Smith, Mary | Daniels, Abner | Feb 22 1828* | 2/8 |
| Smith, Mary | Freeman, William A | Feb 13 1851 | 11/122 |
| Smith, Mary | Payson, Lewis | Apr 30 1852 | 11/244 |
| Smith, Mary | Blalock, Allen B | Oct 8 1855 | 14/248 |
| Smith, Mary | Witt, Charles | May 10 1853 | 12/275 |
| Smith, Mary Ann | Cirode, Daniel W | Nov 11 1843 | 5/303B |
| Smith, Mary Ann | Bates, John G | Feb 11 1839* | 3/156 |
| Smith, Mary J | McAuley, John C | Dec 5 1854 | 13/401 |
| Smith, Mary P P | Jewett, Adams | Jul 1 1841* | 5/141 |
| Smith, Matthew B | Henry, Nancy | 1826* | OIB |
| Smith, Melancthon | Forney, Mary E | Mar 8 1853 | 12/187 |
| Smith, Michael | Gibbons, Catherine | Jan 19 1854 | 13/89 |
| Smith, Michael | Cairnes, Bridget | Feb 25 1854 | 13/140 |
| Smith, Murry F | Deshan, Phebe Ann | May 30 1840* | 5/25 |
| Smith, N Henry | Kilfir, Sarah | Oct 21 1850 | 11/91 |
| Smith, Nancy A | Lundy, Charles P | Aug 28 1855 | 14/219 |
| Smith, Nathaniel J | Brashears, Louisa Z | Jan 4 1850 | 11/31 |
| Smith, Nicolas | Harris, Sarah | May 7 1845 | 8/93B |
| Smith, Patrick | Steers, Susan | 1827* | OIB |
| Smith, Patrick | McFall, Catharine | Sep 20 1848 | 8/324 |
| Smith, Patrick I | Roonen, Ann | May 2 1845 | 8/91B |
| Smith, Pevico | George, Sophie | Feb 10 1848 | 8/282 |
| Smith, Philip A | Canedy, Jenette B | Dec 21 1841* | 5/163B |
| Smith, Ralph S | Ruiz, Maria D | May 26 1853 | 12/299 |
| Smith, Richard Jr | Allen, Elizabeth | Jul 13 1848* | 8/316 |
| Smith, Robert | Lucey, Elmira R | Jan 11 1848 | 8/277 |
| Smith, Robert | Harrington, Mary E | Apr 19 1855 | 14/109 |
| Smith, Robert M | Tetlow, Matilda | Jul 4 1849* | 8/397 |
| Smith, Rose | Levelle, Patrick | Feb 2 1854 | 13/107 |
| Smith, Samuel | Smith, Barbara | Jun 29 1853 | 12/335 |
| Smith, Sarah | Turner, John | 1836* | OIB |
| Smith, Sarah | Neil, John | Sep 20 1836* | 3/59 |
| Smith, Sarah | Forbes, Gifford | May 5 1846 | 8/164B |
| Smith, Sarah (wid) | Moore, Thomas J (wid) | Oct 8 1853* | 12/412 |
| Smith, Sarah A | Riggle, Henry A | Feb 20 1854 | 13/127 |
| Smith, Sarah E P | Ball, John T | Apr 18 1848* | 8/299 |
| Smith, Sarah Jane | Russell, Henry C | Dec 7 1848* | 8/338 |
| Smith, Sidney | Merritt, Alabama W | Mar 28 1835 | 3/13 |
| Smith, Sylvester | Buckley, Rosa | Jun 7 1837* | 3/85 |
| Smith, Theresa | Tucker, John A | Aug 21 1854* | 13/317 |
| Smith, Thomas | Duggan, Ann | Feb 16 1855 | 14/55 |
| Smith, Thomas Brown | Preston, Sarah | May 15 1848* | 8/304 |
| Smith, William | Hudson, Ataline | Sep 27 1854 | 13/342 |
| Smith, William A | Henson, Sarah L | Oct 5 1837* | 3/93 |
| Smith, William H | Leroux, Caroline | Dec 4 1849* | 11/22 |
| Smith, William P | Davidson, Margaret A | May 7 1855* | 14/133 |
| Smith, William M | Mayrant, Mary M | Nov 19 1835* | 3/31 |
| Smith, William T | Kerry, Helena S | Jul 25 1848* | 8/318 |
| Smith, Wilson A | McKiernan, Mary | Nov 27 1850 | 11/99 |
| Smoot, Adeline | Montgomery, Elijah | Dec 28 1837* | 2/2 |
| Smoot, Anna Mary | Hall, Henry | Apr 19 1853 | 12/244 |
| Smoot, Edward M | Reynolds, Annette | Aug 2 1841* | 5/145B |
| Smoot, Ellen | Waring, Moses | Mar 22 1832* | 2/1631 |
| Smoot, Emma A | Deshon, Charles A | Aug 13 1850* | 11/79 |
| Smoot, Joseph H | Buckhotts, Martha | Jun 12 1855 | 14/171 |
| Smoot, Lavenia C | Lyon, James G | Feb 9 1833* | 2/1141 |
| Smoot, Margaret | Jennings, Sebeastian S | Dec 27 1836* | 3/66 |
| Smoot, Susan | McLean, William B | Aug 14 1840* | 5/43B |
| Smoot, Virginia A | Rolston, John | Sep 23 1846 | 8/190 |
| Smullen, Mary | Merrina, Louis (Mersina) | Jan 21 1842 | 5/171B |
| Smullhy, William (Smallhf) | Anderson, Catherine ? | Feb 1 1841* | 5/83B |

| Smullur, Mary | Herhey, Thomas | Jan 15 1837* | 3/97 |
| Snedicor, Platt | Smith, Eliza | Mar 7 1838* | 3/114 |
| Snediku, Samul (Snedecor) | Parker, Ann | Nov 29 1838* | 3/150 |
| Snell, Samuel | Rogers, Martha | Oct 4 1824* | 1/40 |
| Snelling, Ephram | Conely, Jane | Jul 20 1840* | 5/35B |
| Snider, Elizabeth | Webaka, Frederick | Mar 21 1845 | 8/80B |
| Snider, John | Goulding, Ellen | Jan 30 1842* | 5/176B |
| Snow, Emily | Ruder, Alfred A | Apr 9 1839* | 3/166 |
| Snow, Freeman | Vaughan, Eliza | Apr 4 1848* | 8/296 |
| Snow, Harvey | McGill, Margaret | Feb 16 1852 | 11/218 |
| Snow, Harvey | Autrey, Catherine A | May 21 1844 | 8/21B |
| Snow, Minerva E | Allen, William | Jul 4 1849 | 8/396 |
| Snyder, Agnes | Wheeler, Joseph | Dec 19 1821* | CM |
| Snyder, Christine | Maxwell, John | Dec 31 1846 | 8/208 |
| Snyder, J Otto | Gabert, Maria | Oct 14 1852 | 12/29 |
| Snyder, Margaret | Pontappidan, George | Apr 30 1842* | 5/196B |
| Snyder, Risit | Emily, Andre | Mar 15 1825 | 1/67 |
| Snyder, Rosina | Swager, John | 1825* | OIB |
| Snyder, Theobold | Gilbert, Elizabeth M | Feb 19 1844 | 5/323B |
| Socier, Bazelia (Saucier) | Lassabe, Renny (Remy) | Feb 14 1838* | 3/113 |
| Soger, Helena | Ray, James | Sep 2 1848 | 8/322 |
| Soger, John | Kehler, Helena | Mar 9 1848* | 8/291 |
| Sogey, Marie | Decuy, Stanislaus | Jul 17 1851 | 11/165 |
| Solle, William Robert | Greening, Mary | Jul 1 1852 | 11/268 |
| Sollinger, Catherine | Peters, Michael | Aug 4 1853 | 12/375 |
| Somer, Elizabeth | Farmer, John | Sep 25 1834* | 2/121 |
| Somers, Deborah Ann | Quigley, Nathan C | May 5 1831* | 2/167 |
| Somers, John D | Trainer, Ellen | Nov 10 1855 | 14/276 |
| Sondano, Giebbe (Londano) | Nugent, Mary | Dec 31 1841 | 5/166B |
| Sonergain, John | McDonald, Ann | Aug 25 1846 | 8/185 |
| Song, Mary Jane | Keates, Thomas S | Jul 11 1846 | 8/177 |
| Songfield, Jacob ? | Falk, Jeddah (Folk) | Apr 19 1843* | 5/262B |
| Soobert, Stephens | Hubert, Maria | Oct 18 1847* | 8/259 |
| Sooney, Margaret | Mulholland, John | Jul 27 1850 | 11/77 |
| Soost, Andrew Daniel | Nelios, Catharine Ann ? | Oct 9 1844 | 8/43B |
| Soost, Andrew Daniel | Nelson, Catherine Ann ? | Oct 9 1844 | 8/43B |
| Sordin, Ellen | Collins, Andrew B | Jan 26 1836* | 3/38 |
| Sorely, James | Stone, Mary J | 1847* | OIB |
| Soren, Caroline | Gaston, Matthew A | Feb 18 1843* | 5/249B |
| Sorner, Elizabeth | Farrner, John | Sep 25 1834* | 2/121 |
| Sossaman, Adeline | Lonony, John (Lowary) | Nov 25 1842 | 5/229B |
| Sossaman, Augustus A | Joullain, Louise | Jan 26 1848 | 8/279 |
| Sossaman, Blount | Julien, Caroline C | Dec 9 1851* | 11/193 |
| Sossaman, William | Fourcard, Clara | Jan 8 1855 | 14/4 |
| Sossoman, Caroline | Goodman, James W | Dec 20 1837* | 3/103 |
| Sossomon, John F | Pittman, Emily | Feb 16 1837* | 3/72 |
| Soto, Camilla | Reneaud, Adolph | Feb 20 1841* | 5/106B |
| Soto, John | Rondeau, Constance | 1827* | OIB |
| Soto, Merced | Mansony, Charles G | May 22 1824 | 1/33 |
| Soto, Merced | Kennedy, James | Mar 3 1851 | 11/127 |
| Soto, Raymond | Etienne, Julia | Sep 12 1843 | 5/295 |
| Soto, Zero | Jones, Adelle | Oct 19 1850 | 11/90 |
| Sott, Elizabeth | Denmark, Bryant J | Sep 10 1842 | 5/219B |
| Souchet, Amelia | Brownejohn, Thomas | Mar 19 1825 | 1/69 |
| Southerland, Barbara | Watson, William | Jan 10 1855 | 14/10 |
| Southworth, Edward C | Rouse, Louise F (Roux) | Feb 24 1842 | 5/183B |
| Spalding, Caroline J | Tramel, Albert G | Sep 8 1851 | 11/177 |
| Spalding, Elizabeth | Boyle, William | 1839* | OIB |
| Spalding, Laura | Bell, William | 1827* | OIB |
| Spalding, Martha M | Gardner, David B | Mar 12 1851 | 11/129 |
| Spam, Eleanor N (Spann) | Richardson, Richard C | Nov 16 1838* | 3/147 |
| Span, Anna | Reiners, Mathias | Feb 9 1852 | 11/214 |
| Spanagel, George | Pfeiffer, Margaret | Oct 18 1854 | 13/350 |
| Sparanberg, William | Croslent, Sarah | Oct 1 1848* | 8/326 |

| BRIDE OR GROOM | SPOUSE | DATE | BK/PAGE |
|---|---|---|---|
| Sparks, Lora | Pensill, Charles J | 1837* | OIB |
| Spaulding, Rufus | Wingate, Elizabeth | Jan 19 1833* | 2/1201 |
| Spaulding, Stephen | Myers, Nancy | Sep 16 1813* | WB 1/8 |
| Speake, James | Walker, Cornelia | Sep 25 1850 | 11/87 |
| Spear, Lucy T | Mayland, Daniel | 1838* | OIB |
| Spears, Edward | Campbell, Eliza | Feb 13 1849* | 8/356 |
| Spears, Isaac D | Reynolds, Sarah B | Dec 18 1838* | 3/A152 |
| Spence, Mary | Munnerlyn, Benjamin C | Dec 14 1852 | 12/91 |
| Spence, Nancy | Dubose, James | Oct 2 1852 | 12/16 |
| Spencer, Ann | Graves, Benjamin H | Dec 24 1830 | 2/145 |
| Spencer, Ann B | Hutchisson, James F | Sep 19 1836* | 3/59 |
| Spencer, Margaret | Cann, John | Dec 1 1852 | 12/80 |
| Spencer, Martha | Roberts, R W | Mar 23 1839* | 3/161 |
| Spencer, Richard | Nixon, Martha | Oct 6 1849 | 11/9 |
| Spencer, Richard | Root, Margaret A | Oct 2 1855 | 14/245 |
| Spensler, John B | Phillips, Martha Ann | Aug 3 1844 | 7/363B |
| Sperry, John J | Chapman, Abby Anne | Apr 10 1843 | 5/260B |
| Speth, Ferdinand | Camphmuller, Catherine | Jul 22 1854 | 13/291 |
| Spikes, Angeline | Roussell, Edward | Oct 26 1852 | 12/36 |
| Spillard, Catharine | Lynch, Thomas | Apr 13 1842 | 5/196B |
| Spillard, Mary | Morrison, John | Feb 24 1840* | 3/194 |
| Spilleoon, Mary | McNamara, Daniel | Apr 12 1849* | 8/368 |
| Spillings, James | Berry, Jane Louisa | Apr 17 1845* | 8/87B |
| Spillings, Jane Louisa | Perkins, William | Apr 2 1849* | 8/365 |
| Spillins, Ellen | Cowly, Timothy | Dec 9 1840* | 5/73 |
| Spindler, John | Engleman, Margaret | Sep 11 1855 | 14/228 |
| Spinkles, Henry (Sprinkles) | Stone, Rose Anna | Sep 4 1852* | 11/282 |
| Spiver, Francis A | Conners, Margaret | Dec 15 1842* | 5/234B |
| Spotswood, William A W | Eastin, Mary Ann | Nov 28 1842* | 5/230B |
| Spriggs, Erastus S | Cleveland, Harriet | Feb 9 1838* | 3/110 |
| Spriggs, Harriet | Howard, Joshua | Mar 10 1843 | 3/253B |
| Springer, Francis E | Graham, William | Sep 14 1853 | 12/405 |
| Springer, Isaac B | Rusher, Eliza | Dec 31 1845* | 8/134B |
| Springer, John C | Magee, Ann | Feb 22 1854 | 13/129 |
| Springer, Mark | Austin, Jane R | Feb 9 1843 | 5/248B |
| Springstale, Mary Ann | Mudge, A | Apr 19 1842 | 5/192B |
| Sprinkles, George | Stewart, Elizabeth | Nov 17 1854 | 13/384 |
| Sprinkles, Peter | Mills, Catharine | Nov 7 1850 | 11/95 |
| Spullen, Stephen (Spuller) | Girard, Julia (Joanna) | Jan 25 1842* | 5/174B |
| Spurre, Gustaf (Sparre) | Frank, Mary Matilda | Jun 12 1843 | 5/281B |
| Stackhouse, William D | Jones, Sarah Ann | Jul 10 1848* | 8/314 |
| Stafford, Ann | Hays, Charles | Jan 23 1832* | 2/1731 |
| Stafford, Charles | Dowd, Maria | Nov 6 1854 | 13/369 |
| Stafford, John F | Davis, Elizabeth | Mar 3 1842* | 5/185B |
| Stafford, Mary | Martin, Frank | Sep 24 1849 | 11/6 |
| Stafford, Nancy | Boyne, Samuel (Bozone) | Jan 23 1832* | 2/1721 |
| Stafford, Susan | Clagg, David | 1826* | OIB |
| Stafort, Susan | Pallise, Diego (Palliser) | Jul 27 1854* | 13/295 |
| Stall, Frederick | McRae, Catherine | Sep 3 1853 | 12/400 |
| Stallworth, Benjamin J | Goode, Mary Ann | Apr 23 1850* | 11/55 |
| Stanford, Eliza | Laniers, Michael (Lanius) | Feb 14 1843 | 5/249B |
| Stanford, Isaac | Young, Eliza | May 3 1836* | 3/45 |
| Stanley, Edward | McNally, Bridget | Jan 16 1854 | 13/81 |
| Stanmire, William (Stanley) | Latson, Winifred | Feb 20 1820* | CM |
| Stanter, Margrethee | Schirtterle, John | Oct 17 1836* | 3/61 |
| Stanton, Alice | Pollard, John | Jan 27 1834* | 2/501 |
| Stanton, Patrick | Drury, Elizabeth | Apr 3 1839* | 3/164 |
| Stanton, William Jr | Newbold, Sarah Louisa | Apr 9 1845 | 8/85B |
| Stanton, Zachariah A | Monk, Elizabeth A | Jan 9 1855 | 14/7 |
| Starck, Margaret | Pizzini, Domonique | Aug 16 1852 | 11/276 |
| Stark, Charles R | Carroll, Margaret Jane | Apr 5 1849 | 8/365 |
| Starke, Grace | Evans, William | Jan 30 1855 | 14/29 |
| Starkes, Sarah | Pursell, Charles Jones | 1839* | OIB |
| Starks, Eliza | Hall, Ephraim L | Feb 8 1842 | 5/178B |

| BRIDE OR GROOM | SPOUSE | DATE | BK/PAGE |
|---|---|---|---|
| Starkweather, Asher | Clark, Nancy | Dec 1 1831* | 2/1801 |
| Starr, George D | Conway, Sarah | 1826* | OIB |
| Starr, Richard T | Deene, Mary E | May 18 1846 | 8/167B |
| Starr, Sarah | Howland, Jeremy | Aug 12 1835* | 3/24 |
| Stauder, Magdalena | Fink, George | Feb 10 1847 | 8/215 |
| Stauter, Catherine | Lallemant, Anthony | Aug 12 1841 | 5/147 |
| Stauter, Margrethee | Schirtterle, John | Oct 17 1836* | 3/61 |
| Stav, Ola | Gilpin, Ann | Jan 5 1848* | 8/275 |
| Staylor, William | Monk, Rhody | Sep 19 1825 | 1/91 |
| St Clair, Willis | Moore, Margaret | Oct 22 1850 | 11/91 |
| Steal, Barbara | Marshall, Thomas | Dec 15 1842 | 5/234 |
| Steck, Ellen | Fitzgerald, Maurice | Feb 28 1854 | 13/146 |
| Steel, Emile | Valle, Andre | May 17 1825 | 1/78 |
| Steele, Hellen | Shepherd, James | 1840* | OIB |
| Steele, John D | Cox, Elizabeth Harriet | Apr 23 1847 | 8/229 |
| Steele, Joseph | Hobart, Euphrosyne P | 1826* | OIB |
| Steele, Martha J | Partridge, Daniel | 1823* | OIB |
| Steele, Martha M | Hutchisson, James H | Jan 31 1855 | 14/34 |
| Steele, Mary L | Lewis, Rupel W (Russel) | 1822* | OIB |
| Steele, Michael | Gedder, Carolina | Jun 3 1852 | 11/260 |
| Steele, Parmelia (Slute) | Marshall, James | Jan 29 1842 | 5/175B |
| Steele, Samuel A | Green, Elizabeth | Jun 16 1842 | 5/207B |
| Steers, Mary | Coneham, James | Jun 11 1828* | 2/33 |
| Steers, Susan | Smith, Patrick | 1827* | OIB |
| Steers, Susan | Hays, George | Dec 16 1823* | 1/16 |
| Steger, Henry | Loftin, Susan | Dec 21 1840* | 5/77B |
| Steil, Christine | Mendel, William | Apr 9 1842* | 5/191B |
| Stein, Catherine | Kosmensky, Abraham | Jul 26 1855 | 14/199 |
| Stein, Henrietta | Gremer, Isaac | Jun 12 1850* | 11/66 |
| Steinbeck, Sophie | Kuhns, August Wilhelm | Jul 28 1851 | 11/170 |
| Steinberg, Louisa | Diesher, Harman | May 11 1842 | 5/199B |
| Steiner, Hannah | Wetzler, Albert | Jan 14 1851 | 11/112 |
| Steiner, Henry | Corbies, Marie Ann | Jun 28 1841* | 5/140B |
| Steiner, Henry | Hourre, Louise (House) | Aug 28 1848* | 8/322 |
| Steinheart, Christina | Arhart, John | Apr 19 1851* | 11/140 |
| Steirn, Tette | Epstein, Joseph | Feb 27 1854 | 13/144 |
| Stephani, Martha | Billirey, Felix | Oct 14 1845 | 8/119B |
| Stephens, Esther | Thornton, Willis | Aug 13 1835* | 3/25 |
| Stephens, Margaret | Stokes, Hughis N | Jun 16 1852* | 11/263 |
| Stephens, William | Bones, Elizabeth | Apr 15 1835* | 3/22 |
| Stephens, William | Johnson, Lucy | Feb 4 1837* | 3/96 |
| Stephens, William | Disoney, Catherine | Apr 20 1840* | 3/198 |
| Stephenson, John | Bridges, Ann M | Dec 18 1838* | 3/A152 |
| Stephenson, John H (Joshua) | Mann, Marianna | Feb 12 1845 | 8/73B |
| Stepson, Love | Walker, Samuel | Jun 11 1838* | 3/131 |
| Sterling, Mary Ann | Williams, John | Aug 20 1844* | 8/39B |
| Stern, Eva | Marcus, August | May 1 1843* | 5/266B |
| Steve, Mary J (Sterie) | Saely, James (Sorley) | Mar 4 1847* | 8/220 |
| Stevens, Andrew | McNiell, Jane | Mar 21 1843 | 5/254B |
| Stevens, John | McLaughlin, Catharine | Jun 11 1845 | 8/102B |
| Stevens, Mary O | Grimlar, Samuel H | May 14 1852 | 11/249 |
| Stevens, Rasberry | Morgan, Elizabeth | 1826* | OIB |
| Stevenson, Betsey | Bruce, Robert | 1822* | OIB |
| Stevenson, Joseph (widr) | DeShears, Elizabeth (wid) | Jun 27 1853 | 12/331 |
| Stewart, Alexander | Stewart, Mary | Apr 13 1830 | 2/123 |
| Stewart, Alexander | Moore, Mary | Jan 1 1848 | 8/274 |
| Stewart, Aloysius | Barney, Elizabeth | May 13 1819* | CM |
| Stewart, Charles A | Page, Sarah | 1827* | OIB |
| Stewart, Charles H | Fontaine, Mary E | Dec 12 1844 | 8/58B |
| Stewart, Columbus | Harrison, Adolph | Jun 28 1842 | 5/208B |
| Stewart, Elizabeth | Sprinkles, George | Nov 17 1854 | 13/384 |
| Stewart, Gershom N | Busby, Milinda | Aug 17 1854 | 13/314 |
| Stewart, James | Newberry, Eliza | Jan 30 1835* | 3/4 |
| Stewart, James | Mason, Eliza | Aug 20 1850 | 11/81 |

| BRIDE OR GROOM | SPOUSE | DATE | BK/PAGE |
|---|---|---|---|
| Stewart, James | Donald, Ann O (O'Donald) | Oct 15 1845 | 8/120B |
| Stewart, Jane | Cook, Henry | Feb 29 1852 | 11/223 |
| Stewart, John | Barnard, Sarah | Apr 19 1824 | 1/27 |
| Stewart, Louisa A | Benjamin, Walter C | Nov 9 1850 | 11/95 |
| Stewart, Mahala | Frasier, George | Nov 5 1831 | 2/183 |
| Stewart, Martha | Torrans, Charles F | Aug 22 1850 | 11/82 |
| Stewart, Martha | Butler, Samuel | Sep 2 1853 | 12/398 |
| Stewart, Mary | Stewart, Alexander | Apr 13 1830 | 2/123 |
| Stewart, Mary Ann | Tardy, Augustus J | Jun 3 1843 | 5/277B |
| Stewart, Sarah | Copley, William | Apr 22 1853 | 12/250 |
| Stickney, Caroline A | Hammond, William P | Jul 9 1842* | 5/211B |
| Stickney, Daniel H | McVoy, Isabella | Feb 1 1841* | 5/99B |
| Stickney, Hannah Jane | Jones, Emanuel | Nov 28 1842 | 5/230B |
| Stickney, Mary Eliza | Wragg, George | Jul 12 1832* | 2/1401 |
| Stiehl, Mary | Hofer, August | Aug 8 1855 | 14/206 |
| Stikes, Augustus | Biddle, Sidonia | May 11 1846 | 8/165B |
| Stikes, John | Saynick, Caroline ? | May 20 1845* | 8/96B |
| Still, Charles (Strill) | Pringle, Virginia | Oct 23 1854 | 13/360 |
| Stiller, William | Cramer, Catherine | Jun 9 1853 | 12/314 |
| Stillman, John F | Hobart, Hannah Anneta | Jul 20 1841* | 5/143B |
| Stincen, Samuel | Hill, Elizabeth Caroline | Dec 22 1842 | 5/237B |
| Stinnett, George W | Reeves, Nancy | Jun 30 1849 | 8/394 |
| Stinnitt, George W | Reed, Nancy (Sarah) | Jun 30 1844 | 8/29B |
| Stinson, Joseph | Logan, Maria E | Jun 1 1848 | 8/307 |
| Stirling, Daniel | Murray, Catherine | Oct 20 1854 | 13/357 |
| Stiver, Peter | Holborne, Mary | Jan 3 1846 | 8/136B |
| St John, Catherine | Trenier, John | Jan 27 1831* | 2/149 |
| St John, Clairre | Durette, Isidore | Mar 16 1831* | 2/154 |
| St John, Eliza | Gleeson, Michael | Feb 17 1852 | 11/218 |
| St John, Newton | Pope, Maria Jane | Feb 24 1835 | 3/10 |
| St John, Richard | Campbell, Mary | Sep 5 1854 | 13/331 |
| St John, Richard Jr | Kimball, Martha Ann | May 4 1840 | 5/21 |
| St John, Richard Jr | Woollard, Cynthia A | Nov 30 1848* | 8/336 |
| St John, Thomas | Gaines, Ellen Frances | Dec 20 1843 | 5/310B |
| St Laurence, Mary A | Casey, Michael | Oct 23 1855 | 14/263 |
| Stocking, Maria Helen | Magee, James P | Feb 14 1842 | 5/180B |
| Stockman, Rebecca | Schulz, Deiterick | Mar 24 1853 | 12/204 |
| Stockton, Philip A | Bostwick, Rebecca McK | Jul 14 1836* | 3/53 |
| Stoddard, Gridley B | Farrell, Julia | May 4 1843 | 5/267B |
| Stodder, Marcia | Austin, William | Nov 25 1824 | 1/50 |
| Stokes, Caroline A | Shelton, John Jefferson | Mar 15 1845 | 8/78B |
| Stokes, Elizabeth J | Farrow, Henry | Oct 27 1853 | 12/426 |
| Stokes, Hughis N | Stephens, Margaret | Jun 16 1852* | 11/263 |
| Stokes, Jane A | Gibson, Stephen | Mar 11 1854 | 13/156 |
| Stoll, Nancy | Meiners, Diedrich | Apr 5 1850 | 11/51 |
| Stone, Caroline E | Martin, Frederick | Oct 18 1853 | 12/417 |
| Stone, Edward | Lyons, Mary | May 1 1837* | 3/82 |
| Stone, Mary | Collier, John | Jul 1 1844 | 8/29B |
| Stone, Mary J | Sorely, James | 1847* | OIB |
| Stone, Rose Anna | Spinkles, Henry | Sep 4 1852* | 11/282 |
| Stoppin, Leopald (stopper) | Glargon, Sarah (Glasgow) | Jul 21 1838* | 3/137 |
| Storer, Mary Ann Louisa | Mighall, Joseph | Jul 5 1848* | 8/312 |
| Storey, Harriett (Strong) | Winter, Charles | Nov 21 1840* | 5/67B |
| Stork, Sara | Parcell, Charles J | Nov 4 1837* | 3/100 |
| Story, Abraham | Shay, Julia Ann | Dec 11 1849 | 11/24 |
| Story, Abraham | Monore, Fanny (Monon) | May 22 1854 | 13/232 |
| Stoude, Adolphe D | DelBecco, Margaret S | Apr 10 1855 | 14/101 |
| Stouder, Elizabeth | Burgun, Jacob | Jul 2 1844 | 8/31B |
| Stouder, Frances | Burgan, Adeline | Sep 26 1844 | 8/41B |
| Stouter, Christina | Swinderman, Thomas | Jul 2 1847* | 8/244 |
| Stoyer, Mitchell | Pelez, Barbary | Dec 3 1836* | 3/63 |
| Strachan, George | Walton, Martha (Watters) | Aug 25 1840* | 5/43B |
| Stramler, Frances A | Hall, Howard | Jan 27 1852 | 11/210 |
| Stranber, Gracomo | Bou, Mary | Mar 6 1838* | 3/114 |

| BRIDE OR GROOM | SPOUSE | DATE | BK/PAGE |
|---|---|---|---|
| Strang, Agnes | Wilson, Hugh | 1827* | OIB |
| Strang, Lavinia | Carver, Thomas J | Mar 29 1849 | 8/364 |
| Stratkins, Richard | Cunningham, Charlotte | Nov 5 1839* | 3/190 |
| Straub, Godfred | Sheirmann, Theresa | Oct 21 1854* | 13/359 |
| Straus, Babeth | Metzger, Adam | May 13 1850* | 11/61 |
| Straus, Rosina | Beck, Samuel | Nov 16 1850* | 11/98 |
| Strawbridge, Harriett | Fitzgerald, John | 1826* | OIB |
| Strawbridge, Susanna | Fallon, Bernard | Dec 12 1854 | 13/411 |
| Strayhorn, Nancy Jane | Taylor, William | Jul 18 1851 | 11/166 |
| Streach, David | Marrow, Eliza | Jul 29 1849* | 8/319 |
| Street, Martha | Lee, Josiah B | Jul 11 1837* | 3/89 |
| Strein, John | Murphy, Ann | May 20 1840* | 5/23 |
| Stribling, William C | Yonge, Ann C | Jul 9 1855 | 14/192 |
| Strike, Francis | Hickman, Joseph M | Apr 2 1840* | 3/197 |
| Strike, John (Stuke) | Scharden, Mary (Scherman) | Oct 24 1840* | 5/57B |
| Strill, Barbara | Williams, Charles | Feb 10 1845 | 8/72B |
| Strill, Elizabeth | Davis, John | May 9 1848* | 8/303 |
| Strimple, Mary | Andrews, Edmund | Dec 27 1845 | 8/133B |
| Stringer, Frances Ann | Knight, William | Jan 19 1837* | 3/70 |
| Stringer, George | Wilhelmi, Maria | Apr 9 1853 | 12/230 |
| Stringer, Larry | Kelly, Nancy | Jan 14 1853 | 12/131 |
| Stringer, Thomas | Garrahan, Ann B  (Mrs) | Jul 17 1843 | 5/289B |
| Stringer, William W | Powers, Abbey M | Feb 26 1846 | 8/148B |
| Stringfeller, Sarah | Pierce, Lewis | Dec 22 1849 | 11/26 |
| Stringfellow, Ellenor | Howell, Benjamin | Jun 5 1829* | 2/88 |
| Stringfellow, Harmon | Hambleton, Jemimah | Sep 8 1834* | 2/171 |
| Stringfellow, James | Baxter, Rachel | Sep 22 1828* | 2/41 |
| Stringfellow, John | Ward, Nancy | Aug 29 1833* | 2/801 |
| Stringfellow, Mary Ann | Pearce, Silas | Jul 10 1839* | 3/182 |
| Stringfellow, Susan | Goleman, Wilson C | Dec 15 1841 | 5/161B |
| Stringfellow, Tomzil | Pierce, George | Oct 9 1843 | 5/298B |
| Strong, Hannah L | Ross, John B | May 30 1825 | 1/80 |
| Strong, Hercules | Baptiste, Catharine | Sep 7 1847 | 8/255 |
| Strong, William A | Mitchell, Julia A | Apr 11 1844 | 8/12B |
| Stroud, William | Meazles, Mary Jane | Aug 27 1850 | 11/82 |
| Strouse, Simon | Marx, Ester | Jan 30 1855 | 14/30 |
| Struberg, Magmus Peter | Doland, Bridget | Feb 26 1848 | 8/287 |
| Stryhn, Hans R | Weyman, Catharine M | Apr 18 1848* | 8/300 |
| St Shackleford, Ruth  ? | Demerritt, J S | Jun 28 1838 | 3/134 |
| Stuardi, Amanda | Poitevin, Eugene | Aug 13 1855 | 14/194 |
| Stuart, Caroline E | Gillespie, Clayton C | Nov 17 1847* | 8/265 |
| Stuart, Delphine | Points, George W | Nov 8 1853 | 13/9 |
| Stuart, Eliza | Collins, Robert | Nov 22 1848 | 8/333 |
| Stuart, Eliza S | Cooper, Thompson H | May 14 1833* | 2/1011 |
| Stuart, John A | Vos, Mary F | Jun 11 1836 | 3/50 |
| Stuart, Rosalie | Gomez, Francis | Aug 5 1847 | 8/250 |
| Stuart, Rose E | Savage, George P | Nov 21 1854 | 13/387 |
| Stuart, Sarah | Bowen, John | Dec 31 1850 | 11/107 |
| Stuart, Sarah A | Woolf, James | Dec 5 1855 | 14/299 |
| Stuart, William (Stewart) | O'Connor, Cecilia F | Mar 8 1843 | 5/252B |
| Stubbs, Matthew | McDonald, Ellen | Jan 18 1852 | 11/205 |
| Stuckman, Rebecca | Schulz, Deiterick | Mar 24 1853 | 12/204 |
| Sturken, John Henry | Silvin, Ann | Sep 14 1849 | 11/5 |
| Sturtevant, Francis E | Jayne, Harriett A | May 18 1833* | 2/1001 |
| Sturtevant, Rebecca | Blue, Uriah | 1827* | OIB |
| Sturtevant, Thomas | Hinson, May | Aug 3 1825 | 1/88 |
| Stute, Benjamin C (Steele) | Kimball, Emma Pauline | Sep 15 1851 | 11/178 |
| Stutz, George | Herlinger, Catherine | Nov 14 1855 | 14/281 |
| Suarez, Joseph | Foster, Elizabeth | Jul 15 1819* | CM |
| Suhn, Metta Lucie | Baklmann, Gerhard | Nov 26 1851 | 11/190 |
| Sullivan, Bridget | Dea, John O (O'Day) | Feb 11 1847* | 8/216 |
| Sullivan, Caroline | Williams, Samuel | Dec 29 1843 | 5/312B |
| Sullivan, Cornelius | Barret, Margaret | Feb 19 1855 | 14/59 |
| Sullivan, David | Buckley, Mary | Dec 3 1837* | 3/102 |

| BRIDE OR GROOM | SPOUSE | DATE | BK/PAGE |
|---|---|---|---|
| Sullivan, Eliza | Crabtree, Jackson | Mar 11 1843 | 5/253B |
| Sullivan, Ellen B | Cahall, Alfred B | Aug 20 1855 | 14/214 |
| Sullivan, Jane Ann | Williams, R G | Oct 27 1837* | 3/99 |
| Sullivan, Jemimy | Bufkins, Benjamin F | Feb 9 1854 | 13/114 |
| Sullivan, Jeremiah | Meinhin, Catherine | Mar 13 1837* | 3/74 |
| Sullivan, Jeremiah | Calahan, Julia | Mar 23 1842 | 5/187B |
| Sullivan, John | Turney, Margt. (Tierney) | Jul 15 1850 | 11/73 |
| Sullivan, John | Flannigan, Mary Ann | Jan 16 1849* | 8/347 |
| Sullivan, Julia | Judge, Anthony | Oct 22 1850 | 11/91 |
| Sullivan, Julia | Harrington, Cornelius | Nov 11 1851 | 11/187 |
| Sullivan, Leonard M | Boyden, Angelina | May 10 1847 | 8/234 |
| Sullivan, Mark | Tedder, Jemimah | Oct 28 1829 | 2/98 |
| Sullivan, Mary | Fellonil, Louis | Nov 3 1843 | 5/302B |
| Sullivan, Mary | Harrington, Cornelius J | Sep 28 1854 | 13/345 |
| Sullivan, Mary | Farley, Phillip | Nov 25 1852* | 12/75 |
| Sullivan, Matilda | Crabtree, Alfred | Jul 27 1844 | 8/36 |
| Sullivan, Nancy | Wilkinson, James | Apr 7 1831 | 2/161 |
| Sullivan, Priscilla Mahala | Gallagher, James | Feb 20 1846 | 8/146B |
| Sullivan, Richard | Healy, Margaret | Dec 27 1852 | 12/105 |
| Sullivant, Emiline | Miller, John | Aug 18 1840 | 4/3961B |
| Summer, Amelia | Winkel, Henry | Nov 25 1853 | 13/28 |
| Summer, Sarah | Glasgow, Stephen | Nov 26 1834 | 2/1851 |
| Summerland, Matilda | Jordon, Samuel T | Jul 16 1842 | 5/211B |
| Summerlin, David | Foarte, Elizabeth | Jul 3 1849* | 8/395 |
| Summers, Barbara | Allen, Joseah T | Feb 7 1839* | 3/155 |
| Summers, Mary Ann | Ryan, Michael | Apr 30 1853 | 12/263 |
| Sumrall, Moses S | Lott, Dorcas | Apr 3 1834* | 2/401 |
| Sumrall, Sarah | Mason, Caldewood | Apr 30 1832 | 2/1571 |
| Sumrall, Sarah | Mason, Caldewood | May 3 1832 | 2/1571 |
| Sumrall, Susanna | Holland, Robert S | Jul 15 1844 | 8/32B |
| Sumwalt, James M | Test, Martha | Dec 12 1839* | 5/3 |
| Sunter, Joseph | Garraway, Elizabeth | Nov 12 1855 | 14/280 |
| Surtell, Ann | Lecatt, Littleton | Jul 19 1813* | WB1/8 |
| Sussusant, Sophie ? | Gasulle, Lawrence | May 10 1838* | 3/125 |
| Sutherland, Alexander Jr | Cumming, Jane | Sep 1 1854 | 13/327 |
| Sutherland, Eliza | Nye, Henry | Jun 19 1843 | 5/283B |
| Sutten, John D | Dodds, Sarah | May 14 1845 | 8/95B |
| Sutter, William | McGahee, Martha Ann | Mar 1 1851 | 11/126 |
| Sutton, George | Tucker, Sarah | Mar 12 1828 | 2/14 |
| Sutton, James | Chumperios, Julia ? | Mar 8 1847 | 8/220 |
| Sutton, James | Champenois, Julia ? | Mar 8 1847 | 8/220 |
| Sutton, John S | Lewis, Julia A | May 6 1845* | 8/92B |
| Suzor, Andri | Cooly, Mary Ann | Mar 16 1837* | 3/75 |
| Swager, John | Snyder, Rosina | 1825* | OIB |
| Swaglich, Joseph | Mulligan, Cecilia | Jul 28 1849* | 8/384 |
| Swain, Isaac | Scully, Mary | Jul 14 1847 | 8/245 |
| Swain, Mary E | Lott, Elisha B | Jan 21 1845 | 8/67B |
| Swain, Stephen | Prescott, Nancy Ann | Mar 24 1825* | 1/70 |
| Swainey, George | Marshall, Harriet L | Feb 26 1844 | 5/325B |
| Swasey, Henry R | Moses, Elmira (Elvirna) | Aug 4 1845 | 8/114B |
| Swear, Peter | Gamble, Margaret | Aug 31 1818* | CM |
| Sweat, Martha | Odom, Vincent | Feb 22 1853 | 12/179 |
| Sweeney, Elisabeth | Howard, James | Nov 8 1852 | 12/52 |
| Sweeney, Maria | Burke, Thomas | Dec 11 1841 | 5/161B |
| Sweeney, Rose | Bastable, Richard | Jul 27 1852 | 11/273 |
| Sweeny, John | Meley, Elisabeth | Jul 26 1850 | 11/272 |
| Sweetser, Henry C | Folke, Christian | May 8 1852 | 11/247 |
| Swift, Ann | Kelly, Thomas | Aug 18 1853 | 12/384 |
| Swift, Elizabeth | Davidson, William | Dec 23 1845 | 8/132B |
| Swift, Mary | Kelly, Patrick | Apr 15 1854 | 13/183 |
| Swift, Samuel G | Maguire, Catherine C | Aug 30 1833* | 2/811 |
| Swiler, Virginia | Yost, Richard S | Dec 19 1836* | 3/65 |
| Swindermann, Thomas | Stouter, Christina | Jul 2 1847* | 8/244 |
| Swiney, Thomas (Sweeney) | Forlay, Ellen (Farley) | Jun 12 1852 | 11/261 |

| BRIDE OR GROOM | SPOUSE | DATE | BK/PAGE |
|---|---|---|---|
| Swink, Barbary | Brocker, John | Feb 10 1852 | 11/214 |
| Swis, John | Smith, Almeda | Apr 1 1840* | 3/197 |
| Switt, Caroline B | Meader, William E | Sep 18 1839* | 3/187 |
| Sylas, Joseph (Salas) | Larrey, Malies | Aug 24 1853* | 12/394 |
| Sylva, Mary Ann | Eckstine, Jacob | Jun 20 1848* | 8/310 |
| Sylvester, Mary | Jones, Edward | Sep 16 1841 | 5/152B |
| Sylvia, John | Lee, Mary Ann | Aug 17 1841* | 5/148B |
| Synott, John C (Lynott) | Tice, Eliza | Jan 28 1845* | 8/69B |
| Sysuan, Edward B | Oxenham, Mary Ann | Dec 18 1835* | 3/33 |

T

| | | | |
|---|---|---|---|
| Tabele, Maria A | Sands, Abra L (Capt) | Aug 16 1820* | CM |
| Taben, Winney | Baro, Pierr | Jul 2 1853 | 12/338 |
| Tabott, Emma (Talcott) | Norman, John Moore | Nov 21 1843 | 7/37B |
| Tachoir, Francis | O'Hara, Sarah | Jul 28 1846 | 8/182 |
| Tachoir, Francois | Hainsworth, Martha | Jul 15 1846* | 8/179 |
| Tachois, Francois ? | Sea, Margarette | May 14 1838* | 3/125 |
| Tachoir, Francois ? | Lihy, Margarette (Leahy) | 1838* | OIB |
| Tagart, Jacob A | Miller, Margaret | Mar 12 1853 | 12/191 |
| Taggard, Elijah (Taggart) | Carnvella, Sarah Jane | Oct 11 1849 | 11/9 |
| Taggart, Eliza Jane | Wood, Alexander M | Oct 25 1852 | 12/35 |
| Tait, Robert | Erwin, Mary J | Dec 2 1851 | 11/191 |
| Talbot, James | Conley, Margarett | Aug 28 1848* | 8/321 |
| Talbot, John | Prentice, Mary | Feb 18 1825 | 1/64 |
| Talcott, Emma | Norman, John Moore | Nov 21 1843 | 5/306B |
| Talcott, Virginia | Sager, Edmund M | Aug 24 1841* | 5/132B |
| Tallent, Patrick | Murphy, Mary | Apr 17 1854 | 13/186 |
| Tally, Anne | Temple, S C | Jul 11 1837* | 3/90 |
| Tally, Horace | Millise, Elizabeth | Apr 18 1838* | 3/119 |
| Tally, Sarah Jane | Humphrey, William D | Aug 22 1845 | 8/116B |
| Tanebaum, Amalia | Epstein, Isaac | Apr 29 1853* | 12/259 |
| Tankersley, Caroline A | Barnewall, Henry | Oct 19 1852 | 12/31 |
| Tankersley, Frederick A | Dades, Agnes W | Nov 20 1851 | 11/188 |
| Tankersley, Gertrude | Wanroy, John I V | Oct 18 1842* | 5/225B |
| Tankersley, Richard | Mottus, Gertrude | Apr 3 1818* | CM |
| Tankersly, Gertrude E | Miller, Robinson | Dec 5 1848 | 8/336 |
| Tannebau, Dora | Emanuel, Baruch M | Nov 10 1852* | 12/57 |
| Tanner, Elizabeth A | Fraser, William M | Mar 17 1853* | 12/196 |
| Tanner, Franklin | Holcomb, Maria L | Jan 24 1849 | 8/349 |
| Tanner, Sally M | Goff, James | Feb 28 1834* | 2/451 |
| Tapineo, Valentine (Tassin) | Close, Adeline | Mar 8 1849* | 8/360 |
| Tapp, Anna M | Butler, George B | Jan 13 1831* | 2/146 |
| Tappia, Manuel Jose | Lamas, Alice Frances | Mar 2 1848* | 8/288 |
| Tappler, Lydia | James, Joel C | Jan 15 1853 | 12/134 |
| Tarditto, Isabella H | Rodrigues, Joaquim | Oct 23 1837* | 3/93 |

| BRIDE OR GROOM | SPOUSE | DATE | BK/PAGE |
|---|---|---|---|
| Tardy, Augustus J | Stewart, Mary Ann | Jun 3 1843 | 5/277B |
| Tardy, Balthazar | Austin, Clara H | Feb 1 1836* | 3/39 |
| Tardy, Cecilia F | O'Connor, Edward | Sep 24 1834* | 2/141 |
| Tardy, Edwin | Broughton, Elsey M | Jul 20 1852 | 11/270 |
| Tardy, Virginia M | Van Kleek, Henry D | Dec 19 1836* | 3/65 |
| Tarleton, John | Collins, Nancy Ann | Mar 24 1838 | 3/117 |
| Tarlton, Caroline M B | Mackay, Robert | May 10 1852* | 11/248 |
| Tarnaker, John (Tumaker) | Orange, Annie | Apr 20 1846 | 7/414B |
| Tarobocchia, Thomas | Scopinich, Antonia | Aug 25 1854 | 13/320 |
| Tarrant, Catharine | Bissardon, John C | Oct 20 1848* | 8/328 |
| Tartt, Thomas E | Riggs, Martha A | Jun 20 1840* | 5/29B |
| Tarvin, Margaret | Anger, Mathew B | Apr 27 1813* | WB1/7 |
| Tate, David | Coleman, Penny | Jun 26 1814* | WB 1/19 |
| Tate, Zachariah | Wisener, Barbara | Mar 18 1824 | 1/26 |
| Tatem, Alabama | Eichar, Peter | Nov 10 1853 | 13/12 |
| Tatum, Claudia C | Church, Thomas B | May 15 1838* | 3/126 |
| Tatum, Mary G | Scattergoods, Benjamin F | Oct 12 1842* | 5/222B |
| Tatum, Sarah E | McIlvain, Andrew | Jul 25 1844 | 8/34B |
| Tautchton, Sandsley, C | Parker, Caroline C | Oct 8 1836* | 3/60 |
| Tavernier, Elizabeth | Fenouil, Francis | Apr 17 1855 | 14/106 |
| Tayler, Catharine | Provincial, E Paul | Jan 13 1851 | 11/111 |
| Tayler, Mary | Davis, James | Aug 5 1839* | 3/184 |
| Taylor, Betsey | Liblenjohns, John | 1826* | OIB |
| Taylor, Catherine | Rossette, Peter | May 31 1842* | 5/190B |
| Taylor, Champe | McGowin, Cynthia | Sep 26 1839* | 3/187 |
| Taylor, Charlotte M | Garrett, Richard W | Mar 24 1847* | 8/222 |
| Taylor, Cynthia Ann | Hamilton, George M | Jul 4 1855 | 14/187 |
| Taylor, Eliza E | Backus, Joseph B | Dec 21 1841 | 5/163B |
| Taylor, Elizabeth | Doran, James | Nov 13 1843* | 5/303B |
| Taylor, Henry A | Jameson, Narcissa | 1838* | OIB |
| Taylor, James | Anderson, Susannah | Mar 11 1821* | CM |
| Taylor, James H | Hendrix, Neomi | Aug 14 1850 | 11/80 |
| Taylor, John C | Trust, Sarah Ann | May 24 1851 | 11/152 |
| Taylor, John M | Gunnison, Clementine F | Dec 4 1850* | 11/101 |
| Taylor, John W | Huston, Louisa J | Dec 10 1838* | 3/151 |
| Taylor, John W | Meeker, Louisa | May 4 1847 | 8/233 |
| Taylor, Loisa (wid) | Gartman, Henry A | Jan 29 1853 | 12/154 |
| Taylor, Margaret | Simpson, Frederick | Feb 1 1853 | 12/159 |
| Taylor, Martha Ann | Hendrix, Joel | Oct 16 1840* | 5/49B |
| Taylor, Martha M | Sandiford, John B | Jun 15 1848* | 8/309 |
| Taylor, Mary | Warren, John Carter | Apr 22 1839* | 3/168 |
| Taylor, Mary A | McRae, Malcolm I | Aug 24 1842 | 5/217B |
| Taylor, Mary Ann | Abrahams, Tobias | Apr 1 1840* | 5/16 |
| Taylor, Mary Jane | Reese, Jacob | Mar 10 1849 | 8/361 |
| Taylor, Olivia A | Mather, Thomas | 1827* | OIB |
| Taylor, Stephen B | Simmons, Francis R E | Dec 1 1840* | 5/69B |
| Taylor, William | Huffman, Alvina | Mar 3 1848* | 8/289 |
| Taylor, William | Mead, Eliza H | May 27 1828 | 2/27 |
| Taylor, William | Strayhorn, Nancy Jane | Jul 18 1851 | 11/166 |
| Taylor, William | Graves, Charity | Jun 30 1842* | 5/209B |
| Taylor, William | Whalen, Bridget | Sep 6 1852 | 11/283 |
| Taylor, William F. | Holcombe, Virginia A. | Apr 20 1841* | 5/125B |
| Taylor, William H. | Tilghman, Hannah H. | Oct 17 1850 | 11/89 |
| Tazhf, Napoleon | Murphr, Ellen | Jan 30 1841 | 4/31B |
| Tease, Nancy | Johnson, Charlie H. | Mar 1 1842 | 5/185B |
| Tedder, Jemimah | Sullivan, Mark | Oct 28 1829 | 2/98 |
| Tegan, Margaret | Reilly, James | Mar 29 1851 | 11/132 |
| Temple, Anne | Fairley, Archibald G. | Oct 17 1848 | 8/328 |
| Temple, S C | Tally, Anne | Jul 11 1837* | 3/90 |
| Tendral, Amanda | Mondrano, Paul | Feb 17 1849 | 8/358 |
| Tenemy, Paul (Tierney) | Hogan, Catherine | May 24 1843* | 5/275B |
| Tenier, Annette | Charley, Francis | Mar 22 1841 | 4/701B |
| Tenis, Drederick | Harns, Catharine | Aug 10 1842 | 5/215 |
| Tensdale, Mary | Cleveland, George, Jr. | Jun 9 1841* | 5/136 |

| BRIDE OR GROOM | SPOUSE | DATE | BK/PAGE |
|---|---|---|---|
| Tereice, William J | Hiren, Catherine A | Jan 10 1855 | 14/11 |
| Terisis, Rebecca | Hunter, Charles | Oct 14 1840* | 5/55 |
| Terle, Maria | McCartney, Patrick | Mar 31 1855 | 14/93 |
| Ternan, Thomas | McCabe, Susan | Apr 19 1855 | 14/112 |
| Terrenes, Louisa | Casabuena, Gabriel | Jun 14 1847 | 8/242 |
| Terril, William | McGary, Ann | Apr 5 1845 | 8/84B |
| Terry, James | Draper, Mary | Apr 30 1855 | 14/126 |
| Teschemacker, Julia | Goldslig, William | Feb 2 1850 | 11/37 |
| Test, Edward F. | Goodman, Emma Francis | May 24 1841* | 5/132B |
| Test, Martha | Sumwalt, James M. | Dec 12 1839* | 5/3 |
| Tetlow, Matilda | Smith, Robert M. | Jul 4 1849* | 8/397 |
| Tew, Caroline M. | Moore, Edward W. | Mar 15 1848 | 8/292 |
| Tew, Elenor H. | Rogers, Bethel T. | Jan 3 1848 | 8/275 |
| Tew, Thomas R. | Moore, Mary W. | Mar 14 1848 | 8/292 |
| Thacher, Lucy S. | Van Antwerp, Henry | May 31 1841* | 5/134B |
| Thary, Margaret N | Debrier, Antonie | Apr 27 1853 | 12/257 |
| Theben, Marian | Beck, Louis Nelson | Feb 1 1849 | 8/352 |
| Theman, Henry (Thomas) | Harris, Mary | Jan 6 1843* | 5/241 |
| Theodore, Mary | Calderon, Francis | Jun 2 1831 | 2/175 |
| Thierriat, Ambrose | Hall, Sarah Ann | Apr 8 1837* | 3/80 |
| Thomas, Amanda J | Bazemore, William J | Mar 1 1854 | 13/147 |
| Thomas, Amazon C | Mansker, James E | Apr 11 1854 | 13/178 |
| Thomas, Ann Elizabeth | Myer, John H. | Mar 28 1840* | 3/196 |
| Thomas, Benjamin T | Smith, Epsey C | Dec 26 1855 | 14/317 |
| Thomas, Edgar | Perryman, Martha E. | Feb 4 1852 | 11/212 |
| Thomas, Henry | Harris, Mary | Jan 6 1843* | 5/241B |
| Thomas, John | Monk, Francis M | Oct 26 1847 | 8/261 |
| Thomas, John F | Blocker, Virginia M | May 2 1855 | 14/127 |
| Thomas, Lewis A. | Moore, Elnora | Apr 8 1846 | 8/156B |
| Thomas, Louise S | Fisher, John H | Nov 17 1854 | 13/383 |
| Thomas, Margaret | Thomas, Seth | Dec 31 1841* | 5/166B |
| Thomas, Mark | Goodman, Sarah | Feb 21 1844 | 5/324B |
| Thomas, Martha Ann | Saxon, Jacob J. | Jul 30 1845 | 8/113B |
| Thomas, Miranda Catherine | Holly, Hilleary C. | Mar 10 1849* | 8/361 |
| Thomas, Missouri Jane | Wilcox, Jeremiah Briggs | Mar 17 1845 | 8/79B |
| Thomas, Norah | Venn, George (Finn) | Apr 4 1843 | 5/258B |
| Thomas, Norah | Finn, George (Venn) | Apr 4 1843 | 5/258B |
| Thomas, Seth | Thomas, Margaret | Dec 31 1841* | 5/166B |
| Thomas, Susan | Silburn, James | Apr 28 1855 | 14/121 |
| Thomas, William | Peters, Mary E | 1822* | OIB |
| Thomas, William M | Brannan, Eliza | Mar 6 1855 | 14/74 |
| Thomas, Young (wid) | Miller, Presteline (wid) | Mar 13 1855* | 14/83 |
| Thomason, James H. | Flinn, Mary Ann | Jun 23 1842 | 5/207B |
| Thomison, Mathew D. | Schroebel, Louisa A. | Mar 22 1848* | 8/295 |
| Thompkins, Caroline ? | Hartley, Michael | May 17 1840 | 4/4151B |
| Thompson, Aaron | Smith, Elizabeth | Aug 30 1851 | 11/174 |
| Thompson, Alexander | Morris, Mary Jane | Sep 19 1845 | 8/118B |
| Thompson, Andrew | Sims, Mary J | Oct 21 1853 | 12/424 |
| Thompson, Ann | Cameron, John R. | Dec 14 1846 | 8/205 |
| Thompson, Ann | Loveridge, Charles E. | May 28 1844 | 8/23B |
| Thompson, B W | Hughs, Martha Ann | Oct 21 1845 | 8/121B |
| Thompson, Benjamin | Burgess, Phebbe (Burgs) | Jul 28 1842 | 5/212B |
| Thompson, Betsey | Tims, Peter H. | Aug 10 1842 | 5/215B |
| Thompson, Betsey | Dennis, Peter H ? | Aug 10 1842 | 6/183 |
| Thompson, Catharine | Wilson, John | Jun 3 1846 | 8/170 |
| Thompson, Catharine | Woods, William | Dec 17 1840* | 5/77B |
| Thompson, Catherine | Gurley, Leonard | Jan 1 1842* | 5/166B |
| Thompson, Charles | Orkerk, Elizabeth | 1849* | OIB |
| Thompson, Charles J | Miller, Amanda | Jul 2 1853 | 12/344 |
| Thompson, Clarinda Sophia | Lowell, Marlin | Jun 1 1846 | 8/170 |
| Thompson, Cornelia J | Marlow, George F | Oct 16 1839* | 3/188 |
| Thompson, Drury | Conway, Eliza F. | Dec 5 1829* | 2/106 |
| Thompson, Edward | Russell, Ellen | Jan 29 1840* | 5/10 |
| Thompson, Eleanor | Brantley, Ethlebert | Apr 30 1831* | 2/164 |

| BRIDE OR GROOM | SPOUSE | DATE | BK/PAGE |
|---|---|---|---|
| Thompson, Eliza | Davis, John L | Apr 29 1850 | 11/56 |
| Thompson, Eliza H. | Keys, J.R. | Jan 15 1841* | 5/89B |
| Thompson, Elizabeth | Priester, Rudolph | Mar 12 1841* | 5/116B |
| Thompson, Elizabeth | Joseph, Anthony | Mar 29 1844* | 8/8B |
| Thompson, George | McGee, Johana | Jun 18 1845 | 8/104B |
| Thompson, Jane | Miller, Francis W. | Jul 26 1845 | 8/112B |
| Thompson, Janet | Montgomery, William S. | Jun 2 1849 | 8/379 |
| Thompson, Jeremiah R. | Brown, Margaret | Sep 26 1844 | 8/42B |
| Thompson, John | McDonald, Catharine | Jun 2 1841* | 5/134B |
| Thompson, John | Murfree, Sarah | Jun 22 1852* | 11/265 |
| Thompson, Joseph P. | Alvarez, Gertrude | Jan 6 1842 | 5/169B |
| Thompson, Lawrence H. | Gaffney, Ann | Jun 8 1846 | 8/171 |
| Thompson, Margaret Ann | Coleman, Henry F. | Jul 1 1846 | 8/176 |
| Thompson, Margetta ? | Jorette, John (Toretto) | Sep 22 1840* | 5/47B |
| Thompson, Margarett | Toretto, John (Jorette) | Sep 27 1840* | 5/47B |
| Thompson, Martha E | Hanscom, Frank D | Apr 12 1854* | 13/179 |
| Thompson, Mary | Johnson, Peter I. | May 12 1841* | 5/130B |
| Thompson, Mary | Quinland, Andrew | May 16 1854 | 13/226 |
| Thompson, Mary Ann | Martin, John | Sep 18 1852* | 12/7 |
| Thompson, Pholley (Phalbey) | Foster, George | Apr 10 1846 | 8/156B |
| Thompson, Samuel | Walters, Rehama A | Dec 18 1855 | 14/306 |
| Thompson, Samuel J. | Rhan, Margaret | Jun 29 1840* | 5/30B |
| Thompson, Thomas | Burnes, Mary | Mar 7 1849 | 8/360 |
| Thompson, Thomas | Exton, Ellenor C | Aug 7 1854* | 13/305 |
| Thompson, Thomas I. | Burke, Margaret | Jun 24 1835* | 3/18 |
| Thompson, William | Mellon, Eliza | Aug 13 1847 | 8/253 |
| Thompson, William | Horn, Eliza | Aug 17 1854 | 13/313 |
| Thomson, Margaret McRobie | Borrowscale, Fearon W. | Jun 9 1842* | 5/205B |
| Thomson, Mary | Dade, Robert R. | Jun 14 1820* | CM |
| Thomson, Walter | Dugan, Mary | May 9 1849* | 8/375 |
| Thormerhlen, Claus | Post, Anna Catharina | Jun 6 1844 | 8/26B |
| Thorn, Mary | Judson, Lewis | 1826* | OIB |
| Thornton, Benjamin | Trenier, Zatrede | Sep 1 1844 | 8/40B |
| Thornton, Rosanna | Murray, John | Oct 13 1847* | 8/259 |
| Thornton, Thomas | Lynes, Mary | Sep 6 1852 | 11/283 |
| Thornton, Willis | Stephens, Esther | Aug 13 1835* | 3/25 |
| Threefoot, Abraham | Levi, Terese | Nov 13 1850* | 11/97 |
| Threefoot, Ridgell ? | Weiss, Abraham J | Aug 20 1853 | 12/390 |
| Thrower, Sterling | Barnes, Sarah E. | Feb 5 1855 | 3/7 |
| Thurber, William K | Bolling, Julia C. | Dec 23 1848* | 8/340 |
| Tiarney, Paul | Hogan, Catherine | May 24 1843 | 5/275B |
| Tibble, John L (Tribble) | Hall, Missouri | May 28 1842 | 5/204B |
| Tiblin, Victor | Bossorge, Elizabeth | Nov 20 1839* | 5/1 |
| Tice, Eliza | Synott, John Carroll | Jan 28 1845* | 8/69B |
| Tice, Eliza | Lynott, John Carroll | Jan 28 1845* | 8/69B |
| Ticknon, Mary E | Boardman, Benjamin F. | Jul 30 1851 | 11/171 |
| Tierney, Paul | Hogan, Catherine | May 24 1843* | 5/275 |
| Tierney, Ellen | O'Neal, Patrick G. | Jun 7 1838* | 3/131 |
| Tighe, Philip | Dowdell, Mary | Dec 1 1843* | 5/308B |
| Tilghman, Hannah H. | Taylor, William H. | Oct 17 1850 | 11/89 |
| Tilghman, John H. | Hollinger, Octavia | Dec 20 1849 | 11/26 |
| Tillman, Martha | Mizell, James | Feb 11 1845 | 8/72B |
| Tillman, Richard | Wheeler, Elizabeth | Apr 29 1845 | 8/89B |
| Tilman, Gideon | Bounds, Mary Ann D. | Aug 15 1832 | 2/1371 |
| Tim, Esther | Hermann, Moses | Jan 6 1855* | 14/1 |
| Tim, Sarah | Huchberger, Lehman | Dec 3 1855 | 14/298 |
| Timm, John | Unknown | Jul 22 1841* | 4/441B |
| Timmons, Jane | Lynch, John | Oct 15 1839* | 3/188 |
| Tims, Peter H. (Tenis) | Thompson, Betsey | Aug 10 1842 | 5/215 |
| Tine, Caroline | Cohen, Herman M | Jan 10 1853 | 12/119 |
| Tingman, John | Mitchell, Sarah Ellenor | Apr 1 1844 | 8/8B |
| Tipton, William B | Lacoste, Irene C | Nov 19 1853 | 13/17 |
| Tisdale, Eliza | Magee, Jacob | Dec 4 1834* | 2/1842 |
| Tisdale, Hannah C. | Smith, James M. | Apr 12 1836* | 3/44 |

| BRIDE OR GROOM | SPOUSE | DATE | BK/PAGE |
|---|---|---|---|
| Tisdale, Henry | Bancroft, Harriett | Feb 3 1846 | 8/144B |
| Tisdale, John B. | Read, Virginia M. | Feb 15 1849* | 8/358 |
| Tisdale, Mary Eliza | Magee, Jacob | Dec 4 1834* | 2/1841 |
| Tisdale, Nathan O.I. | McCrae, Maria Louiza | Sep 29 1838* | 3/142 |
| Tisley, Henrietta | McGarr, Peter | Jun 7 1844 | 8/26B |
| Titley, Henrietta | McGurr, Peter | Jun 7 1844 | 7/293B |
| Titter, Margaret Ann | McKay, John | Jan 3 1848 | 8/274 |
| Titus, Joseph | James, Elizabeth | Jun 5 1837* | 3/85 |
| Titus, Victoria | Wilson, William | Oct 20 1855 | 14/257 |
| Tobias, Theodore | Putcher, Fanny | Mar 15 1852* | 11/226 |
| Tobin, Thomas | Foley, Elizabeth | Apr 22 1854 | 13/201 |
| Tobler, Paul | Kroner, Margaretta | Dec 18 1832* | 2/1251 |
| Toca, Joseph A. | Jacob, Catherine | Dec 3 1833* | 2/661 |
| Todd, John B. | Colina, Louisa | May 23 1845 | 8/97B |
| Todd, Martha B. | Smith, Charles | Aug 6 1840* | 5/39B |
| Todd, William | Monk, Rebecca | Apr 19 1823 | 1/0 |
| Todd, William L. | Lewis, Mary E. | Mar 30 1843 | 5/256B |
| Todenere, Virgine (Ladnier) | Guton, Jean Batiste | Nov 23 1836* | 3/63 |
| Toemey, Bridget | McTeirnan, Patrick K | Oct 25 1855 | 14/264 |
| Tohal, Ann | Collaton, Martin | Feb 27 1854* | 13/143 |
| Tolle, Charles H. | Jones, Ellen | Jan 15 1852* | 11/204 |
| Toman, Mary | Scott, Henry H. | Jun 17 1836* | 3/51 |
| Tomby, Susannah | Murray, James | Mar 7 1843 | 5/252B |
| Tomley, Susannah | Murray, James | Mar 7 1843 | 6/292B |
| Tomlinson, William | Clawdes, Mary | Sep 24 1828 | 2/42 |
| Tompkins, Caroline | Hartley, Michael | May 17 1840* | 5/28B |
| Tompkins, Harriet | Brown, Morgan D. | Dec 23 1824 | 1/57 |
| Tompkins, Thomas G. | Hobart, Carolina M. | Apr 24 1828 | 2/23 |
| Tompkins, William Q | Johnson, Lavinia | May 31 1855 | 14/154 |
| Tonar, Patrick | Cournell, Ann (Connell) | Nov 6 1838* | 3/146 |
| Tool, Bridget (O'Toole) | McCowen, Robert | Jun 2 1851 | 11/154 |
| Toole, Margaret | Feely, William | May 9 1855 | 14/135 |
| Toomey, Bridget | Philan, Edward | Nov 2 1839* | 3/190 |
| Toomey, Margaret | Mulholland, James | Jan 12 1854 | 13/74 |
| Toomey, Mary | Hyde, James | Dec 31 1844* | 8/64B |
| Toomy, Julia Ann | McKay, William | Jan 7 1846 | 8/137B |
| Toomy, Margaret | Brown, John | Aug 21 1852 | 11/278 |
| Toomy, Mary | Cameron, Alexander | Jan 4 1845 | 8/65B |
| Torbin, Alice | Davis, George | Apr 29 1854 | 13/210 |
| Toretto, John (Jorette) | Thompson, Margetta | Sep 22 1840 | 5/47B |
| Tormey, Marie L | Remacle, Joseph | Aug 9 1853 | 12/379 |
| Torrance, George W | Tuite, Cara (Pinto) | Jul 6 1848* | 8/313 |
| Torrance, George W | Pinto, Cora (Tuite) | Jul 6 1848* | 8/313 |
| Torrance, Thomas J | Bateman, Margaret A. | Nov 8 1847* | 8/264 |
| Torrans, Charles F | Stewart, Martha | Aug 22 1850 | 11/82 |
| Torrans, William H | Charpen, Huldah | Jan 16 1851 | 11/113 |
| Torrans, William P | McCann, Catherine D. | Apr 5 1851 | 11/135 |
| Tortes, James | Hollinger, Margarett | Apr 8 1839* | 3/165 |
| Tosch, Margaret | Pettroff, Conrad | Feb 25 1854 | 13/139 |
| Tosch, Mary Ann (Fosch) | Flannory, William | Feb 2 1844 | 5/319B |
| Tosh, Lewis Prosper | Anderson, Mary Jane | Mar 22 1843 | 6/302B |
| Tosh, Peter | Collins, Mary Jane | Sep 23 1846 | 8/190 |
| Touart, Louis | Quina, Margaret | Nov 18 1833* | 2/701 |
| Toulmin, Edmund P. | Bowers, Francis E. | Apr 10 1849* | 8/367 |
| Toulmin, Emma M | Poe, George Jr | 1827* | 0IB |
| Toulmin, Frances E. | Poe, George W. | Feb 1 1833* | 2/1171 |
| Toulmin, Frances Helen | Toulmin, Joshua M.S. | Mar 23 1846 | 8/153B |
| Toulmin, Jane | Robertson, William H. | Jan 1 1821* | CM |
| Toulmin, Joshua M.S. | Toulmin, Frances Hellen | Mar 23 1846 | 8/153B |
| Toulmin, Louisa Anna | Bowers, Lloyd | Jun 11 1846* | 8/172 |
| Toulmin, Lucinda | Dobson, George | Dec 30 1833* | 2/631 |
| Toulmin, Mary C. | Campbell, James | Jan 14 1824 | 1/19 |
| Toulmin, May | Gaines, Edmund P. | Feb 12 1847 | 8/216 |
| Toulmin, Susan | English, Thomas M. | Nov 25 1833* | 2/681 |

| BRIDE OR GROOM | SPOUSE | DATE | BK/PAGE |
|---|---|---|---|
| Toulmin, Theophilous L | Juzan, Arminth (Arminta) | May 13 1821* | CM |
| Toulmy, Ann | Finch, John | Feb 21 1852 | 11/220 |
| Toulnot, Jacob N (Poulnot) | Wylie, Mary Jane | Dec 22 1845 | 8/113B |
| Toutchston, Landsley C | Parker, Caroline C | 1836* | OIB |
| Toutchstone, Mary | Poso, Frances | Mar 30 1829* | 2/79 |
| Tower, Luther F | Yuille, Catherine | Jul 4 1853* | 12/345 |
| Towers, Susan | Britton, Alexander | May 21 1832* | 2/1481 |
| Towle, Amos | Alvarez, Louisa M. | Jan 10 1846 | 8/139B |
| Townsend, Amelia | McTyeire, Holland N. | Nov 8 1847 | 8/264 |
| Townsend, George | Green, Margaret | Jun 15 1843 | 5/282B |
| Townsend, John W | Everett, Jane | 1827* | OIB |
| Townsend, Lemuel R | Herpin, Urania M | May 1 1850 | 11/57 |
| Townsend, Margaret | Hall, John S | Jul 23 1855 | 14/197 |
| Townsend, Thomas | Williams, Caroline | Jun 1 1850 | 11/64 |
| Townsley, Francis | Smith, Catherine | Jun 12 1855 | 14/170 |
| Townsley, Louis O | Barclay, Mary E | Apr 16 1852* | 11/237 |
| Townsley, Marie Coralie | Andouy, Charles | Jul 4 1843* | 5/286B |
| Tracey, Ann | Scott, William | Sep 12 1839* | 3/186 |
| Trachy, Edward | Kemmer, Johanna C.H. | Apr 5 1852 | 11/232 |
| Tracy, Ann | Scott, William | Apr 17 1851 | 11/139 |
| Tracy, Ellen | O'Connor, Morris | Nov 29 1840* | 5/69B |
| Tracy, Ellen | Byrnes, Charles | Apr 30 1855 | 14/125 |
| Tracy, George | Finnegin, Mary | Aug 20 1849* | 8/398 |
| Tracy, James | Coil, Catherine | Jun 2 1836* | 3/49 |
| Tracy, Mary A | Hansberry, Joseph | Nov 22 1853 | 13/23 |
| Traicy, Anne (wid) | Labernedie, John (widr) | Nov 17 1853 | 13/16 |
| Trainer, Ellen | Somers, John D | Nov 10 1855 | 14/276 |
| Traino, William | Davidson, Margaret | Dec 15 1851* | 11/194 |
| Traites, John (Trailer) | Brown, Matilda | Aug 6 1843 | 5/291B |
| Tramel, Albert G. | Spalding, Caroline J. | Sep 8 1851 | 11/177 |
| Tranier, Charles W. | Bernard, Mary A. | Apr 5 1851* | 11/134 |
| Trask, Frederick | French, Jane | Sep 27 1843* | 5/298B |
| Travers, Patrick | Higgins, Mary Ann | Apr 13 1852 | 11/236 |
| Travis, Enoch | Dade, Harriet E. | Mar 19 1839* | 3/160 |
| Travis, John H | Caldwell, Mary A | May 17 1854 | 13/227 |
| Travis, Mary S. | Beck, Robert | Jan 29 1846 | 8/142B |
| Travis, Rebecca (Terisis) | Hunter, Charles | Oct 14 1840* | 5/55B |
| Treefoot, Ridgell | Weiss, Abraham J (widr) | Aug 20 1853 | 12/390 |
| Tremir, John B | Meigs, Louisa | Jan 5 1841* | 5/85B |
| Trenier, Annete | Charly, Francis | Mar 22 1841* | 5/118 |
| Trenier, Fermin | Bazile, Bazelice | Jan 27 1834* | 2/491 |
| Trenier, Ferron | Durette, Elizabeth | Apr 23 1845 | 8/88B |
| Trenier, John ? | Henry, Mary | 1826* | OIB |
| Trenier, John ? | Henry, Mary | 1827* | OIB |
| Trenier, John | St. John, Catherine | Jan 27 1831* | 2/149 |
| Trenier, John Jr. | Andre, Delphina | Apr 29 1849* | 8/370 |
| Trenier, John B | Meigs, Louisa | Jan 5 1841* | 5/85B |
| Trenier, Sabine | Nicholas, Augustus | Feb 4 1834* | 2/481 |
| Trenier, Zatrede | Thornton, Benjamin | Sep 5 1844 | 8/40B |
| Treuathem, Elizabeth | Ewing, William (Eqing) | Jul 9 1838* | 3/135 |
| Treynor, Martha | Carminetti, John | Mar 25 1844* | 8/7B |
| Tribb, Margaret | Brown, William | May 31 1839* | 3/175 |
| Tribble, Mary | Hall, Namon | Aug 7 1844 | 8/38B |
| Trinier, Annete | Charly, Francis | Mar 22 1841* | 5/118 |
| Troost, Lewis | Evans, Carolina B. | Apr 15 1846 | 8/157B |
| Trotter, Ann | Hall, Daniel E. Jr. | Feb 5 1845 | 8/71B |
| Trouillet, Louise | McDieauerette, Thomas | Jul 1 1835* | 3/18 |
| Trouillet, Marceline | Krebs, Joseph | 1826* | OIB |
| Trouillet, Peter L. | Fisher, Marcellite | Feb 6 1819* | CM |
| Troy, Margaret | Hickey, Thomas | Feb 19 1855 | 14/60 |
| Truker, Engelberg | Holdinberg, Maria L | Jul 22 1844 | 8/34B |
| Trull, D C | Serra, Angelina J | May 9 1853 | 12/274 |
| Trust, Sarah Ann | Taylor, John C. | Mar 24 1851 | 11/152 |
| Truwit, Patrick | Daniel, Ellen | Jun 22 1853 | 12/328 |

| BRIDE OR GROOM | SPOUSE | DATE | BK/PAGE |
|---|---|---|---|
| Truwit, William L. | Richardson, Harriet C. | Jan 31 1843 | 5/247B |
| Try, William W. | Jones, Martha E. | Jun 30 1838* | 3/134 |
| Tucker, Aceline | Brown, Brinkley J | Aug 9 1855 | 14/207 |
| Tucker, Elizabeth | Rayford, William | May 27 1845 | 8/99B |
| Tucker, John A | Smith, Theresa | Aug 21 1854* | 13/317 |
| Tucker, Joseph | Acre, Elizabeth C. | Feb 9 1847 | 8/214 |
| Tucker, Margaret | Mott, James S. | Jan 24 1845 | 8/68B |
| Tucker, Mary | Prescott, James E. | Aug 20 1835* | 3/25 |
| Tucker, Mary | LeFebre, Isaac | Jul 20 1837* | 3/98 |
| Tucker, Polly | Lefefere, Isaac | Jul 20 1837* | 3/98 |
| Tucker, Sarah | Sutton, George | Mar 12 1828 | 2/14 |
| Tucker, William | Davidson, Mary | May 1 1824 | 1/29 |
| Tuite, Cara (Pinto) | Torrance, George W | Jul 6 1848* | 8/313 |
| Tulane, Artemise Julie | Bates, Jared | Mar 17 1842* | 5/186B |
| Tulee, Thomas | Lee, Margaret | 1827* | OIB |
| Tully, John | Hart, Ellen | Mar 7 1846 | 8/150B |
| Tumaker, John | Orange, Anna | Apr 20 1846 | 8/159 |
| Tuney, Mary Ann | Butler, William | Apr 5 1847 | 8/224 |
| Tunnage, Henry | Clarke, Ann | 1826* | OIB |
| Turcher, James | Light, Catherine E. | Oct 28 1835* | 3/31 |
| Turken, Frina | Breswitz, Christian F. | Jul 26 1844 | 8/36B |
| Turn, John | Barns, Mary V. | Feb 22 1841* | 5/108 |
| Turnbit, Nancy | Kennedy, John | Dec 29 1841 | 4/1181B |
| Turner, Amasa | Morse, Julia | 1826* | OIB |
| Turner, Catharine | Adde, William | Apr 14 1852 | 11/237 |
| Turner, Charles | Pfeiffer, Sarah | Apr 26 1854 | 13/206 |
| Turner, Cordelia | Clark, Spotswood W. | Jan 26 1852 | 11/208 |
| Turner, David | McGill, Harriet | Mar 29 1842* | 5/190B |
| Turner, George W. | Wainwright, Eliza Jane | Feb 14 1841* | 5/103B |
| Turner, Harriet | Simpson, Thomas | 1822* | OIB |
| Turner, Henry | McCaskill, Maria | Apr 22 1846 | 8/160B |
| Turner, Henry | Calloway, Mary | Aug 4 1835* | 3/21 |
| Turner, James | Hickey, Bridget | Feb 23 1846 | 8/146B |
| Turner, James | Davidson, Julia | Jul 11 1833* | 2/851B |
| Turner, Jarvis | Ewers, Marcia H. | Dec 11 1847 | 8/269 |
| Turner, Joel L. | Perkins, Rebecca | Jan 28 1841* | 5/95B |
| Turner, John | Smith, Sarah | 1836* | OIB |
| Turner, John | McNaughton, Florian | Jan 15 1834* | 2/551 |
| Turner, John D | Turner, Mary | Sep 24 1855 | 14/238 |
| Turner, John Edward | Cole, Hannah | Jan 27 1849* | 8/350 |
| Turner, Lafayette (Taylor) | Celestine, Josephine | Mar 3 1851 | 11/126 |
| Turner, Leonon | Wilson, J.B. | Feb 13 1839* | 3/157 |
| Turner, Malinda | Crenshaw, Jefferson | Feb 5 1849 | 8/353 |
| Turner, Martha | Box, George W. | Dec 23 1847 | 8/272 |
| Turner, Martha | Goff, William P. | Jun 6 1851 | 11/156 |
| Turner, Martha | McLean, Daniel | Feb 3 1845 | 8/70B |
| Turner, Martha W | Dunning, Edward | 1834* | OIB |
| Turner, Mary | Shand, William | May 18 1842* | 5/201 |
| Turner, Mary | Turner, John D | Sep 24 1855 | 14/238 |
| Turner, Noel | Farrell, Mary (Harrell) | Feb 16 1833* | 2/1121 |
| Turner, Oliver | Calloway, Frances Amanda | Apr 21 1841* | 5/125B |
| Turner, Polly | Corley, Thompson | Feb 12 1844 | 5/321B |
| Turner, Rebecca (Terisis) | Hunter, Charles | Oct 14 1840 | 4/2181B |
| Turner, Samuel Coote | Goodman, Martha Bennett | Jan 28 1847 | 8/213 |
| Turner, Samuel M. | Howell, Emily H. | Apr 10 1849* | 8/367 |
| Turner, Sarah | Rolls, William H. | Nov 13 1846 | 8/199 |
| Turner, Sarah L. | Morton, John C. | Jan 7 1851 | 11/109 |
| Turner, Susan | McCormick, Benjamin | Sep 10 1847* | 8/255 |
| Turner, Virtue | Gillespie, George W.C. | May 5 1845 | 8/91B |
| Turner, William | Woodbury, Maria | Sep 30 1840* | 5/49B |
| Turner, William E. | Broughton, Mary Ann | Sep 18 1850 | 11/86 |
| Turner, Wright ? | Crosby, Margarett | Oct 13 1840* | 5/55B |
| Turney, Lucy | Quin, Nicholas | Jan 2 1847 | 8/209 |
| Turney, Margaret | Sullivan, John | Jul 15 1850 | 11/73 |

| BRIDE OR GROOM | SPOUSE | DATE | BK/PAGE |
|---|---|---|---|
| Turnstall, Phoebe Ann | Kirby, Richard L. | May 11 1843 | 5/270B |
| Turpen, Rosealie A | Sarradait, John | Mar 11 1854 | 13/159 |
| Turpey, Winneford ? | Brady, Michael | Feb 14 1854 | 13/121 |
| Tuttle, Charles S | Hepp, Sarah A | Oct 19 1838* | 3/144 |
| Tuttle, Emily W. | Ogden, Cornelius A. | May 6 1845 | 8/92B |
| Tuttle, George R. | Hodges, Virginia A. | May 29 1849* | 8/378 |
| Tuttle, Mary L | Richardson, John E | Nov 27 1852 | 12/77 |
| Tuttle, Stephen | Malone, Emily W. | Mar 5 1829* | 2/74 |
| Tuttle, William H. | Nelius, Mary Margaret | Mar 18 1852 | 11/228 |
| Twelves, Margaret | Davidson, Samuel | Dec 22 1843 | 5/310B |
| Twelves, Robert | Lichen, Margaret | Jul 9 1841* | 5/143 |
| Twelves, Robert | Brown, Francis T. | Jul 7 1841 | 4/411B |
| Tye, Rosana | Burke, Thomas | Oct 20 1842 | 5/225 |
| Tylee, Horace (Tyler) | Murphy, Margarett Ann | Sep 3 1851 | 11/175 |
| Tylee, Mary | Fincher, John | Feb 4 1836* | 3/2 |
| Tyler, Elizabeth R | Nieth, Jacob H | Aug 5 1854 | 13/302 |
| Tyler, Rosa | Hogan, Daniel | Apr 1 1850 | 11/49 |
| Tyner, Benjamin | Miller, Margaret M. | Aug 16 1842 | 5/217B |
| Typpenhowers, Mary Ann | Etheridge, John | Jun 7 1843 | 5/280B |
| Tyrrell, William (Gyrell) | Devin, Margaret | Jul 21 1838* | 3/136 |
| Tyson, Anthony | Weaver, Sarah M | Feb 16 1854 | 13/122 |

## U

| | | | |
|---|---|---|---|
| Ullman, Barbara | Burk, Martin | Aug 8 1843* | 5/291B |
| Ulrick, John G | Chiles, Isabella C | May 17 1842* | 5/201B |
| Underman, Mary | Nicholes, Michael | Nov 15 1841 | 5/157B |
| Underwood, Nimrod | Nelson, Elizabeth A. | Apr 12 1851 | 11/137 |
| Underwood, Thomas | Smith, Catharine | Jun 28 1832* | 2/1431 |
| Uneiland, Jonas W. | Johnson, Amanda M. | Dec 9 1846 | 8/204 |
| Unger, Rebecca | Pake, Sigfried | Mar 19 1852* | 11/228 |
| Unknown | Timm, John | Jul 22 1841* | 4/441B |
| Unknown | Williams, W | Jul 23 1841* | 4/461B |
| Unruh, Mary J. | Walker, George W. | May 10 1851 | 11/148 |
| Unsworth, John | Wooten, Marceline | May 2 1842* | 5/197B |
| Untrener, Peter | Miller, Dorice | Jan 17 1852 | 11/204 |
| Urquhart, Frances | Conway, James | Jan 19 1843 | 5/244B |
| Urquhart, Henry | Philips, Missouri Ann | Jun 13 1855 | 14/172 |
| Urquhart, Polly | McDonald, Philip H. | Feb 3 1829* | 2/69 |
| Urtman, Phillip | Klien, Louisa | Feb 12 1852 | 11/217 |

V

| Bride or Groom | Spouse | Date | BK/Page |
|---|---|---|---|
| Vail, Ann E | Houston, Moses W | Dec 30 1854 | 13/425 |
| Vail, Lovick B. | Smith, Anna E. | Dec 2 1839* | 5/2 |
| Vail, Lovick B. | Austin, Sarah R. | Apr 5 1830* | 2/120 |
| Valero, Francisco | Gallagher, Amelia | Feb 28 1854 | 13/145 |
| Valette, Antoine L. | Veillon, Mari Cecile | Jun 25 1844 | 8/30B |
| Vallance, Jeremiah | Hendrix, Lydia | May 21 1853 | 12/294 |
| Vallat, Jeanne J (wid) | DeJanvry, Pierre P G | Jun 12 1848 | 8/308 |
| Valle, Andre | Steel, Emile | May 17 1825 | 1/78 |
| Valle, Joseph E. | Madot, Catherine (Pradat) | Oct 23 1838* | 3/144 |
| Valpey, Edward | Brannon, Ann | Aug 4 1840* | 5/37B |
| Van Antwerp, Henry | Thacher, Lucy S. | May 31 1841* | 5/134B |
| Van Bibber, Flabins | Hunt, Saphronia A | Mar 7 1853 | 12/185 |
| Van Buren, Thomas W. | Colbertson, Frances | May 24 1849 | 8/377 |
| Vandalson, James H. | Johnston, Margaret | May 22 1852 | 11/254 |
| Vandergriff, Earle | Browne, Elizabeth | Feb 12 1855 | 14/48 |
| Van Dorn, Earl | Godbold, Martha C. | Dec 23 1843* | 5/311B |
| Vanford, Emily A (Sanford) | Brown, Thomas G | Aug 5 1840 | 4/3981B |
| Van Fossen, Thomas L. | Alvarez, Mercelete | Apr 10 1844* | 8/11B |
| Van Hook, Marcus A. | George, Henrietta E. | Jun 22 1852 | 11/264 |
| Van Houton, Cornelius P. | Lansdalle, Abigail | Oct 28 1834* | 2/41 |
| Van Kleek, Henry D. | Tardy, Virginia M. | Dec 19 1836* | 3/65 |
| Van Kleek, Virginia M. | Read, Joshua H. | Mar 16 1843 | 5/254B |
| Vannatta, Mary E. | Burns, Thomas | Feb 3 1851 | 11/119 |
| Vanness, Jacob | Ellison, Eliza | Sep 20 1824 | 1/38 |
| Vanness, James | Leslie, Carolina F.I. | Jan 27 1836* | 3/38 |
| Van Vleek, G.W. | Lee, Mary C | Oct 31 1838* | 3/145 |
| Van Wanroy, John I | Tankersley, Gertrude | Oct 18 1842* | 5/225B |
| Varie, Rosalie V. | Nicholas, William | Oct 3 1848 | 8/326 |
| Vaughan, Eliza | Snow, Freeman | Apr 4 1848* | 8/296 |
| Vaughn, John B. | Daughdrill,_____ (Only) | Jul 9 1839* | 3/181 |
| Vaughner, John | Bush, Hannah | Jan 10 1834* | 2/561 |
| Vautrot, Gustavus E S | Pillet, Mary Josephine | Jul 21 1851 | 11/168 |
| Vedrenne, Louis H.N. | D'Aubert, Elizabeth A. | May 27 1846 | 8/170 |
| Vegoureux, Julia | Wiener, Eugene | Apr 4 1850 | 11/50 |
| Veillon, Mari Cecile | Vallette, Antoine L. | Jun 25 1844 | 8/30B |
| Veira, Louisa | Porter, William | Jul 14 1847 | 8/245 |
| Veit, Seef | Sallahamus, Chust | Feb 25 1838* | 3/158 |
| Veldaiser, Joseph | Davidson, May | Apr 9 1840* | 5/18 |
| Vengertsman, Conrad | Otte, Christina | Aug 12 1850 | 11/79 |
| Venier, Ann | McDougall, William | Jan 3 1848 | 8/274 |
| Venn, George (Fenn) | Thomas, Norah | Apr 4 1843 | 5/258 |
| Veque, John B.G. | Nicholas, Seraphine T | Jan 27 1829* | 2/66 |
| Verde, Franciso Benito | Rameras, Seraphine | Feb 21 1848 | 8/285 |
| Verdi, Luigi | Di Andrea, Harietta | Mar 13 1841* | 5/119B |
| Verndorn, Earl | Grabold, Martha Caroline | Dec 23 1843 | 7/67B |
| Verneuille, Eliza | Shea, Thomas | Dec 26 1853 | 13/53 |
| Verneuille, Jacinth Louis | Martin, Amelia Ann | Apr 15 1851 | 11/138 |
| Verneuille, Joseph | Harwell, Martha J | Jan 17 1854 | 13/85 |
| Verneuille, Marie P | McGraw, Thomas | Apr 5 1853 | 12/222 |
| Vickery, Leander J | Elliott, Elizabeth A | Apr 21 1854 | 13/200 |
| Vidal, John | Volon, Margaret | Jul 13 1853 | 12/351 |
| Vidmer, Adele | Rabby, Jacob M | Aug 30 1855 | 14/220 |
| Vielli, Joseph Victor | Loker, Mary | Mar 7 1838* | 3/114 |
| Vienne, Honore Tacite | Hutton, Charlotte Anna | Feb 24 1846 | 8/147B |
| Vignroe, Francois | Henry, Ellen | Dec 21 1824 | 1/55 |
| Vigo, Raymond | Lyons, Abbe | Jul 12 1849* | 8/389 |
| Vilaceca, Marie | Borgan, Francis | Jun 17 1832* | 2/1461 |
| Vincent, David H | Boone, Frances | Oct 24 1854 | 13/361 |
| Vincent, Joseph | Maxwell, Catharine | Jun 11 1840* | 5/27B |

| BRIDE OR GROOM | SPOUSE | DATE | BK/PAGE |
|---|---|---|---|
| Vines, Catherine | Beebe, Gustavus A. | May 23 1842* | 5/213B |
| Vines, Charles | Buckley, Rebecca | Mar 7 1835 | 3/10 |
| Vines, Charles | Ayres, Catherine | Dec 25 1837* | 3/105 |
| Viney, Charles | Reardon, Eliza T | Jan 7 1854 | 13/65 |
| Vink, Martha | Clarke, James | Jul 17 1846* | 8/179 |
| Violet, Matilda | Saink, Spencer | Apr 17 1834* | 2/301 |
| Violette, Louis A. | Gorman, Jane Sarah | Jun 11 1844 | 8/27B |
| Violette, Sarah J | March, Andrew | Aug 8 1854 | 13/307 |
| Viollet, Pierre | Wilson, Margaret | May 9 1847 | 8/233 |
| Virger, Thomas J | Elder, Sarah J | 1850* | OIB |
| Vis, Bornard | Joseph, Felicianna | Mar 31 1829* | 2/80 |
| Vitaceca, Marie | Borgen, Francis | Jun 17 1832* | 2/1461 |
| Vitman, Michael | Cuete, Marchtalena | Feb 14 1849 | 8/357 |
| Vivare, Louis | D'Olive, Catish | Nov 2 1832* | 2/1321 |
| Vivaret, Mannette | Serra, Vincent | Jan 5 1846* | 8/136B |
| Vivere, Catherine | Durette, Joseph | Mar 26 1831* | 2/158 |
| Vlaho, Emanuel | Case, Mary Ann | Mar 13 1852 | 11/226 |
| Volek, Susannah | Johnson, Peyton | Feb 24 1844 | 5/324B |
| Volkining, Frederick Wm. | Burn, Jane (Burr) | Jan 24 1842 | 5/173B |
| Volon, Margaret | Vidal, John | Jul 13 1853 | 12/351 |
| Vonars, John | Groseman, Anna | May 29 1852 | 11/256 |
| Voorhis, Peter | Sharp, Missouri A. | Apr 21 1852 | 11/240 |
| Vorsien, Cesarine | Coma, Noel Etienne | Mar 21 1851 | 11/130 |
| Vos, Mary F. | Stuart, John A. | Jun 11 1836 | 3/50 |
| Vose, Scottana R. | Graham, Charles W. | Mar 8 1828* | 2/16 |
| Vreeland, Jonas W | Johnson, Amanda M | 1846* | OIB |

W

| BRIDE OR GROOM | SPOUSE | DATE | BK/PAGE |
|---|---|---|---|
| Wachn, Lucy (Thacher) | Van Antwerp, Henry | May 31 1841 | 5/134B |
| Wacker, Ann (Walker) | Dale, Thomas J. | Jan 9 1846* | 8/138B |
| Wackernah, Christopher | Sanders, Mary M (wid) | Jul 2 1853 | 12/341 |
| Wade, Caroline M.T. | Cummings, David L. | Sep 4 1851 | 11/176 |
| Wade, Sarah Ann | Sears, George H. | Jul 5 1848 | 8/312 |
| Wadley, Nancy | Lyons, John | Jun 15 1853 | 12/320 |
| Wafford, James H | Cummings, Elizabeth J | Apr 8 1848 | 8/297 |
| Wagenbrennor, Michael | Wesh, Harriet (West) | Dec 6 1851 | 11/192 |
| Waggaman, Henry B. | Debritton, Emma | Jul 31 1849* | 8/385 |
| Waggoner, Coleman | Powell, Mary | Apr 25 1852 | 11/241 |
| Waggoner, Doras | Kraiger, Gustavies | Feb 18 1850 | 11/40 |
| Wagner, John | Schnekelberger, Carolina | Oct 28 1841* | 5/155B |
| Wagner, Louis | Fleckner, Marie Rose | Jul 24 1844 | 8/35B |
| Wainwright, Alexander | Dismukes, Nancy M. | May 29 1843 | 5/276B |
| Wainwright, Charles C | Goff, Lorrena | Sep 12 1855 | 14/229 |
| Wainwright, Eliza Jane | Turner, George W. | Feb 14 1841* | 5/103B |
| Wainwright, Isaac | Shea, Margaret | Jun 10 1854 | 13/252 |
| Wainwright, Luck | Roue, Eliza A (Rone) | Dec 7 1846 | 8/202 |
| Wainwright, Nancy M. | Cobb, Oliver S. | Feb 9 1848 | 8/282 |
| Waits, Esaias | Foster, Elizabeth | Jan 11 1836* | 3/34 |
| Waldaner, Leon | Cohen, Sarah | May 3 1847 | 8/232 |
| Waldrip, Hillen | Bates, Elizabeth M. | Feb 4 1828* | 2/7 |

| BRIDE OR GROOM | SPOUSE | DATE | BK/PAGE |
|---|---|---|---|
| Waljamott, Thomas L. | Parmentier, Amelia | Oct 22 1851 | 11/183 |
| Walker, Allice B | Pyor, Christopher J D Jr | Sep 15 1853 | 12/406 |
| Walker, Benjamin Franklin | Jones, Sarah | Apr  3 1837* | 3/77 |
| Walker, Charles | Garner, Matilda | Dec  6 1845 | 8/135B |
| Walker, Cornelia | Speake, James | Sep 25 1850 | 11/87 |
| Walker, Daniel | Youngblood, Nancy | Aug  4 1830* | 2/133 |
| Walker, Emma L | Alembert, Willoughby D | Apr 29 1853 | 12/260 |
| Walker, Francis | Simerson, Eliza Ann | Jun  4 1855 | 14/159 |
| Walker, George | Johnson, Sarah J | Oct 23 1852 | 12/33 |
| Walker, George W. | Unruh, Mary J. | May 10 1851 | 11/148 |
| Walker, George W. | Wheeler, Silester | Jul 13 1846 | 8/179 |
| Walker, Granville | Brown, Mary | Nov 27 1843 | 5/307B |
| Walker, Jacob B. | Youngblood, Susan | May  2 1833* | 2/1031 |
| Walker, Jane | Longhy, Patrick | Dec 16 1841 | 5/162B |
| Walker, John | Lampford, Rebecca | May 27 1844* | 8/33B |
| Walker, John W. | Berhok, Ann | Feb 15 1840* | 5/12 |
| Walker, Laura | Peno, Felix | May 31 1853* | 12/303 |
| Walker, Mary | Hulyr, Thomas | Sep 19 1842 | 5/220B |
| Walker, Mary | Moneagle, Edward | Feb 21 1854 | 13/128 |
| Walker, Mary Ann Paulina | Weibis, Fredrick S | Nov 29 1851 | 11/191 |
| Walker, Mary Isabella | Fiske, Thomas S. | Dec 24 1844* | 8/62B |
| Walker, Percy | Lipscomb, Ellen | Dec 27 1836* | 3/67 |
| Walker, Robert L. | Kennedy, Glorvina A. | Nov 10 1833* | 2/731 |
| Walker, Robert S. | Gascoigne, Maria S. | Dec  7 1842 | 5/232B |
| Walker, Samuel (Lemuel) | Stepson, Love | Jun 11 1838* | 3/131 |
| Walker, Virginia L | Garrow, William M | 1838* | OIB |
| Walker, Wilson | Dikeman, Susan | Nov 12 1834* | 2/11 |
| Walkinson, Isaac | Gordon, Maria | May 12 1838* | 3/125 |
| Wallace, Charles | Ladnier, Carmilite | Nov 15 1847 | 8/265 |
| Wallace, George W. | Ferguson, Anne | Jun 10 1851 | 11/157 |
| Wallace, James | Develin, Anna | Jun 26 1820* | CM |
| Wallace, Thomas S. | Hall, Mary Jane | Jul 17 1842* | 5/211B |
| Wallace, William | Fox, Maria | Aug 22 1846 | 8/185 |
| Walley, Thomas | McFadden, Mary | Mar 13 1844 | 5/327B |
| Walsh, D.R. | Barnes, Sarah | Nov 22 1836* | 3/62 |
| Walsh, Michael | Sheridan, Ellen | Mar 11 1839* | 3/159 |
| Walsh, Thomas | Bosc, Mary (Box) | Feb 14 1825 | 1/63 |
| Walter, Elizabeth | Cooper, Samuel G. | Aug 28 1851 | 11/174 |
| Walters, Rehama A | Thompson, Samuel | Dec 18 1855 | 14/306 |
| Walton, Ginyo (George) | Grica, Jane | Jun 22 1838* | 3/132 |
| Walton, John M. | Patterson, Elizabeth | Oct 18 1847 | 8/260 |
| Walton, John M | Barckley, Anna | Jun 29 1854* | 13/269 |
| Walton, Laurence | Bragg, Catharine A. | Apr 15 1847 | 8/228 |
| Walton, Martha | Strachan, George | Aug 25 1840* | 5/43B |
| Walton, Mary | Nethercott, Edward H. | May  3 1844 | 8/19B |
| Walton, Octavia C.V. | Levert, Henry S. | Feb  6 1836* | 3/40 |
| Walton, Richard | Griffin, Margaret A. | Feb 24 1845 | 8/75B |
| Waltz, Martha Elizabeth | Rouse, Layfield | Jan 10 1853 | 12/121 |
| Waltz, Sophronia | Williams, James | Jan  1 1855* | 13/428 |
| Wanroy, John I V | Tankersley, Gertrude | Oct 18 1842* | 5/225B |
| Ward, Catherine | Collins, Peter | Dec 24 1841 | 5/164B |
| Ward, Eliza | Johnston, George | 1823* | OIB |
| Ward, Harriett R. | Homer, William H. | Dec 27 1843* | 5/311B |
| Ward, Margaret Ann | Quinlan, P | Sep  4 1849 | 11/2 |
| Ward, Mary | Wilson, Charles | Apr  4 1841* | 5/126B |
| Ward, Mary | Devine, James | Apr  7 1849* | 8/366 |
| Ward, Nancy | Stringfellow, John | Aug 29 1833* | 2/801 |
| Ward, Nancy J. | Nelson, Washington | Mar 26 1852 | 11/231 |
| Ward, Rian (Brian) | Sanford, Mary F. | Dec 25 1851 | 11/198 |
| Warder, Henry | Sibley, Ellen | May 28 1831* | 2/173 |
| Wardue, Patrick | Byrnes, Ann | Feb 17 1854 | 13/123 |
| Ware, John | Johnston, Nancy | 1825* | OIB |
| Ware, Loretta E | Forrest, George | Dec 23 1839 | 5/5 |
| Ware, Mary | Hampshire, Richard | Jun 15 1854 | 13/259 |

| BRIDE OR GROOM | SPOUSE | DATE | BK/PAGE |
|---|---|---|---|
| Waring, Moses | Smoot, Ellen | Mar 22 1832* | 2/1631 |
| Warner, Caleb | Beardsley, Epsey | Feb 26 1824* | 1/22 |
| Warner, Harriett W | Irvin, Ramson P | Sep 15 1854 | 13/336 |
| Warner, Janet (Warren) | Coin, Patrick | Apr 13 1846 | 8/157B |
| Warner, Moses C | Goodwynn, Harriett W | Dec 23 1850 | 11/105 |
| Warren, John Carter | Taylor, Mary | Apr 22 1839* | 3/168 |
| Washington, Celest | Rosette, Pier | Jul 5 1845* | 8/109B |
| Waterman, Thomas S | Leich, Emma C F (Leech) | Oct 25 1849 | 11/11 |
| Waters, Charlotte | Murphy, William | Mar 23 1842 | 5/187B |
| Waters, Elizabeth | Gause, Austin B. | Dec 3 1845 | 8/128B |
| Waters, Eunice | Sloan, Thomas | Feb 11 1838* | 3/111 |
| Waters, Frances E | Fry, Budd H | Jan 3 1842 | 5/167B |
| Waters, Leaven | Gibbs, Mary | Jan 21 1850 | 11/34 |
| Waters, Mary | White, Robert | Aug 12 1842 | 5/216B |
| Waters, Mary | Scamerorn, Solomon | Jan 13 1843 | 5/243B |
| Wating, Charlotte ? | Murphy, William | Mar 23 1842 | 6/100B |
| Watkins, Elizabeth | George, William | Aug 8 1840* | 5/39B |
| Watkins, Maria | Leland, Stephen | Jun 28 1833 | 2/901 |
| Watkins, Martha | Lynsh, Cullen | May 13 1847 | 8/234 |
| Watson, Agnes | Caing, John | Jun 26 1854 | 13/265 |
| Watson, Artinus J | Chapman, Jane | Jan 30 1854 | 13/103 |
| Watson, Augustus F | Lorey, Susan | Dec 29 1854 | 13/423 |
| Watson, Charles | Dowdle, Rebecca | Jun 6 1833* | 2/951 |
| Watson, Gavin G | Cummings, Jesse J | Aug 23 1854 | 13/319 |
| Watson, William | Southerland, Barbara | Jan 10 1855 | 14/10 |
| Watters, Martha (Walters) | Strachan, George | Aug 25 1840 | 4/2381B |
| Wattes, Ann | Hughes, William | Dec 18 1837* | 3/93 |
| Wattey, Reuben (Watley) | Lyle, Sarah | Sep 2 1852 | 11/281 |
| Watts, David | Helverson, Harriet | Sep 10 1849 | 11/3 |
| Watts, Martha | Copeland, Henry | Jul 19 1847 | 8/246 |
| Watts, Sarah J | Harris, John M | Dec 13 1853 | 13/38 |
| Watts, W. I. H. | Windham, Martha | Jun 4 1838* | 3/131 |
| Waugh, Joanna | Gaines, Henry T. | Nov 12 1850 | 11/96 |
| Waverly, Mary | Bowman, John | Jan 8 1846 | 8/138B |
| Weatherall, Emma | Rayman, John | Apr 21 1846 | 8/159B |
| Weathers, Becky | Brannan, Samuel | Aug 21 1819* | CM |
| Weathers, Elizabeth | David, Simon | 1826* | OIB |
| Weathers, Harriet | Chastang, Augustus | Dec 22 1828 | 2/57 |
| Weathers, Hypolitte | Alvarez, Diego | Dec 22 1823 | 1/18 |
| Weathers, Rebecca | Bancroft, Charles | Jan 6 1820* | CM |
| Weathers, Thomas | Barnett, Betsy | Aug 25 1819* | CM |
| Weaver, George | Maura, Susan | Dec 12 1846 | 8/204 |
| Weaver, J | Allen, Minerva | Apr 8 1853* | 12/223 |
| Weaver, James | Woody, Ellen | Apr 28 1842* | 5/194B |
| Weaver, James C. | D'Olive, Modiste E. | Nov 1 1848 | 8/331 |
| Weaver, Sarah M | Tyson, Anthony | Feb 16 1854 | 13/122 |
| Webaka, Frederick | Snider, Elizabeth | Mar 21 1845* | 8/80B |
| Webb, Caroline | Dakin, Charles B. | Mar 20 1837* | 3/76 |
| Webb, Harriett | Carthy, Thomas L. | Dec 14 1824 | 1/52 |
| Webb, Hetty | House, Reubin | Sep 15 1836* | 3/58 |
| Webb, Isabella | Morrison, John | Jan 15 1853 | 12/135 |
| Webb, Nathaniel | Baxter, Mary | Nov 5 1855 | 14/272 |
| Webb, Patsey | Drew, Levi | Aug 11 1855 | 14/208 |
| Webb, Sarah | Lucas, William | Jul 7 1825 | 1/83 |
| Weber, Mary | Kockler, Phillip | Feb 12 1851 | 11/120 |
| Webster, Eden | Ballinger, Elizabeth | Feb 19 1835* | 3/9 |
| Webster, James | Mullen, Catharine | Jul 7 1849* | 8/387 |
| Weed, Edward H | Green, Agnes C | Sep 4 1855 | 14/225 |
| Weekes, Delphine | Dailey, Thomas W | Oct 12 1815* | CM |
| Weekes, Samuel K | Morgan, Seley | 1826* | OIB |
| Weekley, Elizabeth | Davis, Samuel | Dec 8 1819* | CM |
| Weekley, Joseph P | Floid, Catherine A | Jan 2 1855 | 13/431 |
| Weeks, Louisa | Cook, John | Mar 8 1831 | 2/153 |
| Weeks, Nicholas Jr | Chaudron, Melanie | Feb 21 1833* | 2/1101 |

| BRIDE OR GROOM | SPOUSE | DATE | BK/PAGE |
|---|---|---|---|
| Weeks, Sarah | Cottrill, William C. | Aug 5 1847* | 8/249 |
| Weibis, Frederick S. | Walker, Mary Ann Paulina | Nov 29 1851 | 11/191 |
| Weicke, Henry (widr) | Cramer, Charlotte (wid) | Dec 23 1853 | 13/49 |
| Wein, Mary E. | Cluis, Frederick V. | Nov 1 1851* | 11/185 |
| Wein, Mary E | Chris, Frederick V | Nov 1 1851* | 11/185 |
| Weinberg, Mina | Frohlickstein, Henry | Feb 10 1854 | 13/117 |
| Weinheimer, Otilia | Franelich, Thomas | Jul 26 1851 | 11/169 |
| Weinschenk, Apalonia | Berg, Tobias | Dec 15 1846 | 8/205 |
| Weinscheuk, Catharina | Kumpfmiller, Auguste | Jul 31 1846 | 8/182 |
| Weir, Rachel M | Bosworth, Abel W. | Feb 14 1844 | 5/322B |
| Weir, Sarah J. | Belknap, Jackson O. | Apr 10 1851* | 11/136 |
| Weiss, Abraham J. | Goldsteiker, Babes | May 4 1847 | 8/232 |
| Weiss, Abraham J (widr) | Treefoot, Ridgell | Aug 20 1853 | 12/390 |
| Weiswall, Catherine | Hobby, Uriah | 1826* | OIB |
| Welch, Ann | Carpenter, James | Oct 5 1840* | 5/51 |
| Welch, Anna Mrs | Mack, Thomas | Jan 17 1850 | 11/33 |
| Welch, David | Floherty, Mary | Sep 25 1849 | 11/7 |
| Welch, Ellen | Parkhurst, John | Jan 3 1853 | 12/110 |
| Welch, Johanna | Armstrong, Michael | Jun 4 1853 | 12/310 |
| Welch, Matthew | Bany, Catherine | Jul 8 1835* | 3/19 |
| Welch, Michael | Eloirt, Bridget (Elvert) | Sep 14 1850 | 11/85 |
| Welch, Shady Ann (wid) | Poalk, Joseph (widr) | May 23 1853 | 12/295 |
| Weldin, Elizabeth | Irwin, Richard | Nov 5 1842* | 5/226B |
| Wells, Elizabeth | Scott, Thomas | Apr 26 1837* | 3/96 |
| Wells, Emeline | Hamilton, Frederick | May 21 1852 | 11/253 |
| Wells, John H | Dawson, Elizabeth Ann | Jun 4 1828 | 2/31 |
| Wells, Mary | Danley, Dennis | Jul 31 1844 | 8/37B |
| Wells, Parmelia | Pace, William J | Jan 16 1851 | 11/114 |
| Wells, Richard | Jackson, Mary Ann | Feb 24 1849* | 8/359 |
| Wells, Sally | Williamson, John | Sep 6 1849 | 11/2 |
| Welman, Catherine J | Reid, Robert | Apr 17 1854 | 13/188 |
| Welsh, George W | Williams, Hannah J | Jan 10 1854 | 13/71 |
| Welsh, Jane | King, Thomas | May 26 1848* | 8/306 |
| Welsh, Joanna | Kennedy, Michael | Jan 29 1853 | 12/155 |
| Welsh, Levina | Galligher, Martin | Aug 29 1850 | 11/83 |
| Welsh, Margaret | Fogerty, Thomas | Jun 17 1852 | 11/264 |
| Welsh, Mary | Byrnes, Andrew | Nov 22 1852 | 12/69 |
| Welsh, Mary | Devine, Colman | Feb 20 1855 | 14/61 |
| Welsh, Michael | O'Brien, Joanna | Jan 25 1842 | 5/173B |
| Welsh, Michael | Hughes, Sarah (wid) | Feb 27 1855* | 14/69 |
| Welsh, Rebecca | O'Birrim, William ? | May 10 1855 | 14/137 |
| Welsh, William | Johnson, Sarah | Apr 20 1850* | 11/55 |
| Weltz, Rika | Bondlemann, Henry | Sep 13 1852* | 12/1 |
| Wemberly, Elizabeth J | Gehr, Joseph W | May 13 1853 | 12/281 |
| Wemberly, Jane | Smith, George | Apr 26 1853* | 12/255 |
| Wendham, Joseph W. | Hag, Sarah | Apr 10 1839* | 3/166 |
| Wendover, Simeon D. | Horress, Mary | Jul 5 1843 | 6/392B |
| Wentworth, William Jr | Goodrich, Elizabeth A. | Dec 4 1844 | 8/56B |
| Werner, Amalia Elise | Boling, Henry | Feb 2 1846* | 8/143B |
| Wernoth, Morton | Rhodes, Sophia | May 6 1850 | 11/60 |
| Wesh, Harriet | Wagenbrennor, Michael | Dec 6 1851 | 11/192 |
| West, Anna Helen | Condon, Alfred | Jan 18 1855* | 14/19 |
| West, Dorothy | Martin, Bernard | Oct 28 1835* | 3/31 |
| West, George | Bassett, Mary | Apr 4 1849 | 8/365 |
| West, James Jr | De Vendel, Melanie A | Oct 27 1841 | 5/155 |
| West, Louis | Jones, Anna H | Dec 22 1851 | 11/197 |
| Westbrook, Adaline | Gurlott, Victor | Sep 21 1855 | 14/236 |
| Westson, Marie | Zinck, John F. | Jul 17 1845 | 8/111B |
| Westfeldt, Reinhold | Crothers, Mary E | Feb 22 1854 | 13/133 |
| Wetherby, Alvan | Seawell, Elizabeth A | Apr 7 1836* | 3/44 |
| Wetherwax, Jacob A. | Dickson, Mary T. | Jan 14 1847* | 8/212 |
| Wetzler, Albert | Steiner, Hannah | Jan 14 1851* | 11/112 |
| Weyman, Catharine M. | Stryhn, Hans R. | Apr 18 1848* | 8/300 |
| Whalen, Bridget | Taylor, William | Sep 6 1852 | 11/283 |

| BRIDE OR GROOM | SPOUSE | DATE | BK/PAGE |
|---|---|---|---|
| Whaler, Elizabeth | Tillman, Richard | Apr 29 1845 | 7/651B |
| Whatley, Lucy | Smith, John | Feb 24 1855 | 14/68 |
| Whatley, Mary | Batiste, Beels | 1828* | OIB |
| Whatley, Rebecca | Byrnes, William | 1827* | OIB |
| Wheat, Chancey C | Williams, Malinda E | Oct 22 1853 | 12/423 |
| Wheat, Martha | Wheat, Solomon | 1827* | OIB |
| Wheat, Solomon | Wheat, Martha | 1827* | OIB |
| Wheeler, Ausman | Lewis, Sarah | Jan 27 1846 | 8/141B |
| Wheeler, Charles J. | Robb, Jane G. | Dec 12 1837* | 3/102 |
| Wheeler, Elizabeth | Collins, Christopher B. | Jul 4 1832* | 2/1421B |
| Wheeler, Elizabeth | Tillman, Richard | Apr 29 1845 | 8/89B |
| Wheeler, Emily | Hunt, Thomas | Nov 30 1848 | 8/335 |
| Wheeler, Jane | Collins, Christopher B. | Jun 3 1834* | 2/231 |
| Wheeler, Joseph | Snyder, Agnes | Dec 19 1821* | CM |
| Wheeler, Judy Eveline | Cooper, Ferdenand | Sep 4 1837* | 3/98 |
| Wheeler, Nancy | Goff, Arnal | Mar 20 1849* | 8/362 |
| Wheeler, Nancy | Lane, George | Apr 21 1853 | 12/248 |
| Wheeler, Sarah | Rolls, James A. | Jul 21 1845 | 8/112B |
| Wheeler, Seleter | Collins, Joseph | Dec 3 1831* | 2/1791 |
| Wheeler, Silester | Walker, George W. | Jul 13 1846 | 8/179 |
| Wheeler, Simeon | Maples, Rebecca | Jul 16 1850 | 11/74 |
| Wheeler, William | Palmer, Delphia | Jul 11 1843 | 5/287B |
| Wheeler, William F. | Elliott, Martha J. | Jun 4 1842* | 5/204B |
| Whelm, Mary | McCalmoil, James | Oct 24 1851 | 11/184 |
| Whitaker, Sarah J | Windham, Jesse | Nov 26 1855 | 14/289 |
| White, Abel | Cotter, Hanora | Jan 17 1849* | 8/348 |
| White, Alexander H. | McKay, Nancy (Mary) | May 5 1836* | 3/46 |
| White, Caleb E | Files, Emily F | Mar 9 1854* | 13/153 |
| White, Charles | Eley, Catherine | Feb 14 1833* | 2/1131 |
| White, Elizabeth | Lallhamon, Christ | 1839* | OIB |
| White, Elizabeth | Rowell, Franklin | Feb 12 1851* | 11/121 |
| White, Elizabeth | Eggart, Robert | Aug 25 1855 | 14/216 |
| White, Fisher A. | Cooper, Susan | Dec 26 1836* | 3/66 |
| White, Hiram J. | Field, Hester | Nov 7 1840 | 5/61B |
| White, Hiram J. | Field, Hester | May 4 1842 | 5/198B |
| White, Joseph | Law, Sarah | May 26 1854 | 13/235 |
| White, Lucy | Cowles, John A. | Feb 16 1830* | 2/112 |
| White, Mary | Mortimer, Thomas V | 1838* | OIB |
| White, Mary | McClay, David | Nov 30 1842 | 5/231B |
| White, Mary | Oliver, William Jackson | Dec 9 1843* | 5/309B |
| White, Peter | Neagle, Bridget | Mar 30 1855 | 14/92 |
| White, Rebecca | Jones, William | Jan 13 1836* | 3/35 |
| White, Robert | Waters, Mary | Aug 12 1842 | 5/216B |
| White, William J. | Madigan, Mary | Aug 26 1843* | 5/293B |
| Whitehall, Joseph | Smith, Anna | Jul 7 1851 | 11/162 |
| Whitehead, John | Sellers, Artemesia L | Jan 6 1854 | 13/62 |
| Whitfield, James K. | Buckman, Mary A H | Feb 1 1848 | 8/280 |
| Whiting, Caroline | Perley, George H | Mar 6 1855 | 14/75 |
| Whiting, Oscar | Quinn, Ann | May 6 1854 | 13/217 |
| Whitley, James J | Nicholas, Josephine | Jun 26 1854 | 13/266 |
| Whitley, Nancy | Courtney, John | Jun 3 1854 | 13/240 |
| Whitney, Catharine | Short, John | Mar 1 1837* | 3/73 |
| Whitney, John S. | Hodges, Ann Maria | Aug 21 1847 | 8/252 |
| Whitney, William L. | Correjolles, Emily | Aug 9 1847* | 8/250 |
| Whitstom, Sarah | Fitzgerald, John | Jun 10 1841* | 5/136B |
| Whittaker, Benjamin A. | Hazard, Mary | Apr 25 1848* | 8/301 |
| Whitten, Asberry | Martin, Ann Matilda | Oct 24 1850 | 11/93 |
| Whyte, William J | Chastang, Josephine | Dec 25 1855 | 14/316 |
| Wiathers, William | Branham, Nelly | Apr 28 1840* | 5/21 |
| Wickes, Charles | Emslie, Margaret R | Jun 21 1847* | 8/243 |
| Wickes, Delphine W | Barnard, Jerome W | May 9 1855 | 14/136 |
| Wickes, William H. | Calvert, Mary | Aug 1 1840* | 5/37 |
| Wickham, James C. | Hadaway, Ann | Apr 5 1848 | 8/297 |
| Wickwin, Charles W. | Hollinger, Mary J. | Oct 17 1849 | 11/10 |

| BRIDE OR GROOM | SPOUSE | DATE | BK/PAGE |
|---|---|---|---|
| Wickwire, Moses | McKee, Ann | Dec  5 1828* | 2/53 |
| Wiehelhansen, Regine | Rosenberg, Marcus | Oct 30 1852* | 12/40 |
| Wiener, Eugene | Vegoureux, Julia | Apr  4 1850 | 11/50 |
| Wier, William W. | Hellen, Abby | Dec  9 1851 | 11/193 |
| Wigan, William (Mryan) | Monroe, Abby | Apr  8 1839* | 3/165B |
| Wiggins, Permelia E (wid) | Fisher, John E | Aug 17 1853 | 12/383 |
| Wilcox, Jane | Russell, Edward | Mar 23 1849* | 8/363 |
| Wilcox, Jeremiah Briggs | Thomas, Missouri Jane | Mar 17 1845 | 8/79B |
| Wilde, Christina | Propell, Thomas | May  1 1845 | 8/91B |
| Wildermain, Philip | Elliston, Anna | May  3 1825 | 1/74 |
| Wileford, Mary A | Harris, John | 1827* | 0IB |
| Wilhelm, Jacob S. | Mansker, Sarah J. | Feb 27 1846 | 8/149B |
| Wilhelmi, Maria | Stringer, George | Apr  9 1853 | 12/230 |
| Wilkerson, James | Riley, Mary | Dec 29 1852 | 12/107 |
| Wilkerson, Nancy | Gardner, William A. | Jul  4 1845 | 8/108B |
| Wilkes, William H. | Calvert, Mary M. | Aug  1 1840 | 5/37B |
| Wilkey, Catherine | Rose, John | Jan 20 1852 | 11/205 |
| Wilkie, Ferdinand | Aesart, Catharine | Aug  4 1846 | 8/183 |
| Wilkie, James | Milton, Sarah (Miller) | Dec 17 1842 | 5/235B |
| Wilkins, Benjamin | Ryder, Jane | Mar 26 1828* | 2/19 |
| Wilkins, Georgette | Flash, William | May 20 1850 | 11/62 |
| Wilkins, Hennrietta M. | Montague, Joseph H. | May 17 1832* | 2/1491 |
| Wilkins, James | D'Olive, Mary M. | Sep 15 1841 | 5/151B |
| Wilkins, Martha J. | Serrill, George L. | May 10 1845 | 8/94B |
| Wilkins, Mary Eliza | Forsyth, Richard T. | Dec  3 1845 | 8/128B |
| Wilkins, Richard R. | Sherwood, Emily (Sherron) | Apr 28 1830* | 2/124 |
| Wilkinson, Catherine E | Gibbs, John H | May  4 1854 | 13/214 |
| Wilkinson, James | Sullivan, Nancy | Apr  7 1831 | 2/161 |
| Wilkinson, John | Duffie, Mary | May 13 1842 | 5/200B |
| Wilkinson, Mary Jane | Robertson, Daniel | Nov 27 1838* | 3/149 |
| Wilkinson, Rebecca A. | Coneh, Alexander B. | Jan 20 1836* | 3/37 |
| Wilkinson, William L. | Sly, Eliza | Aug  7 1847 | 8/250 |
| Wilkinson, Zelphia | McIntire, Peter | Jan 26 1835* | 3/6 |
| Willan, Julia | Jarvis, Francis R | Dec 29 1852 | 12/106 |
| Willcox, William W. | Malone, Mary M. | Feb 25 1852 | 11/221 |
| Willeford, Charity | Baxter, James | Jun 14 1828* | 2/34 |
| Willey, Mary E. | Chapman, Lewis T. | Jun 11 1852 | 11/261 |
| Williams, Alfred | Bozarge, Mary | Aug 30 1854 | 13/325 |
| Williams, Andrew J. | Reynolds, Anna Carolin | Oct 25 1849 | 11/12 |
| Williams, Andrew Jackson | Davis, Julia Ann | Feb 23 1843 | 5/250B |
| Williams, Benjamin C | Bryan, Rebecca Ann | Jul  3 1844 | 8/31B |
| Williams, Camerene | Powell, Elisha | Oct  4 1837* | 3/92 |
| Williams, Caroline | Townsend, Thomas | Jun  1 1850 | 11/64 |
| Williams, Catherine | Fyffe, John | May 28 1821* | CM |
| Williams, Catherine E | Fetters, John George | Dec 27 1842* | 5/238B |
| Williams, Celina | Cordis, William | Sep  2 1852 | 11/282 |
| Williams, Charles | Hursted, Ann | Jun 10 1841* | 5/137B |
| Williams, Charles | Pinkham, Hannah | Jul 10 1851 | 11/163 |
| Williams, Charles | Strill, Barbara | Feb 10 1845 | 8/72B |
| Williams, Daniel W | Griffin, Sarah Ann | Nov 18 1850 | 11/98 |
| Williams, Eleanor | Forster, John | May 12 1823 | 1/3 |
| Williams, Eliza E | Merlin, Thomas P | May 20 1843* | 5/274B |
| Williams, Elizabeth | Faggard, Jackson G | Jan 19 1847 | 8/213 |
| Williams, Elizabeth Ann | Harkins, James | Dec 14 1840* | 5/75 |
| Williams, Emilins | Pervis, Adelaide Ursula | Jun 18 1840* | 5/29 |
| Williams, George | Geiler, Catharine | Nov 23 1848 | 8/334 |
| Williams, George | Golden, Catherine | Mar 24 1842 | 5/188B |
| Williams, Hannah J | Welsh, George W | Jan 10 1854 | 13/71 |
| Williams, Henry | Monk, Mary | 1825* | 0IB |
| Williams, Henry | Loring, Ann | Jul 20 1841* | 5/143 |
| Williams, Henry | Cates, Betsey | Nov 26 1852* | 12/76 |
| Williams, James | Christian, Mary | Jun 22 1824 | 1/34 |
| Williams, James | Waltz, Sophronia (Watts) | Jan  1 1855* | 13/428 |
| Williams, James | Johnson, Ameline | Jul  5 1854 | 13/274 |

| BRIDE OR GROOM | SPOUSE | DATE | BK/PAGE |
|---|---|---|---|
| Williams, James E | Dyess, Elizabeth Ann | Feb 27 1850 | 11/43 |
| Williams, Jeremiah | Randall, Unito Minerva | Jun 26 1850 | 11/69 |
| Williams, John | Gage, Rosanna | May 2 1851 | 11/144 |
| Williams, John | Bawldin, Francis | Nov 18 1823 | 1/13 |
| Williams, John | Sterling, Mary Ann | Aug 20 1844* | 8/39B |
| Williams, John | Henry, Martha N (wid) | Oct 29 1853 | 12/427 |
| Williams, John | Wooster, Mary J | Jan 19 1854 | 13/88 |
| Williams, Jonathan C | Mason, Lucretia | Aug 15 1833 | 2/831 |
| Williams, Joseph N | Adams, Mary E | Jul 2 1841* | 5/142B |
| Williams, Levi | Shelton, Louisa | Nov 10 1841 | 5/155B |
| Williams, Lewis | Price, Phedre Matilda | Jan 1 1847 | 8/209 |
| Williams, Lewis | Gratrix, Martha | Feb 3 1844* | 5/320B |
| Williams, Libby E | Markham, William H | Jun 26 1854 | 13/264 |
| Williams, Louisa | Beaver, Seaborn Jones | Feb 1 1842 | 5/176B |
| Williams, Louisa | Field, George | Jun 3 1847 | 8/240 |
| Williams, M Susan | Pope, William L | Jan 28 1853 | 12/153 |
| Williams, Malinda E | Wheat, Chancey C | Oct 22 1853 | 12/423 |
| Williams, Mary Ann | Dwyer, Patrick | Apr 23 1823 | 1/1 |
| Williams, Mary Ann | Keho, John | Jan 25 1825 | 1/61 |
| Williams, Mary E | Seaberry, James H | Jul 26 1850 | 11/76 |
| Williams, Mary E | Hulen, Samuel | Apr 30 1839* | 3/170 |
| Williams, Mary E | Howell, Charles F | Mar 6 1851 | 11/128 |
| Williams, Nancy | Batiste, John Pierre | Apr 19 1824 | 1/28 |
| Williams, Nancy J | McCullough, George | Jul 4 1853 | 12/346 |
| Williams, Nathaniel F | Dobson, Elizabeth | 1827* | OIB |
| Williams, R G | Sullivan, Jane Ann | Oct 27 1837* | 3/99 |
| Williams, Rebecca M | Moffett, Gabriel | Sep 6 1841 | 5/150B |
| Williams, Samuel | Sullivan, Caroline | Dec 29 1843 | 5/312B |
| Williams, Sarah | Neal, West | Nov 7 1829* | 2/102 |
| Williams, Sarah Ann | Pitts, John G W | May 26 1845 | 8/98B |
| Williams, Seaborn | McGahee, Nancy D | Jun 25 1846 | 8/175 |
| Williams, Susan K | Higgin, Robert | Mar 20 1832* | 2/1641 |
| Williams, Susanna | Pierce, Jeremiah | Jun 17 1845 | 8/104B |
| Williams, Tamsen | Howell, Benjamin | Apr 4 1844 | 8/9B |
| Williams, Thomas | Dailey, Bridget | Mar 6 1852 | 11/225 |
| Williams, Thomas | Maley, Ellen | Apr 10 1852 | 11/235 |
| Williams, William | McKinsey, Margueretta | Jul 31 1855 | 14/202 |
| Williams, William F | Barren, Julia | Nov 15 1840* | 5/63 |
| Williamson, John | Wells, Sally | Sep 6 1849 | 11/2 |
| Williamson, John | Rogers, Catherine | Jul 30 1844 | 8/37B |
| Williamson, Sarah | McKeever, Hugh | Oct 18 1854 | 13/351 |
| Willing, Daniel | Duvas, Sarah | Nov 27 1849 | 11/19 |
| Willis, David | Coward, Elizabeth | Aug 7 1839* | 3/184 |
| Willis, Julius | Grant, Isabella Q | Apr 2 1850 | 11/49 |
| Willison, Edward F | Gaillard, Mary Ann | Apr 19 1853 | 12/245 |
| Willrich, Christina | Hippler, Frank | Nov 9 1854 | 13/374 |
| Wills, Nelson | Burk, Eliza (Bush) | Feb 20 1847 | 8/218 |
| Wilson, Amelia | Jones, Edward A | Jun 6 1846* | 8/173 |
| Wilson, Ann E | Godbold, George | Jul 19 1836* | 3/54 |
| Wilson, Ansaline | Duffy, John | Jan 4 1849* | 8/344 |
| Wilson, Benjamin | Smith, Clarissa | May 9 1833* | 2/1021 |
| Wilson, Bridget (Mrs) | Dearing, Michael | Apr 21 1851 | 11/140 |
| Wilson, Charles | Ward, Mary | Apr 4 1841* | 5/126B |
| Wilson, Davis | Shaw, Narcissa T | Dec 18 1850 | 11/104 |
| Wilson, Ellen | Jepay, John (Jessay) | 1839* | OIB |
| Wilson, George | Jarvis, Mary Ann | Jan 29 1841* | 5/139B |
| Wilson, George F | Kifer, Mary A | Oct 17 1855 | 14/253 |
| Wilson, Henry | Manogin, Ellen | Jan 27 1853 | 12/152 |
| Wilson, Hugh | Strang, Agnes | 1827* | OIB |
| Wilson, J B | Turner, Leonon | Feb 13 1839* | 3/157 |
| Wilson, James | Byrne, Ann (Berry) | Dec 11 1823* | 1/15 |
| Wilson, James B | Randall, Margaret Ann | Sep 10 1825* | 1/90 |
| Wilson, James D | Graves, Rebecca | 1827* | OIB |
| Wilson, James H | McHugh, Mary Ann | Sep 3 1855 | 14/224 |

| BRIDE OR GROOM | SPOUSE | DATE | BK/PAGE |
|---|---|---|---|
| Wilson, Jane | Hanford, Charles | May 16 1840* | 5/22 |
| Wilson, John | Kinsey, Mary | Apr 8 1851 | 11/135 |
| Wilson, John | Thompson, Catharine | Jun 3 1846 | 8/170 |
| Wilson, L Madison | Cuaudler, Sarah Ann | Dec 20 1837* | 3/104 |
| Wilson, L Madison | Chandler, Sarah Ann | 1837* | OIB |
| Wilson, Margaret ? | Kidney, John | Jul 31 1832 | 2/1381 |
| Wilson, Margaret | Viollet, Pierre | May 9 1847 | 8/233 |
| Wilson, Margaret Maria | Moore, Robert | Oct 23 1844 | 8/45B |
| Wilson, Mary | Curtis, Harvey | Mar 31 1831* | 2/160 |
| Wilson, Mary Jane ? | Kidney, John | Aug 3 1832 | 2/1381 |
| Wilson, Newton J | Longfield, J Alabama | Aug 18 1849* | 8/391 |
| Wilson, Rebecca | Lord, John | Apr 21 1832 | 2/1591 |
| Wilson, Sarah | Caleb, John | Feb 28 1843 | 5/251B |
| Wilson, Seymour S | Hurdle, Caroline | May 30 1843* | 5/277B |
| Wilson, Susan A | Powers, Paul | Nov 25 1839* | 5/2 |
| Wilson, Thomas | Johnson, Lavinia | Jan 25 1848 | 8/279 |
| Wilson, William | Hughes, Mary | Sep 26 1849 | 11/7 |
| Wilson, William | Scanlon, Catharine | Apr 13 1843 | 5/260B |
| Wilson, William | Titus, Victoria | Oct 20 1855 | 14/257 |
| Wilson, William | Crosby, Mary | Sep 22 1852* | 12/10 |
| Wilson, William Matthew H | Chamberlain, Elizabeth R | Jan 30 1849* | 8/350 |
| Windergast, Christopher | Egghart, Louisette | Nov 11 1852 | 12/61 |
| Windham, Cynthia | Colbark, George | Apr 15 1835 | 3/22 |
| Windham, G W | Ezell, Sarah | Apr 9 1853 | 12/227 |
| Windham, Jesse | Ellis, Armississi | Jul 18 1844 | 8/32B |
| Windham, Jesse | Whitaker, Sarah J | Nov 26 1855 | 14/289 |
| Windham, John | Andrews, Sara Ann E | Aug 12 1847* | 8/251 |
| Windham, Joseph W | Hays, Sarah | 1839* | OIB |
| Windham, Martha | Watts, W I H | Jun 4 1838* | 3/131 |
| Windham, Patience | Myers, George W | Mar 9 1840* | 5/14 |
| Winechink, Margaret | Witt, Joseph | Mar 4 1844 | 5/326B |
| Winecore, Lavinia | Riley, Owen | Dec 30 1842* | 5/236B |
| Wingate, Caroline | Moore, Joseph | Mar 21 1845 | 8/82B |
| Wingate, Elizabeth | Spalding, Rufus | Jan 19 1833* | 2/1201 |
| Winkel, Henry | Summer, Amelia | Nov 25 1853 | 13/28 |
| Winkler, Eliza | Andre, Outin | Jan 3 1854 | 13/60 |
| Winship, Bathia | Dawson, Robert | 1827* | OIB |
| Winship, Lydia | Ashton, James M | Apr 22 1834* | 2/281 |
| Winslow, Giovanni | Lagomaggiore, Anna E | Nov 28 1850 | 11/100 |
| Winston, Mary A | Goldsby, Thomas J | Apr 24 1855 | 14/117 |
| Winston, Mary Jane | Brown, John M | Jan 7 1843 | 5/242B |
| Winter, Charles | Storey, Harriett | Nov 21 1840* | 5/67B |
| Winter, Charles | Laws, Catherine | Apr 12 1854 | 13/180 |
| Winter, George | Curry, Keren P | Nov 25 1851 | 11/189 |
| Winter, Harriet | Lloyd, Joseph C | Sep 8 1854 | 13/334 |
| Winter, Julia A | O'Rain, Gregory | May 23 1838* | 3/128 |
| Winterhalter, Perpetua | Knoblock, Frederick | May 2 1837* | 3/82 |
| Winterhalter, Thomas | Farley, Catherine | Feb 12 1851 | 11/121 |
| Wintzill, Ellen | Brace, Thomas W | Jun 12 1837* | 3/86 |
| Wisdom, Patrick | Dailey, Norah | May 27 1847* | 8/237 |
| Wisdom, William | Noonan, Margaret | May 26 1849* | 8/378 |
| Wisener, Barbara | Tate, Zachariah | Mar 18 1824 | 1/26 |
| Wiswall, Catherine E | Hobby, Uriah | 1826* | OIB |
| Wiswall, Joseph | Montgomery, Eliza F | Mar 14 1829* | 2/76 |
| Withers, Margaret | Duplessis, James | May 29 1830 | 2/126 |
| Witherspoon, Ann Louisa | Anderson, William H | Dec 24 1851 | 11/197 |
| Witherspoon, Daniel M | Casey, Mary Jane | Feb 21 1835 | 3/9 |
| Witling, Daniel | Dukes, Sarah | 1849* | OIB |
| Witpen, Dederick | Kelley, Amanda | May 19 1846 | 8/167B |
| Witsman, Catherine | Nelius, Jasper | Dec 20 1851 | 11/196 |
| Witt, Charles | Smith, Mary | May 10 1853 | 12/275 |
| Witt, Joseph | Winechink, Margaret | Mar 4 1844 | 5/326B |
| Wittmann, Jacob | Haffler, Caroline | Oct 29 1855 | 14/267 |
| Wolcott, Francis Jane | Lewis, Barbour | Jan 2 1849* | 8/344 |

| BRIDE OR GROOM | SPOUSE | DATE | BK/PAGE |
|---|---|---|---|
| Wolcott, John | Bunch, Mary | Nov 1 1851 | 11/185 |
| Wolf, John | McClelland, Mary | May 24 1853* | 12/298 |
| Wolfe, Jane | Rood, John S | Dec 27 1849* | 11/29 |
| Wolfe, Udolph | Burke, Anna | Jan 11 1842* | 5/170B |
| Wolfkul, Herman H | Derenbesher, Elizabeth | Jan 27 1855 | 14/23 |
| Wommack, Sarah Ann | Crump, Thomas M | Mar 22 1853 | 12/199 |
| Wood, Alexander M | Taggart, Elisa Jane | Oct 25 1852 | 12/35 |
| Wood, Edward | Hooken, Frances | May 21 1844 | 7/265B |
| Wood, George | McKinsey, Caroline | 1834* | OIB |
| Wood, Ida S | Ashley, John (widr) | Mar 23 1853 | 12/202 |
| Wood, Jesse S | Pelham, Sarah | Oct 20 1848 | 8/328 |
| Woodall, Eliza E | Irwin, John | Sep 26 1843 | 5/297B |
| Woodall, Tarlton | Magee, Hariett | Jun 13 1832 | 2/1521 |
| Woodburry, Maria | Turner, William | Dec 30 1840 | 5/49B |
| Woodcock, Abraham S | Montgomery, Adeline | Dec 11 1834* | 2/1841 |
| Woodcock, Caroline M T | Bright, Chas J L | Mar 5 1841 | 5/112B |
| Woodline, Peter | Riles, Elizabeth | Dec 24 1850 | 11/105 |
| Woodruff, H T | Smith, Charity | Nov 2 1842* | 5/226B |
| Woods, Catherine | Agnew, Thomas S | Feb 2 1846 | 8/143B |
| Woods, Charles | Garner, Matilda | Jan 11 1848* | 8/276 |
| Woods, Charles P | Nevins, Mary | Sep 10 1850 | 11/84 |
| Woods, Ellen | Weaver, James | Apr 28 1842* | 5/194B |
| Woods, Malinda | Simonds, James | Mar 31 1851 | 11/133 |
| Woods, Mary | Garland, James | Feb 8 1842 | 5/178B |
| Woods, Sarah | Goodman, James M | May 10 1850 | 11/60 |
| Woods, William | Hill, Nancy | Jan 22 1844* | 5/316B |
| Woods, William | Thompson, Catharine | Dec 17 1840* | 5/77B |
| Woodwik, Abraham S | Montgomery, Adeline | Dec 11 1834* | 2/184B |
| Woody, Ellen | Weaver, James | Apr 28 1842* | 5/194B |
| Woody, Rublarc | Lyons, Martha | Apr 4 1837* | 3/96 |
| Woolard, Hugh ? | Davison, Elizabeth (wid) | 1819* | OIB |
| Woolard, Milly | Griffin, Riley | 1826* | OIB |
| Woolerd, Hugh ? | Dawson, Elizabeth (wid) | Feb 23 1819* | CM |
| Wooley, James | Barrow, Margaret A | Oct 15 1855 | 14/252 |
| Woolf, James | Stuart, Sarah A | Dec 5 1855 | 14/299 |
| Woollard, Cynthia A | St John, Richard Jr | Nov 30 1848* | 8/336 |
| Woolsey, Emily | Heard, Franklin C | Oct 16 1839* | 3/188 |
| Wooster, Mary J | Williams, John | Jan 19 1854 | 13/88 |
| Wooster, Olive A (Wid) | Hoyle, Alexander M | May 27 1854* | 13/236 |
| Wooten, Marceline | Unsworth, John | May 2 1842* | 5/197B |
| Wooton, Jesse | Carroll, Catherine | Mar 25 1852 | 11/230 |
| Worcester, Olive A (wid) | Hoyle, Alexander M | May 27 1854* | 13/236 |
| Worcester, Samuel | Overton, Olive Ann | Jun 6 1843 | 5/279B |
| Wortherington, Mariah | Harper, Samuel | Jul 5 1851 | 11/162 |
| Wotten, Elizabeth | Rhodes, John | Aug 20 1839* | 3/185 |
| Wragg, George | Stickney, Mary Eliza | Jul 12 1832* | 2/1401 |
| Wren, Maria | Ross, Daniel | Dec 29 1855 | 14/320 |
| Wrey, Julia A | Rawlins, Thomas | Feb 14 1850 | 11/39 |
| Wright, Achilles E A | Humphrey, Martha A | Jan 21 1841* | 5/93B |
| Wright, Ann | Oliphant, William | Feb 3 1852* | 11/212 |
| Wright, Benjamin H | Roane, Sarah A | Jan 15 1840* | 5/8 |
| Wright, Charles | Gascoigne, Elmira D | Nov 16 1846 | 8/199 |
| Wright, Ellen A | Foster, Levi | May 30 1851 | 11/153 |
| Wright, Henry | Anderson, Margarette | Feb 14 1838* | 3/112 |
| Wright, Jane | Semon, Hans | Sep 12 1846 | 8/188 |
| Wright, John | Hightower, Emeline | 1827* | OIB |
| Wright, John H | Coloith, Margaret | Jun 10 1842 | 5/205B |
| Wright, John H | Colville, Margaret | 1842* | OIB |
| Wright, Mary Ann | Barterigue, Henry | Jun 12 1847 | 8/241 |
| Wright, Rachel | Eakle, William B | Nov 8 1854 | 13/372 |
| Wright, Reuben T | Meeker, Barbary R | Nov 17 1855 | 14/284 |
| Wright, Richard | Bolton, Artemissa | Jan 31 1850 | 11/36 |
| Wright, Samuel | Leadon, Mary Ann | Mar 3 1841* | 5/112B |
| Wright, Sarah Ann | Campbell, James W | Jan 4 1849 | 8/345 |

| BRIDE OR GROOM | SPOUSE | DATE | BK/PAGE |
|---|---|---|---|
| Wright, William | Knox, Eliza | Jan 16 1850* | 11/33 |
| Wright, William C | Huggins, Louisa (wid) | Apr 9 1853 | 12/228 |
| Wright, William W | Henderson, Martha M | Nov 26 1846 | 8/201 |
| Wroten, William H | Moore, Martha | Mar 22 1849 | 8/363 |
| Wulff, Henry | Mullen, Martha | Jun 15 1842 | 6/161B |
| Wulff, Richard | Reed, Jeanett T | Aug 20 1855 | 14/213 |
| Wyatt, Elizabeth | Pruitt, Thomas L | Dec 30 1851 | 11/199 |
| Wyatt, Martha Ann | Fair, Elisha H | Apr 26 1849* | 8/370 |
| Wyatt, W R R | McKenzie, Amelia Jane | Apr 7 1843 | 5/259B |
| Wyatt, William | Blatchley, Laura A | Aug 16 1837* | 3/91 |
| Wylie, Mary Jane | Poulnot, Jacob W | Dec 22 1845 | 8/131B |
| Wylie, Mary Jane | Folk, James | May 9 1843 | 5/269B |
| Wyman, Nancy | Frost, Eben H | Nov 16 1854 | 13/381 |

## Y

| Yeend, John F | Smith, Elizabeth | Apr 2 1850 | 11/50 |
|---|---|---|---|
| Yoist, Francis M (Yost) | Pearl, Elizabeth J | Nov 10 1855 | 14/277 |
| Yonge, Ann C | Stribling, William C | Jul 9 1855 | 14/192 |
| York, Eliza A | Mellen, Charles | Jan 23 1849* | 8/349 |
| Yost, Frederick | Hoy, Margaret | Jun 8 1850 | 11/65 |
| Yost, Richard S | Swiler, Virginia | Dec 19 1836* | 3/65 |
| Youman, John W | Denison, Ellenah | May 27 1847* | 8/237 |
| Young, Alexander | Busby, Maria | Aug 30 1852 | 11/280 |
| Young, Charles | King, Mary Ann | Jan 16 1849* | 8/347 |
| Young, Charles T | Gratrex, Elizabeth | May 17 1845 | 8/95B |
| Young, Daniel | Pie, Mary Ann (Prie) | Jan 13 1852 | 11/203 |
| Young, Eliza | Stanford, Isaac | May 3 1836* | 3/45 |
| Young, Elizabeth | Goodwin, William Henry | Dec 11 1852 | 12/86 |
| Young, Emma | Russell, James H | Jun 23 1853 | 12/329 |
| Young, Hellen | Baxter, Andrew | Jul 23 1841* | 5/144B |
| Young, John | Gates, Rose | May 7 1849* | 8/373 |
| Young, John | Peter, Elizabeth | Apr 22 1839* | 3/169 |
| Young, Joseph H | Howard, Isabella Holmes | Dec 14 1842 | 5/234B |
| Young, Mary | Bauer, Charles | Dec 13 1847 | 8/270 |
| Young, Susan | Erwin, John | Oct 3 1833* | 2/771 |
| Young, Susan | Cox, George | May 1 1835* | 3/23 |
| Young, Thomas H | Judah, Eugenia | Dec 2 1845 | 8/127B |
| Youngblood, Nancy | Walker, Daniel | Aug 4 1830* | 2/133 |
| Youngblood, Susan | Walker, Jacob B | May 2 1833* | 2/1031 |
| Younger, Mary | Boldz, Henry | Feb 16 1841* | 5/104B |
| Yuille, Catherine | Tower, Luther F | Jul 4 1853* | 12/345 |

Z

| Bride or Groom | Spouse | Date | BK/Page |
|---|---|---|---|
| Zahn, Sophia | Paasch, Henry | Mar 10 1845 | 8/78B |
| Zaph, Charles | Ladel, Amelia | Feb 12 1849* | 8/355 |
| Zertehel, Barbara | Harris, Frederick | Jul 7 1851 | 11/16 |
| Zinck, John F | Westson, Marie | Jul 17 1845 | 8/111i |
| Zurban, Phedora | Monk, Menon | Sep 29 1849 | 11/8 |